OFFICE
MANAGEMENT
AND
CONTROL

By

GEORGE R. TERRY, Ph.D

School of Business,
Northwestern University, and
Management Consultant, Chicago

THIRD EDITION

1958

RICHARD D. IRWIN, INC.

HOMEWOOD, ILLINOIS

THIRD EDITION

First Printing, January, 1958
Second Printing, December, 1958
Third Printing, July, 1959
Fourth Printing, August, 1960

Library of Congress Catalogue Card No. 58–5805

PRINTED IN THE UNITED STATES OF AMERICA

To
My Mother

Preface

THE changing and dynamic dimensions of office management demand that the student, manager, or trainee in this field be alert and responsive to the latest developments in this fascinating management area. Attuned to this progressiveness and benefiting by comments and experience of many teachers and students using the previous editions of the book, this third edition of *Office Management and Control* features an improved arrangement of the subject matter and much new material.

However, with all these additions and changes, the basic objective of the book remains the same—to present fundamental principles and successful practices used in getting office work accomplished. This is essential and remains the stabilizer of office management study. But new ways of accomplishing office tasks, new techniques, and new ideas have been dispersed throughout this entire new edition.

Increased emphasis has been given the management approach to office work and less has been devoted to what might be termed the descriptive approach. The underlying thesis includes the office managerial viewpoint encompassing the task of deciding what is necessary and should be done and then taking the proper and necessary measures to see that it is accomplished efficiently through the efforts of others.

To this end, the theme or continuity of this third edition is built around the concept that office management is a distinct activity, training for which can be given and skill in which can be acquired. This activity of office management consists of specific fundamental functions which when applied constitute a process—a management process. The major parts of this book relate respectively to these fundamental functions of office management as applied in getting office work accomplished. Under each part is included the various activities and practices pertaining to that particular fundamental function. This arrangement has the advantage of supplying a logical and readily followed presentation that is easy to understand and helps orientate the student or trainee. Also, the status of office management is increased by this approach. Ability to apply the office management process successfully is the distinguishing mark of the professional office manager.

Eight new chapters have been added. Prominent among them is the chapter, "Automation and the Office," a subject that is arousing tremendous interest in office work and its management. All the material has been reworked, latest developments have been included, and information believed nonessential has been discarded. This approach was followed in order to provide a compact, helpful, modern, and comprehensive office management book.

New thought-provoking questions have been added at the end of each chapter. They provide a means for an effective review of the material. Also, nearly fifty new case problems, carefully selected from many existing circumstances, appear in print for the first time in this new third edition. The better of the former cases have been retained. Selection was made primarily on the basis of what many office management teachers considered descriptions of pertinent situations requiring analysis, decision, and application of office management knowledge and skill.

Many sources have helped in the preparation of this revision. They have made information available, shared viewpoints, and stimulated thinking about office management. Their assistance and co-operation is most gratifying and deeply appreciated. Space forbids inclusion of the long list of their names and companies, but special acknowledgment is extended Professor Lyle Maxwell of Michigan State University for reviewing the manuscript and offering valuable suggestions. Informal talks with my colleagues and associates, comments by practicing managers of paper work, ideas advanced by executives of various companies, and suggestions by office management teachers appear to unify toward this goal: To improve our present management of office work, to encourage qualified people to enter this field, and to advance our knowledge and practices in this important segment of our economy. Under this motivation, influence, and encouragement, this third edition has been developed.

January, 1958   GEORGE R. TERRY

Table of Contents

PART IV. ORGANIZING THE WORK OF THE OFFICE

PART V. ACTUATING OFFICE EMPLOYEES

APPENDIXES

INDEX

PART I......

Importance of Office Work and Office Management

The study of office management logically begins with the use and importance of office work, its management and the make-up of these managerial efforts, and the basic approaches in performing office management. These fundamental subjects are discussed in the following three chapters.

Chapter · 1

Office Work in Modern Enterprises

Wisdom comes not from experience but from meditating on experience and assimilating it.

—J. E. MORGAN

IN TODAY'S modern business operations, office work is both a vital and an integral part of management because most activities are preceded, accompanied, and followed up by a piece of paper. But before discussing the meaning of management and its application in the office, and vice versa, it is desirable to point out the important distinguishing features about office work and its performance so that a better concept of what is being managed can be gained. Accordingly, this chapter is devoted to the work of the office and the next chapter to the role of office management.

A FACILITATING FUNCTION

Office work is a facilitating function. It is the essential medium through which the various activities of an enterprise are fused together; it is the lifeblood of any enterprise. In a sense, office work can be called the "catalytic agent" of modern management.[1]

Information is the product of the office. Most office work deals with collecting, processing, recording, and transmitting information. Because having the necessary information upon which to base decisions is one of the prime prerequisites of effective managerial action, the importance of the office and its work cannot be overemphasized. The work of the

---

[1] "Catalytic agent" is a term used in chemistry and means an element the presence of which is necessary to bring about a desired reaction between other elements but which does not itself enter into the reaction. In a similar manner, office work brings about a desired reaction of business elements but does not enter into the reaction itself.

office assists in efforts to increase output, lower costs, stimulate employees, pay wages, purchase materials, ship orders, and communicate with others.

This concept along with the attitude to take toward paper work are clearly stated in the following:

It is time management people saw the role of records as an integral part of our production-consumption economic cycle. Records are not a by-product of our economic activity; they are not something to be apologized for. They are an essential part of our economy and therefore, something to be managed, and to manage is not to fear, not to destroy, but properly to use and profitably to make.[2]

Office work has sometimes been referred to as the nervous system of an enterprise or the memory of transactions in that the office serves to trigger desired actions and provides useful records of past and present accomplishments. In this sense, the work of the office represents the nerve or brain center of an enterprise.

In addition, the individual work of practically every department in an enterprise is implemented by office work. For example, a credit department cannot operate successfully without current records of creditors, amounts and dates due, lists of delinquent accounts, credit histories of customers, and a quantity of correspondence.

NATURE OF OFFICE WORK

Another distinguishing feature of office work is that it is a service work. In and of itself, office work serves little purpose; it is performed to help others do their work more effectively. For example, office work is a service to the top executive officers, to the production department, to the sales department, and to the finance department. It helps supply top executives with data which are necessary in order to manage the enterprise. By means of records the production department is helped to improve its service and to lower costs; the sales department is aided in its work of selling the product; and the finance department is assisted in maintaining written evidence of the financial status of the enterprise.[3]

Service is also the primary objective of the office manager. Consideration for office costs, as well as for the utility, quality, and quantity of the office services, is also important; but these should be recognized

---

[2] John P. H. Dethman, of the Ford Motor Company, paper delivered to the Office Management Association of Chicago, February 15, 1956, entitled "Co-ordinated Records Management."

[3] See Policyholders' Service Bureau, Metropolitan Life Insurance Company, *Functions of the Office Manager* (New York, undated), pp. 5–6.

as secondary objectives. An eagerness to slash all costs or a decision to compile only records which the office believes are useful might result in the failure to provide the necessary office services to the other departments. Thus, losses occur in these departments that probably far exceed the savings in operation. However, the service should be evaluated in terms of cost; elaborate and excessive service usually means waste, while, on the other hand, inadequate service represents false economy.

The second important factor concerning the nature of office work is that its volume is determined by factors outside the office. These factors include the number of shipments, the amount of collections, the number of open accounts, the quantity of sales letters, the number of factory employees, and the number of items manufactured or sold —all factors outside the control of the office.

In addition, no profit is realized directly from office work, since it acts through the operative departments, such as the production, sales, and finance departments.[4] In this sense, office work contributes indirectly, not directly, to the profit-making ability of the enterprise. However, some feel that office work produces profit. This belief stems primarily from considering the office as a complete unit within itself.

Furthermore, office work has certain distinctive characteristics. It is chiefly "paper work" of a detailed type, the mental effort is commonly important, and the visual effort is normally quite high. Office work constitutes a large portion of the total work in enterprises such as banks, governmental agencies, insurance companies, mail-order houses, and advertising agencies.

CONTENTS OF OFFICE WORK

Data on the approximate percentage of total time spent by office employees on each of their basic activities provide a pattern of the make-up of office work. This information was obtained in a nationwide representative study and helps to identify specifically the basic work operations of the office.[5] Figure 1-1 shows the data. For example, the work of typing or writing accounts for nearly one fourth of all office time. At first, this may sound high, but it should be remembered that a great deal of paper work necessitates typing or writing— reports, letters, bulletins, and memorandums, plus the fact that even

---

[4] "Profit" as used here is the residual income accruing to the owner of an enterprise after he has paid all the economic aids of production—that is, rent on all land used, interest on all capital used, and wages to all labor used.

[5] The study, *Paperwork in American Business,* by George R. Terry, for Ditto, Inc., Chicago, Illinois, April, 1957.

with office mechanization, typing is required to get much of the data on a card or tape. Calculating is next highest, accounting for 19.5 per cent. Next and in this order come checking, filing, telephoning, duplicating, and mailing. These seven major activities make up nearly 90 per cent of the total office time.

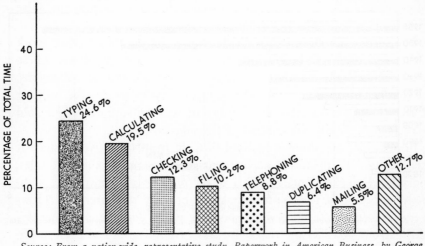

Source: From a nation-wide, representative study, Paperwork in American Business, by George R. Terry, for Ditto, Inc., Chicago, Illinois, April, 1957.

FIG. 1–1.   Major activities making up office time.

Part II of this book, consisting of Chapters 4–11 inclusive, deals with these major office activities. A complete discussion is presented of writing, of calculating and checking work, of filing, and so forth.

FACTS ABOUT OFFICE PERSONNEL

One of the interesting developments among office workers is the increasing proportion of women in this category. There was a time when almost all office workers were men. Back in the year 1870, for example, nearly 98 per cent of office workers were men. By 1930 the distribution was about 50–50, with the number of women approximating that of the men. However, by 1950, the number of women office workers outnumbered the men by a 3 to 2 ratio, and within a few subsequent years they pushed their majority decisively so that, in 1954, the ratio was 2 to 1; that is, there were two women office workers to each man office worker. To win this plurality, women acquired 85 per cent of the additional office jobs during the four-year period, 1950–54. Figure 1–2 shows these data in graphic form.

Another characteristic of office personnel is that there is a tendency for certain office jobs to be occupied by men. These include accountant, collection clerk, credit clerk, and correspondent. Other office jobs are commonly held by women. In this group are the jobs of file clerk, machine operator, receptionist, typist, stenographer, and telephone operator. Still other jobs are held by either men or women and include those of bookkeeper, cashier, mail clerk, and private secretary.

Source: Compiled from Special Report (Washington, D.C.: U.S. Department of Commerce, Bureau of the Census, 1950).

FIG. 1–2.   Clerical workers by sex in the United States, 1870–1955.

Office workers are widely dispersed. They are found in practically every industry. Their number, however, varies widely in different industries. Figure 1–3 shows the industries in which office workers are located. To illustrate, of the total number of office workers, 23.2 per cent are in manufacturing industries. This is the highest concentration, followed in turn by wholesale and retail trade, 17.5 per cent; transportation, communication, and public utilities, 14.8 per cent; and so forth as indicated in the figure.

Also, the proportion of office workers to total workers varies considerably with different industries. For example, nearly one half of the workers in finance, insurance, and real estate are office workers. In contrast, the proportion is about 11 per cent in manufacturing and only 0.3 per cent in agriculture, forestry, and fisheries. This is illustrated by Figure 1–4 which shows, for each of several selected industries, the total number of workers and the percentage of the total represented by clerical workers.

OFFICE WORK DISPERSION WITHIN AN ENTERPRISE

Data on office workers do not give the complete picture of the extensiveness of office work. The work is not performed exclusively in any one department; some of it is performed in every department. There is considerable paper work in a purchasing, engineering, or inspection department. A milling machine operator in a factory, for example, performs some clerical work in the normal course of his daily duty. Where financial incentives and production control are used, the operator may be responsible for a considerable amount of clerical work, yet he is not classified as an office worker. Likewise, most salesmen are

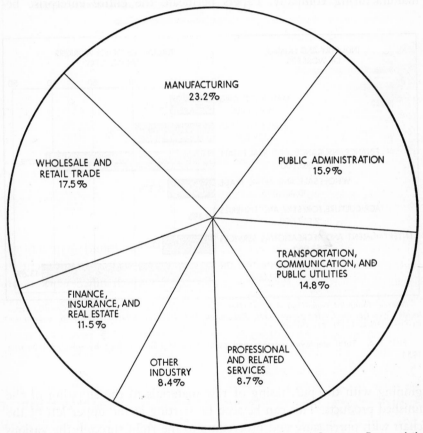

Source: Compiled from Reports of the United States Department of Commerce, Bureau of the Census, 1950.

FIG. 1–3. Respective percentage of total office workers by type of industry for one year, 1950.

accountable for sizable amounts of paper work, and the same is true of many employees of a personnel department who are quick to point out the voluminous paper work used in the execution of their tasks.

The fact is that to a great or less degree, almost every job has some paper work in its make-up. It may be incidental to the chief activity, but it is an essential part of performing the job satisfactorily.

This universality and dispersion of paper work can make for difficulty in its management. The paper work may be neglected by supervisors because their primary job responsibility is something other than paper work which is viewed as a nuisance and unproductive. However, this dilemma can be solved satisfactorily through proper office organizing efforts as discussed in a subsequent chapter.[6]

Figure 1–5 indicates clearly the dispersion of paper work in a typical manufacturing company. Papers permeate the entire enterprise be-

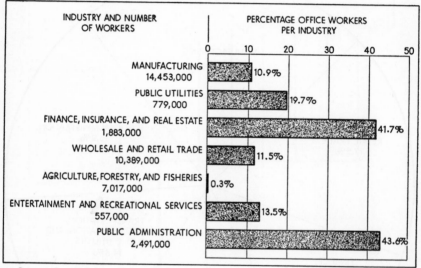

Source: Compiled from United States Department of Commerce, Bureau of the Census, Seventeenth Census of the United States: 1950, Population, Vol. III (Washington, D.C.; U.S. Government Printing Office, 1954), pp. 267–68.

FIG. 1–4. Total employed persons and percentage of office workers by selected industries, 1950.

ginning with the purchasing of raw materials to the shipping of the finished products. This can be seen by starting at the upper left of the chart with purchasing and proceeding to the right through the various activities, such as receiving, storing, processing, assembling, and shipping. In addition, the records of the corollary factory functions, including production planning and engineering, toolroom, tool crib, tool inspection, and personnel, are shown at the bottom of the chart. The records of the important corollary office functions under accounting, selling, billing, and payroll are shown at the lower right of the chart.

---

[6] See Chapter 19, especially pages 377–81.

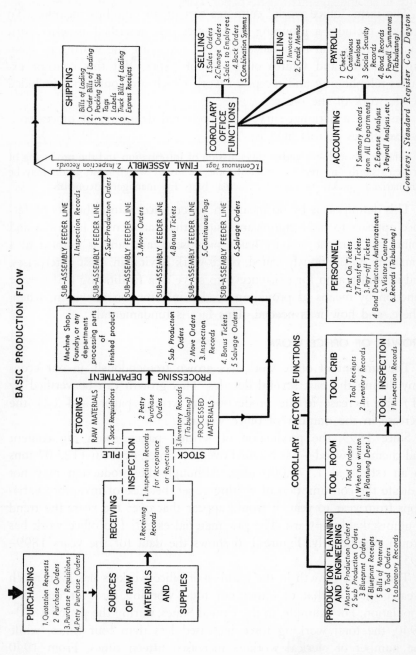

FIG. 1–5. Records permeate an entire enterprise. This chart shows the places in a typical manufacturing plant where records are used.

Courtesy: Standard Register Co., Dayton

DEFINITION OF OFFICE WORK

The term "office work" connotes sort of an omnibus meaning. To many it includes a grouping of activities best described as *miscellany.* Some will say that it includes all work involving the writing or reading of words and figures on pieces of paper. But this concept excludes telephoning and reception work which are commonly included in the work of the office.

Based on a national survey the preferred definition of office work by executives in this field is:

Office work includes verbal transmission of information and the producing of written records and reports providing the means by which many items may be summarized quickly to supply a factual basis for managerial controls.[7]

This definition is by no means in general acceptance, but its preference appears to have significance since the statement is inclusive and points out that the activity has a purposeful aim and is helpful to a manager. As previously stated, office work is vital in most enterprises, and its real reason for existence is to serve as a facilitating and service function by means of providing needed information to whom, when, where, and how it is needed. This fact is fundamental.

GROWTH OF OFFICE WORK

The amount of office work has grown tremendously in our economy during the past several decades. This growth can be verified by (1) the increase in the production of writing paper, and (2) the increase in the number of office workers.

Since 1899, the production of writing paper—both rag content and chemical wood—has zoomed over ten times, or from 112,707 tons to an estimated 1,175,000 tons. Although the production may not indicate the consumption of writing paper, because of inventory variations from year to year, it would appear that over the years the trend is unmistakably upward. The raw material essential to office work has grown significantly. Figure 1–6 shows the data for the years 1899–1955.

The rate of growth in the number of office workers has been much greater than in that of either our total working force or our total population. For example, in the United States, during the period 1870–1940, the total working force increased less than four times, while the number of clerical workers increased fifteen times. From 1940 to 1955, the total population increased 24 per cent, the total work-

---

[7] Terry, *op. cit.*

Year	Writing Paper (Total A + B)	Rag Content A	Chemical Wood B
1955............	1,175,000	135,000	1,040,000
1954............	1,053,000	125,000	928,000
1953............	1,033,542	130,904	902,638
1952............	1,051,193	132,097	919,096
1951............	1,093,378	160,889	932,489
1950............	957,909	138,236	819,673
1949............	805,515	119,819	685,696
1939............	594,594	83,897	510,697
1929............	607,590	......	......
1919............	325,183	......	......
1909............	198,213	......	......
1899............	112,707	......	......

Source: United States Department of Commerce, Bureau of the Census, Special Reports Dated 1939, 1949, and 1956.

FIG. 1–6.   Production (in tons) of fine papers for the years, 1889–1955.

ing force expanded 38 per cent, and the number engaged in clerical occupations increased approximately 80 per cent.

The basic information concerning the growth in total population of the United States, in the total working force, and in clerical and kindred workers is set forth in Figure 1–7. The ratio of clerical to

Year	Total Population of the United States	Total Working Force	Clerical Workers	Percentage—Clerical to Total Working Force
1955.......	163,916,000	60,183,770	7,932,978	13.1
1950.......	151,230,000	55,835,340	6,866,374	12.3
1940.......	131,950,000	45,166,083	4,612,356	10.2
1930.......	123,080,000	48,829,920	4,025,324	8.2
1920.......	106,970,000	41,614,248	3,111,836	7.5
1910.......	92,410,000	38,167,336	1,718,458	4.5
1900.......	76,090,000	29,073,233	1,068,993	3.7
1890.......	63,056,438	22,735,661	801,505	3.5
1880.......	50,262,382	17,392,099	518,439	3.0
1870.......	39,904,593	12,505,923	305,502	2.4

Source: 1955 Annual Report on the Labor Force (Washington, D.C.: U.S. Department of Commerce, Bureau of the Census, March, 1956) pp. 3–5.
    United States Department of Commerce, Bureau of the Census, 1950 Census of Population—Population Vol. I (Washington, D.C.: U.S. Government Printing Office, 1953), pp. 110–12.
    United States Department of Commerce, Bureau of the Census, Sixteenth Census of the United States: 1940, Population, Vol. III (Washington, D.C.: U.S. Government Printing Office, 1943), p. 76.
    United States Department of Commerce, Bureau of the Census, Fifteenth Census of the United States: 1930, Population, Vol. V (Washington, D.C.: U.S. Government Printing Office, 1933), pp. 10–22.
    United States Department of Commerce, Bureau of the Census, Twelfth Census of the United States: 1900, Special Reports: Occupations (Washington, D.C.: U.S. Government Printing Office, 1904), pp. l and li.

FIG. 1–7.   Total population of the United States, total working force, number of clerical workers, and percentage of clerical workers to total working force for the years 1870–1955.

total working force has been calculated for each year, and these values are shown in the last column to the right. For example in 1870 the ratio of clerical to total working force was 2.4 per cent, whereas in 1955 this ratio had increased to 13.1 per cent. Each decade since 1870 has shown a greater percentage of the total working force performing clerical work. Stated differently, in 1870, about one worker in forty was an office worker; in 1955, about one in seven was an office worker.

REASONS FOR GROWTH

This increase in office work and in office personnel is attributable to many forces. The industrial growth of the United States is a major cause. With it has developed the concentration and specialization of efforts with the resultant more intricate relationships between major segments or occupations making up the working force, which circumstance pointed the need and use for more paper work. For example, during the period, 1900–1955, the number engaged in manufacturing occupations increased from 6 million to 16 million, and the number engaged in "service industries" spurted from 4 million to 12½ million. These growths emphasize the necessity and the use of more paper work. In addition, the employment of more factual information by managers has influenced the growth of the office. Demands for statistics, accurate information, and carefully prepared statements can be cited as examples. Then, too, as more information of a general but applicable nature has become available, the tendency is to get this information into the hands of interested persons thereby increasing the office work of recording and communicating this information.

Another contributory cause is the influence of a tremendous expansion in legislation, especially that pertaining to business. On the part of private enterprises, this increased government-business activity has made for more office work and employees in order to fulfill the requirements of the numerous statutes and governmental regulatory bodies. And from government's side, both the amount of governmental clerical work and the number of governmental office employees have been stimulated. There were nearly 2½ million office workers in public administration work in 1950.[8]

Finally, some portion of the growth in office work is undoubtedly

---

[8] United States Department of Commerce, Bureau of the Census, *Seventeenth Census of the United States: 1950, Population,* Vol. III (Washington, D.C.: U.S. Government Printing Office, 1954), p. 285.

due to inadequate efforts to control it. The preparation of essential paper work only, the extended use of efficient office machines, the adequate motivation of office employees, and the development of proper procedures and methods are examples of efforts which assist in reducing the amount of paper work.

WILL GROWTH CONTINUE?

Opinions differ regarding the future growth of office work. Some believe it will continue to grow at a rate exceeding that of all other types of work. They view it as basically a self-perpetuating situation —more people, more paper; more paper, more people. They point out that we have become attuned to the use of the products of the office.

In contrast, many believe that the upward trend in office work cannot continue. They insist we are drowning in a sea of paper and that some office work has become a ritual performance for its own sake. They observe that the past increase in office work has resulted in an overwhelming increase in overhead costs, and this process cannot continue indefinitely.

AMOUNT OF UNNECESSARY OFFICE WORK

Waste office work is a $5 billion loss.[9] This is a shocking amount. Stated another way, it is the equivalent of a working force of 1½ million for an entire work year. The gains to be won by eliminating just a portion of this unnecessary office work stagger the imagination.

No doubt some of this waste is the result of the rapid growth of the office, and some is due to the unawareness and indifference of some managers. But regardless of its source, the challenge to office management is quite clear.

Much of this unnecessary office work could be eliminated without serious consequences. One or both of two major approaches can be utilized: (1) determine what office work is necessary and what is not, and (2) utilize greater efficiency in performing the office work. Under the first approach the criteria becomes what office work serves effectively a definite and essential need. Opinions, of course, will differ in this evaluation. The second approach stresses such things as simplification of the office processes, training of office employees, and more office mechanization. In other words, the emphasis is on getting the work accomplished in less time, with more accuracy, and at less cost.

---

[9] Terry, *op. cit.*

OFFICE MECHANIZATION

The use of more and better office machines is believed by many to be the answer to greater efficiency in office work. With the increasing office work volume and the development of efficient office machines of all sorts, especially the high-speed electronic office machines, the affinity for office mechanization is readily understandable. Chapters 13 and 14 are devoted to office equipment and office machines, but the inclusion of certain factual information at this time appears appropriate.

For a number of years it appears that office equipment and machine expenditures have remained within a range of approximately 9–13 per cent of total expenditures for all equipment. Figure 1–8 shows these data. The figures in column (4) show the range from a low of 9.1 per cent in 1953 to a high of 13.6 per cent in 1933.

What interpretation can be given to these data? The fairly constant relationship can mean one or all of several conditions. First, mechanization is not as intensive in the office as in other areas. Intensity is measured here by dollar expenditures for machines per employee. Since the expenditures for office mechanization have kept a constant pace with total equipment expenditures, and, during the same time, the number of office employees has increased more rapidly than that of any other group, the above interpretation can be made. Had office mechanization kept pace, instead of a constant percentage, column (4) of Figure 1–9 would show an increasing percentage.

Second, if we accept the premise that in the year 1915 the office had a lower degree of equipment utilization than did the factory, it can be stated that office mechanization lags behind that of factory mechanization. However, this premise would be difficult to prove, but in judging what the office of 1915 was like and that at this same time assembly line production and precision machines were employed in the factory, the deduction seems logical.

Third, many office techniques have remained practically the same for several decades. For example, the work of writing mechanically has undergone few fundamental changes, whereas basic cutting tools in factory production have witnessed tremendous improvement. Better means of performing basic operations in the office seem to be required for significant progress in the future.

THE FUTURE OF OFFICE WORK

Many executives believe the office will become more mechanized and more office work will be accomplished electronically.[10] Some be-

---

[10] *Ibid.*

(1) Year	(2) Capital Expenditures New Equipment (000,000 $)	(3) Production of Office Computing, Accounting, and Typewriting Machines (000,000 $)	(4) Col (3) Divided by Col (2)
1955...............	6,970	...	...
1954...............	6,707	...	...
1953...............	7,080	643	9.1%
1952...............	6,623	...	...
1951...............	6,411	...	...
1950...............	5,151	...	...
1949...............	4,821	...	...
1948...............	5,515	...	...
1947...............	5,153	558	10.8
1946...............	3,712	...	...
1945...............	2,173	...	...
1944...............	....	...	...
1943...............	....	...	...
1942...............	....	...	...
1941...............	....	...	...
1940...............	1,619	...	...
1939...............	1,230	144	11.7
1938...............	1,102	...	...
1937...............	1,534	183	11.9
1936...............	1,172	...	...
1935...............	930	120	12.9
1934...............	713	...	...
1933...............	493	67	13.6
1932...............	456	...	...
1931...............	781	78	10.0
1930...............	1,292	...	...
1929...............	1,777	172	9.7
1928...............	1,455	...	...
1927...............	1,406	162	11.5
1926...............	1,535	...	...
1925...............	1,384	161	11.6
1924...............	1,260	...	...
1923...............	1,427	147	10.3
1922...............	1,009	...	...
1921...............	971	95	10.2
1920...............	1,916	...	...
1919...............	1,409	136	9.7
1918...............	1,547	...	...
1917...............	1,231	...	...
1916...............	703	...	...
1915...............	428	...	...
1914...............	....	55	...

Source: Column (2) from United States Department of Commerce, Historical Statistics, 1955. Column (3) from U.S. Facts for Industry, January 14, 1955, Series H 35 R 03; and Census of Manufacturers, 1921–47.

FIG. 1–8. Expenditures for total new equipment and for selected office machines for the available years, 1914–1955.

lieve that paper itself as an instrument will be supplanted to a great extent by drums, tapes, and wires. Payroll checks might be replaced with information fed by wire from the emloyer's machine directly into the bank's machine for credit to the individual employee's account. Collectors will receive payment by drawing on their customer's checking account. Whether these things come about is conjectural. The trend, however, toward greater mechanization appears plausible.

As office mechanization increases, it would seem that clerical personnel will become more technically proficient, require more training, and become more productive. Real wages are likely to increase,[11] but the many problems stemming from the relationship of employee to a machine, specialization of work, and employee work satisfaction are likely to be multiplied.

Increased emphasis will probably be placed upon analysis and interpretation of information made available by the office. As more facts are needed and can be made available within a reasonable period, the task of determining what data are necessary, and why, will take on new and increasing meaning. But the facilitating and service elements of office work will remain of prime importance. Determining and providing essential information effectively, and thus contributing to the success of the entire enterprise, will continue to be the task and the challenge of office management.

QUESTIONS

1. Do you feel the analogy is sound to compare the office to the total enterprise as the nerve or brain center is to the entire body? Elaborate on your answer.
2. Would you say that office work is an end in itself? Why or why not?
3. If no direct profit is realized from office, why is it performed?
4. Is office work always performed in an office? Discuss.
5. In your own words explain the meaning of Figure 1–5.
6. Give examples to show your agreement or your disagreement with each of the following:
    a) Most office work is performed more efficiently than most factory work.
    b) Office work is vital in the execution of present-day business.
    c) Office work is becoming less and less important as the economy of the United States changes.
7. Can office work do a service job without being facilitating? Can it be facilitating without doing a service job? Explain.
8. As you see it, briefly discuss what are probably the most important reasons why a larger and larger proportion of office workers are women.
9. To the office manager what are the implications with regards to the changing percentage of men versus women clerical employees?
10. What are the major reasons for the increase in the number of office workers during the past fifty to sixty years.

---

[11] Real wages are the goods and services that money wages will buy at any given time.

11. In your opinion does the statement, "The success of an enterprise depends upon effectiveness in executing the paper work," apply equally to—
    a) Large and small enterprises?
    b) Various types, i.e., manufacturing, service, and governmental enterprises?
    c) Local and national enterprises?
    Explain your answers.

12. What is your opinion regarding the future growth of office work?

CASE PROBLEMS

CASE 1–1.   THE OLSON-HALL COMPANY

Recently consummated is the merger between the Olson Company and Hall Products, Inc., to form the new Olson-Hall Company. At the time of the merger, the Olson Company employed 125 office and 807 factory employees, and Hall Products, Inc., 15 office and 128 factory employees. Both companies manufacture a similar line of products, and Mr. Robert Tiffany, president of the former Olson Company and now of the Olson-Hall Company, believes the merger will prove beneficial to both companies. He considers the Hall Products, Inc., operation as quite profitable—for the past three years its percentage of profits on sales was higher than that of the Olson Company. The physical plant and offices of each of the merged companies are located about three miles apart in the same city. Mr. Nathaniel Rothsyck, president of the former Hall Products, Inc., is retiring and does not wish to be active in the new company.

Assisting Mr. Robert Tiffany in the administering of the Olson-Hall Company is an executive committee consisting, in addition to Mr. Tiffany, of Mr. Bernard Young, vice-president of production, Mr. Carl Brand, vice-president of finance and records, and Mr. Harold Flowers, vice-president of sales. All the committee members except Mr. Flowers are former Olson Company executives. Mr. Flowers was sales manager of the former Hall Products, Inc.

At the suggestion of Mr. Bernard Young, and subsequent approval of the executive committee, a program has been instituted requiring the production foremen of the former Hall Products, Inc., plant to make out daily records and reports on production, spoilage, and material usage; labor reports; tool requisitions; and machine work load assignments. Mr. Young believes such information is necessary to operate the plant effectively, and it is a practice followed for many years at the old Olson Company. However, after four weeks of operation under the new program, the foremen of the Hall Products, Inc., plant have complained bitterly. They claim that they are overloaded with paper work, that they can't concentrate on production, and that such records were never prepared before by them, yet the plant operated efficiently as Mr. Rothsyck had told them on many occasions.

Mr. Carl Brand, mainly for economy reasons, intended to establish the main office of the Olson-Hall Company in the old Olson Company building. However, three of the four office supervisors from the former Hall Products, Inc., were women—one was a key person in performing the office work. Since it was a long-standing policy of the former Olson Company to employ only men for supervisory jobs, Mr. Brand was faced with the decision of how best to handle the situation.

At the present time each production department of the Olson-Hall Company operates on a separate budget and maintains its own inventory, submitting a report on Friday of each week. Sometimes a department requires materials from another department, and a transfer order becomes necessary. This involves a trip to Mr. Silverman's office (head of supplies and services), which is located in the former Olson Company building. Once his signature is obtained, the order goes through the inner-company mail to the Production Planning Board, and from there to the head of the department presently owning the material. The transfer order is then sent back through the inner-company mail to the department head requesting the material. The department head then makes his own arrangements for the physical transfer of the goods. Usually this means he uses the services of one or two of the men in his department. This arrangement normally requires about three days to get the required material into the hands of the requesting department.

PROBLEMS:

1. From the viewpoint of paper work, what is the major problem here?

2. In your opinion, is the office work, in connection with the transferring of materials from one department to another, satisfactory? Discuss.

3. What suggestions do you offer Mr. Brand for handling the women office supervisors? Elaborate on your answer.

4. What over-all action do you recommend this company take? Why?

Chapter · 2

The Role of Office Management

Plenty of people have a good aim in life, but a lot of them
don't pull the trigger.

—ANONYMOUS

THE EXTENT and distinguishing characteristics of
office work, as described in Chapter 1, suggest the essentiality of its
proper management in order to obtain effective office operations. The
managing of office work so that it is accomplished with the right personnel, in the right manner, and at the right time, place, and cost
constitutes the essentials of office management.

THE MEANING OF MANAGEMENT

The field of management is very broad; it encompasses all enterprises, including those of business, government, school, public utilities, and social organizations. Management has a universal presence,
and its influence upon human welfare and most activities is tremendous.

Management is vital for the success of most enterprises. In a few
instances, chance or a happening of favorable events play a significant
role in the success, but even in these cases, sooner or later, management emerges as the essential for continued satisfactory accomplishment. Management contributes to the effectiveness of human efforts,
points out improved applications of technology, and provides for orderliness in human endeavors.

The word "management" stems from the Italian *maneggiare,*
which means "to train horses," or literally "to handle." The French
words *ménager,* meaning "to direct a household," i.e., "to economize,"
and *ménage,* "an act of guiding or leading," have also influenced the
present-day concept of the term "management." Hence, based on lin-

19

guistics, it can be stated that management has to do with handling, economizing, guiding, and directing.

As knowledge, techniques, and skill of management have evolved, many specialized areas of management have developed. Examples include factory management, sales management, personnel management, finance management, farm management, city management, credit management, and office management. Although the areas of application differ, the concept of management is the same regardless of its area of application. That is, management is a universal concept. Furthermore, it is made up of definite functions or activities. These are discussed in the immediate following pages. The discussion, however, is centered around office management since this is the subject area of this book.

OBJECTIVES

To clarify the meaning of office management, it is helpful to begin with consideration for the predetermined objective or objectives. Office management concerns the achievement of certain desired goals or results, and basically the efforts of the office manager center around ways and means to accomplish these goals. There is a mission to perform, a project to initiate, a service to supply.

The predetermined objectives may be specific or general, written or unwritten, long- or short-term, temporary or permanent, or applicable to certain segments of the office only. Whatever their form or content, these predetermined objectives are set and accepted, for without them the meaning of management becomes nebulous and there is no satisfactory basis for determining the effectiveness or management.

To provide examples of predetermined objectives of office management, the following are presented:

1. To furnish all necessary and complete information to whom, when, and where it is required for the efficient operation of the enterprise.

2. To provide adequate records and reports at lowest possible cost.

3. To assist the enterprise in keeping competitive.

4. To supply accurate paper work and assist in rendering service to the customer.

5. To make better and better written records at lower and lower costs.

Such statements may sound purely academic, but they serve a practical purpose in that they point out the sought-for goal. They define the target. Other objectives, subordinate but related to the over-all goal, can be used to designate the aims for specific office groups or individuals.

In the office, predetermined objectives can be conveniently classified as pertaining primarily to (1) service, (2) social responsibilities, or (3) profit. Service is of foremost importance in the objectives of office management because, as pointed out in Chapter 1, office work is service work; it is intended to assist others in doing their work more effectively. Also of significance is the objective dealing with social responsibilities which stress the attainment of the goal in accordance with certain moral and ethical codes as set forth by the industry and society in which the enterprise operates. Lastly, predetermined objectives emphasizing profit or gain to the owners or to the operators can be assisted tremendously by office management. Performing the office work more effectively can mean more profit inasmuch as less expenditures for clerical work are made. Greater emphasis of the importance of the office to management and profit is in order. Acceptance of this obligation by office management members would strengthen their status and identify their role.[1]

OFFICE MANAGERIAL FUNCTIONS

Objectives can be achieved only through action. The determining, initiating, and carrying out of definite and purposeful actions to achieve a predetermined objective is the content of management. This content is made up of a process—called the management process—consisting of fundamental functions or activities.

These fundamental functions of management include:

1. *Planning*—to lay out a means or a course of action giving consideration to the factors influencing the particular situation.

2. *Organizing*—to distribute the planned work to be done among the members of the work group, establish proper work relationships among them, and supply the proper work environment.

3. *Actuating*—to start and maintain the desire of the members of the work group to execute their respective work enthusiastically in order to achieve the predetermined objective in accordance with the plan.

---

[1] The concept of profit as the objective of any enterprise or segment of an enterprise is actually quite limited. Profit, as such, can be the indirect or direct aim, depending upon the thinking of the particular company involved. Profit is residual in nature, a by-product resulting from goals such as rendering the greatest service, providing the most reliable quality of product or service, or being the lowest-cost producer of a product or service. In a private, competitive economy, profits are necessary for the long-range existence of most enterprises.

4. *Controlling*—to determine what is accomplished, evaluate it, and apply corrective measures, if needed, to insure results in keeping with the plan.

These four fundamental functions are the distinguishing characteristics of management. They apply universally to production management, sales management, finance management, or office management. Specifically, they are the means used by an office manager to perform office management. They identify the office manager from the non-office manager.

OFFICE MANAGEMENT IS A DISTINCT ACTIVITY

It follows, therefore, that like all management, office management is an activity. It is a distinct entity, it can be studied, and proficiency in it can be attained. Management is not a person or a group of people. One who performs the activity of management is a manager. Hence, those who perform this activity of management in the office work area are office managers.

The concept of management as an activity and of those performing this activity as managers helps to clarify thinking on this subject. Unfortunately, many common expressions used to describe the work of the office manager are not very helpful. For example, identifying an office manager as the one who "runs" an office or the person who sees that office work is accomplished does not provide much assistance. Also the condition that a person has subordinates reporting to him does not make that person a manager in the true meaning of management. Having a group of faithful followers is not a guarantee that management exists.

To reiterate, an office manager, to qualify as an office manager, performs four fundamental functions making up the management process. The use of this management process marks the essential difference between a clerk and an office manager, or between an accountant and the manager of the accounting department. Knowing how to write letters, for example, is not sufficient knowledge to manage the correspondence department. Office management is a distinct entity, it is an activity in itself, and it requires the use of certain knowledges, skills, and practices.

OFFICE MANAGEMENT PLANNING

The fundamental function of planning in office management includes the methodic technique of looking ahead and selecting a course from among alternative actions in order to accomplish a predetermined aim. It is a foreseeing action—related facts and assumptions are considered and established for the purpose of determining what must be done, when, by whom, where, and how. Planning requires visualization of future action. It includes determination of proposed actions and knowing what steps will produce the desired results and in what sequence they should be taken.

Effective planning necessitates creative, reflective, and imaginative thinking. Such vision marks the progressive office manager, and in today's office, planning is rapidly becoming even more and more important. It is the core of much modern managerial thinking. Perhaps more than ever before office management planning contains a dynamic element due to the pace at which technology and innovations are being made available to the office and introduced into our economy. In these changes, office managers should contribute, not simply adjust, to the plans, thus adding to the progress and advancing the status of the office management field. Good planning emphasizes prevention rather than correction of delays. It anticipates and defines future possible difficulties and makes provision to care for them.

OFFICE MANAGEMENT ORGANIZING

Organizing means literally to make organic—i.e., serviceable or helpful—by means of establishing a structure or a definite operating relationship among various components of the entire entity. An office manager organizes the work for which he is responsible by apportioning it in an orderly fashion among the various structural units for achieving the task. The personnel for each structural unit are selected, delegated appropriate authority, and held responsible for the satisfactory completion of their respective work. In addition, the personnel are provided proper workplaces, that is, the appropriate equipment, machines, lighting, and area. In brief, organizing deals with the establishing of proper relationships among the components of the work to be done, designating the people who are going to do it, and providing the work environment in which the tasks will be done.

Knowledge and skill in organizing are vital in office management. Organizing makes it possible for the office manager to spread his influence and to get goals accomplished effectively through a group. Organizing is a key to group efficiency. It helps the group serve as a unit with all its efforts blended together toward a specific objective.

OFFICE MANAGEMENT ACTUATING

The fundamental function of actuating includes the creating and continuing of the desire by each member of the work group to achieve the objective in accordance with plans. The work of planning and organizing does not accomplish the predetermined goal. The plan must be put into effect through the organized relationships. This requires people working willingly at prescribed tasks and at given times and places. To accomplish this, people must be properly motivated to work along these guided lines. This activity constitutes managerial actuating.

The type of person, the component activity to be performed, the facilities provided, and the manager's judgment determine the measures utilized to execute this actuating function. Leadership, human-relations practices, sound selection and training programs, and proper communication are among the more common means.

Actuating concerns intangible subject areas, but success in these areas brings high rewards. When members of the work group are inspired to use their highest attainable skills and capacities, when they are genuinely interested in their work, when they are enthusiastic about accomplishing their assigned task, and when they believe in and understand the plan and how the objective is to be accomplished, the burden of management is lightened and the accomplishments attained frequently are startling even to the experienced manager proficient in actuating efforts.

OFFICE MANAGEMENT CONTROLLING

A long-standing practice of a manager is to check results in order to see if the work is progressing satisfactorily and in keeping with what is expected. This "follow-up" is an essential part of management and is included under the term "controlling." The best plan, accompanied by proper organizing and actuating may not bring about the desired results. Variances, misunderstandings, and unexpected events may occur. Such contingencies must be quickly ascertained so that corrective action can be taken.

In order to apply controlling to any activity, measurable performance factors must be established. These include such things as quantity, quality, cost, or time bases. The actual performance is compared with the expected or pre-established standard. For example, the number of payroll cards processed per hour is compared to the number expected for acceptable performance, and deviations from the established base are subject to analysis and evaluation.

Much of the office manager's contribution to the entire enterprise is in the area of controlling. Records and information help provide answers to the question, "How well is the work being done?" However, controlling within the office area is the chief consideration of this book, since it is an essential part of office management. Controlling must be exercised by the office manager to carry out his office management activity successfully. In instances where the office manager is in charge of all office work, some of which is done by people other than those in the office, the function of office management controlling takes on added importance. Also, when people in organizational units throughout the enterprise decide certain matters involving paper work, the problem of proper control in office management and how to maintain it becomes one of major significance.

INTERDEPENDENCE OF FUNDAMENTAL FUNCTIONS

The four fundamental functions of office management are interdependent—they should never be thought of as being mutually exclusive. Each depends upon the others. Actually there is no sharp delineation designating the terminating of one function and the starting of another in the process. For instance, planning constitutes a part of determining the work-to-be-done components, an activity included under organizing. And the establishing of proper relationships among the organizational units (organizing) has an influence of controlling.

Nor is there a definite sequence of the functions which the office manager must follow. In presenting the fundamental functions, the logical sequence of planning, organizing, actuating, and controlling was followed. But a manager performs only the function or functions required by the situation and in the order deemed advisable. Thus, actuating efforts may be employed, followed by planning and subsequently by controlling.

PROFESSIONAL ROLE OF THE OFFICE MANAGER

Recognition and application of the office management process by those in the office management field help to raise the status of office management and to give those practicing it a professional standing. To an office executive, training and experience are beneficial, but they become of even greater usefulness when the approach and application of the management process is employed.

The management process of planning, organizing, actuating, and controlling gives distinguishing substance to management, points up the need and application of specialized knowledge, stresses skill in applying this specialized knowledge, and sets management apart as an entity. Acceptance of the process serves as a practical basis for guidance in preparing people for office management work both in schools and in various enterprises. Furthermore, the necessary, meaningful management system of thought and practices is provided.

OFFICE MANAGEMENT AND THE BASIC ELEMENTS

A manager has six basic elements to which he can apply his activity of management. These basic elements, commonly referred to as

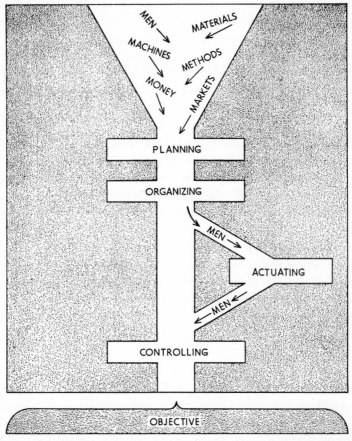

FIG. 2–1. To achieve the objective of the office, the six M's—Men, Materials, Machines, Methods, Money, and Market—are subjected to planning, organizing, and controlling; and the men to actuating.

the "six M's," include Men, Materials, Machines, Methods, Money, and Markets. In other words, a manager by the application of the management functions, i.e., planning, organizing, actuating, and controlling, determines what is done with these basic elements.

Figure 2–1 shows this concept in graphic form. To manage effectively requires a knowledge of the objective, i.e., knowing what is to be accomplished is a prime requisite. In most cases, planning helps to set forth the objective. With the stated goal as a background, an office manager utilizes the six M's in achieving the objective. These basic "M's" are intertwined as shown at the top of the figure. They are subjected to planning and organizing. The men, or members of the work group, are actuated to want to achieve the objective, and all the basic elements are submitted to controlling to help insure that the end result will be the stated objective.

DEFINITION OF OFFICE MANAGEMENT

In Chapter 1, office work was defined as the "verbal transmission of information and the producing of written records and reports . . . ."[2] Keeping this in mind to avoid redundancy, office management can be defined as *the planning, organizing, actuating, and controlling of office work and of those performing it so as to achieve the predetermined objectives.* The predetermined objectives include such things as getting the office work accomplished within reasonable limits of time, effort, and cost expenditures; supplying adequate information (both written and verbal) to manage effectively; and implementing the performance of other major functions of the enterprise by providing the required service and facilitating activity of written and verbal information.

Several observations should be noted concerning the definition given above. First, office management is considered in the broad, inclusive sense. It includes managerial efforts over office work anywhere in an enterprise. It is not confined to efforts of the person called "the office manager" or some similar title, nor to the work performed in "the office" only.

Second, office management is not a purely mechanistic activity. The effective application of the fundamental functions of office management is fraught with great difficulties. No fixed formula can be followed in all cases. There is an art of management as well as a science or body of knowledge of management.[3] The art of management deals with skill or the application of knowledge. This is of especial importance in management. One may have all the facts and pertinent relationships but fail to use them effectively due to a lack of applying the art of management. Good judgment, understanding, ability to work with people, practice in management, and an intense desire to succeed in management work are the keys to acquiring proficiency in the art of management.

---

[2] Page 10.

[3] Science and scientific management are discussed in detail in the following chapter.

Office management necessitates the ability to make decisions. Each of the fundamental functions of management requires decision making in its execution. Determining the course of actions to follow (planning) or appraising a situation (controlling) involves decision making. Decisions should be based on adequate facts, and these facts are often difficult to obtain. The successful manager carefully distinguishes between facts and opinions and utilizes only those data which are definitely related and pertinent to the problem at hand. Frequently all the facts cannot be secured, in which case the best decision based on the known facts should be made with the realization that future adjustments may be necessary. Normally, decisions should be based on a logical or reasoned approach, with due regard given to the intent of the enterprise.

Lastly, office management members must be able to exercise ingenuity. To a considerable extent, all managerial progress is dependent upon the creation and the development of successful ideas. Most improvements start as ideas—for example, a better way of performing an office task, a simplified means of securing applicants, and the rearrangement of data on the paper form to make calculating easier. Such ideas stem from observation and thinking and are not subordinated to custom, tradition, or experience. In many offices the employees are encouraged to turn in suggestions or ideas which will help to improve the office work. While it is true that, in this case, the employees originate the ideas, the fact remains that the ideas must be analyzed and implemented by managers.

OFFICE MANAGEMENT ACTIVITIES

Office work should always be appraised by the results which it accomplishes; to consider it in and of itself leads only to confusion. To reiterate, office work is the means to a desired end; it is not the end in itself. There is little value in records and communications as such. They are made to expedite the work of producing or selling the product or of giving better service.

The activities included in office management are quite numerous, among which are the following:

I. Maintaining adequate office services and communication facilities.
   1. See that correspondence work—stenographic and typing—is performed.
   2. File records and reports.

      3. Handle incoming and outgoing mail.

      4. Supply reception and messenger services.

II. Determining the complete course of action to accomplish the office work.

      1. Keep informed of latest developments in performing office work.

      2. Select office methods and procedures.

      3. Co-ordinate the work of the office with that of the nonoffice.

      4. Maintain proper balance among the various office activities.

      5. Specify and purchase office furniture, machines, and supplies.

      6. Select the office location.

      7. Arrange the office layout—location of office furniture and machines.

      8. Determine effective work environment—adequate lighting, elimination of noise, and proper ventilation.

III. Providing an effective office organization.

      1. Apportion the work among the organizational units.

      2. Identify the organizational units.

      3. Establish definite and known relationships among organizational units.

      4. Know the individual jobs in the office.

      5. Assign proper personnel to organizational units.

      6. Delegate authority.

      7. Fix responsibility among personnel.

      8. Provide for proper work facilities.

IV. Inspiring the office personnel to do their best of which they are capable.

      1. Motivate office employees.

      2. Give adequate supervision.

      3. Analyze and evaluate office jobs.

      4. Select new office employees.

      5. Give office training programs.

      6. Provide adequate communication among office employees and between office and nonoffice units.

      7. Administer office salary plan.

      8. Promote office safety.

V. Measuring and evaluating quantity and quality of office work.

      1. Apply work simplification to office work.

      2. Time study office operations.

      3. Establish standards for office work.

      4. Maintain quality of office work.

5. Schedule and dispatch office work.
6. Write office manuals.
7. Keep office costs within acceptable limits.
8. Prepare office budget.

EXTENT OF OFFICE MANAGEMENT ACTIVITIES

In order for all office management activities to be carried out to their full extent, it is necessary that top management members recognize office management as a vital activity in the efficient over-all operation of the enterprise. Not only must the top managers believe fully in the importance of managing office work but they must also insist that effective ways and means of performing the necessary office work be found and applied.

Office management, like other special branches of management, reflects the light of the top management of the enterprise. If top managers, for example, believe that an office manager should confine his efforts, without exception, to the handling of the mail, the supervising of correspondence work, and the providing of reception and communicating services, it is quite obvious that that is what the office manager will do. He may venture, strictly on his own, into other activities, but by and large he will try to please and satisfy the top managers.

While there is no definite line of demarcation, it is nevertheless generally agreed that to employ an office manager an enterprise should have a minimum of fifty clerks. This figure may be increased or decreased, depending on the type of work performed by the clerks. If all the office work is identical or very similar, the number of clerks required may be higher. On the other hand, if a whole cycle of office activity is carried out by twenty-five clerks and their work is essential to the success of the enterprise, it is very probable that an office manager can be employed advantageously.

OFFICE MANAGEMENT IN THE SMALL OFFICE

In the United States there are many small offices, government figures showing nearly nine out of every ten offices employ seven or less. Characteristically an employee in a small office does many different clerical jobs, including opening the mail, answering correspondence, computing and checking, handling the payroll, and answering the telephone. Also the volume of the work may not warrant the entire time of one executive to office management activities. Under such conditions the management of the small office may be divided among several officers, and this may result in each individual officer subordinating the office work to his main executive function. As a consequence, there is frequently a curtailment of possible office management activities or a lack of utilizing to the fullest extent all possibilities for improvement.

However, the practices and principles of good office management are the same no matter what the size of the office. It is only the application of the practices and principles that change, but this is commonly not as clearly defined for the small as for the large office. Handling accounts payable is basically the same work in a small as in a large office. For example, the receipt of the goods is verified, the due date is noted, the check payment is written and mailed to the vendor. With its particular volume, the small office must adopt the best procedure for handling this work, determine who is going to do what, and check the results. In the large office it is the same, but the means of doing it may differ because more accounts payable and more employees are included.

WHO IS THE OFFICE MANAGER?

Since office work is present in every phase and level of management, it follows that most executives have something to do with office work, although this is not their primary responsibility. Any department head or other executive can improve the management of the office work under his direct supervision by applying the principles of office management as developed in this book. He need not necessarily have a large clerical staff. However, when the scope and extent of activities are limited, the degree of specialization may be somewhat reduced.

The scope of the office manager's job is quite flexible. Strictly speaking, the one in charge of managing office work is the office manager. As already stated, in some enterprises the office manager has charge of the work done by all the departments of the office; in other enterprises, he is the general manager not only of the office work in the office but of all office work, whether it is done in or out of the office.

In actual practice, the one in charge of managing office work is not always titled "office manager." He may have the title of "controller," "auditor," "head accountant," "chief clerk," "systems analyst," or he may have no title at all. In a nation-wide study conducted by the author, the title of the person in charge of paper work was found to be as follows:

Title Used	*Used by*
Controller	22.1%
Office manager	7.8
Vice-president	7.1
Treasurer	4.7
Miscellaneous titles	36.9

That is, the title "controller" is three times as prevalent as that of "office manager." In about one out of every three enterprises, a miscellaneous title is used. The terms "controller" and "office manager" are found more commonly in manufacturing, wholesaling, and retailing enterprises; "vice-president" is relatively most common in financial enterprises; and "treasurer" in transportation and public utility enterprises.[4]

From the same study, information was found concerning the organizational level of the person with the title of "office manager." In nearly one half of the respondents, the office manager is located in the top-intermediate organizational level. Another 20 per cent of the respondents are in the top bracket, while the remainder are in the low-intermediate or low organizational levels.

BASIC QUALIFICATIONS OF AN OFFICE MANAGER

The successful execution of the office manager's work requires probably a broader background and scope of activity than are required for most other executives in an enterprise. The office manager must have a general knowledge of every major part of the enterprise, and he must have a very intimate knowledge of some portions. He must solve problems involving practically every activity of the enterprise. He must be a combination serviceman, research worker, diplomat, engineer, interpreter, salesman, motivator of people, and—probably most important—a manager with a genuine insight and ability in managerial work.

It is extremely difficult to list and to describe all the qualifications which are necessary to satisfy completely the requirements of an office manager's job. However, to understand more clearly the requirements needed, as well as the type of individual probably best suited for office-management work, it can be stated that the fundamental qualifications

---

[4] A nation-wide, representative study, *Paperwork in American Business,* by George R. Terry for Ditto, Inc., Chicago, Illinois, April, 1957. It should be noted that titles, in and of themselves, can be misleading, and their concept varies among different enterprises. In the study a check was made to see if the respondent, due to the title of his own position, permitted this situation to bias or influence his response. No such bias was disclosed.

include: executive ability, a practical background, managerial training, ability to express oneself, an open attitude, curiosity, creativeness, sound judgment, sales ability, patience, emotional control, and co-operativeness.

THE CHALLENGE OF OFFICE MANAGEMENT

Opportunities are abundant in the field of office management. The rapid growth in the amount of work and in the number doing it have emphasized the need for managers trained in this field. Also, there is much to be done in order to advance the management of office work and to raise it to the level warranted by its importance and essentiality. As the importance and contributions of the office with reference to the entire enterprise gain greater recognition, the status of the qualified office manager should increase.

Challenges are indeed numerous for the executive specailizing in the managing of office work. The following list is representative rather than exhaustive. Among the significant challenges is the—

1. Careful analysis and evolvement of remedial actions for coping with mounting office costs.
2. Preparation for the "electronic office."
3. Unwarranted application of office mechanization in certain areas.
4. Extent of specialization in individual office jobs.
5. Reduction in the amount of unnecessary paper work performed.
6. Development of better means of motivating office employees.
7. Increasing the number of office executives with the management viewpoint.
8. Greater delegation of authority by the office manager to his subordinates.
9. Attracting and acquiring the better graduates from schools for office jobs.
10. Simplification of office practices and operations.
11. Establishment of more and better office work standards.
12. Upgrading the status of office management.

There exists in companies almost everywhere vast possibilities for qualified executives. This is especially true for office managers. The future is brilliant for the qualified office manager who recognizes the real importance of office work, can manage it effectively, and can contribute to the successful operation of the entire enterprise.

QUESTIONS

1. If a person performs only a portion of the activity defined as management, is it satisfactory to designate that person as a manager? Substantiate your answer.

2. In your opinion is there any relationship between—
   a) Planning and organizing?
   b) Planning and controlling?
   c) Organizing and actuating?

3. Is management necessary? Why?

4. Do you agree with the statement: "To achieve objectives requires action. This being true, planning can be considered nonproductive because nothing is achieved simply by planning." Elaborate on your answer.

5. Why is knowledge of the objective the first requisite of effective management?

6. Explain how the size of an enterprise affects the extent of office management activities.

7. Visit an office with which you are familiar and find out its major objectives. What do you deduct from the information obtained?

8. The office manager of company "ABC" is not in the top management group of his company. What might he do in order to increase his managerial status?

9. Office management is defined by some as the accomplishment of office work by others. Does acceptance of this definition mean that actuating office employees represents and is the same as office management? Discuss.

10. Discuss the personal qualifications and experience desirable for the job of office manager.

11. Do you feel that the future possibilities and opportunities of office management, compared with those in other fields of management, are (a) greater, (b) about the same, or (c) smaller? Give reasons for your answer.

12. Briefly relate your reaction to this statement: "The key to being an expert office manager is to know how to practice effective controlling. It is the results that count and managerial controlling gets the results."

CASE PROBLEMS

CASE 2–1. THE SULLIVAN-CULBERT COMPANY

This company, a manufacturer of kitchen utensils, has enjoyed a considerable increase in sales during the past twelve months. Many new items have been added to the company's line of products, and distribution has been expanded to a national basis, resulting in the selling of a large number of accounts by the company. Sales are made direct to dealers. The officers of the company include Mr. Daniel Sullivan, president; Mr. Neal Culbert, vice-president; and Mr. Theodore Buffington, secretary-treasurer.

Mr. Culbert, in charge of sales, has received many dealer complaints during the past several months. Delays in billing, incorrect invoices, and mistakes in pricing and discounts are mentioned most frequently.

Mr. Culbert has spoken several times about these complaints to Mr. Buffington, who is in charge of the office. Mr. Buffington states that there is a sufficient number of employees in the office to get the work out promptly and correctly. The difficulty is that they just don't work. He has repeatedly cautioned them about the quality of their work, but it does no good. Office help is difficult to find, so he cannot be too severe. Probably the whole condition is a part of growing pains which the company is now experiencing.

The office force totals twelve men and forty-two women. Most of the men have been with the company four years or longer, while nearly 80 per cent of the women have been with the company less than one year—some 40 per cent having been hired within the last four months.

Mr. Culbert also spoke with Mr. Sullivan about the complaints and the general condition of the office. Subsequently Mr. Sullivan had a talk with Mr. Buffington, at which time it was decided that Mr. Buffington should procede to correct the office situation using all reasonable and necessary means.

Mr. Buffington took the following measures:

1. Hired an additional six male clerks and eight female typists.

2. Announced by means of a personal note to each office employee that the quality of the office work must be improved and pointed out that far too many errors were being made.

3. Stated that all office supervisors would become working supervisors in order to locate sources of mistakes in papers being prepared. Any employee caught preparing an incorrect billing or an invoice would be given 5 demerits by his supervisor. A total of 15 demerits means automatic employment termination.

4. Appointed Mr. Herbert Welsh as his assistant to whom all office supervisors would report. However, carefully stated that decisions involving major issues remain his (Mr. Buffington's) perogative.

5. Indicated a greater activity on his (Mr. Buffington's) part in work of credit extensions, collecting accounts, and trying to keep sufficient cash and funds on hand to meet the needs of the expanding business.

6. Made it clear that if quality of the office work did not improve, changes in personnel would be made.

7. Informed both Mr. Sullivan and Mr. Culbert that adequate means have been taken to improve the management of the office work.

PROBLEMS:

1. What is the main issue in this case?

2. What is your opinion regarding the measures taken by Mr. Buffington?

3. After talking with Mr. Buffington, do you believe Mr. Culbert did the correct thing in seeing Mr. Sullivan? Why?

4. What is your recommendation to Mr. Sullivan? Discuss.

CASE 2–2. THE NATIONAL INSURANCE COMPANY

Mr. James R. Fisher has just turned in his resignation as office manager of this company's branch office in Houston, Texas. He plans to open a gift shop in Gallup, New Mexico. He is fifty-three years old; his salary has been $600 per month; he has been with National for nearly seventeen years and is considered a very satisfactory office manager by the company, which regrets his leaving.

The main office of the National Insurance Company is located in San Francisco, California, with branch offices maintained throughout the United States. In the Houston branch office, for example, there are sixty-five office employees who send out premium notices and credit payments, handle correspondence, write policy forms, and perform various other types of office work in connection with the insurance business.

Of the office employees in the Houston office, about 55 per cent are women between the ages of eighteen and thirty and 25 per cent are women between thirty and fifty-five years of age. The remaining employees are men, the majority of whom are less than thirty years of age.

The immediate problem faced by the company is to secure a replacement for Mr. Fisher. Among the various possibilities, three candidates are considered to be the best; they are Miss Hilda Baker, Mr. Roland Stiles, and Mr. Anthony Cerno.

Miss Hilda Baker, age forty-eight, has been with the company for twenty-one years. She is supervisor of the correspondence department of the Houston office and is well liked by the employees. She has demonstrated extremely high ability in finding and hiring competent stenographers and typists. Currently her salary is $4,800 per year.

Mr. Roland Stiles, age thirty-one, has been employed for the past two years as office manager for a wholesale grocer in New Orleans, Louisiana. Prior to this he held, for four years, the job of accountant for the same company. There are thirteen people in the office. Mr. Stiles was graduated from high school and college (liberal arts), served 34 months in the United States Army with overseas service, and at present receives a salary of $4,200 per year. He wishes to make a change in order to gain advancement.

Mr. Anthony Cerno, age forty-four, is one of the successful field representatives of the National Insurance Company. At present he spends the majority of his time out of Houston. He wishes to remain in town with his family, and this, plus a desire for a change, has prompted him to ask for serious consideration in filling Mr. Fisher's job. Mr. Cerno now receives approximately $6,000 a year and is considered a reliable, honest, and loyal employee. He was graduated from high school, attended Lorenzo Business College for one year, and has been employed as a correspondent, cost clerk, payroll clerk, and at several sales jobs before coming with National about eleven years ago.

PROBLEMS:

1. Which candidate do you feel should be given Mr. Fisher's job? Carefully point out and develop the major reasons for your selection.

2. From an ideal viewpoint and based on the facts given, what training and background do you think a candidate should have for a branch-office manager's job with the National Insurance Company?

Chapter · 3

Scientific Office Management

There will always be a Frontier where there is an open mind
and a willing hand.

— CHARLES F. KETTERING

IN APPLYING the management process, an office manager can follow one of several general approaches. Among these are
the scientific approach, the conventional approach, the observational
approach, and the systematic approach. Office managers who use the
scientific approach, or what is commonly termed "the scientific
method," are scientific office managers. They utilize the scientific approach and accumulated knowledge resulting from the application of
the scientific method. Most of this chapter is devoted to scientific office management because it has done more to advance and improve
the status of office management than has any other approach. Scientific knowledge and methodology are the foundation of modern efficient office management.

MANAGEMENT AND SCIENCE

Owing chiefly to social and personnel influences, scientific knowledge about management cannot qualify unreservedly as a science in
the same sense that mathematics and chemistry are considered sciences. Yet there exists a scientific body of knowledge in the field of
management for which general principles have been developed as in
the physical sciences. Also, it is entirely feasible and practical to apply
the scientific method to management problems.

"Science" is a body of knowledge discovered by means of the scientific method, which knowledge has been accumulated and accepted
in reference to the discovery or understanding of truth. The facts
which make up this body of knowledge are expressed by statements
or data generally believed to be representative of the phenomena and

37

supposedly free from bias and prejudice. Science is entirely objective; there is no place in it for personal influence, likes, and dislikes.

SCIENTIFIC METHOD

The scientific method consists of well-defined steps, including (1) experimentation, (2) observation, (3) classification, and (4) accurate generalization; in other words, this body of scientific knowledge derived by the scientific method is obtained by means of experiments conducted to confirm or to disprove the proposition under consideration. The proposition is tested under carefully controlled conditions. During these experiments, observations are made and records are kept to show what happened, when, and how. Furthermore, the observations from these and perhaps many similar tests are then classified or sorted into similar groups in order to expedite the interpretation of these data. From these classified data, accurate generalizations are made; they may include the formation of a basic law, or they may constitute a statement to the effect that when certain things take place under stated conditions the results will be of a specific sort.

STEPS IN SCIENTIFIC METHOD

It is important for the student of office management to have a very clear concept of the successive steps taken in the scientific method. There are ten definite steps which can be viewed as basic action to create, prove, and conclude, as illustrated in Figure 3–1. Each step is important, as well as the indicated sequence.

To illustrate how these steps are carried out, assume the case of an office manager who is interested in increasing the amount of output per office worker. The office manager wants to employ the scientific method. What does he do?

1. *Recognize the problem.* He must first recognize the specific problem about which he wishes to secure facts. Suppose that, after careful thought, the office manager feels that increase in worker output can be accomplished by any of the following: (1) a better arrangement of the employee's work area, (2) a more even flow of the work to the worker, (3) an improvement in the design of the paper form used, or (4) a training program designed to increase the skill and efficiency of the worker. The influence of each of these factors upon the worker's output constitutes a separate problem.

Suppose that the office manager decides to investigate the training program as the means for accomplishing his objective. This action constitutes step 1, namely, recognition of the problem. Other problems

BASIC ACTION	STEPS	
CREATE	1. RECOGNIZE THE PROBLEM	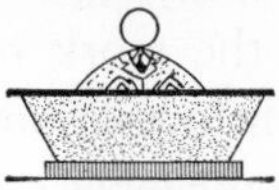
	2. MAKE PRELIMINARY OBSERVATIONS AND ANALYSIS	
	3. DRAW UP A HYPOTHESIS OR TENTATIVE SOLUTION TO THE PROBLEM	
PROVE	4. MAKE A THOROUGH AND DETAILED ANALYSIS	
	5. COLLECT ADEQUATE DATA	
	6. CLASSIFY THE DATA COLLECTED	
	7. MAKE A TENTATIVE ANSWER TO THE PROBLEM	
CONCLUDE	8. TEST THIS SOLUTION OR ANSWER	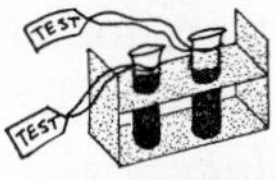
	9. ADJUST IN LIGHT OF RESULTS UNDER STEP 8.	
	10. STATE THE ANSWER TO THE PROBLEM	

FIG. 3–1. The scientific method consists of well-defined steps.

such as better arrangement of the employees' work area upon productivity are excluded.

2. *Make preliminary observations and analysis.* The problem having been recognized, the next step is to make preliminary observations and analyses. In this step, definite information is secured showing the causal effect of various factors upon the particular problem being investigated. For example, the office manager might seek published literature, reports of tests, or other investigations which show any rela-

tionship between a training program and office employee's output. Furthermore, in his own office the office manager would probably study the work records of his employees or actually observe them to gain information on employees' productivity. Then, by comparing each employee's output with that of the respective employee's training, any apparent relationship between output and training could be detected. In addition, the office manager would observe what types of training seem to be present among the high-output workers and what types of training seem to be lacking among the low-output workers. Also, the office manager might inquire of friends, educators, trade associations, and others as to what advantages usually were derived from specific types and courses of training.

3. *Draw up a hypothesis or tentative solution to the problem.* A hypothesis or tentative answer, based partly on the general information accumulated under step 2 and partly on individual experience and background, is now made. The hypothesis for the illustration might be something like the following: The employees who achieve the greatest work output are those having thorough training in (1) office production methods, and (2) application of office policies.

The implied suggestion here is, of course, that this training *is related* to high output and that employees who do not have this training are not, by and large, highly producitve. But it is not known whether this is true, for at this step of the scientific method the statement is only a suggested solution which must be proved or disproved.

4. *Make a thorough and detailed analysis.* "Analysis" means the examination of components in relation to the whole. To carry out this step means to break up the whole of the hypothesis into its component parts and to examine each part separately and carefully. For example, in the hypothesis given above, training in office-production methods would be analyzed separately. The exact content of training work, including such things as the type of training material, the methods of instruction, the size of classes, and the caliber of the instructors, would be carefully studied.

5. *Collect adequate data.* The office manager is now ready to collect adequate data on the various compenents isolated in the above step. These data may be classified as either primary or secondary. Primary data are those obtained direct from people or from current experiments for the specific problem in mind; secondary data are those obtained from records or published sources, such data having been obtained originally for a problem other than the present specific problem.

In the example, primary data might be obtained by the following procedure: Select a worker who has never had any training on the subject of office-production methods and measure his work output. Then, give this worker a definite training course on the subject of office-production methods. At intervals during the course and also following the course, take measurements of the worker's output to determine the relationship between the training course and the worker's output.[1]

Secondary data would also be gathered to help supplement the primary data. These would include such information as published governmental data and available records of private companies showing the relationship of training and office employees' output.

6. *Classify the data collected.* It is necessary to classify the data in order to make accurate interpretations. To "classify data" means to sort or put like data together; i.e., facts pertaining to the same aspects of the phenomena are put in the same class. For example, data pertaining to office-production methods are put in one class, while data regarding the application of office policies are put into another class. Most data can be classified into a number of different groups, but for convenience and clarity it is usually best not to make too many groups.

7. *Make a tentative answer to the problem.* From all these classified data the tentative answer to the problem is interpreted by means of induction and deduction.[2] In the illustration, suppose that employees having thorough training in office-production methods are definitely workers of high-work output. This is the tentative answer to the problem.

Note that this conclusion does not include all the components in the hypothesis under step 3; the component "application of office policies" does not appear in the tentative answer. This simply means that the original training program of several components which would be related with high-work output is not related to as great a degree as a training program of one component, specifically the one listed in the tentative answer. It is important to observe that the hypothesis made in step 3 was a basis from which to work toward an answer.

8. *Test this solution or answer.* The contents of a training program

---

[1] Actually, other factors besides the training program may affect the worker's output. The scientific manager must constantly be aware of changes in relationship due to the unmeasured variables. In the illustration above, it might be possible to isolate a *group* of workers in order to eliminate, as far as possible, the influence of factors other than that of the training program.

[2] These acts of reasoning are discussed in the section immediately following.

have now been determined, and they should show a very close relationship with the output of the worker. However, there may have been some slip-up in arriving at this particular training program. The data may have been read incorrectly, or some error may have been made in their interpretation. Therefore, the tentative answer is tested.

One way to do this is to select several newly recruited workers of equal skill and ability and then divide them into two groups. Give one group the prescribed training program and then compare its output with that of the other group which has not been given the same program.

9. *Adjust in light of results under step 8.*   As a result of testing the prescribed training program, it will probably be found that minor changes should be incorporated in the program in order to show more accurately and correctly the relationship between the training program and worker output. For example, it may be found in the tentative answer, shown under step 7, that training in certain office methods can be eliminated, since they have little relationship with worker output.

10. *State the answer to the problem.*   This is the final step in the scientific method. In the illustration the answer is a program which includes thorough training in office-production methods. Workers who are given this course of training will be closely related with workers who have records of high output. Thus, this program is the answer to the originally recognized problem regarding the relationship of training programs with worker output, and the solution was arrived at not by chance or rule of thumb but by means of the scientific method.

It is important to note that the answer is confined solely to the recognized problem, namely, the relationship of training program to worker output. The answer is not conclusive in regard to the relationship of other important aspects in increasing the amount of output per worker, aspects such as importance of the employee's work area and the flow of work to the worker. These are different problems and can be solved scientifically only by the use of the scientific method for each individual problem.

INDUCTION AND DEDUCTION

The scientific manager utilizes *induction* in order to add knowledge to the existing body of knowledge. "Induction" is the explaining and justifying of a finding by the use of a sufficient number of adequately controlled and appropriate demonstrations on the basis of concrete experiences. It is the process of reasoning from the part to the whole, or from the result of a few experiments concerning a certain phenomenon to the probable result of many experiments concerning the same phenomenon.

Likewise, *deduction* is used in the scientific method. "Deduction" is the explaining and justifying of a finding by the application of the truth of the entirety to the identical segments making up that entirety; it is reasoning from the general to the particular.

It is well to point out that the scientific worker frequently uses induction and deduction interchangeably in order to achieve the scientific truth. Induction tends to give general principles or expressions of fundamental scientific truths and to show the basic underlying relationships among various phenomena. In contrast, deduction tends to give explicit knowledge, the complete scientific truth concerning a particular part of the entirety.

THE IMPORTANCE OF CAUSAL RELATIONSHIP IN SCIENTIFIC METHOD

The scientific method is used to discover *causal relationships* existing among the parts of a phenomena, *not a cause-and-effect relationship*. The scientific office manager is not, for example, perplexed by the question of whether office training causes certain personnel selection or whether certain personnel selection causes office training. But he is interested in the relationship of the two and the precise extent and characteristics of that relationship. A moment's reflection will show that determining the cause and effect of most phenomena is an endless job and usually results in merry-go-round thinking. What is really important to know are the relationships existing inwardly, among the parts of the phenomena, and outwardly, between these phenomena and various other phenomena. It is to these objectives that the scientific manager directs his attention and effort.

It is also important to note that, in seeking new knowledge by means of the scientific method, customarily all variables affecting the final result are kept constant, except one. The effect of this one variable upon the final result is isolated and can thus be more readily ascertained.

SCIENTIFIC MANAGEMENT AND PROGRESS

Applying the scientific method to office management may be perturbing because it implies a constant seeking to improve management. The so-called "best" management is always being sought but never permanently attained; however, this should cause no alarm, for reasons well expressed in the following statement by the late president of the American Management Association: "A constant ferment is characteristic of the science of management, and our particular American type of management, with its fluidity, flexibility, and democracy, will *always* 'have something wrong' with it. Our job is to find *orderly methods* for discovering and correcting mistakes. That is management."[3]

TAYLOR—THE FATHER OF SCIENTIFIC MANAGEMENT

Frederick W. Taylor is generally credited with the beginning of the application of scientific knowledge and the scientific method to management. He is called the "Father of Scientific Management." He was a man of great foresight and ability, and his contributions to management are significant.

About 1880 Taylor started working for the Midvale Steel Company and soon became intensely interested in increasing the output of work. He ultimately discovered that there were two major obstacles in achieving this goal: fear by employees that increased work output would result in wage reductions, and suasion by managers as the popular means of securing greater worker output. Taylor believed that the real essence of the whole difficulty was expressed by this question: "What constitutes an honest day's work?" He reasoned that if this question could be answered specifically then both management and nonmanagement members would have a common basis of understanding which could help answer the problem of increasing output.

Accordingly, Taylor conducted many studies or tests under controlled conditions, i.e., employed the scientific method, and obtained vast new funds of knowledge. Among his important conclusions were that high wages were compatible with low unit costs, that standards were needed to control production, that employees, materials, and procedures should be scientifically selected, and that co-operation between management and nonmanagement members was required for highest productivity.[4]

THEME OF GOOD MANAGEMENT

The fundamentals developed by Taylor, and subsequent additions and improvements contributed by other scientific managers, have evolved into what might be summarized as the main theme of most

---

[3] A. E. Dodd, news item under "The President's Scratch-Pad," *Management News* (New York: American Management Association), May 27, 1944, p. 4.

[4] These fundamentals are expounded in F. W. Taylor, *Scientific Management,* which comprises the previously published works *Shop Management, The Principles of Scientific Management,* and *Testimony before the Special House Committee* (New York: Harper & Bros., 1947), pp. 1–47 and 130–31.

effective management. This theme includes the following eight steps:

1. Establish a simple and precise understanding of the work to be done.

2. Determine the exact manner and conditions under which the work will be performed.

3. Assign specific work to each employee and delegate to him commensurate authority for its performance.

4. Let each employee know exactly his organizational relationship to others in the enterprise.

5. Inform each employee what he is to do and the manner in which it is to be done.

6. Encourage each employee's best efforts by means of positive leadership, praising when deserved, displaying fairness and firmness in dealings, and helping each employee to help himself.

7. Develop for each task a statement of results that will be accepted as satisfactory, and make this information known to management and nonmanagement members alike.

8. Check each employee's actual performance with the expected results and, if necessary, take corrective action.

OTHER BASIC APPROACHES TO MANAGEMENT

As already stated, there are several basic approaches, other than the scientific, which an office manager can use. These include (1) conventional, (2) observational, and (3) systematic approaches. Although none of these are as important as the scientific, they exist and are used. Knowledge from these other approaches is nonscientific and might best be identified, for example, as conventional knowledge, or observational knowledge. Figure 3–2 outlines the distinguishing characteristics of various types of management in tabular form.

CONVENTIONAL MANAGEMENT

Conventional management is characterized by its adherence to custom. It follows the manner and method which have been handed down from the past; emphasis is placed on doing a managerial task in a manner similar to that which one's predecessor used. The fundamental theme is expressed by the statement: "What was good enough for my father is good enough for me." The follower of conventional management seldom asks why or questions the purpose of a particular managerial activity. He is little concerned with efforts to discover new managerial techniques.

Type of Management	Approach Used	Basis	Contribution to Advancement of Management	Management Characteristic
SCIENTIFIC.......	Science	Science—the body of knowledge plus scientific method—a process including experimentation, observation, classification, and accurate generalization	Seeks to find the best way	Dynamic
CONVENTIONAL...	Custom	Custom and tradition—"How did our predecessors do it?"	Very little if any	Static for the most part
OBSERVATIONAL...	Observation	Observations and imitations—"How do other managers with similar problems meet them?"	Affords the greater distribution and exchange of current techniques and principles	Somewhat dynamic
SYSTEMATIC......	Systems	Standardized methods and procedures to cover all major activities of the enterprise	Standardizes respective procedures and makes for efficient execution of the work	Static for the most part

FIG. 3–2. Comparison of the various types of management.

OBSERVATIONAL MANAGEMENT

This type is characterized by the use of observations as the basic media for managing an operation. The observational manager observes how other managers achieve their goal and uses this information in determining his own course of action. He copies and attempts to select what he believes to be the best of his fellow-managers' techniques and then applies them to his own particular problems. The observational manager's attitude is: "Find out how the other fellow performs a managerial task similar to one which you have—then solve your managerial problem by using the same approach and method."

Observational management helps to distribute managerial ideas and techniques among managers. Furthermore, it requires little effort. Most managers like to discuss their activities, especially those in which they are successful. Also, observational management offers dynamic sources of information for the changing managerial problems. The solutions to these problems might require training and experience which neither the office manager nor any other member of the company possesses; and, as a consequence, attention is turned to what others have done under similar circumstances.

However, observational management as such does not necessarily contribute to the improvement of managerial techniques. It is but slightly dynamic. An office practice which works well for one office might produce poor results for the firm which copies it, as a result of differences in objectives, in the size of the office, or in the personnel of the two firms. Nevertheless, observational management is used by many managers of small offices where the facilities and time may make other approaches difficult to follow. When adequate analysis in selection and care in installation are practiced, observational management usually gives satisfactory results.

SYSTEMATIC MANAGEMENT

A systematic manager strives to manage mainly by means of systems. These automatically encompass the plans, policies, relationships, and controls used by the managers and provide the required written managerial records. Systematic management differs from both conventional management and observational management more in degree than in kind, for there is usually some systematic management in every type of management. Actually, it is a necessary supplement to each of the other managerial types.

For the most part, systematic management is static because it tends to fix or to stabilize a given procedure and attitude. It tends to keep things as they are and to develop definite and rigid habits for handling the work. When this approach is the over-all guide, serious limitations in a manager's operation and breadth of vision may result.

QUESTIONS

1. What is your concept of a scientific office manager?
2. To which type of work do you feel scientific management can be applied with the least effort: (*a*) factory work, (*b*) sales work, or (*c*) office work. Give reasons for your answer.
3. Is there any difference between what might be termed "experimental management" and scientific management? Explain.
4. "The best management is always being sought but never permanently attained in the application of the scientific method to managerial problems." Does this imply that there are elements of futility and defeatism in scientific management? Explain.
5. It has been said that a competent scientific manager should possess above-average ability in creative thinking, reasoning power, and showing relationships using data as a basis. Point out and discuss three steps of the scientific method that require respectively probably the greatest amounts of the three abilities mentioned above.
6. Give an example to show how the scientific method can be used in perform-

ing the managerial work for each of the following: (*a*) planning, (*b*) organizing, (*c*) actuating, and (*d*) controlling.

7. Comment on the following quotation: "We are excessively conscious of being scientific and are giving an unwarranted degree of accuracy, insight, and finality to actions reputedly based on science. Many decisions are stated to be scientific when, in fact, such is not the case. But the fact that they are represented as scientific frequently gains general acceptance. It is for this reason plus the desire for managers to want to be known as scientific that our present status of science in management exists."

8. According to the fundamental functions of management, classify the eight steps listed in the text as the theme of good management.

9. Would you advocate the establishing of scientific management centers throughout the country for use by managers of small offices? Why?

10. Assume you are employed on any one of the following office jobs: (*a*) telephone switchboard operator, (*b*) accountant, (*c*) receptionist, and (*d*) file clerk. Explain in not over 300 words how you could apply the scientific method to your job.

11. Is there any relationship between—
    a) Scientific management and observational management?
    b) Conventional management and systematic management?
    c) Scientific management and systematic management?
    Explain your answers.

12. Is there anything basically wrong about the use of observational management by a manager? Explain.

CASE PROBLEMS

CASE 3–1.   THE HANLEY COMPANY

The Hanley Company is a manufacturing company with yearly sales of approximately $2½ million. On an average, 500 customers' orders are handled a week, with peak periods being the May–June and October–December. Currently orders are processed as follows.

Credit is checked, and if satisfactory the order is written in quadruplicate. A shipping label is also prepared. Copies No. 1, 2, and 3 and the shipping label are sent to the stock room where they are used to fill the order. Copy No. 4 is kept in the office and is entered numerically in an order book whenever one of the clerks has some free time. It is then filed numerically in an "order-pending" file.

When an order is received in the stock room, it is also entered in a book which has a page for every item the company handles, arranged alphabetically by name of item. The order is entered by item so that at a glance the stock room clerk and foreman can see how many of a particular item are being ordered by customers. When the orders are sent to the shipping room, they are checked off in the book and the date noted. Copies No. 1, 2, and 3 go to the shipping room. Copy No. 2 is used as a packing slip. Notations are made on Copies No. 1 and 3 as to shipping information—date of shipment, how shipped, and amount of shipping charges. These entries are made by a clerk in the shipping department. Copy No. 3 is kept in the shipping room as a memo of shipment, and Copy No. 1 is sent back to the office for billing purposes.

In the office, the billing is done in triplicate. Copy No. 1 is the customer's invoice, Copy No. 2 is the accounts receivable record, and Copy No. 3 is used for entering in the sales journal. If the customer wants to be billed in duplicate, it is necessary to insert an extra copy of the invoice with the three initial copies. The company has six salesmen, and they receive a copy of all invoices to the customers in their respective territories.

Copy No. 2, the accounts receivable record, is kept in a subsidiary ledger. As they are paid, Copies No. 2 are removed from the book, or they are held until the books of the company are balanced once a month.

The company maintains a file of customers. Each customer has a 5 by 8 card on which certain information from Copy No. 2 is entered. Information such as the item the customer received, the date it was shipped, and the invoice number under which it was billed is entered on this card. Copy No. 2 is then filed alphabetically by customer's name. This customer file is a convenient reference showing items purchased by each customer since the company started in business. This information from Copy No. 2 is supposed to be entered on the customer's cards once a month, but sometimes, due to the pressure of business, several months will pass before it is entered and Copies No. 2 are filed away.

Attached to Copy No. 3, the sales journal copy, are the customer's original order, Copy No. 1 of the original order which was sent to the stock room, and any shipping papers. This copy with the substantiating papers are kept on file by invoice number. Periodically, as someone has the time, the invoice numbers on these copies are entered opposite the order numbers which were entered previously in the book kept in the office. This is done to be sure no orders are written up and lost.

The sales manager believes that the office work should be kept more current to be of maximum value in promoting sales efforts. He has expressed a desire to have an arrangement whereby each salesman is informed daily or weekly of what customers are sending orders and what the items and dollar amounts are. He agrees with the office manager that all the office employees are working hard, but feels that unnecessary work is being done in handling customer's orders.

The office manager resolves to look into the present processing work and find a better way if it is at all possible.

PROBLEMS:

1. Do you feel there is any merit in the contentions of the sales manager?
2. What specific actions do you suggest the office manager take? Explain.
3. Assume you have been requested to improve the customer order processing by using the scientific method. Describe in detail what you would do.

PART II......

The Work of Office Services

The basic work operations of an office include typing or writing, calculating, checking, filing, telephoning, duplicating, and mailing. As a group, these activities or a major portion of them are sometimes referred to as office services, and they are commonly included in the concept of the work managed by the office manager.

In each of the following eight chapters the application of the management process—planning, organizing, actuating, and controlling—is included so that a practical conceptual pattern of management operation in these major office areas is provided.

The order of the chapters is (1) typing or writing as exemplified by office work pertaining to reports, (2) office correspondence, (3) calculating and checking, (4) filing, (5) record retention, (6) duplicating, (7) handling the mail, and (8) communicative services (including telephoning).

Chapter · 4

Office Reports

Half knowledge is worse than ignorance.
—MACAULAY

ONE OF the most powerful factors in the world is helpful ideas, in the minds of energetic men of good will, presented to others in writing so that they can understand and use them. Clear thinking is a requisite of clear written communication. Most newly created thoughts and ideas are fuzzy and must be put in writing which is edited and rewritten before clarity is obtained. Skill in writing can be developed. It is not an ability with which some are blessed and others can never hope to achieve. A strong will-to-do plus the application of basic principles underlying all forms of effective written communications are fundamental in getting messages across clearly, concisely, and simply.

THE CHALLENGE OF WRITING

For many managers the phase of their work they enjoy least is writing. They feel competent in performing their other activities, but the effective transferring of information on paper is too frequently assigned to a subordinate who does not possess the depth of knowledge or firsthand, practical experience in working with the subject. Further, the subordinate may not write clearly and concisely. Hence, the value of the communication rendered to others is diminished, and the criteria of how well the job has been done is obscured.

Many studies have been conducted to determine the extent to which the written matter of American business is understood by employees and customers. The results seem to indicate that intended easy-to-read prose is in reality hard to read and to understand. It isn't comfortable and voluntary; readers must try hard to ferret out the meaning. The key findings of one such study are shown in Figure 4–1. Writing for business is segregated into four types, with pertinent data on the effectiveness of each type. For example, required writing for employees, such as shop manuals and accounting procedures (line 3), is within the reading grasp of only 2 per cent of all American adults, whereas it should be within the group of 53 per cent. In other words, the effectiveness is only 4 per cent, as shown in the last column. Apparently the most effective writing is that termed "voluntary for employees" (line 2), where the effective penetration reaches 75 per cent.

CATEGORIES OF WRITING IN BUSINESS	EXAMPLES	PERCENTAGE WITHIN THE READING GRASP OF ALL AMERICAN ADULTS		EFFECTIVE-NESS
		Is	Should Be	
1. Writing for customers..........	Public relations copy Sales correspondence	12%	60%	20%
2. Writing for employees (voluntary).....................	Plant papers Letters to employees Bulletin board	40	53	75
3. Writing for employees (required)	Shop manuals Accounting procedures	2	53	4
4. Writing for stockholders.......	Letters Annual report	6	40	15

Courtesy: Readability Associates, New York City

FIG. 4-1. Extent of understanding written material by American adults.

REPORTS AND MANAGEMENT

Reports are very important in managerial activity. The work of carrying out the functions of planning, organizing, actuating, and controlling is greatly aided by reports. For example, the work of planning requires information on what must be accomplished, and within what time periods. Reports help to supply this needed information or to suggest possible avenues of approach which might reveal potent information.

As an enterprise grows, various levels of management develop, and many management members find they cannot keep in personal touch with all phases of the enterprise. As a result, reports are used to keep executives informed, to develop favorable interdepartmental relationships, and to help get the work accomplished through the work force.

A report can be defined as *a written statement based on a collection of facts, events, and opinions, and usually expresses a summarized and interpretative value of this information.* A report may deal with past accomplishments, present conditions, or probable future developments.

PLANNING AND EFFECTIVE REPORT WRITING

By means of planning, the necessary objectives, guides, and policies required for effective report writing can be established. Planning assists in writing necessary reports only and in making them terse and meaningful. In this respect the following eight important considerations should be carefully evaluated:

1. *Make only reports having a definite purpose.* The aim of the report should be known to the person preparing it. This knowledge serves as a guide to the writer and helps him point the report toward its intended uses. Informing the writer of the purpose is extremely important, for without this information the report is almost certain not to bring about the mutual satisfaction of writer and receiver.

Furthermore, it is well to write the report from the viewpoint of the reader. Reports that answer his questions have a good chance of being thoroughly read and used. An effective procedure to follow is to tell the reader what he wants to know; the purpose of a report is to inform, not to impress, others.

In some instances reports tend to satisfy the vanity and prestige of the receiver more than to fulfill any other purpose. A large number of reports coming to an executive's desk, and many others in his files, are quite impressive and probably give him a feeling of great importance. But reports prepared with this purpose in mind are impediments to effective office management and should be eliminated as quickly as possible.

2. *Include statements and data that will aid in reaching a clear understanding of the subject.* The aim of the report stands a much better chance of accomplishment if the text of the report is understood. Associated considerations should be brought to the receiver's mind so that he can compare with what he knows. This in turn greatly increases his interest and comprehension of the material.

To illustrate, suppose a report on expenses written for the sales manager shows that company-wide traveling expenses have increased 12 per cent over a six-month period. If this is the only information reported, the sales manager probably would ask questions. He may find that during this six-month period there was an 8 per cent increase in sales personnel. Further questioning might reveal that sales have increased 17 per cent during the same period. Hence, by piecing the information together, he gains a unified picture of the results. But the report should be inclusive and show information on sales, expense, and sales personnel so that the report is meaningful and places the sales manager in a position to reach a decision.

A reader acquires from a report only such knowledge as he brings to it. That is, a person who has broad training and an extensive background in a particular subject will acquire more from a report in that subject than the individual who does not possess such training and background. Irrelevant details should be excluded. What is basic to the purpose of the report should be in the report. Likewise, information which is incomplete and not essential to the purpose of the report should be avoided.

3. *Be factual and unbiased.*   Accuracy is essential to good report writing regardless of the scope, subject, media, or level for which it is intended. The facts should be relevant to the subject; opinions should be identified as such.

The motive and the ideas should be presented without bias. The objective viewpoint should be stressed. The report is not a writing to sway the reader to the writer's subjective beliefs but to inform the reader of the situation or subject as it is. The report can be colorful, yet not filled with emotional statements. Remember that the content and the words of the report should be tools of straight thinking not stumbling blocks.

4. *Follow a logical order.*   There is no one best way to organize all reports. In some instances a standardized format is well established and accepted, but in many cases the writer is free to choose the make-up. Material should be presented logically. Aids which will help in the reading should be provided—for example, simple statements, sectional headings, summaries at the beginning, and a table of contents. A reader often glances through a report, noting the various headings and reading a sentence here and there. For this reason it is advisable to make it possible to obtain a "quickie" on what the report is all about and what it includes. This approach will maintain the reader's interest and lead him to correct conclusions and proper actions.

Every report should follow a carefully developed general outline. The first step in preparing such an outline is to select the information to be included in the report. This is ordinarily dictated by the purpose of the report, what information is available, or what can be uncovered. Next, the items of information should be classified under headings which normally are grouped as major and minor, or as many groups as judgment suggests.

There are a number of general outlines for reports; the following is preferred by many:

1. Summary of findings.
   a) Objectives.
   b) Results.
   c) Conclusion.
2. Methodology.
   a) Techniques.
   b) Sample.
3. Detailed results.
4. Appendix.

Another outline which is effective and adaptable for many subjects, especially those of a technical nature, includes:

1. Summary.
2. Objective and scope.
3. Equipment used.
4. Methodology.
5. Data obtained.
6. Conclusions.
7. Recommendations.

The following has also won considerable favor:

1. Introduction and definition of problem.
2. Conclusions and recommendations.
3. Discussion of procedure and results obtained.
4. Summary.

5. *Use simple words and short sentences.* Word choice is vital; words are the media which identify the concept to the reader. It is desirable to refrain from the use of words stemming from verbs. For example, if a sentence contains "argumentation," try to reword it using the verb "argue" or "discuss." Also, select words that focus sharply on the intended subject matter. Call a parking lot a "parking lot," not a "temporary car depository." Remember Benjamin Franklin's sage advice, "Never use big words when little words will do." This is well illustrated by a story. When still a lad, Benjamin Franklin told his mother, "I have imbibed an acephalous molluscous." His mother believing young Franklin had swallowed something poisonous forced him to take a large dosage of medicine to induce vomiting. When he got over the effects of the medicine, he explained to his mother, "I

have eaten nothing but an oyster." Whereupon his mother thrashed him for deceiving her. Franklin vowed never again to use big words when little words would do.

Clear sentences are one of the most helpful ingredients of clear reports. Although variety in sentence length is desirable, short sentences are normally preferred. Unity, coherence, and correct sentence structure are more readily achieved in short than in long complex sen-

---

THE PERIOD (.)
At the end of a complete declarative or imperative sentence.
Always inside of quotation marks.
To close a request.

THE COMMA (,)
To separate a series of words, phrases, or clauses.
In a series of three or more nouns, adjectives, or adverbs, the last of which is connected by a conjunction (as well as a comma).
To set off the name of person addressed.
Before and after a non-restrictive clause begun by "who," "which," or "that."
After words used to give emphasis in a sentence — for example, "oh," "no," "well," "therefore."
Before and after words in apposition.
For emphatic setting-off of part of a sentence.

THE COLON (:)
After the salutation in a letter.
To set off a lengthy quotation, statement, or list.

THE SEMICOLON (;)
To break up complicated sentences of unusual length which involve commas.

THE DASH (--)
To show a definite break in thought. When repetition is used for emphasis.

THE HYPHEN (-)
In compound words—e.g., "feather-light," "an up-to-the-minute bulletin."

THE INTERROGATION POINT (?)
Always follows a direct question.

THE EXCLAMATION POINT (!)
Following a sentence or phrase, expresses emotion, surprise, or command.

THE APOSTROPHE (')
Signifies possession when coming before the "s" in possessive nouns.
Shows omission of letters in contractions.
To enclose a quotation within a quotation.

QUOTATION MARKS (" ")
To enclose a direct quotation.
To indicate a word that is defined.

FIG. 4–2. A list of usable punctuation.

tences. There is no rule to state the exact number of words to include in a sentence. It should be long enough to convey the thought. One practical suggestion is to fit the sentence to the reader's span of attention. That is, put no more words in a sentence than you can speak in a normal breath. Correct punctuation also helps. Figure 4–2 shows a list of usable punctuation.

6. *Interpret findings adequately and clearly.* Care must be exercised to avoid exaggeration or the inclusion of unqualified interpretations which cannot be reasonably derived from the available data. It is usually best to understate rather than to overstate conclusions. Also, recommendations must be practical and sound.

Charts, drawings, maps, and illustrations help to convey the meaning to the reader, but they must be carefully selected and employed in "reasonable" amounts for maximum assistance to be derived. The accuracy and completeness of the illustrative material must be carefully checked. In many cases the chart or drawing must be explained and significant developments and relations pointed out to the reader, because the exact meaning may not be gained simply by looking at the illustrative material.

7. *Summarize briefly.*   Normally it is best to state the results, findings, or highlights in a summary statement. Supplementary data can be included to explain the items in this summary, and when necessary, adequate amplification of information should be included. The report should be inviting to read and should convey the essentials to the reader easily; under no circumstances should the receiver be required to dig through quantities of words and figures to find out what the report discloses. In the case of statistical tables and other data, for example, the heading should convey the precise meaning of the information.

8. *Make specific recommendations.*   The usefulness of a report is enhanced by the writer stating what should or should not be done about the particular subject. Presumably the writer is or has become thoroughly familiar with the information he has worked with and his recommendations have value. This does not mean necessarily that the recommendations will be followed, but they provide a springboard for action.

In presenting a single co-ordinated proposed action, do not hedge. Avoid double meanings. Long, qualified explanations usually offer little help. Strive to set forth the recommendations so clear and clean that they will be followed.

TYPES OF REPORTS

Reports can be classified into many different types, including private, public, company, departmental, restricted, nonrestricted, technical, and nontechnical. However, for purposes of office usage the three groups of executive, periodic, and special are quite satisfactory.

Executive Reports.   Under this classification are the following:

1. Balance sheet.
2. Statement of cost of goods sold.
3. Statement of profit and loss.
4. Budgetary statement.
5. Annual departmental report.
6. Report to stockholders.

Executive reports stress broad concepts and results rather than details, usually covering a three-, six-, or twelve-month time period. For the most part, they are prepared for members of top and intermediate management levels. Figure 4–3 shows a portion of an executive report.

FINANCIAL POSITION AND CREDIT

The company's balance sheet at the close of this year shows current assets of $98,498,565 and current liabilities of $58,435,388, with a consequent net current asset position of $40,063,177. The banking credit of $40,000,000 had been drawn on at the close of the year to the extent of $26,000,000. The aggregate of capital stock, capital surplus and undivided profits at the end of the year amounted to $63,765,421 or approximately $27.40 per share of stock outstanding.

EMPLOYMENT

Approximately 38,000 employees are on our current payrolls. This employment had increased from about 31,000 at the beginning of the year. Such expansion in employment poses many problems, including training of new people and reassignment of management and supervisory responsibilities. Harmonious labor relations have continued, which is a credit to the individual workers, their representatives, and the supervisory and managerial personnel.

FACILITIES

In addition to the approximately 2,300,000 square feet of space in the company's plant in California, the company has under lease in adjacent areas an additional approximately 750,000 square feet of plant area. Also about 250,000 square feet were recently added to the plant at a cost of about $2,638,000. This additional space was necessary to handle efficiently the expanding work of an increasing engineering and research department.

FIG. 4–3. A portion of an executive report.

Periodic Reports. These deal mainly with departmental activities. Included under this classification are:

1. Monthly reports on operation.
2. Departmental records of performance.
3. Monthly credit reports.
4. Purchasing reports.
5. Material handling reports.
6. Salesmen's reports.
7. Advertising and sales promotion reports.
8. Personnel management reports.

Periodic reports typically cover weekly, monthly, or quarterly periods. Usually they contain some detailed information which is pertinent to the operation of the particular department.

Commonly, a printed form is used to assist in obtaining the needed data for a periodic report. Figure 4–4 shows a portion of such a sheet.

				CURRENT OPERATING REPORT		
Month of_____ Year_____ Days Reported_____ Days in Month_____						

ITEMS	SHIP-MENTS LAST MONTH	SALES QUOTA THIS MONTH	INVEN-TORY FIRST OF MONTH	OPERATIONS THIS MONTH		
				Sales Orders	Ship-ments	Pro-duction
Panels						
Switches						
Sockets						
Transitors						
KLE						
Miscellaneous						
Total						

SALES ORDERS	ACTUAL LAST Month	BUDGET THIS MONTH	NEW ORDERS ENTERED		ORDERS OUTSTANDING	
			This Year	This Month	First of Year	This Month
Custom products—current						
—future						
Standard products—current						
—future						
Total						
Standard products—future						
Custom products—est.						

FINANCIAL RESULTS	CURRENT MONTH				THIS YEAR	
	Dollars		% to Shipment		Budget	Actual
	Budget	Actual	Budget	Actual		
Orders received						
Shipments						
Basic cost—product						

FIG. 4–4. Portion of form sheet used to collect data for periodic report.

In this case the data deal with monthly sales operations of an electronics manufacturer. The top section gives information, by product groups, for the current and for the previous month. In this case, the manager is interested in shipments, sales quotas, and inventory, as shown by the column headings. The other sections give concise information regarding sales efforts and related matters.

Special Reports.   Activities not regularly covered by other reports are covered in special reports. These are published at infrequent intervals, because they deal with special subjects and are of a noncontinuous type. A portion of a special report dealing with the findings of a market research study is shown by Figure 4–5.

| 35–E | X Research Company | N 58 |

SUMMARY OF FINDINGS

OBJECTIVE:

To obtain a measure of consumer acceptance of Product Y.

RESULTS:

1. Product Y is not as well liked as Product No. 17.
2. The market potential of Product Y is somewhat between 50% and 80% of the market for Product No. 17. These are the limits indicated by consumers' stated preferences and test-package consumption.
3. The preference for Product No. 17 over Product Y prevails in all geographical areas and among all types of consumers. The greatest liking for Product Y was found among women.
4. Product No. 17 is preferred chiefly because it is crisp, easy to eat, and has a sweet, mild flavor.
5. Product Y is preferred by those who like a harder and heavier cereal than Product No. 17. Most cold cereal users, however, thought Product Y too hard to chew.
6. While food value is not a dominant factor in consumers' preferences between cereals, Product Y was the choice of consumers who emphasize this point.

CONCLUSION:

There is a limited market for an expanded cereal that is harder and heavier than Product No. 17. The potential volume of one such cereal—Product Y—is between 50% and 80% of the Product No. 17 market.

FIG. 4–5. A portion of a special report.

ORGANIZING AND REPORT WRITING

In a typical enterprise, many employees have the task of report writing. In some cases the total job content is report writing, while in others a report is required but once a week or month. Report writing can be found in almost any organizational unit—it is not confined to "the office." For example, the assistant sales manager may have the responsibility of writing the monthly sales report, the technician a research report, and the personnel manager a report on the company's industrial relations.

When the amount of report writing warrants, an organizational unit made up of report writers only is established. When anyone in the enterprise wants a report written, the task is assigned to a member in the report writing unit. This arrangement called "centralization" implies certain managerial advantages such as greater proficiency of employees, better utilization of equipment, and improved supervision.[1] When duplicating or reproducing machines are used to handle the volume and to supply the needed number of copies, a centralized organizational unit is commonly employed. On the other hand, since the work of report writing is a requirement of many different parts of an enterprise, it is believed by some managers that centralization should not be followed. They contend that permitting report writing to be dispersed provides for technical familiarity of the writer with the subject matter, reduces communicative problems in giving needed explanations, and insures privacy of confidential material.

TYPEWRITERS

In Chapter 2, it was stated that under the fundamental function of organizing was included "supplying the proper work environment." Since the managing of reports usually includes work involving the use of typewriters and in some instances office composing machines, a brief discussion of each will now be given.

Typewriters are the most widely used of all office machines, are easy to operate, and speed the handling of all written work. A convenient classification of office typewriters is: (1) standard, and (2) electric.

The standard typewriter is actuated by hand or human energy, i.e., by the depression of a key. While typing, the carriage is moved to the left by action of a spring. In contrast, the electric typewriter is motivated mainly by electricity. Manual energy is still used to touch the keys, but the energy input is about one fifth that required for manual machines. Work done on an electric typewriter is of uniform type impression, and a greater number of copies can be obtained without any increase in manual energy.

Design Features.   Most typewriters on the market today are excellent machines and have many common features which are recognized as standard equipment. Most are equipped with the "set" and "clear" tabulators, either of a single or decimal key type. Tabulators are very helpful for the rapid movement and alignment of the carriage which

---

[1] Centralization is thoroughly discussed in Chapter 19.

is required in reports and other written work that have frequent indentations. Typewriter platens are available in different degrees of hardness. A soft platen should be used where the number of copies are few and quietness is desired. Conversely, a hard platen is recommended when a large number of copies is required. It causes more noise, however, than does the soft platen.

Various type styles are also available. Whatever the job, there is a type face designed to handle it. The styles vary somewhat among manufacturers. Figure 4–6 illustrates a few of the various type styles

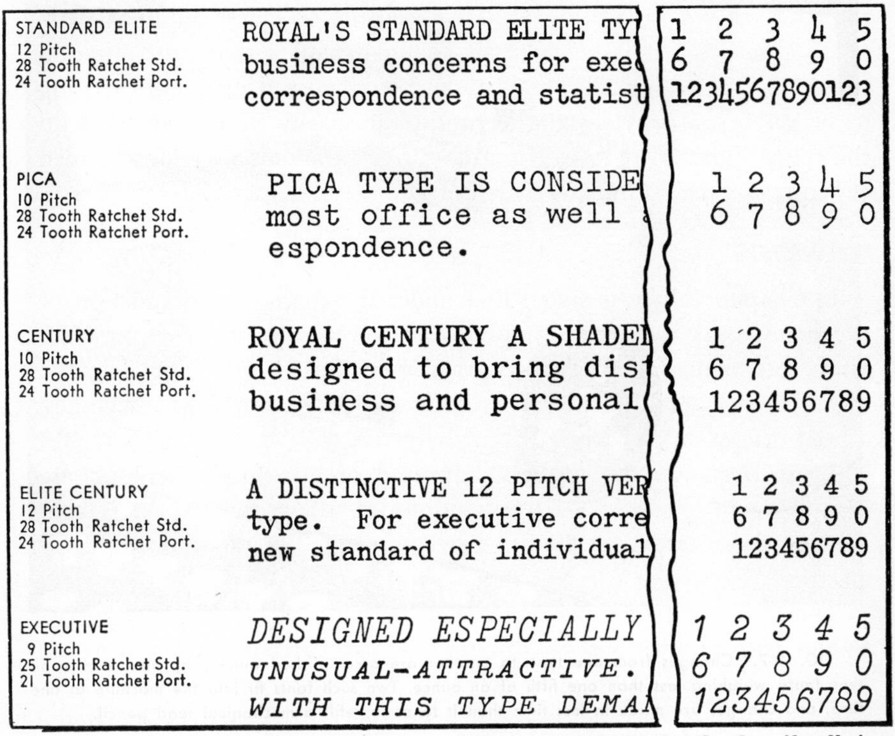

STANDARD ELITE 12 Pitch 28 Tooth Ratchet Std. 24 Tooth Ratchet Port.	ROYAL'S STANDARD ELITE TY business concerns for exe correspondence and statist	1 2 3 4 5 6 7 8 9 0 1234567890123
PICA 10 Pitch 28 Tooth Ratchet Std. 24 Tooth Ratchet Port.	PICA TYPE IS CONSIDE most office as well espondence.	1 2 3 4 5 6 7 8 9 0
CENTURY 10 Pitch 28 Tooth Ratchet Std. 24 Tooth Ratchet Port.	ROYAL CENTURY A SHADE designed to bring dis business and personal	1 2 3 4 5 6 7 8 9 0 123456789
ELITE CENTURY 12 Pitch 28 Tooth Ratchet Std. 24 Tooth Ratchet Port.	A DISTINCTIVE 12 PITCH VE type. For executive corre new standard of individual	1 2 3 4 5 6 7 8 9 0 123456789
EXECUTIVE 9 Pitch 25 Tooth Ratchet Std. 21 Tooth Ratchet Port.	DESIGNED ESPECIALLY UNUSUAL-ATTRACTIVE. WITH THIS TYPE DEMA	1 2 3 4 5 6 7 8 9 0 123456789

Courtesy: Royal Typewriter Co., Inc., New York

FIG. 4–6. Some of the many and varied type styles for typewriters.

offered on the market. Most typewriters are equipped with a standard keyboard. Special keyboards, or parts of keyboards such as engineering, mathematical, chemical, or foreign language signs and marks, are available at an additional cost.

OFFICE COMPOSING MACHINES

These machines are used primarily to prepare master copies for reproduction by various duplicating processes that are discussed in

Chapter 9. Actually in some cases the machines are located in the duplicating department. However, they are so closely tied with office reports and their preparation that discussion of them is included here. Different sizes and styles of type, bold headings, and straight left and right margins are provided. In short, the versatility of a well-equipped printing shop is brought to the office by use of these machines. They have found wide use in the preparation of all types of reports, bulletins,

Courtesy: Vari-Typer Corp., Newark, N.J.

FIG. 4–7. Changes from one type to another are accomplished quickly by means of small type fonts, weighing less than one fifth of an ounce. Two such fonts fit into the machine at one time, and changes are made in less time than it takes to refill a mechanical lead pencil.

booklets, catalogues, price lists, and house organs, where variety in composition is desired.

Figure 4–7 shows an office composing machine. It resembles a typewriter in both appearance and operation. Each type face is on a removable disk which can be quickly inserted into or removed from the machine. Each disk is complete with capital and lower-case letters, numerals, and symbols. Over 600 different sizes and styles of type, ranging from 5½-point newspaper style to 14-point Heavy Gothic type, and including boldface headings and italics, are available. The machine has different impression adjustments to provide the proper intensity of typing. Various vertical spacing choices permit the desired space between lines. In addition, all kinds of rule work—single, double, and vertical lines as well as dots and dashes—can be produced by the machine.

Even margins on both the left and the right, similar to those of regular type set composition, are obtained by typing each line twice. To illustrate: line 1 of the copy is typed in the regular manner on the left half of the piece of paper. Then it is retyped on the right. The machine spaces the second typing so that both margins are even. The procedure is repeated for each line. When completed, the typed material on the right half of the paper constitutes the finished or master copy.

ACTUATING AND REPORT WRITING

Getting report writers to want to improve their writing efforts can be a difficult task, yet it need not be. A number of avenues are open; the discussion here will be confined to what might be considered the major approaches.

First of all, the importance of reports must be established. This will add prestige to the writer as a doer of work that is needed and is beneficial to all members of the enterprise. More specifically, it should be pointed out to the writer how report writing will help him, that reports can be a means to desirable ends—to get certain actions started and others curtailed. The reading of good reports is also helpful. A study of expressions, choice of words, and organization of material can be especially beneficial. In addition, contests stimulating competitive efforts to write effective reports can be used. Regular meetings to encourage the exchange of ideas helpful to writers are another effective media. Also, writers should be told to draft their material currently—while it is on their mind. Make a brief written note when you think of an idea which you can use in your writing. Ideas come when least expected and are easily forgotten unless noted.

Training in report writing is needed just as is training in running a particular machine, or in any other particular type of task. As already stated, the ability to write good reports is seldom a natural gift; it must be developed, and this is best accomplished by means of specific training. Reluctance by managers to do something about improving report writing exists for several reasons. Some managers do not bring up the subject for fear that the responsibility of developing such a program will be added to their already full schedules. Others have never thought about improving report-writing efforts, while still others are reluctant to start an activity which might subject them to criticism of their own handling of written words.

CONTROLLING AND REPORT WRITING

Unnecessary reports are a tremendous waste of time, money, and energy. The office manager should see to it that only necessary reports are prepared and that they fulfill a vital need.

The habit of writing reports frequently tends to remain long after the original need for the report has ceased. It is well to check periodically and to re-evaluate the importance of and necessity for all reports. This practice will not only weed out the reports no longer necessary but will also help to bring about improvements in the reports which are deemed necessary. Progress requires that a critical attitude be taken toward current report writing.

Also, distribution of reports should receive close attention by the office manager. Too often distribution is made to a long list which includes names of persons who neither need or read the report. Many practices reputed to be truthful are told in office management circles regarding efforts to screen the distribution of reports. One such practice is to review the distribution list and remove the names of certain individuals believed nonessential as report receivers. No notice is given those whose names are removed. Subsequently, in most instances, the absence of the report is not noticed by the new nonreceiver; seldom is a complaint or inquiry about the report made.

COST OF REPORTS

An important means of managerial controlling of office reports is cost. All reports require an expenditure for preparation, and, from the managerial viewpoint, it is important to compare their cost with the estimated or real value of the report. A development of cost-consciousness by the office manager and the promotion of this attitude among report receivers will assist greatly in eliminating unnecessary reports and in combining and improving others. An effective technique in this respect is first to determine the total cost of preparing a report; then to attach to each copy delivered a statement similar to that shown in Figure 4–8. Another approach is to advise the recipient of the cost of preparation and to indicate that in the future his unit or department will be charged for this work, with records being maintained in the company's internal bookkeeping accounts. If the costs do not justify the use made of the reports, the recipient will request his name to be withdrawn from the distribution list. Discretion and judgment must be exercised in this approach, but it is effective.

It may be argued that the additional cost for running off extra copies of a report is relatively small; that is, to make 24 copies costs little more than to make 14 copies. But while the cost of labor, paper, and machine time for the differential 10 copies may be relatively small, the fact still remains that 10 more people receive the report. They take

Dept. _____   Report _____
                                                            Date _____

PLEASE NOTE

Dear_____:

The cost of preparing this report for you is $ _____. Is it worth this much to you?
We wish to eliminate, simplify, or combine reports which "cost more than they are worth."
Will you let us have your comments on the following lines?

_____
_____
_____
_____
_____
_____
_____
_____
_____

Return to *Neal Graham*   Sign your name here_____
             Office Manager   Your title_____
                                                 Department_____

FIG. 4–8. Suggested form to be attached to all reports to make receiver cost-conscious and to eliminate unnecessary report work.

time to look it over, become interested in functions or problems which may not be their concern, waste some of their time on these "foreign activities," and require additional filing space and help to retain the reports for some doubtful future reference.

Reducing Report Costs.   In order to reduce expenses incurred in preparing reports, the following questions might be asked:

What is the purpose or aim of this report?
Is its cost justifiable?

Are parts of the report duplicated elsewhere? If so, can this be eliminated?

Is the best reproducing process being employed in making the copies?

To whom are copies sent?

Does each present recipient need a copy? Why?

Are there instances where one copy can serve several present recipients, thus reducing the number of copies needed?

Should the report be continued in its present form? If not, what is your recommendation?

Can the general format be improved? How?

Can the readability be increased by illustrative material and better grammer and English?

When given sufficient thought and properly applied, the answers to these questions will assist in writing better—not bigger—reports. And office managers will have achieved a noteworthy accomplishment.

QUESTIONS

1. Does the use of the scientific method in office management require reports? Explain your answer.
2. Define "office report," and relate why it is utilized in office management.
3. Would you say that a report based on opinions is of little or no value to an office manager? Why?
4. In your opinion how is the best way to get report writers to want to improve their writing efforts?
5. Are reports likely to prove more beneficial in certain types of enterprises than in others? Elaborate on your answer.
6. Discuss the use of planning in report writing.
7. Most managers agree that reports are vital to their work. Why aren't managers more active in efforts to improve reports and make them more meaningful and helpful? What practical suggestions can you make to correct these conditions?
8. State six specific ways of making reports effective.
9. Briefly describe the use and operation of "office composing machines."
10. Do you agree with the following? "Admittedly some reports cost a lot of money to prepare, but the cost is usually minor when the report is viewed in light of its importance. Reducing the funds allocated for report writing is foolish economy. Greater and more tangible savings can usually be acquired elsewhere in an enterprise." Elaborate on your answer.
11. Should a report be written in accordance with the wishes of the writer? The receiver? Justify your answer.
12. Secure a report written for an executive. Study its contents and determine the main purpose it is intended to serve. Assuming that the purpose is a

valid one, explain in what specific ways you feel this report can be improved.

Sources for reports are friends in business, government reports, and various articles in newspapers and magazines available in the library.

CASE PROBLEMS

CASE 4-1. MANNING, INC.

The president of Manning, Inc., asks you to prepare his report to stockholders for the company year just ending. He requests that you give the facts, using a friendly informal style. A length of 300–500 words is suggested. Although some unfavorable conditions have developed for the company during the last twelve months, the president does not feel these should be stressed, nor should they be ignored. To quote his own words, "Give the stockholders all the facts, point out the favorable as well as the unfavorable factors, but I do not think it wise to stress the unfavorable aspects of our business."

Data based on the recently released Statement of Income reveal the following:

	Year Just Ending	Previous Year
Net sales	$61,371,290	$71,285,342
Gross profits	9,843,530	20,055,410
Net income	3,751,017	8,002,688

The president feels that the long-term outlook is good, that stockholders should not lose faith in Manning, and that the expanded research by the corporation points to a favorable and sound future.

A new pension plan has been established lowering the elective retirement age to 62, and compulsory retirement at 65 years of age. Both employee and the company contribute to the plan. Payment of regular quarterly dividends of 25 cents per share payable April 10 has been voted by the Board of Directors. If the present business trend continues, the amount of dividend will have to be curtailed.

Competition is extremely active, and some price cutting is taking place. To date the company has been unable to obtain higher selling prices, although it is paying higher labor, material, and transportation costs.

Two months ago the Crosby plant, one of the company's oldest, was shut down for an indefinite period. The labor efficiency in this plant has been quite low for the past several years.

Lower demand for the company's products is evidenced by reports from sales representatives and studies by the market research department. The present demand level is believed to be temporary, reflecting customers' inventory positions and market adjustments taking place. The demand appears to be increasing for "C-1272." Completion of the new plant designed to produce "C-1272" within the next three months should enable the company to improve its sales position. This new plant will cost approximately $55,000 more than anticipated due to rising construction costs.

Heavy advertising expenditures are being carefully considered in order to increase sales. Two new district sales managers have been appointed during the past sixty days.

PROBLEMS:

1. Prepare the report requested by the president of Manning, Inc.
2. Point out what you believe to be the strong points of your report.

CASE 4-2. ERIC GUNDERSON

Eric Gunderson, training director of a large manufacturer, has just completed a training course for foremen. A total of fifteen meetings—two hours each—were held from 9:30 A.M. to 11:30 A.M. each Wednesday. Twelve foremen comprised the group, member-participation was emphasized, and situations required foreman's attention were taken from the shop, analyzed, and possible actions to take, resolved.

At the last meeting, Eric Gunderson had each member of the group fill out a questionnaire form. The tabulated results show:

	Yes	No
Did you benefit from the course?........	10	2
Did you become familiar with practical principles that you can use in your work?............................	6	6
Did you get any direct benefit traceable to these sessions?...................	8	4
Do you favor any formalized training in the future for yourself?............	11	1
Do you have any suggestions for improving the course content?..........	3	9

In addition, "open comments" brought forth these remarks:
"Enjoyed all the sessions."
"The attitude of the participants was good."
"I think more about planning now."
"Believe the discussions rambled and were too broad."
"All right for classroom, but it's different in the shop."

In the opinion of Mr. Gunderson, the training program worked out very satisfactorily. He felt it was a success and believed an advanced course in foremanship should be recommended for this group with the exception of two members who, in Mr. Gunderson's opinion, were not of foreman caliber. He had no substantiating data for this opinion except his observations during the fifteen meetings.

PROBLEMS:

1. Write the report that you feel Mr. Gunderson should prepare for his superior.

2. What additional information do you believe Mr. Gunderson should have obtained in order to supply a complete report. Discuss.

Chapter · 5

Office Correspondence

Many blunder in business through inability or an unwilling-
ness to adopt new ideas. I have seen many a success turn to
failure because the thought which should be trained on big
things is cluttered up with the burdensome detail of little
things.

—PHILIP S. DELANEY

IN EVERY enterprise much of the work of writing
deals with getting out letters. This work of correspondence usually
represents a significant portion of the toal paper work and efforts to
improve, to simplify, and, in certain instances, to eliminate letters are
a challenge to every office manager.

Letter writing can be stimulating. A person you have never seen
will send an inquiry, a check, or an order—as a result of a letter. That
should inject a pride of accomplishment in writing really good letters
and to be satisfied with only the best.

TOO MANY LETTERS

In modern business there is little doubt that there are too many
letters. When the sender keeps a copy of the original and the receiver's
reply, and the receiver the original and a copy of his reply, there are
a total of four letters in company files. In certain cases, a reply to the
sender is not necessary. In other cases, the reply is not clearly stated
necessitating a follow-up letter with subsequently more letters to be
written. In some cases, the reply consists of notations made on the
original and returned to the sender who destroys his carbon, leaving
one letter in the sender's file and none in the receiver's file. Think
of the time saved by this latter practice.

PLANNING THE WORK OF CORRESPONDENCE

Perhaps the initial step to take in planning office correspondence is
to consider the fundamentals such as the purpose of the letter, the

manner of writing the message, and general writing practices found to be effective. This leads to discussion of the fundamentals of letter writing.

Many business letters do not produce the desired results. Most letters can be improved by following these fundamentals of good letter writing:

1. *Set a definite goal.* Know exactly what is to be accomplished by the letter. Do not confuse the issue; settle on one main point and concentrate on it. Letters pertaining to a single subject are easy to understand, and they expedite filing.

2. *Use the "you viewpoint."* This stresses the needs, wants, and interests of the recipient, who is put in the center of what is written. Look at the subject from his viewpoint; visualize the reader while writing and tailor the letter to him. For example:

Write:

"You may have quick service if you'll just telephone ORchard 1–7777."

Do not write:

"We wish to call attention to the fact that we are in the dry-cleaning business and have a fifteen-year record of excellent service."

Or write:

"Thanks for your letter of May 14. Your order will be shipped today by parcel post."

Do not write:

"We have received order dated the tenth and in reply we wish to state delivery is being made today under separate cover."

3. *Employ positive expressions.* Greater acceptance and motivation are gained by writing in an optimistic tone. Write, "We can send you tickets for the November 27 performance," instead of "We cannot send tickets for any performance prior to that of November 27."

4. *Make the letter clear.* This requires planning and knowing what must be included in the letter. The writer should express each thought so clearly that the reader is certain to understand it. Normally the transcriber helps in acquiring clarity by straightening out improper sentence structures and switching words.

5. *Use short words and sentences.* Short words are bold and clear and say just what they mean. Some business-letter writers, quite er-

roneously, never use a short word if they know a long one of the same or similar meaning, and such practice weakens a letter. The term "goozler" has been used to identify such writers.[1] Omit involved phrases and weed out the extra words. Say it simply, but do not sacrifice completeness for sake of brevity. Tabulate lists for greater clarity. Practical punctuation will help considerably.

6. *Refrain from doubling.* In modern letter writing the trend is toward brevity. Say it and go on to the next subject. Occasionally, the use of two adjectives or two verbs of about the same meaning adds emphasis, but in most cases, this doubling detracts from the letter. For example, writing, "We are trying to be tolerant and considerate," is weak. To be tolerant is to be considerate and vice versa. Why waste time? Note the doubling in the following and the fact that nothing is gained by this practice.

> To request payment is right and proper.
> Settlement on this basis will be satisfactory and agreeable.
> It is unfair and unjust for you to make such a request.

7. *Be friendly.* Let the letter reflect your own natural self. It is well to remember that a letter is written to a human being, not merely to a name. Write naturally and humanly. Avoid the use of so-called "whisker" expressions and dead diction. Examples of "whisker" expressions, along with suggested improvements, are:

Do not use	*Use*
I am not in a position	I cannot
My attention has been called	I notice
Enclosed please find	We enclose
Has come to hand	Referred to me
Acquaint me with the facts	Tell me
Under separate cover	Separately
Contents duly noted	I have read
At this time	At present
We have reviewed our records	We find
It is our opinion	I believe
At all times	Always
Take pleasure	Are pleased
We have yours of the 10th	Your letter of November 10
Your esteemed favor of the 6th and its enclosures	The papers you sent

---

[1] L. E. Frailey, *Handbook of Business Letters* (New York: Prentice-Hall, Inc., 1948), pp. 41–48. This is an excellent source for the how-to-write technique of preparing effective business letters that attract attention and get results.

March 15, 19--

Dear Sir:

Your letter addressed to our Chicago plant has been referred to the undersigned for reply. We wish to advise that it is our long standing policy to limit our sales promotion efforts to ideas originating with our advertising agencies. Therefore, we cannot accept your suggestion.

Enclosed herewith is your letter and under separate cover your display unit is being returned.

Needless to say, we want to extend our thanks to you for your interest in our products and their sales.

Very truly yours,

March 15, 19--

Dear Mr. Hayes:

Thanks for your suggestion concerning the display unit for our products.

Our executive committee has decided not to change the current means of display. This was decided in view of our present sales and the costs for changing our sales program at this time. There are also some legal difficulties to which the use of this display unit might expose both you and ourselves. We would want to clarify these legal points before considering your suggestion for future action.

We will keep you informed of developments.

Very truly yours,

FIG. 5–1. *Top:* A letter written in a stilted manner. *Bottom:* An improvement over the letter above.

The top of Figure 5–1 illustrates a letter written in a stilted manner and using whisker expressions; an improvement is shown in the bottom portion of this figure.

8. *Make the letter helpful.* Be sure you are giving all the information requested or needed. Be informative. Give factual answers.

9. *Make the letter conclusive.* Be certain to include what action, if any, is desired of the reader, what the writer will do, or what the

writer wants done. Be decisive; let the reader know exactly the recommended course or disposition.

FORM OF THE LETTER

A business letter should make a favorable first impression. To do this, it should be placed well on the page, have margins as even as possible, have a uniformity of typing or print, and give a clean and neat appearance.

There is probably no one best form for a business letter. Usually a general pattern is in common usage, but slight variations are the rule, depending upon the particular needs and wishes of the writer. Most readers are accustomed to the general pattern and look for certain information in certain locations. Figure 5–2 shows the forms of several

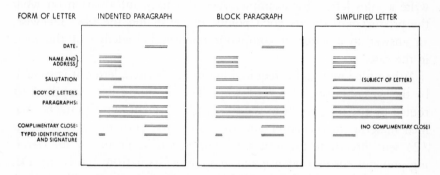

FIG. 5–2.   The respective forms of three different letters used in business.

different types, including (1) block paragraphs, (2) indented paragraphs, and (3) simplified letter. The difference between indented paragraphs and block paragraphs is that in the latter the paragraphs are started at the left margin. In the simplified letter, all material starts at the left margin, the salutation is omitted—in its place the subject of the letter is written—and the complimentary close is omitted. Slight variations from these three forms of letters are employed. One large national distributor, for example, uses the block paragraph form with open punctuation, that is, commas and periods are omitted at end of date, address, and close.

PROCEDURE IN CORRESPONDENCE WORK

A definite procedure is required to handle correspondence work effectively; the work cannot be left to chance. Relying upon haphazard methods or hoping that all correspondence work will be written promptly is wishful thinking. A way of getting letter writing accomplished effectively and economically must be established and followed. The following is suggested:

1. *Get letters to those who answer them.* Letters on ordinary and routine subjects can be quickly routed to the proper party for reply. In contrast, letters dealing with out-of-the-ordinary subjects frequently offer some difficulty. The eternal question in such cases is: "Who handles matters of this sort?" Frequently these letters are addressed to the wrong person within the enterprise and must be rerouted. The task of getting letters to the proper persons for answering is usually the responsibility of the head of the Mailing Department or of the office manager.

2. *Get facts to the correspondent.* In order to compose an intelligent letter, it is necessary for the writer to have all the facts. To write a sales letter, for example, one must have information on what the product will do, its good points, its price, and the like. Likewise, an answer to a letter of complaint requires knowledge of the facts in the case.

When filed material is required in order to write a letter, it is secured by the writer in one of several ways. The incoming letter my be (1) routed by the mail room to the Filing Department, which attaches the filed material to the letter and then forwards both to the writer; or (2) sent directly to the writer, who decides if he needs the file covering previous correspondence and, if so, requests it from the Filing Department. In some cases, both the writer and the file are located in the same area, so that the writer can himself secure any filed material he needs. If there is no file, or if the required information is not in the file, the necessary data might be obtained by making telephone calls or by circulating in the office a simple form requesting the needed information.

3. *Permit correspondent to analyze facts and to organize letter.* To a considerable degree, every letter is an effort to have the recipient believe and act toward a subject as the writer does. Hence, the writer should try to visualize the type of reader to whom he is writing and select an approach that will invoke the reader's response to action. Sometimes this necessitates guessing or taking a chance. However, the opening statement should be designed to get the reader's attention. Following this, the reader's interest should be developed. Then lead this interest into a desire and finally culminate the entire letter with action—to order the service, to accept the adjustment, to pay the bill, or whatever the case might be.

4. *Provide correspondent with a stenographer or a dictating ma-*

chine when ready to dictate.   The assignment of stenographic help to a writer is done by the stenographic supervisor or by the office manager. For best results, the stenographer should report to the correspondent at stated times throughout the day; this permits better organization and execution of work on the part of both the stenographer and the correspondent. In actual practice, however, the task of regulating stenographic work is not this simple. Most offices have a certain amount of irregular correspondence which is best handled by adapting it to a schedule setting definite hours when emergency dictation can be handled. This helps accomplish all the work with a minimum of confusion. On the other hand, emergency work can be sandwiched in with the regular work. However, when this is done, allowance must be made in the regular schedules.

5. *Get letters written and in the mail.*   The final step in getting letters out is the actual physical work of typing the letter, and this is by no means a small job. When the typing is completed, the letters are sent to the correspondent, who reads and signs them. They are then returned to the stenographer for enclosure in envelopes or, in many cases, are sent direct to the mail room, where they are prepared for mailing and posted.

ORGANIZING AND OFFICE CORRESPONDENCE

Like most writing in the office, letter writing is done by different employees located in many different departments. Many top executives prefer to handle their correspondence work in their own unit, i.e., by their secretaries and themselves. However, the bulk of correspondence work is usually performed by personnel designated as correspondents who either have transcribers permanently located in the various departments performing letter writing or the transcribers are in a centralized transcribing department or "pool." In some companies a centralized correspondence department works out extremely well. For example, in a prominent insurance company about 80 per cent of the some 150,000 letters per year were being answered within three business days after their respective arrival. However, this percentage was raised to 98 per cent when a centralized letter-writing unit was established.[2]

Whatever the organization arrangement, the producing of letters consists of dictation and transcription. Each affects the other, for the dictator must correct or redictate if the transcriber's work is in error,

---

[2] Harry V. Odle, "Effective Program of Correspondence Improvement," *Burroughs Clearing House* (Detroit, May, 1955), p. 39.

and the transcriber cannot be efficient if the dictator does his work poorly. The organizational relationship should encourage the needed co-ordination among those engaged in letter-writing work.

Correspondence work can be accomplished either on a personal basis or on a machine basis. In the former case, the dictator talks to a stenographer, who manually takes down the statements in shorthand. Later these notes are transcribed. When a machine is used, the dictation is recorded and subsequently played back to the transcriber, who types the letter.

The choice between the personal and the machine bases rests upon the relative evaluation of the advantages of each in each particular case. No standarized formula can be applied, and the comparison cannot be made wholly on factual data—certain indeterminate subjective factors enter into most decisions covering this subject.

Advocates of the personal are quick to point out that a feeling of close co-operation, better understanding of the type of letter to be written, and consideration for the important human element are in-duced when letters are dictated to a stenographer. Second, the personal basis permits the transcriber to work from written notes which are usually easier to comprehend than audible data. Third, shorthand is not difficult to learn, and satisfactory speeds suitable for most office work are attainable by most employees. Fourth, dictation is possible anywhere. A special machine need not be available. Fifth, the cost of a machine is avoided as well as the costs of operation, special supplies, and maintenance.

It is possible for the transcriber to use a machine for recording dictation. The notes are printed in letters on a tape in accordance with a special code. The machine looks like a small typewriter and requires special training for proficient operation.

The important advantages of the machine basis include: First, dic-tation is expedited—material can be dictated when it is on the dictator's mind. His thoughts can be recorded as they occur to him. Second, the distribution of work among transcribers can be balanced. Steady and even work throughout the day frequently minimizes the number of transcribers needed. Third, the transcriber's time is saved, since her presence is not required while the dictation is being recorded. Fourth, convenience is provided. The dictator can work independently; he can dictate at his convenience; he need not wait for his stenographer. Fifth, the dictator is alone; thus concentration and clearer and better thinking are encouraged.

DICTATING MACHINES

When the machine basis is used, a selection is offered from modern machines employing electronics to provide clear, high-fidelity recording of the human voice. A recorder unit is used by the dictator and a transcriber unit is used by the typist to play back the recorded dictation, or a combination unit featuring both recording and transcribing can be used. The latter is practical when the dictator and transcriber can plan their day for separate periods of dictation and transcription.

The recorder is equipped with either (1) hand microphone recommended for ordinary dictating practices or when the surroundings are somewhat noisy, or (2) desk microphone for recording over-the-desk conference discussions or important telephone conversations, assuming the consent of both parties has been obtained. Furthermore, when the recorder is equipped with a foot-control device, the desk microphone permits free use of both hands during correspondence dictation. It is possible to start and stop the recorder as desired and to listen to what has been dictated. A signaling device is also provided whereby the amount of dictation and places of correction can be indicated.

Transcribers are equipped with special features which assist the typist, including special headphones, foot or hand controls for starting and stopping the machine, backspacer for repeating dictation, voice-control adjustments to regulate speed, volume, and tone, and a signaling device to inform the transcriber of length of dictation and places of correction.

Dictating machines can be classified according to the type of medium used, including (1) plastic belt, (2) plastic disk, and (3) wax cylinder.

PLASTIC BELT

In this type the recording medium is an endless belt of thin, tough plastic, $3\frac{1}{2}$ inches wide and 12 inches in circumference. This belt withstands rough handling, provides constant recording qualities, and permits uniform backspacing for convenient and accurate corrections. Every recorded groove on the belt is the same length and of the same recording quality. One belt will accommodate about 15 minutes of dictation and serves as a permanent, one-time recording medium. As many as five belts, nested one within the other, will fit into a small business envelope and can be mailed for about 3 cents.

The machine is a recorder-transcriber, sturdy and compact; it weighs only 20 pounds and covers a desk area slightly larger than a standard business letterhead. The units may be used in the office or, in the case of the portable model, are especially convenient for traveling representatives who send communications to the home office. A close-up view of the machine with the plastic belt partially removed is shown in Figure 5–3.

Courtesy: Dictaphone Corp., New York

FIG. 5–3. Close-up of the recorder-transcriber "Time-Master," which records on a small, flexible-plastic belt.

PLASTIC DISK

As the name implies, the plastic disk method of voice recording employs a thin disk of plastic material. The disk can be used once, then thrown away or filed for future reference. One hundred disks are approximately 1 inch in thickness; and three sizes are available— 3, 5, and 7 inches in diameter, respectively—for 4, 15, and 30 minutes of recording. The disks are light, tough, and unbreakable, which makes it possible to send them conveniently through the mail. They can thus be used to improve the communication between salesmen and the office, executives and their associates, and the main office and its branches.

WAX CYLINDER

This is one of the oldest means of recording and transcribing used in the office. The equipment consists of a recorder and a transcriber with various features such as hand or desk microphone, foot control device, and special headphones, described above, plus a shaver. This latter unit is used to shave or cut off the engraved surface of the used cylinder so that it can be used again for dictation. The shaver works on the same principle as a lathe. Each wax cylinder will record about eight one-page letters and can be shaved about sixty-five times.

AUTOMATIC TYPING MACHINES

The automatic typing machine has won wide adoption for the typing of similar letters when they are in (1) large quantities, and (2) similar format having slight changes only such as name and address and dates. It consists of a regular typewriter to which a special mechanism has been attached. The paper is inserted in the machine in the same manner as in a regular typewriter, and the date, name, and address are typed in by hand. At the touch of a button, the machine takes over and automatically types the letter, stopping at the first place where a special fill-in is required. This is typed in by hand, and then, after another touch of the button, the machine continues typing the letter to the next stop. Figure 5–4 shows a letter typed in this manner. All

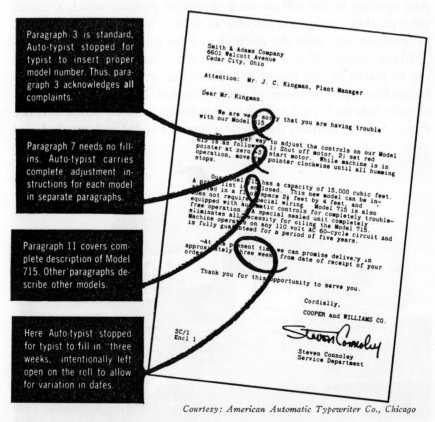

Courtesy: American Automatic Typewriter Co., Chicago

FIG. 5–4. A letter typed by an automatic typewriter. Paragraph selection and individual fill-in material are easily handled as described in the illustration.

paragraphing, spacing, and the like are handled by the machine. If possible, the location of each fill-in should be at the end of a line or paragraph, to provide the required elasticity in space. Words or numbers of varying lengths can be inserted without difficulty. The entire letter has been typed automatically by machine, with the exception of the individualized parts as noted on the illustration.

As many as 200 short letters a day can be typed with this machine. Multiple combinations of machines requiring one operator can produce approximately 500 short letters a day. Such a battery is a mass producer, flexible and efficient. Figure 5–5 shows a battery of four automatic typing machines.

Form letters or paragraphs are originally cut on either a (1) record roll, or (2) a tape. This perforating work is done in the individual office or at the local service office. The record roll, resembling that used on a player piano, is mounted in the machine and, when released, passes over a trucker bar in which a vacuum is maintained. Any opening in the roll causes a change in pressure which actutates the type, thus causing the machine to write. The capacities and details of operation vary with the machine and the manufacturer.

About twenty different letters or an equivalent of form paragraphs can be placed on one record roll. The operator selects the material to be machine-typed by means of simple controls. In one method a series of push buttons is used to make the operation entirely automatic. See Figure 5–6. In another, the operator inserts a coded and punched card

Courtesy: Robotyper Corp., Hendersonville, N.C.

FIG. 5–5. Four automatic typewriters are operated by one employee.

Courtesy: American Automatic Typewriter Co., Chicago

FIG. 5–6. An automatic typewriter featuring push-button controls.

indicating the desired material into a selecting device and presses the "start" button. The desired material in the proper sequence is typed automatically. It is possible to switch from one letter to another or from one paragraph to another by simply turning a dial to the identifying number of the material to be typed.

Courtesy: Commercial Controls Corp., Rochester, N.Y.

FIG. 5–7. An automatic writing machine that is actuated by a punched tape.

When a perforated tape is used, the operation of the automatic typewriter is quite similar to that described above. Such a typewriter unit is illustrated in Figure 5–7. The holes in the tape cause the mechanism to operate specific typewriter keys which result in the desired letter. Perforated tape is being used more and more to operate office machines automatically. Its growth has been stimulated by the application of integrated data processing (IDP) which will be discussed in Chapter 15.

PRODUCING LETTERS BY DUPLICATION PROCESS

To produce a substantial quantity of letters exactly alike, any one of several duplicating means described in Chapter 9 is satisfactory. Duplicating is fast and economical. Frequently the name and address is omitted, and simply "Dear Sir" is put on each letterhead, with the name and address on the envelope only. As an alternate the name and

Courtesy: Addressograph-Multigraph Corp., Cleveland

FIG. 5–8. Machine for writing a complete letter—from blank paper to the finished product.

address can be typed carefully on the letter, but it will not match precisely the duplicated part of the letter. However, with typing skill and experience, satisfactory results are possible.

A machine is available that will write a complete letter from blank paper in one run—individual name and address, salutation, letterhead in color, date, text, and facsimile ink signature—all with one operator. Since the same basic process is used at the same time, the name and address are perfectly matched with the text of the letter. In addition, the machine will print and personally identify a reply card. Figure 5–8 illustrates the machine. Beginning with the automatic feed on the left, the work progresses to the right being printed with name, address, and salutation, then moves further to the right where the letterhead, date, and text are printed, and finally to the extreme right where the signature is affixed and the finished letter collected in the receiving tray. The machine speed is 100 letters per minute.

Another possibility for volume mailings is to use a "window letter." A pre-addressed card is attached to the back and top of the duplicated letter, so that the name and address appear at the normal location and can be read through a window opening in the letterhead. The card also serves as a business reply card with necessary postage and

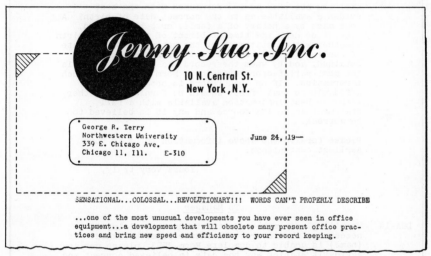

FIG. 5-9. A "window letter" which features the use of a pre-addressed card to individualize a form letter. The card, also used as a business reply card, is held in place either by a pocket in the back or by slots into which opposite card corners are inserted (as illustrated). The name and address appear through a window opening in the letter. The mailing can also utilize window envelopes.

name and address of the sender on the reverse side. This arrangement is illustrated in Figure 5-9.

ACTUATING THE WORK OF CORRESPONDENCE

A program which acquaints all correspondence personnel with effective letter-writing fundamentals, specific practices preferred by the enterprise, and supplies the best writing tools will help tremendously in attaining effective letter writing. Many actions can be taken. For example, Mutual Of New York undertook a comprehensive correspondence simplification program and among other things drafted a series of "guide letters" for its correspondents. Figure 5-10 shows an example. These letters were meticulously prepared to give customers the answers they wanted, in understandable terms, and in a friendly, helpful manner.

Example of The "Long" and "Short" of It

DEATH CLAIM - EXPLAINING AGE ADJUSTMENT

Original

We are enclosing a letter addressed to the payee under
the above numbered policy, explaining the adjustment
which we made because of a difference in the Insured's
age.

Will you see that we are furnished with the best
evidence available as to the correct date of birth? A
copy made by a notary of a family or public record,
made at or near the time of birth, of the date of birth
together with a statement by the notary as to the date
of publication of the book from which the record is
obtained, and by whom the record was made and when, is
the most satisfactory evidence. Form 3593 covers such
information. If no such record is obtainable, an
affidavit to that effect should be furnished together
with the best information available with a full
statement as to its source and why it is believed to
be correct.

Please forward the above information to us at your
earliest convenience.

                                  Yours very truly,

                          Revised
                          To Manager

DCA-14   We will gladly make adjustments on this claim, if
         necessary, when correct birthdate is established. If
         (name) is unable to complete Form 3593, please get an
         affidavit stating why the date is believed correct and
         return with the best evidence available.

         Also, kindly give the enclosed letter* of explanation.

                                  Thank you.

         * Key No. DCA-15

         Original 160 Words: Revised 53 Words: Saving 67 Per cent

         Note: The Original is a splendid example of a letter
                that goes to great unnecessary length in stating
                the obvious. Notice that the Revised states all
                that a manager need be told to know how to proceed.

Courtesy: Mutual Of New York

FIG. 5–10. A guide letter furnished company correspondents to assist them in writing more
effectively.

It frequently is helpful to appoint a correspondence counselor. He
or she may be selected from among present employees, or the services
of a consultant may be used. The duties of the counselor include those
of an adviser, a teacher, and a salesman for effective writing within
the enterprise. He is the nominal head of the program for correspondence improvement.

Also, weekly or semimonthly meetings at which correspondents will discuss the principles of good letter writing should be established. The counselor acts as the group leader, and letters written by the employees can be criticized. It is also possible to hold conferences with individual employees. Frequently this method is more effective than the group meetings, for samples of the employee's work can be inspected and personalized help given.

BETTER DICTATING PRACTICES

Dictation can be made effective by following a few simple suggestions that reflect, for the most part, ordinary common sense. In the first place, the dictator should have complete information at hand. He should organize his thoughts before dictating, preferably making notes on the points to be emphasized and how best to express them.

Second, in so far as is practical, the dictator should refrain from unnecessary interruptions. Long telephone conversations should be avoided during the times set aside for dictation. Likewise, other activities should not be permitted to break the continuity of the dictating work. Good dictation requires concentration of thoughts and efforts.

Third, the dictator should speak crisply, clearly, and correctly. Care should be taken to articulate carefully and to pronounce each word correctly. The use of "ah" and "oh" should be omitted when thinking about the next sentence. Candy or chewing gum should not be in the mouth.

Fourth, be concise. The dictator should express his thoughts completely but in the fewest words possible. Avoid unnecessary details and repetition. Words should be chosen carefully to be sure they give the intended meaning; unusual words should be spelled out. The dictator should assume the responsibility for proper sentence structure and grammar.

Finally, complete information should be given regarding the work requirements, including such things as the number of copies, the general make-up of the letter, and whether the material is to be typed as rough draft or final copy.

BETTER TYPING PRACTICES

Typing proficiency can be developed most quickly by proper instruction, adequate supervision, and regular practice. There are no substitutes for these essentials. The office manager should do everything possible to promote these factors. In addition, he can provide a good working area, including adequate space, good light, a posture chair, a desk or stand which insures that the base of the typewriter is about 13 inches above the chair seat, and supplies within easy reach. The office manager should also give encouragement to and co-operate completely with efforts designed to improve typing technique, including the development of fast finger strokes, rhythm, and proper touch.

FULL UTILIZATION OF CORRESPONDENCE PERSONNEL AND FACILITIES

Each correspondence employee should be kept busy at the level of skill for which he or she is hired. Stenographers should not be tied down to typists' jobs. Correspondents should not spend a great deal of their time filing. High-salaried executives should not dictate letters in those cases where a correspondent will do an equally effective job. Full utilization of all correspondence facilities is the goal. In addition, the machines must be kept in good repair to insure high volume and quality of work.

CONTROLLING THE WORK OF CORRESPONDENCE

A study of the correspondence in any enterprise will reveal that most letters can be classified into one of several major groups such as those dealing with complaints, employment, purchasing, sales, or credit. In turn, letters in each of these major groups can be classified further according to individual type. To illustrate, the following major groups along with their respective types are included.

Complaints—replies are usually of four types:

1. Acknowledgment of complaint and promise to investigate and report later.
2. Adjustment of complaint giving date and amount, and thanking addressee.
3. Refusal to adjust complaint, with reasons explaining why.
4. Request that the goods be returned for inspection and advise that further consideration will be given.

Employment—three types of replies are generally given:

1. Acknowledgment of application, stating no opening at present.
2. Acknowledgment of application and request to report for work.
3. Welcome to newly hired worker of the company and explanation of company policies.

Purchasing—three kinds of letters are commonly originated in this group:

1. Request for prices and delivery dates.
2. Request to trace shipment.
3. Inquiry about disposition of order.

FORM LETTERS

The fact that most letters can be classified into a relatively small number of types has led to letter standardization or the use of form letters. A form letter is *a standardized letter that is used by an enterprise to answer all correspondence of a similar and recurring subject, or which is used to give the same information to many addressees.* A form letter may be sent to accounts past due. Such a letter, keyed "Delinquent Collection Letter No. 1," is sent to all accounts in arrears, with the appropriate name and address added at the top. After a certain amount of time, a "Delinquent Collection Letter No. 2" may be sent to those accounts which remain unpaid.

Benefits in Use of Form Letters. The chief advantages in the use of form letters are that they (1) afford a uniform operation, (2) conserve both the dictator's and the typist's time, and (3) help reduce letter costs. On the other hand, there are disadvantages in the use of form letters, including these: (1) they are not keyed to the requirements of individual cases; (2) they may be a little stilted; and (3) they are very often discounted by the receiver because of the lack of a personal touch.

Generally speaking, form letters serve a very useful purpose. They are tailored to fit certain conditions and are usually worked over by several correspondents to create the best possible results. They need not be impersonal, and it is not necessary to send the same letter again and again to the same customer. When properly handled, there should be no objection to form letters.

FORM PARAGRAPHS

Form paragraphs are similar in idea to form letters but apply to standardized paragraphs only. Under this practice letters are composed of form paragraphs plus individual ones. Experts are frequently engaged to develop the form paragraphs.

It is customary for the dictator to use several variants of a form paragraph. This permits some diversity. The approved form paragraphs are listed, keyed, and indexed and are made available to all correspondents.

DEVELOPING FORM LETTERS AND PARAGRAPHS

Form letters and form paragraphs can be "armchaired" from handy references or they can be determined by the scientific method. The latter procedure is recommended. To do this, simply take these steps:

1. For a period of four weeks, make an extra copy of every letter written.

2. At the end of this period, sort the copies by major subject and further by types under each major heading.

3. Determine the types of letters most frequently written and also, under each type, the most frequently used paragraphs.

4. Select the best reply to each frequently-asked question and also the best expression of the necessary information.

5. Standardize these forms and incorporate them as form paragraphs and form letters.

6. Repeat this entire procedure every twelve months; then adjust and improve form paragraphs and letters as suggested by findings.

The office manager should enlist the services of all letter-writing people in his office in this work. Participation will not only help win acceptance of the program of improving correspondence but will also utilize the best personnel for this work, raise morale, and increase the efficiency.

COST OF LETTERS

Office letters cost more than most people realize. Each business letter that is individually composed and typed costs its sender about 80 cents, perhaps more. The time of the dictator and stenographer, the office overhead, and the mailing and filing costs make up the bulk of this total. A rough estimate based on an allowance of 10 minutes for dictation and 15 minutes for transcription gives a labor cost of around 65 cents, to which must be added the cost of paper, envelope, and postage plus office overhead costs. The cost varies, of course, depending on the length, difficulty of material, method of transcription, and non-productive time.

For large quantities of almost identical letters the cost can be reduced considerably by using the automatic typewriter. One operator with four machines will produce approximately 500 short letters a day. For this arrangement the cost data are as follows:

DAILY COST

Depreciation on four machines (five-year basis)...........	$6.25
Overhead expenses (floor space, heat, interest on investment)..	0.70
Electricity..	0.20
Maintenance...	0.30
Supplies...	1.05
Labor..	12.00
Total..	$20.50

$20.50 divided by 500 letters equals 4.1 cents a letter.

Likewise, the cost for identical letters produced by a duplicating process is less than those individually typed, the exact figure depending mainly upon the process used and the quantity involved. Of course, a comparison of costs for a letter individually typed to that for a duplicated letter is not strictly comparable, since it is unlikely that quantities of identical letters would be individually typed.

The cost of letters stress the necessity for control over letter-writing activities. The expenditures should be compatible with achieving the objectives and plans for the correspondence work. The pertinent question may be asked: "Are the letter costs consistent with the plans and achievements? Usually the manager has two alternatives: (1) strive to gain the same goals but at less cost, or (2) improve the present quality and effectiveness at the same or, if possible, at lower cost.

In any particular case, an office manager may determine the importance of letter-writing costs by the following simple program: Determine the payroll for one month for employees engaged in letter-writing activity in the office. Add to this the monthly investment in machines, space, and supplies. This total will give some idea of the importance of letter writing in the office. If compared with the total office expenses, this figure becomes even more meaningful; in most cases it represents quite a sizable percentage.

FURTHER CORRESPONDENCE CONTROL CONSIDERATIONS

The use of an office manual is an effective means of controlling office correspondence. Manuals provide the employee with standard practices and instructions in a form that is convenient and easy to use. They help the employee to help himself and assist in eliminating many needless errors.

Some measurement of correspondence quality and output should be determined, for only by such means will a manager be able to determine the success of efforts toward improving correspondence. Consideration for such factors as accuracy, clearness, conciseness, completeness, and naturalness can be used to rate the quality of the letter. Output might best be determined by sorting the letters according to type and counting the number of each type written during the period of a week or two weeks.[3]

It is helpful for the manager to keep an accounting of such things as what machine is assigned to each correspondent, the amount of work turned out by each machine, the extent of machine idleness, and the amount and frequency of repairs. These data plus proper follow-up will help to improve the work output. Also, in certain instances it is desirable to keep a daily record or chart for each stenographer, showing the amount of work completed, the amount currently being handled, and the amount scheduled to be done. This information can be used to distribute the work evenly among all stenographers and to check accomplishment with task.

QUESTIONS

1. In connection with office correspondence, give examples of (a) doubling, (b) whisker expressions, and (c) positive expressions.
2. In your opinion why do not more companies adopt the practice of writing a longhand answer at the bottom of a letter?
3. Discuss the cost of letters.
4. Give circumstances under which a form letter can generally be used to advantage.
5. Is it possible to use form paragraphs rather than form letters? Explain.
6. Which form of letter—(a) block, (b) indented, or (c) simplified—do you favor? Why?
7. Under what specific conditions would you recommend the use of the personnel basis—stenographer and shorthand—to accomplish correspondence work? Of the machine basis—a recording and transcribing machine?
8. Why should an office manager know the fundamentals of good letter writing when qualified help is available?
9. Point out the essential differences between producing letters by automatic typing machines and by duplicating process.
10. In general, how can dictating practices be improved? Typing practices?
11. Summarize the media of control which an office manager should usually exercise over correspondence work in an office.
12. As the recipient, do you object to the use of a—
    a) "Window letter"?

---

[3] Measuring office work output is of vital importance and is discussed in detail in Chapter 36.

b) Form letter addressed to "Dear Sir"?

c) Form letter with "nonmatching" inserts or phrases?

d) Nonconventional form of letter?

Give reasons for your answers.

CASE PROBLEMS

CASE 5-1. HIRSCH DISTRIBUTING CORPORATION

Miss Ethel Morrison is chief of the centralized typing section in the office of the Hirsch Distributing Corporation of Omaha, Nebraska. On Thursday morning she received a memorandum indicating that at the weekly management meeting held Wednesday (the day before), several executives and department heads had expressed dissatisfaction with the typing work being done. Specifically they had complained of quite a few erasures and bad spacing on many letters. Several department heads said that they had mentioned these shortcomings informally to the typists but that nothing had ever come of it. A resolution was offered and passed at the meeting to engage the services of Mr. Samuel Thorsen, a management consultant.

About a week later, Mr. Thorsen surveyed the office and found the following conditions:

1. Several of the typists indicated that the material being typed was quite complicated. They did not understand the meaning of some of the material which was technical.

2. Pay of the typists averaged about $5 more per week than comparable jobs in the community.

3. Of all the typists, one-half think Miss Morrison gives more desirable work to her favorite typists, the other half feel the work is distributed without prejudice.

4. Most of the typing work is wanted in a hurry.

5. During the past six months the typists have not worked overtime.

6. From time to time some of the typists are asked to copy certain excerpts from speeches, publicity items, and magazine articles. They feel that little use is made of these copies.

7. The typists appear to be satisfied with their jobs and have a favorable attitude toward the company.

PROBLEMS:

1. What do you believe the major issue is in this case?

2. Did the company do right in calling in Mr. Thorsen? Discuss.

3. What recommendations do you believe Mr. Thorsen should make?

4. What obstacles do you feel will be encountered in putting the recommendations, given in your answer to question No. 3, into effect? How would you prepare to overcome these objections? Explain.

CASE 5-2. HILL AND DOOLEY

Arnold Hill and Patrick Dooley are partners in a law firm. Mr. Hill is physically handicapped and is unable to attend any court proceedings or to perform any field work. Cases are assigned to Mr. Dooley and the two associates of the firm, Mr. Roger Brun and Mr. Edgar Eden. Full-time secretaries are assigned to Mr. Dooley and Mr. Brun. Two part-time court-reporting students from a nearby school handle the dictation of Mr. Hill. These students rank high in their class and work from 1.30 P.M. to 4.30 P.M. each workday. Mr. Eden reports to Mr. Hill by means of memorandums dictated to the part-time students. However, the amount of this work is small and is usually done after 4.00 P.M., when Mr. Hill leaves the office for the day.

Upon arrival in the afternoon, the two part-time students alternate in taking dictation from Mr. Hill. He insists on using these court-reporting students and wants them to become fully acquainted with legal work before they go out and do court-reporting work. Based on past experience the part-time girls remain with the law firm of Hill and Dooley for about eighteen months.

Mr. Hill demands exacting and perfect work in every detail. He has the work first "rough typed," then after he has made all necessary corrections, the work is typed in final form. An afternoon of a part-time student is spent in taking dictation, checking the rough draft with Mr. Hill, and waiting while the other part-time student is taking dictation. Statistics show that the full-time secretaries are able to perform over three times the transcription accomplished by either of the part-time court-reporting students.

Mr. Brun believes the employment of the part-time students reflects poor management. Mr. Dooley feels it is a question to be decided solely by Mr. Hill.

PROBLEMS:

1. As you see it, what is the problem to be solved in this case?
2. Justify both the expressed and what you feel are the implied viewpoints of Mr. Hill? Of Mr. Brun?
3. Outline a plan for improving the correspondence work of the Hill and Dooley law firm. Justify the actions you propose.

CASE 5–3. OAKWOOD-WYMAN COMPANY

Ten private secretaries are employed for ten executives of the Oakwood-Wyman Company. The salary of each secretary is $3,600 a year. Currently each secretary handles all correspondence and other secretarial duties for the executive to whom she is assigned. Letters and memorandums are taken down in shorthand and later transcribed.

For some time the office manager, Mr. William Harris, has believed that the use of dictating machines costing $375 each and a centralized secretarial unit could handle more efficiently the work which the secretaries now do.

The president of the company has told Mr. Harris that under no circumstance will he (the president) approve a change which affects his private office. He states that his secretary is working all day long and there cannot possibly be any saving in moving her to a centralized secretarial pool. However, if the other executives have no objections and a saving is involved, he will approve the centralized plan for the other nine executives.

From the records maintained by Mr. Harris, data were derived which can be considered typical of a day's work for each of the ten private secretaries. These data are shown below. A working day is 7 hours with two ten-minute rest periods, one in the morning, the other in the afternoon. For the past several months overtime pay to the secretaries has totaled $138 a month, but this time is excluded from the data shown.

The office manager states that by adopting a centralized setup and providing each executive with a dictating machine, only six secretaries excluding the president's, and a total of four transcribing machines costing $375 each, would be required. Mr. Harris explains that actually only three transcribing machines would be needed, but to take care of possible overloads and additional dictation, believed quite likely with machines, the purchase of four transcribing machines is recommended.

Mr. Harris further states that the use of machines and a centralized arrangement will provide more flexibility to cope with absenteeism and vacations,

Secretary for Executive	Taking Dictation	Transcribing Shorthand Notes	Other Secretarial Duties	Rest Periods	Idle Time		Total
1 (president's)	2 hrs. 50 min.	3 hrs. 40 min.	—	20 min.	—	10 min.	7 hrs.
2	1 " 10 "	1 " 45 "	2 hrs. 40 min.	20 "	1 hr.	5 "	"
3	1 " 25 "	2 " —	2 " 10 "	20 "	1 hr.	5 "	"
4	2 " —	2 " 50 "	1 " 40 "	20 "	—	10 "	"
5	1 " 25 "	1 " 55 "	3 " 15 "	20 "	—	5 "	"
6	2 " 35 "	3 " 10 "	— " 10 "	20 "	—	45 "	"
7	— 50 "	1 " 30 "	2 " 5 "	20 "	2 hrs.	15 "	"
8	2 " 10 "	2 " 55 "	1 " 25 "	20 "	—	10 "	"
9	2 " 45 "	3 " 50 "	—	20 "	—	5 "	"
10	1 " —	1 " 30 "	3 " 15 "	20 "	—	55 "	"

eliminate an executive's waiting for his secretary, and permit telephone messages for executives to be recorded and transcribed if necessary. He also believes that most of the overtime can be eliminated, because the executive could work overtime and record in the machine, making it unnecessary for the secretary to stay after the regular closing hour.

PROBLEMS:

1. How much importance do you feel should be given the president's objection in arriving at a decision of what to do in this case?

2. Justify the statement of Mr. Harris that exclusive of the president's, only six secretaries, and a total of four transcribing machines, would be required. Show all calculations, and point out your assumptions.

3. Assuming that Mr. Harris is correct, what action do you recommend be taken to gain the acceptance of the executives? Of the secretaries?

4. From the information available, which secretaries would you recommend retaining? Why?

Chapter · 6

The Office Work of
Calculating and Checking

Live only for today, and you ruin tomorrow.
—C. SIMMONS

Iₙ EVERY enterprise there is calculating and checking work. Figuring of some kind is necessary during the ordinary
course of normal operations. Costs must be estimated, sales must be
added, discounts computed, and interest rates figured. In addition, the
work must be checked to insure that the invoices are correct, the
calculated quantities balance with each other, and the written copy
is accurate. Material requisitions, sales analysis, prorating, percentages,
labor distribution, and inventories, all require calculating and checking work.

TYPES OF CALCULATING

In most businesses the great majority of calculating consists of the
simplest computations—adding, subtracting, and multiplying. The
tasks involving this work are many, but relatively simple. Except for
scientific and research work, the typical office is not concerned with
complex calculations. Estimates reveal that about 95 per cent of the
calculating work in everyday business consists of adding, subtracting,
and multiplying—only 5 per cent is made up of dividing, figuring
square root, and substituting values in mathematical formulae.

Typical of calculating work done in may offices is the writing or
the checking of an invoice illustrated by Figure 6–1. To determine the
amount for each item, multiplication or extension work is performed,
for example, in line 1 of the illustration, 3 items at $0.62 each equals
a total of $1.86 (3 × $0.62). The sum of these extensions is determined by means of addition. This is illustrated by the amount of

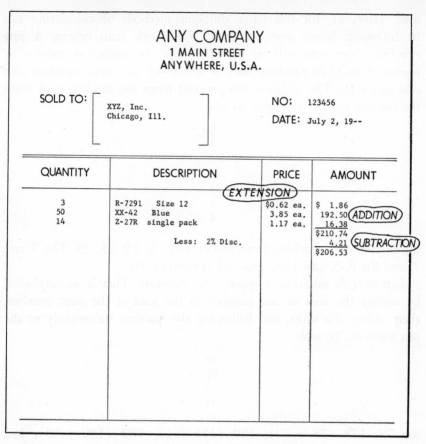

ANY COMPANY
1 MAIN STREET
ANYWHERE, U.S.A.

SOLD TO:

XYZ, Inc.
Chicago, Ill.

NO: 123456

DATE: July 2, 19--

QUANTITY	DESCRIPTION	PRICE	AMOUNT
	EXTENSION		
3	R-7291 Size 12	$0.62 ea.	$ 1.86
50	XX-42 Blue	3.85 ea.	192.50 *ADDITION*
14	Z-27R single pack	1.17 ea.	16.38
			$210.74
	Less: 2% Disc.		4.21 *SUBTRACTION*
			$206.53

FIG. 6–1. Typical calculating work includes extension or multiplication, addition, and subtraction.

$210.74 in the figure. Applying the discount entails subtraction in order to determine the total net amount due.

METHOD TO USE

In the modern office much calculating work is done by machine, but other methods are also employed. These include performing the work mentally, working it out longhand with pencil and paper, utilizing tables and charts of various kinds, and using a slide rule. For convenience the discussion here will be viewed from two bases, including use of the (1) mental or personal basis, and (2) machine basis.

CALCULATING BY MENTAL OR PERSONAL BASIS

In most offices there is a considerable amount of short and relatively simple calculating work for which the personal basis is commonly used. However, for this basis, different methods of calculating can be followed. Some represent much less work than others. A few effective short cuts will be included here. *In adding a column of figures, it helps to combine pairs or groups of successive numbers that add up to 10.* The addition can proceed from the top down or from the bottom up. For example, to add:

$$5$$
$$3$$
$$7$$
$$6$$
$$3$$
$$1$$
$$\underline{4}$$

say to yourself (working from top down): 5, 15, 25, 29. The 3 and 7, and the 6, 3, and 1 are grouped as units of 10.

Left-to-right addition is speedy and accurate. This is accomplished by adding the tens of one number to the tens of the next number, then adding the units, and following this pattern successively to the last number. To add:

$$78$$
$$81$$
$$33$$
$$\underline{45}$$

say 78, 158 (78 + 80), 159 (158 + 1), 189 (159 + 30), 192 (189 + 3), 232 (192 + 40), 237 (232 + 5).

Horizontal addition is helpful in adding numbers not arrayed in column form. Assume the total is wanted from a number of billings, including $42.50, $1.11, $34.77, $9.81, $7.83, $25.40, and $17.08. It is not necessary to arrange the numbers in the form of columns. Simply add the units, then the tens, then the hundreds, and so forth, and write the sums of the successive additions in the form shown below, then add.

Sum of		
Units	20	(0 + 1 + 7 + 1 + 3 + 0 + 8)
Tens	33	(5 + 1 + 7 + 8 + 8 + 4 + 0)
Hundreds	35	(2 + 1 + 4 + 9 + 7 + 5 + 7)
Thousands	10	(4 + 3 + 2 + 1)
Total	$138.50	

Multiplication by near number is simple, yet it is not commonly practiced. By this procedure multiplying quickly by numbers near 10,

100, or 1,000 is possible. For example, 368 multiplied by $0.98 consists of

$$368 \text{ times } \$1.00 = \$368.00$$
$$\underline{\text{less } 368 \text{ times } 0.02 = 7.36}$$
$$\$360.64$$

In other words, multiplying by 100 is accomplished by simply adding two zeros to the end of the number being multiplied, then adjusting this figure for the amount the multiplier deviates from 100. If the multiplier had been $0.12, the multiplier used would be 10 and the calculation would be

$$368 \text{ times } \$0.10 = \$36.80$$
$$\underline{\text{plus } 368 \text{ times } 0.02 = 7.36}$$
$$\$44.16$$

The breakdown method of multiplication is a timesaver when the personal method of calculating is followed. Actually this is similar to multiplication by near number and differs in degree, not in type. To multiply by 50, for example, multiply by 100, which is easily done, and take one half, since 50 is one half of 100. Likewise, to multiply by 25, take one fourth of that found by multiplying by 100. To illus-

Number	Reciprocal	Number	Reciprocal
1........	1.000000	11......	0.090909
2........	0.500000	12......	0.083333
3........	0.333333	13......	0.076923
4........	0.250000	14......	0.071428
5........	0.200000	15......	0.066666
6........	0.166666	16......	0.062500
7........	0.142857	17......	0.058823
8........	0.125000	18......	0.055555
9........	0.111111	19......	0.052631
10........	0.100000	20......	0.050000

FIG. 6–2. Numbers from 1–20 inclusive and their reciprocals.

trate, $1.95 times 25 equals one fourth of $195.00, or $48.75. In multiplying $1.95 times 26, an additional amount for 1 unit, or $1.95, would be added to $48.75, giving $50.70.

The use of reciprocals represents another short cut. A reciprocal of a number is one divided by that number. The reciprocal of 4, for example, is $\frac{1}{4}$. Figure 6–2 shows the reciprocals for numbers 1–20 inclusive. Calculating work involving percentages and prorating can be expedited by the use of reciprocals. For example, 1 day of a 31-day month is the reciprocal of 31, that is, $\frac{1}{31}$, or 0.03226: 1 day of a

365-day year is equivalent to the reciprocal, 0.00274; 1 ounce of a pound to 0.0625. Assume from the following data, the percentage figures are to be calculated:

Department	Sales	Percentage Total
A................	$3,905.40	
B................	7,041.62	
C................	2,052.98	
Total........	$13,000.00	100.00%

The reciprocal of 13,000.00 is 0.000076923. Multiplying the sales for each department by this reciprocal gives the respective percentages of 30.04, 54.17, and 15.79.

To divide by any number is to multiply by that number's reciprocal. The problem, 159.5 divided by 5, can be solved by looking up the reciprocal of 5, Figure 6–2 shows this is 0.2, and multiplying 159.5 by 0.2 which gives 31.90. When this method is followed, tables of reciprocals are usually made readily available. The method is quite effective when the divisor is not an uneven or uncommon figure, such as 156.18. Also the method is used for division work by means of machines that multiply only, or where it is deemed desirable to have the operator stay with multiplying work only, that is, not mix the work of multiplying with that of dividing.

Calculating of discounts is another area where short cuts can be used. Discounts are an important feature in the transaction of exchange of goods or services. Among the important discounts and the reason for granting them are:

Discount	Reason
Quantity................	Less expensive to handle large orders
Trade....................	Different types of buyers perform different marketing functions
Cash....................	Inducement for prompt payment

Customarily a full or list price is used as the base from which the discount, or discounts, are applied. When two or more discounts are in effect, each is applied to the net amount remaining after the previous discount has been taken. For example, with a list price of $25.00 and discounts of 30 per cent and 10 per cent, denoted as 30 and 10, the net price is $15.75, calculated as follows:

List price......................	$25.00
Less 30% (first discount)........	7.50
Balance........................	$17.50
Less 10% (second discount)......	1.75
Net price......................	$15.75

This method is too cumbersome. A simple method follows. A 30 per cent discount means 70 per cent $(100 - 30)$ remains, hence the amount can be determined by multiplying the list price by 70 per cent. Likewise, a 10 per cent discount means 90 per cent applies. In the above example the calculation is therefore

$$\$25.00 \times 0.70 \times 0.90 = \$15.75 \,.$$

Another simple method is to determine the single rate equal to the two discounts. To do this, add the discounts and subtract the sum obtained by multiplying the discounts:

$$0.30 + 0.10 = 0.40$$
$$\text{less } 0.30 \times 0.10 = 0.03$$
$$\text{Equivalent discount } \overline{0.37}$$

or $(1.00 - 0.37)$ remains, applying to $25.00 equals:

$$0.63 \times \$25.00, \text{ or } \$15.75 \,.$$

Where the calculating work includes various discounts, it is common practice to make up a table showing the equivalent single discount and the net that is applicable. Such a table is illustrated by Figure 6–3.

Discount Per Cent	Equivalent	Net
10..............	0.10	0.90
10 & 5...........	0.145	0.855
10, 5, & 5........	0.1878	0.8122
20..............	0.20	0.80
20 & 10..........	0.28	0.72
20, 10, & 5.......	0.316	0.684
40..............	0.40	0.60
40 & 5...........	0.43	0.57
40, 5, & 10.......	0.487	0.513
40, 10, & 5.......	0.487	0.513
50..............	0.50	0.50
50, 10, & 10......	0.595	0.405

FIG. 6–3. Discounts, their equivalents and net amounts.

CALCULATING BY MACHINE BASIS

Modern office machines have reduced calculating work to very simple tasks. Lengthy columns of figures can be added in a matter of seconds, and if wanted, a written record is available for checking the accuracy or for future reference. Errors due to handwriting figures incorrectly, carelessly, or out of column are eliminated by the machine basis. In this chapter adding machines and calculating machines will be discussed. Although other types of machines such as punched-card, billing, and accounting machines perform calculating work, discussion of them is made in Chapter 14.

ADDING MACHINES

Basically these machines are of two types: key driven and crank driven. In the former case the machine mechanism is actuated by depressing a key; in the latter case the number is "put in the machine" by depressing the key, and the mechanism is actuated by pulling a lever or pressing a motor bar.

These two basic types are subject to important possible variations, which include the following:

Listing or Nonlisting. This simply means that the former type lists or provides a written record of the figures on a tape. This can serve as a machine record, for visual comparison, or as proof of work. Where a long column of numbers, over 500, for example, is involved, a listing is usually desired. However, when a nonlisting machine is used and proof of work is required, the work can be checked by going through the addition twice and comparing answers. In some instances this method is as quick as checking a tape record. The nonlisting type is excellent for short batches of numbers and for totaling columns and running cross column checks.

Full Keyboard or Ten Keyboard. A full keyboard machine provides a column of keys from 1 to 9 for each digit position. Thus a five-row machine can handle a number like 628.47. The full keyboard permits high speeds where numbers of four or less digits are involved, such as 4.67, 3.26, 9.00, or 12.95, because the keys can be depressed simultaneously. For best results a skilled operator is necessary. There are many short cuts available in the over-all use of this type of machine. The latter type or "ten key" has, as the name suggests, ten keys from 0 to 9. Within the machine capacity, all numbers are recorded by means of these ten keys. The number 629.43 would be handled by first pressing the key 6, then 2, and then 9, and so on until the number is completed. The ten-key machine is usually very satisfactory for large numbers. The hand travel is small, since it is confined to ten keys. Numbers with five or more digits are quickly handled on this machine.

Manual or Electric. In a manual machine the mechanism is actuated by hand; in the electric machine, by electricity. In both cases the keys are depressed by hand. Comparing these two machines, the manual usually has lower maintenance cost, is lighter, and no electric cords are necessary; the machine can be operated anywhere. In contrast, the electric machine is faster and saves the operator's energy; however, its initial cost is usually greater. Most adding machines can also be used for subtracting, and a number are adaptable for work involving multiplying and dividing. Illustrations of several different types of adding machines are shown by Figure 6–4.

Courtesy: Monroe Calculating Machine Co., Inc., Orange, N.J.

Courtesy: Burroughs Corp., Detroit

FIG. 6–4. Adding machines. *Left:* Listing ten-key model. *Right:* Listing full keyboard ten-column capacity machine.

CALCULATING MACHINES

These machines are specially built for multiplication and division work, which is really repetitive addition and subtraction respectively; that is, 3 times 3 is the same as 3 plus 3 plus 3, and 9 divided by 3 is equal to the number of times 3 can be subtracted from 9, i.e., 9 less 3, less 3, less 3. The same considerations apply to calculators as discussed above under adding machines.

Most calculators are nonlisting, but some feature several answer dials to show accumulated amounts automatically. Figure 6–5 shows such a machine and an illustration of the type of calculating it performs. For example, extension of the third item, $2,982.00, is shown in the lower dial of the machine, and the total amount of the invoice is accumulated in the upper dial. At the same time, proof of the multiplier used and the total weight are indicated in the middle dial of the machine. In calculating this invoice, multiplication, addition of several columns, and subtraction are performed by the machine. Observe that this machine has a full keyboard.

A fully automatic calculator that prints a record of the work done is

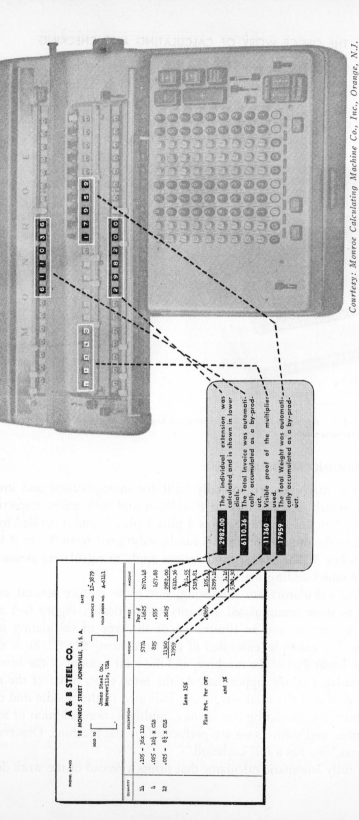

Courtesy: Monroe Calculating Machine Co., Inc., Orange, N.J.

FIG. 6–5. A typical example of the work performed by a versatile high-speed calculating machine that accumulates extensions and multipliers while giving individual answers and individual multiplier proof.

shown by Figure 6–6. In multiplying there is no repetition of figures on the tape—just the problem and the answer as shown in the upper right of the figure. The same is true for division—the answer is read directly from the tape. Likewise, calculating work of addition and subtraction is simplified as illustrated by the lower right portion of the

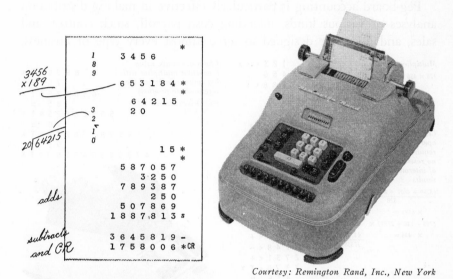

Courtesy: Remington Rand, Inc., New York

FIG. 6–6. A fully automatic printing calculator with an example of its work.

figure. The machine is available with capacity up to one trillion dollars.

There is also available a listing calculator featuring wide range of application, high speed, and interoperation transfers making it possible to perform sequences of combined operations such as storing data in the machine and recalling for use in subsequent operations. An illustration of this machine and several examples of the calculating work it can perform are shown by Figure 6–7.

PEG-BOARD AND PAPER STRIPS

Figures must be available to managers promptly and on time to have maximum value. Peg-board, also known as shingle strip accounting, and summary strip accounting is a simple method for accumulating or summarizing a large number of items with minimum time, maximum accuracy, and convenience. The equipment consists of a special board and ready-made paper strips, about 2 to 3 inches wide and 16 inches long, fastened to the board. Original data are written on the strips. These strips are held in alignment by means of holes across the top which fit into a peg-strip at the top of the board. The arrangement of the paper strips is offset so that a vertical margin of each strip is exposed, thus disclosing a column of figures. Quick summaries and recaps can be run off. A movable horizontal bar is used to guide the eye to the proper line across the forms.

Peg-board accounting is particularly effective in making distribution analyses of various kinds, including cost, payroll, stock control, and sales, and it can be designed to serve almost every type of business.

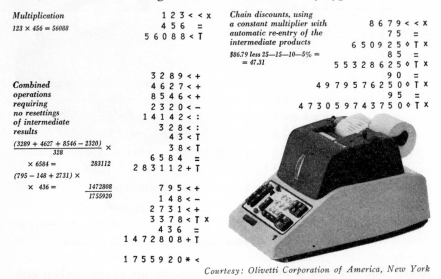

Multiplication

$123 \times 456 = 56088$

```
1 2 3 < < x
    4 5 6  =
5 6 0 8 8 < T
```

Chain discounts, using a constant multiplier with automatic re-entry of the intermediate products

$86.79 less 25—15—10—5\% =$
$= 47.31$

```
      8 6 7 9 < < x
            7 5  =
      6 5 0 9 2 5 ◊ T x
            8 5  =
5 5 3 2 8 6 2 5 ◊ T x
            9 0  =
4 9 7 9 5 7 6 2 5 0 ◊ T x
            9 5  =
4 7 3 0 5 9 7 4 3 7 5 0 ◊ T x
```

Combined operations requiring no resettings of intermediate results

$$\frac{(3289 + 4627 + 8546 - 2320)}{328} \times$$

$\times 6584 =$ 283112

$(795 - 148 + 2731) \times$

$\times 436 =$ $\dfrac{1472808}{1755920}$

```
    3 2 8 9 < +
    4 6 2 7 < +
    8 5 4 6 < +
    2 3 2 0 < -
1 4 1 4 2 < :
    3 2 8 < :
      4 3 < T
      3 8 < T
    6 5 8 4  =
2 8 3 1 1 2 + T

    7 9 5 < +
    1 4 8 < -
    2 7 3 1 < +
    3 3 7 8 < T x
      4 3 6  =
1 4 7 2 8 0 8 + T

1 7 5 5 9 2 0 * <
```

Courtesy: Olivetti Corporation of America, New York

FIG. 6–7. An automatic calculator new in concept, in speed, and in rang of applications. Illustrations of the printed tape supplied by the machine are shown.

The boards are made in various sizes ranging from approximately 20×18 inches to 36×18 inches. The advantages of the use of peg-strips include the following: copying of the data is eliminated—the original forms are used to obtain final results; accurate information can be provided; flexibility is permitted, since variations in the number and kind of distributions are possible; and the cost is economical—there is a minimum of handling, and the equipment required is simple.

UNIT ANALYSIS COMPARATIVE REPORTS

Another strip type of statement especially helpful for comparing figures is the unit analysis comparative report. Data are written on special designed forms held in place by binder rings through holes at the top of each form. At the close of each period, such as a month, the data for the current month are posted in the left-hand column of a strip and the year to date figures in the right-hand column, the center of the strip is used for identifying information. By properly positioning the newly completed monthly strip in the binder, comparisons between figures for the current month and those of previous periods are supplied. In Figure 6–8, for example, comparisons are expedited between (1) April this year and previous months of this year, (2) April this year and April last year, and (3) the year to date this year with the same period last year. The unit analysis method assists in determining trends, measuring the efficiency of the operations, and highlighting the status of different components making up the entire activity. It assists in presenting calculated data in a convenient and usable pattern.

CHECKING WRITTEN MATERIAL

Reading handwritten or typed copy and columns of numbers for accuracy accounts for a sizable portion of office workers' time. Progress in reducing these checking efforts has been made as evidenced by proofing devices on office machines, short-cut means for checking calculations by personal method, and proofing masters only of duplicated material. For the most part, material to be checked falls into two categories: (1) material that requires exact comparison with original, and (2) material that necessitates general checking for correctness of intended meaning and satisfactory appearance.

When exact comparison is required, it is common for one employee to read from the original while another employee checks the material. A word-for-word comparison is made. The employee reading indicates headings, quotations, punctuation marks, and spells difficult words. Care must be exercised by the employee checking to catch omissions, misspelled words, and incorrect syllabifications. Along with this an examination is made to see that the general format, margins, and appearance are correct.

Material requiring general checking is carefully read, but a word-for-word comparison is not made. Frequently general checking work is done by one employee—commonly the one who wrote the material. The meaning of the material must be clear and the general appearance satisfactory. Especial attention should be given dates and amounts. In this respect, comparison with the original is recommended.

The checking of numbers is best performed by reading the columns vertically. Placing the original list side by side to the written list so that the numbers are matched on the same line helps to eliminate possible error. Also, the doubling of figures and using the comma division should be practiced whenever possible. For numbers that repeat use the expression 2 times, 3 times, and so forth. To illustrate:

PERIOD JANUARY THIS YEAR	PERIOD FEBRUARY THIS YEAR	PERIOD MARCH THIS YEAR	PERIOD APRIL LAST YEAR	PERIOD APRIL THIS YEAR	OPERATING REPORT	% OF SALES	TO DATE APRIL THIS YEAR
					SALES		
60,125	62,411	63,147	51,675	57,355	PRODUCT A	55.2	243,038
51,312	61,387	62,298	44,375	55,467	PRODUCT B	44.8	230,464
111,437	123,798	125,445	96,050	112,822	TOTAL	100.0	473,502
					COST OF SALES		
42,066	42,439	43,571	35,643	41,295	PRODUCT A	69.9	169,371
35,462	43,279	43,921	30,234	38,272	PRODUCT B	70.0	180,934
77,528	85,718	87,492	65,877	79,567	TOTAL	70.0	330,305
					GROSS PROFIT		
18,059	19,972	19,576	16,032	16,060	PRODUCT A	30.1	73,667
15,850	18,108	18,377	14,141	17,195	PRODUCT B	30.0	69,530
33,909	38,080	37,953	30,173	33,255	TOTAL	30.0	143,197
					COST OF SALES ADJUSTMENTS		
1,211	657	752	418	458	INVENTORY ADJUSTMENTS		3,076
2,075	1,947	1,846	1,157	1,411	OVER OR UNDER ABSORBED BURDEN		7,279
3,286	2,604	2,598	1,575	1,867	TOTAL	1.9	10,355
30,623	35,476	35,355	28,598	31,388	GROSS PROFIT AFTER ADJ.	28.1	132,842
					GENERAL EXPENSES		
6,317	7,185	7,321	5,732	6,930	ADMINISTRATIVE – SCHEDULE A		27,753
8,245	9,345	8,580	7,048	6,742	SELLING – SCHEDULE B		32,892
3,612	4,762	5,121	3,848	4,637	SHIPPING – SCHEDULE C		18,132
2,098	2,417	2,860	2,461	2,420	BRANCH – SCHEDULE D		9,795
20,272	23,709	23,882	19,089	20,729	TOTAL EXPENSES	18.7	88,572
10,351	11,767	11,493	9,509	10,659	NET PROFIT FROM OPERATIONS	9.4	44,270
					OTHER INCOME		
251	187	252	142	210	INTEREST EARNED		900
516	518	675	567	572	DISCOUNT ON PURCHASES		2,281
122	158	145		112	DIVIDENDS RECEIVED		537
		250			PROFIT ON SALE OF ASSETS		250
218					PROFIT ON SALE OF INVESTMENTS		218
1,107	863	1,322	709	894	TOTAL OTHER INCOME	.9	4,186
					OTHER DEDUCTIONS		
376	112	87	123	75	INTEREST PAID		650
678	458	567	482	420	DISCOUNT ON SALES		2,123
	100				LOSS ON SALE OF ASSETS		100
					LOSS ON SALE OF INVESTMENTS		
1,054	670	654	605	495	TOTAL OTHER DEDUCTIONS	.6	2,873
53	193	668	104	399	NET	.3	1,313
10,404	11,960	12,161	9,613	11,058	NET PROFIT BEFORE TAXES	9.7	45,583
					TAXES		
55	55	55	45	55	CAPITAL STOCK		220
145	152	159	127	121	STATE INCOME		577
3,675	3,742	3,815	2,655	3,420	FEDERAL INCOME		14,652
3,875	3,949	4,029	2,827	3,596	TOTAL TAXES	3.1	15,449
6,529	8,011	8,132	6,786	7,__	NET PROFIT FROM ALL SOURCES	6.6	30,134

JUST LIFT UP

FIG. 6–8. Comparative and accumulative operating and financial information are presented in an effective arrangement.

TO DATE APRIL LAST YEAR	TO DATE MAY LAST YEAR	TO DATE JUNE LAST YEAR	TO DATE JULY LAST YEAR	TO DATE AUGUST LAST YEAR	TO DATE SEPT. LAST YEAR	TO DATE OCTOBER LAST YEAR	TO DATE NOVEMBER LAST YEAR	TO DATE DECEMBER LAST YEAR
212,966	265,648	322,377	380,739	441,106	508,089	576,913	651,284	716,671
195,033	238,744	286,557	334,678	387,159	442,183	501,494	559,179	615,890
407,999	504,392	608,934	715,417	828,265	948,272	1078,407	1210,463	1332,561
150,092	188,548	228,527	271,129	313,991	358,719	407,341	458,628	503,750
136,676	168,147	202,572	236,256	272,467	310,328	351,012	390,713	429,433
286,768	356,695	431,099	507,385	586,458	669,147	758,353	849,341	933,183
62,874	77,100	93,850	109,610	127,115	147,370	169,572	192,656	212,921
58,357	70,597	83,985	98,422	114,692	131,855	150,482	168,466	186,457
121,231	147,697	177,835	208,032	241,807	279,225	320,054	361,122	399,378
1,723	2,234	2,711	3,161	3,886	4,268	4,822	5,643	6,264
4,318	5,578	6,735	7,615	9,199	10,360	11,676	12,894	13,881
6,041	7,812	9,446	10,976	13,085	14,628	16,498	18,537	20,145
115,190	139,885	168,389	197,056	228,722	264,597	303,556	342,585	379,233
21,906	27,338	32,972	38,783	44,604	50,539	56,786	63,284	69,205
27,909	34,726	41,868	48,805	55,740	62,860	70,244	77,826	84,741
15,607	19,327	22,846	26,691	30,515	34,283	38,450	42,837	46,757
10,361	12,933	15,249	17,767	20,734	24,878	29,328	34,483	39,569
75,783	94,324	112,935	132,046	151,593	172,530	194,808	218,430	240,272
39,407	45,561	55,454	65,010	77,129	92,037	108,748	124,155	138,961
541	707	853	1,035	1,228	1,400	1,581	1,737	1,864
2,081	2,773	3,288	3,900	4,525	5,337	6,102	6,724	7,439
110	110	110	110	325	465	595	595	595
163	163	163	163	287	287	287	487	487
251	251	251	251	251	251	251	251	251
3,146	4,004	4,665	5,459	6,616	7,740	8,816	9,794	10,636
505	615	702	817	911	1,021	1,206	1,378	1,535
1,680	2,055	2,483	3,045	3,583	4,085	4,647	5,372	5,993
215	215	215	215	361	361	361	361	361
2,380	2,885	3,400	4,077	4,855	5,447	6,214	7,111	7,889
766	1,119	1,265	1,382	1,761	2,293	2,602	2,683	2,747
40,173	46,680	56,719	66,392	78,890	94,330	111,350	126,838	141,708
180	225	270	315	375	430	498	570	637
479	601	725	850	1,002	1,183	1,377	1,587	1,774
11,107	13,687	16,504	18,685	22,103	25,791	29,813	34,093	37,958
11,766	14,513	17,499	19,850	23,480	27,404	31,688	36,250	40,369
28,407	32,167	39,220	46,542	55,410	66,928	79,862	90,588	101,339

When the number is	*Say*				
157	One	fifty-seven			
2157	Twenty-one	fifty-seven			
2,157	Two	one	fifty-seven		
3,845,157	Three	eight	forty-five	one	fifty-seven
341	Three	forty-one	—three times		
341					
341					

CENTRALIZED COMPUTING GROUP

When the volume of calculating work warrants, it is usually economical and satisfactory to have a centralized computing group with all the proper machines operated by skilled employees. If established, the centralized unit should be the department having the largest quantity of calculating work—probably the bookkeeping section which utilizes calculating machines of various types and is staffed by employees competent in calculating work. In most offices, however, it is not feasible to have *all* the calculating work done by a centralized group; some appears to be handled better by employees throughout the organization. Such employees are familiar with the particular material and the calculating work represents a relatively small portion of the total.

TRAINING OF EMPLOYEES FOR CALCULATING AND CHECKING WORK

Basic training is paramount to acquire proficiency in calculating and checking work. Many people have the background for acquiring acceptable competency, but this ability remains dormant until properly developed through training. To develop skill in calculating necessitates the acquiring of a *number sense,* that is, an ability to recognize relations that exist between numbers and to think of numbers in their broad relations. Basic training in the use of calculating machines is also important. While not difficult to operate, the use of a machine is limited by the knowledge of the operator. The machine calculates only what the operator puts into it. Instructional material is helpful, but to provide maximum benefits it should be prepared. in a step-by-step, easy-to-follow plan, and amply illustrated. Finally, it takes practice and a sincere determination to perform calculating work speedily and accurately. The techniques must be understood, but skill in applying them is essential.

QUESTIONS

1. By the near number or breakdown basis, multiply each of the following:
    a) 427 by 13
    b) 728 by 25
    c) 956 by 9
    d) 6,131 by 50

2. Give a brief description identifying each of the following:
   a) Shingle strip accounting.
   b) Horizontal addition.
   c) A number sense that a person should acquire.
   d) The reciprocal of a number.

3. Calculate the total of the following numbers using left-to-right addition. (State the intermediate numbers as you procede.)

$$15$$
$$82$$
$$36$$
$$93$$
$$\underline{47}$$

4. Calculate manually the net price to a buyer extended a chain discount of 25, 10, 10, and 5 per cent from a selling price of $48.00. Extended a discount of 50 per cent from a selling price of $48.00. Extended a chain discount of 25, 10, 10, and 5 per cent from a selling price of $24.00. What basic observations do you make from your answers?

5. Give several examples to demonstrate that calculating work involving either percentages or division is expedited by the use of reciprocals.

6. Explain the following terminology used in connection with adding machines:
   a) Listing and nonlisting.
   b) Key driven and crank driven.
   c) Full keyboard and ten keyboard.
   d) Manual and electric.

7. As an office manager would you favor training of employees for calculating work? Give reasons for your answer.

8. Discuss the use of peg-boards and paper strips in the office. For what specific types of work do you feel this equipment is best suited?

9. In your own words, explain the purpose and use of a unit analysis comparative report as illustrated in Figure 6–8.

10. Do you agree with the following, "Calculating and checking work comprise important aspects of office work, but their importance will decrease as the wider adoption of recent improvements, and in some instances almost unbelievable developments, in office machines take place."

11. In general, would you say that centralization probably works out better for corresponding work than for calculating work? Why?

12. In your opinion could all checking work in the office be considered controlling work? Explain.

CASE PROBLEMS

CASE 6–1. THE VITEK COMPANY

Upon receipt of a customer's order, it is entered in two ledgers, one is by item, the other is by salesman. This is done in order to determine total weekly sales for each item and for each salesman.

Wendell Adams, office manager of the company's New York sales branch believes this method of tabulating sales data involves excessive entry work and increases the chances for committing errors in copying and adding the figures. He suggests that printed strip tickets be used to simplify the work and at the same time increase the accuracy. According to his idea, the tickets could be shingled several different ways as desired and only one entry of each order received would be necessary.

The Vitek Company manufactures and distributes nationally toilet preparations, including a well-known soap, hair shampoo, a men's hair grooming preparation, nail polish, tooth paste, tooth powder, mouth wash, and a liquid deodorant. Most of the items are offered in several different sizes. The total number of products, including the various sizes of each, is thirty-eight. The company has a sales force of fifty-four salesmen operating out of four branches. Main offices are located in Detroit. Weekly reports by each branch are sent to the main office where they are analyzed and made up into a final company report.

Data on the quantity and dollar sales of each item and the items sold and dollar sales by each salesman and to what customers are required. Many of the items are sold in lots of a dozen, in which case the quantity entered is 12. To illustrate the present work, suppose an order for ½ dozen hair shampoo size No. 2 and 2 dozen tooth paste giant size is received from the Baker Drug Store, located in the territory of John Doe, a Vitek Company salesman. Entered in the hair shampoo size No. 2 ledger is date, salesman's name, quantity, and the amount of sales dollars. In the tooth paste giant-size item ledger is entered date, salesman's name, quantity, and sales dollars. Also in the John Doe salesman ledger is entered date, code number of the Baker Drug Store, quantity, item, and sales dollars.

PROBLEMS:

1. Do you agree with the viewpoints expressed by Wendell Adams? Discuss.
2. Write the proposed means for handling this work according to Wendell Adams, giving sufficient details to convey complete understanding of the proposed plan. Include the design of the printed strip ticket and explain how it would be used.

Chapter · 7

Work of Filing

Success usually comes to those who are too busy to be looking
for it.

—THOREAU

FILING CONSTITUTES a major segment of office work.
Pertinent written information concerning decisions, thoughts, contracts,
obligations, drawings, and transactions must be available, when needed,
in order for the office to provide its needed service.

*Filing is the placing of papers in acceptable containers according to
some predetermined arrangement so that any paper, when required, can
be located quickly and conveniently.* Emphasis is upon the "finding,"
not the "storing," aspect. The written information is retained for future
possible use. Placing it in safekeeping is important; being able to find it
promptly, when wanted, is vital. One needed paper lost or mislaid can
delay a dozen employees in their work.

The word "papers" in the above definition is used in a broad sense.
It includes such diverse written material as:

bills of lading	memoranda
blueprints	orders
catalogues	personnel records
checks	price books
contracts	purchasing records
credit information	quotations
insurance policies	reports
invoices	requisitions
letters	sales quotas
mailing lists	tax statements

ARRANGEMENT OF PAPERS IN FILE

Consideration for the type of material handled, the nature and size of
the enterprise, and the peculiarities of the particular business influence
the selection of the filing arrangement. There are numerous ready-
made filing arrangements from which to choose. Different manufac-

113

turers stress different features. The arrangement adopted should provide for distinct classifications or divisions of the material, allow for possible expansion, and be inclusive of all the material to be handled. Fundamentally the arrangement should stress this condition: when searching for information there should be as few places to look as possible, preferably one.

Material can be filed according to four basic arrangements: alphabetical, numerical, geographical, and chronological. Various combinations of these are possible and, in fact, are commonly used. For example, an alphabetical-numerical plan is often employed, and in many alphabetical files the material in each subdivision is arranged chronologically, i.e., the latest paper always on top. Likewise, the usual filing practice under the geographical plan is to arrange subdivisions alphabetically.

ALPHABETICAL

The alphabetical arrangement is the most widely used form of filing. It stresses the name or topic as the important item; and it can be considered the foundation of practically all filing, since in most instances

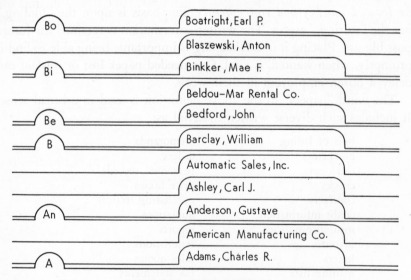

FIG. 7–1. Alphabetical filing.

when other forms are used the arrangement of the smaller units is usually alphabetical.

Under the alphabetical arrangement all material is filed in dictionary order. If the first letter is not sufficient for determining the proper place of the material, the second and, if necessary, the third and fourth succeeding letters are used. See Figure 7–1. For any given total of names the probable number which will occur in each subdivision of the alphabet is known. For example, names beginning with the letters S, B, M, and H, respectively, are most common; those beginning with X, Q, and U occur least frequently. For a given quantity of names, there are usually about three times as many names under B as under A, twenty times as many under H as under I, and ten times as many under T as under U. Information of this sort is utilized scientifically in determining filing guide subdivisions which can be purchased as standard equipment. Sets ranging from 24 to some 2,600 subdivisions are available.

The advantages of alphabetical filing are that direct reference is provided, a quick check is offered on misfiled material, and common names are grouped. It is sometimes considered "the natural way to file." Figure 7–2 illustrates a modern alphabetical filing arrangement for correspondence. From this illustration the following can be observed:

1. The primary guides, or partitions segregating the material, give the chief breakdowns of the alphabet and are identified by green tabs occupying the first three positions which are shown along the top left portion of the guide.[1] These tabs are marked with letters and numbers, i.e., $A = 1$; $Abr = 2$; $Ad = 3$; $Ag = 4$; etc. The number expedites the filing work. When considering the letter d, it is a little difficult to recall that d is between c and e. In contrast, no thought is required to remember that the number "3" is between "2" and "4".

2. Individual folders containing regular correspondence are filed behind their proper primary guide and tabbed in the fifth or the extreme right position: "1. Aaron, Carl," "1. Abbott, A. M.," etc.

3. Miscellaneous folders, used for occasional and miscellaneous correspondence, are marked with red tabs in the first three positions. These folders correspond in identification and number with the primary guides and are placed in the back of each primary-guide spacing. When regular material is moved to the transfer file, the miscellaneous folders are moved also and serve as primary guides in this file.[2]

4. Auxiliary guides, tabbed in the fourth or right-center position, are used to simplify and to speed the filing by dividing primary guide spacings according to individual needs. Auxiliary guides may include: (1) common titles and names, such as "American," "Brown," "Smith," and "United States"; (2) alphabetical listings which segregate the

---

[1] Tabs are located by position along the width of the guide. At the left is first position, and moving to the right are the second, third, fourth, and fifth position, which is at the extreme right.

[2] The transfer of filed material is discussed in Chapter 8.

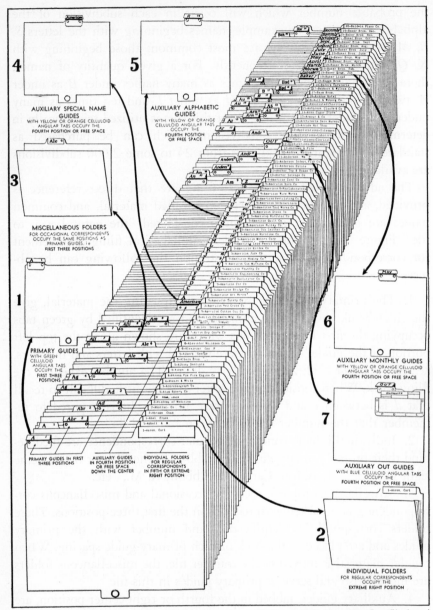

Courtesy: Globe-Wernicke Co., Cincinnati

FIG. 7–2. Filing arrangement under a modern alphabetical correspondence-filing plan.

material under the common title or name—"American Art Works,"
"American Bridge Co.," for example; and (3) monthly listings which
separate the material under the common title or name by months—
"Baker Bros.—Jan.," "Baker Bros.—Feb.," and "Baker Bros.—March."

5. Out guides are tabbed with blue in the fourth position and are inserted in the file when any folder is taken out. Each out guide is equipped with a holder device for a charge-out card. Entries on this card show when a folder is removed, by whom, and when returned. Out guides are also available in folder form, in which case spaces are ruled on the side in order to record data on removals.[3]

SUBJECT FILING

A modification of the alphabetical arrangement is subject filing, in which the arrangement of material is according to subject or descriptive feature instead of name. For example, all material pertaining to insurance is put in one main division and all material on taxes in another division. If necessary, subdivisions of each subject are made. For Insurance the subdivisions might be Accident, Fire, and Group, and the material is usually filed alphabetically under each classification. The choice of subject heading should be inclusive and descriptive of the contents.

Subject filing is helpful in indicating the main classifications for separate files in an office. To illustrate, a separate file may be used for each main subject, such as costs, orders, personnel, purchases, and taxes. Subheadings are included under each main subject, for example, under ORDERS are Adjustments, Collections, Complaints, Correspondence, and Shipments. In addition, subject filing places all material of a common descriptive feature together so that it can be used conveniently. Common examples of subject filing include executive files, files of material going between home office and branches, interdepartmental written material, research data, clippings, and notes.

NUMERICAL

In this filing arrangement each item filed has a number, and location of the material is by numerical sequence. Numerical files are used for such material as bank checks, invoices, and papers pertaining to freight cars. However, the numerical arrangement is not confined to prenumbered material. Items such as letters, memorandums, and notices are also filed according to this plan; and, in such cases, an auxiliary alphabetical card file is employed to learn the proper filing number. The system of numbers can be basically one of two types: (1) serial —to provide unlimited expansion; or (2) coded—to indicate specific types of items. An illustration of the latter type is given below:

---

[3] The subject of charging material out is discussed on page 125.

Divisions

100. *General Sales*	200. *Production*	300. *Research*
110. Recap of orders booked	210. Purchasing	310. Consumer studies
120. Recap of sales shipped	220. Payroll	320. Radio ratings
130. Expenditures	230. Budget	330. Television surveys
140. Budget	240. Recap of items completed	340. Readership records
		350. Product testing

The numerical plan offers simple provisions for expansion, some degree of secrecy, ease and speed of operation, and an effective means of identification. Numbers are easy to work with; in fact, most alphabetical filing systems use numbers on the file guides, in addition to the letters,

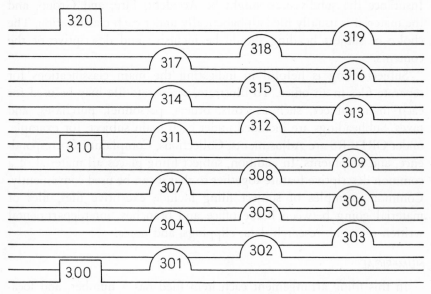

FIG. 7-3. Numerical filing.

in order to expedite finding. Figure 7-3 shows the arrangement of a numerical file.

Terminal-Digit Filing. Although ordinary numerical filing is a conventional way to file numbered records, it has certain serious disadvantages. Among these are: (1) "misfiles" increase as the filing personnel must read numbers of six or more digits; and (2) the newest records, usually those referred to most frequently, are placed at one end of the file, thus causing filing activity to be concentrated and congested in the newer sections.

Terminal-digit filing eliminates these difficulties, yet retains the benefits of the numerical file. In terminal-digit filing, numbers are used, but they are read from right to left instead of the conventional left to right. Hence, records are filed according to the last digit or, more commonly, the last two digits, then the next two or subdivision thereof.[4] To illustrate:

In Numerical File	In Terminal-Digit File Last-Two Number Breakdown	In Terminal-Digit File Last-Two Number Breakdown with Sub-divisions Thereof
160 79	3 25 41	5 17 41
174 63	5 17 41	3 25 41
325 41	1 74 63	1 74 63
517 41	1 60 79	1 60 79

GEOGRAPHICAL

The main filing divisions in the geographical arrangement include states, counties, cities, branch-office territories, and salesmen's areas. Usually the subdivisions are arranged alphabetically; for example, a sales area by cities in alphabetic order, and each city by customers' names in alphabetic order.

The geographical arrangement is easy to understand, simple and direct, and can cover the over-all work division, particularly that of sales. The files are generally less wieldy than is frequently the case with the other basic arrangements. Also, several people can work at the files simultaneously—for instance, one in the Philadelphia file for "Cupper Manufacturing Company" and the other in the Los Angeles file for "Cizzla Sales Corporation." In addition, the geographical arrangement makes it comparatively simple to compile mailing lists by states or cities; and the segregation of material for tax, political, or mailing reasons is readily provided.[5] Figure 7–4 shows a geographical plan of filing.

CHRONOLOGICAL

The chronological filing arrangement simply arranges material according to its time sequence. The main divisions are either months or weeks, with the subdivisions being days. Some correspondence, bills,

---

[4] An interesting explanation of this useful method is given in William H. Hillyer, "Digit Filing: Terminal and Specific," *The Office* (New York: Office Publications Co.) October, 1950, p. 10.

[5] For a thorough discussion of geographic methods of filing, see B. M. Weeks, *How to File and Index* (rev. ed.; New York: Ronald Press Co., 1951), chap. vi. This book presents the principles and practical aspects of office filing in a concise and understandable manner.

and pending accounts payable can be handled on a chronological plan.

The advantages of this plan are simplicity, ease of filing, and a convenient signal or reminder of unfinished work, which is shown by the material in the file with reference to a specific date. Figure 7–5 illustrates chronological filing.

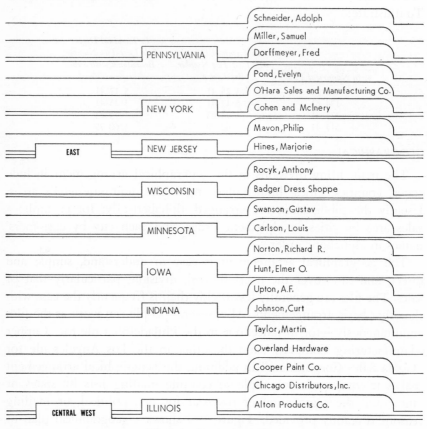

FIG. 7–4. Geographical filing.

Tickler File. The "tickler file" is an adaptation of chronological filing. Future matters requiring attention within fairly well-defined time limits are filed under due dates or the time when action should be taken. A glance at the file shows for any given time what matters are to be followed up, what ones are behind schedule, and what ones must be handled in the near future.

FILE INDEXING

The file index furnishes the key to how the materials are arranged. For any given set of material, a choice is made from several possible

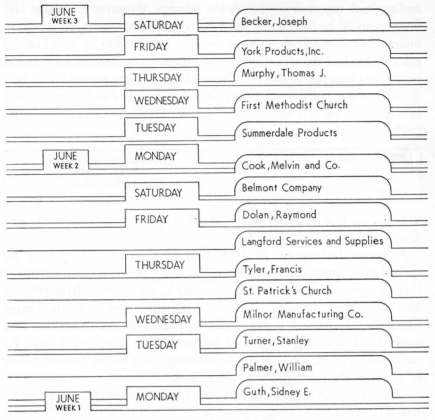

FIG. 7–5. Chronological filing.

indexes. In some cases the subject is the best index; in others the name of the customer or the point of destination might be most useful. To illustrate, the following material could be indexed in any one of the several different ways indicated:

Material	*File according to*
Catalogues	Date, name of company, or name of product
Correspondence	Date, subject, name of company, name of customer, name of seller, point of destination, or point of origin
Invoices	Date, name of customer, or number
Personnel application forms	Name of applicant, or type of work (subject)
Purchase orders	Date, name of vendor, name of product, or number
Tax reports	Date, subject, or name of taxing body

Cross Indexing. Cross indexing is used when more than one subject is covered by the material or when several indicators are helpful in finding it. A report dealing with the subjects of market expansion and finances could be filed under the subject of markets, sales, future sales, finances, or costs. Cross indexes provide information as to where to place and to find the report; however, numerous cross references should be avoided in order to simplify the work as much as possible. It is best to have these indexes on reference cards which can be maintained in a separate file. To find material on WAGES, the index card might read:

Wages	*See also* Compensation
	Fringe Benefits
	Job Evaluation
	Salary

This means that material on WAGES may be found under all five terms.

Phonetic Indexing. In a great many instances a name can be spelled in different ways, thus causing a filing problem when extensive lists of names are included. For example, the name "Barnett" can also be spelled "Barnet," "Bornet," "Bornett," and so forth. Under which spelling is such a name filed or found? Poor handwriting and errors in transcribing might add further to the filing perplexity. To meet this problem, a system of file indexing based on the pronunciation or sound of the name has been developed.

Under this system all names are coded by use of the "Soundex Code," which is:

Code Numbers	Key Letter Equivalents
1	*b, f, p, v*
2	*c, g, j, k, q, s, x, z*
3	*d, t*
4	*l*
5	*m, n*
6	*r*

The letters *a, e, i, o, u* and *w, h, y* are not coded. In addition, the following practices apply:

1. The initial letter is not coded but is used as a prefix to code a number which always has three digits.

2. The zero is used where there is no key letter equivalent.

3. Doubled key letters are coded as one, that is, *rr* as *r*.

4. A key letter and its equivalent are likewise coded as one, that is, *ck* as *c*.

To illustrate, the name "Barnett" would be coded B-653, "Barnet," B-653, and "Bornet," B-653. Thus all names which sound alike, although spelled differently, have identical index numbers. This means that they are in the same classification or grouping in the file and, hence, quickly located. Among the important advantages of phonetic indexing are: 90 per cent of all family names are grouped automatically; duplications are detected; unlimited expansion and flexibility are provided; the effect of transcribing errors is minimized; and a uniform and precise indexing method is provided.

FILING PRACTICES

Certain filing practices have been found helpful and adherence to them will probably bring best results. However, in certain individual cases, slight deviations might work out advantageously depending upon the circumstance. A complete list of these filing practices is beyond the scope of this book, but the more important ones include the following:

1. Use a sufficient number of guides to help place and find the material quickly. This usually means a guide for each inch of filing.

2. File material *behind* the guides.

3. Use colored tabs and labels to increase identification and to prevent misfiling.

4. Provide, with reference to correspondence files, individual folders when five or more papers have accumulated. Crowded miscellaneous folders frequently indicate that more breakdowns of the alphabet are needed.

5. Arrange material in folders chronologically, the latest at the front.

6. Leave 3–4 inches of working space in the file drawer to avoid jamming the files and wasting time in obtaining materials.

7. Use top drawers for current filing, bottom drawers for most recent transfer. This expedites quick reference.

8. Transfer material to inactive file regularly and at stated intervals.

9. Sort material alphabetically by first segregating into four groups, such as *A-F, G-L, M-R,* and *S-Z;* then sort each group according to the first letter. Likewise, with numeric material, first sort 0–2, 3–5, and 6–9; then sort each group by the first digit. This procedure usually saves a great deal of time.

10. File each name according to (*a*) surname, (*b*) given name or initial, (*c*) middle name or initial, and (*d*) title, if important to retain.

Alexander, Charles D. (Dr.)

11. File "nothing before something."

> Carter
> Carter, George
> Carter, George L.

12. File alphabetical material in exact sequence of letters, *A* through *Z,* to the last letter of the last word.

> M & A Stores Inc.
> Maag, Robert C.
> MacArthur, Thomas P.
> Mack, Henry
> MacTavish, Sam W.
> Maleski, Franck C.
> McGuire, William F.
> Mead-Carters Co.

13. Treat compound words as one word.

> Cohen, Julius I.
> Co-operative Sales
> Co-Workers Order of Bart
> Cutter, Frederick J.

14. Spell out abbreviated names.

> Safety Tool and Tire Company
> Saint Louis Poultry and Egg Company
> Saint Paul Club
> Salk, Meyer L.
> Street, Theodore P.

15. Spell out numerals and abbreviations.

> First National Bank
> Three Thirty-Three Lake Building
> Young Women's Christian Association

16. When names are identical, file by city; then state; and, if necessary, by street address in city.

> Carson, John M.
>   Bangor, Maine
> Carson, John M.
>   Springfield, Mass.
> Carson, John M.
>   3719 Lyndale Road
>   Springfield, Ohio
> Carson, John M.
>   5127 Western Street
>   Springfield, Ohio

FILING PROCEDURE

After the filing arrangement, indexing, and practices have been selected, the next requirement is to establish a definite filing procedure. This entails six steps as follows:

Checking Release for Filing.   Before any material is prepared for filing, it must first be checked to be sure it is released for filing. Material which is still being processed or referred to, or which, because of policy, is not retained by the company, should, of course, not be placed in the files.

Reading the Material.   The material must be read or examined to determine the proper filing classification. This work should be done by trained and careful persons, because improper classification might easily result in a "misfile" or temporary loss of material.

Marking for Filing.   Next, the material must be marked in order to identify its classification. This marking can be done by underscoring or circling a word or two on the paper or by stamping or writing the proper file data in the upper right-hand corner. A colored pencil usually works very satisfactorily, as the contrast aids future reference. If the filing is by subject or there is a possibility for filing under several headings, a cross-reference card should be made out and placed in the separate cross-reference file. Also, if the material requires a follow-up —a fact frequently noted on the letter by the correspondent—a follow-up slip is made out by the file clerk and placed in the tickler file behind the proper date guide. The letter or material itself is filed in the usual manner.

Sorting.   The fourth step consists of sorting the material to be filed. Usually this is done progressively, i.e., all materials sorted first according to major divisions, then each major division by subdivisions, and finally, each subdivision as required.

Filing Material.   Each piece is filed under the proper classification with the newest addition always on top or at the front of the contents in its respective folder.

Charging Material Out.   The last step, charging filed material out, deals with the removal of papers from the file. A procedure to handle this work is necessary in order to know where items are, in the event that several people want the papers at the same time, and also to minimize indiscriminate removals from the files with the resultant high loss of material. Records of charged-out materials can be handled in any one of four ways: by substitution card, out folders, out guides, or multiple charge-out forms. Figure 7–6 illustrates these different media.

When the removed material is a single card or piece of paper, its place in the file can be occupied by a substitution card showing the name of the person to whom the material is issued, along with the date and the initials of the file clerk issuing the material. Upon return of the

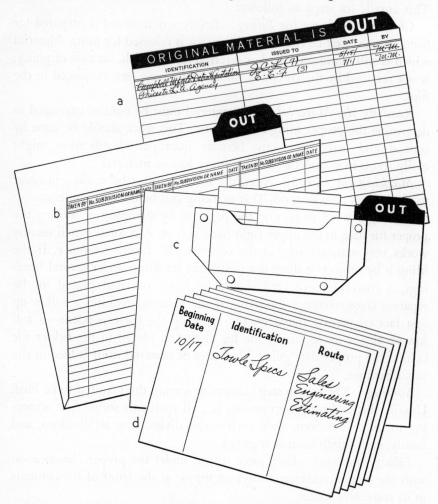

FIG. 7–6. Media used in controlling charge-outs from filed material: (a) substitution card, (b) out folder, (c) out guide, and (d) multiple charge-out form.

material, the entries on the substitution card are lined out and the card is reused.

The "out folders" are ordinary file folders with one side printed for the recording of data concerning removals. The out folder serves as a substitute for the regular folder and permits the removal of only single papers.

When an entire folder is removed, either the out folder or the out guides can be used. The "out guide" is a pressboard guide with tab printed "OUT" and a pocket or device to hold a charge-out slip. The out guide replaces the material taken from the file and serves both as a record and as a marker for the borrowed material.

Multiple charge-out forms are used to keep a record of the transfer of charged-out material from one user to another. The date, identification, and route of material are written on the card. Depending on the system used, one copy of the form is attached to the substitution card, placed in the out folder, or inserted in the pocket of the out guide. A second copy is filed in a tickler file for follow-up. Other copies are attached to the material so that, as each individual or department using the material finishes with it, a line is drawn through the name or department on the route list; the top copy is returned to the Filing Department; and the remaining copies and material are forwarded to the next name on the route list. The returned copy received by the Filing Department is attached to the tickler file copy; thus there is a record of who has the material, without clearance of the filed material each time through the Filing Department.

CENTRALIZATION AND DECENTRALIZATION OF FILES

One of the major issues in the area of filing and the fundamental function of managerial organizing is the question of whether to have centralized or decentralized filing. Convincing arguments can be stated for either side of the question. The trend, however, appears to be toward centralization from the viewpoint of management operation and decentralization regarding the physical files. This combination stems from the fact that with centralized managerial activity the best of filing knowledge and practices from the over-all company viewpoint can be put into use. At the same time, decentralized physical records provide accessibility for those needing the files, flexibility in arrangement, and a satisfactory cost of operation.

However, the decision to centralize or not depends upon the requirements of the particular enterprise. Filing needs differ. Adequate thought must be directed to the type of material, the work habits of the people using the records, and the normal manner in which they are used, i.e., the flow of work, frequency of records use, and information required.

FILING CABINETS

Filing cabinets are available in many different sizes and types designed to fulfill every filing need. In the so-called "common filing cabinet" the material is filed vertically, and hence the term "vertical file" is frequently used. Vertical files are made to accommodate many different sizes of material, but those for cards—3 × 5-inch or 5 × 8-inch—letter, and legal size papers are most popular. The equipment is available in sizes from one to six drawers. The one- and two-drawer models are used on a desk or table; the three-drawer is desk height and is usually used beside a desk, providing ready accessibility to papers frequently used. Four-drawer models are used for counter purposes. The five- and six-drawer files provide extra large filing capacities for the floor space occupied. A standard file drawer holds about 5,000 sheets of paper, 300 file folders, and 26 file guides. Figure 7–7 shows the different heights and dimensions of vertical file cabinets.

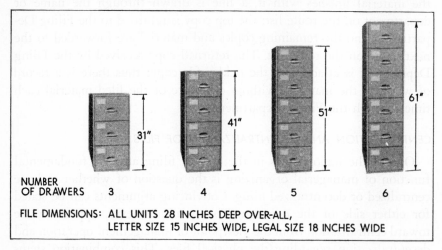

NUMBER OF DRAWERS   3   4   5   6

FILE DIMENSIONS: ALL UNITS 28 INCHES DEEP OVER-ALL, LETTER SIZE 15 INCHES WIDE, LEGAL SIZE 18 INCHES WIDE

FIG. 7–7. Vertical filing cabinets showing different sizes and dimensions.

The mechanical details of files differ with the manufacturers. Most files feature a ball-bearing, full progressive side-arm suspension which provides smooth rolling action of the drawer and permits easy opening and closing. A sliding, adjustable device known as a "follower" holds the papers upright in the drawer. It can be pulled up tight and snapped or locked in position; a slight force releases the device and permits it to be moved to another position. In some files when the drawer is opened, the front of the drawer tilts forward and, at the same time, the back of the drawer tilts backward, thus opening the filed material like pages of a book. This permits easy and rapid access to the filed materials. Steel cabinets have won general acceptance and favor. The equipment is available with or without locks, insulated for fire protection, and in several colors and finishes to harmonize with the color scheme of the office.

SIDE-FILING CABINETS

Filing cabinets are also available in which the compartments swing open sideways as illustrated in Figure 7–8. They are also termed "Pro-File" compartments. Advantages claimed for filing equipment of this design include: (1) permits full and easy accessibility to all materials; (2) conserves energy, since the folders can be slid instead of lifted

Courtesy: Yarman and Erbe Mfg. Co., Rochester, N.Y.

FIG. 7–8. When the Pro-File compartment is swung open, its entire contents are exposed on an open-faced shelf providing increased visibility and accessibility. This equipment is available in standard-letter and legal size in two-, three-, and four-compartment units.

out; and (3) saves floor space—the file depth is approximately 12 inches and the projection of an open compartment is 7 inches, much less than in the case of a vertical file drawer. Side-filing cabinets have won extensive favor in executive officers. The two-compartment model can form a part of an executive L-shaped desk unit and works in well with the executive decor.

MOTORIZED CARD FILES

When the work requires access to a large number of filed cards, a motorized card file may be useful. It is electrically operated and brings in a few seconds any desired tray of cards in the unit at convenient writing height to a seated operator. The cards are filed vertically, and the trays are removable. Units are available in various card sizes and

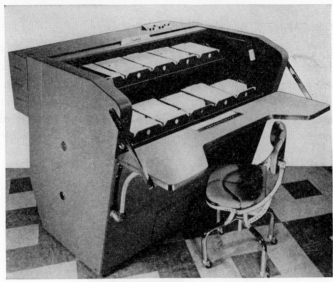

Courtesy: Wheeldex and Simpla Products, Inc.
White Plains, N.Y.

FIG. 7–9. An electrically operated, fully automatic motorized card file that positions the desired tray of cards conveniently before the operator.

capacities. Savings in time and effort result from the use of motorized card files. A motorized card file unit is shown in Figure 7–9.

ROTARY FILES

In this equipment the material is held to the periphery of a wheel which, when revolved, affords ready and quick means for locating any record at writing height. Posting is convenient without removal of card. The unit provides speedy handling, enormous savings of motions —up to 75 per cent has been estimated—and compactness.

Many different models are available. The range of sizes is from small units about the size of a telephone to large units approximately 36 inches high. The capacity varies, of course, with the size of the wheel; for example, a unit having a 21-inch diameter wheel, handling 5 × 8-inch cards, has a capacity of 6,000 cards. Both single- and multi-wheel units are offered, as well as a special mechanism for stabilizing the rotation. A four-unit model is illustrated by Figure 7–10.

In the majority of cases, the cards have a slot-punched opening at the bottom in order to provide a gripping effect of the card to a retaining rod. For large cards double openings and two rods are used. However, revolving file units are also available in which plain cards, i.e., not slotted or punched, can be used. Since no mechanical fastening is em-

Courtesy: Wheeldex and Simpla Products, Inc., White Plains, N.Y.

FIG. 7–10. A multi-wheel unit of rotary filing equipment.

ployed, it is possible to file the same type of material as that used in a vertical file, including such items as file folders, sketches, photographs, and folded drawings.

RECIPROCATING FILES

The employee can either go to the work, or the work can be brought to the employee. This latter situation is stressed in reciprocating file equipment. Figure 7–11 shows an installation of this type of equipment. The employee remains comfortably seated, and the file can be moved forward and backward as required. Use of this type of file (1) reduces employee fatigue, (2) eliminates travel time, (3) minimizes waiting time at files, and (4) allows full supervision, since all equipment is at desk-level height and under full view of the supervisor.

VISIBLE FILES

The name "visible file" reveals its outstanding feature, namely, providing, at a glance, visible information in the files to the user. Visible files are very important means of filing. For convenience, the types of visible files can be divided into three groups: (1) filed strips, (2) cards filed horizontally, and (3) cards filed vertically.

FILED STRIPS

This type of visible file is used when quick reference to records containing a small quantity of data is needed. It is useful for maintaining lists which undergo changes, such as names and addresses of customers, prices, rates, bin locations, directories, reservations, hospital indexes, telephone and switchboard data, and routings.

Either of two methods can be followed. The first consists of (1) typing or otherwise writing the data on scored and special sheet material which is made of resilient veneer covered on both sides with paper; (2) separating the sections by breaking along the scored line; and (3) placing the strips in a frame by bending them slightly and snapping

Courtesy: Rol-Dex Division, Watson Mfg. Co., Jamestown, N.Y.

FIG. 7–11. Reciprocating filing equipment in which the file can be moved back and forth in the long, troughlike container. This is known as the "lateral-type file," since the work is to the side of the operator. A "left-right" arrangement, in which the file moves across the front of the operator, is also possible.

the ends under the side channels of the frame. The second method consists of writing the data on small die-cut cards which snap or button on a receiving device or runway in the frame. This places the cards in an offset arrangement with the upper margin of the card exposed or plainly visible. With either method the frames can be suspended on desk stands, wall brackets, and rotaries. Figure 7–12 shows illustrations of this equipment.

To indicate special conditions applying to a particular name or account in a list, signaling devices can be used. These signals are either opaque or transparent and are available in several contrasting colors. They are either slid over, or attached to, a record and thus serve as a warning or indication of a special consideration applicable to that account. Different-colored strips and cards are also available and can be used for signaling purposes if desired.

Courtesy: Remington Rand, Inc., New York

FIG. 7–12. Two types of visible reference record equipment used where the amount of data is small and where fast, frequent reference is required.

CARDS FILED HORIZONTALLY

In the second type of visible files, cards are filed horizontally in a shallow slide or tray in such a manner that the bottom margin of each card is exposed, providing for quick visibility. In this margin are pertinent data concerning the information on the major area of the card. Varying widths of margin exposure may be used; standard equipment provides $\frac{3}{16}$-inch to $\frac{5}{16}$-inch margin visibility. Card capacity per tray depends upon the card size and the margin exposure used, but 80 cards per tray is a good average figure. Each card is fastened in such a way that it can be raised and flipped by pivoting about the top edge. Thus the complete information on any card can be viewed in full, or additional data can be written on the card with the tray used as an armrest. Units are available with different numbers of trays. Figure 7–13 shows the position of the tray when withdrawn, open, and ready for posting on a card.

Mechanized Units. Mechanized visible file units (cards filed horizontally) are also available. Stooping, reaching, pulling out trays, writing at inconvenient levels, and pushing trays back are eliminated by this mechanized unit. It excludes many causes of operator fatigue, raises productivity, and saves floor space. One popular unit holds sixty

Courtesy: Remington Rand, Inc., New York

FIG. 7–13. Visible equipment of the cabinet-posting type in a railroad office.

trays, counterbalanced in two equal banks which travel up and down when the unit is actuated. Figure 7–14 illustrates a series of such units.

Fastening of Cards. Several arrangements are available for fastening the card into the tray. In some equipment the top edge of the card is fastened directly onto the tray, while in other equipment "pockets" made of strong Kraft paper are fastened directly onto the tray. In the latter case, a card is held in place by inserting the bottom edge into a flap made by a U-shaped plastic strip at the bottom of the pocket. The top of the card is held by inserting the corners into slots pre-cut in the pocket. Each arrangement offers benefits. Fastening the card directly into the tray is advantageous in that markings can be made directly on the exposed visible margin of the card; the tray is utilized solely for cards. In contrast, the use of pockets with the plastic material at the margins affords protection for the visible margin of the card, prevents cards from getting dog-eared, and affords a uniform space for signal devices. Figure 7–15 illustrates pockets used in visible record equipment.

Signals on Card. Effective signaling to denote certain information on the card is one of the outstanding features of visible filing equipment using cards filed horizontally. By sliding different-colored plastic

Courtesy: *Remington Rand, Inc., New York*

FIG. 7–14. By selecting and pressing one of the bars in the row as shown in front of the operator, the desired tray comes out of the unit at writing height in a matter of seconds.

markers along the visible margins, definite dates or quantities, which are signals for specific actions, are brought out in bold relief. By such signals a whole tray of cards can be scanned and the items requiring immediate attention quickly spotted. Figure 7–16 illustrates a signaling system for accurate follow-up.

Book Form. It is also possible to secure visible equipment which is suitable for keeping all card information in book form. Approximately 2,000 cards can be kept in one binder. The book form affords

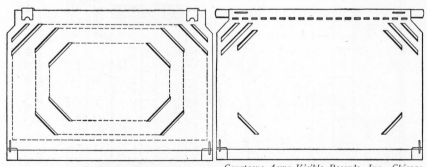

Courtesy: *Acme Visible Records, Inc., Chicago*

FIG. 7–15. Pockets are slotted to take care of various-sized cards. *Left:* The use of the hinge and hanger pocket method. *Right:* The use of the bar-pocket method.

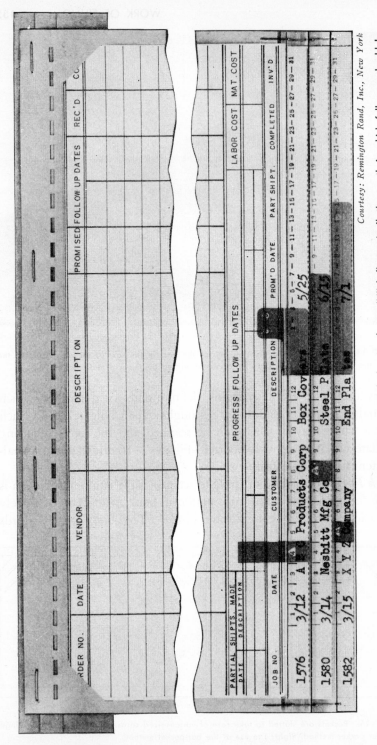

FIG. 7–16. An effective follow-up signaling system. On the top card, the signal over "4" indicates April, the month in which follow-up should be made. The signal at the right of the card at "3" indicates the day of the month on which the follow-up is due.

Courtesy: Remington Rand, Inc., New York

portability and a posting surface always at desk height. Binders are made to lie perfectly flat when open, to lock against any possible accidental shifting of record sequence, and to lift and guide sheets into proper position when the binder is closed. Figure 7–17 shows a binder offering these features.

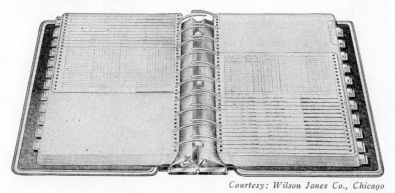

Courtesy: Wilson Jones Co., Chicago

FIG. 7–17. Shif-Dex Visible Record Binder.

CARDS FILED VERTICALLY

The third type of visible files to be discussed is that designed for use where cards are filed vertically in an open-tub type of file. The cards vary in size from about 4 to 20 inches in width and 6 to 12 inches in height. They are similar in appearance to the printed forms for machine- and hand-posting work. One or both of the upper corners of the card are cut away in order to provide diagonal indexing margins; in addition, the horizontal and one of the vertical margins of the card are used for indexing.

Cards are placed in the file in an offset arrangement so that the top, diagonal, and side margins of the card are exposed or visible. The card is held in position by means of a notched arrangement at the bottom of the card which fits into a receiving device at the bottom of the file, and the design is such that cards can easily be inserted or removed. Both sides of the card can be used, and signaling devices similar to those already discussed can be employed. Figure 7–18 shows the arrangement of cards in the file. With this equipment, the finding time is minimized, thumbing through cards is eliminated, and exceedingly quick scanning over large numbers of cards is possible—for example, nearly 7,000 cards, 10 × 5 inches in size, can be accommodated in one file unit.

FILING SUPPLIES

Guides, tabs, file folders, plastic signals, labels, and printed cards are among the items designated as filing supplies. For each item, assorted

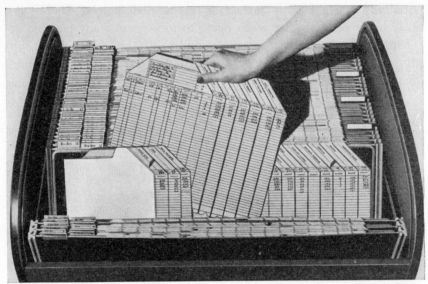

FIG. 7–18. The arrangement of cards in a file. Groups of cards can be removed and re-placed just as easily as one card.

sizes and forms are available. Figure 7–19 shows several popular styles in tabs for file guides and the choice of offset cuts at the top of file folders.

FILING AND PERSONNEL

Better placement of personnel for filing work is needed. In too many instances the attitude prevails that the untrained office employee who cannot be fitted in elsewhere because of the lack of some office skill should be given filing work. Entirely overlooked is the fundamental truth that filing personnel should possess certain attributes, including a sense of orderliness, accuracy, manual dexterity, quick reading comprehension, and a liking for detail.

A realistic approach consisting of four facets appears in order. First, appoint one person to be in charge of all filing. This will help promote needed study and improvements in filing. Second, establish what can reasonably be expected from the filing personnel. For example, are all requests clear and complete? Frequently, the file clerk is expected to have an ability to find a piece of paper even though she's never seen it, don't know what it was about, who it was from, or when it was written. Third, take sincere efforts to upgrade filing. All key and office personnel should be made aware of the importance of filing and of the helpful contributions of those performing this work. Fourth, adjust

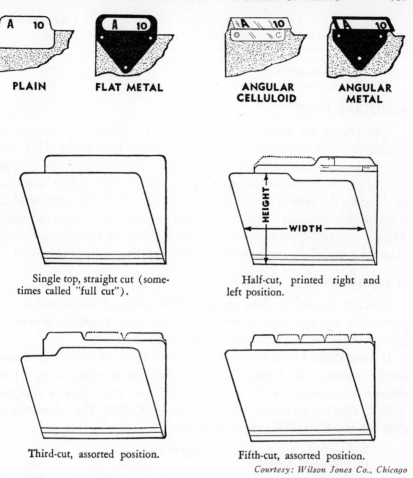

PLAIN   FLAT METAL   ANGULAR CELLULOID   ANGULAR METAL

Single top, straight cut (sometimes called "full cut").

Half-cut, printed right and left position.

Third-cut, assorted position.

Fifth-cut, assorted position.

Courtesy: Wilson Jones Co., Chicago

FIG. 7–19. *Top:* Styles of tabs for file guides. *Bottom:* Offset cuts at top of file folders.

wages of the filing personnel. Of the total cost for filing, most is for labor, and filing can never be more efficient than the people doing the filing.

STANDARDS AND FILING

If possible, production standards for filing operations should be developed. With these as a guide, the manager can determine whether the proper amount of filing work is being obtained. Standards will vary among different companies due to the type of records and the conditions surrounding the work. However, to give an idea of what can be done, expectancies are shown based on data from a number of companies:

Task	Units per Hour
Sorting letters and filing alphabetically	180
Filing 5 × 8-inch cards in an alphabetical vertical file	315
Locating and pulling letters from an alphabetical file	110
Filing vouchers numerically	700
Marking one-page letters for filing	220

AUDITS AND FILING

Spot checks for neatness and accuracy of a company's files are advisable in order to administer adequate control over filing. Also, periodic inspection can be made to determine if misuses of filing equipment exist or if new or different equipment is needed. This work can be done by the person in charge of filing, but a better practice is to use a committee or council. With the latter arrangement, more interest in filing is generated, prestige is added, the thinking of a number of people is utilized, and the awareness for needed improvements is enhanced.

COST OF FILING

Data on the cost of filing are hazy. Not too much attention has been given the subject, and where calculated, the amounts depend so greatly upon the circumstances of the individual office.

It costs about 1 cent for each paper filed in an ordinary four-drawer correspondence file. Stated differently, the cost of filing using a four-drawer correspondence file is about $200 per year. Thus a company with 25 files has an annual filing expense of $5,000. The substantiating data for one file cabinet per year follow:

Rent for 5½ sq. ft. per cabinet and aisle at $2 per sq. ft.	$ 11.00
Depreciation on cabinet	6.00
Transfer cases	8.00
Labor	140.00
File guides and folders	8.40
Overhead and supervision	15.00
Miscellaneous	3.00
Total	$203.40

Cost data such as illustrated by the above can be helpful in controlling filing. From cost information a basis for satisfactory filing can be established and subsequent filing operation costs compared to this base in order to determine if filing operations are satisfactory.

QUESTIONS

1. What are the basic arrangements for filing papers? Which one can be considered the foundation of nearly all filing? Why?
2. Identify each of the following and explain how it is used:
   a) Tickler file.
   b) Terminal-digit file.

c) Primary file guide.

d) Individual file folder.

e) Shif-Dex Visible Record Binder.

3. Discuss a system of file indexing based on the pronunciation or sound of the name.

4. Draw up a tabular chart showing the file indexing used in connection with various types of material handled in your school office or in some other office with which you are familiar.

5. For each of the following filing troubles, suggest a feasible solution:

a) Correspondence papers piled up in miscellaneous folders.

b) Necessity of fingering many folders before finding the right one.

c) Search through many papers in a folder to find the one wanted of a certain date.

d) Saint Louis correspondence may be found under "St. Louis," "Saint Louis," or "Missouri."

e) File drawers jammed tight with material.

f) Too many files in which a needed paper might be found.

6. It is desired to use a convenient signaling system in connection with a visible file (cards horizontal) for items in an inventory. For each item a minimum and a maximum quantity has been calculated. An ordering point has also been established, and it is the quantity on hand at which additional units should be ordered, so that the quantity on hand will always remain between the minimum and maximum levels determined. Using Figure 7–16 as a guide, sketch a signaling system to show the minimum, maximum, and ordering points. Also include an indicator for the present quantity on hand. This will vary between the maximum and the minimum as units of the item are withdrawn from inventory. When the stock-on-hand indicator coincides with the ordering point, a requisition to purchase is made. Explain the operation of your suggested signaling system.

7. Discuss a filing procedure that you would recommend to an office manager.

8. Explain several means for the charging out of filed material, i.e., for controlling the removal of papers from the files.

9. What are the major arguments for centralized filing?

10. Discuss the cost of filing. Do you feel that cost is an adequate means of controlling filing work? Why?

11. The filing work in the office of the Chestnut Sales Company is admittedly inefficient. Investigation by the office manager shows that the difficulty apparently centers around the filing personnel. In general, what action do you feel the office manager should take to help remedy the present situation?

12. Relate eight filing practices that you feel are of major significance.

CASE PROBLEMS

CASE 7–1. CHARLESTON VENEER COMPANY

Manufacturers of tropical and domestic wood veneers, with general offices located in Chicago, the Charleston Veneer Company is considered one of the largest in the industry, producing over one hundred million feet of veneer annually. Three manufacturing plants are located in Suffolk, Virginia; Kansas City, Missouri; and Sisters, Oregon. Warehouses and sales offices are located throughout the United States. The company employs thirty-four salesmen operating out of Chicago and six district sales offices.

To maintain records of veneer is a task of considerable magnitude and must be done accurately. Each log, when cut, is identified by a number. The log is cut into segments, called flitches, and designated alphabetically. To illustrate, a customer may buy flitch K from log 8932. The company manufactures about 60 species of wood veneers.

As the veneer is manufactured, samples are drawn from stocks, graded, priced, and sent to the various sales offices. The salesmen in turn sell from these samples. When the veneer is cut, sample sheets are sent to the Chicago office and the footage and price for each flitch is entered on inventory cards. There is one card for each log. These cards are filed numerically by log number. So-called "slicer reports" are sent daily to the Chicago office by the manufacturing mills showing the amount and type of veneer cut. When a sale is made, the flitch is canceled on the inventory card. This information is taken from sales orders at the beginning of their processing in the Chicago office. A cancellation notice is sent by the Chicago office to all sales offices notifying of the depletion of the particular veneer.

However, too often a flitch is resold before the cancellation notice of its depletion reaches the various sales offices. In addition, the Chicago office keeps no record of total footage on hand of each species of wood. In the event of a large order the customer usually wants the same type of wood, although the veneer pattern will vary due to the make-up of the log itself. To take care of this sales contingency, it would be well to know how much veneer of a certain type or at least flitches from the same log are on hand at any given time. Furthermore, there are no adequate records of salesman's sales. Who is selling what is not known accurately, and it is believed such information would be helpful in guiding sales efforts.

PROBLEMS:

1. Recommend specific improvements for recording and filing information concerning sales and inventory records which the company needs.

2. What are the major disadvantages to your recommendations and how would you try to minimize them?

CASE 7–2. OGDEN INSURANCE COMPANY

The arrangement of work in the Filing Department of a branch office of the Ogden Insurance Company was changed several months ago. At that time double-check files of policyholders were established. In one file the policies were arranged alphabetically by name of policyholder. In the other, reference cards were filed numerically, each card bearing the same number as the policy represented by the card.

The office manager, Mr. Joseph Sarbarneck, believed that all was not going too well in the Filing Department, so he made a quick survey and discovered the following facts:

Each morning the policies were brought to the Filing Department. They are sorted in strict alphabetical order. The two girls with the longest service with the company (four years and three years, respectively) do not sort any policies. They feel that they should not have to do this sorting work because of their seniority. While the other girls are doing the sorting work, the two seniority girls look over material in the files and appear to be checking the general arrangement of it.

After all policies were sorted, each girl was given approximately the same number of policies to file. In the case of a new policy, a reference card had to be filled out which was then filed in the numerical file. In contrast, an old policy, which had been removed for purposes of reference by members of other departments, did not require a reference card, since such a card was already in the numerical file.

The work of filing was frequently interrupted by other office employees searching through the files. Telephone calls, which were answered by file clerks, commonly required considerable time while the requested information was looked up.

Substitution cards were used in the event material was removed from the files. However, the file girls complained that the substitution card was of little significance, as material removed often passed on to a third or fourth party without the knowledge of the Filing Department.

It was further found by Mr. Sarbarneck that most of the filing personnel had been with the Ogden Insurance Company less than one year. Several had been with the company from one to three years, and one over three years. In addition, every filed policy was considered active. None of the filing personnel could remember the last time the files were culled to eliminate inactive policies.

PROBLEMS:

1. What do you suggest Mr. Sarbarneck do in order to improve the current situation in the Filing Department? Briefly elaborate on the major points in your recommendation.

2. What major obstacles would you anticipate in putting your recommendations into effect? How would you plan to overcome these obstacles? Explain.

CASE 7–3. THE BROADWAY CORPORATION

The office manager of the Broadway Corporation is very much concerned with a problem of voucher filing. The present system has been in use for some time. After receiving the vouchers, they are stapled and folded in order to fit into old file drawers which measure about 13 inches wide and 6 inches high. Extra large vouchers are folded separately, and a rubber band is placed around each one to hold it together.

Inspection of these voucher files showed about 750 vouchers are crowded into one file drawer. They are placed in numerical order. No tabs or index are used as it is believed a simple matter to find a numbered voucher from a pack. Approximately 12,000 vouchers are filed each year. Vouchers are retained in the files for four years, then transferred to a storage area in the basement. The managers do not wish to change this practice. There is plenty of unused office space in the filing department. About seventeen references to the voucher files are made daily. Anyone in the office can refer to the file if he so desires; however, practically all the reference is made by three employees whose work requires reference to voucher information. From time to time a needed voucher cannot be found in the file. This causes some inconvenience and places the company at a disadvantage in handling certain office work. Sometimes "lost" vouchers are later found in the file—misplaced, although in many instances they are never located and must be considered permanently missing.

PROBLEMS:

1. How do you suppose a situation such as this came about in the office of the Broadway Corporation?

2. What is the problem of the Broadway Corporation?

3. Justify the specific program of action that you recommend.

Chapter · 8

Records Retention

I hold this to be the rule of life, "Too much of anything is
bad."

—TERRENCE

IN THE typical enterprise, too much material is filed.
Papers that should be discarded are filed because someday somebody
may ask for them. Copies of bulletins, sales orders, routine replies, and
memoranda are zealously guarded and duly filed, in many cases by
several departments. The result is row upon row of filing cabinets,
many useless documents retained, and needless office expense.

The National Records Management Council, Inc., a nonprofit organization, estimates that corporate records occupy office and storage
space valued at $350 million a year. This is the space equivalent of
about 200 buildings the size of the Chrysler Building in New York
City. Furthermore, according to the Council, 95 per cent of the corporate records over a year old are never used, and 95 per cent of the
references made deal with records less than five years old. The problem
is clear: Keep worthless materials out of files and periodically review
filed materials to eliminate what is no longer necessary. In many instances one half of the filed papers can be destroyed and half of the rest
can be transferred from the office to storage space.

MEANING OF RECORDS RETENTION

*Records retention deals with the disposition of records and concerns
filing those that must be retained and destroying those that are or that
become worthless.* The time to effect a records-retention program is before the materials are filed. Permit only carefully defined "useful
materials" to be filed. Keeping worthless materials out of the files is
easier and more realistic than getting worthless materials removed
once they are filed. In addition, periodic checks should be made in

order to remove and dispose of filed materials that have become worthless.

Records retention is an essential part of records management, including the entire life span—the birth and death—of a record. The work of records retention must be co-ordinated with that of other office management activities so that the necessary paper work is done at lowest cost and yet provides the necessary information quickly and accurately.

CONTENT OF RECORDS-RETENTION PROGRAM

Included in the activities of a sound records-retention program are provisions to—

1. Establish a tight schedule of retention periods for every type of record and all its copies.

2. Remove from files all material that has become useless, employing well-timed and orderly procedures for this work.

3. Establish and maintain a convenient, low-cost, and safe area for records storage.

4. Index the exact location of each type record, showing where it is stored, and in what type of container.

5. Take charge of all microfilming of records to insure that necessary copies only are made.

6. Show facts on volume of records, how much is in office, how much is in storage area, and how much is discarded.

7. Revise schedules of records-retention periods based upon facts derived from analysis of the use made of the records, by major types.

8. Participate in purchasing decisions for new filing equipment and supplies.

ADVANTAGES OF RECORDS-RETENTION PROGRAM

Such a program can be quite extensive. It requires good management, foresight, judgment, and especially a steadfastness of purpose. The rewards, however, are high. Better filing efficiency is gained since inactive material is removed, thus reducing finding time. Space savings are also achieved—throwing out records that have become useless means less space is needed. Also, storing useful but inactive records in an inexpensive storage area means dollar savings. Furthermore, the retained records are better protected and safeguarded. Equipment designed especially for storage can be utilized, and the records are not subject to possible mutilation as a result of frequent handling.

Several examples will be cited to reveal the benefits gained by eliminating vast accumulations of unnecessary records. The manager of a large bank in New York City found that 62 per cent of all filed material could be eliminated, thereby releasing nearly 55 per cent of its file room space for other purposes. Carloads of useless old records were destroyed. The case of an airline company is stimulating. After review and appraisal of the records, it was decided to clean out the files, and disposition was made as follows:

> 55% sold as waste paper
> 19% placed in storage area
> 26% permitted to remain in office area
> 100% Total

Think of it. Over one half of the carefully filed and retained records could be discarded as waste paper. Only one paper in four remained in the office files. Imagine the savings in finding time and space. In another example, that of the federal government, record-cleaning efforts were directed upon the government's nearly 20 million cubic feet of files. Within several years, federal agencies were destroying over 2½ million cubic feet of records annually—the equivalent of over 1½ million file drawers. In addition, nearly 1 million cubic feet of paper was being transferred from active to storage areas at centers.

TRANSFER OF MATERIALS TO INACTIVE FILES

A systematic transfer of materials to inactive files is desirable in order to prevent current files from growing unmanageable. Material cannot remain in files indefinitely—the physical space becomes exhausted.

In a four-drawer filing cabinet, the top two drawers can be used for current material and the bottom two for inactive material. This arrangement affords convenient reference to inactive material, necessary from time to time in every office.

The transferring of material can be done in one of two main ways: (1) the entire unit, or periodically; and (2) the individual, or perpetually.

The entire-unit method requires that all material be transferred at a scheduled time. Usually this is done on an annual basis and at the beginning of the calendar year, fiscal year, or busy season. The material remains in the original folders and is moved bodily. New folders are used for the new material in the current file.

The individual or perpetually method places time limits on individual papers by appropriate marks on the folders. Then, periodically, at intervals of about two or three months, or perpetually at irregular intervals, the files are screened, and papers found to have been in the file past the allowable limit are transferred to the inactive file. In cases where the transaction is terminated, i.e., a settlement granted or a sale closed, the material is transferred immediately, regardless of date.

DETERMINING THE RECORDS-RETENTION SCHEDULE

Many offices are confronted with the problem of how long to retain inactive file material. The answer lies in knowing what to save and how to store it. This, in turn, depends primarily upon the usefulness of the material to managers, and the legal requirements. The period of retention differs among companies, but there is a tendency toward the development of standard practices.

Each company should strive to develop its own retention schedule based on an analysis of the actual use made of its own records. To copy what another company has decided or to adopt a "canned schedule" frequently results in serious shortcomings. The analysis might begin with a cursory review of the entire enterprise to obtain background and understanding of the current work and to spot what records are used and what ones are filed for satisfactory operation. Following this, a survey is in order to determine (1) what is filed; (2) how much is filed—its size and quantity; (3) where it is filed—including the copies, if any; (4) how often was it used during specific preceding periods; (5) when, if ever, it is permanently removed from file; and (6) what is done with permanently removed material. In some instances this survey work is expedited by classifying the material by type or by department. Information applicable to several departments can be studied as a group, thus relating the types of information common to several units.

From the survey data, the value of each record is weighed. Questions decided are, "Should this record be filed at all?" "How long should this record remain in the file?" "Is it advisable to retain this record in storage?" Particular attention is paid to records presently having long-term retention. Experience shows that many retention times can be cut measurably below the periods formerly believed necessary.

Results of this work will show the records of varying importance from the viewpoint of retention. For convenience they can be grouped into four classes: (1) nonessential, (2) helpful, (3) important, and (4) vital.

Records classified as nonessential should never be filed. They may have value for a relatively short period—perhaps as little as a few seconds—but retaining them is wasteful. Included in this category are penciled notations, routine inquiries, announcements, and acknowledgements.

Helpful records are those that can assist, but only for a very limited time, perhaps four to five weeks. After this period, their usefulness is completed. If filed, they should be placed in a separate drawer or cabinet and destroyed as their helpfulness ceases. In this group is general correspondence, most of which has a useful life of not over four weeks.

Important records include those containing information of value for relatively long periods—up to five or six years. They should first be filed in the office for handy reference, but ultimately, as they lose their current usefulness, they should be transferred to storage. How long they remain in the office depends upon the type of record and the policy established. Many firms keep records such as invoices, accounts receivable, sales records, quotations, and financial statements in active files for one to two years, then transfer to storage. With sufficient time, important records lose their essentiality and should be discarded. As stated above this may take place at the end of five or six years. However, in this connection, the Statute of Limitations must also be taken into account. It specifies the length of time a record is alive according to law. This period varies for various documents and among states, as shown by Figure 8–1.

Vital records, as the name implied, are paramount. They are retained permanently. They may be transferred to the storage area after a given period of time, but they are never destroyed. Vital records include legal papers of incorporation, titles to ownership, deeds, reports to stockholders, and insurance policies.

If placed in storage, many records managers suggest marking the destruction date on the material at the time of its transfer to storage. This may be a date stamped on the material or a notice to destroy in "one year," "two years," or "retain permanently." In any event all transferred material should be classified, properly labeled, and indexed so that it can be found if needed.

Studies by the National Records Management Council disclose that of the records of a typical company—

> 10 per cent or less must be kept permanently.
> 20 per cent must be retained currently.
> 30 per cent should be transferred to less costly space.
> 35 per cent should be destroyed.

State	Open Accounts	Contracts in Writing	
		Under Seal	Not Under Seal
Alabama	3	10	6
Arizona	3	6	6
Arkansas	3	5	5
California	varies	4	4
Colorado	6	6	6
Connecticut	6	17	6
Delaware	3	20	3
District of Columbia	3	12	3
Florida	3	20	5
Georgia	4	20	6
Idaho	4	5	5
Illinois	5	10	varies
Indiana	6	20	10
Iowa	5	10	10
Kansas	3	5	5
Kentucky	5	15	15
Louisiana	varies	varies	varies
Maine	6	20	6
Maryland	3	12	3
Massachusetts	6	20	6
Michigan	6	6	6
Minnesota	6	6	6
Mississippi	3	6	6
Missouri	5	10	10
Montana	5	8	8
Nebraska	4	5	5
Nevada	4	6	6
New Hampshire	6	20	6
New Jersey	6	16	6
New Mexico	4	6	6
New York	6	6	6
North Carolina	3	10	3
North Dakota	6	6	6
Ohio	6	15	15
Oklahoma	3	5	5
Oregon	6	10	6
Pennsylvania	6	20	6
Rhode Island	6	20	6
South Carolina	6	20	6
South Dakota	6	20	6
Tennessee	6	6	6
Texas	2	4	4
Utah	4	8	6
Vermont	6	varies	6
Virginia	3	10	5
Washington	3	6	6
West Virginia	5	10	10
Wisconsin	6	varies	6
Wyoming	8	10	10

FIG. 8–1. Statutes of limitations, in years, for specified documents.

This means that 65 per cent of all records, or two out of every three, should be either put in a less costly location or destroyed. However, they cannot be indiscriminately discarded. Some are valuable and worthy of retention; others must be weeded out as useless.

A RECORDS-RETENTION PROGRAM

Figure 8–2 shows a sound program of records retention. As previously stated, material classified as nonessential should never be filed but destroyed immediately. "Helpful" material is filed in a separate file for the limited period that it is helpful, then destroyed. Material considered important or vital is filed (step No. 1) and subsequently transferred to inactive file as a normal procedure (step No. 2). Periodically all material is removed from the inactive files and sorted (step No. 3). It is either important or vital material. The former is handled in three different ways: (step 4A) microfilmed, records destroyed, films placed in storage, and ultimately destroyed; (step 4B) the records are placed in storage and eventually destroyed; or (step 4C) the records are destroyed having lived their span of importance. If the material is classified vital, step 4D consisting of microfilming, destroying records, and placing films in storage can be followed, or step 4E placing the material in storage can be adopted.

This program may vary somewhat in individual applications. For example, microfilm may not be used at all, or it may be found more practical to eliminate step No. 3 (sort), microfilm all records, and use the microfilms for reference in all cases.

For records in storage, a system of indexing should be adopted so that all such material can be located quickly. The information can be kept on small index cards or on sheets in a loose-leaf notebook. It should include subject classification, shelf number, box number or name, and scheduled date for ultimate destruction. It is important that each container be labeled plainly.

At least once a year a list should be prepared showing what stored original records should be destroyed. It can be compiled readily from data on the index cards. The list is then submitted to the office manager or designated executive for approval and authority to proceed. When this has been granted, the material is destroyed and the list filed permanently for future reference.

HEAD OF RECORDS-RETENTION PROGRAM

In most cases it is best to have one person in charge of a records-retention program. The person should have adequate authority to

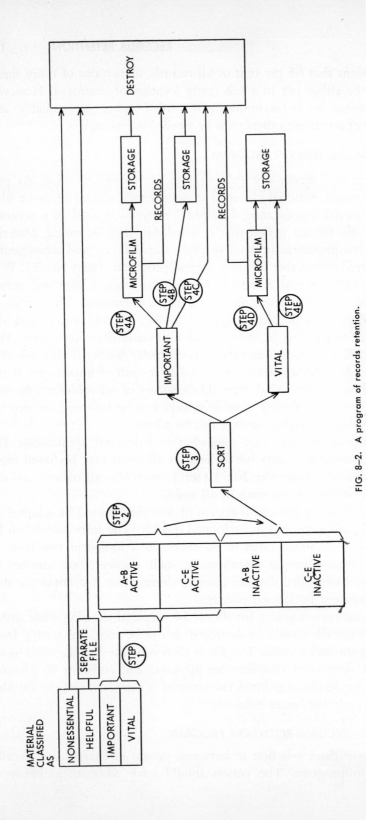

FIG. 8-2. A program of records retention.

direct and maintain the program. To a great extent the success of the program is throttled by the caliber of person heading the unit and the relationship of the records-retention unit to the other office units. Preferably this head should report to an executive in a high enough organization level to get top management support and opinions.

Committees have been used successfully in records-retention work, but this approach is not always effective. Quality rather than quantity is needed. A committee representative is usually well qualified to decide on his own records but will refrain from commenting strongly about practices in other departments. Furthermore, service on a records-retention committee is commonly a part-time job, and this fact can be a deterrent in the program management. Committees for records retention can be used in an advisory, but preferably not in an executive, capacity.

THE PHYSICAL WORK ENVIRONMENT

A clean, dry area should be designated for records retention. Proper conditions of temperature, circulation of air, and humidity should be provided. Traditionally storage rooms have been the attics of business; they should be regarded as attractive work areas. The floor area must withstand a relatively high weight per square foot. For example, about 200 pounds per square foot may be required. This is based on a full drawer holding 75 pounds of records, drawers stacked eight high, occupying a floor area of about three square feet.

Various types of equipment can be used for storing records. The following are of special interest: (1) open-shelf file units, (2) storage boxes on shelving, and (3) specially designed fiberboard drawer files. An open-shelf file unit is illustrated by Figure 8–3. Such a unit provides instant accessibility to records at low cost. It is available in various sizes, is completely prefabricated, and is easy to assemble without tools. Follower blocks keep records upright for convenient reference. Another common storage means are storage boxes on shelving. These boxes are built of high-test corrugated fiberboard especially designed to withstand rough usage and to prevent mildew and damage from dirt or moisture. A variety of sizes is supplied so that the stored material fits snugly in the box. The shelving is assembled quickly without tools and can be extended by adding extensional units. The shelving can be dismantled and reassembled in a new location in a matter of minutes. In the third and last method, specially designed fiberboard drawer files combine the drawer, shelving, and base all in one unit. A steel framework carries the entire weight load. The drawer files are interlocking, as illustrated by the insert in Figure 8–4. It will be noted that a single drawer is within a steel shell. The drawers are locked together solidly each locking to the others around it. The unit "builds its own steel framework as you stack it." As many as twenty drawers can be stacked in one tier. There is no buckling, sagging, or warping. In this method space is entirely devoted to drawer units. Also different available drawer sizes and separators for inside the drawers mean

Courtesy: Bankers Box Co., Franklin Park, Ill.

FIG. 8–3. A ready reference open-shelf file unit.

practically no waste space. The result is a compact, efficient use of space. With space utilization expressed as a ratio of cubic feet of records to square feet of space, the specially designed drawer files method can easily reach a ratio of eight to one. Many storage areas do not attain a ratio of five to one. From actual measurement, one New York bank after installing fiberboard drawer files for storage reported a 30 per cent savings in valuable floor space.

MICROFILMING

"Microfilming" is a photographic means of retaining the information given in office papers. The materials are first photographed on film at reduced sizes; then the film is developed, to serve as the permanent record. To see a paper, the film is placed on a machine called a "reader" or "viewer" which enlarges the picture. See Figure 8–5.

One of the first commercial applications of microfilming was in banks, where it was used in connection with checks. The list of applications grew steadily, and microfilming is now associated with many types

Courtesy: Bankers Box Co., Franklin Park, Ill.

FIG. 8–4. Interlocking fiberboard drawer files for a compact and substantial storage file.

of paper materials. It is an accepted part of many record-retention programs. The records classified as "important" or "vital" which are needed for continuance of an enterprise can be microfilmed and stored in a safe or in a remote area, in order to avoid the loss of these records in case of disaster.

Microfilming is available to the small as well as to the large enterprise. Outside concerns specializing in microfilming work will microfilm records either in the office of the company or in their own plant. The cost for this service, including film and developing, varies from $4 to $6 for each 1,000 pieces, depending upon the size and quantity of the material, whether hand or automatic feed can be used, and whether one or two sides are to be microfilmed.

Advantages. The use of microfilming effects a great savings of storage space. About 98–99 per cent of storage space can be saved, since one to two file cabinets of film hold the equivalent of a hundred cabinets of original records. In addition, the chances for losing a document are minimized. The photographs on the film are in sequence like links of a chain; once a paper is photographed, there is no danger of the photograph being lost unless the whole roll of microfilm is lost.

Courtesy: Diebold, Inc., Canton, Ohio

FIG. 8–5. *Left:* A camera and film-developing machine for microfilming office papers. It is fully electronic in operation. Exposures are made at the rate of 1,500 to 3,000 per hour, depending upon the type of material being filmed. *Right:* A reading projector for reference work. About 100 feet of film can be scanned in one minute. This is equivalent to material in two full regular-file drawers.

Furthermore, with microfilm, the retained materials are clean and easily handled, and they reduce the fire hazard, because the film is of the acetate, noncombustible type.

Disadvantages. On the other hand, microfilming has its drawbacks. The courts usually prefer original documents but will accept microfilmed material when failure to produce the original is adequately explained. Usually, microfilming must be established as a regular procedure and one not motivated by any suspicion or fraud. Microfilming may perpetuate the habit of keeping old records. It is easier to microfilm all records and file the films than it is to decide what should be saved, sort the material, and retain only what has future use. Also, the use of microfilming requires special equipment; a viewer is the minimum requirement. Furthermore, employees must be trained for the specialized techniques required, and these skills are somewhat different from those required for most office work.

INSTILL CONFIDENCE IN RECORDS RETENTION

The manager of records retention must instill a feeling of confidence in the records-retention activities and results. All office personnel, as well as key management people, must believe in the accuracy, completeness, and usefulness of the filed material. Unless they do, they are quite likely to keep important records in their own desks or special files than to trust them with records retention.

A manual supplying information on the procedures and practices of the records-retention group is also helpful. Data on the type of material stored, the indexing system, retention schedule, and specific duties of records-retention personnel should be clearly written and made available to anyone whose work is affected by records retention. Such a manual is extremely beneficial for obtaining better understanding and for training new employees in records-retention work.

CONTROLLING AND RECORDS RETENTION

An effective means of control is to limit the quantity of records per employee. The amount permitted will depend upon the type of business operation. The National Records Management Council suggests these amounts:

Type of Business Operation	Cubic Feet of Records per Employee on Payroll
Clerical—such as accounting or purchasing	10–15
Industrial—such as aircraft factory or assembly plant	1
Public utilities, government agencies	5

Cost is used by many companies to keep records-retention work within reasonable limits. Cost for labor and space will vary depending upon the particular location, but cost for equipment is relatively much more uniform. For this latter, an average cost figure is $2 per cubic foot of records stored. If the amount of records-retention equipment is higher than this amount, remedial attention is probably in order.

Additional cost information that adds to the need to control the amount of records retained is revealed by the fact that it costs about $1,000 to create the contents for one file drawer of correspondence.

Assuming 5,000 papers in one file drawer, one fifth the papers being letters produced at a cost of 80 cents each, the remaining papers carbon copies at a cost of 4 cents each, the calculations are:

$$1,000 \times 80¢ = \$800$$
$$4,000 \times \ 4¢ = \underline{\ \ \ 160}$$
$$\text{Total} \quad \$960$$

Helpful ratios can also be derived. To illustrate, a "usage" ratio reveals the extent to which the materials stored are being used. The formula is:

$$\text{Usage ratio (in \%)} = \frac{\text{Requests} \times 100}{\text{References filed}}$$

For example, if last month 200 requests were made from 20,000 items stored, the usage ratio in percentage would be 200×100 divided by 20,000, or 1 per cent. This ratio for stored materials will seldom exceed 5 per cent. For active materials in the office files, it should run about 15–20 per cent. Further analysis of usage ratios can be made taking into account the rate of reference by type of record versus the age of the record. Such studies assist in better controlling of records-retention efforts.

Another ratio is the "accuracy" ratio which is calculated by this formula:

$$\text{Accuracy ratio (in \%)} = \frac{\text{No. of items not found} \times 100}{\text{No. of items found}}$$

For 10 items not found and 10,000 found, the ratio is 0.1 per cent. For a rating of excellent the accuracy ratio should not be greater than 0.5 per cent. A value of 3 per cent or more signifies remedial action is required.

QUESTIONS

1. Define "records retention" and discuss its importance in office management.
2. What activities are included in a complete records-retention program?
3. Do you favor the use of a well-selected committee to handle a records-retention program? Why?
4. Explain Figure 8–2 in your own words.
5. For how long a period do you suggest each item in the following list of filed material be retained:
    a) Sales prospect lists?

b) Samples of advertising?

c) Real estate deeds?

d) Payrolls and pay rates?

e) Production routing lists?

f) Quotations to customers.

Give reasons for your answers.

6. What, if any, is the difference between indexing for filing and indexing for records retention? Elaborate on your answer.

7. Do you favor the entire-unit or the individual method in the transferring of filed material? Why?

8. Write a two-sentence, identifying description of each of the following:

a) Fiberboard storage box.

b) Fiberboard drawer file.

c) Microfilming.

d) Statute of Limitations.

9. What conditions in an office indicate that advantages might be derived from the use of microfilming?

10. Can you see anything wrong with using old vertical filing cabinets for the storing of records? Discuss.

11. Do you agree with the following: "The availability of reliable microfilming machines and supplies solves the retention of records problem for most offices. This is substantiated by the fact that accurate copies at a cost of a fraction of a cent each and a savings of over 95 per cent storage space are obtained through microfilming."

12. You have been asked to give a ten-minute talk on "Managerial Controlling in the Area of Records Retention." Outline the major points of your presentation.

CASE PROBLEMS

CASE 8–1. GATES MANUFACTURING COMPANY

Supervising the filing department of the Gates Manufacturing Company is Mrs. Herma Penfield, a stern, serious-minded employee who has been with the company for twenty-two years. She permits no one but filing personnel to consult, remove, or insert materials of the company's files. Six file clerks report to Mrs. Penfield. The morale of the department is high. Both within and outside of her department, Mrs. Penfield has a reputation for supplying efficient service, handling her subordinates firmly and fairly, and "running her department."

Every January and July, filed material, classified as current, is transferred from the top two drawers of each file to the bottom two drawers. The material in the bottom drawers is gone through and it is decided what to retain. Mrs. Penfield is in charge of this work. Almost all the decisions in this respect are made by her using past experience and judgment, or abiding to specific requests to save certain materials. In those cases where there is some uncertainty in her mind, Mrs. Penfield calls the party or parties whom she believes is most vitally concerned with whether the material is retained and arrives at a decision qualified with what suggestions are given her.

Materials for storage are removed to old files in the company's warehouse about 150 yards from the general offices. The space is poorly lighted, but it is readily accessible, free from excessive dirt and moisture, and is of ample size— far in excess of what is needed for storage purposes. The material is stored in old files in the same general arrangement as that followed in the filing department. Like requests for material in the filing department, all inquiries for stored paper records are handled by Mrs. Penfield who either personally or through one of her subordinates locates the material in storage and charges it out to the requester or informs him that the material is not available having been destroyed at the transfer time.

There has been "no incident" to focus attention to the present filing and storage practices followed. Informal chats by a management trainee with various key people in the company reveal no complaints. These chats were suggested by the office manager with the statement "to look things over." Statements made during responses included (1), "Mrs. Penfield is a little difficult to understand at times, but I'm certain she means well." (2) "The work is done efficiently I suppose. However, to me, our retention of records seems a bit archaic, but I'll have to admit they have always come through and found the old records that I wanted." (3) "I get along with her all right, but she surely runs her department."

PROBLEMS:

1. Based on the limited information supplied, comment on the present retention of records practices of this company.

2. What is your opinion regarding Mrs. Penfield? Justify the viewpoint taken.

3. If requested to make recommendations to improve the company's records retention, what would you suggest? Enumerate your major point or points elaborating and substantiating your recommended action.

Chapter · 9

Duplicating

Those are fortunate who borrow experience instead of buying it.

—MARGUERITE BLESSINGTON

DUPLICATING IS a basic office operation and is increasing in importance as the work of the office is being modernized. Single copies of papers rarely suffice in the modern office, duplicated copies are needed—in some instances several copies, in other cases thousands.

The task is commonly to make or "run off" copies of a report, form letter, bulletin, price lists, charts, drawings, or financial statements. However, duplicating is not limited to this area. It also is important in many procedures in which basic information is put on a master and subsequently duplicated as needed onto paper forms designed to direct and control a particular business activity. For example, in purchasing, master sheets for duplicating can be prepared. When an item is to be purchased, its master is withdrawn from the file, and the needed information duplicated on all the purchasing forms. These forms are then processed, and the master is returned to the file for future use. The result is accurate, fast work and much savings in writing time.

PLANNING IN DUPLICATING WORK

Two areas are usually the main concern in the planning of duplicating; they are (1) determining the sequence of the duplicating work to be done, and (2) deciding what duplicating process to use. Regarding the first, consideration must be given to the urgency of the material, but in general a first-come first-serve basis is satisfactory. The grouping of work and establishing its sequence for each duplicating machine gives orderliness to the duplicating efforts. Effective is the use of a requisition form showing the duplicating process preferred, the number of copies, size of paper, date needed, destination, and general comments.

Deciding what duplicating process to use is relatively simple when the question is the selecting of one of the existing duplicators within the company. To decide what new duplicating machine, if any, should be added, brings up the question of what basic types are available, what are the trends in duplicating equipment, and what choice will best meet the particular requirements. The following discussion is a concise explanation of each basic duplicating method.

DUPLICATING MACHINES

There are numerous reproducing processes available to the office. Aside from the carbon copy method, by which means from one up to about twelve copies can be made on a standard typewriter and about twenty on an electric, the more common reproducing processes are: (1) stencil, (2) direct or liquid process, (3) indirect or gelatin process, (4) multigraph, (5) photocopy, (6) contact, (7) whiteprint, (8) dry electrical, and (9) offset.

As stated above, individual considerations should determine the reproducing process to use, but the following is offered as a general guide. The stencil process is relatively low in cost and widely used for routine office work. The direct and indirect processes are effective for up to 300 copies. Multigraph provides a clean durable print resembling original typing and is most practical for large runs of perhaps 5,000 copies and over. The photographic processes meet the need for obtaining exact copies of drawings, illustrations, charts, and tabulated data, which may be difficult to obtain by other duplicating means. Also, several copies of a letter can be run off in a matter of seconds. The offset process provides high-quality work—having the appearance of a printed sheet—and is well suited for production runs of from 300 to 30,000 copies. A discussion of each process follows.

Stencil. This is a common method and consists of "typing a stencil," either by typewriter with ribbon removed or nonoperative, by special hand tools (styli), or by a die-impressed operation performed by the manufacturer. The openings thus made in the stencil, i.e., openings caused by the stencil coating being pushed aside and exposing the base fiber, permit ink to pass through so that paper held against the surface receives the image. Even, sharp, and clear stokes on the stencil give the best results. Corrections can be made on the stencil by using a special fluid to reseal the surface and then retyping. It is also possible to block out and remove an area and replace it by attaching a new portion of stencil. For the stencil process the paper should be slightly absorbent so that the ink does not smudge or blur. A 16-pound bond, when one side is used, and a 20-pound bond, when both sides are used, generally give satisfactory results. A quick-drying ink is available, and its use minimizes the possibility of the ink blurring. The image or printing is usually in a jet black color, although several other colors are also available. It is possible to store the stencil for use at a later time; about 5,000 copies can be made from one stencil. Machines are available which provide such features as accurate registration for fill-in material, a capacity of 200 copies per minute, and the use of several colors at the same time. Such a machine is shown in Figure 9–1.

Courtesy: A. B. Dick Co., Chicago

FIG. 9–1. A duplicating machine using the stencil process.

Direct or Liquid Process. In this process the material to be reproduced is put on a master sheet which has behind it a special carbon sheet. The carbon places the image in reverse on the back of the master sheet. Different carbons are used for different colors. The master is placed in a machine, and copies are made direct from it in this manner: the copy sheet is slightly moistened with a special fluid before contacting the back side of the master, and as the copy sheet presses against the master, a very small layer of the carbon is removed and impressed on the copy sheet. Four colors can be reproduced in a single machine operation, and about 300 copies can be made from one master. Production rates of about 100 sheets a minute are possible with a fully automatic machine. Master sheets can be stored for reruns. Figure 9–2 shows a liquid duplicator.

Indirect or Gelatin Process. From a technical viewpoint this process is similar to the one above, with the exception that an intermediate agent, gelatin, is used. The material to be reproduced is put on a master sheet made of special paper; the master sheet is pressed against the gelatin, thus depositing the image on it. Copies are then made by pressing the sheets against the image in the gelatin. The ink remains concentrated long enough to permit the duplicating of several hundred copies, but gradually it is absorbed and dispersed by the gelatin. This makes it possible to use the gelatin over and over again. However, new impressions on the gelatin are required for reruns. The form of the gelatin is that of either a continuous roll or separate flat sections, depending upon the design of the machine. Since the middle 1950's, the manufacture of gelatin process duplicators has been reduced. Today it represents a smaller proportion of the duplicator business than that of former years.

Courtesy: Ditto, Inc., Chicago

FIG. 9–2. A direct or liquid process duplicating machine.

Multigraph. Machines using this process of reproduction are either of an imprinting or a ribbon process. In the imprinting method it is possible to use type, rubber strips, or electrotypes. Ink is applied to the type by an inking attachment which controls and furnishes the exact amount of ink needed. The paper, coming in contact with the wet type, forms the copy.

In the ribbon process the duplicating is done through a ribbon similar to that used in standard typing. Type is composed directly onto a blanket or railed segment. Approximately 65 to 70 lines of type are held by one blanket. The ribbon goes between the blanket and the paper, so that when the paper is pressed against the type it receives the impression and the copy is made. Work made by this process closely resembles original typing, and when such appearance is considered important, this method is commonly used. Direct mail and multiple letters can be cited as examples.

Signature attachments are also available, changes or corrections can easily be made in the type, and the process is speedy, as up to 6,000 copies can be run in one hour.

Photocopy. Photocopy machines are so constructed that readable negative paper prints are obtained by directly photographing the original material. By a photocopy of the negative, it is possible to make a positive paper print (black lines with white background). Photocopy prints can be made in the same size as, or larger or smaller than, the original. The use of this process is normally confined to one or at most perhaps a half-dozen copies of an existing original.

Contact. This method is rapidly growing in popularity and consists basically of placing a sensitized paper in contact with the material to be reproduced, inserting into machine which exposes, develops, and fixes the copy sheet. For purposes here three types of contact reproduction will be included: (*a*) Apeco, (*b*) Verifax, and (*c*) Thermo-Fax.

a) Apeco. This method gives a finished and exact copy of any office record, regardless of type or color; for example, a black on white copy just like the original is produced in less than half a minute. Two machines are used, each about the size of an ordinary typewriter. The advantages in using the Apeco method of contact reproduction include the following: the method is simple and clean, and no chemicals are required; it is fully automatic, and the machines require no special installation. Figure 9–3 shows a unit of two contact reproduction machines.

Courtesy: American Photocopy Equipment Co., Chicago

FIG. 9–3. Illustrating two contact reproduction machines and an employee peeling the sheets apart after use of the contact reproduction process.

The steps in this process are: (1) Place the original face to face with a specially prepared sensitized No. 1 negative medium (sheet of paper or cloth) and insert into the first machine. (2) Permit to remain in the machine for about ten seconds being exposed to bright light. (3) Remove the original and the No. 1 negative medium from the machine. (4) Set aside the original. (5) Place the No. 1 negative medium face to face with a No. 2 positive medium and insert into the second machine. (6) Wait for these sheets to feed through the machine, automatically emerging in about eight seconds. (7) Separate the sheets by peeling them apart. The No. 2 sheet is the duplicate. Sheet No. 1 can be discarded or filed as a reverse reading file copy.

b) Verifax. Figure 9–4 shows a secretary operating a Verifax Signet Copier. A unit such as this can prove a very valuable tool in industry. Experience indicates that increased efficiency and tangible savings pay for such a unit in about a month or two. Exact copies of letters including original letterhead and signature can be obtained; other material of interest to more than one member of a company can also be copied.

To operate, place the material to be reproduced in contact with a sheet of sensitized paper, expose to light for a few seconds—controlled by light switch of the machine—place exposed sensitized paper with developing paper, insert in developing and fixing bath, remove and permit copy to dry. It is possible to secure several usable copies from the same negative.

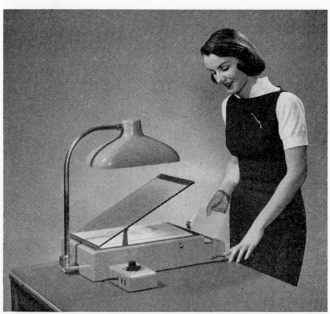

Courtesy: Eastman Kodak Co., Rochester, N.Y.

FIG. 9–4. A Verifax Signet Copier is an effective and economical machine for copying papers.

c) Thermo-Fax. Thermo-Fax Copying Machines make direct copies in a matter of seconds. Figure 9–5 shows such a unit. The machine is turned on with the flick of a switch, exposure timing set on a dial, the original and sensitized papers are placed together, inserted into the machine, the material is quickly processed, and rolls out of the

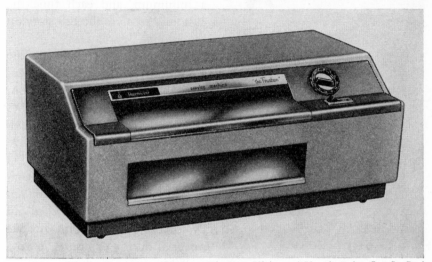

Courtesy: Minnesota Mining and Manufacturing Co., St. Paul

FIG. 9–5. This Thermo-Fax "Fourteen" Copying Machine copies originals up to 14 inches wide—important in accounting and legal departments—and features speed, economy, and convenience.

machine. An interesting application is the short note reply to relieve correspondence work. The answer or comment is written in the margin or at the bottom of an incoming letter. A copy is then made and sent to the interested party, the original letter being retained for the files.

Thermo-Fax Copying Machines require no special training to operate, are ready for instant use, give dry ready-to-use copies, and emit no detectable odor of any sort. The process is effective wherever carbon is present in the writing, such as with pencil or typewriter.

Whiteprint. In this process, positive prints are produced directly from translucent originals. This process features the feasibility of making additions or corrections on a master. For example, its use in certain types of cumulative reports is illustrated by copies of a payroll sheet containing constant data such as name, social security number, and department being made from a master. Subsequently, for each payroll period a copy is used to which has been added the variable information, such as gross earnings, deductions, and net earnings for each employee. Likewise, customers' statements can be typed on a translucent paper and retained as permanent copies by the company. At the end of each month, a whiteprint is made of the entire statement and is sent to the customer. Important advantages include: no copying work is required, errors are held to a minimum, and each time the customer receives the full story on his account.

Courtesy: Charles Bruning Company, Inc., New York

FIG. 9–6. The Bruning Copyflex Model 14, illustrated above, makes direct, positive, errorproof copies of practically any original comprised of the opaque markings from typing, printing, writing, or drawing on paper or on cloth.

Additional advantages of the whiteprint process include speed; flexibility; low cost of operation; capacity for large sizes—42 inches and almost any length; color coding—a choice of white and five colors of tinted paper in addition to four colors for lines; and convenience of blocking out—any unwanted lines may be blocked out by covering them with opaque material during exposure.

Whiteprint machines employ either of two development processes. In one process the copy is given a light coating of a special solution which permanently develops the copy. In the other, the copy is developed by exposure to controlled aqua ammonia vapors. The machines are made in a variety of sizes. Figure 9–6 illustrates a whiteprint machine.

Dry Electrical Process. The reproducing units required in this process include a fuser, a copier, and a special camera. Each unit is a little larger than an ordinary typewriter.

"Xerography" (pronounced zē-rŏg′rȧ-fē) is a combination electrical and mechanical process using powder but no ink or sensitized paper. A specially coated plate is charged with positive electricity and is subsequently exposed to the material to be reproduced, "A," by means of a camera. As a result, the reflection of "A" on the plate is retained and remains charged positively. The remaining area of the plate loses its charge because of light exposure permitted by the camera. Then a negatively charged powder is adhered to the positively charged "A." A sheet of paper is placed over the plate and given a positive electric charge. The positively charged paper draws the powder from the plate, forming a direct copy which is heated in a few seconds to fuse the powder into a permanent print.

Copies of pages for reports and other written work are made quickly and accurately by this process. The copy is permanent, and the same plate can be used hundreds of times. Although not yet commercially available, the xerography principle applied to printing is being studied. The feasibility of a printing process based on the attraction of powder to an electrostatic charge provides interesting speculations.

Offset.   The offset process is subject to many variations. Basically the principle involved is that the material to be reproduced is (1) prepared on a plate, which is (2) transferred to an intermediate agent, which is (3) printed on the paper. Frequently the intermediate agent is made of rubber.

One important offset process is photo-offset. The material to be reproduced is photographed, and the negative is transferred to a sensitized plate. This plate is then used in a photo-offset printing unit. Slight variations in this method are commonly termed "planographing" and "offset lithography."[1]

A well-known process known as "multilith" is based on this offset principle. Either metal or paperlike masters can be used. The latter is more widely used since it can be handled like a piece of paper. That is, a regular typewriter plus pencil, pen, ink, brush, or crayon furnished by the supplier are used in preparing the master. Erasures and corrections are handled as with ordinary paper, and the paperlike masters can be filed in the office like paper sheets. The process is recommended for quantities of from 500 to 10,000 copies. A machine for performing this type of work is shown in Figure 9–7.

ORGANIZATION OF DUPLICATING

Duplicating lends itself toward a centralized organizational unit. Such an arrangement makes for better utilization of the necessary equipment and machines, encourages adequate supervision, fixes responsibility, and expedites the development and the retaining of efficient operators in duplicating work. Depending upon the individual circumstances, however, duplicating is found as a part of the correspondence organizational section, or whatever unit utilizes duplicating the most. Also, in recent years with the availability of low-cost, easy-to-operate machines, such as those using the contact process giving

[1] The dry electrical process is also frequently used for making offset master paper plates.

Courtesy: Addressograph-Multigraph Corp., Cleveland

FIG. 9–7. Duplicating machine using the multilith process. The unit illustrated has the six-tray "work organizer" attachment.

several copies of letters, billings, or notices that are needed in a hurry, the trend is to disperse these machines throughout the office placing them at the locations where they are used frequently and are convenient to the person needing the copies.

ACTUATING IN DUPLICATING WORK

Much duplicating work is of a routine repetitive nature, and managerial efforts usually must be made to maintain the employee's interest and desire to turn out good quality duplicating work within reasonable time periods. At least a modicum of training in the proper use of the duplicating equipment is necessary. Instructions should be provided and required. It is erroneous and wasteful to place an employee in duplicating work and assume that she knows how to operate the duplicating machines. Many of the manufacturers of such machines supply voluminous material on the proper operation of their respective units, and quite a number will provide training help free of charge through their sales representatives.

Employees in duplicating work need definite work goals. The nature of the work seems to require that a sense of accomplishment be emphasized by management. Also the employee's desire to have the manager know what is being achieved in duplicating must be satisfied. The practice of establishing work objectives helps to fulfill these basic desires.

Full utilization of the employee's time should be stressed. Either not enough or too much duplicating work can result in a dissatisfied employee. Or expecting the work to be accomplished within practically no time at all can dull the duplicating employee's enthusiasm. Members of a duplicating department must work as a team with the various members performing several different jobs throughout the day. It is therefore especially important to maintain a congenial group.

CONTROLLING THE DUPLICATING WORK

The controlling efforts over duplicating work need not be uneconomical, but they should be thorough and understood by all affected by them. Material and handling costs are the two big items to watch in controlling duplicating work. Rigid controls over the issuance of paper are usually in order. Likewise, an accurate accounting of how much time is spent on each duplicating job lot is normally needed to exercise really effective control. Reasonable levels of performance should be established and made known to each duplicating employee so that she knows what is expected of her. Making the duplicating employee cost-conscious about her work is a strong, positive force toward achieving adequate control. However, when corrective action is required, it should be taken immediately.

MISCELLANEOUS ACTIVITIES

Affiliated with duplicating work are collating and binding of the duplicated material. Collating is the assembling of several different sheets of paper to form a report or booklet. This work can be done manually or by a hand or electrically operated machine. Figure 9–8 shows collating machines.

In many cases the material is held together by a binding of which there are many different types. First, is side wire stitching, i.e., on the side. Also, there is saddle wire stitching, i.e., through the fold at the back of the booklet. Usually the latter is preferred, since it enables the sheets to remain flat and open once they are placed in that position. Mechanical fasteners are used extensively, including ring or looseleaf binders, prong fasteners, or screw-post fasteners.

The use of wire and of plastic bindings has won widespread favor. Wire binding is spun or coiled onto the packet of punched paper; plastic binding is fastened onto the paper via punched holes by means

of a clasping action. Plastic bindings are available in diameters ranging from ⅛ to 1¼ inches and in a variety of colors. Binding equipment, consisting of a punching machine and a binding machine, each
about the size and weight of a portable typewriter, is commonly used
where it is preferred to bind various manuals and booklets in the office.
This practice offers definite advantages, including: (1) a variety of
stock such as stiff divider pages, metal foils, samples, photographs, and
maps can be bound together; (2) various page sizes can be securely

Courtesy: Collamatic, Wayne, N.J.   *Courtesy: Thomas Collators, Inc., New York*

FIG. 9–8. The collating machine on the left is electrically operated. A feed roller at each
bin ejects one sheet of paper, the operator grasps the sheets, gathers them, and staples each
pack with the electric stapler. The unit on the right is an effective hand-operated collator; as
many as thirty-two sheets can be gathered in one continuous operation.

bound in one manual; (3) revisions and renewals in the manual can
be made conveniently and quickly right in the office; (4) the cost is
reasonable—the two units of equipment and the binding are popularly
priced—and one girl can bind approximately 100 manuals in an hour;
and (5) the binding is sturdy and durable.

HANDLING PAPER AND OFFICE SUPPLIES

An important, but sometimes neglected, office activity is the handling of paper and office supplies. Office employees need proper tools
and supplies if maximum productivity is to be attained. The lack of a
typewriter ribbon, an order pad, envelopes, or letterheads might cause
serious delay in getting out important office work. In addition, supplies
represent an investment of capital. An office of 100 employees might
easily have $10,000 worth of stationery and office supplies on hand,
and unless these are properly looked after, deterioration and waste
might take place.

Whether the handling of paper and office supplies should be included in the duplicating organizational unit will depend upon individual considerations. Since the duplicating unit normally handles large quantities of paper, it is logical to have it include office paper and supplies. On the other hand, it can be argued that better management will probably be exercised over office paper and supplies when they are handled by office organizational units such as reports, correspondence, or mail, or even its own organizational unit, if its size and importance warrants.

In any event, to provide the best possible service and to eliminate needless waste the following steps appear essential:

1. Locate the stock room in a convenient space that is not desirable for clerical work. Be sure it is clean and dry. Enclose the area and keep it under lock and key. Provide adjustable shelving, arranged for easy accessibility to supplies and most effective use of space.

2. Arrange the stock according to some orderly plan. Index all items by number or code and have a handy reference available to locate any item quickly; arrange forms by their numbers. Place heavy items on the lower shelves and light items on the upper shelves.

3. Determine ordering points for each item. These can be based on judgment guided by past experience. The analysis of the requirements for each item will help attain a balanced inventory of supplies. As a normal practice, it is usually best to buy small quantities at frequent intervals. For each item, the amount purchased should be in line with the rate of consumption, the time required to receive a replenishment from the supplier, the quantity considered minimal for the functioning of effective management, and the savings in cost, if any, which are achieved through larger-quantity purchases of the item. Some companies find it desirable to carry a one-, two-, or three-months' supply of the principle items. When delivery is made, a reorder with specific date of delivery is immediately issued in order to maintain an adequate and balanced amount of stock.

4. Limit the quantity of supplies issued at any one time to about a two-weeks' supply. Large quantities of supplies encourage waste; too-small quantities involve excessive requisitions and trips to the stock room. Also, in many cases it has been found that the practice of packaging supplies in small units helps to economize their use. Furthermore, all issuance of supplies might be confined to one day out of the week or to certain dates during the month. This tends to promote planning the need for office supplies and to concentrate the work of control over supplies. In the event that supplies are needed in the in-

terim, a special requisition and approval from the office manager can be required. This practice tends to discourage requests for supplies at irregular times.

5. Place one person in charge of the stock room and delegate complete authority and responsibility to him.

6. Issue supplies only upon authorized written requisitions, which should be made out, in most cases, by the department head or by the supervisor of the unit receiving the supplies. File these requisitions in case they are needed for future reference. Maintain a journal or record by departments of what is issued, when, and to whom. Make a periodic inspection of this record to ascertain if consumption of supplies appears to be normal in the light of past requirements and volume of work handled.

7. Inform supervisors, by means of monthly statements, of the costs of office supplies issued to their respective units. This will help to keep the supervisor conscious of the importance of office supplies, and the supervisor, in turn, will reflect this attitude to the individual employees.

8. Exercise periodic follow-up to help insure that the supplies are needed and meet requirements. An effective practice is to select at random a requisition for supplies and investigate it thoroughly. Find out how the item is used, who uses it, whether it is the best for the specific use, and whether the price paid for it is reasonable and in line competitively. Answers to these questions will either confirm that a satisfactory job of acquiring supplies is being done or will uncover areas which require remedial action.

QUESTIONS

1. Does duplicating work lend itself more to a centralized or to a decentralized organizational arrangement? Justify your answer.
2. As you see it in the management of duplicating work which is most important: planning, organizing, actuating, or controlling?
3. Discuss the use of duplicating work in the modern office?
4. What are the main considerations in the planning of duplicating work?
5. Discuss the managerial work of actuating as applied to duplication.
6. Point out the difference between the items in each of the following pairs:
    a) Side wire stitching and saddle wire stitching.
    b) Offset process and stencil process of duplicating.
    c) Prong-fastener binder and screw-post binder.
    d) Collating and filing.
7. Visit a medium or large office and inquire regarding the duplicating processes utilized along with the respective reasons given for the adoption of

each respective process. What deductions do you make from your investigation? Elaborate.

8. Describe concisely five common duplicating processes found in offices today.

9. In selecting the type of duplicating machine, how much emphasis should be placed on the number of usable copies which the machine will normally produce from the original or master? Why?

10. Enumerate the main advantages in an office having its own bindery equipment.

11. What duplicating equipment would you recommend for each of the following:
   a) Eight copies of a chart 8½ × 11 inches.
   b) Copy of a letter.
   c) A company president's speech of fifteen pages, copy to be made for each of 8,000 employees.
   d) Copy of photograph.
   e) 100 copies of a one-page announcement.
   f) A copy of a map 8½ × 15 inches.

12. As an office manager what steps would you take to provide adequate management over office supplies?

CASE PROBLEMS

CASE 9–1. BASIC BUSINESS RESEARCH INSTITUTE

A considerable quantity of stencil-duplicated material is used by the Basic Business Research Institute of Boston, Mass. Last year, for example, approximately the following amount was used:

From 20-line stencil:

433 reports of 6 pages,
220 reports of 8 pages,
171 reports of 10 pages,
 97 reports of 22 pages.

From 36-line stencil:

516 reports of 5 pages,
289 reports of 8 pages,
370 reports of 12 pages.

From 62-line stencil:

245 reports of 10 pages,
415 reports of 18 pages.

The cost records of the Institute show that stencils cost about 25 cents each, paper $1.00 for 500 sheets when purchased in quantity, and labor $1.50 an hour for typing stencils and operating the machine. Total overhead is $50.00. Ink and accessories cost about $35 per year. It requires approximately twenty minutes to prepare a 20-line stencil, thirty-five minutes for a 36-line stencil, and forty-five minutes for a 62-line stencil. The Institute estimates that it takes ten minutes to put the stencil on the machine, adjust it, and later remove and file it. An operating speed of 100 sheets per minute is used for their cost estimates. A flat rate of 5 cents per report is used to cover collating and stapling. An electric operated machine is used, and it was worth about $1,100 when new.

The Carpenter Letter Service Company has quoted the Basic Business Research Institute the following rates for preparing stencils and running off copies:

No. of Copies	Lines per Sheet		
	To 20	21 to 36	37 to 62
1 to 499...........................	$2.50	$3.00	$3.50
500 and over.....................	3.00	3.50	4.00

Collating and stapling charges for one hundred reports:

To 25 pages...........$3.00

26 pages and over...... 3.75

Charge for paper 50 cents per hundred sheets or fraction thereof.

PROBLEMS:

1. Basing its decision on costs, should the Institute continue to do its own stencil-duplicating work? Substantiate your answer. Assume that the requirements of the Institute will continue at the same volume.

2. In addition to costs, what other important factors should be considered by the Institute in arriving at a decision?

3. What should be the decision of the duplicating manager of the Institute? Why?

CASE 9–2. KLINGER ENTERPRISES, INC.

Miss Adele Kovak is head of the office services of Klinger Enterprises, Inc., a construction company specializing in the design and erection of small commercial buildings. Established in 1947, the company has shown steady growth. During the past year it has averaged about seven buildings being constructed at any one time.

Present practices are to give a weekly progress report every Monday afternoon to each of the company's nine executives. Currently these reports are typed by Miss Kovak and average about four pages in length. In addition, Miss Kovak types lists of materials that are sent to prospective bidders for supplying the company's needs. These lists vary greatly in length. Few are less than three or over sixteen pages. Each copy must be checked to insure accuracy because buying the right material at satisfactory prices is essential to the company's success.

Mr. Burt Udell, treasurer of the company, secures exact copies of legal papers from an outside source. The work and service is satisfactory and costs the company 15 cents per page. A count shows that approximately fifty such pages are used each week.

Miss Ethel Ramsden, a competent stenographer working with Miss Kovak, suggests that some of the correspondence could be handled by writing the answer in a sentence or two at the bottom of the letter received. She claims that many of the replies are, in essence, a simple "Yes" or "No." Miss Kovak is inclined to agree with Miss Ramsden but points out that jotting the answer on the letter received and returning it to the sender leaves the company without a copy of the correspondence.

PROBLEMS:

1. What is the problem of this company and what action do you recommend to solve it?

2. Point out the probable obstacles in getting your recommendation accepted and put into action. How would you minimize these obstacles? Elaborate.

Chapter · 10

Handling the Mail

Action may not always bring happiness; but there is no happiness without action.

—BENJAMIN DISRAELI

SUCCESS OF any enterprise depends in great measure upon the ability to use communicating devices effectively. Man's ability to convey his ideas and thoughts accurately to another person adds immeasurably to managerial accomplishment and to the satisfaction of the employee, the employer, and the consumer or general public. The office manager normally has charge of the various communication services in an enterprise, services such as the mail handling, messenger, and telephone. It is up to him to see that the services selected are the best for his individual company and that they are operated in an efficient manner.

Sustained high office production requires prompt handling of the mail, intelligent reception of visitors, reliable messenger service, and courteous handling of telephone calls. There are no substitutes for these office services. They must be provided if the office work is accomplished effectively.

WHICH COMMUNICATIVE MEANS?

First, the real communicative needs of a company must be determined; after this the proper means can be selected. Various considerations enter into the need, for example, the size of the company, the office and plant layout, and the type of business. Unless careful analysis is made of the genuine needs, there is likely to develop a hodge-podge, overlapping, and nonco-ordinated communicative system that is not tailored to serve best the requirements of the company.

Answers to the following questions serve as guides in determining communicative needs which, in turn, direct the decisions as to what specific means should be used.

177

1. What quantity and type of communications are or should be provided? This information segregated for supervisors, salesmen, customers, vendors, and the general public will provide helpful, factual, and basic information.

2. Should written or oral communications be utilized? The former tend to be more specific, provide evidence, if needed, for future reference and help to lessen misunderstandings. On the other hand, oral communications are quicker, cost less, and are superior when the exchange of ideas to reach a mutual agreement is desired.

3. Is cost a prime consideration? An approximate cost range from the minimum to the maximum will assist in selecting the communicative device. The cost should be related to the service provided so that the "cost-service" concept is emphasized.

4. How long is the average communication? Certain devices are ideal for lengthy communications, while others are designed for short, terse messages. Consideration for length is especially important for written communications.

5. Are there peak periods of communicative activity? If so, the capacity of the selected communicative means must satisfy this load. Quite commonly the number of messenger calls to distribute and pick up mail are maximum during early morning and late afternoon working hours. In some instances, peak periods may be due to the frequency of communication between two employees in different parts of the building. Such a situation raises the possibility of providing a communicative device specially adapted for this condition, for example, employing an intercommunication system rather than using the telephone or installing private telephones between the two stations.

6. Is speed of major importance? Certain devices transmit messages very quickly—in a matter of seconds—but the cost is relatively high. Adequate planning in management reduces much of the need for speed in communicative devices.

IMPORTANCE OF MAIL

The balance of this chapter will be devoted to that vital communicative means in any office—handling the mail. The following chapter will include discussion of other important communicative devices such as reception service, messenger service, teletypewriter, telephone, and intercommunicative system.

Estimates indicate that over one half of all business decisions, suggestions, recommendations, and results of calculation are consummated in the form of some type of mail. It is doubtful that a modern enterprise could exist without mail; it is imperative that some written means of offering the services of the enterprise and of issuing answers to inquiries, statements, and invoices be available. Promptness and accuracy are the major requisites of the mail service. Procedures for the mail room conveniently divide into those pertaining to incoming mail and those pertaining to outgoing mail.

INCOMING MAIL

The procedure for handling incoming mail is fairly uniform. Primarily it consists of receiving, sorting, and distributing; the detailed steps, however, may differ slightly among companies, depending upon the nature of the business, its size, and the quantity of mail.

Receiving the Mail. The handling of incoming mail starts with the mail delivered to the office by the postman or a company representative who calls for it at the post office. The latter is preferred by many large enterprises, especially in the case of the first morning mail, because when called for at an early hour, it can be distributed by the time the office formally opens. In this event, it is well to have the employees handling incoming mail report for work about one-half hour before the regular opening office hour.

Sorting by Class. The mail is then sorted by classes. First-class mail is put in one pile, direct-mail advertising material in another, packages in another, and catalogues and circulars in another. Sorting is done by quick observation of the material so that priority can be given the most important mail, which is usually first class.

Opening the Mail. The third step is to open the mail. This can be done either by hand or by machine, depending upon the volume of mail and the number of available employees. An efficient mail-opening clerk can open by hand about 15 pieces per minute. Machines of various models and capacities are also available for opening the mail; some will open as many as 500 letters per minute. Figure 10–1 shows a letter-opening machine.

Mail which is marked "Personal" or addressed to specific individuals is not company mail and may or may not be opened, whichever is the policy of the company. The more common practice is not to open it, and delivery is made with the regular office mail. However, in some instances, mail so addressed is forwarded immediately to the employee's home address.

Sorting by Content. The next step is to remove the contents of the envelopes and, at the same time, sort them into (1) letters containing remittances—"money mail," and (2) letters not containing remittances—"ordinary mail." The money mail can be handled in several ways. In some cases, all the money or checks are put together, and a listing showing the customer's name and address and the amount enclosed is made out by the Mailing Department. The cash and checks, along with the listing, is later sent to the Cashier Department. In other instances, the check is attached to the letter, or, in the case of cash, the money is placed in a small envelope and attached to the letter with appropriate notation. The checks and cash are then delivered to the Cashier Department. After the remittances have been removed

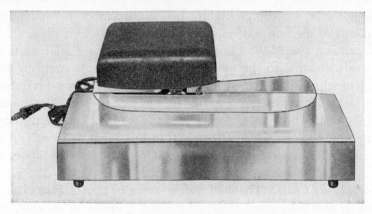

Courtesy: Industrial Molded Products Co., Inc., St. Paul

FIG. 10–1. A letter-opening machine which features a manual adjustment for width of slice across top of envelope; it is easy-feeding and self-sharpening, has cutting wheels, and is light in weight. Letters are fed lengthwise into the machine, with the top edge of the envelope toward the machine. The opener illustrated handles one hundred letters a minute.

by the Cashier Department, the money mail is returned to the Mailing Department.

All mail is sorted according to who handles the particular type of mail under question; this might be a department, a division, or an individual. To expedite sorting, labels are commonly put on the shelves of the sorting rack. The general pattern of the various compartments in the rack is similar to that of the mail stations in the office, for in this way the sorted mail can be kept in a logical order for ultimate distribution.

Usually the name of the person or of the department to whom the letter is addressed determines where it is to be delivered. When this is not given, a quick glance or scanning of the paper is necessary to determine its proper destination. In some cases the entire contents must be read. The mail reader should be instructed to read a letter only once, and if the destination cannot be determined in this single reading, the letter should be referred to the head of the Mailing Department or the office manager for proper routing. This practice will save considerable time.

Figure 10–2 shows a portion of a large mail room. The man in the foreground is opening letters by means of a machine. The man in the background is sorting to the proper compartments in the sorting racks.

Courtesy: First National Bank in Dallas

FIG. 10–2. Handling the incoming mail in a large bank.

Handling Mail Referring to Previous Correspondence. A letter referring to previous correspondence can be handled in one of two ways. It can be delivered to the department concerned, which, if necessary, requests the file from the Filing Department. Or the letter can be sent to the Filing Department, where the needed file is attached and forwarded to the proper correspondent. The method used depends chiefly upon the number of such letters received and the system of filing used. The practice of attaching previous correspondence to new incoming letters should be confined to those cases where the file is absolutely necessary; otherwise an undue burden is placed on the filing staff.

Stamping Time and Date of Receipt. At the time the mail is read and sorted, it is customary to stamp the hour and date received on each piece of correspondence. This provides a timed receipt that can be used as evidence in controversial matters regarding the correspondence. It can also be used for checking the efficiency of mail distribution in the office. Figure 10–3 shows a machine which automatically stamps a time identification, illustrated by the figure, upon insertion of the paper into an opening in the machine.

Courtesy: International Business Machines Corp., New York

FIG. 10–3. A machine to print pertinent data on office papers upon receipt or dispatch. Imprinting is effortless—performed electrically when the paper is inserted in the machine. Use of a machine like this helps to place responsibility for the acceptance of papers, their issuance, and progress through proper channels.

Distributing the Mail. This is the final step in the handling of incoming mail and is usually done by messengers, although other means, such as conveyor belts and pneumatic tubes, may be utilized. Discussion of these latter services is in the following chapter.

OUTGOING MAIL

Usually the same employees handle both the incoming and the outgoing mail. A typical procedure for handling outgoing mail follows.

Collecting the Mail. This is generally done by messengers. To help in collection, outgoing mail is usually placed in special boxes or trays on the desks specified as mail stations.

Grouping by Destinations. Upon receipt at the mail room, the mail is first grouped according to geographical area; then by city; and then by name of addressee. Sorting racks are commonly used for this purpose. All mail of a similar class, and addressed to the same wholesaler, branch, or company, is put together so that it can be mailed as a single piece. Frequently, large manila envelopes with the address printed or stenciled thereon are used for these large firm mailings. In some instances, each of the outgoing sorting racks contains an addressed envelope which is handy for instant use. Replenishments are made either the first thing in the morning or at regular intervals throughout the day, depending upon individual circumstances and requirements.

Folding and Enclosing.   Third, if this is done by the Mailing Department, the material is folded and enclosed. Particular care should be taken that this work is done neatly, so that a favorable impression is given the recipient. Also, when ordinary envelopes are used, the name and address on the material must be checked with that on the envelope.

Sealing and Stamping.   Next, the mail is sealed and stamped. This can be done either by hand or by machine; the volume of mail should determine the method used. It is possible to seal and stamp around 350 letters an hour by hand. When manual operations are used, the stamps are usually kept in an out-in-the-open manner, and this may result in stamp losses owing to carelessness in handling and borrowing. To minimize these losses, an accounting should be maintained to show the number of letters mailed in comparison with the amount of stamps purchased. Special care must be exercised in the case of packages. It is advisable to appoint one mail-room employee as sole custodian of the stamps. He should control their use either by placing the stamps on the letters or packages personally or by seeing the letters or packages the stamps are going on before issuing them to someone else.

Postal Regulations.   The head of the mailing department must know the postal requirements, so that the proper amounts of postage —no more and no less—are affixed. Knowledge of the various classes of mail is basic. In general, first-class mail includes correspondence, securities, and documents; second-class mail, newspapers, magazines, and other periodicals; third-class mail, unsealed printed matter and form letters; fourth-class mail, packages and parcels.

For acceptance by the post office, certain classes of mail require sorting, bundling, and the filling out of forms. Preparing the material for mailing with consideration for the postal regulations can help realize considerable savings. For example, bulk third-class letters can be sent for as little as 2 cents each, whereas first-class letters cost 4 cents each; thus a saving of 50 per cent can be realized. This is a sizable amount on a large mailing.

Weight is also an important consideration in determining proper postage. A mail room should be equipped with an accurate postal scale. Many different models are offered on the market.

Mailing the Material. The final step is to mail the material. It is advisable to post mail at regular intervals throughout the day. This practice smooths out the work load, minimizes the usual late afternoon peak, and helps the post office to deliver mail promptly. On distant mail, this practice might save a day. Also, knowledge of train and plane schedules is helpful in expediting mail. It is necessary to deliver certain classes of mail to the post office.

MAIL-ROOM EQUIPMENT

In addition to the mail-room equipment mentioned above, there are available a considerable number of units designed to facilitate the flow of mail to, through, and from the mail room. Investigations by the office manager should be made in order to find out what these various units will accomplish for his particular office. The facilities will depend mainly upon the volume, but regardless of the size of the daily mail load, the mail room should be adequate for the particular office in space, equipment, and personnel. In addition, consideration should be given such things as the importance attached to prompt mail handling and the value and type of mail.

A list of the more commonly used equipment in a modern, well-planned mail room includes:

Tables	Sealing machine
Automatic letter opener	Date stamp
Sorting racks	*U.S. Postal Guide*
Postal scale	Airmail guide
Utility cabinets	Atlas
Stamp affixer or meter mail machine	Hotel directory
Mailbags and mailbag holder	Miscellaneous items, such as scissors, twine, labels, wrapping paper,
Envelope trays	and crayon

MAIL-ROOM LAYOUT

Proper arrangement of the equipment in the mail room will help keep the mail moving in and out of the office without interruption or confusion. The work of the mail room can be greatly simplified and performed quickly and smoothly by using the proper number of units, correctly arranged.

Figure 10–4 suggests a layout for a modern mail room. The equipment has been arranged in a room with dimensions of 12 × 16 feet.

Beginning at the lower right of the figure, the route of incoming mail is first to the table where the mail is opened and the time stamped; then to the adjacent tables and sorting racks where it is sorted. It is then delivered to the proper stations throughout the office.

Outgoing mail is first taken to the outgoing-mail sorting racks and tables, shown at the upper left of the figure, where it is grouped with

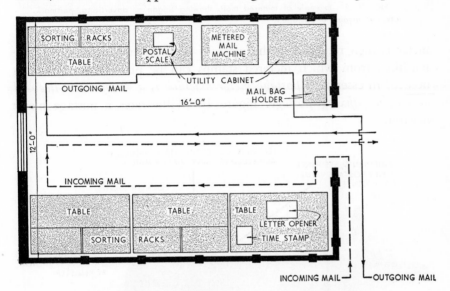

FIG. 10–4. Arrangement of mail-room equipment.

other mail having the same destination. When necessary, each piece is weighed and proper postage determined; then it is put through the metered mail machine and finally into the mailbag located at the upper right portion of the figure. Mail is delivered to the post office in these bags.

METER MAIL MACHINE

A meter mail machine imprints the postage seal either directly on a letter or, in the case of a package, on an adhesive paper tape which is affixed to the package. At the same time the postage seal is imprinted, a slogan, postmark, and date are also imprinted. This is illustrated by Figure 10–5. The machines are offered in an array of capacities and designs; many seal as well as stamp the envelope.

An important part of this machine is the meter, which is a detachable, portable unit containing the printing die for the postage and a recording mechanism. In buying postage, the meter is taken to the post office and set for a lump sum which is paid in advance. The set

Courtesy: Pitney-Bowes, Inc., Stamford, Conn.

FIG. 10–5. Example of metered mail, showing slogan or advertising, postmark, date, and amount of postage.

meter is then returned to the place of business and inserted into the machine, from which metered stamps can be printed as and when needed. In essence, *a postage meter machine is a government-licensed device for affixing postage.* Figure 10–6 illustrates a postage meter machine.

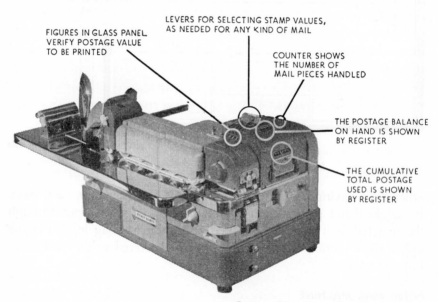

Courtesy: Pitney-Bowes, Inc., Stamford, Conn.

FIG. 10–6. A postage meter machine, with the important operations of the meter illustrated.

Metered mail has many advantages including:

1. Time and effort are saved—the machine does the work. Units having capacities of 300 letters per minute are available.

2. Stamp losses are stopped—the meter stamp can be used only by the licensed firm identified by the number in the stamp itself.

3. Accurate accounting of postal expenditures is provided—the amount of postage and the number of pieces mailed are registered in the machine.

4. Date of mailing is shown—an important consideration for parcels sent out, to prove that the promised shipping date was complied with.

5. Quicker handling is provided by the originating post office—metered mail requires no canceling, often catches earlier trains or planes.

6. Prestige is increased—metered mail helps create the favorable impression that the user is a substantial, progressive company.

7. Postmark, slogan, and advertising is added—individualized reminders can be put on the envelope or package.

MAIL HANDLING USUALLY CENTRALIZED

In the typical office, both the management and the physical facilities of mail handling are centralized. This condition is a logical outcome due to the very nature of the mail-room work. Whereas other office services may be decentralized, this is rarely found in mail handling. The responsibility for the mail function should be fixed, and the person in charge given adequate authority to assure the work is performed effectively. This is especially important in the small office where the mail-room operation frequently requires only the part-time services of one person.

PERSONNEL OF MAIL ROOM

Competent help must be employed if the activities of the mail room are to be performed satisfactorily. Manual dexterity, dependability, and an ability to read rapidly are among the important attributes desirable in mail-room employees. Training designed to inform about postal regulations, company policies affecting mail handling, and the company's organizational units and specific types of work done by each is strongly suggested and will usually pay big dividends. Some managers hold periodic meetings with the mail-room personnel, briefing them on regulations, postal data, the importance of accuracy, neatness, and care in handling all mail. After investigating and establishing effective mail-room practices and procedures, the work of handling the mail will normally undergo relatively few changes. They will be more of degree than of kind. Hence, a manual carefully outlining the directions and instructions to be followed will prove highly beneficial.

CONTROL OF MAIL-ROOM OPERATIONS

Most control efforts affecting mail-room operations deal with either cost or conformity with postal standards and requirements. From this viewpoint, the following suggestions should be adopted:

1. *Include zone number in the address.*   The number should follow the name of the post office. Showing of the zone number speeds delivery, and the post office will indicate zone numbers on mailing lists free of charge. To receive this service, it is necessary to segregate the addresses by cities that have zone numbers and then turn these lists in to the local postmaster. He will zone the local addresses and forward the others to the respective proper cities where they will be zoned and returned at no charge.

2. *Use standard-size envelopes.*   Standard-size envelopes are best suited for most purposes. The No. 9 or No. 10 envelope for correspondence is preferable, since only two horizontal folds in the enclosed material are necessary. Smaller envelopes require annoying vertical folds that the reader has to read over.

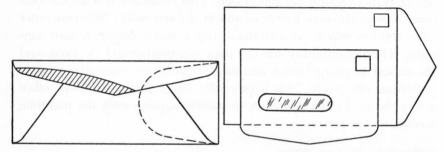

A postage-saver envelope requiring only third-class rate can be top-sealed like a first-class envelope. One end of flap remains unsealed to permit postal inspection.

With the two-in-one combination envelope, first-class mail in one compartment and third-class or fourth-class mail in the other can be mailed as a unit.

FIG. 10–7.   A postage-saver envelope and a two-in-one combination envelope.

The postage-saver envelope permits third-class rates, yet gives the appearance of first-class mail. Also, the two-in-one combination envelope is recommended where a folder or booklet is sent with a letter. With this type of envelope, the letter or other first-class mail is in one compartment, while the folder or other third-class mail is in another compartment. Illustrations of the postage saver and the two-in-one envelope are shown in Figure 10–7.

3. *Use window envelopes when feasible to do so.*   The risk of getting a letter in the wrong envelope and the necessity of sending individually addressed envelopes to the mail room are eliminated by the use of window envelopes. There is also a saving in cost. With regular envelopes the labor costs for addressing are about $8.25 per thousand (assuming a rate of 3 a minute and wages at $1.50 per hour). Window envelopes cost about $2.00 per thousand more than regular en-

velopes, so the net saving realized by using window envelopes is $6.25 ($8.25 less $2.00), per thousand, or 75.7 per cent.

However, some people believe that window envelopes are less attractive and dignified than regular envelopes. Certain types of correspondence are probably best handled by regular envelopes. The final decision in this matter rests with the manager.

4. *Employ enclosed business reply envelopes to increase returns and lower costs.* A permit, for which no fee is paid, must be obtained to use these envelopes. The postage for such envelopes is the first-class rate, plus 2 cents additional for each article. In other words, they are of a collect-on-delivery type for which the recipient pays 6 cents for each reply, based on a 4-cent regular charge plus 2 cents for return privilege. The use of business reply envelopes results in substantial savings when the return is less than 67 per cent of the original mailing, a condition which usually exists. When regular stamped envelopes are enclosed, the postage for 100 replies is $4.00; postage on 67 business reply envelopes is $4.02.

5. *Have posters, books, and guides available to mail personnel so that they can find out and apply the proper mail procedures.* The *United States Postal Guide* (which can be obtained from the Superintendent of Documents, Washington 25, D.C.) is especially recommended. It is extremely important that the mail personnel know the different classes of mail thoroughly—when to use each and what rates to apply. Appendix B in this book (see p. 744) contains pertinent information on the important regulations of the United States Post Office. The office manager should cultivate close co-operation with authorities of his local post office. They are always very helpful and can greatly assist in solving mailing problems.

QUESTIONS

1. Do you feel that handling the mail is vital to the proper functioning of an office? Why?
2. Discuss a satisfactory means of determining the communicative needs of a company?
3. Do you agree with the statement, "The mail reader should be instructed to read a letter only once"? Why?
4. What practical suggestions would you give to a newly hired head of the mail room of an office in order to help him succeed on the job?
5. Point out upon what bases you would favorably recommend the use of each of the following for the handling of incoming mail:
   a) Purchase of machine to open letters.
   b) Early starting hours for employees of mail room.

c) Late quitting hours for employees of mail room.

d) Stamping the time and date of receipt on the mail.

6. Suggest a procedure for handling of outgoing mail in an office of 250 employees.

7. State concisely the difference between each of the following:

  a) A window envelope and a business reply envelope.

  b) Mail and interdepartmental memos.

  c) Metered mail and nonmetered mail.

  d) Postage-saver envelope and regular standard envelope.

8. What is a postage meter? Explain in nontechnical language what must be done in connection with its use in an office.

9. Enumerate and briefly discuss five advantages of using a postage meter machine.

10. As an office manager, would you favor using window envelopes exclusively? Why?

11. In your opinion which three of the following attributes would you emphasize in managing the mail room: (1) speed, (2) cost, (3) economy, (4) dependability, (5) training area for other office jobs, and (6) accuracy. Justify your selections.

12. Enumerate and discuss briefly the minimum activities you feel necessary to insure adequate control of outgoing mail in a large office.

CASE PROBLEMS

CASE 10–1. HOOSIER PHARMACEUTICS, INC.

This company sells a variety of pharmaceutics to a large number of customers, including hospitals, drugstores, and physicians' supply stores. Distribution is nation-wide, and the company is well known and established. About 75 per cent of the company's shipments are in small packages—not over 8 × 8 × 6 inches.

Many of the packages are sent by (1) air mail, (2) special delivery, or (3) special handling, because the customer usually wants the pharmaceutics as soon as possible. Mailing the packages in this manner incurs additional fees charged by the post office. Special delivery provides immediate delivery at the post office of the addressee; special handling applies to fourth-class mail only and insures prompt and expeditious handling by the post office. Starting at 3 P.M., several truckloads of packages are taken to the post office. The last load leaves the company building at 4:30 P.M.

A careful investigation by Mr. Charles Meyers, the office manager, showed that a great majority of the packages could be sent by regular mail, provided the packages were ready to go at stated times throughout the day, and would reach their destination as quickly as by the use of special mailing services. Mr. Meyers estimates the savings from planned scheduled mailing and the use of regular mailing service at about $65 a day.

He feels that some loss is suffered due to stamp pilferage. Currently, stamps are kept in a desk drawer of the packing room and distributed by Mr. James Lange, the foreman. However, this distribution is loosely handled in the opinion of Mr. Meyers. The foreman contends that he cannot sit at the desk all day long to issue the proper amount of stamps, nor can he check each package mailed for correct postage. He has suggested that the company get a postage meter machine, but Mr. Meyers has not taken this suggestion seriously as quite frequently emergency letters or packages must be sent out during nonregular working hours, that is, at night or during Saturdays and Sundays. Mr. Meyers contends that under such conditions, a key to the postage meter machine would have to be given to each of several people and, subsequently, control over its use would be diluted.

It is also believed that orders to the same customer on the same day could be grouped and packed in the same box, thus reducing handling expense, as well as being more convenient for the customer. Mr. James Lange disagrees with this suggestion, pointing out that the postage will be about the same and the time spent in grouping orders to the same customer will slow the work of his men.

PROBLEMS:

1. Do you agree with the viewpoints advanced by Mr. James Lange? Why?
2. What action do you recommend be taken? Justify your viewpoint.
3. How should Mr. Meyers proceed in this situation?

Chapter · 11

Office Communicative Services

One thing I know; the only ones among you who will be really
happy are those who will have sought and found how to serve.
—Dr. Albert Schweitzer

THERE ARE many different communicative means
available to the office manager. A discussion of each of these major
types will now be given following this order: reception service, personal method for carrying messages, mechanical methods for *carrying* messages, mechanical methods for *transmitting* messages, and
verbal communicative devices.

RECEPTION SERVICE

To many visitors, the first impression of a company is frequently
gained from the receptionist. It is important, therefore, that courteous
and prompt treatment be continuously extended visitors in order to
build and develop company public relations and good will.

Aside from being courteous and making a favorable impression,
the receptionist has a definite job to perform, which is (1) to find out
with what person, if any, the visitor should talk; and (2) to arrange
for the visitor to see the proper person quickly. Doing this job efficiently saves the time of the caller, the receptionist, and the executive.

A pleasant manner of speech and a winning personality are highly
important, but, in addition, certain standardized procedures have
been found most effective. For example, in securing information from
callers, the receptionist should ask: "What company do you represent?" or "May I help you?" Should the visitor say he is calling about a
personal matter, or words to that effect, it is well for the receptionist
to inquire: "Does Mr. —— know you?" If an evasive or a negative
reply is given, the receptionist should ask if someone has sent the
caller. If no one has, a recommended procedure is to say: "I'll let you
talk with Mr. ——'s secretary, who will try to help you."

The receptionist must be fully familiar with what matters are handled by each employee who has callers. Normally a guide or booklet is available for reference. Practices vary among companies, but there are certain common policies. For example, requests for employment, trips through the plant, and donations are usually referred to the Personnel Department.

Callers are usually announced by telephone. If the person being called on is free, the receptionist is usually requested to have the visitor come in at once. If the person is not free, the visitor is asked to wait until he can be received. If the person being called on does not announce his availability within a reasonable time, the receptionist should call again to avoid unnecessary delay.

When the person called on is too busy to see the caller, the receptionist should address the visitor with: "I'm sorry, Mr. —— is busy and will not be able to see you. Can you come back or phone first for an appointment?" In situations where the person is absolutely not interested in talking with the caller, the receptionist must be tactful and courteous. Refusals to grant short interviews with callers should be held at an absolute minimum, but when necessary, the receptionist might say: "I am sorry, but Mr. —— is not interested in what you have to offer." Under no circumstance should the receptionist suggest that the visitor call later if the person being called upon has no intention of seeing him. Honesty is the best policy.

It is customary for the receptionist to keep a report of callers. The date, the name of each caller, and the name of his company, as well as the name of the person called on, are usually included. These data are turned in to the office manager for review and analysis.

Other work done by the receptionist includes: receiving special delivery mail; fill-in work, such as sorting, checking, stuffing envelopes, and typing; operating the telephone switchboard. If there is too much extra work, the regular duties of the receptionist might be neglected. The office manager should watch this carefully.

MESSENGER SERVICE

In the normal course of office work, many papers are handled successively by several employees, and this entails getting the papers from one employee to another. Notices and memorandums must be distributed, and reports must be sent to the executives. All these activities necessitate adequate delivery services.

The formality with which messenger services is carried out depends mainly upon the size of the enterprise. In small offices it is usually handled informally by the employees. The space is small, the number of employees is not large, and no special setup is required. In medium-sized offices, messenger service is frequently set aside as a separate function and performed by a few employees as a part-time responsibility along with other duties. In large offices the work of getting written materials to the proper persons requires the full-time attention of employees who operate according to a carefully planned system.

Whether a personal or a mechanical method is employed depends upon the specific objectives of the delivery service. Usually the following factors are of prime concern:

1. The total number of messages.
2. The frequency of the messages.
3. The number of delivery points.
4. The number of messages at each delivery point.
5. The distance between delivery points.
6. The maximum allowable time between delivery points.
7. The expense, including investment and operating costs.
8. The flexibility of the service to meet changing office conditions.

PERSONAL METHOD FOR CARRYING MESSAGES

The personal method is the oldest and the most common method of handling messages. To be of greatest benefit, the service must be regular and frequent. Schedules should call for deliveries about every half hour throughout the office. This time interval can be varied, depending upon the needs of the office. In some cases calls every fifteen minutes might be required; in others calls every hour might suffice. Very often, calls are made with greater frequency in the early morning and late afternoon business hours, in order to take care of the peak loads.

Deliveries can be made either on a desk-to-desk or on a departmental basis. The former is preferable and should be used whenever possible. Desk-to-desk calls insure that the person intended to receive the material actually gets it, that messengers do all the messenger work, and that the distribution and collection is accomplished with a minimum of effort and confusion. In constrast, deliveries by departments require further distribution within each department. This often results in costly delays and means that the time of valuable office help is taken away from regular work to do delivery work.

The personal method for carrying messages provides excellent training for new, inexperienced employees. They can quickly learn the names of key employees, location of their work stations, layout of the office and plant, and the work of each organizational unit. Some large companies start all young office help as messengers before transferring them to their initially selected jobs.

Messengers should be given close supervision. Usually it is best to have a middle-aged person as the head, for such a person gives maturity and stability to the work and usually has better control over the efforts and attitudes of the messengers.

Adequate control of the messenger service requires that certain practices and procedures be carried out. These are as follows:

1. The complete route must be established to include all desks designated as stations. The course to be followed must be defined, and the allowable time for one trip must be known. Adequate rest periods between trips are desirable and usually amount to about 20 per cent of the total travel time—i.e., on a twenty-five minute trip a rest period of about five minutes is given.

2. All desks designated as stations must be visited on each trip. Even though there is nothing to deliver, there might be something to pick up.

3. Messengers should confine their efforts to the delivery and pickup of written materials along the prescribed routes. The running of miscellaneous errands for members of the office should be forbidden. The handling of special services for executives should be carefully watched so that the privilege is not abused.

4. Each member should be instructed to sort the papers as they are collected so that on each trip deliveries can be made to stations not yet called upon. Papers designated for stations already called upon are delivered on the next trip. This eliminates backtracking. For intra-office materials, designate envelopes of different colors for different departments, for example, red, order department; green, sales department; blue, accounting department.

5. A designated area or receptacle for "incoming" messages and another for "outgoing" should be used at each station desk.

6. Each messenger should be provided with an accordion file with one section for each station or some similar arrangement. The file should be equipped with shoulder strap for carrying, or mounted on wheels for pushing, from station to station.

7. A card-control system provides a check upon the activities of messengers. Several plans are possible.

a) The messengers can be required to check in, that is, to sign or punch a card at several well-selected stations along the route. These cards can be collected daily and inspected, and any irregularity of service can be investigated and corrected immediately.

b) The messengers can pick up a card and replace it with another at each station on the route. Different cards, identified by number or color, can be used for each trip; and by noting the card in the basket, spot checks can be made at any time to find out if schedules are being maintained. Also, a quick check on the last call made at any particular station is provided. This is helpful in handling complaints about the messenger failing to call or skipping a stop.

8. To inform employees politely of the last trip for the day, the messenger can either say, "Good night," or leave a card printed "Last collection has been made" in the basket.

MECHANICAL METHODS FOR CONVEYING MESSAGES

Under this classification of communicative devices are: (1) mechanical conveyors, and (2) pneumatic tubes. Mechanical conveyors of different types are well suited to conditions where the work volume is large and fairly constant, and where stations remain fixed. Belt conveyors are probably the most common type used in an office. Brush-off stops can be provided at each station in order to permit the delivery of papers at specific points.

Figure 11–1 shows an interesting conveyor application in the office of a mail-order wholesaler. The orders coming down the belt conveyor have been proofed for cash remittance and analyzed, and to each one a form has been attached indicating the station or stations handling stock records for the items on the order. The order-and-form unit is removed by the first clerk who needs the order for stock-record purposes. She posts the proper entries on the control cards at her desk, places a check mark in the appropriate space on the form, and returns the order-and-form unit to the conveyor to travel to the next clerk or clerks concerned. When all stock records have been completed at the end of the conveyor line, the stock-checked orders are returned to the order analyzer and forwarded to the stock room for order picking. A total of sixteen stock-record stations are employed. The conveyor moves at the rate of 12 feet a minute.

Pneumatic tubes are effective, easy to use, and do not require special skill to operate. Material is carried quickly and accurately to its destination. The initial cost of the tubes is rather high, but the maintenance cost is low. The use of pneumatic tubes is most economical where the volume of work is large. Different-sized tubes and tube carriers are offered. For example, a "4-inch tube carrier" is a popular size for moving large volumes of orders, requisitions, and other papers. This carrier is approximately 2¾ inches in inside diameter and has a maximum standard inside length of 14 inches. Larger rectangular-shaped carriers are also available for handling intact such bulky items as blueprints and letters without folding.

Courtesy: Continental Products, Inc., Chicago

FIG. 11–1. Orders for tally-checking are delivered to clerks by means of a conveyor belt.

In the case of a large aircraft manufacturer, the installation of pneumatic tubes linking seven buildings into one unit resulted in annual payroll savings of over $100,000. The manager of a medium-sized metal-processing company reduced messenger services service costs by $4,200 a year by means of pneumatic tubes. Figure 11–2 shows an installation in the scheduling station of a factory office. The employee on the left is holding the tube carrier in her hand.

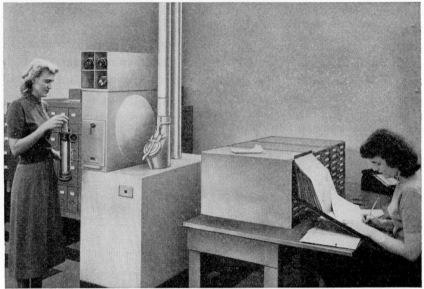

Courtesy: Lamson Corp., Syracuse, N.Y.

FIG. 11–2. Records for scheduling of production operations are sent to this centralized area by means of pneumatic tubes. In the illustration the terminal is a 4-inch up-charge type.

MECHANICAL METHODS FOR TRANSMITTING WRITTEN MESSAGES

This group constitutes those methods whereby the message is converted to energy impulses, transmitted by means of electrical or electronic circuits, and translated to a written or printed form at the receiving end. The original copy of the message remains in the hands of the sender, but the contents of the communication is transmitted to the recipient. Included in this classification are : (1) teletypewriter, (2) telegraph, (3) telautograph, (4) television, and (5) electronic messenger.

TELETYPEWRITER

The teletypewriter, or TWX service of the telephone company, is a machine resembling a large typewriter that transmits messages between stations using telephone lines. The operation is based on the principle of combining the telephone and the typewriter. The machine has basically the same keyboard as a standard typewriter. When the keys are depressed, electric impulses reproduce the message in typed form on one machine or on many similar machines, the number being determined by the number of connections desired. Figure 11–3 shows a teletypewriter.

The machine is used very much like a telephone. To send a message, the TWX subscribers' directory is consulted; the call is placed by number; and the connection is made. Some 12,000 subscribers are listed in the TWX directory. Any two teletypewriters can be connected for communication in the same way as two telephones. However, many teletypewriters are frequently used on a station-to-station basis, for example, between a branch office and its home office. In fact, the service is especially effective over long distances.

Courtesy: Illinois Bell Telephone Co., Chicago

FIG. 11–3. A teletypewriter.

Transmission is at the rate of 75 words per minute. An outstanding feature is that the communication is two-way; a written conversation can be carried out. To illustrate, the following might take place on the same connection: (1) the sender asks a question, (2) the recipient answers, (3) the sender requests certain modifications in answer, and (4) the recipient writes his new answer.

There is no rental charge for teletypewriters to customers offering a substantial amount of business. Charges are made on the basis of time and distance, similar to the long-distance telephone. Rates are approximately one third to one half less than those of the telephone. There is no installation charge, but a minimum service charge is made of about $15.00 per month, depending upon the city location.

TELEGRAPH

Another means of handling messages over relatively long distances is the telegraph. This type of service is fast, reliable, and extensively used. Telegrams secure attention, provide terse businesslike messages, and impel immediate action. They are used for practically all subjects or phases of business activities, such as acknowledging orders, advising salesmen, securing credit information, ordering materials, arranging interviews, and collecting bills.

Telegraphic communications can be sent by any of four main ways, including: (1) over the counter—giving it to the operator at any branch office; (2) by messenger; (3) by telephone—similar to an ordinary telephone call, charges being made to the telephone account or paid by coins dropped into a public pay telephone; and (4) by mechanical tie lines, such as direct telephone connection, and the teleprinter. The direct telephone connection is simply a direct wire between the sender's office and the local telegraph office, and the teleprinter is a device similar to a typewriter which transmits the typed message electrically to the telegraph office. The message is recorded on paper tape both in the sending office and in the telegraph office. The former serves as the sender's reference copy; the latter is used to transmit the message to a circuit for its destination.

The cost of telegraphic communications vary with length of message, distance, and speed of delivery. Domestic messages are classified into the following main types:

1. Full-Rate Telegram.   This is the most expedient service possible. The base rate applies to fifteen words.

2. Day Letter.   This type of telegram is used when messages are relatively long and can be deferred slightly in handling and still serve their purpose. The base rate applies to fifty words or less and is roughly 40 per cent more than that for a full-rate, fifteen-word telegram.

3. Serial.   This includes a deferred message sent in sections to the same addressee during the day. The cost is about 20 per cent more than for a day letter containing the same number of words.

4. Night Letter.   An inexpensive overnight service helpful for long messages, night letters are accepted until 2 A.M. for delivery the following morning. The base rate applies to fifty words or less and is about 75 per cent of that of a full-rate, fifteen-word telegram.

Cablegrams or services to foreign countries are classified as (1) ordinary—the standard full-rate service, (2) urgent—priority over all other messages except government messages, (3) deferred—no priority over other types, and (4) night letter—messages permitting overnight delivery.

Code words are sometimes used for telegraphic communications in order to reduce costs or to insure secrecy. For example, the code word

"ROEUZ" might mean, "What action shall I take?" Commercial codes are available, or a special code can be created.

TELAUTOGRAPH

Another mechanical means for transmitting messages is the telautograph. As the name suggests, it transmits a handwritten message. The writing is electrically reproduced over comparatively short distances, such as between main office and receiving room, department and department, and warehouse and main office. In order to send a message a switch is turned on and the message is written with a metal stylus on a metal platen. In order to see what is being written, the sender watches the pen of the instrument writing on a roll of paper. Figure 11–4 illustrates a telautograph. As the message is written, it is reproduced almost simultaneously at one or a number of connected receiving points.

Courtesy: TelAutograph Corp., Los Angeles

FIG. 11–4. A TelAutographic transceiver that transmits and receives electronic handwritten messages, including special symbols and sketches.

A telautograph provides economical and high-speed transmitting and receiving of messages. Handwritten records are furnished and can be attached to such things as inquiries, notices, and shipping instructions. It is possible to carry on a written conversation—messages can be sent and received.

TELEVISION

One of the newer methods for transmitting written messages is television. Although its current application in business is limited, television holds much promise for the future. By means of closed circuits, it is possible to transmit and have instantaneous receipt at many points. Television presents the message visually and in motion—a series of events. It shows the entire message and is feasible for conveying completely and accurately the entire image—especially important in the case of blueprints, drawings, sketches, or samples.

A television-telephone enabling the caller to see as well as hear the party at the other end of the line is available. When the caller lifts the television-telephone, his image appears simultaneously on one half of his screen and upon one half of that of the party being called. When the party answers, his image appears on the remaining halves of the two screens. The unit is about the size of a conventional television table model set. Maximum effective distance is about one mile. Television-telephone applications include those in large industrial plants to compare drawings and materials, in banks to check signatures, and in penal institutions to serve as an electronic guard.

ELECTRONIC MESSENGER

The electronic messenger transmits exact, permanent copies of a written original over telephone, microwave, or closed circuits to one

Courtesy: Electronic Communications, Inc., Teterboro, N.J.

FIG. 11–5. A machine called "Electronic Messenger" that transmits a copy of a written original over microwave or closed circuits.

or more companion machines in other offices or plants. The machine will handle vouchers, checks, maps, drawings, and letters in any size up to 8½ × 14 inches. It is slightly larger than a standard typewriter and is illustrated by Figure 11–5. To operate, the original material is inserted into the machine and a "transmit" button is pressed. As machine transmits, a "monitor" copy appears in the window of the machine, which copy serves as evidence of transmittal and an extra copy of the original.

VERBAL COMMUNICATIVE DEVICES

Most common in this category are the (1) telephone, (2) inter-communication systems, (3) paging systems, and (4) tape and wire recorders. These devices are among the fastest methods of communicating; they are usually well known and extensively used.

TELEPHONE

Good telephone practices aid in building the good will of any enterprise, save time and energy, and help get work accomplished. The alert office manager recognizes this and does everything possible to see that proper telephone practices are known and applied.

The telephone has come into wide usage because it provides an inexpensive, convenient, and rapid means of communication. However, it is not well suited to convey information concerning drawings, sketches, or dimensions of parts. Conversing over the telephone places the participants in a peculiar relationship. The persons talking can hear but cannot see each other. Thus facial expressions and gestures of the body are eliminated as tools that help to convey the thoughts exchanged. In telephoning, the impression must rely entirely on the voice—its tone, clearness, and pleasantness, the selection of words, and the manner of speaking. All of these factors, properly blended, constitute the art of telephoning, which can be acquired.

Telephone systems can be classified into two types: (1) the outside telephone with extensions, handled through a company switchboard (PBX); and (2) the private internal telephone (PAX). The former provides service for external calls coming into or going out of the office and for internal calls between telephones within the office. Under this system, all calls must clear through the switchboard. In contrast, with the private internal telephone, "inside" calls do not go through the switchboard. Since in the typical company more than one half of the telephoning is internal—between telephones within the company—use of the private internal exchange relieves the regular telephone lines. This clears the way for better service on "outside" calls—those from customers and other important callers.

TELEPHONING BY THE PRIVATE SWITCHBOARD OPERATOR

Certain characteristics distinguish the seasoned and efficient telephone switchboard operator. For convenience, these characteristics may be divided into technical aspects and speech aspects. Under technical aspects are included the best way to handle the levers, the manipulation of the cords, the dialing of numbers, and the writing of messages; each of which constitutes an important segment of switchboard telephone efficiency. The best way of performing these tasks can be found by consulting the telephone company's special representative.

Speech aspects include the proper use of the voice over the telephone, the manner of speaking, and the standardization of certain phases and words in conversations. They help to obtain faster service, better co-operation, and company good will. It may be well to secure the help of a trained consultant in this field, but in many cases the office manager can contribute a great deal. Good results are usually obtained if the following expressions are used in handling the private switchboard:

1. Identify the company immediately. To illustrate, say:

"Good morning. American Manufacturing Company," or
"American Manufacturing."

2. If the party must be delayed, the operator should say:

"The line is busy right now. Will you wait?"

3. When the caller agrees to wait, the operator should report about every thirty seconds, saying:

"The line is still busy."

When able to complete the call, the operator should say:

"I'll connect you now. Thanks for waiting," or, "Here's the line now. Thanks for waiting.

4. When the caller cannot wait, his name and number should be obtained and the call returned. This is handled best by the operator saying:

"May I have your name and number? I'll have Mr. —— call you back."

5. If the party requested is not in, the operator should state:

"Mr. —— is not in at present. Will you talk with anyone else?"

If the caller desires to talk only with the person asked for, the operator should secure his name and number as stated above so that the call can be returned.

TELEPHONING BY THE INDIVIDUAL

The good work of a private switchboard operator must be supplemented by proper telephone techniques on the part of the individual using the telephone. Again, these considerations can be viewed from the technical and also from the speech aspects.

Under technical aspects are the following:

1. To be heard clearly, speak directly into the transmitter with the lips about one to two inches from the mouthpiece.

2. To hear better in a noisy office, place your hand over the mouthpiece, not over your ear.

3. To attract the operator's attention, move the receiver hook up and down slowly and evenly. The signal might not register if hook is moved rapidly.

4. After finishing a conversation, replace the receiver gently on the hook, making certain the receiver is all the way down. Slamming the receiver might injure the telephone and make a disagreeable noise to the other party. Unless the receiver is all the way down, the line is either "out of order" or "busy" to anyone calling.

Speech aspects emphasize the following suggestions in order to gain the most satisfactory results:

1. Answer the telephone immediately and identify the department and yourself. For example, say:

"Cost Department, Mr. Allen," or,
"Cost Department, Mr. Allen speaking."

If answering for someone else, give his name and then yours. Say:

"Mr. Brown's office. Miss Kenny speaking."

2. If the telephone rings while you are talking with someone personally, excuse yourself to the personal caller, and answer the telephone.

3. Handle, if possible, but transfer the call when it requires handling by someone else in the organization. To do this, advise the calling party he is being transferred to another phone. Say:

"I will transfer you to our accounting division. One moment, please."

Then flash and tell the switchboard operator:

"This call to Mr. Kohl."

4. When using the telephone, do not leave the line unless it is necessary. If this is the case, tell why and for how long. Say:

"Will you excuse me for a moment? I must look at our file on this."

5. On outgoing calls, introduce yourself promptly. Say:

> "Hello, Mr. Briggs. This is Spencer of National Sales."

6. If the person requested is not available, information given in a general way is usually best:

> "I'm sorry. Mr. Pearson isn't in the office now," or "Mr. Pearson is busy on another telephone right now. Do you care to wait?"

7. Permit the other party to tell his complete story. An occasional, "Yes, I'm listening" or "Yes" or "I understand" will indicate attention.

The office manager should maintain periodic checkups on the use of the telephone by company personnel. All calls should be handled in the prescribed manner. Data can be obtained on the time required to handle calls and on the manner of speech and use of words. Important activities upon which to focus control efforts include promptness in answering the telephone, helpfulness on all calls, and maintaining a pleasing telephone personality. Employees should be informed that periodic checkups are made. When necessary, remedial action should be taken without delay.

AUXILIARY TELEPHONE SERVICE

It is possible for several executives in different parts of the country to hold a conference by means of a simultaneous telephone hookup known as *conference call service.* The savings in time and trouble from this type of service are obvious. In some instances the connections are monitored or recorded for possible future reference. When this is done, approval by the parties is necessary. The signal that the call is being recorded is a "beep" tone every fifteen seconds.

A perpetual telephone receptionist is afforded by the *automatic answering device.* This unit, about four times the size of a telephone, is linked to the telephone. Incoming calls are answered by a recorded message something like this:

> This is the Avenue Realty Company. Your call is being answered by an automatic answering device. Will you leave your name, telephone number, and message after you hear the "beep" tone? You may leave a half-minute message for me and I'll call you when I return. Thank you.

After returning to the office, all the messages recorded by the unit are audited and the return calls made. The device is especially convenient not only for small one-man offices and for medical doctors but also for large offices during the nonworking hours, thus providing round-the-clock service. The cost is $30 per month after an installation fee of $15 is made.

The *"hands-free" telephone* is another auxiliary service. The equipment consists of a transistor-amplifier type telephone, similar in size and appearance to a regular telephone, and a small speaker unit. A distant talking feature enables the user to carry on a conversation yet have full freedom of movement. Notes can be taken using both hands, files can be referred to, or desk-side conferences can be held. "On" and "off" buttons control the operation of the device. When privacy is desired, the "hands-free" telephone is used in the conventional manner. The cost is $5 per month in addition to the regular telephone rates plus a small installation charge.

Radio-telephone service provides communication between moving units and any Bell System telephone. It is particularly adaptable for use by trucking, taxicab, public service companies, and by police and fire departments.

To call a mobile unit, the regular desk phone is used. A request is made for the mobile service operator who, by means of radio, signals the driver of the mobile unit. This is done over an approved radio channel. The driver answers the call on his dashboard telephone, and the conversation takes place. By a similar manner the driver can call his office from his mobile unit. Control over the radio frequencies used is under the jurisdiction of the Federal Communications Commission.

The above description covers the so-called "two-way" voice communication using a telephone instrument. There is also a one-way signaling service which signals only to the mobile unit. By means of a code, the driver translates the message, such as "Go to Warehouse R immediately," or "Drive to Third and Foster Streets at once."

INTERCOMMUNICATION SYSTEMS

Quick verbal communication is provided by means of intercommunication systems. The various individuals or stations are each equipped with a speaking-talking unit. By turning a switch or depressing a key, instant right of way is obtained with anyone in the circuit, and conversations can be conducted with great clarity of tone. When privacy is desired, the microphone in the unit can be turned off and a handset substituted.

Many different capacities and features in units are available, and usually it is advisable to consult with the manufacturer or sales representative for specific data regarding individual requirements. The units can be connected in various circuit arrangements, depending upon the

Courtesy: Executone, Inc., New York   *Courtesy: Du Kane Corp., St. Charles, Ill.*

FIG. 11–6. Intercommunication units enable the user to converse with any other master station or any staff station in the system. The hand set is optional; it provides complete privacy of conversation.

needs of the particular enterprise. Figure 11–6 shows various models of intercommunication units.

PAGING SYSTEMS

An important adjunct to messenger services, telephones, and intercommunication systems is the means of locating people through the use of flashing lights, tone bells, and buzzers. These paging devices are usually run by the telephone switchboard operator, or they may be a part of a private internal telephone system. The light or noise outlets are located throughout the office and plant so that key personnel are free to leave their desks without fear of missing any calls. By means of a code, such as two long and two short rings for the president, one long and one short ring for the controller, and so on, these men are notified of calls. By telephoning the switchboard operator, the message is obtained. The system is quite effective, for it is convenient and a time-saver to all concerned.

TAPE AND WIRE RECORDERS

These devices are being used for a large number of applications, including the recording of inventory counts, personnel interviews, laboratory tests, and sales talks. In the case of inventory counts, the person taking the count is equipped with a microphone attached to the recorder in the office. As the inventory count is obtained, it is spoken and thus recorded. A typist then plays the recording and types the inventory lists. Intermediate paper work, tally sheets, and the like are eliminated. Likewise, interviews with prospective employees or, in the case of lawyers, talks with clients can be recorded and studied for complete information—a more effective practice than the use of hand-written notes, which often inhibit the speaker. However, when conversations are recorded, approval by both parties is necessary.

Whether tape or wire is used, it travels from one reel to another when the machine is in operation. When tape is used, it is of a narrow, thin, flexible, paperlike material coated on the side with magnetic oxide of iron. The wire recorder uses a special type of wire. The sound is recorded by a magnetic principle rather than by "cutting" a nonmetallic material. A recorder is slightly larger and heavier than a portable typewriter. Figure 11–7 shows a popular tape recorder.

Courtesy: Webster-Chicago Corp., Chicago

FIG. 11–7. A high-fidelity recording and playback tape recorder.

TRAINING IN HOW TO USE COMMUNICATIVE DEVICES

Suggestions for managing the use of various communicative devices were included in the discussion of each device. But before closing this chapter, it is well to reiterate that it is essential to instruct executives and other personnel in the proper use of communicative devices and to point out comparative costs of these devices. Demonstrations by the manufacturer's representative are impressive and should be utilized. Illustrative literature, bulletins, and clinics are also effective. Comparative rates of costs for the different communicative devices should be distributed along with suggestions as to when one type of device is probably more economical than another. Suggestions for improving the service should be encouraged from all employees.

QUESTIONS

1. From the over-all organizational point of view, do you feel that communicative services belong under the office unit? Discuss.
2. What do you consider the essentials of a satisfactory reception service?
3. Under what general circumstances would you suggest that an enterprise use (*a*) the telegraph, (*b*) the long-distance telephone, (*c*) an airmail letter, (*d*) the teletypewriter, and (*e*) the telautograph. Give reasons for your answers.
4. Summarize the pertinent facts concerning the use of pneumatic tubes for the handling of paper work in the office.
5. Figure 11–1 illustrates the use of a conveyor belt for handling customers' orders in an office. For what other office work do you feel conveyors might be recommended? Elaborate on your answer.

6. Point out the significant differences in the various charges made for tele-graphic communication service.

7. Briefly describe each of the following, pointing out for what type of com-munication and under what circumstances it is best suited.
   a) Automatic answering device for telephone.
   b) Electronic messenger.
   c) Hands-free telephone.
   d) Television.

8. Relate how you would apply managerial actuating work to a messenger boy.

9. In your opinion, what conditions make desirable the use of a personal means for delivering messages? Explain.

10. Discuss the proper use of the telephone by an office employee in handling incoming calls.

11. Discuss some major elements of controlling a personal messenger service in an office.

12. The manager of a company already having a signaling system is consider-ing the installation of an intercommunicative system. Do you feel that the addition of the intercommunication system can be justified? Why?

CASE PROBLEMS

CASE 11–1.   STEVENS, INC.

Twelve separate Order and Traffic Departments dispersed over eighteen mid-west states handle all orders with customers for Stevens, Inc., a large petrochemi-cal processor. The head of each of these separate Order and Traffic Departments reports to the main and central office located in Chicago, Illinois. This arrange-ment is followed in order to develop district managers and to provide quick on-the-scene action and service for customers. For some time the belief has been prevalent that employee good judgment and intuition were sufficient to handle the work satisfactorily and was about the best that could be attained.

After observing several of the Order and Traffic Departments first-hand for a period, Mr. David E. Bryant, assistant controller of the general office, believed that all too frequently business telephone calls were terminated by employees without the customer being completely satisfied. He discussed the matter with several office executives in the general office, and after considerable discussion, it was decided to bring the chiefs of the various Order and Traffic Departments together in a training clinic where suggested solutions to this problem and others might be developed.

In planning the clinic, Mr. Bryant spoke with representatives of the tele-phone company who agreed to help set up a workshop session on the proper use of the telephone. Also, each chief was given the opportunity to place a long-distance call to a company Order and Traffic Department other than his own, playing the part of a prospective customer for the duration of the call. The calls were placed in such a way that the receiving office was unable to tell that they were other than local calls. In each case, however, the statement was made by the caller that the conversation was being taken down on a tape recorder and asked if the respondent had any objection. If not, the conversation continued. If an objection was voiced, the call was terminated immediately.

Subsequently at the clinic, all chiefs were gathered in a lecture room. Demonstrations of effective telephone usage were given by the telephone company. Then the recordings of the actual calls were played for them. In each case the entire conversation was played, but no identifications as to what district office or speakers were revealed. Among the interesting outcomes of the calls were:

1. Customer was switched to five different employees in the office in rapid succession without securing a satisfactory answer to his question.

2. A price clerk quoted incorrect prices.

3. A technical man was unable to furnish specific technical information.

4. The majority of those reached failed to identify properly either themselves or their department.

5. In most cases the clerks failed to "ask for the order." In those cases where an order was given, they failed to thank the customer for it.

6. Customer was switched to warehouse when he asked how soon a delivery might be made, although he expressly asked that his call not be switched.

During the recordings, notes were made by the chiefs. Following this, discussions were held regarding how to use the telephone effectively and suggested improvements were developed by the group. Each chief was encouraged to discuss the clinic with his associates and subordinates upon his return to his Order and Traffic office. It was strongly recommended that the aid of the local telephone company be enlisted in the development of such a program at the local level and that it be repeated as often as necessary in order to indoctrinate new employees.

PROBLEMS:

1. Discuss what alternate actions Mr. Bryant might have followed?

2. Do you believe the approach and action taken by the company was appropriate?

3. What results would you anticipate from the steps taken by the company? Discuss.

CASE 11–2. EGGERT CHEMICAL COMPANY

On a tract of 31 acres of land, this company operates three plants in which asphalt products, roofing materials, and naphthalene are respectively manufactured. In addition, a fourth building, housing a control laboratory, is located near the north side of the tract. This laboratory building is about a half city block from the asphalt products unit, a city block from the roofing materials unit, and a city block and one half from the naphthalene unit.

Under the present arrangement, operators from each of the three operating plants bring samples to the control laboratory for testing. Later they return for the results. The work of the laboratory is vital, for the products must meet specific chemical specifications.

Since the samples are brought into the laboratory from different sources, there is no control of the flow of the receipt of this work. At times, peak loads occur and samples cannot be run immediately.

Frequently the operators make several trips to the laboratory to get the results on the samples brought in. If the tests are not completed, the operators may linger in the laboratory waiting for tests to be completed. On some occasions a great deal of unnecessary conversation with the technicians and other operators takes place, thus interfering with both manufacturing and laboratory efficiency.

PROBLEMS:

1. Enumerate the more important possible actions which the manager of the Eggert Chemical Company might take to improve the communicative services within the company.

2. Which action do you recommend be followed? Why?

3. Explain how you would proceed to justify your recommendation.

PART III......

Planning the Work and Environment of the Office

A more thorough study of the management process—planning, organizing, actuating, and controlling—and its application to the office is now in order. This portion of the book, Part III, is devoted to planning.

Included in the fundamental managerial function of planning is the determining of what must be done, where, when, and the course of action to pursue. This activity of looking ahead and of visualizing the complete pattern that brings all proposed actions into a smooth integrated and practical program is vital in the efforts of the modern office manager.

In the seven chapters that follow are discussed various and selected aspects of managerial planning considered of outstanding importance in office management.

Chapter · 12

Planning Office Work and Procedures

There is nothing so wretched or foolish as to anticipate misfortune.

—SENECA

THOROUGH PLANNING requires reflective thinking, imagination, and foresight. It is mental work. It is preparatory and should precede the physical effort. For this reason, planning is sometimes referred to as a "pre-executive" function in that it constitutes work done prior to physical efforts by a manager. The preparatory efforts determine the goal, select the various activities, set their respective scope, integrate them, and identify them to interested parties.

Stated formally: *Planning is the visualization and formulation of proposed activities designed to achieve certain results.* It deals with future or hoped-for actions and is of a predetermining nature.

TYPES OF PLANNING

Planning is of two major types: (1) end-result planning, and (2) means-to-an-end planning. The former determines objectives. It designates goals or sought-for end results. In the case of office management, the basic objectives may be set forth by others such as the Board of Directors, or top managers, this being true since office work is a facilitating and service work as pointed out in Chapter 1. However, with the basic objectives known, the office manager frequently has to determine certain objectives for his organizational unit and their respective subordinate units. This necessitates planning. The immediate objective of each organizational unit must fit into and be part of the basic objective of the entire enterprise so that actually a hierarchy of integrated objectives from top to bottom are stated and known.

Planning of the second type, means-to-an-end, is more commonly associated with managers. As implied by the name, means-to-an-end planning concerns the course of action to follow. It deals with determining the type and timing of work in order to achieve a given goal.

End-result and means-to-an-end types of planning are closely related. What is determined from end-result planning—the objectives —greatly influences the means-to-an-end planning. In other words, the goal affects the course of action to be followed. And, conversely, the means-to-an-end planning affects the end-result planning. This follows because the goal is reached by some means or avenues of action.

PLANNING AND OBJECTIVES

Because objectives are vital, not only to planning but to all management work, it is appropriate to discuss them further. The objectives of office management in most instances is subordinated to the basic objective of the enterprise. Typically the office work is performed to contribute to the effectiveness and economy of the basic objective by helping the production, sales, and finance departments. To illustrate, the basic objective may be to increase the size of the enterprise, in which instance the office manager should plan his objectives and gear his office work to help in obtaining this major goal. In another enterprise, the basic objective may be to eliminate evil influences in a community. With such an objective, the office manager would determine his goals in keeping with this basic purpose and see that various office activities are performed to help in attaining the basic objective.[1]

As time and conditions change, objectives are shifted, adjusted, added, or eliminated. There is, however, a stability about many objectives—they do not change perceivably over long periods. Many changes, if made, are slowly evolved, although some take place relatively quickly as a result of emergencies or major events such as legislative acts, world developments, or economic emergencies. But even in these instances, there are frequently forewarnings or indications that a change is likely to occur.

It is difficult to overemphasize the importance of objectives in management. The whole justification for management existence is to achieve a desired objective. End-result planning helps to establish this goal. It sets the target for the entire management process because as previously stated the fundamental functions of management—organizing, actuating, and controlling—are essentially activities to imple-

---

[1] For specific examples of office management objectives see Chapter 2, p. 20.

ment the plan which in turn is designed to achieve certain objectives. The obvious is frequently soon forgotten, and this is far too often the story with objectives. No one disagrees with the statement that a common goal must be established in order for a group to work together effectively and management to operate efficiently. But in quite a number of cases, the objective is not known, is forgotten, or ignored. This hampers effective management. Periodically, a manager should state his objective and then check his activities to see if he is managing toward the achievement of that objective.

PLANNING—FACTS AND PREMISES

Facts are a basic ingredient of practical and effective planning. The facts should be obtained, carefully evaluated, and possible relationships uncovered before attempting to formulate a plan. Sometimes when the facts are difficult to ascertain or are unpleasant, there is a tendency to discount them or to ignore them in the planning. Such action should be avoided. A planner must face the facts and take into account the actions that the facts dictate. Planning founded upon hopes or opinions may represent wishful thinking and prove impractical in efforts to apply it. Most successful planners stick to the facts. However, this certainly does not imply that visualization of hoped-for achievements cannot be accomplished. As a matter of fact, they are, but the planning to achieve them should be based on facts, on the realities of the things and conditions upon and with which the hoped-for goal is to be attained.

Premises or assumptions about the future facilitate planning. This follows because planning deals with the future which is unknown. To set forth goals or actions for the future necessitates making some assumptions about future happenings. That is to say, premises form the background against which the planner believes future events affecting his plan will take place.

As future events unfold, planning premises change causing, in turn, changes in plans. To illustrate, on the premise that sales would increase 20 per cent during the coming year, an office manager planned his operations to take care of the additional office work resulting from this anticipated increase in sales. The increase in sales materialized and soon exceeded the 20 per cent gain forecast. Concurrently, the office manager had to adjust his plans in keeping with the facts and the new premise established—in this case an additional 10 per cent sales increase.

Typical of planning premises are business forecasts, governmental actions, price structures, population projections, business cycles, quantity of work, quality of work, process used, and market demand studies. These are assumptions about the future and upon which the planning efforts are based. Planning premises within any given enterprise should be harmonious, otherwise integration of the various planning efforts throughout the enterprise will not be achieved. However, different premises can and should be used. This leads to alternate plans discussed in the following paragraphs.

CHOICE OF ALTERNATES

From the viewpoint of management, embracing all planning are alternate goals and courses of action. If there is only one goal, end-planning is superfluous. Likewise, if there is only one means of achieving a goal, means-to-an-end planning becomes a rigid, mechanical activity. The concept of planning in management implies determining a choice from several possibilities. There are a number of worthy goals. Which one or ones should a manager select? There are a number of means to accomplish a given goal. What means should be given preference by the manager? These questions are answered by planning.

Since the future is uncertain and conditions are dynamic, most managers agree that planning should provide alternates so that changes in plans, when needed, can be applied. As stated above, this can be the outcome when different premises are used. A plan based on premises A, B, and C may be dissolved when events show premises B, D, and E are in effect, and a plan substituted which plan is based on these premises B, D, and E. Planning for a range of plans, not just a plan, provides a needed practical aspect and flexibility to plans so that a manager can perform his work better.

PLANNING AND PEOPLE

Although planning is a fundamental function of management and all managers require planning in their work, it is common for a manager to perform planning efforts with others. Consultation with others to gain suggestions, facts, basic information, and advice is a fairly common practice in modern management. This approach is more democratic, helps to gain hearty acceptance and co-operation of those affected by the plan, and probably gives a better plan than if it were conceived by one person. Joint participation gives recognition to the fact mentioned above that no matter what is planned it must be carried out by people and the success of any plan depends in some degree upon people's knowledge, comprehension, and wanting to make the plan work.

In some cases, participation by nonmanagers in planning work is on a highly informal basis, while in other cases it is quite formalized. Committees are used by many enterprises for planning. Customarily they are advisory with the final approval on their recommended plans residing with the manager in charge. Committees provide an excellent means for making employees more aware of the importance of planning and of the difficulties in its formulation.

The success of any plan depends in great measure upon the manner in which employees perform their respective jobs. It is easy to think of planning primarily in a material sort of way—void of the human element influence. But the most effective planners give due consideration to the abilities and skills of the people involved and realize that a workable plan includes preparing the information for use and determining the steps for action by various individuals.

A vital consideration in all planning is the manner in which the plan is applied and the subsequent reaction of people affected by it. The approach should be well thought out, with the timing and details given especial attention. The term "strategy" has been used in this connection meaning the manner in which the plan is introduced or applied in order to help insure its success. There are many strategies employed by planners. Among the more common are:

1. *Strike while the iron is hot.* This stresses proper timing. When a situation appears favorable for adoption of a plan, it should be proposed without delay. Thus, unexpected opposition or difficulties possibly arising in the future are avoided.

2. *Time is a great healer.* This strategy points out that through patience and enforced delay, time is spent and with it acceptance of the proposed plan can be won. In other words, with time, events will happen which will make the plan acceptable and, in some instances, requested.

3. *Camel's head in the tent.* The infiltration approach is followed by offering a small portion of the plan and winning acceptance for it, subsequently successive portions are offered, and accepted, until the entire original plan is in operation.

4. *Mass-concentrated offensive.* Here the belief is to perform a major surgical operation—cut out the old, install the new—and handle the entire change in the shortest practical time. The rapidity and the get-it-over-with aspects feature this strategy.

5. *Sowing seed on fertile ground.*   The best place to gain acceptance for a plan is from those who favor it. Under this strategy, favorable members of a group are endoctrinated with the merits of the proposed action. In turn they explain the plan to other group members, thus enlarging the number favorable to the plan. When sufficient members have been won "to the cause," the plan is formally offered and usually accepted.

The above strategies have been included for illustrative purposes only. The list is not inclusive; there are many, many, different strategies. It should also be observed that some strategies are the direct opposite of others. This follows because the situations to which they apply, especially the human element make-up of the group, may be directly opposite. Considerable skill is required to apply successfully strategy in planning.

STEPS IN PLANNING

Planning is highly individualized and is greatly influenced by such things as the subject area, the type of plan being created, the people who will carry out the plan, the person or persons doing the planning, the wishes of top managers, and the type of work included. However, there is a step-by-step planning process common to all planning work. Although not followed by all planners, close adherence to it assists in evolving effective planning. The steps are: (1) visualize and state the aim of the plan, (2) obtain and classify all facts and information pertinent to all activities that might be affected, (3) establish the premises to be assumed, (4) draw up the alternate plans, (5) decide which plan to adopt, and (6) arrange for the adoption of the proposed plan. Attention is called to the similarity between these steps and those of the scientific method discussed in Chapter 3. Planning is creative and should be based on facts. It is predicated upon certain assumptions or premises. Similar conditions exist in applying the scientific method.

A plan to develop a common course of action includes the following components:

1. *What work has to be done.*   This includes the nature of it, the amount, time allowed to accomplish it, and when it should start and when finished.

2. *What manner or process will be followed.*   For example, will the work be done manually or by machine. If the latter, what kind, etc.

3. *What is the sequence of the work.* How does the work progress from beginning to end? What is the work flow? What organizational unit or units are concerned with the work?

4. *What skill or type of employee is included.* This answers the question, "Who is going to do the work?" The plan spells out this information in detail. For the operative level, instructions to the individual employees should be provided.

TYPES OF PLANS

With reference to means-to-an-end planning, most work can be planned, although some work lends itself more to planning than does other work. Generally speaking, repetitive work is best suited for planning. However, much nonrepetitive work has in its make-up portions of repetitive work, and by analysis it will be found that more repetitiveness and hence more planning is possible than might at first have been believed possible. Also work that is nonrepetitive but is performed frequently can usually be planned successfully.

In office work most concern is usually given these types of plans: (1) objectives, (2) policies, (3) procedures, and (4) methods. Discussion of objectives and planning was made several pages back. Policies are formulated by planning and assist in deciding what work must be performed. *A policy is a basic guide to action.* It sets forth over-all boundaries within which activities are to take place. Policies result from managerial planning, and they, in turn, affect planning. They tell the intentions of the managers in respect to various activities. For example, a company may have a policy of purchasing each year a quantity of office machines based on an amount determined by a percentage of net sales. This establishes that certain activities are to take place and puts limits upon them. However, it does not set forth what machines are to be purchased. That is, a policy permits planning and decision making within the prescribed limits of the policy.

Procedures are of special interest in the management of office work. An "office procedure" can be defined as *a series of related clerical steps, usually performed by more than one person, which constitute an established and accepted way of carrying on an entire major phase of office activity.* Procedures are obtained by preplanning the various steps believed necessary to accomplish the work. Procedures are applied to the handling of such things as incoming orders, accounts payable, purchase orders, making up payrolls, sending out statements, and handling mail. An office procedure is broad in scope and frequently extends throughout a large portion of the entire office.

The term "method" designates *the manner of work performance of a task consisting of one or more clerical acts by an individual em-ployee.* Thus, a series of methods which are cumulative and integrated make up a procedure.

In planning it is more logical to determine first the procedure and then the methods making up this procedure. In this way the broad activities are established, co-ordination is enhanced, and the end result of the total effort is more clearly visualized. Actually, consideration is usually given to the methods while in the stage of planning the proce-dure. It is possible, however, to start with the methods and tie them together for the procedure.

ESTABLISHING A PROCEDURE

This chapter concerns planning, and for purposes here the remain-ing discussion will be confined to procedures, as representative of planning. A certain type and amount of office work can be per-formed in many different ways. The office manager usually has a choice of alternate procedures. In determining the procedure to estab-lish, adequate consideration should be given several important factors, including:

1. *Study the entire office process.* Find out the type of paper work to be handled, its volume, any characteristic peaks and valleys in its normal flow, and the importance of the time limit for getting the paper work finished. Consider also the present office layout and how current arrangement will tie in with the procedural requirements. Keep in mind that procedures are far-reaching—they frequently affect the work of several departments.

2. *Establish the best sequence of the necessary steps.* Use the mini-mum number of steps required to do the work adequately. Each step should make a definite contribution toward the completion of the of-fice work, i.e., each step should be entirely justifiable. There should be no delay, no duplication, and no backtracking.

3. *Hold the writing to a minimum.* As far as possible the work of copying should be eliminated. The operations of checking and com-paring should be the smallest feasible amounts. Likewise, the number of copies should be limited to a quantity necessary only for carefully selected persons or departments—those really concerned in the opera-tion. There is no merit in making copies and in distributing them simply for the sake of doing so or because they are available.

4. *Adopt a procedure best suited to the individual need.* The best procedure is tailored to accomplish a specific and particular goal—no more and no less. Frequently this necessitates modification of a proce-

dure used by another enterprise under similar conditions. "Use by others" is no valid justification for adopting a certain procedure, unless it can be shown, by thorough study, that the procedure will accomplish the objective better than any other procedure that could be devised within reasonable time and cost limitations.

5. *Give consideration to the personal preference of the employees who will do the work.* Consulting with the employees, getting their ideas as to what the make-up of the procedure should be, and incorporating these ideas whenever possible usually results in obtaining better work. The practice of employee consultation helps to raise morale, gives consideration to the small but important details of the work, and provides due regard for custom and tradition in establishing the procedure.

6. *Perform one type of office work with one procedure.* Attempts to secure a general over-all procedure for all types of work result in ineffectiveness. For example, special work processed through a regular work procedure usually results in delaying the former and slowing down the latter.

EXAMPLES OF OFFICE PROCEDURES

In order to give definite illustrations of office procedures, a brief discussion of two separate procedures will be made, including: (1) handling invoices and sales orders, and (2) handling accounts receivable by a unit invoice arrangement.

HANDLING INVOICES AND SALES ORDERS

Enterprises where merchandise is delivered or services are performed in return for compensation have the task of invoicing their customers for this merchandise or service. In many instances the same information is required on both the invoice office forms and the order office forms. This suggests the use of a combination invoice-order form which requires only one writing, reduces the possibility for errors, minimizes the possibility of shipping merchandise without issuing an invoice, and bills each customer immediately after shipment of merchandise.

Figure 12–1 shows graphically a procedure for using the combination invoice-order form. Starting at the top of the illustration, the order is received from any of a number of sources. The first step is to edit the order, i.e., check for correctness of model, part number, description, price, and credit. The order is then written on a stub-type unit-arrangement office form, omitting date shipped, quantities shipped, how

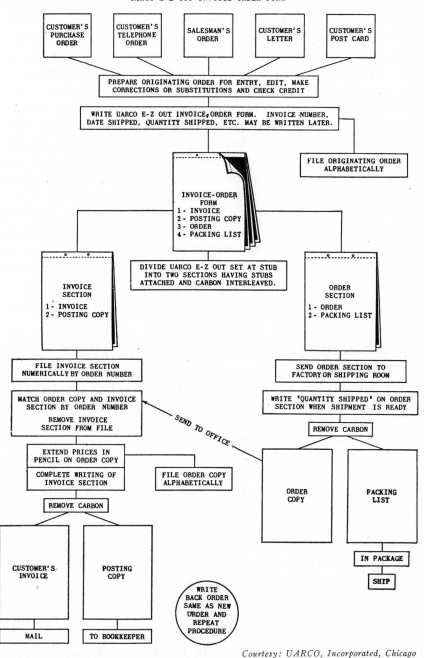

FIG. 12–1. Procedure using a combination invoice-order form.

shipped, total price, and usually the invoice number and invoice date. These omitted items can usually be determined only after the shipment is made. The form is then separated into (1) an invoice section, and (2) an order section. The latter is sent to the factory or shipping room. When shipment is ready, the "quantity shipped" is written on the order section, the packing copy is inserted in the package, and the order copy is sent to the office, where it is matched, by order number, with the invoice section. Prices are filled in on the order copy, and the writing on the invoice section is completed. The invoice copy is then mailed to the customer, and the posting copy is sent to the bookkeeper.

This procedure is simple, effective, and practical. It will give very satisfactory results for most invoice and sales-order handling. However, in some instances, because of the particular details of the operation, the procedure may prove deficient. Among the more common of such cases are: when the description of the merchandise or service frequently changes from the original writing, when descriptions or specifications of service needed on order copy differ considerably from that on the invoice copy, when the number of items is large and many back orders are required, and when a large single order is received for frequent release shipments over a long period of time.

HANDLING ACCOUNTS RECEIVABLE BY A UNIT INVOICE ARRANGEMENT

For this work, the planner conceived the idea of using copies of invoices as the accounts receivable ledger. These copies are filed vertically in what can be described as a vertical file with each major vertical file guide equipped with visible index pockets. About twenty pockets are contained in one major file guide. Each pocket is assigned an account.

The ledger copy of the invoice is filed by name of account into the pocket assigned and behind any older invoice in that pocket. The visible signal on the pocket is then set to reveal the age of the oldest charge. The signal is not moved if another invoice is already in the pocket; it will already indicate the month of the oldest charge. If there is no other outstanding charge, the signal is set over the current month.

Remittances are applied by removing the invoice being paid, date-stamping it "Paid," and noting any discount or allowance. The signal is moved to show the month of the next due invoice, if any, for that account or pocket. Partial payments, underpayments, and overpayments are handled by making out triplicate copies of a debit or credit form as required. For example, on partial payments the original is placed with paid invoices, the duplicate is stapled to the invoice copy and returned to the file, and the triplicate is sent to the credit department. On underpayments the original is placed in the pocket, the duplicate is stapled to the invoice copy and placed in the file with paid invoices, and the triplicate is sent to the credit department.

A daily proofing of the records is made by adding the amounts from the invoice copies removed, noting the under and the overpayments, usually designated by differently colored forms, and comparing the net total with the total receipts represented by cash and checks.

Credit authorization is accurate and fast because, for each account, the credit history is summarized on a card in the visible pocket of that account. An incoming order can be quickly checked to find out whether credit is satisfactory by referring to the credit history card of that account and noting the unpaid invoices and amount outstanding shown by the invoices in the pocket of that account. Figure 12–2 illustrates the credit authorization control. A new order for $18 has been received. An unpaid invoice of $11.50 remains unpaid. This is found by looking at the invoice or invoices in the pocket designated for the customer being considered. The credit history, written on the front side of the pocket divider, shows a credit limit of $75 for this account with sixty days to pay. Hence the credit on the new order is satisfactory. Figure 12–2 also shows the visible signal for each pocket. By these signals the account status is shown graphically, and delinquent accounts are pointed out and sent notices and collection letters.

Among the advantages of this procedure are complete proofs of posting and control figures are offered, transcription errors are minimized, accurate credit authorization and automatic collection follow-up are provided, and the work of debit "posting"—the invoice copies are placed into the pockets assigned them—is simplified.

SELECTION OF AVAILABLE PROCEDURES

There are a number of ready-made procedures which are available to the office manager. Quite a few companies offer pre-planned procedures and engage in the business of selling "office systems." Some can be adopted in total without any alterations, while others require modification in order to answer the specific needs of a given case.

No one type of procedure can be universally recommended. When a ready-made procedure is to be used, the selection depends chiefly upon such things as (1) the volume and regularity of the flow of the paper work; (2) the kind and amount of data; (3) the relative costs, including both installation and maintenance; (4) the policies of the company; and (5) the attitude of top management members, including the influence of key personnel.

The office manager should keep informed of what procedures are available, carefully evaluate them, and study them to determine how

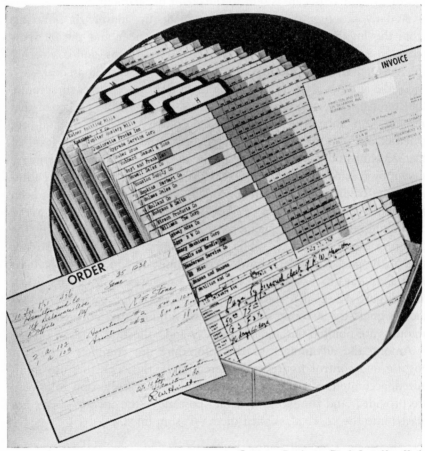

Courtesy: Remington Rand, Inc., New York

FIG. 12–2. The credit for the new incoming order is checked by referring to the credit history of the account summarized on the card and noting the unpaid invoices in the pocket. The visible signals show the age of the oldest open charges by accounts.

they can be modified, if necessary, to improve the operations of his office. For the most part he should neither adopt all ready-made procedures nor reject all of them consistently. Satisfactory results are usually obtained by taking an open-minded attitude, having a will to progress, and comparing what is to be accomplished with what is currently being accomplished, giving due consideration to the total expenditures involved. In brief, he should never forgo his planning work entirely to others.

ADVANTAGES OF OFFICE PROCEDURES

Procedures bring order and a mode of operation to office work. They reduce everyday work to a routine, thus simplifying the execution of the work and minimizing the task of decision making in the handling of that work.

Executives are relieved of many details of execution, making it possible for them to devote most of their time to other work. The carrying out of the usual and frequent tasks is taken care of by the procedure. Thus only the out-of-the-ordinary or exceptional matters are referred to the executive who decides what is to be done in these cases. This practice is referred to as the "exception principle" in management literature.

Uniformity of action is obtained through use of office procedures. Common clerical tasks are handled in an identical manner each time they occur. Work can be easily located, and quick checks on progress can be made. Well-designed paper forms, work habits, and controls can be utilized.

Procedures usually result in savings in costs of office operations. The work is kept moving, delay is minimized, employees are guided in their respective tasks, and unnecessary steps are eliminated.

In addition, the work of training personnel is simplified. The duties and operations of each job are clearly defined. Information is known regarding what the employee must be capable of doing. Selective training programs can be focused on the particular requirements needed by the employee.

Procedures formalize the successive clerical steps, and an omission of any one of them is unusual. Thus, the chances for errors are reduced. Furthermore, the possibility of any inaccuracy in the work at any one point is minimized, since an employee becomes particularly efficient and adept at his operation because of specialization and repetition.

Lastly, procedures improve the service of the office. It is by means of procedures that the modern office is able to meet the large demands placed upon it. Getting the work out, on time, and in an acceptable form are possible through the help of office procedures. They make it possible to render the type of office service desired.

QUESTIONS

1. Discuss the work of planning in relation to the objectives of an office manager.
2. In planning, is there always a choice of alternates? Explain.
3. Name and discuss five advantages in using office procedures.

4. In your opinion, could an office employing five employees carry out its work satisfactorily without any procedures? Give reasons for your answer.
5. What do you understand by the term "premises of planning," and of what importance are they in managerial planning?
6. Summarize the chief points under the subject of "Planning and People."
7. What is meant by each of the following terms:
   a) Policy.
   b) "Camel's head in the tent."
   c) End-result planning.
   d) Method.
8. In establishing an office procedure, why is it important to study the entire office process?
9. Describe a practical approach to the task of selection and installation of an office procedure.
10. For what other types of office work do you believe the unit invoice arrangement would prove satisfactory? Discuss.
11. Explain Figure 12–1 in your own words.
12. Write a short report explaining an office procedure followed for work other than processing purchase orders, which procedure is of the same general type as either example of procedures discussed in this chapter.

CASE PROBLEMS

CASE 12–1. POLAR BEAR PRODUCTS COMPANY

Air-conditioning and refrigerating units and parts are sold and serviced by the Polar Bear Products Company of Chicago, Illinois. The company handles the products of several different manufacturers. Approximately sixteen people are employed in the offices of the company.

Files are kept for each account or customer, and the number of papers for some of the accounts grows quite large because a record of any part sold to the account and a work-order sheet prepared by the service man each time he works on an installed unit, are placed in the respective account file. Over a period, several units can be sold at different times to an account which action increases the number of papers in the file. It is very important that the date of installation for each unit sold be kept in the file as well as any subsequent parts used. This is necessary because a one-year warranty is given; should anything happen to the unit within the first year it is repaired without charge to the customer. Also, certain units carry a two-year warranty and certain parts are sold on a six months' warranty basis.

If more than one unit is installed within one establishment, the location of each unit must also be recorded because if one unit should break down, it is necessary to know whether the warranty is still in effect on that particular unit or part. The company has tried fastening number plates to the units, but these become obliterated, or get loose and fall off. In certain instances evidence seems to indicate that removal of the plate has been made by noncompany personnel. In addition, tagging or marking certain parts is not practical.

When a service request is received from a customer, the office employee has to look in the file of that customer to see when the unit was installed, and, if the customer had several units installed at different times, the location of the unit within the establishment to see whether the warranty is still in effect. Because of the many papers in most of the account files, it is a long, painful process to find the paper that has the necessary information. Quite often the office employee must call the customer back because of the time it takes to find the needed data.

PROBLEMS:

1. What is the problem in this case?
2. Outline the action you recommend the company take and justify your recommendation.

CASE 12–2. WARNER COMPANY

Some 18,000 accounts are handled monthly by the Warner Company of Detroit, Michigan, a distributor of a morning newspaper. The average amount for each account is about $1.75 per month.

Currently the procedure for handling the collection is as follows: A file card is made out for each subscriber, showing name, address, period of subscription, monthly due date, and the amounts of credit, debit, and balance. These cards are filed alphabetically according to the subscriber's surname.

Each collection day the office clerk goes through the file and makes out a list, stipulating the name, address, and amount of accounts due. The collection sheets are given the collectors. Upon collection, the customer is given a receipt, and the amount paid is written by the collector opposite the proper name on the collection list. From these sheets, the office clerk posts the collection date and amount on the proper file cards.

Mr. Henry Madison, the office manager of the Warner Company, feels that the present procedure does not permit sufficient flexibility—for example, when only partial payments or advance payments are made. Furthermore, he believes that the procedure can be simplified and that constant combing through the file and drawing up lists can be minimized or possibly eliminated. At the same time Mr. Madison realizes that the number of accounts is large but that the amount per account is small. He believes that any proposed change must, of necessity, require little or no new equipment.

PROBLEMS:

1. Do you agree with Mr. Madison, the office manager? Why?
2. Indicate the procedure which you recommend for the Warner Company.

CASE 12–3. NORTHWESTERN TYPEWRITER COMPANY

In order to stimulate sales, the Northwestern Typewriter Company encourages its dealers to send in names of prospects, who are then written a letter by the company, offering to send free of charge a booklet entitled, "How to Reduce Your Typing Costs." Likewise, the company sends out letters (offering the free booklet) to names on various mailing lists which it purchases.

If the prospect replies that he would like to receive a copy of the booklet, he is sent one by the company. Subsequently, the company wishes one of the salesmen of the dealer in the particular area to call on the prospect who replied and either (*a*) sell him a Northwestern typewriter or (*b*) get him to use a Northwestern typewriter on a free trial basis. The company has found that a high percentage of "Trials" results in sales.

Ordinarily, the salesman's call should occur within 30 days after the booklet is mailed. Frequently, two calls are necessary—one 30 days after booklet mailing, another 60 days after mailing. Where "Trials" are obtained, a third call 90 days after the salesman's initial call is generally necessary. In some instances a sale is made on the initial call by the salesman.

The sales manager of Northwestern Typewriter Company wishes to have a paper-work procedure installed whereby the handling of the necessary paper work would be reduced to a system, and which would indicate the status of every prospect to whom a letter was sent.

PROBLEMS:

1. Define the company's policy regarding its sales efforts.
2. Discuss the strategy in the planning of this company.
3. What procedure do you recommend for the Northwestern Typewriter Company?

Chapter · 13

Planning for Office Equipment

> Never attempt to do anything which you are not prepared to
> do thoroughly. A little done well is far more satisfactory than
> a great deal done carelessly and superficially.
> —FRANCIS PARKMAN

To PERFORM office work effectively requires suitable
equipment, and machines, in proper condition and operating order.
The office manager cannot reasonably expect full potential output unless employees are provided with the correct means for achieving their
respective tasks.

As pointed out in the previous chapter the initial consideration in
office planning is to determine the work to be done, the manner and
sequence of its accomplishment, and the skill required. Frequently
these decisions necessitate certain types of equipment to implement
them so that knowledge of equipment is essential for office planning.
Actually office planning consists of study and analysis, back and forth,
considering the work to be done, the equipment and machines to be
utilized, and the people to do it. These factors are interdependent.

The discussion of this and the next two chapters pertains to office
equipment and to machines. However, before proceding with office
equipment, attention will be directed to important managerial considerations especially helpful in planning and that apply to all office
equipment and machines.

IMPORTANCE IN OFFICE MANAGEMENT

The use of equipment and machines is one of the most interesting
aspects of modern office work. Suitable facilities have contributed tremendously to the increased efficiency of the office. An idea of the im-

portance of equipment and machines in office management is shown by the capital investment made in them. According to a study dealing with this subject, in 1955, the following degrees of office mechanization were found:[1]

| | Investment of Office Equipment and Machines per Paper-Work Employee |
Degree of mechanization	
High	$1,700
Medium	925
Low	500

In other words a company having 100 paper-work employees and a capital investment of approximately $170,000 can be considered of relatively high office mechanization. As will be shown in the next several chapters, the trend is toward greater office mechanization so that the above figures are probably greater as of the present.

However, the use of office equipment and machines has placed increased burden and responsibility upon the office manager. He must marshal all available facts about possible facilities and help decide for each task the best manner of performance consistent with his particular requirements. Adequate consideration must be given to such important factors as the types of equipment available, the characteristics of each, the cost per unit of output, the initial outlay, the maintenance cost, the accessories to be provided, and the suppliers of equipment and accessories.

SELECTION OF OFFICE EQUIPMENT AND MACHINES

Careful evaluation of several aspects is usually necessary in order to select wisely a particular unit of equipment or machinery. The decision should never be made hastily or impulsively.

The sales representatives of most office equipment manufacturers are excellent sources of helpful information about their particular products. They are very willing to be of service and will cheerfully give or try to find out the information requested. The office manager will do well to work with them, for they can keep him informed of latest developments and advise him of any special applications in other offices. This may prove an important source of ideas for improvements. Furthermore, these representatives can help in working out special applications and uses. The representative should be considered as one who is trying to help. His aggressiveness adds to his merit, as this characteristic is desirable in sales representatives.

---

[1] A nation-wide, representative study, *Paperwork in American Business,* by George R. Terry, for Ditto, Inc., Chicago, Illinois, April, 1957.

On the other hand, the office manager, or whoever selects office equipment or machines, has definite obligations to fulfill. Good management dictates that these objectives cannot be ignored, passed over lightly, or left entirely to the sales representative.

EQUIPMENT AND MACHINE SELECTION FACTORS

In performing the work of office planning, the following twelve factors should be carefully considered:

1. *The Work and the Manner of Accomplishing It.* The purpose of the work should be clearly defined and critically examined, to assure that it is essential and that all unnecessary detail has been eliminated. Knowledge of what is probably the best way of doing the work, along with alternate effective ways, should be determined.[2] Sometimes work of a similar nature, currently performed in the office, can be used as a guide. A careful analysis of the work prior to the purchase or rental of office equipment is always in order. If this is omitted, there is danger that unsatisfactory equipment may be acquired. For example, a desk may have been purchased when a table would have been better, or a different model of machine from the one purchased might have answered the specific requirements of the office more completely.

2. *The Individual Requirements.* The decision to utilize a particular piece of office equipment or machine should be based upon the *individual* requirements of the particular office. Use by others is not sufficient grounds for adoption. The questions of whether to use a certain unit and, if so, what size and type to use are extremely important. They necessitate careful weighing of all the facts to determine the proper plan with a logical and unbiased attitude. Use of the scientific method can be extremely helpful.

This individual requirement approach is especially important in regard to the use of office machines. The efficient office manager does not mechanize an office operation whenever it is possible to do so. Instead, he considers the available machines in the light of the way each one will assist in getting the work accomplished in his particular office. Basing his decision upon these factual data, he decides what, if any, machine to utilize and include in his final plan.

3. *Amount and Value of Total Time Saved.* A new piece of equipment might foster greater speeds of accomplishment, but the important consideration is not comparison of speeds but savings in total time, both in amount and value. The amount will depend a great deal

---

[2] Office methods are discussed fully in Chapter 34.

upon the volume of work. Economies are usually not realized unless the unit is operating a good portion of the time. Volume is affected mainly by the possibility of combining work, the flexibility of the unit for handling various types of work, and its capacity for expansion and contraction in order to handle varying amounts.

In addition to the amount of time, the value of time saved must be evaluated. To be advantageous, time saved should be used for other productive office work. If the time saved is simply dissipated and spread over other tasks, there are no economic benefits.

4. *Flexibility of Use.* The economies gained from the use of office furniture, equipment, or machines are influenced by the extent to which the units can be used for various types of work in the office. Generally speaking, if a unit being considered can be effectively employed for many types of work in the office, justification for use of that unit is usually indicated. Likewise, the feature of expansion and contraction in order to accommodate varying amounts of paper work is normally advantageous.

5. *Price and Investment.* The question of price is always an important managerial consideration. However, price should be considered along with the services provided and made available by the unit. In other words, due consideration must be given what is received as well as what is paid out. In many instances, purchases of equipment are made on the basis that expected savings will recoup the initial investment within about one fourth the life of the unit.

However, the factors which determine how quickly an office unit should pay for itself vary somewhat with the policies of the individual purchasing company and with the importance attached to each factor. In any given case, however, the decision is usually based on an evaluation of such things as (1) the current complete price, including installation and delivery; (2) if a replacement, the make, model, type, and condition of the replaced unit and its probable current market value; (3) the percentage of working time the unit will be used; and (4) the investment percentage return to the company (the effect of income taxes and overhead expenses in reducing the gross earnings should be included in this calculation).[3]

6. *Capacity of Unit.* It is imperative that the unit be of sufficient size to permit efficient operations. Nothing is gained by getting a smaller desk or accounting machine than the reasonable expectancy of work volume indicates is necessary. In the case of many machines, the

---

[3] Depreciation and the influence of trade-ins are discussed later in this chapter.

expected output can be judged from experience of actual users of the machine, data from the manufacturer, and actual test runs in the office. When feasible, this latter source is recommended; in fact, it is always advisable to obtain a demonstration of an office machine. Free trials, however, should be carefully qualified as to purpose, use, and extent of time, for unless this is done a machine originally brought in for trial tends to remain, and eventual purchase may be required, regardless of selection efforts.

7. *Aesthetic Values.* The appearance of the office—a desire to impress by having the latest or the finest in office furniture, equipment, and machines—is an important, although sometimes subdued or concealed, consideration. Aesthetic values are highly subjective and are controlled primarily by one's preferences, not by any factual data. Justification for certain selections is based on personal likes. In some instances benefits resulting from aesthetic values are advanced as considerations; for instance, it may be claimed that an attractive office has a favorable effect upon office morale and makes it less difficult to hire new employees.

Actually, office equipment and machines should be looked upon not only as *physical* means assisting employees to accomplish their work but also as *mental* stimuli, because supplying the proper equipment makes for a positive and co-operative attitude and helps place the employee in the right frame of mind to work efficiently.

8. *Employee Preference.* This consideration is of great significance because the human element is vital in determining whether the equipment is properly utilized or operated. A strong bias against a particular unit prevents maximum benefits from being realized, regardless of the suitability of the unit to the work. The highly successful office manager will not force the use of a particular unit against a prejudice which the employee may have concerning that unit. Most office employees will turn out consistently the maximum work of acceptable quality when they are supplied with the equipment and machines *they feel* are the best available.

9. *Effect upon Personnel Requirements.* In many cases, the installation of office equipment or machines changes the requirements regarding both the number of employees and the level of their skill; and the problems of transferring, reducing, and training the work force must be considered. For example, in the case of machines, trained operators or the availability of those who are trainable as operators are foremost considerations. Furthermore, when machines are adopted to perform monotonous work, the effect upon personnel is also im-

portant, because usually a happier and more satisfied work force is the result.

10. *Forecast of Work Load.* Not only must the current volume and type of work be considered but also the probable future requirements and the adequacy of the unit to fulfill these future needs. Future requirements should be estimated for about five years, and such forecasts are sometimes quite difficult. Good management requires, however, that the unit neither becomes inadequate to handle the work volume several months after its installation nor stands idle a large portion of the time because of a decline in work volume which could have been predetermined.

11. *Quality of Paper Work.* The effect of the unit upon the accuracy and appearance of the papers should also be considered. When a machine is to replace a manual operation, increased accuracy usually will result, for machines tend to make fewer errors than human beings. Also, forms executed by machine generally have a better appearance; they are neater, more legible, and more uniform than papers which are handwritten.

12. *Need for Copies and Statistical Data.* This consideration applies mainly to office machines selection. A contemplated machine may provide more copies of a record, and it may furnish a great deal of data of a sort and in a form not currently available. However, the important consideration is whether these available copies and data are necessary and whether they serve useful purposes which significantly aid management efforts. Unless these conditions are fulfilled, the availability of additional records and papers may lead to inefficient instead of efficient management practices.

DEPRECIATION

There is no one set of answers to the questions of how to figure costs of machine operation, rates of depreciation to use, and when it is economically sound to purchase or to make a trade-in. The accounting practices followed must be referred to by the planner. Most companies consider office equipment and machines as assets, and over a period they write them off because of depreciation. The rate will depend upon the kind and size of product. Figure 13–1 shows the average useful life for selected office equipment and machines. Some companies follow the practice of charging to expenses any equipment purchase of less than a stated amount, for example, $100, and any equipment purchase over this amount is put into an assets account. Other practices are

AVERAGE USEFUL LIFE OF OFFICE EQUIPMENT
AND MACHINES

Time
in Years

Desks.. 20
Fans, electric................................ 10
Files.. 15
Office machines:
   Adding.................................... 10
   Billing.................................... 8
   Bookkeeping............................... 8
   Dictation................................. 6
Pneumatic-tube systems......................... 20
Rugs, carpets, and mats........................ 10
Safes and vaults.............................. 50
Tables....................................... 15
Typewriter................................... 5
Water coolers................................. 10

*Source: "Bulletin F," Federal Income Tax Bureau, U.S. Treas-
ury Department, Washington, D.C.*

FIG. 13–1. **These figures provide guides in determining
depreciation rates on office equipment and machines. The
data are based on averages and do not necessarily apply
in any particular case.**

also followed, but they must be reasonable and within the meaning
and intent of income tax laws.

INFLUENCE OF TRADE-IN

The question of trade-ins further complicates the work of office
planning. Some general over-all guiding policy should be followed,
tempered with certain adjustments based upon the individual circumstances. A trade-in depends mainly upon three factors:

1. The availability of the cash and capital resources of the enterprise. This is always present in any trade-in discussion.

2. The expected cash savings to be derived from the new unit's
use. If these savings will pay for the net outlay within 24 months, a
trade-in is usually in order.

3. The difference between the accrued net depreciation and the expense necessary to keep the unit operating; that is, if the net (present
book value minus trade-in) is less than the cost of repair, a trade-in is
probably best.

MAINTENANCE

All office equipment and machines require attention periodically in
order to keep them in satisfactory condition. Ordinary use results in

wear and tear, making cleaning, oiling, adjusting, and the installing of new parts the rule rather than the exception.

Preventive maintenance, rather than remedial maintenance, should be stressed. The former seeks to catch trouble before it happens; this is accomplished by scheduling inspections at carefully determined intervals. The latter, or remedial maintenance, deals with trouble after it occurs. Preventive maintenance provides the greater employee satisfaction and efficient product performance.

A program of orderly maintenance will eliminate most of the unexpected breakdowns and costly repairs. Uninterrupted service at the lowest cost should be the chief objective. This work can be handled in three ways: maintenance contracts, individual service calls, and company-operated service.

Maintenance Contracts.   Many manufacturers, or their sales distributors, perfer to service their products in order to insure complete satisfaction, and to this end they offer maintenance contracts which call for regular inspection, cleaning, adjusting, and oiling. Charges are made on a predetermined basis, and the rates and conditions for special service calls are usually stated. Advocates of this type of maintenance service claim that the regularity of service, the use of genuine parts, the employment of skilled, factory-trained mechanics, and the overall, long-range low cost warrant its use. Limited research indicates this method is probably the most popular for offices of all sizes, but it represents the highest maintenance expenditures.[4]

Individual Service Calls.   Individual service calls can be thought of as a "when required" type of service. This is sometimes called "no service contract" maintenance. It is of a remedial nature. The age and number of units are the chief factors which influence the choice of this policy. If most of the units are new, it is reasonable to expect that they will not require repair service; likewise, when a large number are in use, it is logical that not all will require maintenance service. However, a service call on an individual basis usually costs more than one under a maintenance contract. Also, the regular cleaning and oiling of most equipment and machines is usually advisable, and this must be provided on an individual service basis when this plan of maintenance is used.

Company-Operated Service.   The third alternative is a company-operated service. Companies which follow this policy do so primarily because of considerations of cost, control, or availability of service.

[4] A. H. Gager, "Facts on Cost of Servicing Office Equipment," *Office Executive* (Philadelphia: National Office Management Association), July, 1956, p. 17.

Maintenance costs may be lower under this plan, providing there are a sufficient number of machines and amount of work to warrant the full-time services of maintenance employees. With a company-operated service it is possible to exercise close control over the progress of the work, the expenses, and the regularity of inspections. Finally, in some instances available outside services are inconvenient, owing to the remoteness of the office—for example, an office located with a factory in an out-of-the-way small town. In such cases it may be desirable to adopt the company-operated service plan.

OFFICE EQUIPMENT

The remainder of this chapter will be devoted to office equipment. As previously mentioned, knowledge of equipment must be obtained before effective planning involving its use can be created. Information on many types of equipment and machines was included in Part II, The Work of Office Services. In the following pages material on additional and important units is included.

OFFICE CHAIRS

The office chair is probably the most important physical facility in an office. It is personal to the employee and vitally affects the ease and comfort with which the work is done. Most office work is of a sedentary nature, a fact which further stresses the importance of the office chair. Some believe that the progress of an office organization can be judged by the kind of chairs furnished clerical employees. This is aptly stated as follows: "The principal blind spot which seems to affect those responsible for furnishing the office is that most indispensable article— the chair. It is safe to judge the degree of progress an organization has made toward modernizing its office by the kind of chairs it furnishes for clerical workers."[5]

CHAIR TYPES AND FEATURES

There are many types of office chairs, including the familiar straight-back chair, the swivel chair, chairs that tilt, the posture chair, plain or upholstered chairs, wood or metal chairs, and chairs with or without armrests. Certain features about chairs require careful consideration by the office manager. Upholstering generally adds to appearance and comfort, but it requires periodic cleaning and, in the case of leather, "dressing" in order to preserve the material. The materials used in the

---

[5] H. J. Ross, "Blind Spots in the 1947 Office," *American Business* (Chicago: Dartnell Publications, Inc.), February, 1947, p. 16.

seat construction and base and the chair balance are further considerations. Caster wheels made from relatively hard material are usually best for use on carpeting, while casters of softer material should be used on composition tile and wood flooring. The self-lubricating type of caster helps reduce maintenance.

In the office, posture chairs are especially important. According to the dictionary, posture means the "relative arrangement of the parts of anything, especially the body." A posture chair helps the user to attain the proper relative arrangement of the body parts in the correct position. Support is provided so that the body weight is properly distributed and correct body balance is maintained. The chair has three adjustments, thereby making it possible to "tailor-fit" it to the occupant. These adjustments include:

1. The seat height—so that the feet are comfortably placed on the floor and no undue pressure is present on the underside of the leg just above the knee.

2. The back-rest height—so that support is provided the small or lumbar region of the back. The swivel joint of the back rest should be approximately one inch higher than the top of the hip bone.

3. The back-rest horizontal position—so that the muscles covering the two pelvic bones, i.e., the glutei muscles, overhang slightly the rear edge of the seat, thus placing the body weight forward on the underside of the leg muscles.

Figure 13–2 illustrates a clerical and an executive posture chair.

The use of posture chairs can improve the appearance of office employees, reduce fatigue, improve morale, and aid in the functioning of important body actions, including breathing, circulation, and elimination. An adequate supply of oxygen for the lungs, a free flow of blood throughout the body, and proper positioning of the vital abdominal organs are seriously retarded by a slumped position maintained for long periods of time.

OFFICE DESKS

The office desk is the workplace of many office employees. Its purpose is to provide a work surface, a temporary storage for materials being processed, and a convenient area for selected tools and machines required in accomplishing the work. However, a desk is more than just a place where work is done; actually it is a basic working tool, and this should be kept in mind when planning. Viewing a desk as a working tool emphasizes the meaning of desk efficiency which is influenced by (1) the design features of the desk, and (2) the person using the desk.

The first factor—the design features of the desk—stresses the old adage, "A place for everything, and everything in its place." The desk and its interior are planned to give maximum service to the user. Tailor-made desk-drawer arrangements are available to aid work production. As new requirements arise, the drawers can be interchanged

Courtesy: Harter Corp., Sturgis, Mich.

FIG. 13–2.   Office posture chairs. The left illustration shows a clerical posture chair; the right, an executive posture chair.

and rearranged as desired. Figure 13–3 suggests efficient arrangement of materials in desk drawers to meet specific requirements. Consideration for these facts assists in achieving better office planning.

Desks are also designed to serve particular needs. Among the most popular are those for executives, junior executives, stenographers, typists, adding and calculating machine operators, and billing clerks. Figure 13–4 illustrates several different types of desks designed to serve particular requirements.

The second factor—person using the desk—emphasizes the influence of the desk user's work habits and attitudes upon desk efficiency. The personnel element is vital and necessitates adequate instructions, training, and supervising. To assist in achieving desk efficiency the following guides are listed:

1. Work on one task at a time and finish it before starting another. Abstain from trying to do several tasks at the same time.

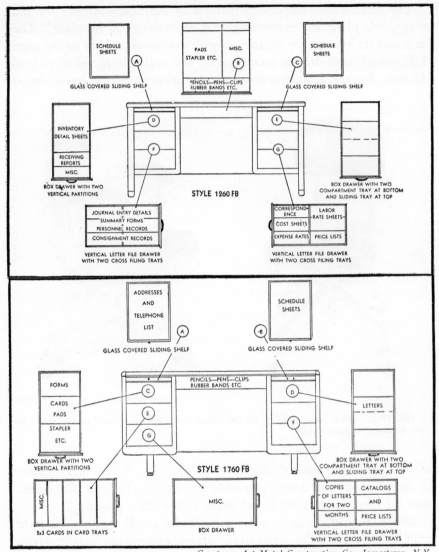

Courtesy: Art Metal Construction Co., Jamestown, N.Y.

FIG. 13–3. Suggested desk-drawer layouts to meet individual requirements. *Top:* For cost accountant. *Bottom:* For Order Department manager.

2. Keep the desk free from excess papers and supplies. Have only those items on the desk that are needed. The desk top is a work surface and should facilitate immediate action.

3. Strive to keep the work moving over the desk. Take action on each paper coming to the desk as quickly as possible.

4. Adopt a convenient standardized arrangement for papers and supplies in the desk drawers.

Courtesy: Art Metal Construction Co., Jamestown, N.Y.

FIG. 13–4. This office features desks designed to meet specific work requirements. Observe in the foreground the fixed-bed typewriter desk; in the left background, the general-purpose desk; and in the right background, the desk with an overhang top.

DESK APPEARANCE AND DIMENSIONS

The trend in desk appearance is toward smooth, streamlined surfaces. Edges are rounded; offsets are not being used to any noticeable degree; the supports touching the floor are recessed in order to conceal them from view, to permit ample toe room when standing near the desk, and to facilitate cleaning the floor. Steel desks are equipped with linoleum, plastic, or composition tops; and lighter colors and finishes seem to be preferred. Many wood desks are finished with light stain and bleached colors; for steel desks, a light gray finish is being used extensively. Hardware and exposed metal parts are of dull finish to avoid annoying highlights.

Generally speaking there is no standard size of desk top, as the dimensions vary with the type of desk, the material used, and the manufacturer. Executive desks are usually the largest, sizes ranging from 76×36 inches to 60×32 inches being the most common. For general office work, sizes from 60×34 inches to 42×30 inches are popular. There is an increasing use of smaller executive desks, especially of general office desks which are 50 to 55 inches wide instead of 60 inches, and 30 inches deep instead of 34 inches. In some companies, however, certain sizes are specified for certain uses. For example, in one company the following applies:

Employee	Desk-Top Size	
Department head............	78 × 38 inches	triple overhang
Supervisor.................	60 × 36 inches	front overhang
Staff......................	60 × 30 inches or	special-purpose desk
Clerical...................	60 × 30 inches	

Desks are made of various heights. At one time the popular height was 30½ inches, but the trend is toward a lower desk, 28½ or 29 inches high. Small adjustments are provided mainly to level the desk due to variations in the floor level. Certain industrial engineers claim for the physical characteristics of the average employee that the lower desk working level is a better height, since it maximizes the employee's comfort.

TYPES OF DESKS

Desks are available in single- and double-pedestal styles. The pedestal is the support or foundation of the desk, and it contains the drawers or a fold-away platform which houses a typewriter or some

Courtesy: Jasper Desk Co., Jasper, Ind.

Single-Pedestal Desk   Double-Pedestal Desk

FIG. 13–5. Two pedestal-type wooden desks. The unit to the left is of a conventional design; that on the right is of a modern design.

special machine. The single-pedestal desk is used in cases where a single tier of desk drawers and a smaller-size top are sufficient. Figure 13–5 shows single- and double-pedestal desks.

Especially where an electric typewriter is used, a great many companies have adopted the machine platform arrangement in conjunction with the ordinary desk. Figure 13–6 shows such an arrangement. The platform can be attached to either side of the desk. Economy and efficiency are gained. Provided is a firmer base than the disappearing platform, more knee space, and desk drawers for supplies.

The term "conference desk" is usually applied to a desk having an oversized top that overhangs the pedestals, at one or both ends and at the back. At meetings, it is possible for five or six people to sit comfortably around a conference desk, since ample work space and leg room are provided. The conference desk has become quite popular. It is impressive and adds prestige to an executive's office.

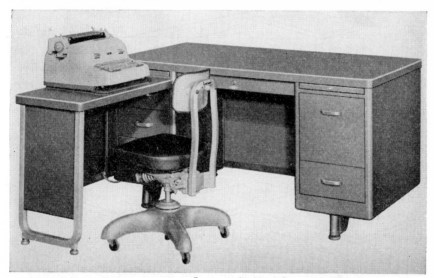

Courtesy: Art Metal Construction Co., Jamestown, N.Y.

FIG. 13–6. A machine platform attached to a steel office desk.

Triangular-shaped business desks are also available. These desks offer great usefulness, efficient grouping, and space saving, particularly for meetings involving small groups of up to six people. The occupant of the desk can direct the group without turning in his chair. The dimensions for one popular model are 72 inches on the working side, with the other two sides of the triangle being 54 inches each. Convenient space for a desk lamp, mail baskets, and books is provided on the forward corner. This type of desk is available in a number of woods including primavera, bubinga, mahogany, and walnut.

MODULAR OFFICE FURNITURE

This type of furniture consists of easily and quickly assembled modular components that, when assembled, comprise an effective functional and modern arrangement. The basic unit consists of a desk top, desk pedestal, auxiliary top, and end supports that form an L-shaped unit. Partition panels for privacy can be added to meet individual requirements. All components are standard and interchangeable, thus supplying flexibility and many various combinations. Figure 13–7 shows several popular arrangements.

The use of modular furniture contributes greatly to the economical employment of space. Some manufacturers claim that savings as great

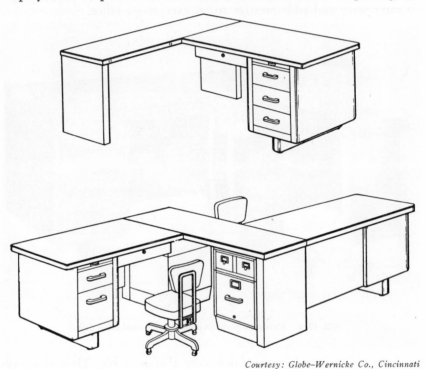

Courtesy: Globe–Wernicke Co., Cincinnati

FIG. 13–7. Modular office-furniture units. *Top:* An L-shaped desk unit with drawer pedestal under desk top. *Bottom:* Two work stations requiring only one auxiliary top.

as 40 per cent are possible. In addition, modular furniture makes a good flow of work possible, contributes to better morale, and affects time savings. Its use appears to be gaining significant headway.[6]

SORTERS

A great deal of office work consists of sorting, and equipment is available to help in this work. In one type of device, the material is handled, for the most part, in a horizontal position. The device consists of dividers properly indexed and hinged, at intervals of about one-

---

[6] See also Chapter 18, pp. 363–64.

quarter up to one inch, to a common base section. Thus a series of pockets is formed, and each item of the material to be sorted is dropped into the proper pocket. Different sizes are available, ranging from around 30 up to as many as 2,000 divisions or pockets. Figure 13–8 illustrates circular sorting devices of this type.

In another type of sorter, which might be called a vertical sorter, the equipment looks similar to a file drawer, with either low or open

Courtesy: Erie Railroad, Cleveland

FIG. 13–8. Sorting waybills in a large office. Approximately 3,000,000 waybills per year are sorted in this office.

sides to permit free movement of the material into the correct pocket. Various sizes and capacities of units are available. This type of sorter is shown in Figure 13–9. The operator holds a group of tickets in the left hand, thumbing each ticket into its proper place.

POSTING-TRAY UNIT

This equipment is commonly used in connection with machine installations and is designed to provide convenient reference to sheets or cards. Rapid removal and return of the material, quick access to accounts, locking in sheets to prevent unauthorized removal, clear vision, and a clean, orderly arrangement of records are among the features of this posting unit. The tray can be purchased separately, or the equipment can be secured as a unit consisting of tray and stand which in some models houses a vertical file drawer. To meet individual requirements, a variety of types, sizes, and capacities are available. Illustrations are shown in Figure 13–10.

Copyholders are especially helpful for stenographers doing copy work, for, as the name implies, they hold papers in place at a conven-

Courtesy: LeFebure Corp., Cedar Rapids

FIG. 13–9. Sorting devices in which the material is primarily in a vertical position.

ient reading level. A horizontal bar guides the eye to the proper line. Correct posture is aided, because the material is held in a proper reading position. Since the copy is held directly in front of the operator at a constant distance, eyestrain, head twisting, and fatiguing refocusing of the eyes are eliminated.

NUMBERING DEVICES

In some instances it is desired to place numbers chronologically on incoming orders, memos, and other papers in order to plan and process the papers more effectively. For this work numbering devices can be used. They are offered on the market in a variety of sizes, capacities,

Courtesy: LeFebure Corp., Cedar Rapids, Iowa

FIG. 13–10. Posting-tray equipment adjustable in height from 31¼ inches for standing position to 22 inches for seated position. The specially designed trays keep the work convenient to the operator and at a distance providing comfortable vision.

and prices. They are well designed and will give satisfactory service for many years.

CHECK PROTECTORS

These devices are employed to make out checks in perforated print so that the chances for altering the words or figures are eliminated. Different styles and types of print are available. Most check protectors are manually operated. Also offered are units that sign checks with official names thus eliminating much laborious and repetitious work for some executives.

QUESTIONS

1. What is your reaction to the following: "When an office manager finds that a certain type of equipment is being used in many other offices, it is fairly conclusive evidence that he should use that equipment too." Defend your position.
2. Rank the following factors—employee preference, price and investment, amount of time saved—used in the selection of office equipment and machines in the order of their importance as you see it. Justify your answer.
3. Would a scientific office manager ever purchase a particular piece of office equipment primarily because of aesthetic values it offered? Explain.

4. Comment on the following quotation: "Trying out the office equipment or machine under actual conditions can go a long way toward determining its adequacy and desirability in a particular office. However, a trial has a tendency to obligate the user and may result in a purchase when such is not in order."

5. What are some major physical considerations in the selection of office desks?

6. Do you think it wise for an office manager to purchase (a) only what he currently needs in the way of office equipment and machines, (b) a little less than is needed—to encourage better production rates and full machine utilization, or (c) more than is needed—to provide for future expansion and possible breakdowns? Why?

7. Evaluate the following information sources for an office manager who is considering the purchase of an office machine which has a list price of approximately $2,000:
   a) Sales representatives of manufacturers.
   b) Present users of the type of machine considered.
   c) Local branches of professional management groups.
   d) Advertisements of manufacturers.
   Give reasons for your answers.

8. Carefully distinguish between each of the following pairs:
   a) A secretarial desk and a conference desk.
   b) Modular office furniture and modern office furniture.
   c) Office chairs and posture office chairs.
   d) Copyholders and desk pedestals.

9. Discuss the subject of depreciation in connection with office equipment and machines.

10. What arrangement to provide for the proper maintenance of a new accounting machine do you favor for a small office employing nine people? Justify your answer.

11. Generally speaking as an office manager what major factors would govern you in determining whether to trade in an old for a new piece of office equipment? Why?

12. You are contemplating the purchase of seven electric typewriters for a centralized stenographic department. Three different manufacturers' makes are being considered. Basing your decision on the following data, which make of machine would you purchase?

	ELECTRIC TYPEWRITER		
	A	B	C
Unit cost	$325.00	$312.50	$339.00
Done business with manufacturer in past	Yes	No	No
Employees' preference	Third	Second	First
Quality of work done by machine	Satisfactory	Satisfactory	Satisfactory
Aggressiveness and competency of sales representative	Very satisfactory	Average	Average

Justify your decision.

CASE PROBLEMS

CASE 13-1. SECURITY INSURANCE OF SAINT LOUIS

For the past several months discussions dealing with modernization of office facilities have been held by executives of Security Insurance of Saint Louis. At the last meeting, approval to proceed was passed and a committee was authorized to formulate a complete plan and submit it to the president of the company within sixty days. Approval of the committee's recommendations would be a routine matter. The prime purpose of the committee was to determine what office equipment to purchase and to keep expenditures within the authorized limits. The committee consisted of the office manager, the controller, and the personnel manager.

Since the prescribed expenditures were somewhat limited, the committee decided to purchase what was probably most important—desks and chairs. It was believed this would be a good start in the company's office modernization program. Suppliers of this type of equipment were called in and requested to submit bids. It soon became apparent that the company's tentative appropriation for this purpose was insufficient to purchase as many desks and chairs as the committee had in mind.

The controller suggested that a survey of the present equipment be made and only the oldest or what was most in need of replacement be purchased. One supplier agreed to make this survey free of charge and to take the used equipment as partial payment on the new equipment. The personnel manager, however, objected to this plan explaining that an office employee with a new desk and chair working alongside an employee with an old desk and chair might cause difficulty and some misunderstanding among employees.

The idea was also advanced that either new desks only or new chairs only be purchased. But disagreement over which should be purchased existed among the committee members. One committee member strongly advocated new desks since these provide the working areas, are in full view, and contribute a great deal toward improving the general appearance of an office. In contrast, it was pointed out that a new comfortable chair probably would mean more to an employee and would result in more favorable comments by the employees.

The office manager rejected the idea that the project be held in abeyance pending the availability of more money to purchase both desks and chairs and perhaps other modernization work. He believes a beginning must be made now and eventually the entire office probably will be improved. In his opinion, to delay will bury the office modernization program indefinitely.

PROBLEMS:

1. Evaluate the viewpoints of the controller. Of the office manager.
2. What alternates are available to the company?
3. What action should be taken? Why?

CASE 13-2. NORTH AMERICAN MAIL ORDER COMPANY

Mr. Edward Hunt, office manager of the North American Mail Order Company, is seriously considering the purchase of accounting machines in connection with the work of billing time payment orders. The company features an attractive credit plan in which purchases, on any order for $25 or more, can be handled by a small down payment and a few dollars each month. This billing work is being done manually by seven girls who are paid $1.85 per hour. They work eight hours a day, five days a week. If office machines are purchased, Mr. Hunt proposes to pay $2.00 per hour.

During the past ten weeks, several girls have quit and new girls have been hired to replace them. Considerable difficulty was experienced in finding suitable help for this work, and this fact, together with the possibility that through mechanization the work might be done at less cost, has prompted Mr. Hunt to investigate the possibilities of machine operation.

He proceeded as follows: The average time to bill a time payment order was calculated by applying the time for each operation and the percentage of occurrence as established by records covering an eight-week period. In other words, the various required operations were listed in proper sequence, and the extent to which each operation occurred was noted. It was found that some of the operations were performed on every order, while other operations were not. An example of the latter is the operation of billing the original time payment order, which is performed only when the account is opened; it is not required when subsequent time payments on that order are made. The records showed that 10,000 time payments orders were handled each week and that the average time taken for one order, based on both original and subsequent orders, was 1.5480 minutes.

Mr. Hunt then called in Mr. Charles Pearson, the sales representative of the Williams Machine Company, and thoroughly explained the work to him. Several days later Mr. Pearson returned to Mr. Hunt's office and submitted data to show that his No. X-3L-972 accounting machine, selling for $2,890, including delivery and installation, would process one order of the company in an average time of 0.9089 minutes.

Mr. Hunt was quite interested in the proposal, and arrangements were made to demonstrate the machine doing the particular work in which Mr. Hunt was interested the following Tuesday afternoon in the local demonstration room of the Williams Machine Company.

The demonstration was held as scheduled, and Mr. Hunt, as well as his assistant, who also attended the demonstration, were convinced that the machine would do the work satisfactorily. Mr. Hunt was informed that the machine would require a new paper form and was quoted a price of $9.20 per thousand for these forms. The form now used in the manual process costs $2.38 per thousand.

During the next two weeks, Mr. Hunt discussed the proposed machine process with both his assistant and the supervisor of the time payment billing unit. There was complete agreement that use of the machine should prove satisfactory.

PROBLEMS:

1. Evaluate Mr. Hunt's approach to his problem of possible mechanization.
2. How many machines do you calculate the company will need and how long will it take them to pay for themselves based on projected savings?
3. Excluding monetary expenditures, what other important considerations do you feel should be taken into account by Mr. Hunt? Elaborate on your answer.
4. Should the company purchase the accounting machines? Why or why not?

Chapter · 14

Planning for Office Machines

Only he who can see the invisible can do the impossible.
—FRANK GAINES

THE NUMBER and type of office machines are very extensive. For simplicity the discussion here will concentrate on the most important units so that fundamental and helpful information is supplied for the planning that is necessary to get office work performed effectively. Mention of certain machines and their use were made in appropriate chapters of Part II, dealing with office services. The machines included in this chapter are in addition to those previously discussed.

PLANNING AND OFFICE MACHINES

Planning is required in connection with the use of office machines both *before* and *after* the machine is adopted. The *before* planning helps decide what machine is well suited to perform the work as set forth by the procedures and methods planning work and is in keeping with company policy. For effective planning it is, of course, necessary to know what machines are available and what can be done with them in addition to the procedures and methods to be followed and the policies that are in effect. However, as mentioned previously, planning is of a back-and-forth type of analysis and decision making for determining future actions. That is, the procedures and methods influence the machine to be used, and, likewise, the machine influences the procedure and method to be followed.

The *after* planning concerns the specifics of performing a given portion of the work. Also, after a company has a machine there is *after* planning efforts to use it for new work as such work arises, assuming machine time is available. Then, too, the work originally intended for the machine may be modified necessitating new and additional *after*

253

planning to perform the modified work with the same existent machine.

PUNCHED-CARD MACHINES

Among the most important and versatile of all office machines are punched-card machines. They are used to punch holes in cards, tabulate desired information by means of these punched cards, and write data based on the information revealed by the holes in the cards. Sometimes these machines are called "Hollerith machines" (International Business Machines Corporation punched-card machines) and "Powers machines" (Remington Rand punched-card machines). Both lines of machines are similar, the chief difference being that the mechanisms of the IBM equipment are activated mainly by electrical means, while in the R-R equipment the activation is primarily by mechanical means.

Punched-card machines put data and information in such a form that it can be easily handled for any of a number of subsequent operations. These machines provide flexibility, accuracy, and rapidity. They are employed for many different uses, including the analyzing and summarizing of statistical data, the writing of invoices, payrolls, inventory control, labor distribution, market research, sales reports, and accounts payable. In fact, punched-card machines can be used for nearly all parts of the accounting function. Furthermore, it is possible to obtain correlated data very easily by using this type of machine. In market research studies, for example, the number of respondents who answered "yes" to a given question, broken down according to age, income, and occupation, can be quickly obtained. Likewise, sales analyses by units, dollars, territories, and months, or manufacturing costs by various types of labor operations, can be easily determined.

Punched Card. The "punched card" is the fundamental and key physical unit about which the whole process revolves. The card size is about $7\frac{3}{8}$ inches long $\times$ $3\frac{1}{4}$ inches high. In the IBM type, the card is divided into 80 vertical columns, each one containing 12 units which, read from the top down, are: 12, 11, 0, 1, 2, 3, 4, 5, 6, 7, 8, 9. The 12 and the 11 zones are frequently called "R" and "X" respectively. Data from original records are put on the cards by means of punched holes; that is, when certain holes are punched in the card, these holes represent definite information. More specifically, the letters of the alphabet number 26 and there are 10 digits (0–9), making a total of 36 characters each of which must be assigned a coded representation by a positioned hole in the card. Since there are 12 units in a vertical column on the card, it requires three different vertical arrangements totaling 36 (3 × 12) characters to represent all possibilities. As discussed in the following paragraphs, a word like "street" abbreviated "st" would require 2 vertical columns—one for the "s" and one for the "t." A number like 122 necessitates 3 vertical columns. To illustrate, the punched holes which represent the letters of the alphabet and the digits from 0 to 9 are shown by the card in Figure 14–1. Observe that the letter "a" is represented by a hole in the 12 or "R" zone and in 1, letter "j" by a hole in the 11 or "X" zone and in 1, while the number 1 is represented by a hole in zone 1.

Arrangement of Data on Card. A vertical column or columns of the card are allocated to different items, depending upon the nature of the data and what information it is desired to include. Information on months may be given two columns so that the "1" in the first column and the "0" in the second can be punched to indicate "10," or the month of October. Figure 14–2 shows the allocation of space on a punched card covering accounts receivable. In this illustration the number "1" punched out in each of the first two columns indicates the eleventh month, or November. The meaning of the punched holes on this card can be studied by using the card in Figure 14–1 as a guide.

The laying out of the punched card or the deciding of what information to punch in the card warrants careful thought. This emphasizes the planning function. Only information which is valuable to management, which will reveal pertinent major relationships, and which will provide the basis for meaningful subanalyses should be included. This is well stated in the following:

. . . But laying out a chart of accounts involves a full appreciation of what use is to be made not only of the final reports but also of the various subanalyses as these become currently available. Failure to foresee the needs of management in developing a chart of accounts need not be commented upon to accountants—satisfactory operation on such a basis can only be an accident.

Designing punched cards presents exactly similar problems; the final results must be anticipated with equal intelligence, but the related subanalyses or by-products frequently attain major importance because the extent of the practical subanalyses or the speed and economy of the by-products may be the very factors that make punched cards desirable.[1]

BASIC PUNCHED-CARD MACHINES

There are three basic machines for a punched-card arrangement. They include a punching machine, a sorter, and a tabulator.

---

[1] Leon E. Vannais, "Punched Card Accounting from the Audit Viewpoint," *Journal of Accountancy* (New York: American Institute Publishing Co., Inc.), September, 1940, p. 4.

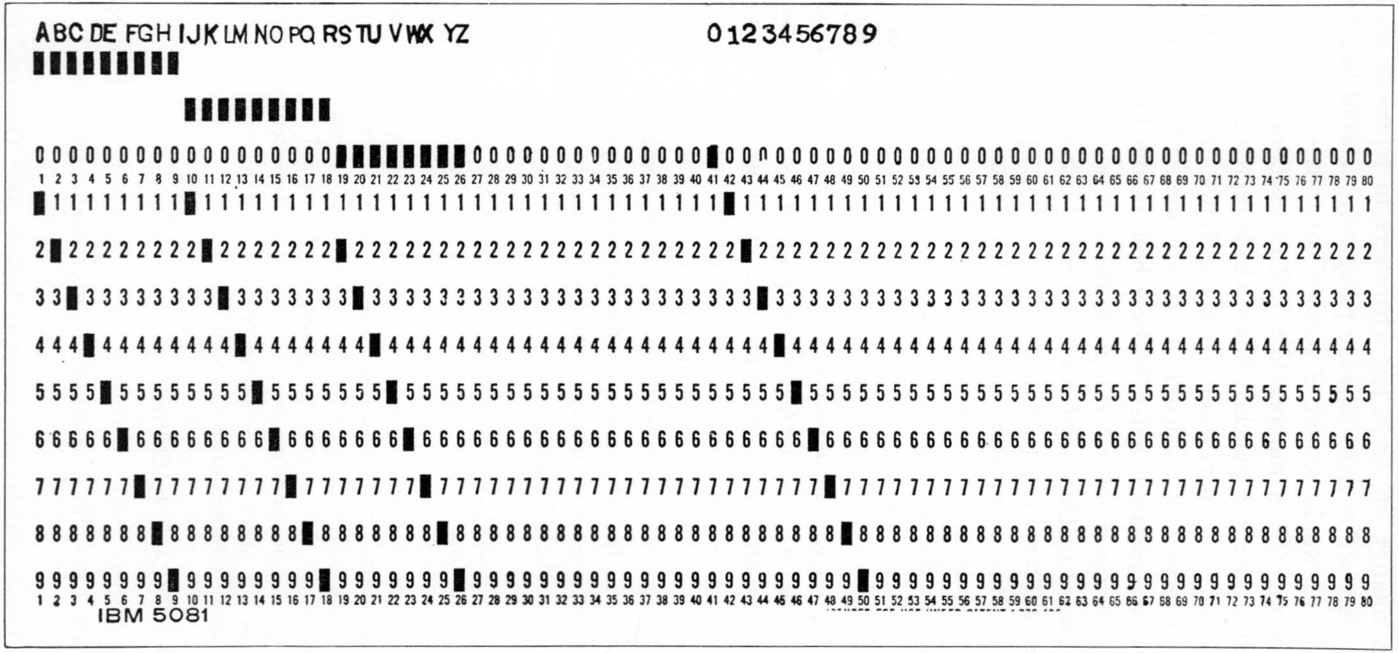

FIG. 14–1. A code used for punched holes which represent letter and figure data.

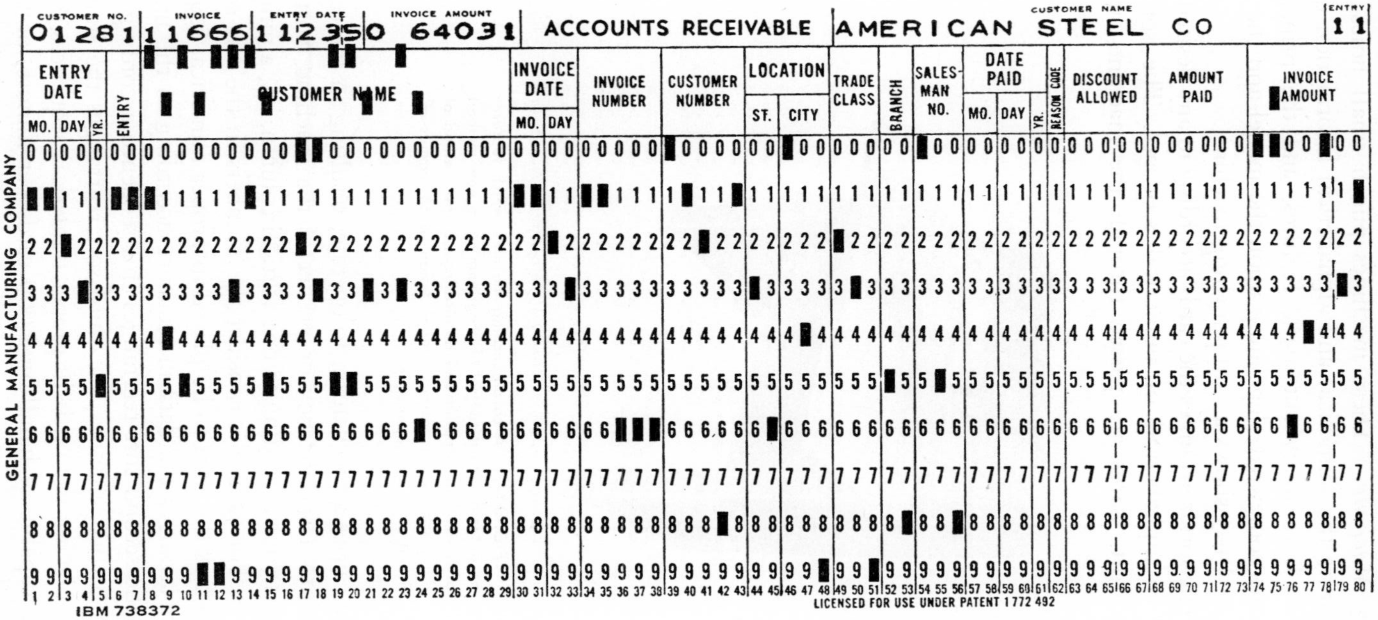

Courtesy: *International Business Machines Corp., New York*

FIG. 14–2. The space on the punched card is allocated according to the needs of the particular study.

Punching Machine. These machines punch small holes in the card representing the numerical and alphabetical information desired. The machines have many automatic features, and the principle of operation varies somewhat, depending upon the model and the manufacture. Figure 14–3 shows a card-punching machine.

Sorter. The sorter arranges the cards according to any desired classification and in alphabetical or numerical sequence. The sorting is really a box sort. Cards are passed through the machine, and the

Courtesy: International Business Machines Corp., New York

FIG. 14–3. A card-punching machine which features an automatic card control of programming (a new method of controlling skipping and duplicating), a fast method of duplication when desired, and a design which permits efficient and rapid operation.

punched hole causes a mechanism to operate, resulting in the card being directed into a specific box or pocket of the machine. Sorting at any one time is done according to one vertical column, i.e., a unit number or a letter. For example, consider the numbers in the left column of Figure 14–4 as the data to be placed in proper numerical sequence. The first sort arranges the data in sequence according to the unit column. Then, the second sort rearranges this sequence according to the tens' column. In like manner, the third sort rearranges the hundreds' column, thus placing the cards in proper numerical sequences. Sorting machines are capable of handling 1,000 cards per minute, or 60,000 per hour. An illustration of a sorter is shown in Figure 14–5.

Unsorted Data	Arrangement after First Sort	Arrangement after Second Sort	Arrangement after Third Sort
	↓	↓	↓
828.....................	750	904	107
107.....................	460	107	191
542.....................	191	212	212
904.....................	542	828	375
212.....................	212	542	388
375.....................	904	750	460
191.....................	375	460	542
750.....................	107	375	750
388.....................	828	388	828
460.....................	388	191	904

FIG. 14–4.

Tabulator. The tabulator prepares printed reports from the data contained on the punched and sorted cards. These machines can print individually or in summary; a great variety of reports is possible. The number of reports that can be printed is almost limitless but depends

Courtesy: International Business Machines Corp., New York

FIG. 14–5. This sorter will put a stack of punched cards, mixed at random, into numerical or alphabetical order at the rate of 1,000 cards per minute.

mainly upon the information to be "read" by the machine, the forms on which the reports are prepared, and the arrangement and rearrangement of the cards. A tabulator, or as it is sometimes called a punched-card accounting machine, is illustrated in Figure 14–6.

Special Punched-Card Machines. Special machines for specific operations are also available. A complete listing of these is beyond the scope of this discussion, but the more common ones should be included. A machine called an "interpreter" prints at the top of the card the

Courtesy: *International Business Machines Corp., New York*

FIG. 14–6. An IBM Electric Accounting Machine, or tabulator. This machine prepares reports and records after the cards have been arranged in the required sequence. The unit shown is equipped with wheel printing and lists 150 lines of information a minute from the cards.

data represented by the punched holes. This information is sometimes desired for quick identification and reference. However, many experienced and skilled operators can read the punched cards as easily as the average person reads normal print. A "verifier" can be used to check the accuracy of the holes punched in the cards. Another machine, called a "gang punch," is designed to punch standardized information on cards. For example, data such as date and location of customer, which are repetitive for a batch of cards, can be punched at one time and not performed individually for each card. There is also a "multiplying punch" which senses, for example, two factors prepunched in the card, computes the product, punches it into the card, and records the factors and the product on a paper.

More in the nature of auxiliary devices then special punched-card machines are the Cardatype and the typewriter card punch. Into the former, prepunched cards are fed thus actuating an attached typewriter to prepare written material as determined by the data in the cards. Just the reverse is accomplished with the typewriter card punch which includes an attachment to an electric typewriter. As the original material is being typed, a punched card is prepared simultaneously.

USAGE OF PUNCHED CARDS

Punched-card machines are employed most commonly for (1) correlating, analyzing, and summarizing data, such as sales by customer, and net revenue by salesman, as illustrated by Figure 14–7; (2) preparing bills or invoices—the data on cards can be easily grouped and totaled; (3) handling accounts payable—each payment to creditor is processed via a punched card; (4) keeping inventory records—purchases and usages by items are simple operations with punched cards; and (5) preparing payrolls and distributing labor costs—checks are prepared from information on card for each employee, and tabular lists can be quickly run as well as labor cost allocated to predetermined groups.

It is strongly recommended that competent help and assistance be secured in the selection, adoption, and use of punched-card machines. The proper and full use of the equipment requires adequate knowledge, ingenuity, and a fundamental understanding of the work and of the objectives to be achieved. The expert in this field can be of great and genuine assistance.

Key considerations in the usage of punched cards include the cost and time of getting the raw data punched into the cards, the intent to which correlated or listed information will be helpful, and the value of additional facts gained from being able to interpret the data in a more feasible form.

The use of punched cards is not confined to large companies. The following quotation illustrates the extent to which punched-card accounting is used in enterprises employing several hundred people:

One company employing less than two hundred people furnishes a fair example of what may, in the future, become more common. . . . Investigation showed that 95 per cent of items ordered were for six different quantities (in cases). This permitted even the punching to be preponderantly automatic. Two files of prepunched cards were set up, one for each popular quantity of each commodity and the other containing master cards for each customer. Orders originate in branches and are forwarded to headquarters. An operator pulls a master code card for the customer and a commodity card for each item ordered. No key punching is necessary except when the quantity ordered is unusual

SALES AND GROSS PROFIT BY CUSTOMER

CUSTOMER		COMMODITY		UNIT	QUANTITY	COST OF GOODS SOLD	SALES AMOUNT	GROSS PROFIT
BR.	NO.	CODE	DESCRIPTION					
13	67		ACE DRUG CO			0		
13	67	0301	BEAUTY SOAP REGULAR	DZ	12	19 80	24 00	4 20
13	67	0302	BEAUTY SOAP GUEST	DZ	12	20 40	25 20	4 80
13	67	0303	BEAUTY SOAP BATH	DZ	12	21 60	27 00	5 40
13	67	1314	SHAVE SOAP LARGE	DZ	24	48 00	69 60	21 60
13	67	1352	BRUSHLESS CREAM LRG	DZ	24	31 20	43 20	12 00
			(FOR THE PURPOSE OF THIS EXHIBIT, ONLY A FEW COMMODITIES ARE ILLUSTRATED)					
						275 00 *	375 00 *	100 00 *
13	105		ADAMS DRYGOODS CO					
13	105	0301	BEAUTY SOAP REGULAR	DZ	24	39 60	48 00	8 __

NET REVENUE ANALYSIS BY SALESMAN

BRANCH	SALESMAN		GROSS SALES	RETURNS AND ALLOWANCES	NET SALES	COST SALES	TRAVEL AND EXPENSE	COMMISSION	NET REVENUE
	NO.	NAME							
13	29	A ANDREWS	5403 00	375 00	5028 00	2960 00	25 70	425 00	1617 30
13	32	G DRISCOLL	6119 00	435 00	5684 00	3825 00	26 40	574 14	1258 46
13	45	R M EDWARDS	3905 00	340 00	3565 00	2240 00	29 00	340 00	956 00
13	47	A H FRANKLIN	7513 00	450 00	7063 00	5135 00	28 00	625 00	1275 00
13	51	J A HOLLAND	6257 00	441 00	5816 00	3855 00	26 25	595 50	1339 25
13	55	L B LAWSON	6120 00	429 00	5691 00	3850 00	25 75	575 25	1240 00

Courtesy: International Business Machines Corp., New York

FIG. 14-7. Samples of the work prepared by a tabulator of punched cards.

(5 per cent of the items). From then on the order analysis, sales accounting including costs, inventory control (factory and five warehouses), accounts receivable, production planning, production explosion (the breakdown of the effect of orders upon raw materials and packages) becomes completely automatic. Of course, cards other than those for orders come into the picture. As a matter of fact, all records of production, including inventories, costs, and payroll, are handled on one set of machines.[2]

And in another case the following:

Another company employing less than three hundred men, in this case a small subsidiary of a national organization, manufactures wire which is distributed through the branch offices of the parent company. Here all payroll, production, sales, and inventory records are handled on one set of machines. The inventory records include control of wire stocks not only at the factory but also at more than fifty branches. The production records are so exact that employees putting rubber coating on insulated wire have their daily production compared with standards daily.[3]

MARGINAL NOTCHED-CARD MACHINES

These machines are used to notch pre-coded holes *along the edge* of a card so that sorting of the data by key classifications can be accomplished quickly and accurately. After sorting, data referring to a similar attribute, such as sales, inventories, or indirect labor costs, can be totaled and used in management reports. The process is versatile; it is applicable to many transactions, including sales orders, stock requisitions, purchase and expense vouchers, and payroll records.

The cards are available in varying sizes, for example, there is a $2 \times 3\frac{1}{2}$-inch card and a $7\frac{1}{2} \times 8\frac{1}{2}$-inch. As on most record cards, pertinent information is written in the center position of the card. Holes located adjacent to one or more margins are assigned definite values or meanings, depending upon their location. Identification with a particular classification is made by notching away the portion of the card between the hole and the edge. For example, in Figure 14–8 the operation number "24" can be identified by the notches in the upper left margin of the card where the "2" under the tens and the "4" under the units have been notched. Likewise, the date, "May 22," is coded in the left margin, indicating that the month is "5" and the day is "22." Observe that for any one segment, the holes of values 7, 4, 2, and 1 make possible any value from 1 through 9.

The cards can be notched either by means of a hand punch similar to that used by a train conductor or a machine especially designed for

---

[2] *Ibid.*, p. 17.

[3] *Ibid.*, pp. 20–21.

that purpose. To hand sort the cards, a single or a multi-prong fork is employed. The prong is positioned so that it slides through a designated hole in a stack of cards. Then, by the shaking of the pack, the cards with notched holes at the prong location fall clear of the other cards. Thus a fast, accurate sort is provided. When large amounts of notched cards are to be sorted a machine called a selector can be used. This

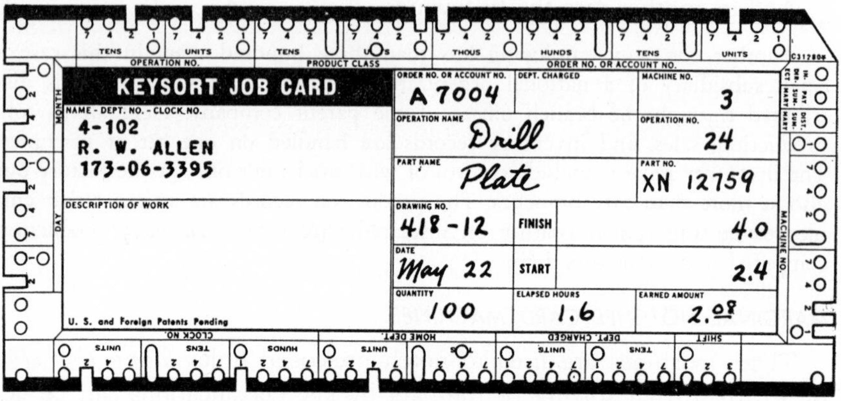

Courtesy: McBee Company, New York

FIG. 14–8. Card punched with holes and notches to indicate definite information.

machine utilizes the same principle as that of hand sorting described above.

ACCOUNTING MACHINES

There are many different kinds of accounting machines. In some discussions the classifications of billing machines, posting machines, bookkeeping machines, and accounting machines are used. However, a clear definition of each type is difficult to state and serves no real practical purpose. In this discussion the one inclusive identity of accounting machines is used. Punched-card machines can be used as accounting machines, but they have been described in the preceding pages.

These machines do not perform accounting work in the same sense that an accountant does accounting work. They are basically mechanical aids which simplify and expedite the paper work. They are not wholly automatic, since such things as the form to use, what numbers to put in the machine, and how the data obtained are used from the accounting point of view remain the task of the human brain and hand.

Although accounting machines are used for a great many different purposes, nevertheless they perform fundamentally the same basic operations, which are writing and calculating. The extent, manner, and combination of these functions found in any one machine type are determined by the main purpose and use intended for that machine. Some billing machines, for example, are designed to write in the name, address, and descriptions, to multiply and to extend, to figure discounts, and to add for the net total. For each entry the proper keys are depressed, but the movement of the machine is automatic. In others, the machine is equipped with a calculating mechanism for multiplying and adding. The operator picks up the number from the reading on the mechanism and types it in the appropriate column.

To minimize errors a checking or proofing device is featured on many accounting machines. These accuracy devices are of several types. In some instances they consist of showing a number which is compared with an original, such as "old balance," or with an entry

John Doe 2124 Dayton Drive					Account No. 342		
Old Balance	Date	Debit	Date	Credit	New Balance	Proof Line
37.85	Nov. 7	8.12			45.97	37.85
45.97	Nov. 30	10.60		20.00	36.57	45.97

FIG. 14–9. Ledger sheet used in machine, showing comparison between old balance and proof line for proof of accuracy.

number, for proof of accuracy; in other cases the machine locks and will not print if old entries have been picked up incorrectly. Figure 14–9 illustrates a ledger sheet showing old balance, date, debit, credit, new balance, and proof line. For each horizontal line of figures, the proof line figure must be equal to that of the old balance; otherwise an error is in that horizontal line. Different machines handle this so-called "direct-proof" feature in slightly different ways.

Many accounting machines are equipped with "heads" or accumulating registers which make it possible to summarize and to distribute accounts. This feature is very valuable in most accounting work, particularly with records dealing with cost, sales, and payroll.

Accounting machines can be classified in a number of ways. One common distribution is whether the machine is descriptive or nondescriptive. In the former, the machine has both typewriter and numerical keyboards permitting the entry of letter as well as figure data. In the latter, the machine is equipped with a numerical keyboard only; if letter material is required with this machine, it is usually accomplished by means of either an addressing or stamping machine. Figure

14–10 shows some common bases for classifying accounting machines along with comments on each type machine.

NONDESCRIPTIVE ACCOUNTING MACHINE

To illustrate further the types of accounting machines and the kind of work done with them, several brief descriptions will be included. The first is the nondescriptive or numerical keyboard accounting machine. Figure 14–11 shows a machine of this type. It provides flexi-

Basis of Classification	Types	
Keyboard.......	*Nondescriptive Machine.* Has numerical keyboard only.	*Descriptive Machine.* Equipped with both typewriter and numerical keyboards.
Bed............	*Flat Bed Machine.* The printing surface and the papers are placed horizontally onto this flat bed. Advocates claim it simplifies insertion of papers.	*Platen or Carriage Machine.* The papers are inserted in the carriage, and platen is turned similar to that of a typewriter.
Print..........	*Single-Print Machine.* Prints two or more copies simultaneously. Papers are inserted into machine as a pack with carbon interleaved.	*Multi-Print Machine.* Papers are placed side by side into the machine that prints one paper then moves over and prints the same data or portions of it on the other paper.
Style..........	*Window Machine.* Papers are placed in an opening or window, machine entries are printed while papers are held in this position. Easily handles entries in booklets as in a bank and expedites visual checking by operator and customers.	*Nonwindow Machine.* Papers are placed in the carriage or on the flat bed—there is no window opening of the machine.

FIG. 14–10.   Common classifications of accounting machines.

bility and automatic machine operations. For discussion, consider accounts receivable work in which the ledger, statement, and proof tape journal are prepared. Figure 14–12 shows these records. To illustrate, for the last entry, the operator inserted the forms into the machine, entered the old balance, the reference numbers, and the charge by depressing the proper keys, then actuates the machine by the motor bar. The machine automatically prints all the needed information including date, reference number, charges, and the new balance on the three forms. To reset the machine for other accounting forms, such as accounts payable, a quick adjustment is provided by turning a knob at either side of the machine. The letter material at the top of the ledger and the statement can be written by means of a typewriter or an ad-

dressing machine. The ledger copy is permanent and retained, a statement is mailed monthly to the customer.

DESCRIPTIVE ACCOUNTING MACHINE

In the discussion of a descriptive accounting machine, the work of
accounts payable can be used. The exact requirements will vary from
industry to industry as well as from company to company. Figure 14–13
(page 269) shows a descriptive accounting machine. It is adaptable

Courtesy: Burroughs Corp., Detroit

FIG. 14–11. A modern nondescriptive accounting machine.

for many different types of work including general ledger, accounts
payable, accounts receivable, and payroll. Frequently, it is applied for
several accounting uses. For accounts payable work shown by Figure
14–14 (page 270), a purchasing journal, remittance advice, and distribution expense ledger are used. They are printed simultaneously. Requiring the machine's typewriter keyboard is the descriptive material
giving the vendors' names on the purchase journal. For example, referring to Figure 14–14, the purchases from Smith Supply Company
are posted January 9, for $16.00 and $8.50, making the balance due
of $170.00. For inventory or expense purposes, the items are distrib-
uted direct to the proper column shown in the upper right of the figure. The first item from Smith Supply Company for $16.00 is charged
to "Miscellaneous" account 84, and likewise the second item of $8.50

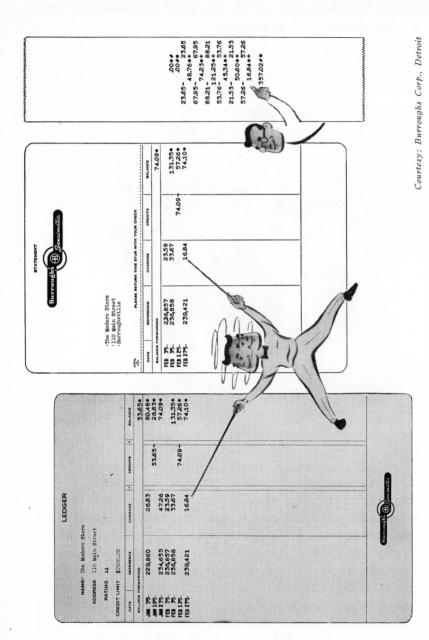

Courtesy: Burroughs Corp., Detroit

FIG. 14–12. Accounts receivable work consisting of original ledger, statement, and proof tape journal. The entries are made by the machine shown in Figure 14–11.

is charged to "Miscellaneous" account 92. These data are printed on the respective distribution ledger as shown by the illustration. Distribution totals are accumulated automatically. The same machine can be used if a voucher check is used instead of a remittance advice. When due, the remittance advice is paid less any discount allowed. Illustration of this work is not included here, but for this payment work a check and a check register are prepared simultaneously by the same

Courtesy: Burroughs Corp., Detroit

FIG. 14–13.   A modern descriptive accounting machine.

machine. A carbon copy of the check is made on the office copy of the remittance notice. Partial payments are handled by posting to suppliers' accounts during the check-writing operation. Checks written that do not affect accounts payable, such as those to replenish the petty cash fund or for transportation charges, are written and distributed direct to the columns affected.

WINDOW-POSTING ACCOUNTING MACHINE

The window-posting cash register type of bookkeeping machine is different in operation and appearance from the majority of others and is especially adapted to use by retail stores, banks, and hotels. With this type of machine, the payment of a bill or a deposit in a bank is handled by inserting the customer's ledger card and statement or book into the machine. The proper keys are depressed, and when the ma-

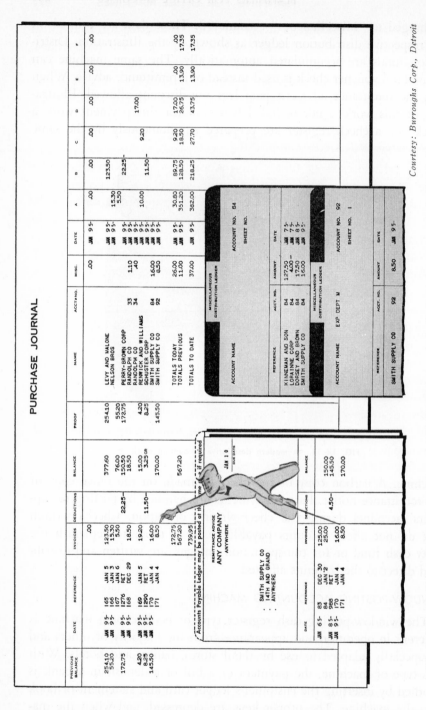

FIG 14-14. Remittance advice, purchase journal with distribution, and distribution ledger prepared simultaneously with machine as illustrated in Figure 14-13.

Courtesy: Burroughs Corp., Detroit

chine is actuated, the entries are printed on the inserted forms and also on a machine audit sheet or roll which shows the total transactions. The necessary calculations are then made automatically by the machine, and the new balances are printed on the forms. The window-posting cash register accounting machine, and the type of work it does, are illustrated by Figure 14–15.

ADDRESSING AND LISTING MACHINES

Affixing addresses or other information in applications where the same information is used periodically typifies one of the popular uses for addressing and listing machines. Their widest application is probably addressing envelopes or advertising literature. The use of these machines is beneficial wherever a small quantity of identical information must be written repeatedly. In addition to mailing lists the following are typical applications: names of employees along with standardized payroll information i.e., check number and social security number, addresses on shipping labels and tags, headings on invoices and ledger cards, listing of customers, items ordered, items of storekeeping, lists of tools, tax roll, names and addresses of stockholders, and the list of dividend recipients.

There are two types of addressing and listing machines: those using metal-embossed plates, and those using fiber or tissue stencils. Metal plates are made in a machine specially designed for that purpose. The plate is stamped thus forcing the required impressions in the metal. Metal plates give very long service; they practically never wear out. The fiber stencils can be prepared on a typewriter equipped with a special platen, last a long time, but should be handled carefully. It is also possible to type or cut a punched tape which when fed through an automatic machine for making plates will produce them at a high rate of speed.

In operating, addressing and listing machines position a plate over the material and impress the data on the plate onto the material. A ribbon is between the plate and the material. One plate is used for each item, or name and address. Machines are available which handle over 100 items or plates per minute, each item consisting of up to 360 typewriter characters. For listing purposes the spacing between impressions can be adjusted from $\frac{1}{6}$ inch to 4 inches. This makes it possible to line up the impression on a ruled form.

Attachments Used. The great majority of the machines using metal plates permit attachments which add considerably to their value for

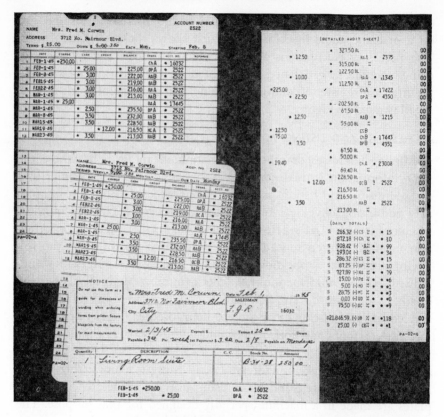

Courtesy: National Cash Register Co., Dayton

FIG. 14–15. A window-posting cash register type of accounting machine. The work illustrated is an installment registration of accounts receivable for a piece of furniture.

specific operations. Among the more common attachments are:

1. A cutoff device which permits only part of the plate to print at one time. This is especially useful where a portion of the information on the plate is printed in the first column of a spread sheet, another part in the second column, a third part in a third column, and so on.

2. A selector which permits certain plates to pass through the machine without writing. This feature is desirable, for example, when certain plates are wanted for a particular mailing. The sequence of the plates remains unchanged.

3. A repeater for printing duplicate impressions from each plate before advancing to the next plate. To illustrate, the name and address might be required on the check stub and on the check, or on the statement and on the envelope. Settings for triplicate impressions are also available.

4. A dating device for entering the date simultaneously with the printing of other data. This is used a great deal in connection with statements and letters.

SPECIAL APPLICATIONS OF ADDRESSING AND LISTING MACHINES

It is also possible to use this type of machine not only for writing but also for distribution and addition of figure information si-

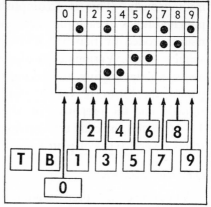

Courtesy: Addressograph-Multigraph Corp., Cleveland

FIG. 14–16. Code for hole punching and keyboard of key punch used in addressing-accounting type of machine.

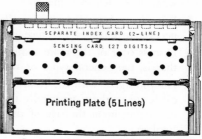

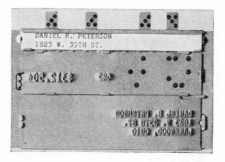

Courtesy: Addressograph-Multigraph Corp., Cleveland

FIG. 14–17. Two different types of plates used in addressing-accounting machines. The plates shown provide index-card and sensing and printing areas; the tabbing sockets at the top provide the primary selective classifications. Many styles of addressing plates are available.

multaneously.[4] This is accomplished by means of carefully located, punched holes in each plate. A sensing mechanism translates the information coded by punched holes into figures which are printed on a suitable form. Various capacities for coded figure data are available, including the writing and listing of annuity checks in insurance companies, the listing of various statistical data, the processing of billing records, and the preparing of payrolls. Referring to page 273, Figure 14–16 shows the code used for punched holes, and Figure 14–17 illustrates several types of plates.

LABELING MACHINES

These machines prepare addressed labels in long continuous length strips. The back of the labels are mucilaged. The strips are cut automatically and individually for each label just prior to its being affixed to an envelope, package, or periodical. The labels are available in a variety of sizes. The speed of the machine is relatively high.

QUESTIONS

1. Generally speaking, does office mechanization tend to increase or to decrease office managerial planning? Why?
2. Discuss the before and after planning necessitated by the use of office machines.
3. Do you agree with the following: "Since various accounting statements such as billings, invoices, checks, and the like can be prepared by punched-card machines, a better identifying name for these machines would be accounting machines."
4. What are the three fundamental machines in a punched-card setup, and what does each machine do?
5. Would you say that the installation of accounting machines frequently necessitate changes in office procedures and methods? Why?
6. Discuss four of the more common uses for which punched cards are used, that is, the general types of reports or information obtained from them.
7. Do you agree with the following: "Marginal notched cards and punched cards are used for practically the same purposes in an office, the selection depending upon the size of the office and the volume of work handled"? Explain.
8. To what extent does an accounting machine simplify office work?
9. For what type of office work are addressing and listing machines usually well adapted?
10. In your own words describe the work being done as illustrated by Figure 14–12.

---

[4] *Selectivity of Modern Business Information* (Cleveland: Addressograph-Multigraph Corporation, 1954), contains much helpful information on this subject.

11. Distinguish carefully between each of the following pairs:
    a) Nondescriptive and nonwindow accounting machines.
    b) Punched card and notched card.
    c) Labeling machine and fiber stencil.
    d) Cardatype and addressing machine.

12. Can addressing and listing machines be used efficiently for any office work other than that of addressing mail and making lists of customers or prospective customers? Explain.

CASE PROBLEMS

CASE 14–1. ROBERTSON AND DAVIS, INC.

The following letter was received by a professor of office management in a large midwest university:

Robertson and Davis, Inc.
6140 Plum Street
Cincinnati

February 3, 195–

Dear Professor:

About six years ago I was a member of several of your most helpful classes and since graduation have realized more and more what you did for me while I was on campus. Probably you will recall that it was through your help that I got a job with Robertson and Davis, Inc. As you can see from this letter I am still with them and like my work very well.

Since a year ago last November I have been supervisor of our IBM Tabulating Department. About two weeks ago the controller of our division, the midwest one here in Cincinnati, requested that I devise a way of handling accounts payable and the general ledger for our division. At present we are using a manual operation consisting of hand posting entries and subsequently typing voucher checks. Although I have no data on the time it takes to handle an account payable under our current system, it appears that a great deal of time is consumed in processing the invoices and in compiling information necessary for the trial balance at the end of each accounting period.

My thoughts are along the following lines and I would appreciate your comments regarding them and any suggestions you care to offer. In this respect my company will gladly compensate you for your time and services.

I propose to layout the tab card so as to include space for all pertinent information including invoice date, number, due date, vendor number, and so forth. Also, suitable paper forms will be designed for an invoice register, cash disbursements register, and an account distribution for running trial balance.

Invoices will be sent to my department after checking and approval by the purchasing department and accounting department. We will code vendor lists, each vendor being assigned a number. Upon receipt of invoices, they will be coded and stamped with a number for reference purposes. This information will be punched into cards, one for entry on invoice register and payment and another for account distribution for the general ledger file. After punching and balancing, this information will be listed on the invoice register from payable cards and then put into a due date file for future payment. The account distribution cards will be filed into the current month's general ledger file.

When payment is due, cards will be pulled from this due date file and machine tabulated on the cash disbursements register. The cards will then be collated by vendor name and the payments or checks run off by the machine.

For each accounting period, journal entries will be prepared and punched for entry into the general ledger file. A trial balance will be run after all entries are made. This trial balance will show account number and entries giving totals by major accounts.

Sincerely yours,

JAH:r

John A. Hemminger (signed)
Manager, Tabulating Department

PROBLEMS:

1. In your own words describe the proposed means for handling the work under discussion.

2. Evaluate the proposed use of the IBM equipment by Mr. Hemminger.

3. Draft the reply that you feel the professor should write.

CASE 14–2.   LaVELLE LUMBER COMPANY

Contractors usually telephone their lumber orders to the company, and as the list of ordered lumber items is written on an order sheet, the cost is also accumulated and a total is taken. A special ink is used in writing these order sheets. The sheet is sent to the contractor, but before this is done, a copy is made for the company salesman of the territory in which the contractor is located.

Each salesman has his own sales record book, a bound book with onionskin pages. When a new order is entered, the back of the last unused book sheet is moistened and the new order is inserted with its face against the moistened surface. Then the book is closed and pressed, causing the special ink to transfer to the moistened page. The order can be read through the thin onionskin paper. This sales record book serves as a reference for the salesman in determining what contractors are giving him business and what prices were quoted.

Customarily, only a portion of the lumber on a contractor's order is shipped at one time. He does not want it in one shipment, but as he needs it in keeping with the progress of the building work. Also, in many cases the quantity of lumber is too large for one shipment; furthermore, the contractor does not wish to tie up too much of his funds in lumber at any one time.

Currently a yard man of the company brings cards into the office that show, by order, what material is loaded on each truck. From these cards or load tickets a clerk writes an invoice in longhand. Usually two carbon copies of the invoice are made at this writing, one the delivery copy given to the contractor, the other the delivery receipt, which is signed by the recipient of the lumber and brought back to the office. Some buyers request two delivery copies; in these cases the clerk has to remember the wishes of the contractor and make the extra copy. The original invoice is held by the office and priced. This work is done periodically as time permits. No pricing is done at the time the delivery copies or receipts are written.

It is not uncommon for five or six drivers with trucks loaded to wait in the office while the clerk laboriously transcribes the information from the load tickets. This condition is especially bad from 10:30 A.M. till noon. A batch of load tickets are turned in to the office at 4:00 P.M., which is the quitting time of the yard help. The clerk usually tries to write all the delivery copies and receipts before leaving for the day, in order that delivery of the orders can take place the first thing on the following morning. Usually the clerk does not leave the office until about 5:45 P.M. He receives overtime pay, but is unhappy about working late every day.

Pricing the orders constitutes a laborious task. Different prices and terms are given to different contractors. Sometimes the shipments on an order are not released until several months after the contractor receives his order sheet. Currently, the copy of the order must be located in the salesman's sales record book; sometimes fifteen to twenty minutes are spent in locating the needed order. On some occasions, the salesmen take their sales record books with them, in which cases the pricing cannot be determined by the office.

The general manager of the company is considering either (1) getting additional clerical help or (2) using machines for handling this work. He is undecided what to do and comes to you for help.

PROBLEMS:

1. Evaluate the present manner of handling the paper work, pointing out the good and bad points of the present system.

2. What is your recommendation to the general manager? Be specific, and indicate reasons for your suggestions.

Chapter · 15

Automation and the Office

A vision without a task makes a visionary; a task without vision makes a drudge.

—MULLENS

THE DEVELOPMENT of electronic devices and their application to office machines are bringing about revolutionary changes and an amazing new era in the performance of office work. Achievements staggering the human imagination, accomplishing office work at fantastic speeds, eliminating monotonous jobs, and streamlining office procedures are among the highlights of this new and fascinating office era. Equipped with electromechanical devices, office machines now in operation control their own performances and complete tasks at speeds and with accuracy which are difficult to comprehend.

EXAMPLES OF AUTOMATION AND THE OFFICE

A few examples will serve to point out the type of accomplishments and their importance in modern economic life. An electronic giant built and in operation multiplies two thirteen-digit figures in 31 millionths of a second, that is, at the rate of 32,000 such multiplications in *one* second. In one day, this unit can perform not millions but hundreds of millions of operations without a single error. This amount of work is equivalent to that accomplished using the entire work life of one thousand people.

In another installation a main office headquarters receives inventory information daily from twelve divisional plants. A total of some 9 million of different items is included. The information on punched cards is fed into an electronic system, processed, and in a matter of minutes provides complete data on what supplies are on hand at each plant, how fast they are being used, and what has to be ordered and in what quantity. As a result of this accurate, fast, and complete information, an inventory reduction of $18 million has been achieved and 160 employees freed for other jobs.

Plane reservations are now handled with the help of an electronic machine. A record of all seats on over one thousand separate flights is contained in the unit. Upon a call for a reservation, a metal card is inserted into a panel board at a particular opening and a proper key is struck. As a result, some lights either do or don't flash, which indicate to the agent whether seat space is available. As reservations are accepted the machine subtracts from the total number for that flight, and likewise for a cancellation an addition is made to the number available. The entire operation requires but a few seconds, and waiting time by the customer is minimized. Formerly the agent was required to do a great deal of telephoning, and behind the scenes, much tallying and sorting were necessary.

MEANING AND IMPORTANCE OF OFFICE AUTOMATION

In performing work of any kind, automation means the arrangement whereby one or more machines are operated without human participation except to press the starter button. It is the regulation of processing by which high-speed, self-correcting instruments or machines control the operations of other machines. In a very real sense, automation is the extension of mechanization. If an office machine can be operated and controlled by other machines or devices, office automation, as commonly conceived, can be said to exist. The situation, however, is primarily one of degree and terminology.

Actually, automatic devices are not new. Nineteen hundred years ago the Romans used an hydraulic float valve to regulate the water level in their reservoirs and tanks. However, today the simultaneous introduction of many electronic devices to control the kind and flow of office work and their outstanding accomplishments are of significant value.

In general and from the economic viewpoint, there must be a sufficient volume of work to justify the use of automation. With an adequate quantity of work, the automated unit becomes feasible. Statements such as, "Automation is not applicable to our office work," or "Automation is too costly," resolve into the question of the volume of work.

Automation is a means; it is not the end in itself. It is created and adopted to achieve an objective which is to increase the productivity of human labor. It may be followed in order to provide a better process or to reduce costs, but the importance of these considerations will vary depending upon the particular case.

In all probability the trend toward office automation will continue to increase, and this, in turn, will produce disruptions and needed adjustments. Actually this is characteristic of a dynamic economy. From the long-range point of view, the changes should be highly beneficial. It is from the short-range point of view that the adjustments pose meaningful difficulties. Essentially they deal with employment. For purposes here the discussion can be considered under the headings of economic and of social effects.

ECONOMIC ASPECTS OF AUTOMATION

As the managerial need for written facts becomes more and more pressing, the means for supplying this information quickly and completely have been stimulated. Managers of present-day enterprises need considerable data to help them make effective decisions and plans. When events happen with increasing rapidity and decisions must be based in part on these events, it is necessary that complete information be compiled, transmitted, and processed as quickly as possible. In the case of supplying scientific and research data calculated from mathematical formulas, electronic units have been especially helpful. Problems requiring years of calculations and projections can now be accomplished in several hours.

Closely allied with this need for data is the requirement of obtaining sufficient help to perform the work. As pointed out in Chapter 1, during the past fifty years the office work force has represented one of the fastest growing groups. The search for competent office help is continuous. Ways of getting out the necessary work with a limited number of people have been eagerly sought.

Furthermore, office automation has represented a satisfactory investment by most users. In a study of the Chicago area, for example, it was found that the average estimated cost of automated equipment per company was about $110,000, whereas the average estimated clerical savings was about $50,000. This means a "pay-out" period of a little over two years—an attractive inducement.

SOCIAL ASPECTS OF AUTOMATION

Social change stimulated by automation emphasizes employment which can be viewed as offering either (1) greater opportunities, or (2) fewer opportunities, even to the point of mass unemployment. The former is indicative of the attitude under which automation will come to maturity. It stresses what will automation help us to better, or assist us to achieve that has never been achieved? There is a problem, however, in adapting to this greater opportunity. In this connection, much human effort will shift from manual to mental work and from menial to more challenging tasks. In the second viewpoint, the dominant force is fear. Employees are quite naturally concerned whether the higher rates of office work performance will result in unemployment or in raising living standards. Past experience seems to indicate that technological advancements have increased the over-all level of employment. New demands have developed—the machines themselves creating a large labor force required for their construction and maintenance. However, many people are *displaced, not replaced* to other areas of duty. For example, a large installation of electronic office machines in a Chicago office required the shifting of several hundred employees to other jobs. Not a one lost his job but was trained and placed in new work. This called for real management ability and, of course, necessitated an adjustment on the part of each employee.

In some cases the adjustment to different employment is difficult, and it is not always possible to fit displaced employees into new openings. Many are of the opinion that the skill requirements will increase for most office jobs as a result of automation. From the over-all viewpoint, this might be, but it is well to observe that many jobs of relatively low skill will remain. The automated office is not a 100 per cent mechanized robot. The best current estimates are that some 30 per cent of the total office work is performed by electronic systems in a typical present-day "automated office."

Undoubtedly the number of irksome, monotonous tasks are reduced by automation. Much laborious and time-consuming office work is done by the machine. This is desirable from the social point of view and is a benefit to mankind. Many feel that we are at the beginning of what might be described, "a second Industrial Revolution," which will substitute machines for human beings in performing mental drudgery, just as the first Industrial Revolution substituted machines for carrying out most backbreaking physical drudgery.

OFFICE AUTOMATION AND OFFICE MANAGEMENT

One of the greatest effects of office automation is and will be upon office management. The function of managerial planning has increased in importance or at least its importance is being brought to the foreground and revealed in its own true vital nature. Underestimates of the planning time and effort that must precede office automation is the main cause of difficulty in harnessing electronic power to office work. Automation in the office stresses managerial problems; in the factory they are technical problems. The use of an electronic system itself requires very careful and thorough planning, as will be discussed later in this chapter under the subject of "programming."

Emphasis is also given to taking a broader viewpoint, or a perspective of the entirety rather than of one single component. As a result the thinking in planning must be broadened and carried out in more sweeping, yet integrated lines.

Objectives too must be more clearly defined. Abundant factual information is available, for example, to establish goals. In addition, the data the office can supply makes for improved aims of the entire enterprise. To illustrate, the sales department can be assisted in making accurate estimates with minimum time and cost expenditures.

The capacity to compile, transmit, and process operating data quickly can be utilized to provide timely control efforts. Thus the functioning of the management process is enhanced, for it is no longer necessary to delay the essential follow-up, evaluation, and corrective measures to insure that predetermined goals are attained. A manager need not wait until the present month is half over to be informed exactly what was accomplished last month and what areas, if any, require managerial attention.

For a given office, automation usually increases relatively the machine cost and decreases labor cost. In turn, the greater machine expenditure spotlights attention upon questions of depreciation, scheduling and maintaining even work flows, and keeping the machanized units in top working condition.

In summary, office management should become more effective with the help of office automation. Faster and better information being available, the office can provide more and more service, more co-ordinating help to the enterprise. At the same time the competent office manager's status will increase because the need for effective management in the office is simultaneously being further emphasized.

THE ELECTRONIC BRAIN

The awe-inspiring electronic business machines with their fantastic accomplishments have led some to refer to them as machines that think. This is not true. The machines do not think. They operate only as instructed and must be told what to do in the minutest detail. Decision making is not their perogative except what decision making is given them. They must follow a predetermined pattern of action.

What these office machines do is enhance the power of the human mind, not minimize its importance. They provide help as never before believed possible or even conceived. Instead of being occupied with the accumulating and processing of data, the human mind is relieved of such work, and freed to think about the data, what they mean, what should be done, and whom to inspire. The opportunity for mental deliberation with adequate facts leading to sound decisions and management action becomes a reality. In essence, the human mind is aided and guided by factual information and afforded a chance to deliberate so that good judgment can be formulated.

BASIC ELEMENTS OF PROCESSING DATA

Processing data means taking a succession of facts, subjecting them to a series of operations according to a pattern or formula, and arriving at a result that shows the information in some standard and more useful form. It means bookkeeping, inventory record keeping, payrolling, accounting, and solving mathematical equations. There are five basic elements into which all processing data can be divided. These elements are classifying, sorting, calculating, summarizing, and recording. Not all five elements are used in each processing, and for a given type of work, various combinations of elements are commonly employed.

The names of these elements are somewhat self-explanatory, but a brief description of each will help to identify them properly. Classifying deals with distribution into groups. For example, digit codes used for geographical separations have gained wide usage. Sorting is separating according to group. It is employed mainly for two purposes: (1) to obtain a distribution by expense, product, or territory; and (2) to arrange by sequence for filing or transcribing purposes.

Calculating includes multiplication and division work. Figuring billings, discounts, and payrolls are examples of calculating work in processing data. For the most part this calculating work is numerous and relatively simple in ordinary office work, but less frequent in occurrence and comparatively complex in engineering and scientific studies. Summarizing means addition and is illustrated by determining the totals of expenses, purchase orders, sales, and other records. Recording includes not only the printing, writing, or transcribing of data but also its reproduction and filing which are usually performed at the same time as the recording.

Office machines to perform these basic elements are not new. To illustrate, a listing calculating machine performs calculating and recording; a descriptive accounting machine does sorting, calculating, and recording; and a window posting accounting machine performs classifying, sorting, calculating, and recording.

AUTOMATIC ELECTRONIC COMPUTER

This leads to the automatic electronic computer which is a group of mechanical and electronic devices connected into a unit or system to process data. It can be viewed as a unit that performs all the basic

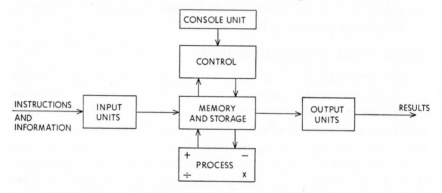

Photo Courtesy: International Business Machines Corp., New York

FIG. 15–1. Basic components of an electronic computer.

elements required for processing data. That is, it performs classifying, sorting, calculating, summarizing, and recording. Actually the electronic computer is the outgrowth of the continued advancement in office mechanization. Here is a unit that can take bundles of facts, process the necessary string of operations including any or all five of the basic elements as required, turn out the answer with fabulous rapidity, without error, and proceed automatically to the next bundle of data and process them.

The top portion of Figure 15–1 diagrams the essential make-up of an electronic computer; the bottom portion, the general appearance of actual units. Different models will vary somewhat in detail and spe-

SIMULTANEOUS CURRENT THROUGH WIRES A AND B WILL REVERSE MAGNETIC CHARGE OF ONLY THE CORE AT THEIR INTERSECTION.

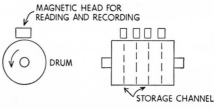

FIG. 15–2. *Left:* Magnetic core provides access to data faster but is presently more expensive than the magnetic drum. Each core holds one binary digit. About 75,000 can be stored per cubic foot of core and are available at the rate of about 50,000 per second. *Right:* Magnetic drum is mounted on its axis and rotates at from 2,000 to 8,000 r.p.m. Infromation is stored on channels around the drum by means of magnetic spots. The desired information is brought to a magnetic head and read. More than 1,000 digits can be stored per square inch of surface and are available at a rate of about 25,000 per second.

cific purposes, but the fundamentals outlined here are common to all computers.

Data in the form of punched cards or magnetic tape are fed into the input units where the data are converted into so-called "computer language," or more accurately electric pulses. Input units usually are either card readers, tape units, or magnetic drums, depending upon the particular design of the equipment. These data, now in computer language, are stored or retained in a memory unit which commonly consists of magnetic cores, magnetic drums, and pulse emitters. They hold standard or current facts and sometimes instructions. When needed, the data are released to the process or computer section. Figure 15–2 gives illustrations of these memory type of equipment.

Directing the entire operation is the control section which issues a program, or chain of instructions, to the process unit for each new group of data. It can send stored data required by the program, examine any step to select the following one, and start the processing of the next group of data. Frequently, a console unit, illustrated by Figure 15–3, permits a human operator to enter data if necessary, to determine the status of the operations, and exercise complete supervision of the processing work. By means of the output units, completed processed data are converted from the "computer language" to a usable form such as printed records, punched cards, magnetic tape, or perforated paper tape. Figure 15–4 shows a printing unit having a capacity of 600 lines per minute—each line approximately 20 words.

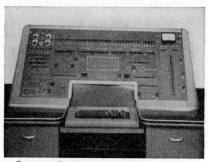

Courtesy: Remington Rand Corp., New York

FIG. 15–3. Panel of a supervisory control console unit of an electronic computer. This is the "nerve center" of the electronic system, giving the operator a continual picture of the internal operation.

PERSONNEL REQUIRED

From what has been stated, it follows that electronic computers are made up of different pieces of equipment working in harmony with one another. They have tremendous flexibility and capacity to perform many office tasks. But their actions must be carefully planned so that they will do what is wanted, remember what is wanted, and reveal what is wanted. This means a competent staff is needed to utilize an electronic system. Expert help in at least three areas is suggested:

1. Analyzing the office work for the electronic processing.
2. Coding the processing work for machine usage.
3. Operating the electronic processing system.

ANALYZING THE WORK

The term "programming" designates the breaking down in most complete detail the work to be electronically processed. The preparing of customers' invoices, for example, may require 1,500 or more steps. The work, usually in the form of a flow chart, lists the precise step-by-step actions to be taken. Programming includes therefore the designing of programs of instructions for electronic systems. Without

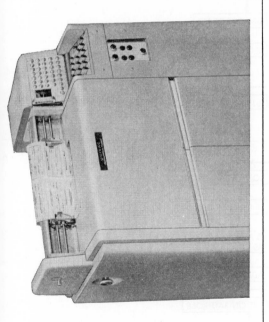

THE UNIVAC HIGH-SPEED PRINTER PRINTS ON PAPER UP TO 78,000 CHARACTERS IN A SINGLE MINUTE - EQUIVALENT TO PRINTING THE
CONTENTS OF THIS PARAGRAPH 60 TIMES A MINUTE. NOW, FOR THE FIRST TIME, IT IS POSSIBLE TO GET UNIVAC RESULTS PRINTED AT
SPEEDS TO KEEP PACE WITH THIS FAMOUS COMPUTING SYSTEM. 7,500 PAYCHECKS CAN BE PRINTED, FOR EXAMPLE, IN LESS THAN ONE
HOUR. OPERATING ON UNIVAC OUTPUT TAPE, THE HIGH-SPEED PRINTER OFFERS A SELECTION OF 51 CHARACTERS - LETTERS, NUMBERS,
AND PUNCTUATION MARKS - ON A LINE 130 CHARACTERS WIDE. ITS EXTREME VERSATILITY PERMITS PRINTING, IN ANY FORMAT DESIRED,
ON SPROCKET-FED PAPER - EITHER BLANK OR PREPRINTED - FROM 4 INCHES TO 27 INCHES WIDE, AND UP TO CARD STOCK IN WEIGHT.
INTERCHANGEABLE PLUGBOARDS PROVIDE COMPLETELY FLEXIBLE CONTROL OVER THE PRINTED OUTPUT. ACCURACY IS ENSURED IN HIGH-
SPEED PRINTER OPERATION, AS THROUGHOUT THE ENTIRE UNIVAC SYSTEM, BY EXCLUSIVE SELF-CHECKING FEATURES. THIS PHENOMENAL
NEW UNIVAC AUXILIARY IS ALREADY AT WORK IN LEADING COMPANIES, PRINTING THE PAYCHECKS AND THE OTHER BUSINESS FORMS NEEDED
IN COMMERCIAL DATA-PROCESSING. NOW, AT LAST, ELECTRONIC COMPUTING IS PRACTICAL FOR OFFICE ROUTINES.

Courtesy: Remington Rand Corp., New York

FIG. 15–4. A high-speed printer complete with control panel. In just one second, the entire paragraph illustrated was printed with this unit. A
total of 7,500 pay checks can be printed in less than one hour.

these instructions the computer would be unable to function. Intimate knowledge of existing procedures, methods, and routines are extremely helpful in performing programming work. The broad over-all picture should be taken, for one large programming job may encompass many small jobs, thus eliminating duplication and needless waste. A background in office procedural analysis and a complete understanding of the purposes for which the finished data are used appear paramount

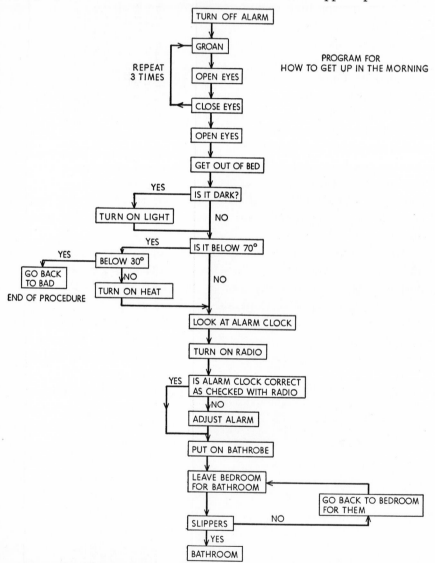

FIG. 15–5. This diagram illustrates how programmers have to instruct the electronic system to work.

in this work. A humorous, but helpful, illustration explaining how a programmer instructs a machine to work is shown by Figure 15–5.

CODING THE PROCESS WORK

Every detail which the machine is to follow must be put into language that the machine can handle. This includes the use of special codes and numbers which, put on or into the data transmitting media, will cause the machine to perform the operation desired. In the case of magnetic tape, for example, the data are recorded on it in the form of magnetic dots or spots on seven tracks. The code employed is illustrated by Figure 15–6. Beginning from the bottom, the first four tracks labeled 1, 2, 4, and 8, respectively, represent numerical characters of 0 through 9. Any number can be recorded by these four tracks; for example, 5 is 4

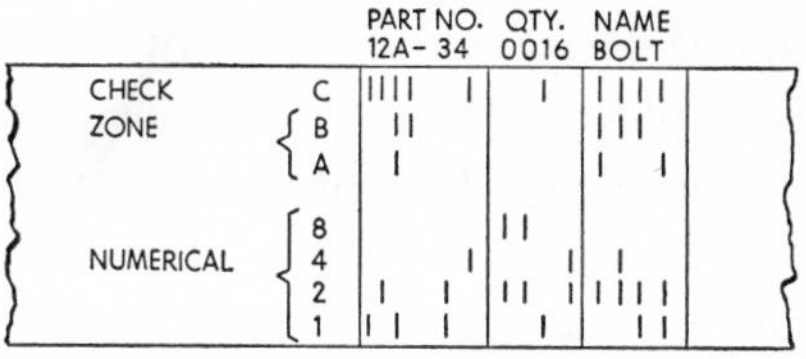

FIG. 15–6. Coding of magnetic spots on tape to transmit information.

and 1, 7 is 4 and 2 and 1, 1 of course is 1. The next two tracks, marked A and B in the figure, are used for recording zones, and the track at the top, C, is for checking.

An electronic system is not infallible; therefore, it checks itself to find any error. The impulses for check on the tape are used for this purpose. For example, every transfer of information from the memory units might be tested on an odd-even basis. If the sum of the group of digits is an even number when it is supposed to be odd, the machine indicates the error and stops.

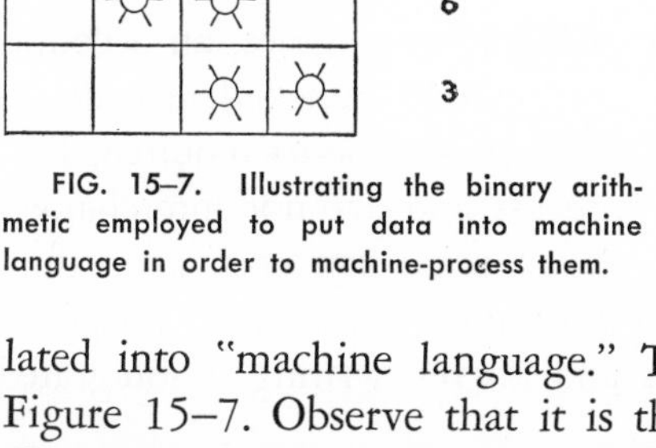

FIG. 15–7. Illustrating the binary arithmetic employed to put data into machine language in order to machine-process them.

The great majority of computers operate in binary arithmetic which is a system having a base of two, just as decimal refers to a base of ten. The two number symbols are zero and one, represented by "off" and "on" conditions in the electrical circuits of the machine. This arrangement plus a columnar pattern enables data to be translated into "machine language." The columnar pattern is shown in Figure 15–7. Observe that it is the same as the numerical tracks of the magnetic tape code shown in Figure 15–6.

This coding work requires a thorough knowledge of how the machine operates and what can and can't be done by it. This knowledge is specialized and is offered by the manufacturers of the machines. A concentrated course of several weeks' duration is usually required. Assistance is also made available by the manufacturers after installation of the machine.

OPERATING THE ELECTRONIC SYSTEM

Competent help is required to operate the electronic system, and the duties of these operators are about the same level of difficulty as those of standard office machines. The proper data must be selected and placed into the machine, removed, and filed away when the job is completed. Certain checks are made to insure that the unit is operating properly, and the work should be so arranged that a high percentage of machine utilization is achieved. Operating the machine properly is vital, but it does not require highly skilled technical help. With the programming and coding phase worked out and servicing of the machine provided by the manufacturer, the actual operating of the machine is a relatively simple matter.

INTEGRATED DATA PROCESSING

Another important aspect of office automation is integrated data processing (IDP). This can be described briefly as automation of source data. The writing for an office operation is put into such a form that subsequent operations requiring this writing can be processed automatically. IDP, therefore, tends to tie office work together, to integrate it, or form a whole from the various parts.

To illustrate, in connection with the processing of a customer's order, certain data such as customer's name and address, terms, shipping instructions, and the items ordered must at one time or another appear on papers including acknowledge, shipping copy, packing list, production order, inventory control, and invoice. The elimination of duplicate writings can be accomplished by using carbon copies, an accounting machine extends and totals, and information punched in code on cards can be used repeatedly to reproduce all documents required. But, in general, these deal with a single process and are not interchangeable among various processes. However, in some instances, as in duplicating copies containing essential information for specific purposes, the copies serve in several processes and all the writing is integrated by use of the one master.

DISTINGUISHING FEATURES OF IDP

The basic concept of integrated data processing is the preservation of data in a mechanical and reusable form from the time of origination so that all subsequent processing of the data can be performed and preserved in this reusable form. This concept applies to all office processing and is distinguished from conventional approaches by the original data being (1) recorded at the point of origin in a mechanical form, (2) processed exclusively in a mechanical form, and (3) utilized in all subsequent operations, where needed, resulting in the integration of the processing work.

To implement this approach all conventional office machines must be adapted to speak the same language, that is, a basic and direct compatibility, so to speak, between different types of machines and between machines of different manufacturers must be achieved. In this manner, data originating on one type of machine can be used later on other types of machines, without human reading, interpreting, and writing.

THE COMMON LANGUAGE LINK

The common language medium joining all machines utilized is the key to integrated data processing. The medium is acceptable to all the machines, permits each to perform its particular task, passes the result

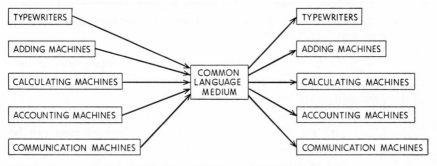

FIG. 15–8. The key to IDP is the common language medium.

on to the next machine which utilizes this information and passes on the accumulated data. In essence the group of conventional machines are connected into a single harmonious system. This idea is shown graphically by Figure 15–8.

There are three common language media in use today: (1) perforated tape, (2) punched card, and (3) edge-punched card. Whatever the medium, it is prepared simultaneously with the initial writing of the data. To reiterate, when a sales order is initially typed, a mechanism attached to the typewriter automatically prepares the medium. As stated above, this medium is then used to operate all subsequent machines required. Normally, each machine is equipped either to prepare the medium or "read" it, or both. Figure 15–9 illustrates a nondescriptive accounting machine connected to a tape perforator. In this application, the following is performed in one operation: a voucher is posted, the voucher check is computed and printed, and a

Courtesy: Burroughs Corp., Detroit

FIG. 15–9. An accounting machine to tape perforator installation providing perforated tape for subsequent integrated data processing.

voucher register is prepared. Integrated with this operation, a perforated tape is made for subsequent preparation of punched cards used in the processing and the analyzing of the data.

The most widely used perforated tape has five rows or channels of perforations, and for technical reasons this five-channel tape can be considered standard. Various combinations of holes in these five channels give a total of thirty-two symbols, including the twenty-six-letter alphabet, letters, figures, space, carriage return, line feed, and blank. A shift symbol provides for numerals. Figure 15–10 shows the five-channel code for perforated tape.

It must not be concluded that perforated tape is limited to five channels. Actually up to eight channels can be used; this permits more characters, check, and control symbols. A seven-channel tape, for example, would require all equipment using this tape to be so equipped for it. As long as the operations are within an enterprise, no particular difficulty would be present, but in dealing with outside firms, difficulty would be encountered because as stated above, the five-channel is standard and by far the type widely used.

Punched cards are also a medium for conveying data in an IDP arrangement. The data are put into punched cards which serve to operate all subsequent machines in the process.

The edge-punched card is, as the name suggests, punched along the edge of the card. The code used is that of the five-channel perforated

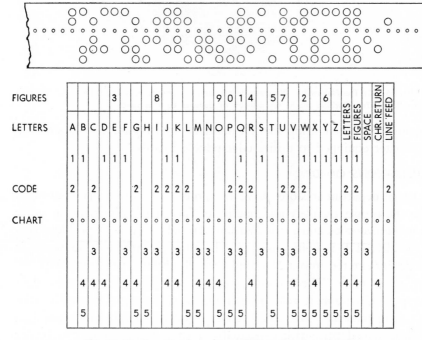

FIG. 15–10. *Top:* Five-channel tape. *Bottom:* Five-channel code.

tape. Cards are easy to handle and file; however, the information on one card is limited by its length, generally about seven inches. This is sufficient, however, for many purposes. Consider a manufacturer with a large number of customers. A punched-edge card is prepared in advance for each customer showing name and address. Also a separate card is prepared for each item sold, such as description, weight, and price. Upon receipt of a purchase order, the customer's name card, and the cards for each of the items ordered are pulled from the file and placed into the typewriter which automatically types the complete order. If it is desired, at the same time a perforated tape can be produced that can be used later for processing such as invoice preparing, label

Courtesy: Commercial Controls Corp., Rochester, N.Y.

FIG. 15–11. The Flexowriter Programatic prepares documents from unit edge-punched cards automatically. The machine reads, reproduces, or punches card or tape.

writing, and distributing market analysis data. Figure 15–11 shows a typewriter equipped to utilize edge-punched cards.

ILLUSTRATIONS OF IDP

Large department stores have the problem of inventory control so that the proper quantity and quality of each item is on hand in order to maximize sales and gross margins. To help solve this problem economically, IDP is being used. At the time a customer transaction is originally entered into a National Cash Register, a perforated tape recording is made. The recording shows whether cash or credit sale; salesperson's number; customer's number; description of merchandise including material, size, style, retail price; and the vendor's number. A prepunched price ticket—actually a small card about 2½ inches wide and 1 inch long—inserted in a unit called a Media Reader automatically starts the tape recorder and produces a detailed record of the item sold. Complete information on inventory control, by units, is thus accurately and economically provided. Figure 15–12 illustrates the machine, tape, and price ticket used for this purpose.

Communications companies are among the largest users of perforated tape. Under the old process, transmitting the message by hand was considerably slower than the capacity of the wire system. With the new process, the operator punches the message on tape and puts it through a transmitting device which sends the communication out at a high speed. On the receiving end a tape is perforated as the message comes in, and is subsequently inserted in a teletypewriter that types out the message.

Figure 15–13 illustrates an interesting application of IDP for a national manufacturer having four widely separated plants. All production scheduling, stock control, receiving and billing of customers' orders, release to manufacture, and routing of shipments are made from the centralized office located in a large city, different from that of any of the plants. All customers' orders sent direct to one of the plants by customers are immediately forwarded to the central office. Referring to Figure 15–13 and beginning at the left, the sequence is as follows. Customers' orders are received, edge-punched cards are pulled for cus-

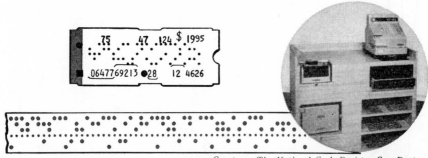

Courtesy: The National Cash Register Co., Dayton

FIG. 15–12. Machine, perforated tape, and price ticket used for effective unit inventory control by large retail outlets.

tomer name and for products ordered, and sent to Flexowriter with auxiliary tape perforator. Insertion of the edge-punched cards into the Flexowriter reader causes a six-part invoice to be typed automatically and two perforated tapes of the transaction. Tape No. 1 is sent to a teletypewriter which, by means of the tape, transmits the order to the proper plant. The tape made at the receiving unit of the plant is used to write a five-part Bill of Lading and packing slip. Tape No. 2 from the Flexowriter is used in a tape-to-punched-card converter. Two sets of punched cards are prepared, one set being used by general accounting accounts receivable, the other set for statistical analysis purposes and tabulated open orders file. Plant shipments are teletyped daily to central office. Upon notice of shipment, the invoice copies are distributed, the accounts receivable copy being sent to general accounting, upon receipt of which, the punched card of the transaction in their possession is pulled and sent to the tabulating where costs and other reports are prepared.

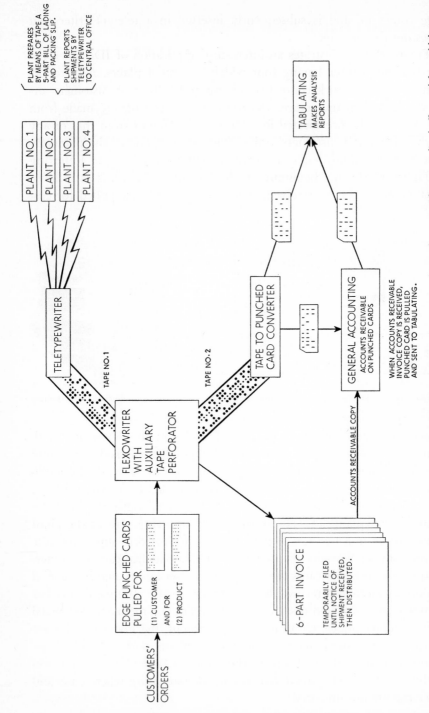

FIG. 15–13. Integrated data processing of order entry, shipping, and billing by a national manufacturer with a centralized office and four widely separated plants.

THE MANAGER'S ROLE IN OFFICE AUTOMATION

In concluding this chapter and at the risk of some repetition, several fundamentals of office automation from the managerial viewpoint will be cited. Whether it is the use of an electronic system or integrated data processing, or both, it is essential to keep in mind what is to be accomplished—what the real need of the enterprise is. This is fundamental. The better approach might be to analyze and know the needs thoroughly, then get the machines that will best do the required work. On the other hand, knowing the machines and what can be done with them can prove a satisfactory approach. With machine knowledge as a background it might be possible to adjust the procedures, the form and type of records to fit what the machine can perform most economically. However, in either event the real need of the enterprise in terms of its paper-work requirements should receive top priority.

Office automation stimulates thinking of office work as a whole, not just a component of it. All the papers and records should be considered, not simply the payroll records, or the inventory statistics, or the order-handling procedure. Automation is geared to volume. There should be a sufficient quantity of work—frequently this means grouping the components and performing the work for all. Elimination of waste and duplication are more easily attained when the entire office work picture is taken. Furthermore, office automation cuts across divisional lines—divisional in the sense of organization structure, problems, and vested interests. The maximum advantage of office organization is seldom realized by adhering to outworn and nonapplicable divisions.

The benefits of office automation are numerous, yet problems are entailed, and greater emphasis is placed on sound, competent office management. To adopt successful office automation requires comprehension, much thought and study. Difficult decisions must be made. Deeply intrenched habits and beliefs may have to be dispelled. The design of office papers may require revision, the retraining of office personnel may be needed, and an extensive educational job conducted with nonoffice personnel and customers. A committee with a member of each participating function represented can prove helpful as an educational means and for the collection of facts, exchange of ideas, and in the eventual steps of installing the new way of doing office work. But keep the committee mainly advisory; specific responsibility for determining the extent and kind of office automation in a given case should be vested in one operating executive. This helps provide leadership, co-ordination, and an enthusiastic, purposeful managerial effort. Office automation is an area in which a manager must manage.

QUESTIONS

1. Are you of the opinion that office automation will continue to increase? Justify your answer.
2. Comment on the following: "Machines in the office have resulted in many simple, repetitive, and monotonous office jobs. At one time, the employee had a variety of interrelated tasks, but now she is expected to do one simple task over and over again in order to utilize an office machine or piece of equipment."
3. Discuss the meaning and importance of automation in the office. Is it more important for the large or small office? Why?
4. Distinguish between each of the concepts in each of the following:
    a) Automation and mechanization.
    b) Magnetic drum and electronic brain.
    c) Magnetic tape and five-channel perforated tape.
    d) IDP and "computer language."
5. Do you feel that the economic aspects of office automation or the social aspects are of greater significance? Why?
6. In your opinion, does office automation tend to increase, decrease, or have no effect upon the caliber and status of the office manager? Elaborate on your answer.
7. Discuss programming as a requirement in the use of an office electronic system.
8. Do you agree with the following: "The over-all net result of office automation is voluminous records of all sorts processed quickly and accurately. But many fail to realize that too many records confuse rather than help and herein lies the essential problem of office automation as well as the major difference between the desirability of automation in the factory, but not in the office." Discuss.
9. Explain Figure 15–1 in your own words.
10. What effect do you believe office automation will have upon office managerial planning? Organizing? Controlling?
11. Describe an office procedure in which the use of edge-punched cards are used to advantage. Make your answer specific and complete.
12. Discuss the possibilities and a manner of using IDP for any series of office tasks with which you are familiar, such as (*a*) processing the purchase orders by a bookstore and its sales to students; (*b*) maintaining students' records in a large university; (*c*) handling the requisitions, purchases, and inventory records of a manufacturer; or (*d*) any selection of office work you care to make. Indicate the process now followed and also the suggested IDP way and why you feel IDP would prove beneficial in the particular application.

CASE PROBLEMS

CASE 15-1. PUBLIC UTILITY SUPPLIERS, INC.

This corporation, in business for over fifty years, manufactures and handles many different types of equipment and maintenance parts used primarily by public uutility companies. About 40 per cent of the business is from products manufactured by the company; the remaining 60 per cent is jobbed and warehoused by the company for some eighteen small manufacturers. General offices are in New York City, but all shipments to customers are made from the corporation's seven warehouses dispersed throughout the United States. Quite a few of the products have a high dollar value and are expensive to handle and ship. Service is important since usually the ordered items represent materials needed for emergency work.

The records of all sales transactions must be quite detailed. This requirement is brought about not only because the corporation wants to have complete information of its business but also because vendors to the corporation wish complete information concerning sales of their products. Also, the customers need complete data on their purchases to comply with government regulations concerning public utilities.

Currently, upon receipt of an order it is typed on a five-page multiple copy form. Copy No. 1 is retained by the general office; copies No. 2, 3, and 4 are airmailed to the warehouse nearest the customer's designated place of delivery; and copy No. 5 is mailed to the customer to acknowledge the order. The warehouse, upon shipment of the order, encloses copy No. 4 with the merchandise. Copy No. 2 is returned to general office, and copy No. 3 is retained by the warehouse for its records. Upon receipt of copy No. 2 by general offices, it is matched with its copy No. 1 which is then completed regarding date of shipment, pricing, etc., and mailed to customer. Copy No. 2 is retained by general offices for their records.

There is considerable writing required to designate the name of customer to be billed and the items of each order. The work, as now performed, requires a skilled and experienced order writer who receives a weekly pay of $104. Present rate is 7 orders written an hour. The average quantity is 382 orders a day. Study shows it takes about four days, on the average, from the time the order is received until it is shipped. There have been cases where copies No. 2, 3, and 4 were delayed in transit to the warehouse or were not sent to the nearest and proper warehouse.

The president of the company wants to mechanize the entire order-handling paper work and asks you for recommendations.

PROBLEMS:

1. What are your recommendations for this corporation?
2. Enumerate the important assumptions made in answering question No. 1.

CASE 15-2. THE ALLEN OFFICE EQUIPMENT COMPANY

Over one thousand different items in various sizes, models, and colors are sold to some 250 dealers by this company. In addition, about 25 national accounts

—usually very large companies—are sold direct by the Allen Office Equipment Company. Incoming orders are sent (1) to the sales department for review and amplification, (2) to the credit department for credit approval, and (3) to the order-billing department where they are first priced and extended—a calculating machine is used for this work—then typed on a six-copy form—this number being required for production scheduling, control, sales, etc. Typing includes such information as the name and address of customer, destination of shipment, date, requested date of shipment, and detailed description of items. This latter practice is followed to expedite shop handling and understanding by the customer. The written order is then checked; about 4 in every 100 are found to contain errors. Usually the writing can be corrected; rewriting is unnecessary. Five copies of the form are used by the company for the production and sales records created by the order handling.

One copy of the order is placed in a binder, and when the bill of lading arrives from the factory signifying order shipment, the copy is pulled and a four-copy invoice is typed including the name and address of customer, where, when, and how shipped, terms, freight charges, complete descriptions of items, and any notes of significance in the transaction. After proofing, the invoice copy is mailed to the customer, and the remaining three copies are sent to the sales, cost, and billing departments, respectively. The six employees in the order-billing department are excellent workers and complete 215 orders and invoices a day.

PROBLEMS:

1. Describe in detail how office automation might be applied to the company's order-billing department.

2. What action should the company take? Justify your answer enumerating specific advantages.

Chapter · 16

Planning of Office Space—
Location and Facilities

Past experience should be a guide post, not a hitching post.
—D. W. WILLIAMS

Up TO this point the chapters on planning have
dealt with the work, the process, the skill of the personnel required,
and the equipment and machines that will be needed. All of these
must be brought together into an effective physical arrangement so
that the work can be performed efficiently and managed properly. In
other words, suitable housing, physical surroundings, and arrangement of the necessary office equipment and machines must be planned
and provided.

TRENDS IN OFFICE SPACE LOCATION

Since about 1945, the trend in office space locations has been characterized by three distinct developments. The first is the moving of
offices to the suburbs of large cities. This is due not only to the relocating of industrial plants, with their offices on the outer edges of
cities, but also to the relocating of office enterprises in suburban areas.
Among the advantages cited are cheaper rents, ample room for expansion, closeness of adequate work force, and a pleasanter, cleaner
place in which to work. However, there are also disadvantages, including the difficulty for executives of attending important meetings
in the downtown area, lack of desirable eating places for employees,
and inconvenience to frequent callers—such as sales representatives—
who may be necessary for the continuance of the enterprise.

The second development is the construction of new office buildings
in the business areas of various cities. In some areas, many new office
buildings have been erected, especially in regions that are enjoying a

basic growth in economic activities. However, in a considerable number of localities, relatively few new office buildings have been constructed recently.

This leads to the third development, the remodeling of existent or old office buildings. The approach has been to modernize the exterior and public areas and services, especially elevators. In this development, relative costs have been an important consideration, for in the early 1920's, a building could be constructed for about one third the cost of a comparable-size building today. By remodeling old buildings, however, many of the new building features can be achieved at lower cost.

SPACE PLANNING

The term "space planning" is used to designate the determination of office space; adoption of an area for specific office work; cognizance of favorable and useful features as well as the drawbacks of a given space for the specific office work; provision of adequate light, proper colors, ventilation, and noise control; and the effective arrangement or space location of all physical units.

Space planning is a broad and important subject. It is being given far more attention and emphasis than in the past, and rightly so because it constitutes a major portion of planning work, represents a somewhat tangible and observable aspect of planning, and affects the management of the paper work. Improper space utilization results in hidden and excessive costs both in direct operation and in maintenance. Furthermore, inflexibility of space is quite likely to result if not planned.

INTEGRATED SPACE PLANNING

For beneficial results it is advisable to take an over-all viewpoint of the various components making up space planning. Serious defects creep in when a piecemeal approach is followed. To illustrate, the location, size, and shape of an office area affects the type and amount of lighting to be provided. The arrangement of the equipment and machines is related to the space utilized. And the physical surroundings provided should harmonize with the units of equipment and machines.

THE INTEGRATED OFFICE

In fact, the over-all viewpoint should include not only the components of space planning but also that of other office planning as well, including the work to be done, the process adopted, the equipment and machines used, and the personnel to do it. And all these considerations should be integrated. This follows because they all exist in the plan for one main purpose—to accomplish the office work satisfactorily.

The integrated office is harmonious and unified toward a common objective. The people, materials, equipment, machines, processes, space, and surroundings are co-ordinated to accomplish the work with a maximum of satisfaction and service, and a minimum of energy and cost. A particular type of desk is provided at a designated area because this location helps most in accomplishing the required work. The chair, the color and treatment of the walls, the location of the office area, the facilities of the space, and the machines utilized all have a common ultimate purpose. Office planning should integrate their separate contributions so that an effective co-ordinated program is attained and unified help is provided in performing the office work.

The integrated office combines the dual purpose of beauty and efficiency. An office can serve practical needs, yet possess distinctiveness and impressive appearance. To the office employee, the work and how it is accomplished are important as a unit. It is well to remember that helpful, workable surroundings make up good design and is never out of style. If an office is workably correct, it can be aesthetically pleasing. In addition, the integrated office is flexible because it is built around the needs of the individual and the work performed.

FUNCTIONAL ANALYSIS FOR SPACE PLANNING[1]

Any office space should help the employee using it do his job better. For this purpose careful study of the space and its use by the individual firm is recommended. To assist in these efforts, functional analysis can be followed. Essentially this is a data-gathering, question-asking approach so that effective space utilization can be evolved into a plan. It includes the type of information to be gathered and digested before calling in the architect or construction engineer.

A list of questions to facilitate space functional analysis is shown in Figure 16–1. This list will be found complete for most studies, but questions can be added or deleted as the situation suggests. They need not be asked in the order given, but it should be observed that as a group they apply to a building, to a space within a building, or to an area within a given space.

---

[1] Mr. William I. Sohl, Business Procedures Department, Inland Steel Company, Chicago, provided expert help and suggestions in this chapter on the subjects of Functional Analysis for Space Planning and of Facilities of the Building Space.

Actually, space functional analysis stresses the use or function to which the space will be put in the normal course of handling the work. But as stated in the previous planning chapters, this functional approach is also used in determining the type of work, the equipment, and the machines. In any event, the work required to be done and the

---

QUESTIONS TO ASK DURING
FUNCTIONAL ANALYSIS FOR SPACE PLANNING

1. What functions are to be performed respectively by what departments, sections, and individuals?
2. What number of employees must be provided for (1) today, and (2) a specified future date?
3. What office equipment, machines, and space does each employee require—based on the functions performed and the standards followed?
4. Does the office space satisfy major location considerations?
5. Will adequate building services be provided—including rest rooms, stairways, elevators, water, and fire protection?
6. Are there adequate ducts for ventilation and also for electrical wiring to meet the needs of office machines, light fixtures, telephones, and intercommunication systems?
7. Will the area provide or can it be made to provide effective physical working conditions, i.e., adequate light, proper color, air circulation, and control of noise?
8. Are the building code requirements known and taken into account?
9. What group and what individual job functions are related and should be located near each other?
10. Does the present grouping of activities give a good flow of office work?
11. What office service groups are intended to serve all other office units?
12. Do the costs involved appear justified?

FIG. 16–1.

---

use made of the space, equipment, and machines are important criterion. Figure 16–2 shows an interesting example of this as applied to a private office. The "before" pictures illustrate the drab, nonfunctional office. The old desk without overhang top did not lend itself to formal conferences required daily, and the old sofa kept visitors at a distance for informal conferences. The "after" views show the functionalization, comfort, and warmth supplied. The L-shaped desk placed along one wall provides ample work, storage, and conference areas. Informal conversational groupings can be held away from the desk

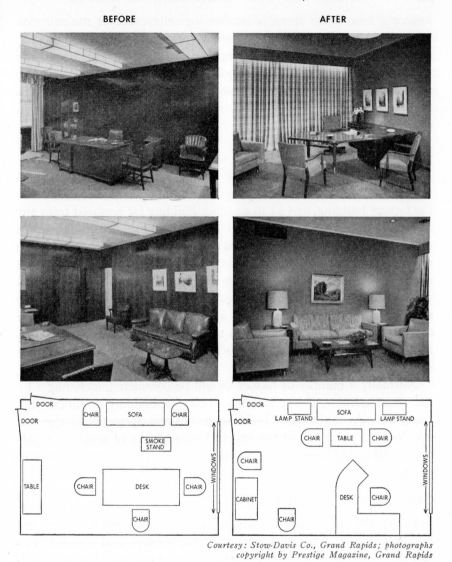

Courtesy: Stow-Davis Co., Grand Rapids; photographs
copyright by Prestige Magazine, Grand Rapids

FIG. 16–2. The before-and-after views of a private office, showing the improvements and better design brought about by space planning guided by functional analysis.

and in pleasant surroundings. Proper lighting, draperies, and carpeting were added to complete the dignified yet functional office.

The selection of space is another example demonstrating the fundamental importance of space functional analysis. Referring again to Figure 16–1, question No. 2 of the list deals with the amount of space required now and in the future. The answer to this question should be determined and used as a guide in selecting the space. That is, knowing how much space is needed logically precedes the selection from available sites. The work resolves into determining the amount of space for each employee, taking into account the equipment and tools required, prestige factors, and space standards for such items as aisle widths, work areas for files, and spacing between desks.[2] For this purpose a detailed listing is beneficial and helps avoid costly errors in estimates.

LOCATING THE OFFICE

Most offices are located in one of the following places: (1) in the factory building, (2) in a separate building adjacent to or near the factory building, or (3) in an office building far removed from any factory building. In the first two cases, the office location depends upon the factory location, which is usually determined with reference to factory needs only. However, in the third case, the office location can be determined in line with the particular needs of the individual office. For any of these three cases, the office space within the prescribed or selected building must also be determined. True a choice of space within a given building is not always available, but study can be conducted to confirm the suitability of a given space or to select a space within a selected building.

Normally a number of factors should be considered, including (1) the characteristics of the building, (2) the building facilities, (3) the proximity of the office building to business factors, (4) the cost involved, (5) stability of tenants, (6) adaptability of space, (7) natural lighting and ventilation provided, and (8) freedom from dirt and noise.

CHARACTERISTICS OF THE BUILDING

Under this heading are included the general appearance of the building, its size, reputation, age, available services, and technical factors. In considering these things decisions are made whether the building is modern or old, whether the building name is in good repute, whether the name and address are easy to pronounce and remember, and whether the building is well advertised. The building services including the elevator service, janitor service, and night protection should also be considered.

An important technical factor is the allowable floor live load. At least 75 pounds per square foot are needed for office operations. A value of 100 pounds is desirable for complete versatility of layout. Also the floor-to-ceiling heights must be taken into account. A minimum

---

[2] Space standards are discussed in Chapter 18.

of 8 feet is usually recommended; however, for large open areas, 10–12 feet may be appropriate. Low ceilings create a feeling of congestion and make the office difficult to ventilate; high ceilings make lighting, noise-reducing, and heating efforts difficult. Furthermore, columnar spacing must be considered for it affects office layout, especially the location of main partitions that are joined to columns. A spacing of 20 × 20 feet or more is acceptable; spans less than 18 feet are normally unsatisfactory for efficient office space. The need for moving partitions, adding offices, and accommodating new pieces of office equipment is best met by maintaining flexibility in the office layout. Designs specifying alternating 4½-foot windows and piers, similar to that of the RCA Building in New York City, or the 5-foot 2-inch center to center of window sections as in the Inland Steel Building, Chicago, provide exceptional flexibility. See Figure 16–3.

THE BUILDING FACILITIES

The meaning of building facilities is sometimes not clearly understood. Normally the term includes any device or feature incorporated in or attached to the building which device or feature assists in using the space with convenience and efficiency. In brief, a building facility must be fastened to the building, or installation is required to finish the building. Building facilities include a long list of items among which are entranceways, elevators, stairways, electrical and telephone facilities and outlets, wiring arrangements, heating and ventilating ducts, air conditioning, hallways, columnar spacing, janitor closets, water accessibility, noise control features, means of fire protection, and other fixed facilities. To highlight the importance of building facilities, a brief discussion follows of telephone outlets, wiring needs, and cellular steel floors.

Telephone Outlets. Modern office space planning should include an adequate number of properly located telephone outlets. This requirement for telephone service should be developed by space planners, equipment people, or telephone company personnel. Knowledge of the building facilities and of the functional needs of the persons using the office, supplies the basic information. Figure 16–4 shows portions of work sheets to assist in determining telephone requirements and locations. Without this planning, it may subsequently be found that telephones have to be changed, outlets are incorrectly located, and unsightly conduits must be attached to the floors and ceilings.

Wiring Needs. Adequate wiring facilities is one of the big considerations in building facilities today. Separate runways are used for (1) low voltage including telephone and communication systems, and

Photo by Hedrich-Blessing, Chicago

FIG. 16–3. The Inland Steel Building in Chicago. Among the many architectural features are approximately 10,000 square feet of clear floor space on each floor—no columnar obstructions, each floor suspended from external columns, zone control heating, floor-to-ceiling windows, electronic elevators, and maximum flexibility of space utilization.

(2) high voltage for normal electrical current as well as that of higher voltages. For electrical current many office buildings are wired for about 2 watts per square foot of floor area, but with the increase in the amount of light and the power necessary to operate electric office

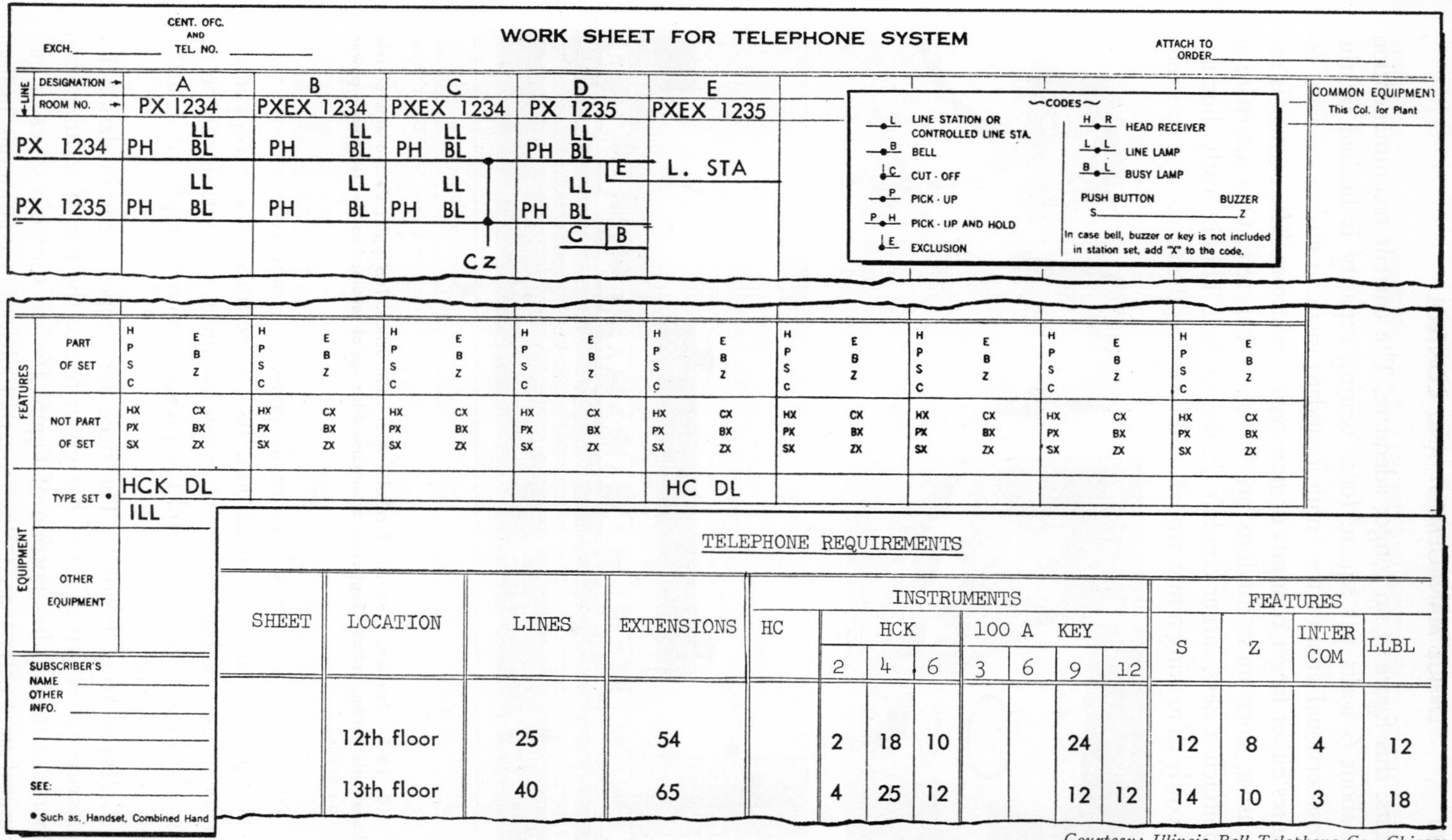

WORK SHEET FOR TELEPHONE SYSTEM

EXCH. _____ CENT. OFC. AND TEL. NO. _____ ATTACH TO ORDER

LINE DESIGNATION → ROOM NO. ↓	A PX 1234	B PXEX 1234	C PXEX 1234	D PX 1235	E PXEX 1235	COMMON EQUIPMENT This Col. for Plant
PX 1234	PH LL BL	PH LL BL	PH LL BL	PH LL BL	L. STA	
PX 1235	PH LL BL	PH	PH LL BL	PH LL BL	E	
			Cz	C B		

CODES:
- L LINE STATION OR CONTROLLED LINE STA.
- B BELL
- C CUT-OFF
- P PICK-UP
- P-H PICK-UP AND HOLD
- E EXCLUSION
- H-R HEAD RECEIVER
- L LINE LAMP
- B BUSY LAMP
- S PUSH BUTTON
- BUZZER —?

In case bell, buzzer or key is not included in station set, add "X" to the code.

	H P S C	E B Z	CX BX ZX
PART OF SET	HX PX SX		
NOT PART OF SET	HX PX SX		

TYPE SET • HCK DL ILL

OTHER EQUIPMENT HC DL

• Such as, Handset, Combined Hand

TELEPHONE REQUIREMENTS

SHEET LOCATION	LINES	EXTENSIONS	HC	HCK 2	HCK 4	HCK 6	100 A 3	100 A 6	100 A 9	100 A 12	KEY	S	Z	INTER COM	LLBL
12th floor	25	54		2	18	10			24			12	8	4	12
13th floor	40	65		4	25	12			12	12		14	10	3	18

INSTRUMENTS: HCK, 100 A, KEY FEATURES

FIG. 16–4. Telephone work sheets used in space planning.

Courtesy: Illinois Bell Telephone Co., Chicago

units, this figure is no longer adequate. The current recommendation is about 6 watts per square foot. Wiring capacity is limited by the cross-sectional area of the conduit, and to increase wiring capacity requires either larger conduits or new-type conductors. The former is expensive, since most conduits are buried in concrete. One alternate is to attach a new, larger conduit on the surface. This is costly, but not so costly as making a new trough and recessing the conduit in concrete.

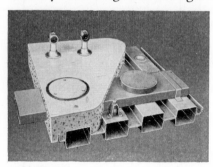 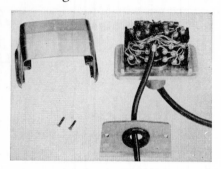

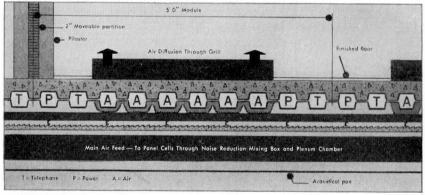

FIG. 16–5. *Top left:* Close-up of cellular floor construction. *Top right:* Components of telephone outlet fitting. *Bottom:* Suggested arrangement for use of cellular floor for telephone, power, and air needs.

Recent developments have made possible a new type of wire with very thin but effecitve insulation. Its use permits greater copper capacity in the conduit; hence, in many instances, old wiring can be replaced with this new type and the present conduits employed. Usually this is an economical practice.

Cellular Steel Floors. The need for proper accommodation for quantities of electrical wires has given rise to the use of cellular steel floors. At the top left portion of Figure 16–5 is shown a series of galvanized steel cells spaced close together providing continuous in-floor passageways throughout the entire floor area. Various cross-sectional areas and spacings of the cells are available. These steel cells serve as a subfloor over which the concrete is poured. However, before pouring concrete, steel headerducts are fastened directly on top of the steel cellular flooring and at right angles to the cells. Headerducts provide passageways from the main distribution points to the cells. Connections between headerducts and cells are made at access units which are spaced as required. The illustration shows the removable top of the access unit featuring a simplified three-screw leveling design permitting exact adjustment to the finished floor level. Outlet fittings connect the cell to the desired point of use. In other words, the main feeder lines in the headerducts are connected to the desired distribution lines in the cells from whence the proper distribution line is connected to an outlet. In the illustration two outlet fittings are shown. Easily installed anywhere along the cell length, they are available in many designs to meet various functional requirements. For example, in the top-right illustration of Figure 16–5 is shown the components of a compact aluminum outlet fitting for telephone service; it features three connecting blocks with a capacity of fifteen pairs or thirty separate telephone wires. Additional flexibility is made available by cellular steel floors in that via conduit underneath the cells, additional wire connections between designated points can be utilized.

However, cellular steel floors provide raceways for purposes other than electrification. The dry, unobstructed, underfloor ducts can be used for heating and air conditioning, as well as other uses. A gain in usable floor and window areas is among the outstanding advantages of the cellular steel floor design. The bottom illustration of Figure 16–5 suggests a combination of air, electrical, and telephone cells.

PROXIMITY OF OFFICE BUILDING TO BUSINESS FACTORS

When an office-building location is to be selected, the following factors should be given careful consideration because office efficiency is greatly influenced by them.

Customers and Others in Same Business. The proximity of the building to those who are in almost daily contact with the office is a very important consideration. In the first place, closeness to customers is generally considered advantageous. This is especially true when personal interviews and associations are frequent. However, in those cases where most activities can be handled by telephone or by correspondence, the importance of proximity to customers is greatly diminished.

Second, closeness to others in the same line is usually considered sound business practice. This closeness of association encourages discussions of common problems among occupants, helps simplify the problems of the building manager, and adds to the convenience of customers and clients dealing with occupants of the building. There is, for example, a tendency for offices of financial houses, law firms, real estate firms, insurance agencies, and public utilities to locate in buildings in the financial district. On the other hand, offices of physicians, dentists, and advertising agencies are frequently found in the shopping districts. Also, in many cities specialized buildings to accommodate particular types of business offices are available; for instance, motion-picture offices may be located in the "Film Exchange Building," grain offices in the "Grain Exchange Building," and physicians' offices in the "Medical Building." It is interesting to observe, however, that with the exception of medical buildings, these specialized buildings become, in time, occupied by a good proportion of general tenants.

Transportation Facilities. In the selection of an office location, it is imperative to determine that the location is served by adequate transportation facilities. Convenient and low-cost means of getting to and from the building must be available not only to employees but also to outside representatives, visitors, and delivery and messenger men. Out-of-the-way places necessitating transferring and long waits for streetcars, busses, trains, or taxicabs are distinct disadvantages. As a result of inconvenient transportation facilities, the enterprise might suffer unnecessarily—frequent association with others in the same business would be limited, and the personnel problem of recruiting and maintaining employees would be greatly increased.

Shopping Centers, Restaurants, and Hotels. Convenience to shopping centers might well contribute to the growth of the business. For example, domestic financing enterprises have found it helpful to locate in or near the shopping areas; medical doctors likewise find that shopping areas are good locations. The availability of restaurants is another consideration. Employees like to have a selection of handy eating places for noon lunch, or for evening meals when overtime work is necessary. A lack of eating places might necessitate the providing of a company cafeteria, dining room, or place where employees can eat their lunches. Also, nearness to hotels is, in many cases, a distinct advantage in the location of an office. In cases where many out-of-town representatives call at the office, the advantage of close proximity to hotels is apparent.

Mail Facilities. The handling of incoming and outgoing mail is of great importance in any office. Good mail facilities should always be secured and given prime consideration in the selection of an office location. Frequent pickups and deliveries with convenient accessibility to a post office can contribute very materially to the operating efficiency.

THE COST INVOLVED

The cost of office space is of cardinal importance; however, it should never be considered the sole basis for selection of the office location or space, but it should always be considered along with the other location factors discussed. The universal unit for expressing the cost of office space is dollars per square foot of floor area per year. To illustrate, assume an office measures 30×40 feet and the rental is $5.00 per square foot. The cost per year is:

$$30 \times 40 \times \$5.00 = \$6,000$$

or, on a monthly basis:

$$\frac{\$6,000}{12} = \$500.$$

The annual cost per square foot varies with many factors, such as the size of the city and general business conditions; but in order to gain some idea of the range in rates, a high of around $5.00 to a low of around $0.25 per square foot can be used. The top figure represents space in the better location and building, while the latter may be converted factory space in a relatively poor location. The following data indicate further some of the spread in rates:

Type of Enterprise	Rate per Square Foot per Year
Financial houses	$5.50
Advertising agencies	5.00
Real estate	4.00
Law firms	4.00
Physicians and dentists	4.00
Insurance agencies	3.50
Public utilities	3.00

The square foot cost usually includes many services such as air conditioning, running water, wall maintenance, and elevator service. In many respects the price is subject to negotiation as to what is included.[3]

STABILITY OF THE TENANTS

It is generally considered advantageous to locate an office in a building where the tenants are stable. Frequent moves by tenants in and

---

[3] See also p. 319 for discussion of provision of Lease.

out and alterations are undesirable from the viewpoint of solid, substantial enterprises. Various studies seem to indicate that real estate companies, law firms, and financial houses are among the most stable. Their office needs remain fairly constant, and they seem disposed to remain in one location for relatively long periods. In some cases their tenure in the same location extends for twenty-five years and longer. In contrast, manufacturer's agents and advertising agencies tend to move more frequently. However, many of these remain in the same location for ten or fifteen years, and while this is relatively less, it still reflects a strong element of stability.

ADAPTABILITY OF THE SPACE

The space chosen should permit suitable arrangement for the various office divisions; it should also be of adequate size and shape to permit the best arrangement of office equipment and machines. For the most part rectangular shapes are best, and where requirements permit, occupancy of an entire floor is usually preferred. Individual circumstances alter cases, but normally it is more economical to travel 10 feet vertically, i.e., between floors, than 150 feet horizontally, i.e., on the same floor. As already discussed in this chapter, the space should be adaptable from the viewpoint of building facilities such as heating and ventilating ducts, adequate soil pipe, water, and electrical wiring.

The difference between "gross space" and "usable space" should be noted. Usually one pays for gross space in some instances called "rental area," which is the area measured between the inside surfaces of the outer boundaries. It includes areas for columns, projections, pilasters, and window arrangements necessary to the building. The usable space is the effective area which can be used for the office. Frequently 10 per cent of the gross space cannot be used, and in some buildings the column locations further add to the uneconomical use of space rendering the space efficiency to as low as 65 per cent. The heavy black portion in the top illustration of Figure 16–6 shows space with low usability. Some of this can be utilized by ingenious arrangements of files or odd pieces, but much will be unusable. Modern buildings omit columnar obstructions on the inner face of outside building walls, and the columns are spaced to permit effective subdivision of the space. This is shown by the bottom portion of Figure 16–6.

As stated earlier in this chapter, the space selected should permit future alteration and office expansion. Attention to future requirements means more than just securing space greater than that needed for current requirements. Consideration must be given to where and how future changes will alter present space provisions. Usually future considerations are taken care of either by leasing entire floors and subleasing what is not now required or by securing options on adjoining areas. In any event it is desirable to provide space arrangements to accommodate a minimum of five years of future expectation.[4]

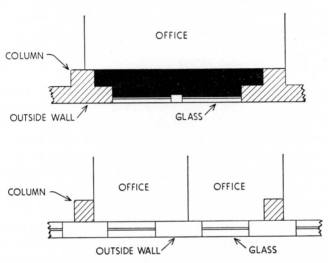

FIG. 16-6. *Top:* The columnar spacing and inside wall offsets make economical use of space difficult. The solid black area has low usability. *Bottom:* Modern building columnar and window arrangement emphasizes maximum usable space and facilitates subdivision of space.

NATURAL LIGHTING AND VENTILATING PROVIDED

Lighting is a significant factor in the selection of any office space. Most office work is very exacting, and the space selected normally should provide the maximum of available daylight. Exposures facing the north are generally preferred, as northern light is of a steady and soft type. Eastern exposures are next in preference, followed in order by southern and western exposures. Normally the outside wall areas should utilize a maximum of glass area and be not less than one fifth of the floor area. Windows extending almost to the ceiling permit a maximum amount of natural light to reach the inner areas of the floor space.

It must be added, however, that in addition to daylight, artificial light is usually required. For this purpose adequate fixtures, electrical outlets, and lighting provisions must be provided. Agreement on the

[4] Albert K. Wilson, "The Design, Construction, and Maintenance of Office Buildings" (Philadelphia: The NOMA Conference Proceedings), 1949, p. 49.

amount of artificial light to be provided and the cost of installing and maintaining the necessary fixtures is a further important consideration.[5]

It is imperative that an office be well ventilated. Careful observation should be made of the prospective space area to determine if adequate ventilation is possible. Spaces with few windows, a small number of openings to air ducts, low ceilings, and window openings on inside courts normally do not provide sufficient ventilation.

FREEDOM FROM DIRT AND NOISE

Certain elements are extremely disturbing to office workers, and these elements should be avoided whenever possible. Dirt, smoke, and soot are very objectionable, and the possibility of their presence in an office location and area should be taken into account. Street noises are very bothersome and interfere with efforts of mental concentration. In addition, noise and vibrations from the operation of machines and equipment are also disturbing and should be avoided if at all possible.

LOCATION AND SPACE SELECTION CHART

In most cases it is difficult to evaluate all the above factors and give the proper weight to each in order to determine the best location and space selection. To overcome these obstacles a location and space selection chart like that shown in Figure 16–7 can be used. The selection factors are listed on the left, and beneath each factor are statements designed to help identify the intended meaning of the factor. Opposite each factor is a series of numbers indicating the range of points or values which have been assigned to that factor.

The factors and weights shown in the illustration are suggestive only. In an actual case, the factors selected and the weights given each one are determined by the evaluator. However, to make comparisons among different possible locations valid, the same chart is used for evaluating the several sites under consideration.

In the chart shown, the values or points assigned to each factor are not equal. The maximum for factor 1 is 24 points; the maximum for factor 2 is 60 points; etc. This simply means that, based on the evaluator's judgment and experience, the relative value of the factors are of different weight or importance.

---

[5] Office lighting is fully discussed in the next chapter.

	Excellent	Good	Fair	Poor
1. Characteristics of the building: Does the building have a favorable appearance, good name and address that are easy to pronounce and remember, and adequate floor load and ceiling height?	24	18	12	6
2. Building facilities: Are entranceways, wiring arrangements, outlets, ducts, fire protection, and other *fixed* facilities adequate?	60	45	30	15
3. The proximity of office building to business factors: Is the building near to customers, to transportation facilities, to shopping centers, restaurants, hotels, and to mail facilities?	44	33	22	11
4. The cost involved: Is the rate reasonable and in keeping with competitive prices?	40	30	20	10
5. Stability of tenants: Do tenants of the building tend to stay put (are moving and transferring the exception)?	20	15	10	5
6. Adaptability of space: Is the space adaptable to the needs of the office? Is there room for expansion?	60	45	30	15
7. Natural lighting and ventilating provided: Is the exposure on the north, east, south, or west? Does it have large glass areas? Do windows face the street or open lots? Are ceilings high?	28	21	14	7
8. Freedom from dirt and noise: Is the general area free from dirt and noise? Is the area itself clean and quiet?	24	18	12	6
Maximum total	300	225	150	75

FIG. 16–7. Chart used to determine location and space selection.

ILLUSTRATING THE USE OF CHART

Suppose five possible office spaces are being considered. To evaluate the various spaces, the chart is used. Assume the total selection points for each location are as follows:

Space	Total Points
Location No. 1	156
Location No. 2	243
Location No. 3	178
Location No. 4	145
Location No. 5	206

Based on these data the decision would be to select location No. 2 with a total of 243 points.

BUILDING CODE REQUIREMENTS

It should be noted that construction and remodeling work is subject to building code requirements which specify the design and the type of construction that is permitted. For example, use of certain materials may be forbidden for certain uses, or stated design principles must be followed for certain structural parts. Requiring all buildings to have at least two entranceways, one on each of two sides of a building, may be included in a building code, the purpose being to reduce the fire hazard. Code requirements are enacted and enforced usually by local government.

Before launching a space planning project it is well to consult the building code requirements. Frequently some flexibility is provided in the code—certain alternates and choices being designated. Portions of some building codes have remained the same for a number of years, while others have been modified from time to time. Keeping informed and up to date on the requirements can prove very helpful.

OWN OR RENT

In most discussions regarding the selection of office space the question usually arises: "Is it better to own or to rent?" This question involves basic policy and can actually be answered only by the top managers. Certain considerations should be made, however, and these are indicated in the discussion following.

Advantages of Owning Office Building. The advantages to an enterprise of owning its own office building can be listed as follows:

1. The building can be tailor-made for, or remodeled within technical limits to meet, the particular needs of the enterprise. However, needs change, and sometimes the building becomes obsolete or at least not as convenient as first planned

2. There is an element of prestige for an enterprise in owning its own office building. The name of the enterprise can be used for the building, and the publicity value can be quite high.

3. There is a possibility of income from renting out a portion of the building. This procedure allows also for flexibility in future expansion.

4. Permanency of location is obtained. This might lend stability to the enterprise and, in addition, permit continuity of desired name and street address.

5. A relatively safe investment is afforded. An office building represents an equity in which the capital invested is fairly secure.

Advantages of Renting Office Buildings. The main advantages of renting an office building are:

1. Freedom of top managers from care and worry in connection with ownership. The problems of building maintenance and repairs are avoided.

2. Finances of the enterprise are more flexible. Large amounts of capital are not tied up in one relatively long-time investment. The renter is free to invest any surplus in the most productive channels.

3. Changes in office location can usually be made more freely. The enterprise is not wedded to one location.

4. A satisfactory arrangement is provided for the small enterprise whose office requirements are not elaborate.

The "sale-and-lease-back" arrangement is being heard more and more frequently. This describes a transaction in which an investor buys a building from a seller and in the same transaction gives the seller a long-term lease on the building. The seller continues to occupy the building, pays rent, and is free of the responsibility of building upkeep and operation. For the seller, the deciding issue to enter into a "sale-and-lease-back" arrangement is his financial position, especially that of taxes.

PROVISIONS OF LEASE

When space is rented, the legal right of a tenant to occupy a given office space is usually consummated by means of a lease. Actually, *a lease is a form of contract by which one party conveys real estate to another party for a period of time at a specified compensation.*

A lease is in effect for a stated period of time. Office leases usually run for one, three, five, ten, or twenty years, and in some instances longer. Payments are usually made monthly, with the first payment due at the time the lease is executed; this first payment customarily applies as rent for the first month or stated period. Sometimes an advance of three months' rent is made at the beginning of the lease period, and this is held by the lessor as evidence of good faith and intentions on the part of the lessee.

It is well to remember that a lease is a legal document; and in dealing with matters pertaining to leases, the services of a competent lawyer are advisable. It is well, however, that the office manager has a general knowledge of a lease, especially of its more common provisions.

A lease may contain many different agreements or clauses. The aggregate depends upon the type and value of the real estate involved and also upon the number of subjects upon which the lessor and the lessee believe definite written agreement is advisable. A lease can be specially written, or it can be a standard form. Normally the lessor provides janitor service, heat, running water, elevator service, window shades, and fire-protection apparatus. On the other hand, the lessee usually provides floor coverings, partitions, Venetian blinds, awnings, ventilators and fans, and intercommunication telephones. In addition, the lessor usually has the right to change the name and street address of building, designate all sources for sign painting, ice, towel service, and the like, have passkeys to the premises, and enter the premises at all reasonable hours for inspection, repairs, and alterations.

QUESTIONS

1. Discuss the trends in office location.
2. What is your understanding of an "integrated office"? Elaborate on your answer.
3. Define each of the following: (a) space planning, (b) gross space of an office area, (c) building facility, and (d) functional analysis for space planning.
4. Various office spaces may be classified as undesirable because of certain factors involved. Discuss briefly some points that may determine that a space is not acceptable.
5. Do you agree with the following, "An office can be functionally correct and at the same time be aesthetically pleasing." Explain your answer.
6. In your own words, explain the bottom illustration in Figure 16–5.
7. Discuss the consideration for telephone outlets and electrical wiring in modern office space planning.
8. Evaluate the statement: "Closeness to others in the same line of business is usually considered unsound business practice."
9. Name six questions that can be asked in making a functional analysis for space planning.
10. Select two office buildings in the community in which you now live and make a survey to determine their suitability with respect to—
    a) The characteristics of the building,
    b) The cost involved,

c) The adaptability of the space,

d) Freedom from dirt and noise,

for each of the following prospective tenants:

a) a sales representative requiring desk space and a room for small samples.

b) an insurance office requiring a total of about 1,800 sq. ft. including a reception room, a room about 15 × 25 feet, for salesmen, and general office space.

c) a medical doctor who needs a reception room, an examining room, and if possible, a small room to one side for his records and library.

Write your results in a suitable form using a sentence outline type of presentation.

11. Enumerate and briefly discuss the major reasons why a company may prefer to rent rather than own its office building.

12. What is a lease and what advantages does it provide for the lessee? For the lessor?

CASE PROBLEMS

CASE 16–1.   THE BOULEVARD BANK

The Boulevard Bank is located in a fast-growing suburb, east of the city of Los Angeles. In 1946 this bank erected a new modern two-story building with ample space and modern equipment to take care of the needs of its customers. The building faces 75 feet on the main street of town and is 150 feet in depth. It does not have a complete second floor but a balcony only, extending all around and designed for small commercial offices. The basement is used for the bank's safety deposit vaults, storage space, washrooms, and building maintenance equipment.

Today the bank has outgrown its present building facilities. More space is definitely needed if the bank's growth is to continue. The bank's managers are conservative and efficient. The bank is financially very strong. To date the managers have not arrived at a decision aimed to solve the problem of expansion.

In an effort to gather some basic facts, the president of the bank has obtained the following information:

1. Additional office space believed needed is 5,600 square feet.

2. No ground is available for purchase or lease on either side of the bank's present building.

3. An additional floor to the bank's present building cannot be made due to the design of the building.

4. Present bank building is owned by bank and is free of debt.

5. Available office spaces in buildings within 200 yards of the bank building include (1) 6,000 square feet at $2.00 per square foot on a ten-year lease basis, and (2) 10,200 square feet at $1.85 per square foot on a five-year lease basis.

6. Size of balcony space in present bank building is 4,000 square feet.

7. Estimated cost of remodeling balcony for bank's use is $8,500.

8. To demolish present bank building and erect a new three-story bank building the cost is estimated at $750,000.

9. Annual rentals from occupants of balcony offices are $10,820.

PROBLEMS:

1. Discuss the arguments for, as well as those against, the erecting of a new building by the bank.

2. Are you of the opinion that the bank should seek a new location? Why?

3. What decision do you suggest the bank managers take?

CASE 16–2.   ATWATER, DIETZ, FITZSIMMONS, AND MURPHY, INC.

Atwater, Dietz, Fitzsimmons, and Murphy, Inc., is a large, prominent advertising agency with main offices in a large eastern city in the United States. ADF and M, as it is commonly called, has a number of nationally known clients and enjoys an enviable reputation for creating highly successful advertising.

Mr. J. Elsworth Fitzsimmons, vice-president and general manager of the agency, feels that the agency is growing but not prospering. It is not, for example, a well co-ordinated, orderly type of operation, but a group of separate units, each housed in overcrowded, scattered locations throughout several floors of a centrally located office building. In all, a total of 51,750 square feet are rented at an average rate of $3.75 per square foot. The present lease expires in ten months and can be renewed for either one or five years at rates to be determined at the time of renewal.

Mr. Fitzsimmons is in favor of relocating in a newer office building where the impression upon clients and visitors would be more in keeping with the quality of work performed by the agency. It is possible to acquire such a site consisting of 60,000 square feet on a five-year lease basis for $4.20 per square foot. The area constitutes five adjacent floors of the building. The lessor will install and pay for new lighting fixtures throughout the entire area. The contemplated site is not as conveniently located as the present one. But Mr. Fitzsimmons points out that the newer building is only about an eight-minute walk from the central business area and offers fairly good parking facilities.

The controller, John B. Goddard, believes that if the agency moves it ought to move into a building of its own. He contends that the present basis, from lease to lease, is insecure and there is no return on the money paid to occupy the space. Estimates secured by him give the cost of a new building, exclusive of land, to meet the company's needs as about $1,000,000. Expenses for taxes, heat, light, interest on mortgage and depreciation would be roughly $100,000 a year. This would mean a saving over present space costs of about $95,000 a year, which could be applied toward paying off the building. In other words, about ten years or so would be required.

Mr. Fitzsimmons does not go along with the suggestion of the agency's buying its own building. He points out that all advertising agencies are confronted with the problem of possible loss of key clients. Should ADF and M lose a client with a large billing, the financial burden of the building might prove serious. In addition, building management is far different from agency management, and he believes that ADF and M should confine its total energy to its business of creating effective advertising.

One of the account executives, Morton A. Symington, upon whose judgment Mr. Fitzsimmons relies a great deal, suggests that the agency seriously consider moving to a suburb. If the agency is going to move, it seems to him wise to locate in a less crowded area and where ideal surroundings could be obtained. He cites several examples of big-named companies moving to suburbs.

PROBLEMS:

1. Enumerate and discuss what additional information or considerations concerning possible relocation that you feel the managers of this agency should find out and take into account.

2. Who should make the final decision, and how should it be determined?

3. What action do you believe should be taken? Why?

Chapter · 17

Office Physical Working Conditions

Setting out well is a quarter of the journey.
—H. G. BOHN

PROVIDING AND maintaining proper and adequate physical working conditions are important in the carrying out of office work. The working conditions should be pleasant, comfortable, and conducive to good work habits, with adequate consideration given to cost.

Among the major factors of physical working conditions in most offices are: (1) light, (2) color, (3) music, (4) air, and (5) sound. As stated in the previous chapter, these factors should be integrated. Light, for example, is dependent somewhat upon the color scheme employed in the area, and sound conditioning of an office influences the effectiveness of music. The benefits of proper air conditioning may be reduced considerably by lack of adequate light in the area.

LIGHT IN THE OFFICE

Adequate light is perhaps the most important consideration in office physical facilities. Many office tasks are of an exacting and close nature. Small print, carbon copies of typed material, and poorly handwritten notes are among the regular hard-to-see materials that must be handled. The successful execution of this paper work requires good light.

Proper lighting-seeing conditions reduce fatigue resulting from eye strain, promote office efficiency, make an office more pleasant, and add prestige to an office. In a number of examples, improved lighting has demonstrated that it not only pays for itself but is a profitable investment. In a two-year test made in the office of the Bureau of Internal Revenue in Washington, D.C., it was found that supplying adequate light and introducing light-colored finishes for balanced brightness resulted in an increased productivity of 5.5 per cent. The work consisted of card punching. The increase in productivity amounted to about $12,000 annually, whereas only $6,500 had been spent in improving working conditions. The dollar investment paid for itself in about six months, not to mention the returns in better employee morale, reduction in absenteeism, and more accurate work.

The cost of lighting is one of the smallest expenses of operating an office. For modern lighting a range of from $0.60 to $1.00 per square foot per year is normally required. The exact figure will depend upon the local prevailing utility rates.

THE TASK OF SEEING

Without light, there can be no sight, and for light itself to be seen it must be *associated with surfaces.* Light and surfaces are closely linked. This means that the entire working environment must be taken into account when considering lighting questions because the surfaces affect the light which, in turn, regulate the ability to see. For an object to be seen, it must stand out from all other things around it. That is, contrast is necessary. The subject of contrast and light is discussed later in this chapter.[1]

It is universally agreed that the smaller the object, the more difficult it is to see. Visual perception of size depends not only upon the dimensions of the object but also upon the distance of the object from the eyes. Hence, the ability to see can be improved by increasing the size of the object, for example, by enlarging the type size of printed material and by adjusting the distance of the eye from the object. Adjustments, from the practical office viewpoint, can only be made within a limited range.

A great deal of physical and nervous energy is required to see. Certain eye muscles can relax only when viewing distances of about 10 feet and over. To read material under normal working conditions of an office requires the eyes to converge and to focus for the near distance. The eyes must also adjust for the brightness of the light; this is accomplished by the contraction and expansion of the pupils of the eyes.

Finally, the ability to see an object varies with the degree of light brightness. Generally speaking, as the amount of light increases, brightness increases, as does also the ability to see easier, faster, and more accurately. But these benefits do not accumulate without limit—a point

---

[1] See page 326.

is reached where more light does not provide improved ability to see. To supply effective office lighting is much more than that of getting offices to use enough light. This is important, but the right kind of light on the right surfaces, the size of the object, the positioning of the light fixtures, and the minimizing of seeing difficulties are additional vital considerations.

QUANTITY OF LIGHT

In order to determine the proper amount of light for any given case and to make reasonable comparisons, a measurement of light is necessary. One such measurement is a *foot-candle,* which technically *is the amount of direct light one foot distant from a standard candle.* A rule of thumb for rough estimating is that, for small rooms, one watt per square foot of area provides 15 foot-candles. Thus a 100-watt bulb in a room 10 feet $\times$ 10 feet will provide approximately 15 foot-candles of light. The amount of light also depends upon the distribution of the light sources; for example, that provided by a single 100-watt bulb will differ from that supplied by four 25-watt bulbs, because of the difference in the light dispersion over the area.[2]

Figure 17–1 shows the recommended values of illumination for office work. To illustrate, for ordinary seeing tasks a quantity of 30 foot-candles is recommended. These values are guides; some variation from them is possible according to individual conditions.

CONTRAST AND DIFFUSION OF LIGHT

Brightness is a quality determined by the amount of light reflected from an object. The effective light for seeing is the reflected light, not the light from the source. If the object to be seen reflects very little light of that cast upon it, the object is relatively difficult to see and in this case possesses a low reflectance value. The ratio of the light a surface reflects, divided by the amount of light it receives, is the reflectance value of that surface. For example, a smooth finish in white has a reflectance value of about 0.90, or 90 per cent, in medium yellow, 0.65, and in dark green, 0.07.

Brightness Contrast. The importance of brightness contrast in a lighting is illustrated by this excerpt: ". . . . Studies by lighting authorities and ophthalmologists show that the eye sees best when all areas within the field of vision (the desk and its surroundings) are approximately of the same brightness.

---

[2] The subject of light dispersion is discussed on page 328.

"The next best situation is when the office desk is slightly brighter than its environment—the walls and floors. The least desirable situation is that in which the environment is greatly brighter than the desk."[3]

RECOMMENDED VALUES OF ILLUMINATION FOR OFFICE WORK

	Foot Candles Recommended
DIFFICULT SEEING TASKS	50

Involving:
    (a) Discrimination of fine detail, such as 6–8-point type
    (b) Poor contrast
    (c) Long periods of time
Such as:
    Auditing and accounting
    Business machine operation
    Transcribing and tabulation
    Bookkeeping
    Drafting
    Designing

ORDINARY SEEING TASKS	30

Involving:
    (a) Discrimination of moderately fine detail, such as 8–12-point type
    (b) Better-than-average contrast
    (c) Intermittent periods of time
Such as:
    General office work (except for work coming under "Difficult Seeing Tasks" above)
    Private office work
    General correspondence
    Conference rooms
    Active file rooms
    Mail rooms

CASUAL SEEING TASKS	10

Such as:
    Inactive file rooms
    Reception rooms
    Stairways
    Washrooms and other service areas

SIMPLE SEEING TASKS	5

Such as:
    Hallways and corridors
    Passageways

Source: "Recommended Practices of Office Lighting," (New York: Illuminating Engineering Society, March, 1956), p. 11.

FIG. 17–1.

For the visual area, which is generally described as about 30 degrees in all directions from the eye, there are certain current guides for brightness contrast. One such guide is that the ratio of the brightness of the task area to its immediately surrounding area should not be

---

[3] H. R. Wells, "Color and Lighting," *NOMA Forum* (Philadelphia: National Office Management Association), July, 1948, p. 10.

greater than 3 to 1. If the ratio exceeds this limit, seeing becomes unnecessarily difficult. The proper selection of material, finish, and color helps to achieve the desired ratio.

Another guide is that the ratio of the brightness of the light source itself to its background should also not exceed 3 to 1. The design of the fixture and its arrangement influence this ratio. From a practical viewpoint too great a brightness contrast can cause glare which comes from either the source of light or from smooth, highly polished surfaces. This means that a lighting plan should include not only the proper type of fixtures but also the light-reflecting characteristics of all surfaces within the office area. In some instances, the correct amount of brightness contrast is obtained by having several, not one, source of light.

Color Contrast. A fundamental factor in seeing is contrast between objects. Greatest visibility is usually reached when there is a maximum color contrast between writing and its background. It is difficult to read when there is little contrast between the paper and the printing, for example, white on white, white on cream, or black on black. On the other hand, white chalk marks on a blackboard or black print on white paper afford a high contrast and help the seeing process.

It is usually recommended that a ceiling be of a very light color with a reflectance value of around 0.80. Walls should be of a material and color having about 0.50 as a reflectance value. The floor should have a reflectance value of at least 0.25, since it is the background against which much work is seen.

Diffusion of Light. Diffusion of light is also important, in order that an object in any spatial position may be seen clearly and easily. Absolutely uniform diffusion is not desired. Some shadow effect is normal to the eye, but harsh, strong, contrasting shadows are annoying and should be avoided. Well-diffused light is sometimes referred to as a "soft" light. Proper diffusion of light is obtained by having light in different amounts come from an adequate number of sources and directions.

ARRANGEMENT OF FIXTURES

Lighting fixtures can be arranged in almost any pattern. Some uniformity or symmetry is usually desirable for better general appearance. Long rows of fixtures may be interrupted or designed with an occasional break, but the foremost considerations are proper lighting without serious glare, the impression of integrated lighting—not a group of individual lights—and cost of installing and of maintaining. Of course, general appearance is also important, and the arrangement of the lighting fixtures should bring out the architectural and decorative features that assist to produce a cheerful working atmosphere. Fixtures can be suspended from the ceiling or recessed in it. The design of having the ceiling completely luminous is gaining favor.

The eyes should be protected from direct glare which often results where the luminaires are not shielded. The normal line of sight is from the horizontal to 45 degrees above the sight line; therefore, the eye should not be able to view directly luminaires within this zone. This is illustrated by Figure 17–2.

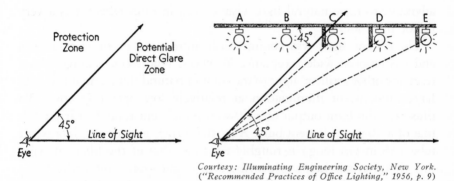

Courtesy: Illuminating Engineering Society, New York.
("Recommended Practices of Office Lighting," 1956, p. 9)

FIG. 17–2. The potential direct glare zone is from the line of sight to about 45 degrees above, and the luminaires in this zone should be shielded in order to protect the eyes. In this illustration, luminaires A and B are outside this zone and need not be shielded, but luminaires C, D, and E should be shielded as shown.

To determine what percentage of persons will find a particular lighting design or arrangement of fixtures comfortable in a specific area, an index called the Visual Comfort Index (VCI) has been developed by engineers at General Electric Company. Factors are considered in mathemathical equations so that the comfort level of a proposed lighting design for a given area can be predetermined. Among the important factors taken into account are: (1) brightness—low brightness gives a high VCI rating, (2) size of the lighting system— VCI ratings decline in large areas, (3) lighting location with respect to a person's eyes—low ceilings cause VCI ratings to decline, and (4) brightness of the general area—light colors give high VCI ratings.

Generally speaking, with fluorescent lighting it is more comfortable to view the fixtures *crosswise,* not lengthwise. Especially is this true in a large office. In a small office this consideration is relatively unimportant. However, there is one important exception—the use of luminous-sided fixtures with glass or plastic sides. These units should be viewed lengthwise for greatest comfort, regardless of the area size.

SOURCES OF LIGHT

Sources of office lighting include natural, fluorescent, and filament bulb. Natural light is probably the best source of light, but it varies throughout the day and from day to day. Usually other sources of light must be used to maintain the required amount of light. Natural light has certain beneficial psychological effects. An employee usually feels better and has a sense of less confinement when he can look out occasionally and see daylight, observe the weather, and the like. It is advisable to have natural light visible even in cases where it is a very minor light source.

Fluorescent light was commercially introduced in the late 1930's and has enjoyed wide acceptance in offices. Fluorescent light is closer than any other artificial light to the color of natural light, and it provides large amounts of illumination at relatively low operating costs. To illustrate, the light output of a 40-watt fluorescent tube is nearly twice that of a 40-watt filament bulb. Also, the surface area of the fluorescent tube (48 inches long) is roughly ten times that of the filament type; this characteristic helps to distribute the light more uniformly.

Filament-bulb light is still an important source of artificial lighting. Improvements in filament bulb shape, type of glass, and length of life have been achieved. However, the filament bulb has certain objectionable characteristics, including the yellowish color of its light that looks different from the color of natural light, the large number of bulbs that are necessary to supply a sufficient amount of light under today's office lighting requirements, and the heat generated from these masses of bulbs.

Sources of light can also be classified as either (1) general lighting, or (2) supplementary lighting. In the former the entire area is lighted to a prescribed level of illumination. The source is usually a number of fixtures in or suspended from the ceiling. The second, or supplementary lighting, consists of illuminating a relatively small area as a desk top or portion of an office machine. Supplementary lighting can be used advantageously not only to provide the desired decor as in private offices, or from lamps on tables and desks, "pull-down" lamps, and lighting effects in reception rooms and hallways, but also for increasing the illumination when the office work is in a fixed position or where the area involved is relatively small.

The central working areas of desks and most office machines meet these conditions. Figure 17–3 shows the distribution of light intensity on a desk top from a one-tube fluorescent desk light. Note that 35 foot-candles of light are provided at a distance of 24 inches from the lamp—the area in which difficult seeing tasks are performed. This is in keeping with recommended values for ordinary seeing tasks, as shown in Figure 17–1.

However, the use of highly lighted local areas with a large surrounding dark area should be avoided because such a condition requires severe eye adjustments when looking away from the local area

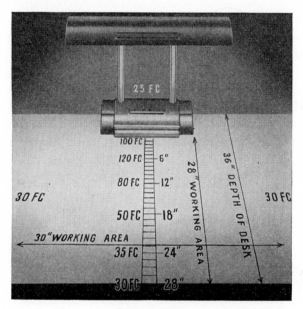

Courtesy: Midwest Naturlite Co., Chicago

FIG. 17–3. Intensity of light on desk top from a fluorescent desk lamp.

and again when the eyes are turned to the relatively bright local area. Such a condition makes the seeing task more difficult and is tiring to the eyes. Normally, local lighting should never exceed five times the light intensity of the general surrounding illumination.

BASIC DESIGNS OF LIGHTING SYSTEMS

The four basic designs are illustrated in Figure 17–4. A description of each follows:

Direct Lighting. Under this arrangement, light from the luminaire is permitted to travel directly to the working surface. This gives a "hard" type of light, and diffusion is not too good. Glare may be high;

shadows are sharp; and the ceiling is usually dark. Generally it is the least preferred type.

Semi-Direct Lighting. This design allows some of the light from the luminaire to travel upward to the ceiling, whence it is reflected downward to the working area. Most of the light, however, travels downward directly to the working area. A semi-direct system illuminates the ceiling and lessens the effect of deep shadows.

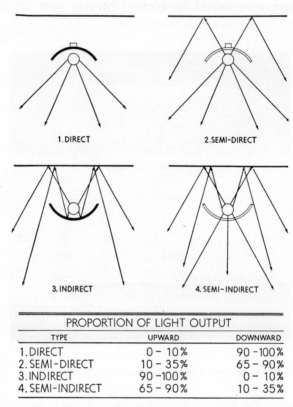

PROPORTION OF LIGHT OUTPUT		
TYPE	UPWARD	DOWNWARD
1. DIRECT	0 – 10%	90 –100%
2. SEMI-DIRECT	10 – 35%	65 – 90%
3. INDIRECT	90 –100%	0 – 10%
4. SEMI-INDIRECT	65 – 90%	10 – 35%

FIG. 17–4. The four basic lighting systems.

Indirect Lighting. In this case the light travels upward to the ceiling where it is reflected downward to the working area. This provides a light which is "soft" and relatively free of sharp shadows. Actually, the ceiling is the source of light to the work area, and, therefore, it should have a high reflection value. But since the employee cannot completely ignore the ceiling, the possibilities of glare and too intense ceiling brightness must be taken into account.

Semi-Indirect Lighting. With this type most of the light travels upward to the ceiling and then down to the work area, but some of the light is allowed to travel directly downward. As with indirect lighting, the ceiling is, in effect, the main source of light. The direct light helps increase the amount of light on the work area, but consideration must be given to its possible contribution of objectionable shadows and glare.

These various arrangements apply to both the filament bulb and the fluorescent type of lighting. An illustration showing a semi-indirect fluorescent arrangement is shown in Figure 17–5.

Courtesy: Day-Brite Lighting, Inc., St. Louis

FIG. 17–5.   A general office with fluorescent lighting troffers 6-foot centers, continuous rows, providing 85 foot-candles.

SELECTION OF LIGHTING FACILITIES

No one type of lighting facilities is best for all offices. Individual requirements and considerations are important. The selection of the lighting facilities should include ample consideration for each of the following:

1. Suitability (for producing the desired result)—Is there adequate illumination, proper protection against glare, both direct and reflected, suitable elimination of shadows, etc.?
2. Efficiency (of the system per unit of light emitted—this directly affects the operating cost)—Is the luminaire efficient compared with others under consideration?

3. Maintenance—Can it be cleaned easily and inexpensively? Can it be easily serviced?
4. Sturdiness—Is the construction such that the luminaires will hold together in service—glass will not be likely to break—the entire assembly will have good wearing qualities?
5. Appearance—Is the appearance, both lighted and unlighted, suitable for the room?
6. Flexibility—Can the light output be increased if at some future time it is desired to increase the illumination? Are the outlets so located that partition changes can be made without expensive relocation of luminaires?[4]

To elaborate on one point, maintenance has a significant influence upon the adequacy of office lighting. Needed are periodic cleaning of the luminaires, proper wattage of bulbs, and correct voltage. In one study involving eight locations, the foot-candle output was raised from an average of 11.8 to 46.2 foot-candles, or an increase of over 350 per cent, by cleaning the dirty fixtures, using color of high reflecting value for the ceiling and walls and keeping them clean, replacing aging bulbs, and supplying the correct voltage.[5] Equally startling results were experienced by other companies when action was taken toward acquiring better maintenance of lighting facilities.[6]

COLOR CONDITIONING IN THE OFFICE

Color not only beautifies an office but also improves conditions under which office work is performed. The gains from proper use of color are, therefore, not only aesthetic and psychological, but economic as well. Color cannot be used indiscriminately. This is especially true in the office where the aim is a dignified yet cheerful and comfortable atmosphere. The intelligent use of color requires constant attention and an understanding of color harmony and compensation.

PSYCHOLOGICAL EFFECT OF COLOR

A full comprehension of the psychological effect of color on human beings must await the more complete assessment of color science and color philosophy. This is taking place rapidly, but precise relationships and complete understandings are yet to be attained. However, it is fairly well established that color affects the human emotions, senses,

[4] Illuminating Engineering Society, *Recommended Practice of Office Lighting* (New York, July, 1947), p. 22.

[5] F. I. Wilson, "More Light without Added Expense," *American Business* (Chicago: Dartnell Publications, Inc.), November, 1945, pp. 30–32.

[6] C. M. Holden, "How to Reduce Lighting Maintenance Costs," *Buildings* (Cedar Rapids, Iowa: Stamats Publishing Co.), November, 1952, p. 27.

and thought processes. For example, color usually has an important influence upon one's blood pressure and disposition to relax.[7] A certain color will impress the minds of some individuals with a particularly favorable feeling or thought; another color will have the opposite effect. Some colors give a lift; others impart a depressed feeling. Some tend to hasten mental action; others to retard it.[8]

Colors in the range of yellow, orange, and red are regarded as "warm" colors; they usually have the psychological effect of encouraging warmth and cheer. In contrast, cool colors, including blue, violet, and dark green, generally produce a subduing effect of restraint and calmness. Tints such as buff, beige, and ivory are moderately stimulating, while pale violets and blues are suppressing.

SELECTION OF COLORS

Colors should be selected very carefully for an office.[9] Warm colors should be used to counteract the effect of a drab, cheerless area. Color seems to change the temperature in that a room with blue walls, for example, feels cooler; this is actually the result of a mental process stimulated by the blue color, which appears to reduce the sensitivity to heat.

For example, during August the walls of a New England office were painted blue. The following winter the employees complained of the office being cold, even though the normal temperature of 70 degrees was maintained. Then the temperature was raised to 75 degrees, but complaints still continued. The blue walls were then redecorated to warm yellow and green. The temperature continued at 75 degrees. Now the employees protested that the office was too warm. A return to the temperature of 70 degrees resulted in the ceasing of the complaints.

The general color scheme of an office can follow one of many arrangements, depending upon the individual preferences. An office of all one color sameness should be avoided. If the one color is a light color, it will create an area which is too somber, tending to induce relaxation. Under such conditions a person is not mentally alert. On the other hand, if all the color or too much of an area is of a strong or brilliant color, the result is excessive stimulation and discomfort—

[7] "How Color Control Can Motivate Workers," *Management Methods* (Greenwich, Conn.: Management Magazines, Inc.), May, 1954, p. 28.

[8] R. H. Evans, *An Introduction to Color* (New York: John Wiley & Sons, Inc., 1948), p. 17.

[9] Robert C. Daly, "The Power of Color," *Buildings* (Cedar Rapids, Iowa: Stamats Publishing Co.), November, 1951, p. 28.

likewise nonconducive for sustained office work output. A proper color balance is needed.

The current trend is toward the monochromatic which describes the use of various shades of one color for floors, walls, and draperies, together with one bright accent color. As a beginning point the desk is selected in a particular color. With this basic color determined, the

When Desk Is—	Use Carpet of—	Use Walls of—	Use Draperies of—	Use Chair, Also Pictures, Desk Accessories, and Lamps of—
Gray	Gray	White	Gray	Red
Gray	Rust brown	Light gray	Rust	Yellow
Walnut or mahogany	Green	Beige	Chartreuse	Dark yellow
Walnut or mahogany	Beige	Light blue	Light blue	Dark yellow
Bleached or blond finish	Light brown	Beige	Beige	Orange
Bleached or blond finish	Charcoal	Gray	Yellow	Coral

FIG. 17–6. Suggested color guide for an integrated color pattern.

floor covering is selected to harmonize correctly with the desk. Then lighter shades of the floor covering can be used for walls and draperies. The accent color can be in the chair or accessories such as pictures, desk pieces, and lamps. Figure 17–6 shows a suggested color guide to obtain an integrated color pattern in an office.

Unless unusual features characterize certain office areas or the man-

Area	Colors Suggested
General office	Ceiling in white, walls faced by employees in soft, cool colors—one or more of the other walls may be in a warm color like light yellow. Wall colors should harmonize.
Conference room	Light and neutral colors are preferable, but some carefully utilized strong colors are usually necessary to stimulate occupants.
Reception room	Neutral colors are usually the best. Avoid sharp contrasts. Limited and careful use of vivid colors are in order.
Corridors	Light colors are usually needed because of lack of daylight.

FIG. 17–7.

ager has strong preferences concerning color, it is usually best to follow basic recommendations regarding colors in the office. These are presented in outline form in Figure 17–7.

PRIMARY, SECONDARY, AND COMPLEMENTARY COLORS

The primary colors are red, yellow, and blue; and they can be located on a color wheel at equally spaced distances. Secondary colors are obtained by mixing adjacent colors on the wheel. For example, red and yellow give orange. (See Fig. 17–8.)

Complementary colors are those directly opposite each other on the wheel. Green, for example, is the complement of red; blue, of orange. When used with discretion, complementary colors tend to enrich each other and afford contrast without a color clash.

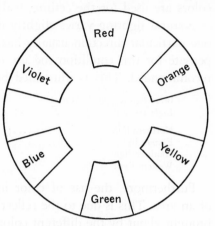

FIG. 17–8. Sketch of color wheel, showing relationship of primary colors—red, yellow, and blue. Secondary colors are made by mixing adjacent colors named on the wheel. A combination of all the colors shown produces a neutral gray.

Pleasant and harmonious color effects are obtained by securing a balance among the colors used. Three ways in which this can be done are described below.

Harmonious Color Effects	Description (Refer to Color Wheel, Figure 17–8)
1. Complementary colors...........	Red and green, the colors directly opposite each other.
2. Split complementary colors—actually a triad, two colors adjacent to the direct complement of the third color....................	Green-blue and green-yellow, the two colors adjacent to green, the direct complement of red.
3. Triads—three colors equidistant from each other................	Red, yellow, and blue.

Color experts usually employ considerable quantities of the grayer shades, i.e., colors toward the center of the color wheel. These are subdued, and their use minimizes the possibility of color violence. The brilliant colors are used here and there to give accent and distinction.

COLOR AND LIGHTING

As mentioned earlier in this chapter, color has a significant influence upon the lighting of an office. Light colors increase the utilization of light; dark colors decrease the lighting intensity. This is because light colors reflect the light rays, whereas dark colors absorb the light rays. For these reasons any normally dark area will lighten up when lighter colors are used for the ceiling, walls, and floors.

Natural lighting varies slightly in color. Light predominantly from one particular direction usually has a characteristic tinge, and to compensate for this condition the use of complementary colors is usually recommended. This is illustrated below:

When Predominant Natural Light Source Is—	Light Is Slightly Colored by—	Recommend Use of—
Northern light	bluish tinge	warm color
Eastern light	neutral	neutral color
Southern light	yellowish tinge	cool color
Western light	reddish tinge	cool color

Furthermore, the use of color influences the apparent proportions of an area. This is due to the reflecting and the contracting light effect brought about by the different colors. Dark colors seem to advance an area, light colors to retreat it. Hence, the dimensional effect of a long narrow room can tend to be equalized by the use of a dark color on the end walls and a lighter shade of the same color, or of a harmonizing hue, on the other walls. Similarly, the proportions of a square area can be made to appear elongated.

MUSIC CONDITIONING

"Music-while-you-work" programs are designed to improve working conditions and create a pleasant work environment. Specifically, in the office they are intended to relieve mental and visual fatigue, reduce nervous tension, and make the employees feel better.

Results from numerous tests involving thousands of office employees, in offices where music conditioning is present point conclusively to extremely favorable benefits being obtained by both the employers and the employees. To illustrate, increased productivity of from 6 per cent to 21 per cent, depending on the type of work, improved employee morale, and a decrease in absenteeism and nonessential employee conversations, are among the important employers' advantages reported.[10] Of over 35,000 employees questioned, 90 per cent stated they liked music while they worked; an equal number credited music with making their work more enjoyable; and nearly 85 per cent said it helped to break the monotony of their work.[11] The types of office

[10] Robert F. Finegan, "Music in the Air—New Style," *Office Management and Equipment* (New York: Andrew Geyer, Inc.), May, 1952, p. 35.

[11] *Muzak in Industry,* 1951 (a booklet published by the Muzak Corporation, New York, N.Y.).

work showing the maximum benefits include filing, mail-room, typing, reception, key-punching, and verifying.

The music is functionally controlled, which means that it is specifically arranged, orchestrated, and recorded to accomplish a specific goal. Distracting and attention-getting music, such as heavy brass effects and solos, are excluded. The music is stimulating and designed to create a favorable and pleasing mood. Neither directly nor consciously does the employee listen to the music just as he does not minutely examine colorful wall designs that help create a pleasant working environment.

Programs are tailored to fit the music to the specific office work as well as to the temperament of the employees. The music selections are based primarily upon the type of music and the "standard energy curve" of employees. For example, maximum low ebbs of energy usually occur at 10:30 A.M. and 3:30 P.M. Around these times music of maximum stimulus is applied. In contrast, music during the first part of the morning consists of a bright opener followed by moderately bright music such as several waltzes. Light classics and slower swing tunes are usually predominant in programs for office employees. A definite schedule is followed—the music is played for specific intervals only, because best results are usually obtained from this type of pattern.

The music is "piped" or transmitted from a central sending studio to the subscribing office. The expense to the office is nominal, especially in view of the results achieved. The cost approximates $1.00 per day for the smaller office and 10 cents per month per employee for the larger office. The inexpensive addition of a microphone to the subscriber's equipment automatically converts the installation to a public-address system. Thus, managerial messages can be conveyed to all or part of the premises.

AIR CONDITIONING

Air conditioning regulates atmospheric conditions by controlling the four basic elements of temperature, circulation, moisture content, and cleanliness. It is possible to control only three, or two, or, in fact, just one of these elements; but such control is more correctly referred to as partial rather than complete air conditioning. In addition to aiding human health and comfort, air conditioning offers economic advantages. Higher productivity and decreases in cleaning and decorating costs are prominent. Reports of productivity gains due to air conditioning are quite common. In one study office employee efficiency showed a 20 per

Courtesy: Frigidaire Corp., Dayton

FIG. 17–9. A well-designed, economical air conditioner in one compact package. Capacities range from 3 to 15 tons of cooling, and the unit is suitable for areas such as a general office. The unit can be used with or without ducts, depending upon the application.

cent gain after air conditioning was installed.[12]

Air conditioning can be supplied from a central unit or from an individual unit. Varying sizes and capacities are available. The individual units for a small group of offices or for part of a floor area have grown in popularity. Some are designed for a single room and are portable. The cost of air conditioning has been greatly reduced. A well-engineered individual unit is now available for as low as several hundred dollars. Figure 17–9 shows a modern air-conditioning unit designed for a general office.

TEMPERATURE, VENTILATION, AND HUMIDITY

The temperature in many offices is too high. This leads to drowsiness and tends to retard the execution of office work. The recommended office temperature is about 70 degrees F.[13]

Ventilation or the movement of air is also important. Lack of proper ventilation can make a person feel sleepy and unduly tired. At 70 degrees F., an adult human body at rest gives off heat at the rate of about 5 b.t.u. sensible heat per minute, an amount about equal to the heat given off by a 100-watt incandescent light bulb.[14] This heat must be carried off by the surrounding air; otherwise the body becomes unduly heated, resulting in discomfort and lack

---

[12] Norris Wells, "Is Investment in Air Conditioning Sure to Pay Off?" *American Business* (Chicago: Dartnell Publications, Inc.), April, 1954, p. 31.

[13] If air conditioning is used, the recommended temperature range is from 68 to 82 degrees F., depending upon the outside temperature. Too great a differential between outside and air-conditioned areas is undesirable.

[14] Herkimer and Herkimer, *Air Conditioning* (New York: Chemical Publishing Co., Inc., 1947), p. 257.

of energy. The normal ventilation requirement is about 2,000 cubic feet of air per person per hour. Drafts should be avoided. Usually the best practice is to have the air circulating from a number of outlets so that it is distributed evenly over the entire area.

Humidity is another important consideration because the amount of moisture in the air definitely affects the comfort and efficiency of a human being. At the same temperature, moist air feels hot and dry air feels cool. Excessive dampness might cause physical discomfort of a respiratory nature and induce a heavy, languid feeling. Likewise, excessive dryness or very low humidity frequently induces a feeling of parchedness and nervous irritability.

The term "relative humidity" is used to describe the intensity of moisture saturation in the air. A recommended relative humidity for an office is from 40 to 60 per cent. For example, when the relative humidity is 20 per cent, the office air is too dry; when the humidity is 70 per cent, the air is too moist.

Courtesy: W. W. Welch Company, Cincinnati

FIG. 17–10. A modern floor-type fan for offices. The unit will produce a uniformly directed circulation of air at the rate of 4,500 cubic feet per minute without disturbing papers on desks or tables.

AIDS IN IMPROVING HEATING AND VENTILATING CONDITIONS

The office manager can follow several simple practices which will assist in achieving desirable heating and ventilating conditions. Regulators should be installed on the heating apparatus so that excessive temperatures are not reached. It is well to become "thermometer conscious" and to keep the office temperature within reasonable limits. Fans and window ventilators will help considerably in providing more adequate ventilation. A modern floor-type fan is shown in Figure 17–10. Window ventilators permit incoming fresh air without direct drafts blowing on any one person. Disagreeable odors can be eliminated by the use of specially designed electrical units and of deodorant air-cleaning products which are available in packaged bottle form. Furthermore, the practice of opening windows and airing the office for short, stated periods during midmorning, noon, and midafternoon will do a lot toward expelling stale air and freshening up the office.

SOUND CONDITIONING

A noisy office is seldom an efficient office. Noise is unpleasant, distracting, and costly. It makes for difficulty in concentrating, in using the telephone, and in turning out accurate office work. The effects of noise on the health and efficiency of employees are explained in this interesting quotation:

Office noises, according to physicians and psychiatrists, may cause many physical disorders such as increased pulse rate and irregular rhythm of the heart, transient changes in blood and brain pressure, and, most common of all, disturbances of digestion. It is a grave error to speak of "getting used to noise." While one may momentarily be aware of its effect, the result is evidenced by the fact that individuals whose work, as such, is not laborious, are completely tired out at the end of eight hours. It is the biological reaction to the tenseness they are under to do their job with any kind of application.[15]

TECHNICAL ASPECTS OF NOISE AND SOUND

Noise can be briefly described as discordant sound. Noise has no definite pitch and quality, whereas in a musical tone these properties are fairly well defined. Sound can be defined technically as "vibrational energy." The oscillation of these waves of energy, or sound waves, traveling through the air, stimulate the auditory nerves, and this in turn results in a perception of the sensation and a consciousness of sound.

The characteristics of sound depend chiefly upon its (1) pitch—the frequency of the vibrations, (2) intensity—the energy of the vibrations, (3) quality—the mode or type of vibration, (4) reverberation—the sustaining qualities after the sound has stopped at its course, and (5) the expectancy and acceptance of the individual. From the practical viewpoint, loudness is probably of greatest concern. Loudness is primarily determined by both intensity and pitch, with emphasis on intensity. Actually the phenomenon of increasing loudness follows a rather complex physical law. For this reason and in order to have a relative measurement of the range of intensities which are handled in noise control, a unit of measurement called a "decibel" is used.

A decibel is approximately the smallest change in sound which it is possible for the human ear to detect. The decibel scale shows the relative values from the lowest to the highest human audible sound

---

[15] George H. Sherwood, "The Noise Factor in Office Fatigue," *The Journal of Accountancy* (New York: The American Institute of Accountants), September, 1946, p. 252.

intensity. For convenience the scale is measured logarithmically. The lowest value is zero, the beginning of human audibility, to approximately one hundred ten, which represents the sound of thunder. Figure 17–11 shows a table of sound identification and the corresponding decibel ratings.

VALUE OF NOISE LEVELS EXPRESSED IN DECIBELS

Threshold of hearing	0
Noise in average home	32
Quiet office	37
Quiet radio in home	40
Noise in city (residential district)	45
Restaurant clatter	50
Noisy office	57
Stenographic room (large office)	70
Noisy factory	85
Boiler factory	97

Source: "Encyclopedia Americana," Vol. I (New York: Americana Corporation, 1955), p. 107.

FIG. 17–11.

MANAGERIAL ADVANTAGES AND MEANS OF CONTROLLING NOISE

In addition to the human comfort benefits, probably the greatest advantage derived from office noise control is increased productivity and, even more important, increased accuracy. In one study of noise control conducted in a large insurance office, the over-all production increased 8.8 per cent, typists' errors decreased 29 per cent, and machine operators' errors decreased 52 per cent.[16]

The means for controlling noise include the following:

1. *Reduce and, if possible, eliminate the source of noise.* Felt pads placed under typewriters and adding machines, and rubber cushions under various types of office equipment, will help considerably in noise reduction. Soundproofing cabinets which fit over the machine like a hood, with a front opening for the operator, can also be used. Adequate maintenance and proper lubrication of file drawers, doors, desks, and chairs contribute further to noise reduction. Appeals to employees can be made, stressing consideration for others and the importance of eliminating unnecessary conversations.

2. *Locate office in a quiet space.* The top floors of a building are usually less noisy, since they are further removed from street traffic. Relocation within the building, so that the office is not directly exposed

---

[16] Celotex Corp., *Twenty-Five Answers to Questions on Sound Conditioning with Acousti Celotex* (rev. ed.; Chicago, February, 1954), p. 8.

or adjacent to objectionable noise sources, is another possibility. Finally, moving to a quiet area should be considered. Less congested areas are usually less noisy than highly congested areas.

3. *Segregate noise sources from the rest of the office.* A great deal can be accomplished by placing all noisy equipment in one place. A separate room to house the noisy office operations works out very well. If this is not feasible, concentrating the chief noise sources in one area is usually better than having them scattered all over the office.

4. *Use sound-absorbing materials for office floors, ceilings, and walls.* Sound travels in waves and is reflected from glazed or non-porous surfaces in the same way that light is reflected. Under these conditions, sound continues to travel in all directions and bounces back and forth until its energy is absorbed; then the sound dies out of its own accord. This condition usually makes for a noisy office.

When acoustic treatment or sound-absorbing material is used, the sound dies out faster. The same identical sounds exist as before, but they are not permitted to reflect repeatedly until dissipated naturally. Carpet eliminates virtually all floor noise such as that from walking or from pushing a chair across the floor, and it serves as an effective sound blotter absorbing most air-borne noises. Office noise is definitely reduced by means of carpeting. Also drapes and curtains made of soft fabrics help to absorb sound.

Ceilings and walls can be covered with acoustic material which is available in many forms. One common and popular type is a fibrous, mineral tile, about 12×12 inches in size and perforated. The tile is available in thicknesses ranging from $\frac{1}{2}$ inch to $1\frac{1}{4}$ inch, and can be attached either by a special cement or by means of nails or screws. Another common variety is a mastic type of acoustic material which is spread on the surface and dries, leaving a porous surface. In some instances a loose, fibrous material is used along with a separate hard facing material that has numerous perforations.

QUESTIONS

1. Discuss the subject "Quantity of Light" as applicable to the field of office management.
2. Of the five major factors of physical working conditions in an office, which one do you believe is most important? Justify your answer.
3. Explain the important relationship between light and color in an office. Explain the relationship between color and temperature.
4. Outline the important considerations to be taken into account in the arrangement of lighting fixtures.

5. Is supplementary lighting desirable in a modern office? Explain your answer.

6. Of what importance is the following statement to an office manager: "The effective light for seeing is the reflected light, not the light from the source"?

7. Discuss the significance of light direction and diffusion.

8. What is the meaning of each of the following terms:
   a) Visual Comfort Index with reference to office lighting.
   b) Decibel.
   c) Color wheel.
   d) Color contrast as factor in seeing.

9. An office manager heard many favorable comments concerning the adoption of music-while-you-work in various offices. Believing this might be desirable in his own office, he arranged, through the office supervisors, to ask his entire office force, if they would like to work to music. The response was overwhelmingly in favor of having music. Accordingly, the office manager purchased a wide selection of long-play records and two record playing machines—one machine for each of the two main office areas. What benefits or difficulties do you feel might result from the office manager's action? Explain your answer.

10. Discuss the psychological effect of color upon office employees.

11. An office is quite noisy, but the office employees have never complained about the noise. Should the office manager make any attempt to eliminate the noise? Why?

12. Specifically, what can an office manager do in order to combat office noise? Discuss each suggested measure briefly.

CASE PROBLEMS

CASE 17-1. THE GIDNEY COMPANY

Charles M. Kingman, assistant treasurer of the Gidney Company, is visiting the regional branch office of the company in Buffalo, New York. During his visit, he observed the physical working conditions of the general office area. In his opinion a satisfactory amount of light is present in one corner of the area. This corner has window openings to the outside permitting daylight to enter. He estimated the lighting in the remaining area to average about 20 foot-candles at the most.

The current lighting fixtures are a filament-bulb, direct lighting type. The luminaires are suspended from the ceiling by means of chains. Mr. Kingman estimates the floor to ceiling height as about 13 feet 6 inches, and the height of the luminaire from the floor as approximately 11 feet. The luminaires, spaced 8 feet center to center, are arranged in rows running the length of the office. There is about 8 feet between each of several rows of luminaires. Each luminaire is equipped with a 100-watt bulb.

Supplementary lighting in the form of desk lamps are used by some supervisors. Upon inquiry, Mr. Kingman found that the lamps were brought in by the employees and do not belong to the company.

The desks have a highly polished dark mahogany finish. The walls of the office area are painted a medium brown color up to a height of 4 feet from the floor, from this level to the ceiling the walls are a medium gray, with the ceiling a grayish white color. The floor is dark green vinyl asbestos tile. Mr. Kingman was informed that it was installed about three years ago.

PROBLEMS:

1. What is the problem in this case?
2. Outline what you recommend to solve the problem.
3. Should Mr. Kingman take any specific action? Why?
4. Explain how you would gain the Gidney Company managers' agreement to act upon your recommendation as stated in Question No. 2 above.

CASE 17–2. LA SALLE TUBE COMPANY

Six weeks ago a planned music program was installed in the offices of the La Salle Tube Company in Pittsburgh, Pennsylvania. During the past few days, the office manager, Mr. Dwight F. Quinn, has conducted a survey to find out the employees' reactions to "music-while-you-work." Judging from informal chats with various employees, Mr. Quinn felt that the plan was well liked, but he believed a more formal means of securing the employees' reactions was desirable.

Accordingly, the purpose and manner of conducting a more extensive survey were explained to the company's fifty-six office employees, and questionnaires were distributed. No signatures were required on the forms—there was no means of identifying a returned questionnaire by employee. The following table shows the tabulated results.

	Punch Cards	Mail Room	Typists	Filing	Accounting	Totals
Total employees in office.........	22	6	9	7	12	56
Makes office more enjoyable place to work.....................	20	5	8	7	5	45
Makes time go quickly...........	15	4	7	6	4	36
Decreases fatigue................	17	1	6	6	3	33
Keeps from getting nervous.......	20	3	7	7	6	43
Breaks monotony of work........	19	3	6	5	4	37
Improves attitude of supervisor toward us...................	15	1	3	4	5	28

At the same time Mr. Quinn held a brief interview with each of the five office supervisors in his office. The supervisor of punch cards doubted if any more work was being accomplished now that they had music, and a similar statement was made by the supervisor of typing. The mail-room supervisor expressed the opinion that unnecessary conversation during working hours had been reduced since the music plan was in effect; however, none of the other supervisors expressed this belief. All the supervisors indicated that, with music, their work seemed more enjoyable.

PROBLEMS:

1. What interpretations do you feel can be drawn from the survey results obtained?

2. The music costs the company $47.50 a month. In your opinion is it worth it? Explain.

3. Do you believe the reactions of the employees will change significantly in perhaps six to twelve months? Why? Are the reactions of the supervisors likely to change? Why?

Chapter · 18

Office Layout

Industry, economy, honesty, and kindness form a quartette of virtues that will never be improved upon.

—JAMES OLIVER

SIGNIFICANT IN the management of office work is office layout. It can be formally defined in a number of ways. The following is satisfactory: *Office layout is the determination of the space requirements and of the detailed utilization of this space in order to provide a practical arrangement of the physical factors considered necessary for the execution of the office work within reasonable costs.*

There is more implied in this definition than appears at first reading. Office layout includes a knowledge of the individual requirements, such as the providing of corridors, private offices, wardrobe facilities, and storage areas; it requires planning as to possible alterations and some provision for effecting them with the least disturbance and cost; it requires some estimate of future office needs, so that ample expansion or contraction provisions can be included according to the planned and accepted program. In addition, good office layout work includes a basic understanding of what work is to be done and the best method, as well as several alternate methods, for getting it done; plus imagination and ingenuity in visualizing practical results from an abstract sketch detailing a plan or a perspective view.

BASIC CONSIDERATIONS OF OFFICE LAYOUT

It should be emphasized that office layout includes more than just arranging equipment and machines. Complications enter into the picture; for example, the presence or the absence of certain building facilities may be the vital issue in deciding upon a layout, the ideal arrangement may not fit in with the physical working conditions, or the consideration for ample flexibility to meet varying needs may overshadow all other aspects. Co-ordinating of many facets is required.

From the viewpoint of layout, most large offices are made up of four separate types of areas, including (1) private offices, (2) general office area, (3) service areas, and (4) storage areas. It commonly helps to keep these in mind when preparing office layouts so that the over-all viewpoint is maintained and the essentials for each type area are included.

In order of their increasing difficulty, office layouts are for either new, remodeled, or currenttly being used areas. New areas normally permit the most effective space utilization; complete integrated space planning is possible. The next group—remodeled areas—sometimes pose difficult-to-solve problems in that the building facilities are inadequate or the space modernization is incomplete. Finally, the planning of existing areas for space improvement can be both fascinating as well as frustrating in that considerable improvement in space utilization can usually be brought about, but certain rigidities prevent a desired level of space efficiency being attained.

Among the major purposes of office layout, efforts are to facilitate an efficient flow of office work, to assist good supervision, to use space effectively, to add to the employees' comfort, and to impress favorably customers and visitors. While all are important, special stress upon the office layout facilitating an efficient flow of work deserves discussion because work flow is sometimes slighted in office layouts.

OFFICE LAYOUT AND FLOW OF WORK

The movement of clerical work through and between departments is a fundamental consideration in determining the arrangement of the physical units.[1] Flow is either by (1) papers, or (2) people. Usually it is better to bring the papers to the person than the person to the papers, although both are and must be used. Careful planning is required to provide a minimum amount of travel from one department to another, from machine to machine, and from desk to desk.

In a large office, the flow of work is usually of a constant pattern, i.e., the sequence of steps, the work volume at the various stations, and the particular type of work performed at each station remain fairly constant. The layout can be designed to accommodate these fairly uniform conditions. In contrast, when the office is small, many different flows must be handled with the same layout. In these cases the layout should be made to handle best the flows representing the largest volumes of work, usually those of orders, accounts payable, invoices, and purchases.

---

[1] Flow of work is discussed on pages 355–59, and means for improving flows of work are fully discussed in Chapter 33.

The relatively minor flows can be fitted to the layout as best as possible.

The flow when plotted on the floor plan should conform to a straight line, circle, or some regular shape. This helps insure that wasteful backtracking or deviation is avoided. In addition, a minimum of time and cost should be required in going from beginning to end of the flow.

IMPORTANCE OF OFFICE LAYOUT

Efforts expended in acquiring an effective office layout are usually very well repaid. Good layout is important for a number of major reasons.

First, an effective office layout assists in accomplishing the work efficiently, while a poor arrangement can seriously retard the work output. Adequate space must be provided and must be properly utilized, for too much or too little office space can make for inefficiencies. In the former case, needless energy is wasted in such things as messenger service and the flow of work through the office; likewise, excessive costs of heating and lighting frequently result. When too little space is provided, it usually results in crowded conditions which not only interfere with the work output but also encourage employee complaints, which are reflected in low morale.

Ineffective use of office space is a continuous liability. It contributes to office inefficiency daily, and it will continue to do so until an improved layout is planned and put into effect. Frequently the individual daily loss is small, but when consideration is given the cumulative amount, for a month or a year, for example, the importance of proper layout is brought into bolder relief.

In addition, it must be remembered that occupancy of office space represents a definite cost. While, in most cases, office space does not represent the largest portion of office expenditure, it usually does represent a sizable outlay; and it must be kept within reasonable limits. Adequate consideration to the office layout helps insure proper space provision as well as space utilization.

SPACE STANDARDS

The amount of space to be allocated for any given quantity of office work is subject to a great many considerations. The type of office work, the physical units, the shape of the area, the general effect desired, and the location of service facilities are examples of factors to be taken into account. Of prime importance are the individual circumstances of each case. Certain guiding data are available, but judgment and experience must be used in determining the correct amount of space.

Desk Space Standards. Fairly uniform space standards have been evolved for common office units, such as desks, chairs, and files. For example, when 60 × 34-inch desks are arranged as single units with aisles adjacent, or when they are arranged in pairs, end for end, with aisles adjacent to each desk, the minimum space standard from back

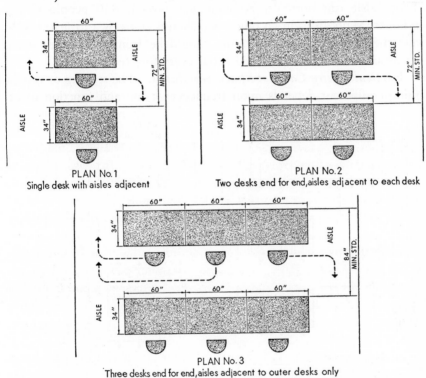

PLAN No. 1
Single desk with aisles adjacent

PLAN No. 2
Two desks end for end, aisles adjacent to each desk

PLAN No. 3
Three desks end for end, aisles adjacent to outer desks only

FIG. 18–1. Minimum standards for back-to-back arrangement of desks under different floor plan layouts.

to back of desks is about 72 inches. See Figure 18–1 (top illustration). These arrangements provide about a three-foot strip for the chair and for getting to and from the desk. However, when three desks are used end for end, with aisles adjacent to outer desks only, the minimum standard for space from back to back of desks must be increased to about 84 inches, thus providing a chair space of around four feet. This extra distance is necessary so that the employee at the middle desk can get in and out without unnecessary disturbance to the occupants at the outer desks. The bottom illustration of Figure 18–1 shows this case.

Generally speaking, the arrangement of two desks end for end, as illustrated by Plan No. 2, necessitates the smallest area per clerk of any conventional desk arrangement. In contrast, the arrangement of desks in single units, as shown in Plan No. 1, requires the greatest amount of space per clerk.

Office Corridor Standards. Main corridors should be from 5 to 8 feet wide, depending upon the amount of traffic to be handled. A 5-foot aisle can normally accommodate around 850 people in five minutes. Main aisles in an office area should be from 4 to 5 feet wide, and the range of secondary aisles should be from 3 to 4 feet wide. Cross aisles should be provided about every fifty feet.

Vertical Filing Cabinet Space Standards. The spacing of vertical filing equipment depends upon frequency of use and function of the

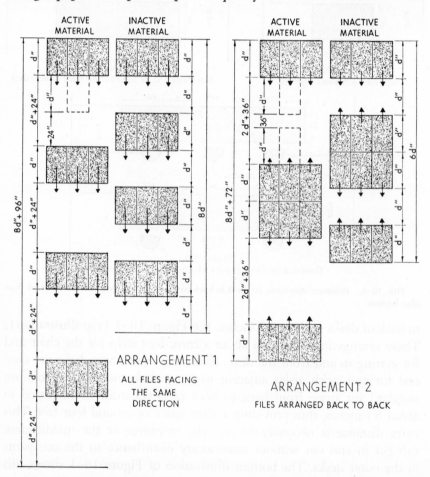

FIG. 18–2. Illustrating the saving in space of arranging files back to back.

material filed. For active material the aisle space should be equal to the drawer depth plus 24 inches if files are facing the same direction, or two-drawer depths plus 36 inches if files are arranged back to back. If the material is storage or inactive, the aisles between filing tiers should be equal to the depth of the drawer, or about 28 inches. As shown in Figure 18–2, to save space, the cabinets should be arranged back-to-back which arrangement, for four files, results in a distance savings of 24 inches for active and 2d, or about 56 inches, for inactive material.

SPACE ESTIMATES

Studies show that a value of 50 square feet of space for each *ordinary clerical employee* is a desirable standard, and when an office layout calls for this amount, the space utilization may be considered highly satisfactory.

The value of 50 square feet per ordinary clerical employee is arrived at in this manner:

```
54-inch desk and chair, 54" x 72"  = 27.00 sq. ft.
Aisle per desk, 18" x 72"          =  9.00 sq. ft.
Miscellaneous (files, aisles, etc.) = 14.00 sq. ft.
                Total................50.00 sq. ft.
```

In actual practice, however, this value is frequently very difficult to achieve. An average of around 60 is probably better. Anything greater than this frequently means that improvements in the layout are possible; anything less probably means crowded conditions. Space estimates for other personnel include:

	Total Square Feet of Space	Approximate Dimensions of Space
Top executive..................	400–450	20 × 20
Intermediate executive..........	275–300	14 × 20
Supervisory executive...........	110–125	14 × 8
Chief clerk....................	75–80	10 × 8

It must be remembered that space estimates are *estimates*. The amount of space that can or should be used is greatly influenced by the available total area, the number and type of equipment and machines, the space standards used, and the location of service areas.

SURPLUS AREA

As far as possible, efforts should be made to determine what amount of space appears to be appropriate, and this amount should be allocated—no more and no less. In cases where the total space available is greater than that deemed necessary, the surplus should either be immediately utilized for other purposes, screened off and held in readiness for future use, or rented to other interests. Following a do-nothing attitude and permitting the space to remain open and idle usually results in current adjacent activities spilling over into these areas, and after this happens, it is difficult to get them back into the area where they belong. Also, any semblance of space control is lessened, and an orderly planned expansion program is ignored.

BASIC LAYOUT GUIDES

Over a period of time there have been developed a number of layout guides which should be followed in order to provide an effective office arrangement. Not all of these can be followed in any one layout, but in general the more that are included, the better the layout. A list includes:

1. Utilize one large area in preference to an equivalent area of small parcels. The single large area permits better lighting, ventilating, supervising, and communicating.

2. Use uniform size desks in any one area. This gives better appearance and promotes the feeling of equality among employees.

3. Keep filing cabinets and other cabinets at uniform height in any one area to improve general appearance.

4. Use straight symmetry in layout. Avoid offsets, jogs, and angle arrangements.

5. Provide for work to flow in straight lines as nearly as possible. Avoid backtracking, crisscrossing, and unnecessary movement of papers. Give major preference to the dominant flows of work.

6. Provide for maximum work loads.

7. Have the work come to the employee, not the employee go to the work. Keep employee flow to a minimum.

8. Place related departments adjacent and keep jobs of a similar nature in close relationship.

9. Anticipate and provide for future changes. Keep the layout flexible.

10. Locate supervisors at the rear of their work groups so that they can easily observe what goes on in the work area.

11. Place all employees so that they face in the same direction. Do not have employees facing one another.

12. Arrange desks so that ample natural light comes over the left shoulder. Do not have the employee facing a window.

13. Avoid private office locations which cut off natural light to the adjacent general office area.

14. Place units requiring noisy equipment and machines in an area with soundproofing to avoid disturbance to others.

15. Locate departments which normally have many visitors from the outside near the entrance or, if this is not feasible, make provisions so that this traffic will not disturb other departments.

16. Put files and frequently used equipment near the employees who use them. Abstain from putting all files at deadwall space.

17. Place filing cabinets back to back.

18. If a corner is required, consider the possibility of providing it with filing cabinets.

19. If possible, provide lounging areas where employees can relax during rest periods, talk informally, and eat lunch.

20. Provide convenient and adequate rest-room facilities.

GENERAL APPROACH IN OFFICE LAYOUT

There is no standardized approach in determining an office layout, but for general expediency and satisfactory results the following twelve recommended steps are discussed.

1. *Secure a drawing or blueprint of the available area.* In obtaining the drawing or blueprint, care should be exercised to insure that the information shown is accurate and complete. In the event that no print is available, the space should be measured and the dimensions indicated on a neatly drawn hand sketch. A convenient scale is $\frac{1}{4}'' = 1'$, which means that $\frac{1}{4}$ inch on the drawing is equal to 1 foot of actual floor dimension. The exact location and size of radiators, windows, building offsets, and door swings, and the location of columns, pipes, electric light outlets and wiring, ducts for telephone wiring, running water facilities, and entrances and exits, are important. Frequently the ability to adapt a suggested layout depends upon the completeness and accuracy of these data. A building offset incorrectly spotted, or the omission of a radiator, can necessitate changes and alterations in a proposed layout and cause an otherwise acceptable layout to be rejected.

2. *Determine the areas of main traffic movement.* These areas will depend upon such things as the size and shape of the space available and the general type of office. The location of building facilities such as entrances and exits, stairways, elevators, rest rooms, and the like will suggest areas of greatest travel. From this information the location of the main corridors, reception rooms, and wardrobe rooms in the layout will be suggested.

3. *Gain a complete over-all picture of the work to be done in the area.* Gaining an over-all picture is not easy, yet at the same time it is not especially difficult. The organization material of the office will assist in determining what unit does what work and, in turn, what employee performs what work.[2] Study of this information will be helpful. In addition, this over-all picture might suggest to the office planner the re-assignment of certain duties among the groups in order to gain a better layout. Subsequently, the suggestions can be evaluated and decided.

As already mentioned, information must be known regarding the flow of work in, through, and out of the office. The importance of this point is brought out by the following: "All parcels of space have a basic circulation plan around which the office layout is built. This is one of the first matters to study in looking over a parcel of existing space, or when planning for new construction."[3] An analysis of the various procedures used, the specific work involved in preparing the number and type of reports, and the various services rendered are among the important considerations to be included. The usual sequence of operations in performing the work should be listed so that the space relationship of desks or machines will be in a convenient, logical order, according to the progressive steps of the work.

4. *Determine the quantity, size, and type of physical units to be included.* There are several ways in which this can be done. For example, they can be calculated by dividing the estimated quantity of work by the accepted standard of performance. To illustrate, for 750 orders daily and a standard of 250 orders per day per unit, the requirements are $750 \div 250 = 3$, which means that provision for three units must be made in the layout to take care of these orders.

Another way is to use a list showing the various types and sizes of the units to be included. Such a list usually is a copy of what has been used in the past or is based on estimates of what probably should be included. There is usually little, if any, scientific determination of the items on such a list, and for the most part it represents an opinion of what should be used. This approach is satisfactory as a temporary expedient, but efforts should be made as soon as possible to determine with some accuracy what items are really needed. This may require close co-operation with the procedures planning and the methods of performing the work.

---

[2] Organizing is discussed in Section IV of this book.

[3] K. H. Ripnen, "Office Space Administration," *Office Management Series No. 114,* American Management Association (New York, 1946), p. 15.

Data should also be available regarding any type of work, machine, or equipment which is exceptionally noisy or otherwise objectionable. Such physical elements should be noted and, as stated in the previous page, consideration given to the possibility of locating them in areas isolated from the office proper.

5. *Identify the basic groups making up the office.* These data can be obtained from the organization structure.[4] Normally they include the top management and various departmental and divisional groups; however, sometimes units smaller than a division can be used, depending upon the individual requirements. Among the more typical groupings are: top management, sales, purchasing, accounting, billing, cost, stenographic, and estimating, and these form the nucleus around which the layout will be made. They serve as small segments for convenience in handling the entire layout.

6. *Consult briefly with the head of each basic group.* This is primarily to gain some idea of what each group leader has in mind regarding his particular unit, and it affords the leaders the opportunity to speak up and to have some voice in the layout work. Frequently very valuable suggestions are received. In some instances conflicts, such as several groups wanting the same space, are encountered, but these can usually be worked out as the entire layout work proceeds. The important point is that by consulting with the group leaders at this step, an opportunity is given for an expression of their space needs and how these needs can be provided for.

7. *Formulate tentative answers regarding the use or nonuse of private offices for each basic group.* A complete discussion on the use of private offices is made in the following section of this chapter. The various factors raised in this discussion should be carefully weighed in arriving at the decision of whether or not to use private offices. For purposes of illustration, assume that, for the time being, the tentative answer is to use six private offices in the top management group and one in each of the five departmental groups. These data are then added to the physical units information discussed previously under point 4.

8. *Make templates to scale of all physical units (or use models), and identify clearly.* A "template" is a scaled pattern, made of cardboard or paper, which is used to represent the floor area occupied by a physical unit. The scale of the templates must be the same as that of the drawing showing the available area; as already pointed out, a scale of $\frac{1}{4}'' = 1'$ is convenient. Frequently the shape of the templates is

---

[4] See Section IV in this book on subject of organizing.

confined to that of a square or a rectangle, and in most cases this is satisfactory; but there are instances where the details of cutoff corners, rounded corners, and the like should be included in the templates, as the final arrangement may hinge upon these considerations. Figure 18–3 illustrates floor-plan symbols which are commonly used in layout work.

A separate template should be made for each physical unit considered in the layout. For purposes of identification, the name of the

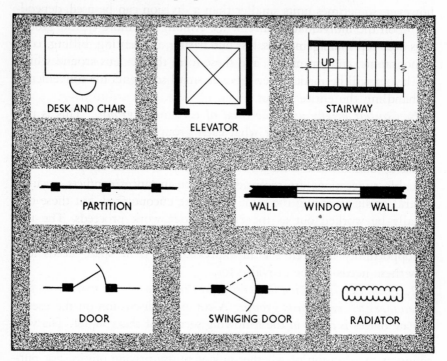

FIG. 18–3. Office floor-plan symbols.

unit and of the basic group by which the unit is to be used should be stamped or printed on each template. It is also possible to use different colors representing different physical units to help visualize the work. Where private offices are considered, templates covering the over-all floor dimensions should be made and clearly identified. Details of the arrangement within the private offices can be postponed temporarily until it is determined if the entire space will be available for use.

Instead of templates, small scale three-dimensional models of the physical units can be used. These models are dimensionally accurate and show at a glance the arrangement of the office. Complete kits, consisting of several hundred pieces including desks, chairs, files, machines, coat racks, and building columns, are available. Magnetic templates and magnetic models can also be used along with steel-covered plywood as the base. Some companies have found sandpaper-backed templates on flannel boards to be highly effective, since they permit vertical display of office layouts and are well suited for meetings.

9. *Arrange templates or models for each basic group within its respective tentative area in accordance with effective office layout principles.* The suggested layout is determined by moving and shifting the templates or models to various positions so as to arrive at an effective arrangement. This phase of layout is a tentative trial-and-error process. It requires considerable time and cannot be rushed. If magnetic templates or models are used, they can be moved about as desired, yet when released they hold a fixed position. When the contemplated layout is completed, a picture of it can be taken and white paper copies made so that convenient reference sheets are provided.

10. *Check entire tentative layout and make minor adjustments as required.* After the units in each group have been arranged in the best manner, the next step is to review the entire layout in order to see that it is a well-knit arrangement which will meet the particular needs. Provision for the smooth flow of all work through the entire office is checked; the extent of complimentary units along common division lines is noted; and the general appearance of the entire layout is reviewed. Usually minor adjustments are made to achieve the over-all effect desired.

11. *Indicate by appropriate markings the major flows of work and the telephone and electric wiring. Also include the name of the employee to be located at each unit.* This information is necessary in order to gain a complete understanding of the layout. The location of electric wiring outlets is especially important where groups of electrically driven machines are used. In many cases some wiring arrangements must be provided for getting current to each desk.[5] The name of the employee at each work unit is helpful to the office executive in visualizing the arrangement.

12. *Recheck related layout with each respective basic group and, after securing respective sanctions, submit the over-all plan to the top managers for final approval.* The first basic group to consult, of course, is the top managers. Point out where the executives will be located, what facilities are provided, and the chief considerations determining the recommended layout. Generally minor changes will be suggested,

---

[5] See pages 307–11 of Chapter 16.

and they can usually be incorporated. The same approach is followed with each group head. If the plan follows closely along the suggested ideas of the group head, as disclosed in step 6 above, it is well to point out this fact. If not, an explanation of the recommended layout should be made, with the reasons carefully pointed out in a simple, logical way. After all groups have O.K.'d their respective layouts, the entire plan is submitted to the top managers with the statement that this layout has the approval of each group head. Acceptance by the top managers is then usually little more than a formality.

THE PRIVATE OFFICE

The subject of the private office warrants special attention, and decisions regarding its use should be made only after ample consideration has been given to the individual circumstances. A private office should be used when its use is dictated by facts and unbiased judgment. It should never be provided simply because it has always been provided for a particular job or because requests and sometimes pressure have been brought to bear.

Justifications for Private Office. A proponent for a private office will usually seek to justify his views upon three considerations: (1) prestige, (2) suitable space for work requiring high concentration, and (3) proper accommodations for confidential work. Because of prestige considerations, most top management members are supplied with private offices. This helps add weight, influence, and respect to this group in the eyes of other employees and of visitors to the office. Aside from top managers there are other members of the office who, for reasons of prestige, probably merit separate private offices. They include department heads and professional people. In many cases, however, the department head prefers and can perform the most effective supervision when located in the general area of his unit with additional individual space.

The second major consideration, to provide suitable space for work requiring high concentration, can usually be determined objectively. Creative work, such as writing advertising copy and preparing difficult reports, usually justifies a private office. Likewise, employees doing intricate analysis, original planning, close mental work, and work requiring exclusive attention with a minimum of distraction merit a private office.

The third important reason, proper accommodations for confidential work, is significant in work involving research, planning, control, and consolidating recaps of important statistics. Likewise, the conversations during personnel selection interviews are of a confidential sort, and it is best to conduct them in a private office. However, the importance of confidential work can be overemphasized by employees, and extreme care should be exercised in determining whether this consideration actually warrants a private office.

Objections to Private Offices. The relative high cost is a paramount objection to private offices because with them space utilization is about 35–50 per cent that of the open-area arrangement. In addition, the buying, erecting, maintaining, and, in case of alteration, moving of partitions entail expenditures which cumulatively amount to quite sizable figures.

Another objection often made is that the use of private offices may tend to slow up the work by interfering with supervisory effectiveness. The closeness of the supervisor to the employees, his familiarity with problems as they arise, and his being at the heart of all happenings in his unit are the types of things that are usually lost when the supervisor is segregated by a private office. In order to see that an order is carried out properly, it is frequently best to be close at hand to give instructions, check performance, and provide encouragement.

Furthermore, private offices complicate the heating, ventilating, and lighting of these areas as well as of adjoining areas. Individual segments of space, set off from the large area, requires special arrangements to supply these services, all of which means additional materials and labor.

Moreover, the use of private offices may prevent other arrangements which work out equally well or better. Such arrangements include the use of dwarf partitions, railings, modular furniture with partitions, and conference rooms. These are discussed in the following paragraphs.

MOVABLE PARTITIONS

For segregating the private offices needed and dividing the office space as the approved layout requires, the use of movable partitions is winning increasing favor. Movable partitions are made from metal or wood and are easily erected, dismantled, and relocated. They are prefabricated and factory finished. Wiring and outlets are laid in the baseboards and joints. A variety of styles, colors, and finishes are offered. Panels with recesses for bookcases, alcoves for drinking fountains, provisions for door openings, and with or without glass (crystal or obscure) in the top areas are among the many available kinds offered to fit requirements for every type of working space. Various heights, ranging from the railing to the ceiling, are available. Door units can be selected from either single or double models; they may be hinged, double-acting, or sliding. The partitions are soundproof, with insulating material in the center or core.

Movable partitions afford great flexibility in office layout; they make it economically possible to fit the available space to new layouts whenever the need occurs. The panels can be used over and over again. Not only space flexibility but also space control and high material salvage are thus realized. Changes in layout can be made overnight or during a week end. In many instances the cost of erecting movable partitions is only 15 per cent of that of immovable tile and plaster walls. Furthermore, the use of movable partitions eliminates objectionable inconveniences such as noise, commotion, debris, dirt, waiting for plaster and paint to dry, and, after partition installation, the cleaning of rugs, draperies, and furniture.

Partitions from about 36 inches to 84 inches in height are very popular. They afford privacy, yet do not interfere with ventilating and lighting as much as partitions extending from the floor to the ceiling. In many cases a 36-inch partition is used to surround the work area of one person, thus affording many advantages of a private office at much less expense and trouble. However, movable partitions creating the effect of private offices have, in some instances in their initial usage, resulted in employees behind the partitions becoming loud and boisterous. In such cases an educational job on how to use "partitioned offices" has corrected the situation.

For partitions higher than 36 inches, the use of clear or crystal glass for the upper portion of the partition is highly satisfactory. This design permits the occupant to look out and see what is going on—an important consideration for a supervisor's office; it also minimizes the obstruction to light, and the cost is reasonable. Sometimes a frosted or obscure glass is preferred. Figure 18–4 shows several examples of movable office partitions. In the top view the use of the low partition is shown, while in the bottom view the panel with the obscure top glass section is illustrated.

Railings are used, especially in banks, with outstanding success. The old layout idea of having executives in private offices concealed in the rear of the bank has given way to the modern plan, whereby executives are in the front, open portion of the bank area, with offices divided by low railings. This arrangement is of relatively low cost, minimizes the need for special lighting and heating facilities, makes a pleasing appearance, and is convenient both for the officers and the customers.

Courtesy: General Fireproofing Co., Youngstown, Ohio

FIG. 18–4. Effective use of movable office partitions.

MODULAR EQUIPMENT

Modular equipment and its availability with partition panels was pointed out in Chapter 13.[6] Such units give a private office effect and satisfactorily meet many privacy and prestige requirements. Figure 18–5 shows several arrangements. The illustration on the left is a popular arrangement for a series of private office areas; the illustration

---

[6] See Chapter 13, pp. 245–46.

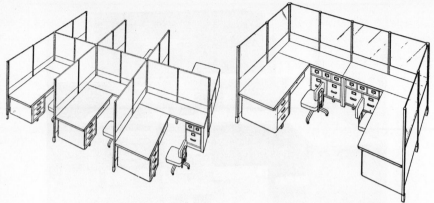

Courtesy: Globe-Wernicke Co., Cincinnati

FIG. 18–5. Popular arrangements made from interlocking, interchangeable component units.

on the right is a U-unit with glass in the upper sections of the partitions.

Modular-type arrangements save floor space and increase efficiency. Figure 18–6 illustrates a comparison between conventional desk units and modular units, with a saving of 22.4 per cent of floor area resulting from the use of the modular units. At the same time, the smaller space is more convenient and provides an adequate work area.

CONFERENCE ROOM

For meetings in privacy a conference room is highly recommended. Many private offices are not suited for the handling of meetings. With a conference room, the participants can be arranged more satisfactorily; a greater number can usually be accommodated; and each one can have a convenient place to write or to take notes. Furthermore, the meeting is placed on a businesslike basis, with a minimum of interference and distractions. The conference room should be located conveniently where traffic in and out of the room will be least disturbing to the other office employees. The top illustration of Figure 18–7 (page 366) shows an effective layout for a conference room.

RECEPTION ROOM

Careful attention should be given to the reception room. It creates the initial impression of the enterprise upon the visitor, and it is true that initial impressions are often lasting ones. The reception room can, therefore, help create favorable reactions and assist in building public good will.

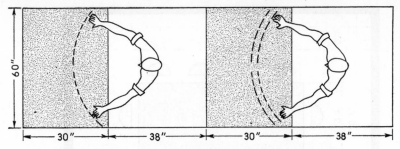

DESK AREAS = 3,600 SQ. IN.   TOTAL AREA OCCUPIED = 8,160 SQ. IN.

CONVENTIONAL DESK UNITS

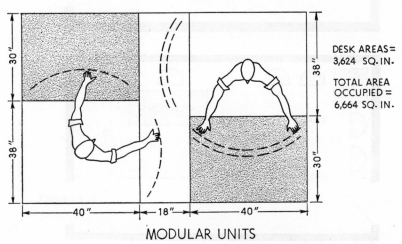

DESK AREAS = 3,624 SQ. IN.

TOTAL AREA OCCUPIED = 6,664 SQ. IN.

MODULAR UNITS

Courtesy: Globe-Wernicke Co., Cincinnati

FIG. 18–6. A comparison of conventional desk units with modular units shows that, for the same number of employees and approximately the same desk areas, the modular units save nearly 23 per cent of floor space (8,160 square inches compared with 6,664 square inches).

The reception room should have an attractive, inviting appearance. Many managers have found that displays of the company's products or illustrations of its services are very effective. Keeping the room clean also helps. Chairs should be kept in a straight line, with newspapers and magazines arranged neatly on a table, and ash trays kept clean.

To add to the caller's comfort it is well to include some sort of cloakroom facilities to the reception room. A convenient place to leave one's hat and coat is appreciated by many callers, particularly in inclement weather and when the call is of fairly long duration. The providing of a telephone and a washroom are additional conveniences, but the decision on them should be based on the requirements and the cost of providing and maintaining them.

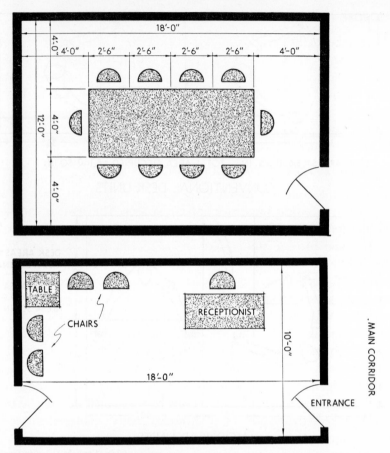

FIG: 18–7. *Top:* Suggested layout of conference room for ten people. The table size is 4 x 10 feet. For each two additional people to be accommodated, add 2 feet 6 inches to table length and to room length. *Bottom:* Suggested layout for small reception rooms.

Whenever possible, the reception room should not handle ordinary and necessary traffic between different areas in the office. Employees walking across the reception room create a disturbing influence and distract from the dignity of the entire office. To prevent this condition, it is best to provide a passage for regular office traffic which bypasses or goes around the reception room.

The possibilities for the arrangement of the reception room are almost endless. The illustration at the bottom of Figure 18–7 gives a satisfactory layout for a small room. Sometimes the work of receptionist and switchboard operator can be combined when the amount of work can be conveniently handled by one person. However, very often this is not the case.

WARDROBE FACILITIES

Wardrobe facilities can be provided either by having separate rooms —locker or cloakrooms—or by placing wardrobe racks in the office areas. If the former plan is used, provision should include separate rooms for men and women. When racks are used, they can be located throughout the office areas. Units are available which provide storage for coats, hats, overshoes, umbrellas, and the like for as many as three persons per square foot of floor area.

CORRECTIVE MEASURES FOR TROUBLE SPOTS

One of the common mistakes in office layout is an arrangement necessitating needless movement of employees. The remedy includes: heed the major flows of papers, bring together employees who work together, and provide the correct space btween desks and machines. Gaps in the flow of work are perhaps best handled by straightening the line of work flow and studying the sequence or steps. Another error is the lack of a co-ordinator for all office layouts within a given enterprise. When such a person is present, the desired uniformity, interrelationships, and equitable space distribution can be gained. A third common error is a tendency to stay with an old inefficient layout thereby retarding progress and making needed layout changes very difficult. Alertness to new ideas, comparison of costs, and strong desires to improve space utilization must be stimulated in order to overcome this keep-the-layout-as-it-is attitude. Lastly, management members in some instances err by not being alert to indicators of employee discomfort caused by physical facilities and evidenced by complaints, drop in work output, and increase in errors. Quite often the solution is revising the layout, getting the physical units in proper repair, improve the lighting, or seeing that better ventilation is afforded.

QUESTIONS

1. Carefully point out the relationship that exists between the flow of office work and the office layout.
2. What are the basic considerations in office layout work? Discuss the one you feel is most important.
3. Explain Figure 18–1 in your own words.
4. Relate eight layout guides that you feel are of major importance.
5. In determining an office layout, discuss the steps of (1) "gaining a complete over-all picture of the work to be done in the area," and (2) "making templates to scale of all physical units or use scale models and identify clearly."

6. In your opinion should an office supervisor be located at the front, rear, or center of his or her group? Should he be facing in the same direction as or in an opposite direction from, the work group? Give reasons for your answers.

7. Carefully evaluate the three considerations upon which the proponent for a private office seeks to justify his views. Which one do you feel is most valid? Why? The least valid? Why?

8. Approximately how much office space would you allot to each of the following:

   a) Two desks end for end (60 × 34-inch desk), aisle adjacent, chair for each desk.

   b) Private office for top executive.

   c) General office space for eight clerks.

   d) A conference room for ten persons.

9. Discuss fully: "The layout of vertical filing cabinets should be of a back-to-back arrangement."

10. Do you favor the use of movable partitions in an office layout? Justify your answer.

11. Comment on the following statement: "Money spent in redecorating and refurnishing a reception room can be better spent in fixing up the office proper. The reception room has little, if any, relationship to the efficiency with which the paper work of an office is accomplished."

12. Select a local business concern which employs about twenty to thirty office workers. Visit this office and make a rough sketch of the present office layout, indicating the approximate dimensions and location of equipment and furniture. Be sure to note the location of such things as electric light outlets, windows, radiators, running water, and doors (also whether they swing in or out, or both).

   Take these data home and make a scale drawing, using a scale of ½″ = 1′. Clearly identify all parts of the drawing.

   Carefully study this layout, and using the principles of office layout as a guide, note the places where you believe the present layout can be improved. Give reasons for your opinions.

   Now prepare a revised layout and support it with a brief discussion, pointing out the effective features incorporated in your improved layout.

CASE PROBLEMS

CASE 18–1.   UNIVERSAL CORK COMPANY

Representatives of this company just signed a ten-year lease for office building space as shown in the accompanying drawing. The area will be used as the district sales office. To meet the company's requirement, an effective arrangement for the following minimum equipment within this space is needed:

Three salesmen's desks, 60 × 32, and chairs
Two stenographers' desks, 60 × 32, and chairs
Two bookkeepers' desks, 60 × 32, and chairs

One 60 × 32 table
One 72 × 38 drafting table and stool
One 44 × 23 blueprint rack
One 36 × 18 telephone switchboard and chair to be located as shown on drawing
Three five-drawer filing cabinets
One private office for district manager
One reception room or area

PROBLEMS:

1. Draw your recommended office layout for the company.
2. Justify your recommendations.

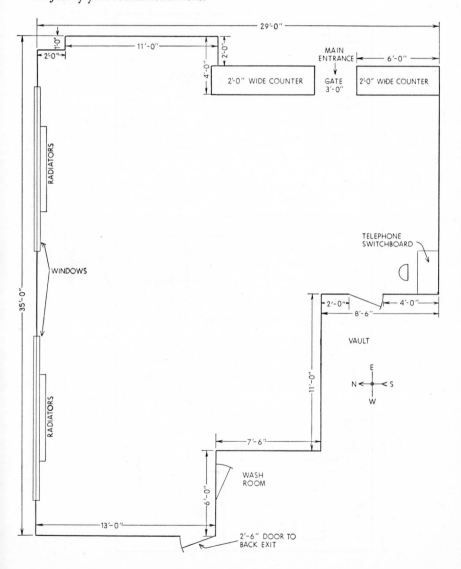

CASE 18–2. HAVERVILLE WEEKLY SENTINEL

The present layout of the front office of this weekly newspaper is illustrated by the accompanying drawing. The over-all dimensions are 30 feet by 16 feet. The increasing amount of work necessitates that within this area provision be made for two additional employees, as assistant bookkeeper and an assistant classified advertising manager. The heat registers and the counter are not to be changed, but the locations of all other units can be changed. The general manager wishes to keep his present desk, and he is agreeable to getting new desks

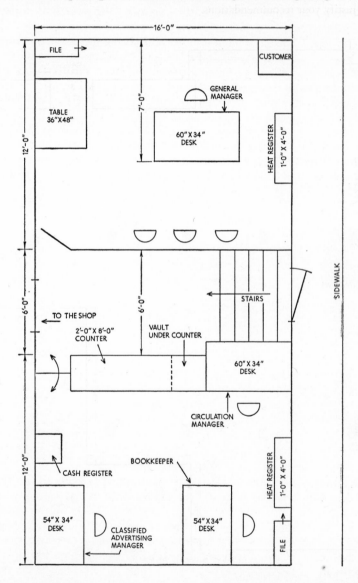

for the others. The minimum desk size to be considered is 42 inches wide by 32 inches deep.

PROBLEMS:

1. Draw a recommended front office layout for the Haverville Weekly Sentinel.

2. Point out the strong points about your layout. The weak points.

CASE 18–3.   EMPIRE STATE MORTGAGE COMPANY

New offices are being laid out for this company. The space is an entire floor of a building, featuring a clear span area 56 feet 10 inches wide by 175 feet 8 inches, without a single column or other obstruction, thereby permitting complete flexibility of office layout. Floor-to-ceiling windows are featured on all sides of the space. A cellular flooring contains raceways for all wiring and affords a maximum of convenient locations for such outlets. The space is designed with 5 feet 2 inches modules center to center both ways. All partitions are to be movable and erected on module lines, thus tying in with the building outside columns and metal portions of the glass window casings. As indicated on the accompanying drawing, leading from a lobby is the entranceway—on the other side of the lobby (not shown) are elevators, washrooms, and service facilities and need not be considered in this case problem.

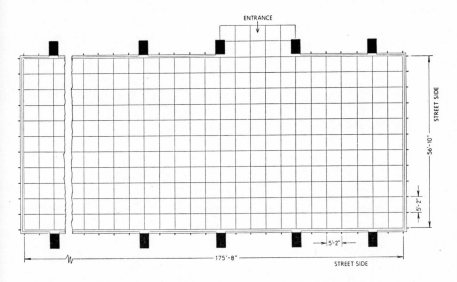

The company specializes in real estate management and mortgages. There is a president with a private secretary and three general vice-presidents with two private secretaries. The offices of these top executives should not be located too far apart. An additional and separate area of about 150 square feet should be furnished for these executives' files. Also, there are four executive vice-presidents, each with a private secretary. Reporting to each of these executive vice-presidents are:

1. To V.P. of Accounting—12 accountants and 2 special staff people.

2. To V.P. of Management—4 clerks and 5 special staff people.

3. To V.P. of Sales—2 clerks and 2 special staff people.

4. To V.P. of Mortgages—9 clerks and 2 lawyers, each lawyer having a private secretary.

Wherever possible, special staff people are to be given preferred locations. Each executive vice-president should be near his particular work group.

Also to be provided are a conference room about 3 × 3 modules in area; a second conference room about 2 × 3 modules; a fairly large reception area; an employees conference room and lounge; areas for storage of employees' coats and hats; an office machine room approximately 3 × 4 modules; a cashier department for three cashiers—made accessible to public for payment of bills—a payroll clerk, a switchboard operator, a mail and messenger boy; a centralized filing area of about 900 square feet including offices for filing manager and her assistant; an area of about 600 square feet for stored filed material and storage of office supplies.

PROBLEMS:

1. Draw your recommended layout for this company.

2. Discuss what areas or requirements you found most difficult to solve before arriving at your final recommendation.

3. Point out the practices of effective office layout that your layout incorporates.

PART IV......

Organizing the Work of the Office

The next fundamental function of office management to be discussed is organizing. This includes apportioning the work to be done as determined by planning, assigning the distributed work to specific members of the work group, and establishing the proper work relationships among them. Effective organizing is essential in managing an office. The four chapters that follow deal with office organizing.

Chapter · 19

Organization of the Office

It is easy to fool yourself. It is more difficult to fool the people you work for. It is still more difficult to fool the people you work with. And it is almost impossible to fool the people who work under your direction.

—HARRY B. THAYER

ORGANIZING BECOMES a necessity when two or more people work together. Decisions must be made regarding who does what work, who reports to whom, and who decides what types of issues. Organizing deals with these basic questions.

MEANING OF ORGANIZING

Organizing is the allocating of the total work to be done among the work group, establishing the relative authority and responsibility of each individual who is placed in charge of each work component, and supplying the proper work environment. In organizing, a manager is concerned with (1) work—how to distribute it, (2) people—who are going to do what work, (3) relationships—what is the relative authority and responsibility among the "organization units" formed by the work distribution and the respective people doing it, and (4) work environment—what tools and workplaces will best contribute toward maximum work accomplishments. From the managerial viewpoint, organizing results in the determination of an "organization structure." This can be thought of as the over-all framework joining the functions of an enterprise and establishing definite relationships among the personnel who perform the respective functions.

Organizing is a dynamic, not a static, process. As a result, changes take place in an organization structure; this is the common occurrence rather than the exception. Changes in organization structure take place for many reasons, such as changes in the objectives of the enterprise, changes in personnel, and changes in the conditions outside the enterprise. The student of management must fully realize that organization structure is a living, present, dynamic entity—it is not a static concept. The effective manager normally changes his organization structure from time to time in order best to meet the current requirements of the enterprise.

IMPORTANCE OF ORGANIZING

Organizing makes possible the effective operation of a group. It is the basis for teamwork. The members can serve as a unit directing all their various efforts toward a common goal. Each member of the group can contribute his maximum and his speciality toward the major objective. A management member can be effective only when he knows specifically what work he is to manage, who is to assist him, to whom he reports, and what members are in his work group. Likewise, a non-management member must know how he and his work fit into the total picture, to whom he reports, what he is to do, when, and who, if anyone, helps him.

Of significant importance is that organizing enables a manager to enlarge his scope of operation or effectiveness. Organizing makes it possible for a manager to accomplish much more than he could as an individual. It provides the means for using effectively the work of other people, and it sets the groundwork for the development of people. In fact, failure to organize properly limits any manager's ability to manage. Many problems of management stem in part from poor organizing—according to various estimates, some one half of all management problems originate from organizational defects.

PURPOSE OF ORGANIZING

From what has already been stated it follows that the purpose of organizing has many expressions. It is to avoid needless duplication of efforts. It is to get individuals to work effectively as members of a team, not separately as single individuals. It is to avoid confusion and misunderstandings as to who is to do what work. It is to prevent buck-passing, an excessive number of managers, and misinformed employees. Organizing assists in the management job of achieving the objective in the best manner by means of a group consisting of an informed and satisfied work force. In short, the major purpose of organizing is *co-ordination*. It is the blending together of all the group's efforts and facilities into a concerted unit directed toward achieving a stated goal efficiently.

From the office manager's viewpoint, this co-ordination must be achieved in two different areas: (1) interdepartmental—among the office and other major organizational units of the enterprise, and (2) intradepartmental—among the activities making up the office. The extent and importance of the required co-ordination can probably best be understood from the interdepartmental viewpoint, that is, considering the relationships of the office organization to the organization of the whole enterprise. This follows because, as pointed out in Chapter 1, the office provides a facilitating service which helps others to perform their work more effectively; it is a service unit for the benefit of other units of the organization. This being the case, it is important to keep in mind the activities performed by the entire enterprise so that a better understanding of the office activities will be realized.

MAIN FUNCTIONS OF TYPICAL ENTERPRISE

In the typical organization there are three major activities to be performed: production, sales, and finance. Each must be done satisfactorily if the enterprise is to survive. The creating of a utility for others is basic for most enterprises. This, in turn, necessitates selling efforts so that the product or service is made available to buyers. The producing and selling efforts necessitate financing activities in that ample capital must be obtained and maintained.

Office work is done to help fulfill these main functions, it is not performed apart from them. Production activities such as cutting, sewing, machining, assembling, painting, drying, and packing are assisted by the work of the office. Likewise, typical sales activities such as merchandising, analysis of markets, and selling efforts are helped by the office. And the same is true of finance in which many records and papers are needed.

ORGANIZATIONAL CONTENT AND PLACEMENT OF THE OFFICE

The questions can now be asked, "What activities should be included in the office?" and, "Where should the office organizational unit be placed in the organization of the entire enterprise?" The answers must be known before effective co-ordination, both inter- and intradepartmentwise, of the office activities can be achieved.

To designate an organizational unit as "the office" can be confusing. Actually it is neither likely to be in one location nor to include all office activities. Office work is not an activity in and of itself but a part of and employed in almost every function. Office work contributes information needed in performing the major functions of production, sales, finance, and other functions, such as engineering and purchasing, that are necessary in a particular organizational structure.

Logically, from the organizing point of view, the required office work should be located where it can be performed at lowest cost and with highest service to those using it. This is determined by giving consideration to a number of factors of which the following are important: (1) the type and nature of the entire enterprise, (2) the importance which top managers attach to office management, and (3) the extent to which office functions are centralized. Each of these will be discussed.

TYPE AND NATURE OF THE ENTERPRISE

The content and the placement of the office function are affected greatly by the dominance of the production, sales, or finance activities. If the enterprise is primarily one for production, a large manufacturer, for example, selling its entire output to several large buyers, the office unit probably will be of relatively small importance. However, in a predominantly financial enterprise the work will be relatively of great importance. To illustrate, in a bank or insurance company office work is usually of much greater importance than it is in a manufacturing company. Likewise, in a governmental enterprise the office unit normally occupies a position relatively high in the organization structure.

IMPORTANCE ATTACHED TO OFFICE WORK

If top managers of an enterprise recognize the work of the office as of relatively high significance, the tendency will probably be to bring it together into one organizational unit and place this unit high in the organization structure. But if office work is considered minor, although necessary, it probably will be performed by the department needing it and co-ordinated as completely as possible with the primary activities of the respective department.

EXTENT OF CENTRALIZATION OF OFFICE FUNCTIONS

Since office work occurs throughout the entire enterprise, from the president's office to the lowest paid clerk, it is possible to have it performed in dispersed locations, under the jurisdiction of the unit in which it arises. When this practice is followed, the office function is dispersed and either combined with, or made subordinate to, other organizational units. In its fullest application, this dispersion extends to the smallest and lowest organizational unit of the enterprise. In contrast, a directly opposite arrangement might be used. In this case, the office work is fully concentrated and is placed in the hands of a single executive who is completely responsible for all office activities in the organization.

These two conditions, however, are extreme. From a practical viewpoint, seldom are either used. An intermediate or modified arrangement between these two extremes is commonly followed. These additional arrangements include the doing and placing of office work by major departments and making each department head fully responsible for the office activities in his own department. Or a modification of this can be used in which the office work is distributed among all departments but one person is placed in charge of this office work in order to achieve reasonable co-ordination. Or certain office work can be centralized in one unit and placed under one manager, the remaining office work is performed in the unit in which it arises and is supervised by the regular department head of that unit. This latter arrangement is quite popular and is discussed further in the following paragraphs.

THE OFFICE SERVICES ORGANIZATION

As pointed out and discussed in Chapter 4, so-called "office services" including writing and correspondence work, calculating and checking, filing, record retention, handling the mail, and communicative work are frequently included in the office organizational unit and placed under the "office services manager" or in some cases the "office manager." However, all these services are not always centralized, the notable exception being writing and correspondence work, and calculating and checking. Furthermore, even when all these services are referred to as being centralized, they are only partially so—some of certain services being performed in various units throughout the entire organization structure.

The adoption of an "office services" unit arrangement means that the manager in charge of office work has a dual managerial task. First, he should manage the services unit, and, second, since office work is being performed in various other units in which it arises, he should counsel with the executives of these various units and help them accomplish their office work in the best manner. This second task is of paramount importance and in many respects establishes the true status of the office manager in any organization structure. Actually it is identifying what office work is and demonstrating to other managers in the organization structure how best to accomplish this type of work. It can also be considered as providing the office work viewpoint to all managers of the enterprise. All use office work and hence help in how to use it effectively constitutes a real service. The situation is analogous to that of a personnel manager. Certain personnel work is performed by the personnel management organizational unit, but a big portion of the personnel manager's job is to get other executives in the enterprise to take the personnel viewpoint and to utilize personnel work as a help in achieving their required objectives.

Figure 19-1 shows this dual managerial arrangement of the office management specialist. Under a unit called "office services" are the following activities: report writing, correspondence, calculating, filing, record retention, mail handling, and communications. The unit providing assistance in office management to various other departments is titled "Procedures Department" in the figure. This title is suggestive only. Many other names are used, including methods department, planning department, business services department or systems department, but none identify completely and clearly the work performed. The specific help rendered and the exact position in the organization vary considerably among enterprises. In the illustration the main units comprising the Procedures Department include: (1) office form analysis and design—to suggest the type of office form to use, its format and make-up to do the job required; (2) office equipment and machine analysis—to advise what type of equipment or machine should be used for a specific type of office work under the prescribed conditions; (3) office layout and working conditions—to recommend the most effective arrangement of office facilities and the physical surroundings to supply; (4) office standards—to relate useful levels of performance or frames of reference in order to evaluate achievement; and (5) office work simplification—to point out ways to eliminate waste of all kinds and get the office work out more effectively.

CENTRALIZATION IS KEY

The essential issue in office organization is the degree of centralization which is adopted. As already indicated the degree of centralization of "office services" varies among different enterprises, and by no means do all or even a majority of enterprises have a department akin to the "Procedures Department" of Figure 19-1. Equipment analysis, for example, may be handled by the executive handling the particular function for which the equipment will be used, and, likewise, the executive of the operating department may have charge of

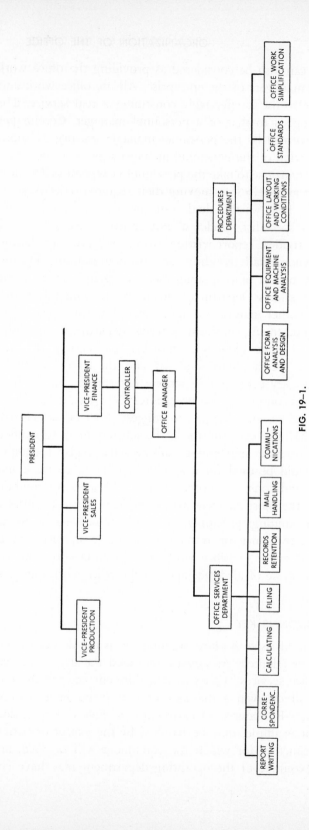

FIG. 19–1.

standards applying to paper work in his unit. The particular organizational pattern followed depends upon many factors, such as the personal preference of top management members, the size and general nature of the enterprise, the quantity of office work, and the repetitiveness of the office work. In the final analysis, the judgment, background, and experience of the manager play very large roles. However, because the key issue is the degree of centralization adopted, further comment on this subject is warranted.

CENTRALIZATION

"Centralization of office activities" means the physical concentration of such activities into a single group, and the management over them vested in one person. For example, in centralized filing, all filing work for an entire office is done by a filing section and managed by a filing chief.

The concept of centralization is well expressed in this excerpt:

"Centralization" means concentration. It may be thought of as a force, directed inward, drawing those things which come within the orbit of its influence toward a common center.[1]

Actually centralization can be of two practical types, namely, from the viewpoint of (1) physical location, or (2) management. Figure 19–2 shows these two practical types illustrated for each of the four possibilities marked "A," "B," "C," and "D" in the illustration.

In the statement above, centralization is considered from both the physical location and management viewpoints. However, to reiterate, *complete* centralization of all office activities from either the physical or management viewpoints is, of course, not practical, but consideration for the type of centralization used helps to clarify office organizational thinking.

EXAMPLE OF DEGREES OF CENTRALIZATION

To illustrate further the effect of centralization upon office organization, assume the activity of filing in an office with four executives in charge of four main divisions. Under a complete centralization arrangement, all filing—including that of the executives and the main divisions—would be handled by the centralized filing unit. All papers and records would be kept in the files of this filing unit, and an executive or any other member of the office would have to consult

---

[1] E. Petersen and E. G. Plowman, *Business Organization and Management* (rev. ed.; Homewood, Ill.: Richard D. Irwin, Inc., 1948), p. 278.

POSSIBILITY "A"

MANAGEMENT: CENTRALIZED
PHYSICAL WORK: CENTRALIZED

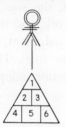

COMMENT: COMMON CONCEPT OF
CENTRALIZATION

POSSIBILITY "B"

MANAGEMENT: CENTRALIZED
PHYSICAL WORK: NOT CENTRALIZED

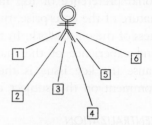

COMMENT: COMMON BUT SOMETIMES NOT
FULLY COMPREHENDED AS A TYPE
OF CENTRALIZATION.

POSSIBILITY "C"

MANAGEMENT: NOT CENTRALIZED
PHYSICAL WORK: NOT CENTRALIZED

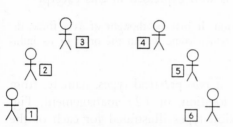

COMMENT: SERIES OF INDIVIDUAL UNITS—ACTUALLY
NO CENTRALIZATION CONCEPT EXISTS

POSSIBILITY "D"

MANAGEMENT: NOT CENTRALIZED
PHYSICAL WORK: CENTRALIZED

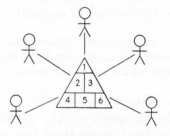

COMMENT: RELATIVELY RARE CONCEPT
OF CENTRALIZATION— LITTLE
USED.

FIG. 19–2.   The four possibilities of centralization.

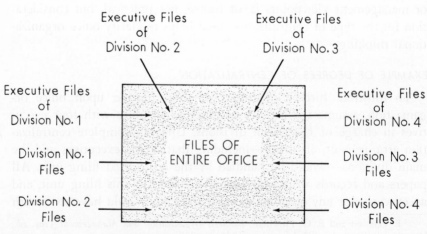

FIG. 19–3.   Illustrative diagram of centralized filing.

these files to secure needed information. Figure 19–3 shows a diagram of centralized filing.

It might be advantageous to have a separate file for the executive of each office division. In each case, this separate file would be managed by the executive himself, or more likely his secretary, and the file would be physically located in or near his office. In addition to these individual files, there would be a central group of files which would contain all material other than that kept by the executives. These central files would be maintained by the personnel of the filing division. Figure 19–4 illustrates this arrangement.

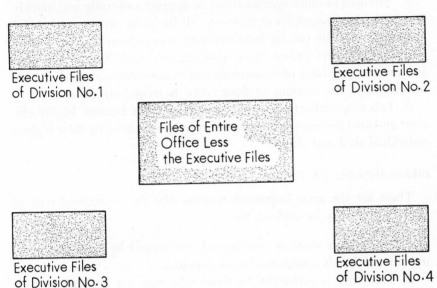

FIG. 19–4. Partial centralization of files.

An arrangement providing less centralization of filing may be followed. The ultimate in this direction is to have the file of each executive and of each employee managed and located near the respective person. This arrangement would give maximum convenience, but at the same time it would undoubtedly encourage duplication, cause high filing costs, and prove impractical for many filing requirements.

ADVANTAGES OF CENTRALIZATION

Since the question of centralization is important and is frequently confronted in office management, the advantages and the disadvantages of centralization will be enumerated. Among the important advantages are:

1. Flexibility is given the organization structure. Work peak loads can be readily handled; office machinery utilized fully; and the effects of labor shortages reduced to a minimum.

2. Equitable wage schedules are fostered. The measurement of office output is encouraged, and comparisons of wages for similar work are possible.

3. Training of office employees is expedited. New employees can be added to centralized groups without seriously affecting the operations of the group. The retraining of old employees for new jobs is also well adapted to a centralized type of organization.

4. Methods of office operation can be applied uniformly and quickly. Standards and procedures common to all divisions can be established, and improvements can be installed with a minimum of effort.

5. Cost of performing office work is decreased. Supervisory costs are lowered; the costs of investment and maintenance on machines are lowered; and the amount of floor space is frequently reduced.

6. Labor specialization is practiced. Employees become highly efficient and are continuously employed on work necessitating their highest individual skill and ability.

DISADVANTAGES OF CENTRALIZATION

These are the most important reasons why the centralized type of arrangement may be undesirable:

1. Much office work is confidential and should be handled by the unit in which this confidential trust is placed.

2. The work is performed by those who may not be familiar with the detailed requirements. Minor changes and corrections cannot be made on the spot.

3. Effective planning and controlling are difficult to exercise since the executives most familiar with the use and purpose of the paper work are not near at hand.

4. Work is done without regard for urgency or importance to the individual office unit. Delays may take place. The efficiency of each unit may be hampered.

5. Costs may increase due to nonproductive transporting and handling time required.

6. Employees of a "generalist" nature are not developed. Some versatile persons with over-all viewpoints are essential in all enterprises.

ORGANIZATION OF THE OFFICE

For purposes of discussion, it is convenient to show the various office activities in chart form and to discuss in turn each major activity. This is illustrated by Figure 19–5. A highly centralized office is considered because it affords a panorama of all office work and simplifies the discussion. However, as discussed above, the extent of centralization in actual practice can be one of many degrees. Few will be of the highly centralized type depicted here. Also, the office manager is shown in charge of the office. Since office work is a service work assisting and affecting practically every part of the enterprise, it can be reasoned that the office manager should report to the president, assistant president, or general manager. Seldom, however, is this the actual case. This can be explained by two considerations: (1) office manager may not be the title of the executive in charge of office work, and (2) the office work may not be of a relatively high centralized pattern. As stated in Chapter 1, many office managers report to the controller who in turn may report to either the president, a vice-president (usually of finance), or the treasurer. In some cases, he might report to an executive at a lower level of management, depending upon the importance and content of the office work in the view of the responsible head of the particular enterprise.

MAIN DIVISIONS OF OFFICE

Under the office manager, Figure 19–5 shows five main divisions of the office. These divisions are: office planning, physical facilities, services and practices, office personnel, and office control.[2] Each of these divisions is headed by a chief, so that the nominal heads of these divisions are, respectively, chief of office planning, chief of physical facilities, and the like.

OFFICE PLANNING DIVISION

Under this division are included those activities dealing with the determining of how the office work will be performed and when it will be done. Employees of this division must have knowledge of all

---

[2] The division of office personnel is sometimes included under the main Personnel Department of the enterprise. This arrangement is satisfactory as long as the personnel activities of the office are similar to those of the entire enterprise. However, where office personnel is significantly different, a separate office personnel division is usually warranted. In order to make this discussion of office organization complete, the office personnel division has been included.

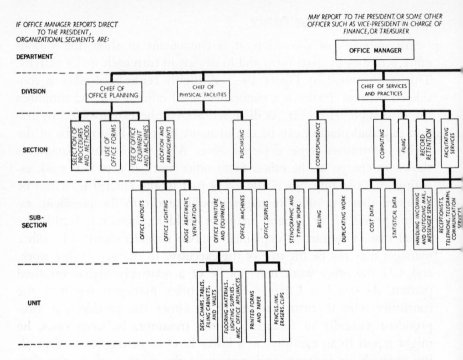

major office tools and be able to select or evolve the best means by which the work of the specific office can be accomplished. As indicated in the figure, the work is divided into three sections: the selection of procedures and methods, the use of office forms, and the use of office equipment and machines.

PHYSICAL FACILITIES DIVISION

The chief of the Physical Facilities Division has charge of those activities dealing with securing, using, and maintaining the physical factors necessary for the efficient performance of office work. The activities of this division are divided into two sections: the location and arrangement section and the purchasing section.

In the location and arrangement section are handled such activities as office layouts, office lighting, noise abatement, and proper office ventilation; the efforts of this section have an extremely important effect upon the general over-all efficiency and operations of any office.

The purchasing section purchases office furniture and equipment such as desks, chairs, tables, flooring materials, typewriters, adding machines, paper forms, pencils, clips, staplers, and punches. It is highly important that the purchasing section work with its allied physical facilities section, the location and arrangement section, as well as with

FIG. 19–5. An office organization chart.

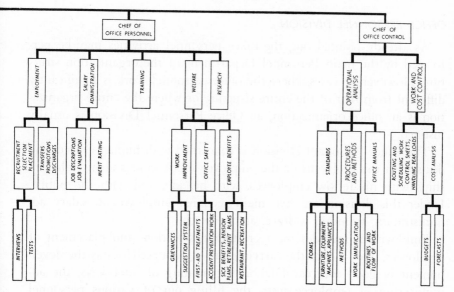

the procedures and methods section of the Office Control Division, in order to buy the forms, equipment, and supplies which are needed and which best conform to the recommended office layout and procedures.

SERVICES AND PRACTICES DIVISION

This division includes activities commonly thought of as dealing with office work, including correspondence, computing, checking, filing, records retention, and facilitating services. Work of this unit is frequently referred to as "office services," discussed in detail in Part II of this book. The correspondence section deals with the work of receiving, and writing replies to, all written communications. Computing includes all types of calculation, including those of costs and statistical data. As managers turn more and more to factual information as a basis for important policy and decision making, the importance of the computing section's work becomes greater and greater. Filing is a very important section of the Services and Practices Division. It deals with the retaining of office papers and the locating of these papers when needed. Records retention includes keeping records which have future possible service and destroying those for which use is no longer anticipated. The work of the facilitating services section includes the handling of incoming and outgoing mail, messenger service, and receptionists; the operating of telephone, telegraph, and outer departmental communication systems; and the storage and issuance of office supplies.

OFFICE PERSONNEL DIVISION

As already pointed out, the office personnel activities may be performed by the main Personnel Department of the organization structure. However, in cases where the office personnel work is significantly different from that of the entire structure or where the entire organization is an office organization, an Office Personnel Division is usually justified.

The Office Personnel Division is concerned with human aspects and deals with the problems of the employee motivation and his relationships with his fellow employees, with his job, and with the public. Under this division are five main sections: employment, salary administration, training, welfare, and research.

Employment includes the recruitment, selection, and placement of employees. This means the carrying out of such activities as the development of good sources of labor, the holding of interviews, the administering of employee tests, the filling out of various personnel forms, and the actual placing of the office employee on the job.

Salary administration efforts are aimed at bringing about and maintaining fair and equitable methods of wage payments. Activities include complete studies of the jobs, in order to know exactly what they require of persons filling them; an evaluation of the relative importance of each job and its relative wage; the determination of personnel ratings for each employee; and continuous studies of the prevailing wage structures.

Training deals with instruction designed to help the employee better fulfill the requirements of his present or future job. Through training, the employee is brought to greater personal effectiveness.

The welfare section is concerned with the general well-being and contentment of the employee. Under this section are found: (1) work improvement, which includes the handling of grievances and the suggestion system; (2) office safety, which includes first-aid treatment, and accident-prevention work; and (3) employee benefits, which include such activities as sick benefit plans, pension plans, retirement arrangements, the employees' restaurant, and various recreational programs and activities.

The research section deals with efforts and studies to improve employee-employer relationships, i.e., labor turnover studies, wage studies, motivation studies, and efforts to improve job-evaluation techniques. This section is frequently assigned special investigations.

OFFICE CONTROL DIVISION

The Office Control Division is a vital unit in the active management of office work. In this division are evolved measurements and comparisons necessary to see that the office work is performed as planned. The two main sections under this division are operational analysis work and cost control section.

The operational analysis section can be conveniently divided into three main subsections: standards, procedures and methods, and office manuals. The standards subsection establishes standards for material, equipment, and methods. An equipment standard, for example, might include a specific type of office machine and attachments which have been found most efficient for performing a specific office task.

The procedures and methods subsection is concerned with the effectiveness of the means used. Studies are made of the successive steps through which the paper passes and how these steps may be improved, consolidated, or eliminated.

Lastly, the office manual subsection puts in writing the policies and rules of the office and gives specific instructions regarding the duties and responsibilities of every office worker. Through the work of the office manual subsection, each employee is informed of such things as his place in the office organization, the over-all background of the enterprise, and its major aims and activities.

Work and cost control is the other section of the Office Control Division. This section deals with the control of office work by means of proper routing and scheduling of paper work and by cost analysis.

The routing and scheduling subsection is interested in the development of office work-control sheets, in seeing that work follows the prescribed channels as set up by the approved systems, and in timing the start of office work to achieve an even and uniform flow of work.

The cost analysis subsection appraises office activities in terms of dollars, and these figures are used as control units in evaluating the relative accomplishments of the various activities. In addition, this work includes such things as the drawing up of various budgets and the making of forecasts.

QUESTIONS

1. What are the four major considerations that concern a manager in his work of organizing?

2. Does it make any real difference whether organizing is considered a dynamic or a static process? Explain.

3. Do you agree with this statement: "Organizing is the work of setting up a hierarchy of managers and determining who supervises whom and what unit does what thing or things." Explain your answer.

4. What is meant by the term "centralization"? Of what importance is it in office organizing? Elaborate on your answers.

5. Explain the meaning of the statement, "The manager in charge of office work has a dual managerial task when an 'office services' organizational unit exists in the organization structure."

6. If specialization helps in getting work accomplished, should not all office work in an enterprise be performed in a centralized location and under the management of one head? Justify your answer.

7. Discuss the purpose of organizing.

8. Justify your answer to each of the following:

   a) Does centralization give flexibility to an organization structure?

   b) Do organizing and organization structure have essentially the same meaning?

   c) Does centralization always mean from the viewpoint of management?

   d) Is co-ordination the main purpose of organizing?

9. Briefly discuss what in your opinion are the four most important advantages of centralization? Of decentralization?

10. Comment on this statement: "In any organization structure, some functions must be on a decentralized basis—otherwise an organization structure would not exist. Hence, the disadvantages of decentralization are present to some degree in all organization structures."

11. Discuss Figure 19–5 in your own words pointing out what you consider the chief points of interest from the viewpoint of organizing.

12. What are some major difficulties you would anticipate in placing one person over all department heads in order to co-ordinate their heretofore separate office management efforts?

CASE PROBLEMS

CASE 19–1. THE WEBB-DOUGLAS COMPANY

Approximately two hundred people including factory and office personnel are employed by the Webb-Douglas Company which has been in business over fifty-six years, has outgrown its original quarters and now occupies two buildings one-half mile apart. Construction is being completed of a new building to house the office and factory. The move into new quarters is expected to begin in about sixty to ninety days.

Currently the major organizational departments include sales, advertising, production, purchasing, accounting, engineering, cost, and general office. With the exception of the latter, many of these major departments have separate offices while the office work for the remaining departments is performed by the personnel of the general office unit headed by Mr. Joseph Van Sant. For example, under the general office unit are activities of credit, collections, reception and intercommunicating services, watchmen and company guards, handling of the mail, corresponding work for the engineering and the accounting departments, and records retention for the entire company. The work of duplicating is presently handled by the production control unit under production, since this unit requires much of this work in the normal course of its activity. Purchasing of all items including office items is handled by the purchasing department. Each major department head does all the hiring of new employees for his department.

With the impending move to the new building, many problems have arisen. Mr. Van Sant is on the planning committee to determine an orderly arrangement for the execution of this work. He has been with the company for eight months and is generally considered competent. He is especially concerned with these issues:

1. Most of the office equipment is quite antiquated, many of the desks and chairs being as old as thirty years. Should this equipment be moved into the new building?

2. What should be the office organization in the new plant? To reduce operating costs and expedite the work, should the general office take in all office work and thereby provide improved service to the other departments?

PROBLEMS:

1. Do you feel it would be wise to centralize all office work as being considered by Mr. Van Sant? Why?

2. Discuss the advisability of timing such an organization change to coincide with the move to the new building.

3. List five questions to which you would suggest Mr. Van Sant secure the factual answers in helping him to reach a decision.

4. What decision are you inclined to believe Mr. Van Sant should reach? Why?

CASE 19–2.   SHARPE PRODUCTS COMPANY, INC.

Mr. Brown is the office manager of the Sharpe Products Company, Inc. Over a period of the last seven years, the office force has expanded from ten to ninety-one people. The production and the sales activities have expanded tremendously, but the expansion percentagewise of the office force has been greatest. There is not, however—and never has been in the company's history—a formal organization of the office employees.

The president of the company requested that Mr. Brown investigate and study the organization of the office force and to improve it in order that the company could operate more effectively. Accordingly, Mr. Brown held several meetings with his key people and discussed the general problem and challenge. It was decided to distribute questionnaires requesting each employee to supply information including a list of his duties and the name of the person he considered as his boss.

The results showed that about 65 per cent of the employees listed Mr. Brown as their boss—the one to whom they bring work for approval and from whom they receive instructions. Some 15 per cent listed as their boss four of the oldest employees, those from whom they had learned their particular job when they first started for the company. Many of the returned questionnaires listed quite a few duties that were identical. This would seem to indicate needless duplication, but Mr. Brown interpreted this to mean the use of the same term by different employees to designate different duties.

A list of the total office force includes:

Position	Number
Office manager	1
Assistant office manager	1
Chief accountant	1
Credit manager	1
Credit clerks	3
Accountants	20
Order clerks	10
Billing clerks	10
Inventory clerk	1
Typists	21
File clerks	5
Calculating machine operators	4
Duplicating machine operators	2
Receptionist	1
Switchboard operators	2
Mail department	3
Messenger service	2
Stockroom clerk	1
Janitors	2
Total	91

PROBLEMS:

1. Evaluate the approach taken by Mr. Brown and the possible usage of the organizational information obtained.

2. Based on the data given in this case, what major organizational units do you recommend be established? Justify your answer.

3. For each of these major units (in answer to No. 2 above), enumerate what activities or people you would include.

4. What other activities might logically be added to each of your major organizational units? Do you recommend that they be added? Why?

Chapter · 20

People and the Work of Organizing

Success or failure in business is caused more by mental attitude even than by mental capacities.

—WALTER DILL SCOTT

IN THE last chapter emphasis was placed upon the
division of the total work to be done, thereby creating clusters of somewhat similar work forming the nuclei of organizational units. Reference was made to the filing unit where filing work would be done, and
to the office machine analysis unit where analysis of office machines
in performing office work would be investigated. This approach along
work lines is helpful in gaining a clear insight to the *initial* task of
organizing. It is sometimes referred to as thinking along functional
lines, but before one can do this, it is necessary to understand what is
meant by "a function."

THE MEANING AND IMPORTANCE OF FUNCTIONS

*A function is the normal or characteristic operation of an activity or
performance.* It may also be thought of as the proper action of anything. Filing, for example, is a function in that it is an activity which
always has characteristic identities, and these identities are usually
considered the proper action of filing. In management, it is common
to speak of "functions," such as the function of producing, the function
of selling, and the function of financing. The function of producing
means the normal or characteristic action of producing goods or services; likewise, the function of selling means the normal or characteristic
action of selling goods or services.

In turn, any function covering a broad scope of action can be broken
up into component functions covering actions of a relatively limited

scope. To illustrate: the broad function of producing can be divided into component functions, such as the function of designing, the function of plant layout, the function of inspection, the function of production control, and the function of purchasing.

In order for the objective of an enterprise to be attained, it is necessary that functions be performed. In fact, the whole operative being of an enterprise is made up of functions. To illustrate: assume that the objective of an enterprise is to provide the public with an economical, smart-appearing, and efficient adding machine. To achieve this objective requires various activities or functions, among which would be the production of the machine, including the component functions of layout of the factory, purchase of materials and supplies, operation of production equipment, assembly of parts, and inspection of the final product. In addition, the function of selling would have to be carried out. This would include personal calls upon prospective buyers, contacts with various distributors, advertising activities, and marketing research. Also, the function of financing, including such activities as the securing of loans from banks, the allocation of funds in the enterprise, and the arrangement of credit and terms with suppliers and buyers, would have to be performed.

PEOPLE AND FUNCTIONS

Although functional analysis is important and is the initial step in most organizing, it must be remembered that it is only one part of organizing. The work must be *performed by people*, relationships established among the organizational units, and proper work environment supplied. It is advisable to think first of functions, then of individuals performing these functions. This approach is effective because (1) a manager must co-ordinate functions, i.e., what is done, not who is doing it; (2) functions are usually permanent, the interests and abilities of personnel tending to change with time; and (3) personnel emphasis often results in unusual combinations of duties that are difficult to manage and for which the securing of replacements is arduous.

It is important to note that the same function may be performed by two or more people. Likewise, the same person may perform two or more functions. The former case may be illustrated by a group of clerks all doing the same work, for example, checking billings in a department. The latter case is illustrated by the receptionist who greets and directs visitors, opens and sorts the mail, and types letters.

Grouping common activities or functions to form an organizational unit is the common approach. However, other means for departmentation are used, including (1) by process, (2) by customer, (3) by product, and (4) by territory. An organizer can use any means he desires, and commonly several means are employed in the same organization structure. The means that best helps to achieve the objective should be used. In a bank, for example, for the top levels, functions may be used, whereas the loan department may be divided by customer —loans to manufacturers of plastics, chemicals, and paper, loans to manufacturers of food processors and package machines—or by product —commercial loans or personal loans.

IMPORTANCE OF PEOPLE IN ORGANIZING

Successful organizing helps provide the means for getting effective results through people's efforts. It provides for the adequate development and placement of people. While both the division and the assignment of work are important, they are not the end objective in organizing. The main goal is to make it possible for a group of people, called employees, to work co-operatively and efficiently as a unit. The total work is segregated by functions so that each individual of the work group can perform a portion of the total work in the best possible manner. The expression, "organization is people," is trite, nevertheless it stresses the importance of people in the work of organizing. It brings out the basic idea that people constitute the center about which the other organizational concepts—the work to be done, authority, and work environment—should revolve.

In the final analysis, the organization structure is a tool—it provides the grouping of specific activities and of people for the purpose of applying management. Work is accomplished by people or machines operated by people. Organizing does not accomplish any work objective; it must be implemented with people. Hence, one of the biggest jobs of a manager is to form or maintain an organization structure which permits the proper placement and the development of employees. Some claim most any organization structure will prove satisfactory as long as the right people are operating it. Others lay great stress on the proper division of work and relationships. No doubt, both are important. However, the point here is that people are vital in organizing; they can make or break any organization structure.

It follows therefore that a sound organization structure is necessary for effective employee performance. This is true because organizing deals with and sets forth such basic issues as what is to be done and by whom, and who decides what. This view of organizing has been compared to that of writing the story for a motion-picture film. It sets the stage and predetermines what is to take place. How well it takes place, i.e., the quality of the motion picture, depends in great measure upon the actors—the personnel element.

Organizing affects and is affected by the human side of group activities. The sought-for co-ordination among different activities is more correctly stated as the co-ordination among *the employees* performing the different activities. After all, the work is divided so that it can be accomplished by the group. How effectively the various members of the group work together as a unified team toward achieving the objective is the paramount consideration.

MANAGER'S ATTITUDE AND ORGANIZING

Organizing reflects a manager's attitude and thinking. That is to say, there is a personal managerial influence in organizing. It reveals the understanding of a manager for the essentiality of the human element and the determining how this element is to be regarded. Just allocating the work, assigning employees to neatly conceived endeavors, and granting carefully defined authority to selected persons are insufficient. The people assigned to what tasks and the creation of what working relation among themselves must be handled with care for they are of great significance in the success of the organizing work. There is genuine skill in having logical work divisions tie in respectively with an adequate consideration for who is to do each respective component of work.

An office manager implements regard for the human element in his organizing work by recognizing and appreciating the value, as well as the limitations, of his employees. This is not a one-shot proposition but a continuing, ever-searching effort to keep up to date on how best the employees available to him can be brought together to work toward a common goal. The supervisor in charge of the mail room, for example, reflects from the human element viewpoint the office manager's thinking organizationwise of the supervisor's value, including his strong and his weak points for his particular supervisory job. The job content, a result of work division, is presumably what the office manager thinks it ought to be, likewise the authority granted is what the office manager thinks it ought to be—all or at least a big portion of it is with reference to the office manager's human element evaluation of the supervisor. In this sense it is sometimes said that an organization structure reflects the shadow of its manager. However, it appears more appropriate to state that the organization structure of any manager reflects the light or understanding of its manager.

CHALLENGE OF ORGANIZATION AND PEOPLE TO MANAGEMENT

In the previous chapter it was stated that "organizing is a dynamic, not a static, process." Too frequently this is forgotten, and after the organizing efforts have been worked out, it is rationalized that only minor adjustments will be needed. But effective organizing necessitates eternal vigilance. The required changes will be of two types, those in (1) objectives with subsequent alterations in functions to be performed, and (2) personnel as a result of labor turnover and the development of people. Both are important, and both ultimately require changes in organizing from the viewpoint of people doing what jobs, in what organizational unit, and with whom.

Three major situations can arise. The first is the revamping or shifting of present personnel. To illustrate, certain office work may be mechanized necessitating the transferring of some employees and the retraining of others. This means that the organization structure will have to be changed. New relationships will be formulated, and, of course, who is going to do what work must be decided.

The second condition is that of expanding activities. Here the emphasis will be upon acquiring co-operative work groups. In addition, it might be necessary to add some new authority relationships and new organizational units. The anticipated permanence of the expansion will regulate the alternatives for handling the increasing work load.

The third and last situation is decreasing the number of people employed. This requires the closest co-ordination of over-all activities and usually affects the organization structure significantly. Some organizational units may be completely eliminated or combined with other units. Lines of authority may be modified considerably—lengthened in some instances, contracted in other areas. Entirely new groupings and relationships may result, necessitating considerable adjustment by some employees and severe hardship by others. It must be remembered that what is done may have repercussions over future years.

Another major challenge of organization and people is to integrate fully the work being done by the people of the various units into a co-operative and co-ordinated whole. This sounds fairly simple, but acquiring it in actual practice is a different story. People are not entirely unpredictable, yet they certainly cannot be considered the same as machines. Based on available knowledge, the intricacies of the human mind are far more difficult to understand than the chemical reaction of several compounds. Consider, for example, an individual working as a member of a group. He is an individual, but at the same time is group-affected. If removed from the group and analyzed, the investigative results would have to be greatly qualified because he is not the same person he was when integrated into his organizational unit.

Another and perhaps eternal challenge is to develop a favorable organizational climate or atmosphere in which people are stimulated and permitted to grow so that they can perform greater quantity and quality of work and assume greater responsibility. The organization structure must supply the needed background. Favorable surroundings conducive to the development of a way of life, operating under the arrangement devised by organizing, must be provided. Competency of an employee may be curbed due to improper organizational relationships, or his full contribution may never be realized if he is placed in the wrong organizational unit or not supplied proper work environment. There is spirit, an attitude of mind, a belief in people and what they can accomplish in the best of organizing work. A solid organization structure is not built on form or body alone.

Finally, in the work of organizing there is the challenge of utilizing all available resources, especially people, to their utmost. The tendency is to create new authorities, new units, and to go out and get "new faces." Adequate regards should be paid the tried and true. It is not always wise to discard the traditional for something new, mainly because it is new. Good organizing requires concentration on fundamentals. From a practical viewpoint, a manager must use in the best possible manner what is available to him. At the same time, changes and newness cannot and should not be avoided for progress demands and is a part of something different.

INDIVIDUAL JOB CONTENT

From the organizing viewpoint, individual job content is the contribution to the objective made by the individual performing the respective job. The activities assigned or the individual job content can be viewed as what the employee is required to perform because of the organizational position and relationship occupied in the organization structure.

Effective organizing requires that each employee has a definite task that he understands, knows how, and can perform. When these requirements are met plus the necessary physical facilities and adequate supervision are provided, the individual is in a work situation where ideal accomplishments can be reached.

The division of work to be done must be carried out to the individual job level. That is, the department functions must be divided ultimately into jobs for each individual. Unless this is done, the managerial work of organizing is incomplete and the group of people connected with the enterprise cannot perform as a whole or contribute with a unity of action.

JOB SPECIALIZATION

Specialization is a demonstrated successful fact. Its benefits are tremendous. Complex work can be segregated into relatively simple components, each accomplished effectively by employees specializing in that single or similar group of operations. Training is simplified and reduced, yet skill in a limited area can be greatly increased. Specialization has been stimulated by the trend toward mechanization which usually necessitates large volumes of similar work, thus creating specialized and concentrated work areas for the attendant operators.

JOB SPECIALIZATION—HOW FAR?

All organizing requires some specialization. Most managers agree that no one person can do everything equally well. Capitalizing upon what he can perform best and the need for allocating total work has resulted in job specialization. The question is not whether to have job specialization but to what extent should job specialization be carried. In organizing, the manager must decide this question as exemplified by determining the work make-up of each organizational unit and what is done by each member of that unit.

Too many and too varied tasks for one employee are generally avoided. On the other hand, a job of very limited scope is not used presumably in order to minimize the problem of monotony and lack of employee interest in his work.

In some enterprises where the organizing has utilized job specialization to a great degree, provisions such as job rotation, music while you work, rest periods, and keeping the employee informed of all major enterprise operations have been adopted to maintain high morale and to make the organization structure effective. For the most part the degree of specialization has not been questioned. However, in some companies an attempt to broaden the job scope has been advanced. This is commonly referred to as job enlargement. The results of these efforts have been surprising. In several interesting examples, job en-largement brought about reduced office costs, improved quality of work, better teamwork, and lower absenteeism. These results, which must be interpreted carefully, indicate that there are both economic and social limits to job specialization. But more specific data are needed to derive definite recommendations. What degree and form of job specialization to follow presumably depends upon the type of work and the individual doing it. However, reconsideration of prevalent ideas concerning job specialization seem in order. Some questions such as, "How far should a manager carry job specialization and "What ar-rangement of job enlargement is desirable" are decided in organizing; they deal with people and organizing. Further discussion on this sub-ject appears warranted and is included in the following pages.

WORK DIVISION ARRANGEMENTS

There are two basic ways of work division arrangements: (1) se-rial, and (2) parallel. These names are self-explanatory. In the serial arrangement the work division is extended to a series of small tasks, each task being performed by a specialist in that particular type of work. Moving progressively from task to task the work advances until completed. The serial arrangement is the same basic plan as the famil-iar factory assembly line, commonly found in production plants. In some quarters, the term "production-line basis" is used to describe the serial arrangement in the office.

The parallel arrangement permits a series of needed and separate tasks to be performed by one individual or a work team. The employee or employees, as the case might be, do not specialize in performing one task but gain proficiency in accomplishing several tasks. Frequently the tasks are related, but this is not necessary. To implement the par-allel arrangement, the total work is divided into two or more major parts, and each part is assigned to an employee or group of employees. The basis for dividing the work into parts can be any of many factors, for example, by letter of the alphabet, number, territory, type of mer-chandise, or major subject. From the individual's viewpoint the scope of the work is relatively large under the parallel arrangement.

Figure 20–1 shows these two basic arrangements in graphic form. The work considered pertains to filing and consists of three separate operations, including (1) scan and mark material for filing, (2) sort marked material, and (3) file the material. Assume a work force of three file clerks, Nancy Brown, Sharon Hewitt, and Virginia Walker. The serial arrangement is shown at the top of the figure. For simplicity each separate operation has been considered a separate task and one file clerk has been assigned to each task. In contrast, the parallel arrangement is shown at the bottom of Figure 20–1. In this illustration the total filing work has been divided into three parts that parallel each other. Each part consists of all three separate tasks of filing work, that is, marking for filing, sorting marked material, and

SERIAL ARRANGEMENT OF WORK DIVISION:

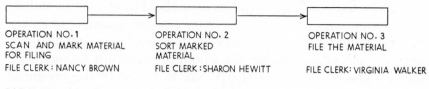

OPERATION NO. 1
SCAN AND MARK MATERIAL
FOR FILING

FILE CLERK: NANCY BROWN

OPERATION NO. 2
SORT MARKED
MATERIAL

FILE CLERK: SHARON HEWITT

OPERATION NO. 3
FILE THE MATERIAL

FILE CLERK: VIRGINIA WALKER

PARALLEL ARRANGEMENT OF WORK DIVISION:

| OPERATION NO. 1 | OPERATION NO. 2 | OPERATION NO. 3 |

FILE CLERK: NANCY BROWN

| OPERATION NO. 1 | OPERATION NO. 2 | OPERATION NO. 3 |

FILE CLERK: SHARON HEWITT

| OPERATION NO. 1 | OPERATION NO. 2 | OPERATION NO. 3 |

FILE CLERK: VIRGINIA WALKER

FIG. 20–1. Illustrating the serial and the parallel arrangements of work division.

filing the material. And each part or breadth of filing work is performed by one employee. As illustrated, employee Nancy Brown performs all three filing tasks or operations, and so do each of the other two employees, Sharon Hewitt and Virginia Walker.

WHAT ARRANGEMENT TO USE

Like many other practices, the question of whether to use serial or parallel arrangement cannot be fully answered with a "Yes" or a "No." It is not a question of black or white but of gray—some compromise between the two extremes. The tendency will be toward one or the other, but it will not be a pure adaption of one or the other. In any given case, the individual circumstances will govern. Included will be such things as the importance of cost, employees' interest in their jobs, quality of work, preferences of managers and by employees, and the over-all objectives.

More specifically, the serial arrangement of work division requires a sufficient work quantity of a particular type to keep an employee fully occupied in its performance. Quantity and specialization are close buddies. Also, mechanization tends toward a serial arrangement. Most office machines handle a large volume of work, and their cost usually points to a high percentage of utilization throughout the workday. In some instances the job content is so complex and the tasks so heterogeneous that some breakdown in the work is necessary to acquire and maintain employees for the work. When this is the case, the serial arrangement is usually followed. In addition, some office work if performed by one employee would incur sizable loss of time in shifting from one operator to another. For example, a job consisting of typing, then calculating, followed by checking, and resumption of typing may show low efficiency. Selecting the serial plan frequently follows when the skill needed is of a special type, due to scarcity or the amount of training that can economically be provided. It is usually not feasible to dilute the efforts of the employee possessing a needed skill in a specialty. An expert in operating punched-card equipment should not type and file letters as a part of her regular job duties. Another condition normally suggesting the adoption of the serial arrangement is when great uniformity in handling certain portions of the office work is required. The signing of checks and bank drafts can be cited as an illustration.

In contrast, the parallel arrangement is usually followed when better work performance appears to be associated with a complete understanding and handling of the particular subject matter. Handling an overcharge in a billing to a complaining customer might best be handled in its entirety by one employee. Furthermore, when the start to finish period for the work performance must be reduced, the parallel arrangement may be superior. Under this pattern, delay in work processing or loss in time by papers traveling from operation to operation is avoided. Less handling and idle time generally results when the papers are processed by employees working under a parallel arrangement. In some cases by keeping the division of work too small, an employee is deprived of helpful over-all checks in the work. When this situation exists, the parallel arrangement automatically provides the solution. It should also be observed that with parallel groups performing similar cycles of work, it is possible to hold contests, compare work accomplishments of each group, and inject other competitive devices in managing the work. Such measures help stimulate high productivity. In addition, the parallel arrangement helps to eliminate duplication of efforts such as reading and checking if such is present when high specialization is followed. Under the parallel pattern, one employee familiarizes herself with the contents of the paper by a single reading and a single checking. Finally the parallel arrangement is suggested where the circumstances indicate that greater interest and enthusiasm by employees probably will be gained from having a greater variety of work in the job make-up.

JOB ANALYSIS

Job analysis is a formal means of determining the job content. It can be defined as follows: *Job analysis is the process of critically examining the components of a job, both separately and in relation to the whole, in order to determine all the operations and duties.* In short, job analysis deals with facts about jobs and what is required for competent performance. Typical of data included are such things as the forms and materials handled, the equipment and machines used, the methods utilized, the frequency of the operations, the amounts and kinds of skill required, and the degree of concentration needed. Such information is extremely useful in management because (1) the scope of the job becomes definite, (2) the identity becomes fixed, and (3) definite association between job title and content is established.

Job analysis is customarily and quite correctly thought of as an activity logically a part of personnel activities because it is basic in the performance of many personnel department functions. For example, job analysis is the basis for determining the relative worth compensationwise of jobs, it facilitates hiring and placing, can be used for formulating training needs, and serves to identify promotions and transfers. These are truly personnel in character or a part of the management fundamental function of actuating discussed in the next section, Part V, of this book. However, inasmuch as job analysis does identify and establish the job and its content, it is included in this discussion dealing with organizing. As pointed out throughout this chapter, really effective and complete organizing work requires specific work divisions at the individual level. Job analysis helps supply this requirement.

OBTAINING JOB ANALYSIS DATA

In the case of new work or a new organizational unit, the manager doing the organizing must decide the characteristics of the newly created job or jobs including their content and relation with other jobs in the enterprise. He may not formalize this work to the extent nor in the detail that is common in the usual job analysis efforts. Nevertheless, information of the job analysis sort is helpful in organizing, and the indicting statement can be made that many difficulties in organizing begin with the manager's failure to make greater use of job analysis information.

In a going office there are three different methods of securing job analysis data: interviews and observations, conferences, and questionnaires. Whatever the method it is advisable to secure, within practical limits, as much information as possible about every job. It is usually better to have too much than too little data. To foresee all the uses to which the data may eventually be put is not always possible. Experience shows it is best to provide for expansion of the job analysis program.

When the interview and observation method is used, the analyst goes to the employee, asks questions about the job, and observes what the content of the job is. While this method is satisfactory for office jobs, it is probably most popular for factory jobs.

In the second method, the employee is called into conference and verbally describes his job to the analyst, who records the information. This method usually requires more time than the others, takes the employee from his job, and may interfere with the work routine.

In the third method, a questionnaire is sent to the employee, who fills in the information. This method is used in cases where the employees can intelligently handle clerical details and are more or less accustomed to paper work. It is commonly used for most office work. The federal government has employed this procedure successfully for over forty years. However, it is frequently advisable to supplement the questionnaires with short observations and interviews, especially on the more important jobs, for this brief contact usually gives the analyst a better idea of the job content.

JOB ANALYSIS REPORT

The data of job analysis commonly are recorded on prepared paper forms sometimes referred to as a job analysis report. The form serves as a reminder to answer definite questions and thereby secure all the needed facts so that no part of the job is overlooked. In addition, it provides a means of recording the data in a standardized manner, thus making it easier to handle and interpret the information. Figure 20–2 shows a portion of a job analysis form.

JOB DESCRIPTION

The information on the job analysis form actually describes the job. However, when this information is written in a more descriptive style, the term "job description" is frequently used.

JOB ANALYSIS

Present title of job _____ Department _____

1. What is the general purpose of this job?
2. What duties are performed in the *usual* course of the work? (Tell from where work is received, what is done with it, and where it is sent.)
3. What duties are performed only at stated intervals? (Group answers by daily, weekly, monthly, etc.)
4. In what organizational unit is this job presently located?
5. Does the job entail supervising other employees? (Explain.)
6. If there are any special courses in school essential in order to perform the duties of this job satisfactorily, name them.
7. What past experience is *necessary* for a new employee to have in order to perform the duties of this job?
8. What are the *most* difficult parts of this job?
9. What are the *least* difficult parts of this job?
10. About what proportions of this job require sitting _____%, standing _____%, moving about _____%.
11. What machines or other equipment are operated?
    Regularly:
    Occasionally:

FIG. 20–2. Portion of questionnaire used for job analysis.

Job descriptions are useful in the work of organizing. The duties and the lines of authority, if any, are clearly set forth. In addition, job descriptions help bring about better understanding within an enterprise because the qualifications required of the successful employee on a particular job are pointed out. Furthermore, job descriptions help in selecting persons best fitted for the requirements of the job, in acquainting the new employee with the job to which he is being assigned, and in crystallizing scattered information into a clear job picture.

Contents of Job Description. The general make-up of job descriptions vary among different enterprises. In most cases, however, a summary of the job, the work performed, and the qualifications is generally considered essential. See Figure 20–3.

Job Statements and Job Titles. Although a universality of terms is not present, current practice tends to use the terms "job description," "job statement," and "job title" for representing progressively contracting descriptions of the job. A job statement is used to furnish a quick picture of the job. To illustrate, in Figure 20–4 the job content of "Stenographer" is condensed to a single paragraph, as is done likewise for the other jobs shown, such as "General Clerk" and "Secretary."

JOB DESCRIPTION

DATE__ August, 195-____

JOB TITLE__ JUNIOR ACCOUNTANT _____GRADE_ VI ____CODE _ _ _ _ _ _ ..

SUMMARY: Under general direction of Comptroller and immediate
supervision of Accountant, performs general accounting
duties and prepares special reports as assigned.

WORK PERFORMED: Maintains records of cash receipts and/or disbursements,
posts related subsidiary records. Posts various journal
entries and adjustments, maintains record of Supply
Department receipts and prepares minor financial statements.

Handles correspondence, verifies tabulations and reconciles
bank statement. Assists in distributing work to temporary
help, prepares monthly reports and special statements.
Performs related work, such as figuring per capita and
expense ratios. Operates office machines as required.

May supervise work of accounting clerks, typists for
temporary periods, etc. and performs similar duties as
assigned.

QUALIFICATIONS: Normally requires three to five years' training and
experience, including two years' general accounting training plus three years' company accounting experience as
an Accounting Clerk.

Courtesy: The J. D. Moore Organization, Park Ridge, Ill.

FIG. 20–3. A job description written in a effective form.

A job title is simply a common name for a job. Job titles are commonly inadequate and do not identify the job satisfactorily. Again referring to Figure 20–4, the material has been arranged to expedite comparison among common job titles. For example, observe, for the common title of "Stenographer," the differences in the three job statements of a stenographer's job. This situation is further illustrated by the following interesting remarks:

Another thing we have found in office jobs is that there is no consistent terminology. What is a clerk? I wish somebody would tell me. In one plant he is the chief accountant and in the next plant he is sorting tabulating cards. They both have the same title. We go into engineering departments—what is a draftsman? One is a detail draftsman and one is a layout draftsman, but they previous training, which involves the performance of routine clerical duties, such as addressing envelopes, keeping simple records, and gathering and delivering messages and assisting in operating office machines.

Stenographer: Takes dictation in shorthand or on a stenotype or similar machine and transcribes this dictation on a typewriter. Also types from written copy and spends a minor part of time on routine or simple clerical work.

Secretary, Class A: Performs general office work in relieving executives and other company officials of minor executive and clerical duties; takes dictation using shorthand or uses a stenotype machine; transcribes dictation or the recorded information reproduced on a transcribing machine; makes appointments for executive and reminds him of them; interviews people coming into the office, directing to other workers those who do not warrant seeing the executive; answers and makes phone calls, handles personal and important mail, writing correspondence on own initiative.

Source: "Clerical Job Evaluation," "NOMA Bulletin," No. 1 (Philadelphia: National Office Management Association), January, 1946.

...degree of difficulty and responsibility, under general supervision, in the conduct of office routines calling for the exercise of initiative and judgment in carrying out established procedures or group leadership of a number of clerical workers engaged in similar office qualifications.

Stenographer: Takes dictation in shorthand of correspondence, reports, and other matter and transcribes dictated material, writing it out in long hand or using a typewriter. May be required to be versed in a technical language and terms used in the particular location in the office.

Secretary: Performs general office work in relieving executives and other company officials of minor executive and clerical duties; takes dictation, using shorthand or a machine; transcribes dictation or the recorded information reproduced on a transcribing machine; makes appointments for executives; answers and makes phone calls; interviews people coming into office, directing to other workers those who do not warrant seeing the executive.

Source: "Wage Bracket Determination, No. 36 (Kansas City, Mo.: Regional War Labor Board VII), Part II (April, 1944).

...exercise of judgment and with responsibility for general assignments, to perform difficult and responsible clerical work of a varied nature, in specialized fields such as production or manufacturing methods, or in the general business fields such as sales, accounting, purchasing, etc. Work involves a fairly thorough knowledge of a restricted field, the use of a wide range of procedures and analysis of facts in situations to determine what action should be taken within limits of standard practice...

Stenographer (I): Under general supervision but with some exercise of judgment and responsibility for carrying out general assignments, to take and transcribe dictation of more than average difficulty involving technical and unusual expressions; to perform associated clerical and typing tasks in the corresponding level of difficulty and responsibility; does secretarial work for division and section heads; familiarity with the terminology peculiar to the unit; and to perform related work as required.

Secretary: Performs general office work in relieving executives and other company officials of minor executive and clerical duties; takes dictation, using shorthand or using a stenotype machine; transcribes dictation or the recorded information reproduced on a transcribing machine; makes appointments for executive and reminds him of them; interviews people coming into the office, directing to other workers those who do not warrant seeing the executive; answers and makes phone calls; handles personal and important mail, writing routine correspondence on own initiative; keeps important files.

Source: Mimeographed material distributed by Office Management Association of Chicago, September, 1944.

FIG. 20-4. Illustrations of office job statements. Notice that the job title is not sufficient identification. The job statement must also be included.

are classified the same. Why? Certainly more is required from the standpoint of skill and experience of a designing draftsman, or a layout draftsman, than of a detailer. Classifications of bookkeepers indicate amazing differences. Anybody running a calculating machine is a bookkeeper, whether he knows anything about accountancy or not. Those who are just following instructions are book-keepers.[1]

The point is this: *The title plus the job content are necessary for accurate identification.* This is true regardless of the fundamental function of management being performed. It is especially important in organizing where work division and organizational unit creation must be decided.

QUESTIONS

1. Do you agree with the following: "Organization structure is a tool, in and of itself it does not accomplish any work objective"? Explain your answer.
2. What do you understand by the expression, "thinking along functional lines"?
3. Discuss the effect of a manager's thinking and attitude upon his organizing efforts.
4. Enumerate the more common bases for departmentation of a large office, giving an example of each.
5. Explain the meaning and the importance of individual job content in organizing work.
6. Explain Figure 20–1 highlighting the main concepts that this illustration shows.
7. Under what general conditions would you recommend the parallel arrangement of work division? Justify your answer.
8. As you see it, is the condition of expanding or of decreasing activities of an office the more challenging to an office manager in his organizing work? Give reasons for your answer.
9. Identify each of the following by means of a concise statement:
    a) Job statement.
    b) Job enlargement.
    c) Job specialization.
    d) Job analysis.
10. How does job analysis enter into the picture of office managerial organizing? Of office managerial actuating?
11. How much emphasis should the office manager give to job analysis? Why?
12. Discuss the use of job descriptions in the managing of an office.

---

[1] C. J. Uhlir, "Job Evaluation—A Tool of Management," *Annual Conference Proceedings, National Office Management Association, 1944* (Philadelphia), p. 19.

CASE PROBLEMS

CASE 20–1.   THE ROZELL BANK AND TRUST COMPANY

An important division of this company is the machine accounting division which prepares reports for all other divisions in the company. At the present time this division is organized as follows: reporting to an assistant manager are three supervisors, one for each of the control section, the machine room section, and the punch section. The assistant manager is a good technician for planning office work for machines. He is an excellent designer of required paper forms for machine operations and is highly respected. He appears to get along best with people interested in operating office machines. He is a poor writer and many do not understand about what he is writing in his memos to the people in his unit or to those in other units of the company.

The control section supervisor is ambitious, a liberal arts college graduate, thinks in broad concepts, and feels that the work of both the machine room and the punch sections should be subordinated to him, since their work is for control purposes, the function his unit performs. In the control section are (1) the cash unit headed by a group leader with six employees reporting to him, and (2) twelve employees working on reports and statements reporting direct to the control section supervisor.

Reporting to the machine room section supervisor are two group leaders. The first directs fifteen machine operators, the second supervises seven file clerks. The general concensus is that the machine room supervisor is a specialist in office machine operations. He has been in this type of work for eight years. He is a detailist, very precise, and ignores verbal orders. He wants and requests that all orders and suggestions affecting him be put in writing. Most who know him agree that he has a very keen mind.

The supervisor of the punch section has ten key-punch operators reporting to him. He is a happy-go-lucky, hard-working man whose chief interest is to keep a steady job so that he can maintain a reasonable standard of living for his wife and three children.

Each time a report is late in delivery or wrong in content, the two supervisors of the control and of the machine sections blame each other. There is almost constant dispute between them and little, if any, co-operation. A sizable amount of overtime work is put in by both sections to complete reports now and then needed.

PROBLEMS:

1. What is the problem in this case?
2. What do you feel should be done? Why?

CASE 20–2.   ABBOTT ELECTRONICS COMPANY

As a result of an extensive study by a management consultant firm, several changes in the Abbott Electronics Company organization structure are being planned. Among the contemplated changes is the formation of a clerical pool under the direction of Mr. Robert D. Reiter, the present assistant office manager. The existent general office clerical group would form the nucleus around which the new group would be formed. It is suggested that two employees now listed as "Payroll Accountants" in the General Accounting unit and three employees each with the title of "Sales Analyst" and currently in the Sales Analysis and Research section of the Marketing Research unit be transferred to the general clerical group. Better supervision, greater utilization of present office machines and greater employee promotional possibilities are the major reasons cited for the proposed move.

Investigation discloses the following information concerning the make-up of each of the jobs under consideration.

Clerk:

Does routine clerical duties, sorts and files papers, addresses envelopes, keeps simple records, picks up and delivers messages within her department. Clear legible handwriting or ability to operate a typewriter is required. Some office training is desirable, and a minimum of two years of high school is necessary.

Payroll Accountant:

Calculates the hours worked and extends for daily amount of pay for each hourly paid employee. Accumulates daily totals on a large or spread sheet. Enters proper deductions for each employee and calculates net weekly pay. Work is then given to Payroll Agent who prepares necessary payroll records and payroll checks. Payroll Accountant work requires accuracy, completing work within prescribed periods, and maintaining secrecy about confidential data. Ability to operate adding and calculating machines is necessary.

Sales Analyst:

Makes studies of company sales in various markets to determine sales effectiveness per product, line, dealer, advertising dollar expenditure, or company salesman. Keeps relatively simple records of sales data. Makes projections of sales and draws comparisons between comparable sales periods. Writes simple reports indicating significance of sales data. Experience in sales work helpful, but not mandatory. Must know all products and parts sold by the company.

Problems:

1. Do you favor the formation of the general office clerical pool? Substantiate your answer.

2. As you see it, discuss one important consideration in organizing that this case brings out in relief.

Chapter · 21

Organizational Relationships

More people are humbugged by believing in nothing than by believing too much.

—P. T. BARNUM

IN THE previous two chapters attention was directed primarily to two aspects of organizing: (1) the task of dividing the work, and (2) the importance of people. Thus, the organizational units are formed, each consisting of definite work to be done and of people assigned to do it. These organizational units must be related so that they make up a unified or concerted group and the various peoples assigned to various tasks can operate effectively in unity. Discussion of this relationship leads to the subject of authority.

AUTHORITY DEFINED

Authority is the right to act or to exact action by others, within a prescribed area. With the concept of authority is associated the power to make decisions and to see that they are carried out. The compliance concept is a vital part of the meaning of authority. However, this compliance need not and, as a matter of fact in office management, is seldom confined to coercion or force; more commonly it is gained by means of persuasion and requests.

Authority as a part of and emitting from organizing has definite limitations. In managerial practice, authority must be used in conformity with the efforts to achieve the accepted goals of the organizational unit as a part of the enterprise. Authority, acting through organization relationships, helps to achieve these goals. Authority is not used by a manager as his whims or wishes might suggest. Also, the use of authority is influenced by the people with whom it is being employed. The exacting of certain actions by others must be within their capacity to perform. To illustrate, trying to enforce a decision impelling an inexperienced file clerk to operate a modern bookkeeping machine is

411

ridiculous and a misuse of authority. Furthermore, the beliefs and habits of the individual over whom authority is being exercised should be taken into account. When the individual is convinced that the action requested is proper and in order, he will respond readily. In contrast, when this condition does not exist, the effectiveness of the authority used may be limited, and in some instances the content of the authority may be altered.

Authority is dynamic. Its make-up changes according to the specific conditions and requirements of the group or the individual case. Authority is a tool, not the end result, of a manager; it exists and is used to accomplish specific work goals.

AUTHORITY AND THE ORGANIZATION STRUCTURE

Within any one enterprise, authority connects the various organizational units, establishes relationships, and gives meaning to an organization structure. Vertical authority relationships are those between different organization levels and concern the superior-subordinate association. Horizontal authority relationships deal with organizational units within an organizational level and concern the manager-to-manager association within the same organization level.

The establishing of authority within an organization structure is usually conditioned by several factors. The relative position in the structure normally indicates the degree of authority from the formal viewpoint. But the amount of decision-making power and ultimate enforcement may be modified by the popularity or acceptance of the one in authority by the person being influenced by that authority. Managerial competence to gain enthusiastic co-operation, to acquire respect, and to inspire may be lacking despite the formal authority established by position in the organization structure.

Furthermore, a person may have little or no formal authority established by reason of position in the structure. Yet that person might actually possess extensive authority due to his integrity, knowledge, and skill. In punched-card accounting, for example, others might seek suggestions from a certain individual and do what he recommends. Although the person may not be formally in charge, he actually possesses significant authority. Situations of this type may be of a temporal nature or may exist for long continuous periods.

In many organizational units, situations of an unusual or emergency nature arise from time to time. They may not be provided for in the regular organization arrangement. In such circumstances the person assuming the authority has derived it from what is called the "authority of the situation." This usually is temporary and exists until the person normally in charge assumes authority over the unusual event.

DELEGATION OF AUTHORITY

By means of delegation an executive spreads his area of operation and makes an organization structure meaningful. Without delegation, an executive restricts his actions from the management viewpoint to those that he himself can perform. In fact, organizing does not become fully effective until delegation of authority is practiced.

Delegation of authority is the act of granting or conferring authority by one executive or organizational unit to another. Delegation is usually thought of as moving from a higher to a lower level. It is important to note, however, that delegation can be from a lower to a higher level and from one level to another on the same plane. Hence, delegation can be downward, upward, or outward, as exemplified respectively by the case of a president and a vice-president of a business organization, by United States citizens and Congress, and by a Congregational Church and the Congregational Board of Authority.[1]

In delegation, the delegator always retains his over-all authority for the delegated duties. He does not surrender or permanently release his authority. He does grant the right for others to act officially within the specific areas. Only the authority needed to carry out successfully the assigned functions is or should be delegated. This makes for the tapering concept of authority and simply means that in most organization structures the authority becomes successively smaller or tapered as successively lower horizontal levels of the structure are considered.

From the practical viewpoint, delegation of authority is either specially granted or inherently implied in the job. In the former case, it is given to an individual in order that he may act to perform the management which is essential in achieving the objective. In the latter case, the authority is inherently tied up with the job, so that whoever holds the job, or performs the delegation function in the organization structure, automatically possesses the authority which goes with that position. In any enterprise, therefore, authority is contingent upon such things as the delegation of those already in authority, the traditional structure of the organization, and the character and mental characteristics of the individual.

---

[1] J. D. Mooney, *The Principles of Organization* (New York: Harper & Bros., 1947), pp. 17–23 and 50–56.

PROBLEM OF DELEGATION

One of the big problems in organizing is to get executives to delegate authority. Ideally the proper delegation should exist at each delegator-to-delegatee level throughout the entire structure, and the delegation should extend as close to the level or point of action as possible. This makes for effective organizational action and encourages initiative by employees at each organization level. But in practice some managers are reluctant to delegate. They fear that if authority is delegated, the right decision may not be made, and the work won't be handled correctly. Their belief is that they must keep in close touch with activities and decide most issues. In some instances they may not fully realize the amount of authority needed by a subordinate to get the work done properly. In other instances, the executive states that he has delegated authority, but at the same time criticizes his subordinates when they make and enforce decisions without his advice. As a result, it is not uncommon for the amount and extent of delegation of authority to be arrived at informally by trial and error. The subordinate makes a decision or tries out a certain practice, and if no reprimand results, he assumes the management work performed is within his province. In many cases the status of delegation of authority is the result of an infiltration process over a long period of time. Slowly but surely authority for certain matters has been turned over to the delegatee. Commonly, verbal statements establish the amount of delegation of authority, and in a relatively few instances, the superior gives specific delegation of authority in writing.

SPAN OF AUTHORITY

In writing of relationships among organizational units and the subject of authority, the question arises: How many immediate subordinates can a manager manage effectively? The number is commonly referred to as "span of control" or "span of management." For purposes here it is believed the term "span of authority" is appropriate and helpful.

Span of authority is based on the concept that there is an optimum number of persons to be immediately subordinate to any executive, which number normally provides most satisfactory results. Although opinions differ widely among managers, a number from four to eight is frequently stated as most desirable. That is, an executive can best utilize his time and ability if he has a minimum of four persons immediately under him to whom he can delegate authority for performing the work to be done. On the other hand, when an executive has more than eight persons reporting to him, there is a good possibility that their work will not be managed as best it can be and that the executive's ability is wasted, owing to dilution of his efforts over too wide a span.

Adequate and conclusive research in this subject, however, is lacking.[2] The proper span of authority depends upon many considerations. The organization level at which the work is performed appears to be important. At the higher levels, few might report to their immediate superior, while at the lower or operative levels, many might report to one superior. Also, the type of work is important. To illustrate, a supervisor of draftsmen might adequately direct the work of fifteen draftsmen, depending upon the particular type of drafting work performed. Generally speaking a relatively broad span of authority can be used. In addition, adequate consideration must be given to whether all the immediate subunits are of equal size and importance, whether they must be given equal attention by the supervisor, and whether the caliber of personnel requires a large or a small amount of supervision. Where the make-up of the work is fairly stable and little communication between units is required, a broad span of authority usually proves satisfactory.

From the practical viewpoint, the trend in organization structures appears to be toward wider spans of authority. In some instances, successful operations are reported with twenty to twenty-five persons reporting to the same superior.[3]

It is interesting to note how the number of relationships increases as the number of persons supervised increases. First, consider a manager, M, with two supervisors, A and B. In this case there are six relationships: M with A, M with B, and A with B, plus the reverse of each, assuming the initiative is taken by the second named party, i.e., the additional three are A with M, B with M, and B with A. Now when a third supervisor C is added, the number of relationships increase to eighteen. The third supervisor makes for these additional twelve relationships: M with C, B with C, A with C, M with AB, M with BC, and M with AC, plus the reverse of these six relationships. This is summarized in Figure 21–1.

[2] See John M. Pfiffner, "The 'Third Dimension' of Organization," *Personnel* (New York: American Management Association), March, 1952, p. 392.

[3] "Bosses Break Rule on Span of Control," *Business Week* (New York: McGraw-Hill Publishing Co.), August 18, 1951, pp. 101–2.

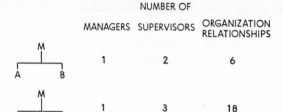

FIG. 21-1. Data showing the rapid increase in organization relationships as the number of persons increase.

RESPONSIBILITY

When a subordinate is delegated authority to perform specific work, an obligation to perform the work is created. The acceptance of this obligation is known as responsibility. Sometimes the responsibility takes the form of a list of duties. These can be assigned, but as stated above, compulsion or persuasion to perform them arises from authority which is the medium through which a manager operates.

Responsibility is the obligation for the carrying out of a duty and what one is answerable for in the execution of an assigned task. That is, responsibility can be viewed as having two parts: (1) the obligation to secure results, and (2) the accountability to a superior—the delegator of authority.

Since an authority delegator retains in the ultimate all his authority, he likewise retains in the ultimate all his responsibility. He cannot elude a failure of a subordinate by saying it was the fault of the subordinate. The superior retains the ultimate responsibility and is accountable for what is or is not achieved by his organizational unit.

LINE AUTHORITY AND STAFF AUTHORITY

There are two major types of authority: (1) line, and (2) staff. An executive can have either or both. An executive having line authority, called a "line executive," exercises direct command over the work of all members in his unit. Characteristically the authority relationship is of a superior-subordinate type forming "a line" from the top to the bottom of the structure.

In contrast, staff authority is of an advisory nature. An executive with staff authority is a staff executive. The word "staff" according to Webster means "a pole carried in the hand for support." Therefore, staff authority relationship pertains to assistance or support. Specifically it assists the line authority relationships by offering counsel or advise. Staff authority is a manager-to-manager relationship and can exist within any organization level.

The use of line authority exclusively leads to the line type of organization structure. When to this line type is added staff authority, the result is a line and staff type of organization structure. Both these types will be fully discussed and illustrated, but before doing so a short digression dealing with the meaning, preparing, and the advantage of organization charts appears in order.

ORGANIZATION CHARTS

An organization chart is a graphic representation of an organization structure. It can be thought of as a picture of the organization structure; it shows the functional relationships and the existing lines of authority.

The drawing of an organization chart is simplified by using the outline approach. First, list the main functions; next, place those functions which are subordinate to the main functions under the proper main function in the outline list; then, place under each subordinate function the minor functions which properly belong under the respective subordinate function. In this way, a list is developed which shows the main functions, the subordinates under each main function, and the minor functions under each subordinate. This outline form is then transformed into the graphic form which makes up the organization chart.

The chart may also be prepared by starting with the person of highest authority in the organization structure and working down by determining who reports to this top person and what activities each person handles. This procedure provides the information for the first level of management below the chief executive and may be followed for each consecutive layer. From the information so gathered, the organization chart can be constructed.

ADVANTAGES OF AN ORGANIZATION CHART

An organization chart insures neither good organization nor good management; it simply helps in visualizing the organization structure and, for this reason, assists in obtaining a better organizational structure. An organization chart compels the organizer to put down in black and white what the structural relationships are. This crystalizes his thinking and clarifies fuzzy, but important, details which might otherwise be overlooked. Specifically, the main advantages of an organization chart can be listed as follows: (1) a clear over-all concept of the organization is obtained; (2) the main lines of authority and responsibility are brought out in full relief; (3) promotional possibilities are provided; and (4) the assignment of titles is simplified.

THE LINE ORGANIZATION

The line, or scalar, type of organization, which was used extensively in our early industrial development, is one of the oldest organization forms. This type is still quite popular and is frequently employed by proprietors of small businesses and for other enterprises where the number of employees is small.

The line organization is characterized by direct lines of authority from the top executive to the various assistants, and direct from them to the employees at the operative level. Each member is fully responsible for the carrying out or the actual performance of the job to be done. Throughout the entire structure, each member is in complete charge of all activities within his particular organization segment. Authority and responsibility are greatest at the top, and reduce or taper as successively lower levels of management are considered.

The line type of organization is illustrated in Figure 21–2. Line authority exists between the president at the top to the employees at the bottom. The line authority may be thought of as a scalar type, in that it reduces by scales or steps. To illustrate, the connection is from the president to the vice-president of production, to the superintendent of steel products, to the foreman of the foundry section, and to the workers of this section. The vice-president of production is in complete charge of production, including the work of the superintendent of steel products and the superintendent of wood products; the superintendent of steel products is, in turn, in complete charge of that particular segment of the organization and specifically over the foremen of the foundry, machine, and assembly sections.

Advantages. The advantages of the line organization include the following: Authority and responsibility are definitely fixed, and the person who has that authority and responsibility is known to all; the structure is very simple and, hence, readily understood by all personnel; discipline is easily maintained, since each worker and each boss knows what is expected of him and in which areas he is to operate; decisions can be quickly reached; the oneness of the boss who is in complete charge makes for a minimum of delay in decision reaching; and, lastly, the line organization offers splendid training opportunities for the development of executive talents. The line officer is charged

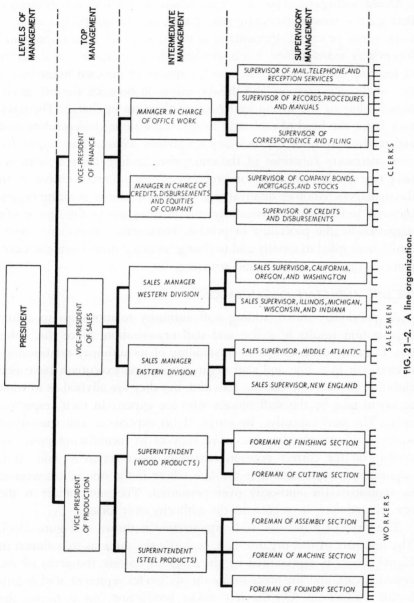

FIG. 21–2. A line organization.

LEVELS OF MANAGEMENT

TOP MANAGEMENT

INTERMEDIATE MANAGEMENT

SUPERVISORY MANAGEMENT

PRESIDENT

VICE-PRESIDENT OF FINANCE

VICE-PRESIDENT OF SALES

VICE-PRESIDENT OF PRODUCTION

MANAGER IN CHARGE OF OFFICE WORK

MANAGER IN CHARGE OF CREDITS, DISBURSEMENTS AND EQUITIES OF COMPANY

SALES MANAGER WESTERN DIVISION

SALES MANAGER EASTERN DIVISION

SUPERINTENDENT (WOOD PRODUCTS)

SUPERINTENDENT (STEEL PRODUCTS)

SUPERVISOR OF MAIL, TELEPHONE, AND RECEPTION SERVICES

SUPERVISOR OF RECORDS, PROCEDURES, AND MANUALS

SUPERVISOR OF CORRESPONDENCE AND FILING

SUPERVISOR OF COMPANY BONDS, MORTGAGES, AND STOCKS

SUPERVISOR OF CREDITS AND DISBURSEMENTS

SALES SUPERVISOR, CALIFORNIA, OREGON, AND WASHINGTON

SALES SUPERVISOR, ILLINOIS, MICHIGAN, WISCONSIN, AND INDIANA

SALES SUPERVISOR, MIDDLE ATLANTIC

SALES SUPERVISOR, NEW ENGLAND

FOREMAN OF FINISHING SECTION

FOREMAN OF CUTTING SECTION

FOREMAN OF ASSEMBLY SECTION

FOREMAN OF MACHINE SECTION

FOREMAN OF FOUNDRY SECTION

CLERKS

SALESMEN

WORKERS

with getting things executed; he must be a doer; he must get the work accomplished.

Disadvantages. The line organization also has its disadvantages. Perhaps the most outstanding one is that, relatively, specialization of work is not practiced. Particularly is this true at the intermediate and supervisory management levels. Another disadvantage is the difficulty of securing co-ordination. Each lord is master of his own house or his unit of the organization, and the co-ordination between the two is obtained solely by the strong leadership of the man in charge. The tendency is for the head of each unit to develop a rather independent unit and to think only of his own unit's activities without due regard for other necessary functions of the enterprise. In fact, some writers believe that the line organization probably places too much emphasis on the managers. Another disadvantage is the difficulty of forming organizational units; this is particularly true in cases where the unit is not suggested by the procedure or process. Frequently, insufficient opportunity is afforded to modify and to change existing units from the viewpoint of the total organization structure.

THE LINE AND STAFF ORGANIZATION

As previously stated, adding staff authority relationships to a line organization results in a line and staff organization. Since this latter type is widely used, a clear understanding of its authority relationships is essential. In a line and staff organization, line executives have line authority for carrying out the activities, but they are advised as to what action to take by the staff officers who are experts in their respective fields. The staff executive, by virtue of his experience and specialized training, affords the line executive support in formulating policy or arriving at the correct decision regarding what action to take. It is important to remember that the line officer is the one who executes; he represents the authority over personnel. The staff officer is the one who advises; he represents the authority over ideas.

The chart of a line and staff organization is shown in Figure 21–3. The line part of this organization, basically the same as that shown in Figure 21–2, is represented by the diagram *outside* the areas of the dotted circles, and the areas *inside* the six circles represent staff organizational functions. On the left, under production, for example, the jobs of plant manager, chief inspector, and methods and standards manager constitute staff activities. Likewise, under the vice-president in charge of sales, the jobs of market development and sales and market research constitute staff functions. The entire portion of the chart to the right, under personnel, is circled, since personnel is a staff function to the entire organization. Areas enclosed by circles 2 and 3 represent staff functions at lower levels of management. Staff functions can exist at all levels. Note in particular that, even though a function is staff, the organization for carrying out that function may be of a line-organization type. To illustrate, under the vice-president of sales, the directorship of the sales and market research division is a staff activity to the organization structure as a whole; but the sales and market research division itself is organized as a line organization, with the work of market potentials and consumer opinions under it.

Advantages. The advantages of the line and staff organization include the following: First, the lines of authority are fairly well fixed; good discipline can be attained; decisions can be reached after desirable deliberation; and the principle of specialization can be utilized to the extent of practical limits. Second, co-ordination can be improved because the line officers are supplied with factual data concerning activities both within and outside their own units. Third, flexibility is provided for the organization structure to expand or contract as conditions warrant. New activities can be added and old ones discarded without seriously affecting the organization structure. Fourth, proper balance among all the activities, line as well as staff, can be maintained. Fifth, more opportunities are afforded to match the desires, capacities, and interests of personnel with the job, since a greater variety of jobs, involving different duties, responsibilities, training, and background, are required.

Disadvantages. The disadvantages of the line and staff organization center around the worker and the relationships existing between the line and staff officers. In the first place, the line officer may tend to ignore the staff officer's advice, so that the expert information provided is never used. Second, the staff officer may tend to ignore the ideas of the line officer simply because ideas are supposed to be under the jurisdiction of the staff officer. Third, the staff officer may feel that the business of advising only is too dull, that something should be done about it; and he may attempt to take over line authority which is out of his realm of activity. Fourth, a considerable number of staff officers are not good salesmen, and many staff findings are not used partly because the line officer is not shown, and convinced of, the merits of the staff's findings. Fifth, line orders and staff advice may be confused by members of the organization structure, with the result that the what, when, where, and how of activities are not clearly known to the managers or to the nonmanagement members.

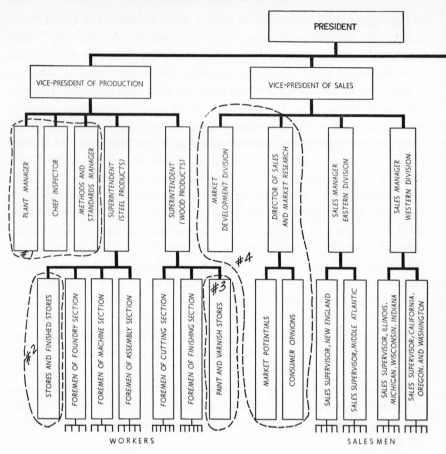

FIG. 21–3. A line and staff organization.

To clarify further the relationship between the line and staff executives it can be stated that the authority to manage the work in order to gain the objectives of the enterprise belongs to the line executive. He exercises his authority *along* the organizational line (not staff) authority. In contrast, the staff executive counsels—in effect he contributes indirectly through the line executive to the objectives of the enterprise. Unlike the line executive, the staff executive exercises his authority *to,* not along, the organizational line of authority. In some companies the practice of "compulsory staff service" is followed. This requires a line executive to listen to his staff executives, but the final decision and enforcement rests with the line executive. When the managers are competent, this practice aids them in their respective tasks. Also, in some enterprises "the completed staff work doctrine" is

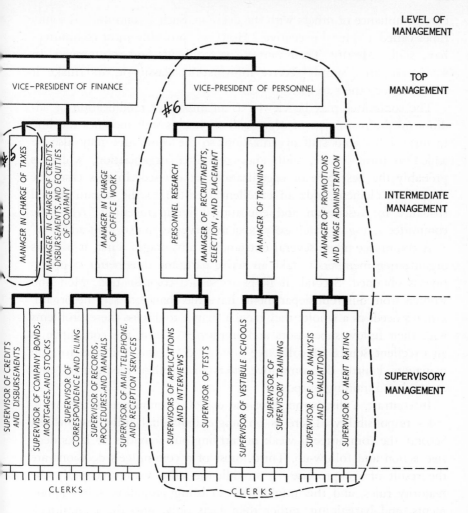

LEVEL OF
MANAGEMENT

TOP
MANAGEMENT

INTERMEDIATE
MANAGEMENT

SUPERVISORY
MANAGEMENT

followed. This emphasizes the presentation of complete solutions by the staff to the line executives. Piecemeal recommendations are avoided, and stress is placed on supplying assistance, not placing the line man in a predicament with questions regarding what he wants investigated or what data should be included in a report. Of course, the line man and the staff man should talk things over, but in a constructive way with each making contributions.

USE OF COMMITTEE

Committees constitute an important part of most organization structures. They can exist at any organization level, be of short or of long time life, and deal with various subjects. Many are delegated line authority, that is, they not only discuss and decide issues but also secure compliance of others with the decision. Such a committee is sometimes called a "plural executive." However, probably most committees have staff authority. Their purpose is to discuss and recommend. In some cases they simply receive information, classify it, and make it available for others to use.

The committee may be viewed as an important modification or addition to the main type of organization. Just as staff modifies the line to form a line and staff organization, so the committee may also be added to form a line, staff, and committee organization, which is probably the best type of organization yet devised. In this case, the committee element adds an excellent medium to the organizational structure for discussion and educational group meetings. Also, the committee acting in an advisory capacity serves as an excellent addition.[4]

A committee offers several outstanding advantages. First, it permits organization members to take an active part, and thus better co-operation is obtained. Second, it helps to secure co-ordination. Men and women from different departments have the chance to see the organization's needs as a whole; they have a chance to discuss these problems with their fellow supervisors and employees. Third, the committee is an excellent source of collective advice, ideas, and opinions for top managers. Fourth, the committee offers an excellent medium for educational and training purposes.

In contrast, a disadvantage of the use of a committee is that it divides responsibility. There is no single individual fully responsible. Second, the committee is weak in carrying out activities. It lacks decisive action and follow-up. Third, most of a committee's decisions are the result of compromise—a straddle-the-fence variety. Usually the majority rules, and this might tend to bring prejudice, secret agreements, and bargaining, rather than facts only, into the committee's decisions. Fourth, committee meetings usually require a lot of the members' time. There appears to be little doubt that a sizable amount of this time is wasted and might better be spent by members on their individual tasks.

FUNCTIONAL AUTHORITY

In office management the use of functional authority is especially common. Functional authority concerns specific functions only and is delegated from one manager to another manager who is not related to the former by formally established authority channels. It can be

---

[4] P. E. Holden, L. Fish, and H. Smith, *Top-Management Organization and Control* (Stanford, Calif.: Stanford University Press, 1941), pp. 59–73.

conferred by a line to a staff manager, or vice versa. To illustrate, a line manager, "L," may delegate to one of his subordinate staff executives, "S," the authority to issue orders directly to one of "L's" subordinate line executives, "E." In this case the authority is functional, because it is limited to a particular activity and applies only to the authority relationship in this activity between "S" and "E." Functional authority expedites efficiency and is convenient. Its use however must necessarily be limited, otherwise established authority relationships are neutralized. Some specialized activities of the office from time to time require a competent office executive to explain and interpret to non-office personnel in order to insure proper handling and good administration. Such situations are solved by the use of functional authority.

SERVICE ORGANIZATIONAL UNITS

When speaking of office organizing, the term "service unit" commonly arises. A service organizational unit is made up by grouping same or similar activities. Its justification is primarily economy and improved work performed or service offered by the unit. Accounting, general office service (mail, telephone, reception service), and legal counsel are examples of service organizational units.

Some units are line, others are staff, depending upon the type of authority relationship. When line authority exists, the head of the service unit commands not only his own unit but also exercises line authority over work, similar to that of his unit, performed in units outside the service unit. In other words, his line authority is both within and without his unit as it pertains to his specialty work. In addition, some service organizational units utilize functional authority when delegated, that is, they have jurisdiction over specific work performed by others not normally or formally under the authority of the service unit. In some instances the service unit's authority is strictly staff. The unit recommends and counsels in work regarding its specialty, but the decision of what to do and its enforcement is not within the province of the service unit.

ADDITIONAL FACTORS INFLUENCING THE ORGANIZATIONAL STRUCTURE MAKE-UP

Before closing this chapter a discussion of additional major factors influencing the organization structure will be given. These factors include:

1. *Size of Organization Structure.* The framework of a small organization is quite likely to be very simple. Frequently many functions

are grouped together under one heading, and the total number of headings is usually small. Under such circumstances, there is no need for an elaborate organizational structure. Quite often the line type of organization is used by a small enterprise. In contrast, when the divisions of functions are numerous, the organization structure may become quite complex. The relative importance and the relationship of the various activities necessitate a different pattern from that of a small organization structure of few segments.

2. *Time Element.* This factor influences the structure of an organization significantly, for a structure set up temporarily to accomplish an emergency task might be far different from one set up to exist over a long period of time. Temporary organization structures are usually very simple. For example, a crowd of people organized to put out a fire in a neighborhood will probably be organized far differently from the firemen of the local fire department. The crowd of people will probably form a line type of organization with every member doing something physical to put out the fire. It is unlikely that there would be any staff or advisory members. Also, speed of action would be paramount, and this consideration emphasizes a line rather than any other type of organization. In contrast, the local fire department probably utilizes a trained staff of experts in the business of fire fighting. Through time, the fire department has developed an efficient, highly co-ordinated structure of the line and staff type, with committees probably used to train members and to discuss phases of fire fighting.

3. *Continuity of Demand for Products or Services.* This factor can be viewed from the point of view of the flow of work and also from that of the type of work. A steady flow of work resulting from a fairly constant demand usually results in a stable organization structure. In this instance the line or the line and the staff functions are usually well defined and known. On the other hand, when demand for the products or services is irregular, the predominant idea is usually to meet current requirements, and generally the organization is of a line type with relatively few staff functions.

Under the second consideration, the type of work, assume that office "A" handles the same work day in and day out and that office "B" handles a certain type of work "X" for a part of a month, work "Y" for another part of a month, and work "Z" for still another part of a month. The structural organization of office "A" will probably differ from that of office "B." Office "A" will emphasize staff elements —advisory services will quite probably be employed. Office "B," on the other hand, will tend toward a line type of organization in which most workers can perform several activities with equal skill.

4. *Space Considerations.* Frequently the location of the office, wholesale house, or plant determines the over-all limits of an organization structure. An enterprise with a plant in New Jersey and one in Illinois will usually have separate organizational structures for each plant. However, if these two plants were located across the street from each other, a single organizational structure would probably be used. Space considerations are particularly important in sales organizations. Frequently the territory divisions constitute the main segments of the sales organizational structure, and the offices serving such organizations are likewise segregated and located throughout the country.

5. *Personnel Utilized.* This factor can have a decidedly marked effect upon the structure of an organization. When, for example, the ratio of skilled to unskilled workers is high, the pattern of the organization structure might be far different from that for one where the ratio is low. The reason for this, in part, is the relative importance of supervision and the placement of different functions at different levels in the two structures. The line type is to be preferred when employees of low intelligence and training are used. In contrast, the employment of persons with high intelligence and broad background and training emphasizes the use of staff units. Also, as discussed in the previous chapter, the organization structure can be built around the available men and women, with secondary consideration being given to the functions. When this is done, the peculiar abilities and likes and dislikes of the personnel utilized tend to shape the pattern of the organizational structure.

6. *Process Used.* One of the most important influences on the structural characteristic of an organization is the process used. Frequently, the main components of the structure are determined by the steps of the process; in handling a purchase order, for example, receiving, costing, billing, and mailing may constitute the main components of the organizational structure. Furthermore, the mechanization of the process influences the structural relationship. The make-up of an organization in which the process is largely manual differs considerably from that of one in which machines are extensively used. In the latter case, functions involving hand labor are eliminated, and in their place other functions are instituted, necessitating different relationships within the organization structure.

7. *Complexity of Functionalization.* In general, when a relatively large number of specialized functions are performed, the organiza-

tional structure tends to stress the staff characteristics. Likewise, when specialized functions are scattered throughout the enterprise, it is quite likely that the staff elements will be numerous, with emphasis on the staff components. Also, in this latter case, if the functions are quite distant and apart, the committee type probably will be extensively used in order to help to co-ordinate the widely separated activities.

8. *Philosophy of Top Management Members.* Lastly, the philosophy of top management members has a very important influence on the organizational structure, for the attitude and thoughts of managers tend to mold the organizational structure used. In the final analysis it is the managers who cast the die and decide, sometimes arbitrarily, what the form of organization will be. Organization structure, therefore, reflects top managers' thinking, and over a period of time the organization structure mirrors the instrumentality through which top managers wish to operate.

There are factors aside from the eight mentioned above which influence the structure of an organization, but it is not the purpose of this book to exhaust the list. However, it should be clear to the student of management that the make-up can differ widely from one organization structure to another. The differences may be minute in some instances, and they may be very great in others.

QUESTIONS

1. Discuss the problem of delegation in office organizing and suggest several possible ways for solving it.
2. Point out the difference between the terms in each of the following:
    a) Span of authority and responsibility.
    b) Functional authority and staff authority.
    c) Tapering concept of authority and horizontal authority relationship.
    d) Compulsory staff advice and plural executive.
3. Evaluate the following statement: "Authority is the force which is exercised to make an organization structure function."
4. Mr. A is a line executive of Department X. Also in this department is Mr. B, a staff executive reporting to Mr. A. Clearly state the organization relationship between Mr. A and Mr. B.
5. Explain this statement: "In delegation, the delegator always retains the responsibility for the delegated duties."
6. Is it possible for an enterprise to have a member without (*a*) authority, (*b*) responsibility, or (*c*) authority and responsibility? Explain.
7. Assuming a choice is possible, under what conditions would you use a line organization? A line and staff organization?

8. Do you agree with the following statement: "The disadvantages of the line and staff organization center around the employee and the relationship existing between the line officers and the staff officers"? Why?

9. Relate the advantages and also the disadvantages in the use of committees in office organization structures.

10. The organization chart of the Stevens-Elwood Company shows that Tom Clements, an office employee with twenty-eight years of service in the mail department, has no formal authority, yet on many occasions questions requiring decisions are addressed to Tom, and the employees of the mail department follow his suggestions. How do you account for this state of affairs?

11. For what reasons does an office manager use an organization chart?

12. Define service units and discuss their importance in office organization.

CASE PROBLEMS

CASE 21-1.   THE RYAN AND HARRISON COMPANY

A total of fifty-two employees are classified as office workers in this company. The office manager is in charge of one telephone operator, two mail clerks, four timekeepers, two billing clerks, two duplicating machine operators, and a receptionist. The controller is in charge of ten accounting clerks, three bookkeepers, a purchasing agent, and three purchasing clerks. The sales manager has a regular force including ten stenographers and three file clerks. The remaining office workers are dispersed throughout the company and report to the chief of their immediate and respective unit.

The office manager believes his unit should include the correspondence work, but the president of the company has done nothing about the suggestion. He is not sure that the office manager could handle it properly, and he does not want to interfere with getting sales correspondence work out promptly nor to offend the sales manager. The controller is a very forceful and conscientious man who keeps in close touch with every operation performed in his unit. He insists that all decisions concerning work of his unit be cleared through him. He justifies this practice as an effective means for keeping costs in line. His work load is very heavy, but he has repeatedly turned down the suggestion to appoint an assistant, explaining it would increase office costs too much. It is common for the controller to work until seven o'clock several evenings a week and to come down to the office for a part of Saturday morning. Some of his associates chide him by telling him, "You can win a promotion in an easier way," or "You should work steady during regular working hours." The controller resents these comments, but says nothing in reply. The sales manager being a very busy man has only limited time to supervise the stenographers so he has the secretary to the president, an elderly woman, take charge of the stenographers and file clerks.

There is very much independence between units with little co-operation between them. The stenographers usually will not type any letters unless they are pertaining to sales. Occasionally the controller comes into the office manager's department and directs people what to do. The purchasing agent doesn't co-operate with the office manager, giving as the reason that the office manager has no authority over purchasing. The general atmosphere around the office spells independence. Some of the clerks feel that they are being picked on because more work is piled on them, while others just sit around and look busy.

PROBLEMS:

1. In your opinion, what are some plausible reasons leading to the present condition of this company's office, that is, what might lead to the formation and existence of this office?

2. From the viewpoint of organizing, evaluate the present office of this company.

3. What action do you feel should be taken to improve the company's office organization?

CASE 21–2.   PAUL LAWRENCE CHADWICK

Paul Lawrence Chadwick is the head of a staff unit, the office procedures improvement unit; he reports to the office manager. In turn, the office manager reports to the president of the company. Chadwick works hard, has a multitude of ideas, and at times becomes discouraged because of the delay and inactivity on many suggestions for improvement made by his organization unit.

What he believed to be an excellent suggestion, both from the viewpoint of less effort required to do the work and lower cost, was submitted to the office manager in a report some six weeks ago. Since that time, Chadwick has asked the office manager several times what he thinks about the suggestion and receives the answer, "We are looking into it." Chadwick feels, however, that the office manager is just stalling.

A few days after the last time Chadwick spoke to the office manager, the latter suffered an injury in an automobile accident. It was announced that he would be unable to come to work for at least four weeks; while he was absent, his duties would be taken over by the assistant office manager. Chadwick has little respect for the assistant office manager's abilities. Likewise, the assistant office manager feels that Chadwick is too precise, and spends company money on a lot of impractical ideas. The two do not get along too well.

Chadwick believed the suggestion embodied in the last report to the office manager to be so important that, in the company's best interests, delay in its adoption should not be tolerated. Based on past experience he was convinced the assistant office manager, now in charge, will take no action on it. Accordingly, he explained the new procedure to the supervisor whose department, direct mail, is affected and to a small number of line employees in that department. The new procedure was installed. For the next several weeks careful records of time expenditures were made by Chadwick, and these were compared with expenditures under the previous procedure. Savings of $23 a day, or approximately $6,000 a year, were indicated through the use of the new procedure. Chadwick wrote the report concerning the installation and the results obtained and submitted it to the president of the company, with a copy of the report being sent to the "office of the office manager."

Two days later the office manager returned to his job, and during the course of "welcome back" conversations, the president referred to the report and asked a few questions about it, which the office manager could not answer, explaining he was not familiar with it. Returning to his office, the office manager called in his assistant and inquired about the new process being used in the direct mail department. The assistant knew nothing about it. The office manager's secretary, overhearing the conversation, located the copy of Chadwick's report to the president and gave it to the office manager.

PROBLEMS:

1. What action do you feel is proper for the office manager to take? Why?

2. Do you approve of Mr. Chadwick's action? Justify your answer.

3. What general impression do you gain concerning the organization of this company?

Chapter · 22

Principles of Office Organizing

It is easier to do a job right than to explain why you didn't.
—MARTIN VAN BUREN

Effective organizing is a challenge to every manager. It cannot be achieved by any mechanistic discipline or technological process. The best approach appears to include knowledge of basic organizing truths plus skill in their application, taking into complete account the individual considerations. Improving organizing practices and maintaining sound organizing concepts are continuous tasks and commonly must be sought amid everchanging economic and social atmospheres. Fortunately, in these efforts valuable aid, based on experience and reasoning, is available in the form of principles of organizing which constitute the subject of this chapter.

PROBLEM OF OBTAINING GOOD ORGANIZATION STRUCTURE

Too often an enterprise expands without any real plan of organization structure. New functions and new personnel are added, and the enterprise just grows. From the viewpoint of efficient management, the absence of any real plan of organizing usually leads to undesirable conditions, including the following:

1. The functions become disproportionate in their relationship to each other when judged by the relative importance of each function to the objectives of the enterprise.

2. Important functions are neglected, or they are subordinated to other functions; either condition makes it difficult to carry out the requisite activities.

3. New functions of a planning nature which might greatly strengthen the organization are ignored.

432

4. Capable men are confined to mediocre jobs.

5. The necessary co-ordination among the major functions is decreased, since the personnel for each major function tend to stress their individual activity exclusively.

THE IDEAL ORGANIZATION STRUCTURE

Theoretically, an ideal organization structure can be set up for each enterprise. Such a structure would include all the desirable characteristics of an organization structure, determined by philosophizing as to what the functional relationships and the personnel performing them should be in order to approach perfection.

In actual practice the ideal organization structure is seldom, if ever, obtained, and there are several reasons why this is true. In the first place, the personal influence of top executives upon the structure of the organization is exceedingly important. Men differ in their beliefs, and not all top executives view an organization structure with identical opinions and convictions. Also, the enterprise may lack the funds required to set up the ideal structure. Certain functions, recognized as important, are not a part of the organization structure simply because top managers cannot see their way clear to finance these activities. In addition, there is a tendency to stay with the old and established form of organization structure rather than to change to a new and untried form. Enterprises tend to build up customary practices, and these traditions tend to maintain an organizational status quo. Finally, the ideal organization structure may never be attained because of agreements, bargains, and favors which exist among members of the enterprise. Contracts with certain individuals to perform certain functions, and understandings among members of an immediate family or relationship, may be cited as examples.

ORGANIZATION PRINCIPLES

Although the ideal organization structure can probably never be attained, it is entirely possible to improve most structures. Over a period of time, definite organization principles have been developed. These principles are general truths and should be viewed as common guides to action. They are universal and apply with equal validity to an organization structure set up for the accomplishment of office work or to one set up to achieve any other major objective. Their specific application to office organizing can be particularly helpful to the progressive office manager.

As already stated, these organizational principles have been proved by experience, but the success obtained from their application in any specific case depends upon the individual circumstances. In certain instances, these principles are merely some of the factors which should be taken into account, along with other factors believed important in the individual case. The principles are as follows:

1. Consideration of the objective of the enterprise.
2. Utilization of functions as essential components.
3. Application of simplicity.
4. Determination of clearly defined channels of authority and responsibility.
5. Establishment of definite and fixed responsibility.
6. Provision for coequality of authority and responsibility.
7. Attention to co-ordination of the activities.
8. Definition of each job.
9. Consideration of the human element.
10. Provision of effective leadership.

CONSIDERATION OF THE OBJECTIVE OF THE ENTERPRISE

The very first principle to be considered is the objective of the enterprise. Answers to the question "What is the aim of the enterprise?" or "What is the enterprise trying to accomplish?" are fundamental considerations in any organizing effort. The objective permeates all activities within an enterprise and influences their number and the extent to which they are carried out.

It is extremely difficult to judge the effectiveness of an organization structure without an adequate knowledge of the objective of the enterprise. What would be considered efficient for one objective might well be considered very inefficient for another objective. For example, the objective of cleaning the streets in a small town after a heavy snowstorm might require an organization structure which is entirely different from the structure needed when the objective is to distribute samples of products in ten cities throughout the United States. Because the objectives are different, the type, number of functions, and personnel of one structure would be entirely different from those of the other.

UTILIZATION OF FUNCTIONS AS ESSENTIAL COMPONENTS

The essential functions of the enterprise should constitute the main elements of the organization structure. The true relationship of the functions gives the true organizational setup. The nature of the enterprise determines the main functions, and these, in turn, determine the essential components upon which the organization structure should be built.

Furthermore, the functional approach provides continuity. Functions remain and can grow almost indefinitely; they are not limited in span of time or in ability as are individuals. Also, the functional approach promotes the objective viewpoint in organizational structures and minimizes the subjective influences of the individual.

The grouping of similar functions together helps to form strong major groups; the tendency to split activities is minimized. Not only does grouping of like functions with like functions afford great strength to an organization structure but it also provides great flexibility; functions may be modified, new functions added, and old functions eliminated easily and simply without disturbing the essential structure of the organization.

In addition, the utilization of functions as the essential organization components helps to define clearly the various functions and to prevent uneconomical overlapping and duplicating. Working directly with functions helps to concentrate attention on them, and clear concepts of activities tend to be developed.

APPLICATION OF SIMPLICITY

Simplicity has been defined as "that delightful perfection between too much and too little," and the best all-around organization structures are those which encompass simplicity in their make-up. A complex structure is almost certain to make difficulties for a manager. Likewise, an organization structure that excludes necessary functions is a serious handicap to the success of the enterprise. A good organization structure includes only the necessary functions, no more and no less, and establishes the relationship among the necessary functions in the simplest possible manner.

The rules of nature are comparatively very simple; the natural way to perform a task, to relate one's work to that of another, or to accomplish a common goal is to do it the simple way; it is against natural instincts to do anything in a complex and involved manner. The true concept of a particular function—what is to be done, when, and how —is best understood by people when they are informed in simple language and in a direct manner.

Efforts to make an organization structure seem profound by adding unnecessary functions, giving old functions new names, and developing complex relationships between the functions make for confusion.

Efficient managers work with things that are simple; they understand them better; and they know that simplicity brings the best results.

At this point, it is very appropriate to quote from a statement attributed to Sir Henry Deterding of the Shell Oil Company, who said:

> There is a master key to success with which no man can fail. Its name is simplicity, simplicity I mean in the sense of reducing to the simplest possible terms every problem that besets us. Almost every man can succeed if only he will simplify everything in his life. That has been my working theory for forty years. As a very young man I stumbled upon this fundamental truth that everything that is complicated is wrong. Simplicity rules everything worth while. Whenever I have met a problem which after taking thought I could not reduce to simplicity, I have left it alone.

DETERMINATION OF CLEARLY DEFINED CHANNELS OF AUTHORITY AND RESPONSIBILITY

In every structure there is some personnel directive which is manifested through the instructions, orders, and procedures that are transmitted through organization channels. This personnel directive is one of the most important means of obtaining effective group effort, and it can operate efficiently only when clearly defined channels of authority and responsibility are provided within the organization structure.

Each member of an enterprise must know not only what to do but also that his work is looked over to determine if it is being done correctly. Definite channels eliminate the so-called "horizontal gaps" in organization structures, i.e., areas at any given organization level which are not covered by a channel of authority and responsibility. When horizontal gaps exist, the functions and activities of the personnel in such areas are not adequately synchronized with those of the other parts of the structure, and inefficient overlapping of personnel control activities is usually present.

ESTABLISHMENT OF DEFINITE AND FIXED RESPONSIBILITY

Responsibility implies an individual trust, a dependence upon an individual to perform an assigned task promptly and efficiently. When one is vested with responsibility, it is up to him and to him alone to see that the job is carried out satisfactorily, and it is this fixed responsibility that tends to develop the individual and to increase his initiative. When an individual knows exactly the task and the activity for which he is being held fully responsible, he tends to overcome common obstacles and to perform his tasks promptly and thoroughly. Human beings like to measure up to the requirements made of them.

Fixed responsibility also aids in getting the work accomplished.

When fixed responsibilities have been placed, it is known who is responsible for each particular activity, and with this knowledge available, the proper person for a specific function can be seen quickly and directly, without waste of time.

Responsibility should be fixed at a level as low in the organization structure as is consistent with the capability of the personnel at that level to assume responsibility. The lower the level, the greater the benefit to the total organization personnel, simply because the merits of fixed responsibility reach a greater number of the personnel. Furthermore, fixed responsibility helps to develop executives and supervisors who will probably be needed in order to meet future needs of the enterprise. In addition, the individual's feeling of worth is increased, and the problems of discipline are minimized.[1]

PROVISION FOR COEQUALITY OF AUTHORITY AND RESPONSIBILITY

Another important principle of organizing is that the authority of any manager should be coequal with his responsibility and, vice versa, his responsibility coequal with his authority. The association between authority and responsibility is intimate and arises from accomplishing the same work. As pointed out in Chapter 21, making decisions and enforcing them regarding specific work (authority) also entails the obligation to perform this work (responsibility) by accepting and using the delegated authority.

Authority and responsibility are therefore akin to an object and its image in a mirror. If one exists, the other exists also in a coequal status. Authority commensurate with responsibility is needed before responsibility becomes meaningful, and, likewise, responsibility without commensurate authority has dubious managerial value. Effective managers keep this principle of organizing in mind and see to it that for any executive coequality of authority and responsibility is present.

ATTENTION TO CO-ORDINATION OF THE ACTIVITIES

Co-ordinating implies the smooth working together of the various activities which make up the total effort expended in achieving the prescribed work. Co-ordination can be thought of as aiming toward a perfect meshing or a harmonious adjustment. By means of co-ordination, a manager obtains a smooth synchronization of all necessary activities, each performed at the desired place and time. The following expression of co-ordination is also helpful: "Co-ordination means con-

---

[1] For a thorough discussion of responsibility in organization, see R. C. Davis, *Industrial Organization and Management* (New York: Harper & Bros., 1940), pp. 62–70.

currence in purpose and performance to secure harmony in action toward a common end."[2] A good illustration of a situation in which coordination is paramount is that of a symphony orchestra, where various musical sounds of many instruments, consisting of different tone qualities, pitches, timbres, and quantities, are all co-ordinated or blended together in such a manner that the end result is smooth, melodious music.

Organizing is intended to provide a vital means for co-ordinating the activities of a group. This integration of efforts, in the opinion of many, is the ultimate deciding factor in organizing. Without order and arrangement there is quite likely to be disjointed efforts and a hodgepodge of mental and physical toil incompatible with the objectives of the enterprise.

Each member of a group should know not only his own immediate goal but also the common goal of his fellow workers, so that recognition can be made of a common interest and the obligation of mutual service. To reach the peak of co-ordination each member must accept the basic purpose of the enterprise, understand why this achievement is essential, know his part in these efforts, and be informed of the progress as it is achieved. This implies a self-imposed type of discipline by each member upon himself in order to win status as a true "mutual server."

DEFINITION OF EACH JOB

To define each job of an organizational structure makes for better organizing. The activities to be performed should be prescribed in complete yet simple language. The duties and the responsibilities should be noted as well as the authority relationship between the job being defined to that of other jobs in the structure. Such work helps the organizer to utilize constructive and creative thought in his efforts and to see more clearly the division of work and the relative organizational position of the person assigned each component work segment.

Organization charts and job descriptions are helpful media in this work, but special attention should be given organization manuals. The format can follow any one of many different patterns, but specific information regarding the title, the organizational unit, responsibility, and authority are usually included. Getting this information down in black and white helps to clarify overlapping operations, eliminate duplications, and assign duties to specific areas. However, when the

---

[2] E. Petersen and E. G. Plowman, *Business Organization and Management* (rev. ed.; Homewood, Ill.: Richard D. Irwin, Inc., 1948), p. 148.

material for an organization manual is collected and written by each manager in charge of each respective unit, interest is stimulated in better organizing work and general understanding among executives throughout the structure is gained. Organization manuals are also helpful in training of the executive incumbent as well as his successor, and they provide official answers to organization questions for the given enterprise.

CONSIDERATION OF THE HUMAN ELEMENT

The motivating power behind any organization structure is the personnel of that structure. For a function to be performed, a responsibility to be assumed, and an authority to be exercised, the presence of human beings is required. Therefore, adequate consideration for the human element of any organization structure is of prime importance.

Psychologically, the fact of individual differences is well established. People differ in their desires, in their capacities, and in their interests.[3] What one person seeks, another abhors. The capacity of one might be unusual for creative work, while that of another is such that he can think of a new idea only after extended and considerable effort. Likewise, the chief interests of one person might be along the line of mathematical details, while those of another are in broad generalities.

The various functions to be performed also differ so that in any organization structure there are many functions to be performed by many different types of persons. This condition is not paradoxical, as might first be expected. Rather, it is extremely fortunate, for it makes it possible to match a person of certain desires, capacities, and interests with the particular function which requires those particular characteristics.

Motivating Power Supplied. This matching of a person with a job and of a job with a person provides an enormous motivating power within the organization structure. In the first place, it makes for overall harmony within the organization. It helps determine whether the person fits into the organizational setup, that is, whether the person's make-up is compatible with such things as the aims and purposes of the organization and the methods of operation. In the second place, it provides for high efficiency among the organization members. A person does his best when he is engaged in a function which satisfies

---

[3] This idea is taken from the excellent discussion of capacities, interests, and opportunities of personnel as developed in *Personnel Management*, by W. D. Scott, R. C. Clothier, and W. R. Spriegel (5th ed.; New York: McGraw-Hill Book Co., Inc., 1955), chap. ii, pp. 9–20.

fully his individual characteristics. When a person finds that his job requires the particular desires, capacities, and interests which he possesses, that person usually becomes a highly efficient and satisfied worker. Thirdly, is the advantage of a better social order. The employee feels that he is doing the things which he believes are worth while and that he is contributing to society according to his individual ability. In addition, he is engaged in work which places him in an environment which gives him social satisfaction.

Building the Organization Structure around Available Personnel. The human element is so important that in some actual cases the entire organization structure has been built around the available personnel, giving minor consideration to the functions. One big advantage in this approach is that all the unique characteristics of all the available personnel are utilized to the very utmost. Good results are obtained. From the practical viewpoint, some very successful organization structures have been built on this personnel hub basis. However, the big disadvantage in such a practice is that the necessary replacements are extremely difficult to make, because it is frequently almost impossible to find a person with the exact characteristics of the person being replaced. This makes for organizational difficulty and frequently results in genuine weaknesses inside the organizational structure.

Dynamic Characteristics of Human Element. Consideration of the human element as an organization principle should always be thought of as a dynamic concept. What is considered the right function for the right person today may not be true six months, one year, or ten years from today, for human beings change in their characteristics. What constitutes job satisfaction for a person twenty years of age may be substantially different when that person is thirty years of age. For good organizational work, it is imperative to keep reviewing the organizational structure from the viewpoint of the human element and to keep men and women on jobs for which they are best suited and which they want to do. This can be accomplished by planning ahead, by training personnel for jobs, and by utilizing the best of what each person has to offer.

PROVISION OF EFFECTIVE LEADERSHIP

Leadership is always outstanding in the success of any enterprise. The structural relationships of an organization may be very poor; yet wonders may be accomplished through effective leadership. On the other hand, the relationships may be excellent; yet little can be achieved if its leadership is poor.

The true concept of leadership is difficult to define. It may be thought of as the process of influencing large numbers of people in important ways or the process of changing the attitudes of many persons.[4] Leadership implies a threefold meaning, including: (1) the skill to direct—to show the way, (2) the ability to win co-operation and loyalty, and (3) the courage to carry on until the assigned task is accomplished. A discussion of each of these points follows.

Skill to Direct—to Show the Way. A leader possesses the ability to guide people—to point out the proper means for attainment. This showing-the-way characteristic of leadership usually means that the leader is out in front leading, not in back pushing. Consider, for example, a piece of ordinary wrapping twine. While this example is not directly applicable, it nevertheless illustrates the principle. When the front end of the twine is directed and guided along desired paths, the rest of the piece of twine will follow. In contrast, when the twine is pushed, it follows no predetermined path and flounders in aimless direction.

Ability to Win Co-operation and Loyalty. A leader is able to get people to act jointly and to work toward a common goal. All efforts of the group are knitted together and concentrated into one large force toward the attainment of the objective. This unity of operation is accomplished by strong and enthusiastic feelings, so that each member has a deep sense of obligation to the leader.

Courage to Carry On until the Assigned Task Is Accomplished. A leader is dauntless and ever confident that the task to be done will be completely accomplished. He has implicit faith in the success of his actions and gives a feeling of confidence and positiveness to all associated with him.

People like to be led by a dynamic leader. They like to be led by a person who clearly envisages the goal, who knows how to achieve that goal, and who goes out after it. Effective leadership is an important entity at all levels of management in an organization structure. It is not confined to top levels alone but is equally important for managerial personnel at lower levels, i.e., for supervisors and group leaders. In these lower levels, the scope of operation is relatively small, but the carrying-out of leadership is essential.[5]

---

[4] Emory S. Bogardus, *Sociology* (New York: Macmillan Co., 1941), p. 510.

[5] For outstanding discussions on the subject of leadership, see O. Tead, *The Art of Leadership* (New York: McGraw-Hill Book Co., Inc., 1935); and A. M. Cooper, *How to Supervise People* (New York: McGraw-Hill Book Co., Inc., 1946), pp. 54–68.

QUESTIONS

1. What is an organization principle and how can an office manager use it? Give example to illustrate your answer.
2. Is there such a thing as an "ideal organization"? Why?
3. A great deal of importance is attached to the objective in evaluating an organization structure. Why is this?
4. For each of the following undesirable organization conditions the application of what principle or principles of organization will probably correct it?
   a) Capable men confined to mediocre jobs.
   b) Some organizational units in the office growing disproportionate in relation to their relative importance.
   c) No tie-in among several organizational units.
   d) Excessive buck-passing when emergency office work fails to be completed on time.
5. Is consideration of the objective of the enterprise applicable to organizing work of the office manager? Explain.
6. As business operations become more complex and the paper work arising from them become more voluminous, do you feel it practical to feature simplicity in an office organization structure? Explain.
7. Why is the establishment of definite and fixed responsibility important in organizing?
8. You have been transferred from a branch to the main office and promoted to assistant general office manager. You discover that one of your supervisors, Mr. Earl Tanner, seems to have authority far in excess in relation to his responsibility, while Miss Yvonne DuVall, another of your supervisors, has little authority but relatively a great deal of responsibility. Relate the specific action that you would take and explain why.
9. Discuss the organizational principle of definition of each job.
10. What basic guide or guides in organizing have been violated in each of the following:
    a) Failing to recognize and include certain functions in the organization structure.
    b) Assigning the responsibility for a single function to three people.
    c) Organizing an office exactly like that of a highly successful office.
    d) Establishing a satisfactory organization structure and subsequently adding functions as and where needed or requested.
11. In your opinion, can effective leadership exist without an organization structure? An organization structure without effective leadership? Elaborate on your answers.
12. What is the meaning of each of the following managerial terms or concepts:
    a) Co-ordination.
    b) Leadership.

c) "Horizontal gaps" in an organization structure.

d) Human element.

CASE PROBLEMS

CASE 22–1. DeKALB MANUFACTURING COMPANY

The top management group of the DeKalb Manufacturing Company consists of Mr. James Bertell, president; his three sons, Henry, Albert, and Theodore; Mr. William Hubbel; and Mr. Carl Atkinson. Competition of the company is keen and becoming more so. As a part of an effort to reduce costs and to operate more effectively, an outside office expert was engaged to study the company's office organization. The expert noted the following facts:

1. Two supervisors have fifteen employees in their respective units while one supervisor has only two employees. The average number of employees per supervisor is nine.

2. Each office unit maintains its own files. The filing arrangements are similar for all except two divisions in which the supervisors explained respectively that "My work is different" and "This is the way it was when I came and so I have continued it."

3. Overtime work is frequent in the payroll processing unit. The supervisor of this unit appears competent, but complains of too much work to do.

4. The employees in both the Billing and the Ordering Departments work overtime during certain periods of the month and are allowed to leave early during the remaining periods.

5. Several of the girls said they received a minimum of instructions as to what constituted their jobs. Most of the office employees had no idea why they are doing their particular jobs.

6. Each of the Bertell sons has a private stenographer, two of whom spend 90 per cent of their time at this duty, while the other divides her time between stenography and computations for the Accounting Department.

7. Eleven of the girls employed in the office said they were considered "unclassified personnel" and were kept busy doing odd jobs around the office. They reported to no one in particular and received orders from the various department heads of the office.

8. Informal chats with the office employees reveal that many feel (1) their supervisor got his or her job by "pull" from one of Bertell's sons, (2) there is little opportunity to get ahead in this office, and (3) the best thing about working in this office is the fact that they are not docked for being late to work.

PROBLEMS:

1. What interpretations do you believe can be drawn from the information collected by the expert?

2. What recommendations for improving the company's office organization should be made?

3. What difficulties may be encountered in putting your suggested recommendations into effect? Explain.

CASE 22–2.   GEORGE C. NANCE COMPANY

The George C. Nance Company manufactures fractional horsepower electric motors and employs a total of three hundred sixty people, of whom forty-seven are office employees. The active head of the business is George C. Nance, now sixty-three years old and sole proprietor.

Mr. Nance is not satisfied with the performance of the office of the company. He feels that the present office manager, Mr. Jerome Cleary, age thirty-seven and with the company for eleven years, lacks decisiveness, shuns responsibility, and neglects some of the six units in his office organization structure by devoting most of his time and interest to several favorite ones.

To correct this situation, Mr. Nance at first thought it best to terminate the employment of Mr. Cleary, but after some consideration believes this would probably be too drastic, even if accomplished on an amiable and mutually agreeable basis. He feels the best solution is to place Mr. Cleary in charge of one office unit along with similar heads of the other office units and have all reporting to him (Mr. Nance).

The personnel manager believes Mr. Nance's suggestion will result in confusion and might cause ill feeling toward the company. He reasons that if Mr. Cleary is demoted, the effect of such a move might be very detrimental to the present office morale, which he judges to be less than average. Also, he questions whether Mr. Cleary will accept the lower-level job.

The sales manager disagrees with Mr. Nance, saying that it would be better to select the most promising man in the office and promote him to the office manager's job. Mr. Cleary's position could be determined later, or possibly his employment terminated as soon as possible.

Mr. Nance countered that, in his opinion, there is no qualified candidate for the office manager's job among the present office employees. The vacancy of the office manager's job might stimulate some present employees to prepare themselves for this opening, but Mr. Nance believes that eventually a man from the outside will have to be hired.

PROBLEMS:

1. In line with Mr. Nance's suggestion, do you feel that having the heads of the various office units reporting direct to Mr. Nance would probably prove successful? Explain.

2. What significance do you give to the statement by Mr. Nance that "there is no qualified candidate for the office manager's job among the present office employees"?

3. What action do you feel Mr. Nance should take? Why?

4. Assuming Mr. Nance's suggestion is followed, should Mr. Cleary (1) accept the demotion, try to improve himself and profit by the experience, or (2) quit the company? Elaborate on your answer.

PART V......

Actuating Office Employees

The discussion of the fundamental managerial function of planning and of organizing now completed, the next function in the management process for study is actuating. To many, this is the vital fundamental function of management.

Actuating includes the creating and the continuing of the desire by each member of the work group to achieve the predetermined goal by working willingly and enthusiastically at prescribed tasks and at given times and places. When employees believe in and understand what is trying to be accomplished, when they are inspired and are called upon to use their highest attainable skills and capacities in work they are genuinely interested in, the task of management is considerably lightened.

This section of the book, Part V, is devoted to office managerial actuating and includes the following eight chapters: (1) motivating office personnel, (2) office job evaluating and salary administration, (3) recruiting and selecting office personnel, (4) training of office employees, (5) office safety, (6) office trade-unionism, (7) office supervision, and (8) developing office executives.

Chapter · 23

Motivating Office Personnel

> The great scientific discoveries of the past hundred years have
> been as child's play compared with the titanic forces that will
> be released when man applies himself to the understanding
> and mastery of his own nature.
>
> —MELVIN J. EVANS

SOME EXPERTS have stated that the most important
skill of an office manager is the ability to motivate people. And the
statement is often heard that motivation accounts for almost all of the
great achievements of all time. There are many who feel that actuating
is the most important activity of management. Certainly it is vital. To
build men and women is management's great role. There is no question that accomplishments are achieved through people—management of people permeates all phases of office management. Every
function in an organizational structure is affected in some way by the
personnel aspect, and in the final analysis, all management is implemented by and through the human element. Materials, equipment,
and machines can all be readily replaced; they can even be insured
against loss. But capable and loyal human beings cannot be replaced,
nor can their loss be adequately insured. Efforts to acquire, develop,
and maintain competent and co-operative human beings must be taken,
and this means that human motives must be understood and actions
taken according to that understanding.

BASIC VIEWPOINTS TOWARD LABOR

The Industrial Revolution brought about centralized production activities, transformed skilled workmen who were their own employers
into employees of others, separated many employees from the buyers of
their products, and widened the gap between the employer and the employee. As a result, the status of the employee and his relationship with
his employer underwent significant changes.

446

At one time the employee was considered in the same light as a commodity—something to be bought on the open market, and of a fairly uniform quality. Later, the so-called machinery conception of labor became prominent; the employee was considered a producing unit and his value measured in terms of the goods produced. After years of struggle and unhappiness, a new concept of employer-employee relationships gradually evolved. It was that an employee is a human being and that his welfare is important; hence, the employer should encourage and supply various welfare services deemed desirable. A paternal attitude toward the employee developed. This represented an improvement over the employee's previous status, but was not the answer to satisfactory employer-employee relations. Many employees were suspicious of these welfare efforts and resented being the children of a paternalistic policy. Since the period of around 1915–20, the concept that an employee is a human entity and must be treated as such has gained headway. This means that consideration for an employee's psychological make-up and recognition and utilization of his desires, attitudes, interests, and motives are as important as attention to his physical efforts, perhaps even more so.

As thinking along this human-entity line has progressed, the basis for a great many current practices developed, including: that individuals vary in their personal aptitudes and interests, that different jobs require different abilities, that the emotional make-up of the employee is important, and that the prevailing spirit or feeling of the work force affects its productivity. A "mutuality of interests" between an employer and employee is being recognized. This means that both have an interest in the well-being of the enterprise and that the relationship between employer and employee should be a harmonious working together toward their common objectives, which are compatible over the long-run period of time.

MOTIVATING EMPLOYEES

The question can be asked, "How do you motivate employees?" A logical approach is to find out the wants of the employees and either satisfy these wants in managerial activities or supply reasonable explanations why they cannot be fulfilled. Many studies have been conducted to discover the important wants of employees. The survival or biological needs, sometimes referred to as economic, include the desire for adequate food, clothing, and shelter. What constitutes adequacy in these areas will differ among people, and likewise the degree of motivations to acquire satisfaction of these needs will vary. However, in normal economic times, these survival needs are met, and when taken care of, much of the employee's concern is then turned to the satisfaction of emotional and social needs. For example, he wants to know that what he is doing is worth while and has merit, that he is accepted and approved by his fellowmen. For most employees, their daily work is expected, at least in part, to supply these needs by providing an opportunity to demonstrate their talent, acquire prestige, and gain recognition.

Studies along this line reveal listings of the psychological and social wants of employees. The wants vary somewhat depending upon the study, but most include the following: job security, opportunity for expression, chance to develop and to grow, be informed about changes that will affect them, equitable pay, personal help when requested, recognition for accomplishments, treatment as human beings, and effective supervision.

Knowing these wants, the next step is to set operations in action in order to satisfy these wants. Here is where the real skill of motivating enters. Employees' wants are not identical for each group or for each member of a group. Furthermore, the wants do not remain constant; they vary from day to day. And the reaction to the same stimuli may differ widely among employees.

SUGGESTIONS FOR EFFECTIVE MOTIVATING

There are, however, certain general guides that in many offices have proven successful in motivating employees. They include:

1. *Belief in yourself and in people.* Effective motivating starts with a genuine belief in both yourself as a management member and in the people under your direction. A manager must sincerely believe that he can motivate and must want to motivate his employees. Belief in employees means thinking and promoting the idea that they can plan better, exercise authority better, do their work better, and giving them the opportunity to do so.

2. *Set a good example.* The management member should demonstrate by his actions the kind of effort he would like his employees to exert. Performance on the part of the leader, his attitude, and work habits tend to set a pattern which employees copy. Important in this consideration is to keep busy—everyone including the supervisor should have enough meaningful work to do. Failure to provide ample work results sooner or later in employee dissatisfaction and a lack of justification for the money spent in their employment.

3. *Place employees in proper jobs.* Employees normally will give their best efforts in work that they like and feel competent to perform.

They need to have assignments they are capable of performing. Finding the field of endeavor best suited for each individual employee's capacity and interest, as well as following up to insure that each member is on the best job for which he is currently adapted, will assist in stimulating the employee's best efforts.

4. *Stress participation.* Rare indeed is the person motivated to unusual achievement without some participation in the planning, discussion, and decision making of the activity in which he is going to take a part. Actually this is the basis for practicing delegation of authority.[1] An employee wants to say something about conditions that affect him. Employees want to be asked their opinions about factors involving their work. They appreciate an audience. By such means, the employee gains the feeling that his employer has an interest in, and cares about, those working for him. Likewise, the desire "to get ahead"—to advance, to win status and prestige—tends to be satisfied when participation is stressed. In some companies weekly meetings among members of a department are held in order to bring the employees into the task of operating the department by seeking their counsel.

5. *Keep employees informed.* It is a natural human tendency to want to know what is going on, why this or that operation is important, and what changes are being considered—in short, to be kept informed. This adds to an employee's sense of belonging and of being an integral part of the organization structure. Employees want to feel they are valued members of the team. Communicating effectively with people is essential in motivating them.

6. *Give adequate incentive and reward.* This can and does take many different forms including the amount of wages, the granting of special privileges, the conferring of titles, and the instilling of competition between departments or among employees. To illustrate, the amount of compensation, as well as a proper differential between jobs, is important. Employees want comparable pay for comparable jobs and salaries that are "in line" with those of other enterprises in the area. They may be less interested in the amount of their own pay than in the relationship of their pay to that of other employees. Individual recognition, awarding of honors, and seniority can be cited as common means of granting special privileges, but these rewards are conferred within the limits of well-publicized policies. Employees can be greatly motivated when the reward offered has significant value to them.

7. *Recognize achievements of employees.* Most employees want to

---

[1] See Chapter 21.

feel useful; they want their efforts to be appreciated. In short, they want recognition. Credit where credit is due and a sincere expression of satisfaction from the employer for a job well done are effective motivating means. The practice of holding periodic talks in private with each employee is also highly recommended. In this way the employee is individualized, he is afforded recognition, he can voice his feelings about aspects of his job, and a better employer-employee understanding can be established.

8. *Develop group spirit.* Motivation is assisted by making employees feel they are a part of the group and needed on the team. In this respect, various employee recreational activities can be used to good advantage. The group spirit among an interested and participating number of employees is also fostered by giving them certain facts and an objective, then let them, working as a team, come up with a recommended course of action. In one company, the employees are given a profit and loss statement based on the work they performed and are requested to tie this in with the major objectives of the company.

9. *Inform about the job itself.* To motivate effectively each employee must believe his work is wholesome and important. The relationship of his assignment to the entire office and to the aims of the company should be clearly brought out. It is helpful to point out why the particular equipment and machines are supplied so that an attitude of pride in performing their work well and in being a part of the enterprise is developed.

10. *Provide an opportunity for job security.* Almost every employee is concerned about having steady work—not being laid off or losing his job. Security is the main reason for demanding restrictions on the type of work that an employee can perform. Also, adequate financial support for old age or to take care of illness or accidents is an important security want of the employee. Providing this wanted security can be a stimulating effect upon the employee. However, it is necessary to keep him aware of it and to point out that work accomplishments effectively attained are the best means of achieving and maintaining job security.

11. *Employ fear judiciously.* Fear is a negative force, but when properly used it can serve as a very strong motivator. The apprehension of not wanting certain happenings to take place can cause a person to exert unusually strong efforts in the direction away from the unwanted event.

12. *Exercise strong leadership.* All normal persons are motivated by competent leaders. The typical employee wants a leader who knows

what he is doing, can speak authoritatively, never makes promises he cannot keep, builds confidence, and takes prompt disciplinary action whenever necessary.

PERSONNEL MANAGEMENT

The task of motivating employees is the duty of every management member. However, in managerial discussions, this task is usually considered under personnel management, since this area is concerned primarily with people. The following definition is simple and useful: *Personnel management includes those activities dealing with the procuring and the maintaining of a satisfactory and a satisfied working force.* The number and the intensity of activities performed to accomplish effective personnel management vary with such things as the size of the office, the general type of office work, the organizational pattern, and the philosophy of the top managers. In a small office of ten employees, the work of personnel management is probably handled on an informal, highly personal basis by the owner. In contrast, in a large office of 1,000 employees, the activities are probably functionalized and definite programs set up and executed in order to provide for the employee's development and for desirable relationships.

It is worth repeating that since the basic objective of office management is to get work accomplished and to do this effectively, good management of personnel is vital. Specifically, the goal of personnel management is to assist in this major objective, i.e., to obtain people capable of doing the work, to motivate them favorably, to develop their abilities, and to help them find satisfaction in, and be satisfied with, their jobs. Personnel management efforts are directed not toward the achievement of one big happy family of employees, as such, but toward the achievement of this happy and contented group as an essential in accomplishing the task to be performed. Or, stated in a different way, such efforts are directed toward making an employee's work life happier by making his work more meaningful to him and hence attaining stated objectives more effectively.

MAKE-UP OF OFFICE PERSONNEL MANAGEMENT

A multitude of activities make up personnel management. This probably follows because any program designed to promote the obtaining and maintaining of a competent and harmonious working group is certain to take in a great many situations and functions. For convenience, included in the following seven chapters of this book are office job evaluating and salary administration, recruiting and selecting office personnel, training of office employees, office safety, office trade-unionism, office supervision, and developing office executives. However, there are other activities in connection with actuating efforts of an office manager that merit discussion. These are included in the immediate following pages.

PROMOTIONS

Promotion affords satisfaction to the average individual in his desire to develop, to advance, and to improve his status. Strictly speaking, promotion implies a change of job. The promoted employee is normally required to discharge the duties of a new job demanding greater assumption of duties and responsibilities. Contrary to popular usage, an increase in wages does not constitute a promotion.[2]

Most companies have the policy of promoting from among their present employees whenever possible. This requires keeping a sharp eye open for the discovery of promotable personnel—those people who demonstrate a desire to advance by qualifying for a better and more responsible job. Quite a few managers, however, feel that the policy of promoting from the ranks should be modified: that some of the vacancies for better jobs should be filled by candidates from outside the enterprise. By this means, it is contended, new ideas, new attitudes, and different methods of operation are brought in which tend to foster an active, healthy condition.

A definite written plan of promotion is helpful toward orderly and purposeful upgrading. Such a plan not only provides the managers with an orderly guide for action but also enables the employee to know the possible steps for promotion and the qualifications that are necessary in order to advance from one job to another.

Promotion implies two-way action. It calls for action by the managers, to open up avenues along which employees can advance, and it calls for action by employees, to qualify themselves for advancement.

The initiative for promotion work belongs with the manager. Without prodding, the manager should see that worthy people are promoted. The knowledge of whom to advance is gained through records covering each employee's merit, competence, and length of service.

ABSENTEEISM

The failure of an employee to report on the job when scheduled to work is one of the difficult personnel problems with which the average office manager must cope. Absenteeism disrupts the smooth flow of

---

[2] Dale Yoder, *Personnel Management and Industrial Relations* (4th ed.; New York: Prentice-Hall, Inc., 1956), p. 383.

work. When an employee fails to show up, the work either stops completely, or extra work is forced upon another employee.

The causes of absenteeism are various and extremely difficult to ascertain correctly. The reasons differ with each employee and cover any one of a number of things. The most common causes, however, include sickness of the employee, illness in the family, transportation difficulties, bad weather, personal business, weddings, and funerals.

There is no single cure for absenteeism, for it is an individual problem. Experience shows it is best to apply the remedy which best fits the specific cause or causes. Records should be kept to reveal who is absent, how long, how often, and why. These records need not be elaborate—a simple card system will prove adequate.

To help motivate the employee to be on the job every day, company policies regarding absences should be explained thoroughly to each employee, who is obligated to notify the company in advance of any expected absence and should understand what disciplinary action the company will take in certain cases. Actions such as these, however, are passive and do little to restrain the "absent without leave" employee.

Among the various motivating means used to reduce absenteeism are pointing out to employees the importance of being on the job, talking with each absentee upon return and thoroughly discussing the cause and explanation offered, checking to see if the right person is on the right job, maintaining a continued health program, allowing a definite number of days off per year, requiring absentees to make up time, and showing some outward thanks and appreciation to those employees who are always on the job.

TARDINESS

The employee who is not punctual makes the task of co-ordinating employees' efforts more difficult. Managerial planning assumes that employees will be available and ready to work at a specific time. Bad timekeeping on the part of employees indicates perhaps a disrespect for others and a lack of dependability. Tardiness is contagious. When one or two continue to come into the office late, the idea gets in the minds of other employees that such behavior meets managerial approval.

Being early is as much a habit as being late. The hour at which work starts has little influence on the problem. The tendency to procrastinate must be corrected, and the importance of keeping time obligations stressed.

An effective motivating means consists of creating a strong employee interest in promptness. Supervisors should set good examples and always be on time themselves. They should also keep reminding the workers about the importance of being on time. Promptness should be recognized in the employee's rating. Also, recognition can be given tardy-free employees by listings on the bulletin board, write-ups in the company paper, or the granting of special privileges in the office. In many instances, the employee simply fails to allow himself sufficient time to get ready and go to work. Dependence upon hairline transportation connections and failure to allow extra time for travel under bad weather conditions are common causes. The means of correction here are self-evident.

In many offices it is purposely made difficult for the tardy employee to get to his workplace. A tardy employee reports first to the office manager or to the timekeeper, where an explanation is given verbally for the tardiness and a form filled out indicating the reasons why. The idea of going through a "lot of red tape" helps to discourage tardiness.

The imposition of a fine or some sort of penalty, such as making up time lost or doing the least desirable work, proves effective. However, before using such a plan, it should meet the approval of the employees, who should agree to "go along with it." One company uses a unique plan which brings surprisingly good results. An employee's name is selected at random from the payroll list and, promptly at starting time, the employee is called on the telephone. If he answers, indicating presence and promptness on the job, he receives a reward of $20.

KEEPING EMPLOYEES INFORMED

A great deal is being said in management circles about communication especially in the area of keeping employees informed. An aggressive and sincere effort in this respect will do wonders toward achieving a co-operative, confident, and enthusiastic working force. An informed employee is usually a good employee. Employees like to be told firsthand about new policies and why they are being adopted, and they feel that they have a right to know about changes to be made in existing conditions.

On the question of what information to give employees, the following is pertinent:

. . . The point is that we must begin our whole thinking by realizing, as nearly as we can, what questions are in the minds of employees. We must be as realistic about our problem as they are about theirs. If we believe that the desired relationship of understanding can be aided by sharing information with employees, we must face the fact that we cannot successfully convey any information to them without meeting these questions which are in their minds. If we can find out what they want to know, we have a priceless opening for our program. But if we ignore, evade or generalize instead of specifically meeting their questions, we have supplied material for building higher the walls of misunderstanding.[3]

Initiative by Managers.   Managers should take the initiative and supply full information to employees. They should not depend upon the "word of mouth" or traditional office grapevine as the dispensers of information. To do so commonly results in the employees' receiving incomplete and, all too frequently, erroneous information.

Classification of Information.   Most information can be classified into three groups:

1. Knowledge of company—including history of the company, products or services offered, current trends and growths, names of departments and their heads, plan of organization, and lines of responsibility.

2. Knowledge of policies—concerning employees and customers, with reasons why such policies are in force.

3. Knowledge of special events—covering the out-of-the-ordinary happenings and developments on controversial issues.

Media Available.   Many media are available. The selection depends chiefly upon the type of information and the type of employees to be reached. Figure 23–1 suggests the features and the organization level for six selected media.

INSURANCE AND BENEFITS

Various plans and services are now available to help the employee gain some measure of security. These plans have been brought about through the efforts of companies and employees and the influence of state and federal law, among which are unemployment insurance regulations, workmen's compensation laws, social security regulations, and fair labor standards regulations. The form, purpose, and content of these various plans vary considerably, but each one is designed to provide an opportunity to the employee to attain some measure of the security he desires.

The discussion here will be confined to three benefit plans: hospitalization, group insurance, and pension. All of these plans require

---

[3] Alexander R. Heron, *Sharing Information with Employees* (Stanford, Calif.: Stanford University Press, 1942), p. 43.

Medium	Features	Organization Level for Which Effective
Conversation	Man-to-man, forthright personal relationship	All organization levels
Letters	Excellent for statistical data and where permanent record is desired	Top managerial and supervisory levels
Pamphlets and booklets	Suitable for large volume of material	All organization levels
House organs	Adequate coverage satisfactory for reminder and announcements	All organizational levels
Motion picture, radio, and television	Dramatizes presentation; helpful in training, relating company history, and special achievements	All organizational levels
Speeches	Impressive for special events and celebrations	Top managerial and supervisory levels

FIG. 23–1. Media available for communication purposes.

special training and experience for complete understanding. It is usually advisable to employ the services of experts in this field; administration of the plan, however, can be handled by the office manager.

Hospitalization Plans. These plans are a form of insurance which pays nearly all hospital expenses resulting from all nonoccupational illnesses or accidents suffered by the employee. Premiums are usually paid by the employee, although in some instances the company contributes toward the plan. Costs are reasonable. To illustrate, a typical plan might call for payment of $3.00 per month by an unmarried employee for semiprivate accommodations. The amount of cost varies with such factors as the number of employees in the plan, their sex and age, and the benefits provided.

Group Insurance Plans. Protection for individual employees as members of a group is provided by group insurance plans. Usually employees are eligible only after a stipulated period of service and in an amount relative to their earnings. The company or the employees may pay the full cost of the plan, or the cost may be assumed jointly. Employees are usually able to secure protection at a cost below that of individually purchased insurance of the same protection. The exact nature of the policy varies with different plans; the basis of all are straight life-insurance coverage, but this frequently is supplemented with other benefits.

Pension Plans. Such plans are orderly processes whereby regular payments are made to one retired from service. The experience of many older companies shows that a great number of employees reach retirement age without sufficient means of support. To meet this condition, pension plans have been set up by quite a few companies. These plans make it possible to give needed relief and to grant rewards for long service. Pension plans also benefit the company, for retirement of older employees permits the employment of younger persons as replacements. This helps to keep the work force alive and vibrant, and

A Typical Profit Sharing Retirement Plan

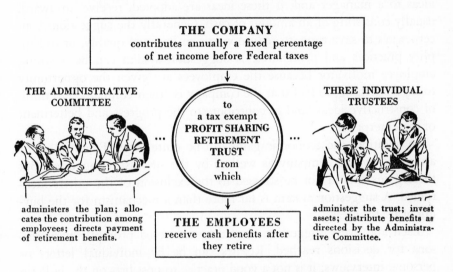

THE COMPANY
contributes annually a fixed percentage
of net income before Federal taxes

THE ADMINISTRATIVE COMMITTEE

to
a tax exempt
PROFIT SHARING RETIREMENT TRUST
from which

THREE INDIVIDUAL TRUSTEES

administers the plan; allocates the contribution among employees; directs payment of retirement benefits.

THE EMPLOYEES
receive cash benefits after
they retire

administer the trust; invest assets; distribute benefits as directed by the Administrative Committee.

Executives of corporations can create a suitable profit sharing retirement plan — easily and inexpensively — by following the simplified procedures outlined above, with the help of the company's own lawyer, accountant and the investment dealer who presents these working documents.

The use of this service entails no obligation except your careful consideration of the merits of mutual investment funds for the Trust investment.

Courtesy: Vance, Sanders & Co., Boston

FIG. 23–2. An employees retirement plan based on a profit-sharing arrangement.

the existence of a retirement pension plan makes for high morale and attracts better employees.

The cost of a pension plan can be paid by either the company or the employees, or by both. Figure 23–2 illustrates a profit-sharing retirement plan. The amount of retirement pay generally provided is about 50 per cent of the average rate for the five-year period preceding retirement. The plan should be based on a sound actuarial basis. It is usually advisable to employ the services of specialists in this field.

The trend in pension plans is toward a reduction in the waiting period for eligibility and the elimination of high age requirements of participants for pensions. Many of the recent plans also make provisions for adjustments in payments in accordance with general economic conditions. Programs under which the employee contributes are also becoming more common.

SUGGESTION SYSTEMS

A suggestion system is a means by which employees can submit their ideas to a manager and, if these ideas are adopted, receive an award, usually consisting of an amount of cash. Generally the suggestions concern ways to save time, to reduce waste, to improve quality, or to simplify practices and procedures. A suggestion system can be a strong employee motivator because the employees are given the opportunity to say something, to feel that the company is "their company," to think of constructive ideas, and to contribute to the progress and betterment of the enterprise.

In addition, the economic gains can be quite large. Financial gains are made by the company as well as by the successful suggester. But these gains should not be stressed to the exclusion of the others mentioned. A suggestion system is far more than a mechanism for the buying of useful ideas.

Each and every suggestion should be answered promptly with reasons for decisions reached. Replies can be by individual letters or personal interviews; it is not a good practice to post lists on the bulletin board. Replies to turndowns, i.e., those suggestions receiving no award, must contain the reasons why such action is taken. This practice is recommended because it (1) lets the employee know that his suggestion was evaluated; (2) reveals whether the judging committee understood his idea; (3) helps him to become better informed, inasmuch as he is told why his idea was not worthy of an award; and (4) prompts him to continue to try and stimulates further thinking. The amount of the reward must be worth while and must offer some inducement to the employee. Many companies have found that $5 is a minimum figure to use and that maximum awards based on 10 per cent of the savings for the first year are satisfactory.

Suggestion systems have a tendency to become dormant and, for this reason, they must be continually promoted. Showmanship, publicity stunts, and promotions can be used to keep the program alive. Devices which have proved successful include the following: attractive suggestion forms; appealing and well-located suggestion boxes bearing the sign "Have you deposited your suggestion in here today?"; attention-getting posters; reminders in payroll envelopes; and notices in company papers.

The suggester's identity is unknown to the investigator in some systems. This anonymity is obtained by means of a numbering and coupon arrangement on the suggestion form. The suggester retains a numbered coupon which corresponds to the number of the suggestion. Under this arrangement, impartiality on the part of the investigators is promoted. In contrast, other systems require the suggester's signature, a practice which affords close contact with the suggester.

Suggestion stimulators can be directed to all employees in order to encourage their participation in the suggestion systems. Letters and announcements can be used or more direct and definite means such as the manager asking, "What can you suggest to save time in the Filing Department?" Employees then start thinking of ways to improve that department. This practice appears to bring usable results, but it does involve a serious disadvantage. A suggestion system is supposed to enable the employee to take advantage of the things he or she already knows but which have not as yet been used to full advantage; directing his attention to new fields, therefore, might mean a loss of excellent ideas stemming from employee-on-the-job knowledge.

EMPLOYEES' RECREATIONAL ACTIVITIES

Recreational activities have motivating influence, but their greatest benefits are in providing a balance between work and play. A well-rounded program of recreational activities is an important part of personnel activities because it improves employer-employee relations, increases efficiency, and makes for healthy, satisfied employees.

Such activities may include the following: archery, baseball, softball, basketball, tennis, horseback riding, golf, bowling, horseshoe pitching, swimming, hiking, band, glee club, photography club, and amateur shows.

The participation of management members in recreational activities should consist of a readiness to furnish advice, to offer suggestions, and to lend assistance *upon request*. Managers should not attempt to force inclusion of certain activities or to run the program. Any semblance of paternalism should be avoided.

In guiding the development of the program, the following approach is usually helpful:

1. Measure the adequacy of the activity to find out the total number of employees who can participate.

2. Examine each existing activity to see if it is attracting a capacity number of employees.

3. Investigate public and private recreational facilities to determine how and when they can be used.

4. Find out what is included in programs of other companies.

5. Publicize the existence of the activities so that all employees who can and want to participate may do so.

RESEARCH IN ACTUATING OFFICE EMPLOYEES

Why is the successful actuating of office employees one of the most helpful of all managerial skills? The answer, in part, is because typically the office employee calls upon only a fraction of his full potentiality in performing his job. Managers commonly do not tap the ultimate of what an employee is capable and able to do. The main reason is because available motivating tools and their application are inadequate. Much more needs to be known about motivating and how to apply it.

It is hoped that research will supply the answer. Research is a lucrative source of new techniques, new methods, and new information. It seeks to appraise by objective means. It strives to answer such questions as "How well is the job now being done?" "Can it be improved?" and "What will happen if certain changes are made?"

Good research starts with basic factual knowledge about each employee—facts that can be used to increase the employee's satisfaction and to help assure a maximum of work output. In addition, personnel records are necessary in dealing with many outside agencies, particularly those of the state and federal government.

Success in maintaining helpful personnel records depends chiefly upon the content and number of records used, the accuracy of the recorded data, and the analysis and interpretation of the facts. Available standardized forms will be found helpful, but these should be evaluated in terms of what is essential for the particular program. Among the common personnel records are the following: personnel history of the employee; employee's application form; physical examination findings; results of selection tests; identification record; data on training; merit ratings; seniority ratings; safety record; first-aid record; record of attendance, warnings, and demerits; salary and earnings; and termination.

In addition, a personnel record folder on each employee is very helpful. This folder consists of a collection of all personnel records pertaining to the employee; it gives the complete story on that employee and makes this information available for instant reference. Normally, it contains the records listed above, but in some cases either more or less records may be retained.

QUESTIONS

1. Relate an experience in which you as an individual or as a member of a group was motivated in accomplishing a task. Indicate the means of motivation and how successful you believe it was. Do you feel other means of motivation would have been more successful? Why?

2. Briefly define each of the following:
   a) Managerial actuating.
   b) Personnel management.
   c) "Office grapevine."
   d) Machinery concept of labor.

3. How important do you feel the actuating of office employees really is? Elaborate on your answer.

4. Of the twelve means of motivating employees given in this chapter, which five, in your opinion, are probably the most effective for most cases? Why?

5. Discuss "give adequate incentive and reward" and "provide an opportunity for job security" as means of motivating office employees. Are these means identical? Explain.

6. Contrast the "paternalistic" viewpoint toward employees to that of the "mutuality of interests" viewpoint. In your opinion which has the greater motivating potential? Why?

7. As an office manager, what policy of promotion would you support? Give reasons for your answer.

8. Six months ago company "XYZ" established a suggestion system which unfortunately has proved to be very ineffective. You were asked to investigate the system and make recommendations for improvements. Describe your approach to and procedure in this assignment.

9. What do you recommend to bring about an awareness among office employees of the importance of (a) being on the job, and (b) being on time?

10. What point of view do you take in regard to managers' keeping employees informed? Why?

11. Discuss the need for research in the efforts of office managerial actuating.

12. Are hospitalization, group insurance, and pension plans effective motivating means for employees? Give reasons for your answer.

CASE PROBLEMS

CASE 23-1. GREENLEAF CHEMICAL COMPANY

Miss Allison was hired by the Greenleaf Chemical Company of Kingsport, Louisiana, directly upon her graduation from high school and was placed in the payroll office as a typist. She was intelligent, quick, cheerful, energetic, and had a pleasing personality; however, she looked delicate and was somewhat lacking in self-confidence. The paymaster had asked for a girl who was good at figures, who could type with reasonable speed and accuracy, and who could take short-hand. Miss Allison more than met these qualifications.

There were twenty girls in the paymaster's office, and Miss Allison readily made friends with all of them. She not only adapted herself quickly to the job but also enjoyed the work. She was usually the first to arrive in the morning and was frequently spoken to for her failure to quit work at noon or at night. She became an asset to the department head, and within a year she had demonstrated to the employment manager that she was in line for promotion. Consequently, when the employment manager received a requisition for a secretary to one of the sales executives, Miss Allison immediately came to his mind. He went to the paymaster and suggested Miss Allison's release for transfer. The paymaster was reluctant to let Miss Allison leave his department because of her efficiency. He at first suggested that he pay her more money, but this was not feasible since she was now receiving the top rate for her present job classification.

The employment manager called Miss Allison into the office and suggested the change to her. She asked for a few days in which to think it over. After three days, there was no answer from her. She seemed to be very upset and unable to do her work and apparently was unable to reach a decision.

PROBLEMS:

1. In your opinion, what are the relative responsibilities of the paymaster and the employment manager in respect to the promotion of Miss Allison? Explain.

2. Evaluate the attitude and action of the paymaster.

3. How do you explain the behavior of Miss Allison after the change was suggested to her? Discuss.

4. What action do you recommend the employment manager to take? Why?

CASE 23–2.   CLINTON-JACKSON COMPANY

The Clinton Company, a progressive growing company located in Baltimore, has recently acquired the Jackson Company of Philadelphia, to form the new Clinton-Jackson Company. The present office of the Clinton Company will be enlarged to provide needed services for the new company. It is estimated that two bookkeepers will be added to the present Clinton Company staff of two bookkeepers, two accountants to make a total of five accountants, and eight general clerks making a total of twenty-two general clerks. The bookkeepers and the accountants will be in the accounting department; some of the general clerks will be in the general office unit, while others will be dispersed among various nonoffice units.

In addition, the present plan is to add one clerk and one supervisor to the order group making an organization unit of this group consisting then of three employees and the supervisor. At present, fifteen men comprising the sales department do all their report work at home on dictating machines and mail their recordings to a stenographic pool consisting of three transcription operators. Each girl handles the correspondence of five salesmen, giving her about seven hours of work daily. Under the new plan, two more girls will be hired to handle the work of ten additional salesmen, and will be supervised by the newly appointed secretary of the assistant sales manager who formerly did not have his own secretary.

Some of the increased office personnel will be transferrals from the absorbed Jackson Company, while others will be new recruits. Quite a few of the Jackson Company office employees expressed desires to remain in Philadelphia and will seek new employment there with other companies.

In enlarging the office, it is believed some difficulties may arise with a few of the present Clinton Company employees, the former Jackson Company employees, and the new recruits. The present Clinton Company office force now has a very high morale, a good spirit of friendship and co-operation, and high individual work productivity. The additional employees will have to be worked into the group, gain their acceptance, and be able to do their work and not slow down the office.

PROBLEMS:

1. In what areas of managerial actuating do you feel the most difficult problems will exist for the Clinton-Jackson Company? Discuss.

2. Set forth your recommended general actions to handle these problems satisfactorily.

Chapter · 24

Office Job Evaluating and
Salary Administration

There is no security on this earth; only opportunity.
—GEN. DOUGLAS MACARTHUR

BOTH JOB evaluation, dealing with the value and salary level that each job warrants, and salary administration, dealing with the establishing and maintaining of equitable compensation, are important aspects of office managerial actuating work. The monetary reward for performing definite work is a fundamental consideration in employer-employee relationships. Although a number of avenues can be followed, the most common and the core of most salary programs is through the media of job evaluation—which determines the relative worth of the job—and merit rating—which determines how well the incumbent is doing his particular job. However, as will be pointed out in this chapter, factors other than job evaluation and merit rating affect the determining of the individual employee's salary level, and, furthermore, merit rating serves many more purposes than solely that of inclusion in salary administration programs.

BASIC CONCEPTS

In other words, the fundamental questions affecting all salary administration plans are: (1) For what is the salary received? and (2) Who receives the salary? The first question concerns the job; the second question concerns the employee. These two concepts, the job and the employee, are the main pivots about which all salary administration plans center.

JOB EVALUATION

The concept of the job and its relative worth are considered in job evaluating which can be formally defined as follows: *Job evaluation is*

464

the determination of the relative value of each individual job in an enterprise and is arrived at by means of a systematic procedure using jobs or selected job factors for comparison or measurement. There are four main methods of carrying out job-evaluation work, including ranking, classification, factor comparison, and point.

Ranking Method. The jobs within an enterprise can be arranged according to their relative difficulty. A ranking of the jobs is thus obtained, and in this manner the relative importance of each one is established. The job at the top of the list has the highest value, and the job at the bottom of the list has the lowest value. The usual procedure is (1) to rank the jobs in an individual department, and (2) to combine all departmental rankings into one composite ranking.

Figure 24–1 illustrates the results which might be obtained from

ARRAY OF JOBS ACCORDING TO RANKING METHOD

Rank No.	Name of Job	Earnings per Week*
1	Accounting clerk I	105
2	Purchasing clerk	101
3	Traffic clerk I	97
4	Cashier	93
5	Accounting clerk II	89
6	Traffic clerk II	85
7	Cost clerk	81
8	Tabulating machine operator	77
9	General bookkeeper	73
10	Correspondent	69
11	Stenographer	65
12	Switchboard operator	61
13	Typist I	57
14	File clerk	53
15	Typist II	49
16	Office boy	45

* In uniform variation from top to bottom.

FIG. 24–1.

this method. For example, the job of "Accounting clerk I" was considered of greater value than the job of "Purchasing clerk," while the job of "Office boy" was ranked lowest in the office. If the weekly salary of the top job is set at $105 and that of the lowest job at $45, then the rank order of the intermediate jobs, assuming a straight line or uniform variation, are shown in the last column in the illustration.

Classification Method. Under this method, a predetermined number of job classes or groups are established and the jobs are assigned to these classifications. For example, the job classes from highest to lowest might include:

Class A. Executive
  Office manager
  Office departmental supervisor
Class B. Skilled
  Purchasing clerk
  Traffic clerk
  Cashier
Class C. Limited skilled
  Tabulating machine operator
  Stenographer
  Switchboard operator
Class D. Unskilled
  File clerk
  Office boy

In this method the jobs within each grade frequently must be further graded to show more adequately the existing relationships. To do this, the ranking method previously described can be employed.

Factor-Comparison Method. Jobs can also be evaluated according to predetermined factors which have been established as a measure of ranking. Customarily, a key-job comparison scale is established and used for this purpose. This is done by ranking the key jobs on each of the factors. The scale also provides the means for applying *salary rates* to job relativities as needed.

Figure 24–2 represents a key-job comparison scale. In this case, the key jobs are eight in number and are ranked on each of four job factors: education, experience, responsibility, and working conditions. Frequently more than four factors are used, but in such cases the factors are generally a modification of the four mentioned. The salary-rating schedule is shown by the column of figures on the left. From this key-job comparison scale, it is possible to determine what portion of the present salary for each job is being paid for each factor. For example, for the "Accounting clerk I" job the apportionment is:

Education	$ 32.00
Experience	24.00
Responsibility	40.00
Working conditions	9.00
Total	$105.00

This scale is the measuring device for evaluating all other jobs in the company. Other jobs are fitted into this scale with the key-job evaluations being used as guides. To illustrate, consider the job of "Tabulating-

ILLUSTRATION OF A KEY-JOB COMPARISON SCALE USED IN THE
FACTOR COMPARISON METHOD OF JOB EVALUATION

Dollars per Week	Job Factors			
	Education	Experience	Responsibility	Working Conditions
46				
45			Cashier	
44				
43				
42				
41				
40			Accounting clerk I	
39				
38				
37				
36				
35				
34				
33				
32	Accounting clerk I			
31			Traffic clerk I	
30				
29				
28		Cost clerk		
27				Office boy
26				
25				Correspondent
24	Traffic clerk I	Accounting clerk I	Cost clerk	
23				General bookkeeper
22		Traffic clerk I		File clerk
21				
20		Correspondent		Traffic clerk
19		General bookkeeper		Cost clerk
18			General bookkeeper	
17	Cashier	Cashier		
16			Correspondent	
15			File clerk	
14				Cashier
13	General bookkeeper			
12				
11		File clerk	Office boy	
10	Cost clerk			
9				Accounting clerk I
8	Correspondent			
7				
6				
5	File clerk			
4	Office boy			
3		Office boy		
2				
1				

FIG. 24–2.

machine operator." The evaluator would first read the job-analysis sheet for this job. Then, concentrating his attention on the factor of education, he judges where under the education column the job of tabulating-machine operator seems to fit. He might decide that this job requires a little more education than "Cost clerk" but less than "General bookkeeper." Hence, he would evaluate the job at "12" under education. In similar manner, the job is evaluated according to the other job factors, and the other jobs in the company are evaluated in a similar manner.

Point Method. In this method, job factors are selected, and each is assigned a maximum number of points or credits. For example:

Education	300 points
Experience	250 points
Responsibility	250 points
Working conditions	200 points
Total	1,000 points

The selection of job factors is qualified by the following: that each job factor (1) exists in all the jobs to be evaluated, (2) varies in amount in the different jobs to be evaluated, and (3) is mutually exclusive from other job factors. The maximum point value assigned to each factor is determined by its relative importance. This is governed primarily by the judgment and experience of the analyst.

Each selected job factor is defined in clear and simple language. The degree or intensity of each selected factor is broken down, and points are assigned for each level of the factor. Figure 24–3 shows these data for the factor "Responsibility for Loss," which has been given five levels: "A" through "E," ranging in value from a low of 3 to a maximum of 50 points. Figure 24–4 illustrates eleven job factors selected for use in the evaluation of clerical and supervisory jobs. In this case the data showing the level and the points of rating, along with pertinent comments for the job of "Junior Accountant," are indicated for each factor. Note that under factor No. 4, responsibility for loss, the rating level of B is valued at 15 points, which was arrived at by referring to the guide shown by Figure 24–3.

Normally, the number of factors used in most studies is from eight to fourteen. For some studies a smaller number, perhaps six, may be considered adequate, while other studies may suggest the use of as high as twenty-five factors. Those most frequently used can be classified under the headings of skill, experience, education, responsibilities, working conditions, effort, and supervisory requirements.

4. Responsibility for Loss

Level	LEVEL DEFINITION	Points
A	Nature of work involves negligible opportunity for loss. Normal or reasonable care required and all work is verified or proved by repeating entire operation.	3
B	Nature of work is such that more than normal or reasonable care is required to prevent loss. However, work is checked by proving against totals or some standard rather than by repetition of operation.	15
C	Nature of work involves moderate but constant opportunity for error, limited only by daily or subsequent spot check or examination. Great care should be exercised to prevent loss. Potential serious loss from errors in transcription or computation.	27
D	Good judgment must be exercised regularly to prevent loss. Work is of such nature that complete and correct performance is hard to control, reliance being placed on the individual. Work subject to general supervision and occasional review.	38
E	Work of such a nature that commitments are made which may involve the entire bank. Work is frequently released without any check being made or is checked only by individual doing the work. A high degree of financial responsibility is involved.	50

Courtesy: The J. D. Moore Organization, Park Ridge, Ill.

FIG. 24–3. Illustrating the different levels of "Responsibility for Loss" and the assigned number of points to each level.

PRICING THE JOB

The ultimate aim of job evaluation is to determine the job price or rate of pay. Jobs of high evaluation should command high rates of pay; in general, the higher the evaluation, the higher the pay. The immediate problem is to determine what the rate of pay should be when the evaluation is a known amount. The job prices to be established must be consistent (1) externally (rates within the enterprise are in line with the rates paid outside the enterprise) and (2) internally

CODE .... SALARY GRADE .... VI ....

JOB TITLE .... JUNIOR ACCOUNTANT ....

CLERICAL AND SUPERVISORY EVALUATION

	NO.	FACTOR	RATING LEVEL	RATING PTS.	JOB REQUIREMENT
SKILL	1	Essential Knowledge	D	84	Requires a knowledge of advanced accounting methods and procedures and a working knowledge of company financial policies.
SKILL	2	Experience and Training	G	73	Normally requires 3 to 5 years' training and experience, including 2 years' accounting training plus 3 years' company experience as an Accounting Clerk.
SKILL	3	Analytical Requirements	C	27	Requires analysis of figures and data which vary in content but follow general patterns of application
RESPONSIBILITY	4	Responsibility For Loss	B	15	Requires more than normal care to prevent loss due to miscalculations. However, work is usually checked against totals.
RESPONSIBILITY	5	Confidential Information	B	6	Involves preparation and use of limited confidential matters in the Accounting Department.
RESPONSIBILITY	6	Contacts Public and Internal	B	28	Involves routine contacts with persons where detailed subject matter must be presented satisfactorily.
RESPONSIBILITY	7	Individual Initiative	B	12	Involves initiative in planning details of own work.
EFFORT	8	Mental Effort	C	15	Requires moderate mental effort to solve problems of accounting.
EFFORT	9	Physical Effort	A	6	Involves light physical effort with intermittent standing and sitting at comfortable intervals.
	10	Work Conditions	A	0	Working conditions are excellent.
	11	Supervisory Requirements	FX	18	Involves immediate leadership over Accounting Clerks and Typists.
		BASE POINTS		400	
		TOTAL POINTS		684	

Courtesy: The J. D. Moore Organization, Park Ridge, Ill.

FIG. 24–4. Job factors, ratings, and comments for the job of "Junior Accountant."

(rates within the enterprise are directly associated within the evaluations).

External Consistency. This is accomplished by securing the current wage rates in the area from private companies specializing in this type of work or from local governmental offices. Sometimes, however, a thorough labor-market survey must be made. It is also well to remember that accurate job descriptions are necessary for meaningful labor-market surveys.

Internal Consistency. This can be determined by comparing the job evaluations with the rates paid. In some cases this can be done by a simple comparison of columnar data. Very often, however, a graphic representation helps to visualize this comparison, especially when the point system of evaluation has been used. Commonly employed is a chart or scattered diagram in which existent wage rates are plotted on the vertical axis and evaluations on the horizontal axis. A curve showing consistent relationship between rates and evaluations can then be drawn on the chart. The deviations of actual rates from this curve can readily be spotted, and jobs overpaid or underpaid with respect to their evaluation can be quickly observed.

Figure 24-5 is a scatter diagram showing the relationship between wage rates and evaluations. The plotted points are indicated by the small circles. Curve *AA* has been drawn in and represents what is considered to be a consistent relationship between rates and evaluations. Curves *BB* and *CC* have been drawn in for reasons discussed in the paragraphs that follow.

JOB PRICE RANGE

From a practical viewpoint the office manager is interested in more than a job price for each job. What he really wants is: (1) *a price range for each job,* not a single price for each job; and (2) *a price range to cover a group of jobs,* not just one job. A price range provides flexibility and makes for a better salary plan. Furthermore, when a group of jobs are within one price range, the entire task of wage determination is simplified.

Referring again to Figure 24-5, a wage range has been indicated by the two curves *BB* and *CC* drawn on the chart.[1] The job of Traffic clerk I, for example, evaluated at 490 points, has a range from $77 to $93 per week, indicated by ordinate *DD* on the chart.

---

[1] Frequently a constant percentage change from the center line is used to establish the outside range lines. For example, for $50 median, the range is $45–$55, for $90 median, the range is $81–$99.

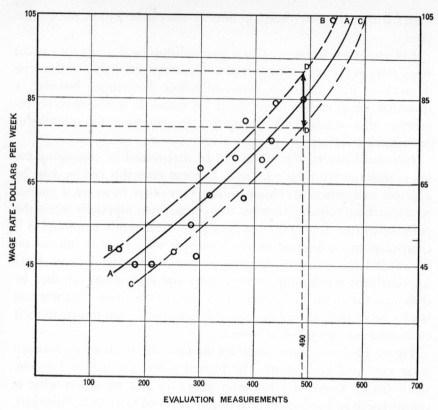

FIG. 24–5. Scatter diagram showing relationship between wage rates and evaluation measurements.

JOB CLASSES

To expedite the handling of job-evaluation findings, it is customary to group jobs into classes so that all jobs in the same class have the same price range. In other words, jobs of the same worth are put into the same class. The number of job classes depends primarily upon the total number of jobs, and the spread between the highest and the lowest job. Usually a total of six to ten job classes is sufficient in most offices.

Formerly, the number of job classes used varied from about twelve to eighteen, but the current trend is toward fewer classes. This has taken place for two main reasons. First, the jobs can be more distinctly set apart with relatively large rate differentials. Upgrading, in order to grant a wage increase, is minimized. Second, the task of finding key jobs for each class is simplified.[2]

[2] Charles W. Lytle, *Job Evaluation Methods* (2d ed.; New York: Ronald Press Co., 1954), p. 135.

As already discussed, the classification method of job evaluation automatically puts the jobs into various classes. On the other hand, when any of the other methods of job evaluation is used, the alignment of jobs is arbitrarily divided into different numbers and levels or classes. For example, with the point system, the range of points for each of the selected classes is determined, with the results shown in Fig. 24–6.

Alignment According to Job Evaluation	Job Class Assigned	Price Range in Dollars per Week
Accounting clerk I	1	90–115
Purchasing clerk	1	90–115
Traffic clerk I	2	77–93
Cashier	2	77–93
Accounting clerk II	2	77–93
Traffic clerk II	3	65–82
Cost clerk	3	65–82
Tabulating-machine operator	3	65–82
General bookkeeper	3	65–82
Correspondent	4	57–70
Stenographer	4	57–70
Switchboard operator	4	57–70
Typist I	5	50–64
File clerk	5	50–64
Typist II	6	42–52
Office boy	6	42–52

FIG. 24–6.

ADVANTAGES DERIVED FROM JOB EVALUATION

A solid foundation for an equitable method of wage payments is supplied by job evaluation because it (1) shows the relative value of jobs within a company, (2) assists in the evaluating of new jobs, (3) helps obtain a satisfactory wage level for all jobs within the company, (4) helps to eliminate salary inequalities by putting jobs having similar requirements in the same salary range, and (5) affords factual data for the settling of salary disputes. It should be pointed out, however, that the work of determining job content, grades, and price ranges should be kept up to date by regular, periodic checkups. The contents of many jobs change with the normal course of events, and this, in turn, frequently changes the relative values of the jobs. Likewise, changes in the general wage levels appear to be the usual rather than the exceptional happenings.

MERIT RATING

Whether the employee receives the maximum, the minimum, or some intermediate level of pay depends in part upon the evaluation of the employee's performance of the job. This rating or evaluation is called performance rating, employee appraisal, or merit rating. To reiterate, merit rating is used for more than helping to determine rates of pay. It is an important tool of managerial actuating. Among the important uses of merit rating are:

1. To assist in developing the supervisor's critical evaluation of the employee's worth.

2. To provide a record of the progress of new employees or those in training.

3. To indicate areas where training is needed.

4. To let the employee know what management members think of his performance.

5. To uncover employees of unusual abilities along specific lines.

6. To guide personnel work in promoting, demoting, or transferring an employee.

MERIT-RATING PLANS

Merit rating is accomplished by rating the employee on a number of predetermined factors. These factors are considered to be directly associated with, as well as indicative of, the employee's performance on the job. Many different forms of employee ratings have been devised. In each case, however, the factors selected are considered to be applicable to the employee, not to the job.

There are four basic types of merit-rating plans: (1) employee comparison, (2) man-to-man, (3) check lists, and (4) charts. The first is an elementary form of ranking in which a comparison of the relative performance of employees is determined. Normally the employees under a given supervisor or in one department are ranked, from the most satisfactory at the top of the list to the least satisfactory at the bottom of the list. The ranking can be by separate traits or on an over-all basis.

In the man-to-man type, the employee is rated by comparing him to another employee believed to exemplify the highest rating of the particular factor being considered. Sometimes a rating scale, established by the highest, middle, and lowest exemplary employees, respectively, is used. Thus, on the quality of dependability, for example, employee "A" is compared with each of the three employees included in the rating scale and is then given a rating it is believed he deserves. The man-to-man basis is not widely used in offices because it is rather complex and time consuming. Difficulty is encountered in selecting the employees to use in the rating scale, and wide variations in the characteristics of those selected appear common.

Check lists consist of a series of statements or questions dealing with the employee's performance. Frequently the statements have different values or weights which are unknown to the respondent. Questions which can be answered either "Yes" or "No," or by "It applies to this employee" or "It does not apply to this employee," are used. The following illustrates a portion of a check list:

Item	Scale Value*
1. She works at a slow but steady pace	5
2. She is usually ahead of her work schedule	3
3. She gets along with fellow employees	8
4. She makes few mistakes in her work	10
5. She asks for considerable time off	7
6. She usually thinks of the company first	4

*Not included in form supplied rater.

Charts are probably the most common type of merit rating used in an office. This is because they are easy to use, readily understood, and accepted by both the raters and the ratees. The chart type consists of a list of selected traits, each accompanied by a scale indicating different degrees of the trait. The rater indicates on each scale the extent to which the employee displays that respective trait in his work. For guidance to the rater, short descriptions for various degrees are usually printed along each scale. Figure 24–7 shows a merit rating of the chart type which features, for each trait, a brief description or definition and statements of various degrees of the trait.

MERIT-RATING FACTORS

The factors used in a merit rating should be carefully selected, although they will vary somewhat with the individual requirements of the office. Only those factors that are necessary to give adequate data about the employee in his or her particular job should be included. Usually six to eight factors are sufficient, as the use of too many factors might lead to carelessness in rating, and too few might distort the ratings. Information which is available elsewhere, such as attendance, punctuality, and length of service data, should not be included in the merit-rating form.

EMPLOYEE RATING REPORT

DATE_____19___

NAME _____ OFFICE _____ DEPT. _____

POSITION (DESIGNATE CONCISELY, SUCH AS FOREMAN, ENGINEER, ETC.) _____

NATURE OF WORK _____

MACHINES OPERATED _____

INSTRUCTIONS TO RATERS

1. READ THE ENTIRE RATING REPORT THOROUGHLY BEFORE RATING ANY EMPLOYEE.
2. BASE YOUR JUDGMENTS UPON THE ENTIRE PERIOD COVERED AND NOT UPON ISOLATED INCIDENTS ALONE. BE OBJECTIVE.
3. RATE ON EACH FACTOR SEPARATELY. DO NOT ALLOW JUDGMENT ON ONE FACTOR TO INFLUENCE JUDGMENT ON OTHER FACTORS. CHECK THE DEGREE OF EACH FACTOR WHICH, IN YOUR OPINION, DESCRIBES THE EMPLOYEE MOST ACCURATELY.
4. USE THE SPACE PROVIDED UNDER EACH FACTOR FOR EXPLANATION, IF EXPLANATION IS NEEDED TO AMPLIFY THE RATING.
5. RATE ON EVERY FACTOR, UNLESS EMPLOYEE HAS NOT HAD AN OPPORTUNITY TO DEMONSTRATE SOME PARTICULAR FACTOR, IN WHICH CASE INDICATE THIS FACT IN THE SPACE ALLOWED FOR EXPLANATION.
6. REMEMBER THAT YOUR OPINIONS ARE ALSO USED AS A MEASURE OF YOUR JUDGMENT. MAKE YOUR RATING AN ACCURATE AND COMPLETE DESCRIPTION OF THE PERSON RATED.

AMOUNT OF WORK					
CONSIDER NUMBER OF ASSIGNMENTS COMPLETED AND VOLUME OF OUTPUT IN RELATION TO NATURE AND CONDITIONS OF THE WORK PERFORMED. DISREGARD QUALITY OF WORK.	Extraordinary Volume of Work Completed	Consistently Turns Out A Good Volume of Work.	Amount of Work Completed is Satisfactory but not Unusual.	Output Barely Acceptable.	Amount of Work Entirely Inadequate.
EXPLANATION					

QUALITY OF WORK					
CONSIDER THOROUGHNESS, ACCURACY, AND ORDERLINESS OF COMPLETED JOB. DISREGARD AMOUNT OF WORK HANDLED.	Work Usually Lacking In Thoroughness, Accuracy or Neatness.	Quality Occasionally Is Unsatisfactory.	Work Is Reasonably Complete, Accurate and Presentable.	Quality Is Of High Grade, But Not Exceptional.	Unusually High Grade Work Is Consistently Performed. Quality Is Exceptional In All Respects.
EXPLANATION					

DEPENDABILITY					
CONSIDER THE MANNER IN WHICH WORKER APPLIES HIMSELF TO HIS WORK. IF HE DOES JOBS ON TIME, AND THE AMOUNT OF SUPERVISION REQUIRED TO GET THE DESIRED RESULTS.	Justifies Utmost Confidence. A Minimum of Supervision Required.	Applies Himself Well But Occasionally Needs Direction and Supervision.	Fairly Reliable and Conscientious. Normal Supervision Required.	Cannot Always Be Relied Upon To Get Desired Results. Without Considerable Supervision.	Entirely Undependable. Needs Constant Supervision.
EXPLANATION					

JUDGMENT					
CONSIDER THE WISDOM OF HIS DECISIONS IN THE ABSENCE OF DETAILED INSTRUCTIONS AND JUDGMENT IN UNUSUAL SITUATIONS. WHERE DISCRETION IS ALLOWED.	Judgment Entirely Undependable.	Makes Frequent Errors in Judgment. Works Best With Detailed Instructions.	Judgment Adequate In Normal Situations Only.	Judgment Usually Of A High Degree.	Thinks Quickly And Logically In All Situations. Judgment Can Always Be Depended Upon.
EXPLANATION					

PUNCTUALITY AND REGULARITY OF ATTENDANCE					
CONSIDER THE EXTENT TO WHICH EMPLOYEE IS ON THE JOB AND AVAILABLE FOR PERFORMANCE OF ASSIGNED DUTIES.	Almost Never Absent Or Late. Spends Only A Minimum Of Time Away From His Work.	Seldom Absent Or Late. Careful About Wasting Company Time For Personal Reasons.	Occasionally Absent or Late But Not To Excess.	Frequently Absent or Late, or Both.	Absent Or Late Too Frequently To Be Depended Upon To Do The Work Required.
EXPLANATION					

APPEARANCE					
CONSIDER THE IMPRESSION MADE UPON OTHERS AS TO PERSONAL GROOMING. NEATNESS OF DRESS AND MANNER.	Slovenly. Lacking In Concern About Personal Grooming and Appearance.	Occasionally Inclined To Neglect Appearance?	Takes Normal Care Of Appearance.	Neat Personal Appearance And Grooming.	Always Extremely Well Groomed And Presents Outstanding Personal Appearance.
EXPLANATION					

Courtesy: The J. D. Moore Organization, Park Ridge, Ill.

FIG. 24–7. A merit-rating form featuring descriptions of each factor and of the various degrees of each factor.

TIMING OF MERIT RATING

Merit ratings are normally made about twice a year. Customarily the total range of a job is expressed as a series, that is, the range of $77–$93 as $77, $81, $85, $89, and $93. An employee starting on this job might be paid $77. If the merit rating of this employee justifies an increase, the pay would be raised to $81; subsequent increases, based on future merit ratings, would increase the salary to $85, to $89, and to $93. Some companies automatically raise, by steps, to the mid-point of the range based on length of employee service. Above the mid-point, however, increases are predicated upon merit ratings.

CARRYING OUT THE MERIT RATING

The supervisor normally is charged with the responsibility of rating employees. Sometimes assistance is given by his superior or by a member of the Personnel Department, and in some instances, several superiors who are in intimate contact with the employee rate him in order that more than one judgment of his performance will be available. In most cases the supervisor knows or should know most about the performance of the employee in his division or unit.

Since judgment and subjective factors are so important in merit rating, it is advisable to supply a training program for raters in order to help secure intelligent and well-considered ratings. Training helps to implement the plan properly and constructively. The rater must understand the purpose of the form and what method to follow. Competent rating work is a key area of satisfactory merit rating. Also, it is important to provide periodically retraining so that new developments in employee rating work and future plans can be brought to the attention of the raters. A retraining program also aids in reviewing the principles of good rating with each rater before each rating period.

IMPROVING THE WORK OF MERIT RATING

It is generally agreed by experts in this field that each factor used should be adequately described. This helps the rater to know more specifically on what factor he is making a judgment. For example, to request a rating on the factor "dependability" is wholly inadequate, because it is vague and different raters might give it widely different meanings. However, the concept of "dependability" becomes clearer and its meaning more uniform when a description is added. For example: "Dependability: Consider the employee's thoroughness, reliability, and application to the duties of the job day by day." As already indicated, the description is frequently included under each factor, as it is, for example, in Figure 24–7. However, in some instances the factor is only named, and the description is confined to the rating scale.

In addition, the so-called "halo effect" in rating is minimized. That is, the tendency is lessened to give a higher rating than is actually justified or to view the employee in an overfavorable light—in short, to place a halo over him.

Employee self-appraisal is another helpful technique. When office employees are fully informed in advance of the purpose, operation, and application of merit rating, they do remarkably accurate self-appraisals. There is some tendency, however, for the better employees to underrate themselves, and the problem employees may overrate themselves. Employee self-appraisal helps to give the how and why of merit rating to the employee. He knows what is expected of him and uncovers areas in which improvements can be made. Self-analysis encourages self-development. Self-appraisals can be recorded on special forms provided for this purpose. They supplement the regular ratings determined by management-designated raters.

An interview between the employee and the management representative affords an opportunity for a forthright discussion on the employee's performance. Each factor of the merit rating can be discussed in a constructive and factual manner. Recognition of the employee as an individual can be increased and employee good will enhanced. The interview can be highly objective, because preplanning and concentrating upon specific topics are feasible.

Review by a management panel is highly successful in many companies. Funneling all ratings within an enterprise through one body makes for better control and greater uniformity of ratings. Employees who are qualified for salary increases, promotions, transfers, replacements, and training are readily identified. A qualitative inventory of the entire work force is thus periodically provided.

APPROVED PRACTICES IN MERIT RATING

At the expense of some repetition, the following list is included, because it is important, and because it shows in an excellent and concise form the approved practices covering the major considerations in merit-rating work.

1. The rater should rate all his subordinates on a single quality or trait before rating any of the subordinates on any other trait.

2. The rater should be challenged to illustrate the type of actions that he regards as characteristic of the ratee.

3. Careful consideration of the description phrases below the line is essential to the accurate use of the rating scale.

4. Ratings should be made in response to a pertinent question.

5. If many persons are rated on a single trait, there would ordinarily be a few low ratings, but most of the ratings would be near the average or median.

6. The trait upon which the employee is to be rated must be a simple trait and not a compound one.

7. The trait should be defined or expressed objectively and not subjectively.

8. The trait should be defined and illustrated in terms of work performed on the job.

9. Any trait that manifests itself in industry manifests itself also in activities away from the workplace.

10. The rater frequently finds that the rating scale fails to include certain traits or certain considerations that are important assets or are serious liabilities in the performance of the ratee. Space should be provided for additional information.

11. In using a rating scale, all judgments should be based on observation of concrete actions.

12. Only those traits should be rated on a rating scale that are of the greatest importance in the progress of the individual.

13. Only those traits should be subjectively evaluated on a rating scale that cannot be measured by an objective test.

14. The executives who are asked to rate their subordinates need to be "sold" by a brief statement issued by the president of the company.

15. Each supervisor or other employee who is to be rated needs to be "sold" also.

16. Each employee should have the protection and the advantage that comes from being rated periodically by three of his superiors who are in intimate contact with his work.

17. Users of the rating scale have more and more come to recognize it as a convenient instrument for improving morale.

18. The rater should take the ratee into his confidence, show him his ratings, and discuss them with him.[3]

OTHER FACTORS AFFECTING AN OFFICE SALARY ADMINISTRATION PLAN

Up to this point, job evaluation and merit rating have been discussed as basic considerations in a salary administration plan. However, there are usually other considerations which are important, including: (1) fringe benefits, (2) career influence, (3) supply and demand for em-

---

[3] W. D. Scott, R. C. Clothier, and W. R. Spriegel, *Personnel Management* (5th ed.; New York: McGraw-Hill Book Co., Inc., 1954), pp. 211–17. Adapted and reproduced here by special permission. See this source for a scholarly discussion on each procedure.

ployees of specific occupations, (4) bonus arrangements, and (5) financial incentive plans.

Fringe Benefits. The amount paid out for so-called "fringe benefits" is an important consideration in wage plans and labor costs. Fringe benefits include such items as vacation with pay, group insurance, hospitalization plans, and sick leaves. Various estimates point to an average of about 10–12 per cent of total payroll costs constituting expenses for fringe benefits.

Many office employees give considerable weight to the fringe benefits included in a job. The dollar take-home pay is adjusted in view of the fringe benefits received, and it is common to find an office employee preferring to work for a particular concern where the dollar salaries are average or even low, but the numerous fringe benefits provided make for an attractive total remuneration.

Career Influence. Career influence is made up of what an employee is looking forward to when he accepts a job and the influence of this ambition on his work. The pay for a job may be too low, in terms of what the job requires, but because of career influence, the employee willingly forgoes the higher and appropriate pay in order to get ultimately to a job he wants. The case of a young law graduate in a law office illustrates this point. On the other hand, the career influence may cause a job to be rated too highly by the employee, based on the actual job requirements. The job might be of the dead-end type and offer no usable training or advancement beyond a well-known level. In this case, sufficient salary must be paid to secure and hold the proper type of employee.

Supply and Demand for Employees of Specific Occupations. For the most part, salary rates are affected by the condition of supply and demand. These economic factors are dynamic; they change with time and exert a push-and-pull effect on salary rates. As a matter of practical consideration, recognition must be given to significant changes in the supply and demand for employees of specific occupations. *Temporarily,* minor adjustments might have to be made in order to alleviate serious labor shortage difficulties. For example, current conditions may make it necessary to start a new employee at a figure higher than the usual starting wage but still within the range of the job. Or, in unusual cases, the rate may be outside the job range; but such a condition usually does not last and might be viewed as an emergency case. If it does persist, however, it is well to revalue the job and change the classification, thus giving reality to the salary administration plan.

This does not mean that the wage structure established primarily through job evaluation and merit rating should be ignored whenever the labor market is either generally tight or loose. It does mean some deviation for some jobs—generally very few—which have become out of line because of the effect of current economic forces. As a matter of fact, the job-evaluating factors, such as education, experience, and responsibility, are themselves functions of time and of the economic forces of supply and demand. It is, therefore, reasonable to expect some minor adjustments in salary rates as a result of the influence of supply and demand for employees of specific occupations.

Bonus Arrangements. There are other special forms of salary payment which should also be mentioned in a discussion of office salary administration. These forms are payment of bonuses on special occasions, such as Christmas, a birthday, or an anniversary commemorating continuous employment. Frequently these payments amount to sizable sums—perhaps an extra month's pay or, in some cases, as much as 20 per cent of a year's salary. They are usually given to share the results of profitable operations, to recognize outstanding service, to continue a traditional custom, or to improve employee morale.

Financial Incentive Plans. Financial incentive plans are another significant consideration that in some cases plays an important part in the wage structure of a company. Financial incentive plans are wage-payment methods of paying the employee to some extent for the amount of work accomplished instead of strictly on the basis of time spent at work.

Financial incentive plans are not common in offices, although for certain office operations in certain types of industry, incentive arrangements are used. Transcribing, order processing, and billing are among the more common incentive office operations.

There are two fundamental concepts in practically all incentive plans: (1) a base or standard amount of work output, and (2) the amount of wage payment which will be given for production below standard, at standard, or above standard. The first concept, the base amount of work output, can be determined by past performance records, by motion and time studies, or by guess. Customarily this standard amount of work is expressed as 100 per cent. The amount of work which is established as standard is extremely important, for it is commonly but not always the point at which the incentive pay begins. The second concept, or pattern of the amount of wage payment, varies with the incentive plan. Some plans guarantee base rates up to standard;

others do not. Some divide the excess above standard equally between employee and employer, while others share the overflow according to various percentages.

To illustrate, assume the plan guarantees the base wage and shares the excess over standard on a fifty-fifty basis with the employee. Consider the job of pulling various records from files for which the standard is 80 pieces per hour, the rate of pay $1.30 per hour, and an 8-hour day is worked. Suppose the employee accomplishes the work at the rate of 100 pieces per hour. The daily earnings are:

$$\text{Earnings} = \text{Base pay} + \text{Incentive pay}$$
$$= 8 \times \$1.30 + \frac{10 - 8}{2} \times \$1.30$$
$$= \$11.70$$

The same general type of plan can be used for a group instead of a single employee. This arrangement can be used when the nature of the work is such that segregation of work by individual employees is very difficult or costly. The group incentive pay is figured first, then divided among the members according to either the individual base wage rates, the number of hours worked by each member, the individual gross base pays, or on some other agreed basis.

The sharing of the pay for accomplishment in excess of the standard may be less or greater than the fifty-fifty basis assumed above. If the employee receives a pay increase of the same percentage as the percentage increase in work output over standard (no sharing with employer), the earnings, based on the same data as above, would be:

$$\text{Earnings} = \text{Base pay} + \text{Incentive pay}$$
$$= 8 \times \$1.30 + (10 - 2) \times \$1.30$$
$$= \$13.00$$

In other words, when an employee does a ten-hour task in eight hours, payment is made for ten hours of work. The employer does not take any part of the overage. It is possible to utilize this type of incentive plan when standards are carefully determined and general overhead costs do not increase appreciably with an increase in work volume.

MAJOR GUIDES FOR INCENTIVE PLANS

Incentive wage plans should be tailor-made to suit the particular office and to achieve the particular objectives desired from the plan. The following guides are helpful:

1. Incentive plans should have the backing of the top managers.

2. The best incentive plan is usually the simple plan. It should be thoroughly understood by all concerned.

3. There should be a close relationship between reward (incentive pay) and results (contribution).

4. An incentive based on the individual employee is generally better than one based on a group.

5. The work output should increase as well as the amount of salaries.

6. The base or standard production amounts should be carefully determined—preferably by motion and time study.

7. The number of temporary standards should be held to a minimum. When standards are temporary, this fact should be known to all concerned.

8. The incentive wage should be neither guaranteed nor limited. In most instances the base wage should be guaranteed.

9. The standards should be reviewed for possible revision whenever any change is made in the material, machine, or method used.

10. If indirect production employees, such as messenger boys, receptionists, and telephone operators, are included in the plan, they should be affiliated on some measurable basis, such as the maintenance of an acceptable ratio between the total indirect man-hours to the total direct man-hours, or the total indirect man-hours to total work output. This tends to keep the indirect man-hours under control.

QUESTIONS

1. Which method of job evaluation do you consider the simplest? The most accurate? The easiest for employees to understand? Substantiate your answers.

2. In what ways are job-evaluation data helpful in settling controversial salary problems confronting an office manager?

3. Discuss the steps of "pricing the job" in job evaluation.

4. For an office employing 750 employees, can the wage rates be externally, but not internally, consistent? Internally, but not externally, consistent? Elaborate upon your answers.

5. Would you say that job evaluation is scientific in its determination of the value of a job? Why?

6. In what specific ways can merit rating be used by an office manager to assist in his efforts of actuating? Elaborate on your answer.

7. Draft a merit-rating chart that to you seems satisfactory for a file clerk. Justify your recommended chart.

8. As you see it, which of the following considerations—selection of factors,

definition of factors, competency of raters, or timing of the rating—do you feel is most important in merit rating office employees? Explain.

9. What steps do you feel might be taken to make an office employee more aware of fringe benefits he or she is receiving?

10. What basic employees' desires does a financial incentive provide? Are these of major or minor importance in office management?

11. What is meant by each of the following:
   a) A bonus payment.
   b) Career influence upon a wage administration plan.
   c) Job price range.
   d) "Halo effect" in merit rating.

12. Relate ten merit-rating practices that normally should be kept in mind for most satisfactory results from the viewpoint of both employee and employer.

CASE PROBLEMS

CASE 24–1.　LAWRENCE P. STRONG CORPORATION

President Strong of this corporation believes that certain salaries of his office personnel are out of line. Accordingly, he brought in an outside group of management consultants to make a job evaluation of the office jobs. After these jobs were evaluated and classified, the data revealed the facts shown in the accompanying table.

MONTHLY SALARIES	JOB CLASS								
	9	8	7	6	5	4	3	2	1
Accountant	475								
Auditor	550								
Calculating machine operator					275				
Draftsman			500						
Expeditor		500							
File clerk A					240				
File clerk B						200			
Junior Accountant			400						
Junior Stenographer A						230			
Junior Stenographer B							230		
Messenger									175
Price clerk				325					
Rate clerk				325					
Receptionist							190		
Senior stenographer					300				
Senior stock clerk									170
Statistical typist						275			
System analyst		450							
Telephone operator							225		
Typist A							220		
Typist B								200	
Voucher-register clerk								195	
Established minimum	530	440	370	310	270	230	200	170	150
Established maximum	620	530	440	370	310	270	230	200	170

PROBLEMS:

1. What are some possible reasons for the various salaries being out of line with the established range?

2. How should salaries falling above or below the established salary range be handled?

3. In your opinion, do any of the salary ranges and respective classifications appear out of line? If so, which ones? If not, how do you explain that they are in line?

4. Graph the data, using "Wages in Dollars" vertically and the nine "Job Classifications" horizontally.

5. Using this chart or graph, what further considerations can you draw from these data?

CASE 24–2.   THE KEYSTONE PRODUCTS COMPANY

After one year in high school, Gilbert Palmer, oldest of three children, found his first job, a sorter in the mailing department of the Keystone Products Company. He received $1.30 per hour with time and one half for working Saturday morning. Three months after the start of his employment, he received a raise of 10 cents per hour upon recommendation of his supervisor who considered Palmer a good worker.

Two months later, Palmer left the company giving two weeks' notice, explaining that he was tired and wanted a rest. Within three weeks he returned seeking re-employment and was re-hired as a messenger at a starting wage of $1.05 per hour.

After six weeks, Palmer did not show up for work. His absence necessitated some shifting of work by the other messengers. Three days later Palmer called at the office of the company for his pay check covering the amount of money due him. At this time he indicated he would like to return to work the following Monday morning. He was informed that the only job open which he was qualified to handle was that of a loader in the mailing department for which the starting rate would be $1.05 per hour.

Palmer related that he had experience in that department and had received $1.40 while there. He did not see why he should start for less. Thereupon, he was informed that his starting rate would be $1.10 per hour. It was implied that he probably could work a full day Saturday and receive time and one half for such work. Palmer accepted the job.

PROBLEMS:

1. Evaluate the salary administration policies and procedures of the Keystone Products Company.

2. How do you explain Palmer's acts?

3. Would you have taken any steps different from those which the company took? Justify your answer.

Chapter · 25

Recruiting and Selecting Office Employees

> People are much more alike inside than they are on the surface.
>
> —VERNE BURNETT

ONE OF the basic needs of every office is to supply and to maintain a satisfactory working force. In order to do this, likely candidates must be located, and those best qualified to meet the needs of the office selected and hired. Recruitment and selection of office personnel are therefore of great importance, for they control the life line of the human element in the office and are fundamental to all actuating efforts.

RECRUITING

The recruitment of employees is a permanent activity. Increased emphasis is placed upon this activity during periods of peak business activity, but the problem of securing the right employees confronts most offices most of the time. There are always forced separations because of marriage, illness, and death. Changes also take place because employees leave or are discharged.

Recruiting is a managerial responsibility and for best results should be subjected to the four fundamental functions of management. Fortunately many office managers now realize recruitment is vital and are doing something about it. More and more it is being recognized that personnel needs cannot be filled by waiting for likely candidates to apply; consistent and well-planned efforts must be exercised to find and interest capable prospects.

Recruiting involves four major aspects: (1) the determining of future needs, (2) the evaluating of the recruiting process for different types of office jobs, (3) the establishing of contacts helpful for referrals of candidates, and (4) the preparing and distributing of appropriate material used to promote recruiting efforts. Knowing the quantity and quality of candidates to seek and when to seek them constitute the first requirement of effective recruiting. People of the skill, attitude, and interest that the office requires should set the background for recruiting efforts. Following this, attention should be directed to the sources utilized and the contacts established. These are discussed in the immediate following pages. The fourth aspect, preparing and distributing appropriate recruiting literature, is also important. Some reasons why the propective employee will enjoy working at a particular company are pointed out in the illustration of Figure 25–1. Most companies report good results from the use of such literature.

SOURCES OF OFFICE HELP

Generally speaking, a variety of labor sources is desirable and needed to meet recruitment goals. "The best source" usually must be qualified regarding the type of office job, the geographical location, the prominence of the company, and the skill with which the recruiter uses a particular source. The proper personnel viewpoint is to work with a number of different sources of office help. Better people usually can be selected if there is a group from which to choose.

Among the more common sources are:

1. *Persons Recommended by Present Employees.* This is usually a very good source, but caution must be exercised to avoid favoritism. Some companies post notices on bulletin boards encouraging employees to recommend friends who might be seeking employment. Other enterprises periodically distribute specially prepared forms to their employees, with the request to give such forms to friends who may be looking for jobs. In a Chicago insurance office, an employee is given $25 for each person recruited and an additional $25 if the recruit stays three months.

2. *Former Employees.* This group constitutes an excellent source. However, careful screening and selection techniques are required to avoid a "come-and-go" atmosphere. Frequently satisfactory part-time employees can be obtained from this source.

3. *New Employees.* The person just hired usually knows somebody else who is looking for a job. Satisfactory results are usually obtained if candidates are put through the regular selection channels.

4. *Government Employment Agencies.* This service is provided mainly by state governments with financial assistance from the federal

- After-hour activities . . . purely optional, of course, include a mixed bowling league . . . annual golf tournament . . . holiday party.

BLUE CROSS and BLUE SHIELD believe in your well-being and security so they provide at no cost to you . . .

Sick leave
Blue Cross and Blue Shield memberships
Health and accident insurance
Life insurance
Pension plan

BLUE CROSS and BLUE SHIELD, believing that vacations are essential, offer, when you have worked for the Plan for six months, one week vacation . . . one year, two weeks and after five years, you'll get three wonderful weeks of paid leisure!

A Credit Union provides both a means of saving and/or borrowing . . . depending on your need.

AND . . . there's a modern clinic with registered nurse . . . supervised by staff doctors.

**START YOUR CAREER PLANS NOW...
AND KNOW YOUR FUTURE IS SECURE...
BE ANOTHER HAPPY PLANITE**

Courtesy: Blue Cross and Blue Shield, Chicago

FIG. 25–1. A page from a circular pointing out the advantages in working for a particular company.

government. It is well to utilize this source, no fee is charged, and jobs of all levels and classifications are handled.

5. *Private Employment Agencies.* Many of these specialize in handling specific types of jobs and applicants. A fee is charged, and the trend is for the employer to pay this charge. Normally, private employment agencies are an effective source; they have broad contacts and experience, and try to supply likely candidates for the jobs to be filled.

6. *Schools—Including Vocational Advisory Boards.* This is one of the better and larger sources of office employees. Some companies keep in close touch with high schools, business colleges, and universities and send representatives to talk with students about to graduate. Many schools have placement offices and will co-operate fully with prospective employers. It is well to develop schools as a source of office help. The candidates usually have formal training but limited business experience.

7. *Institutions for the Rehabilitation of Handicapped Persons.* Frequently very capable people can be secured from this source. The possibilities of using this source should be investigated by the office manager in his particular area.

8. *Voluntary Applicants.* It is a good practice always to see people who come in looking for a job. Frequently this source offers excellent personnel, but it cannot be relied upon as the sole source of help. Applicants from this source should be given the normal employment screening process.

9. *Advertising.* Newspapers, radio, and television advertising are effective media for securing a number of candidates. Good coverage is usually obtained. It is best to be as specific as possible concerning the contents of the job and the qualification requirements. All respondents will not be fully qualified, and the normal weeding-out process must be used.

RECRUITMENT IMPROVEMENT

Based on limited information available it appears that, including all sources, the relationship between the number of applicants rejected to the number hired is about 7 to 1. Somewhere in the neighborhood of $100 is expended for each office employee hired. These data appear to suggest that recruiting can be improved. A number of possibilities for improvement could be mentioned, but among the foremost is the use of more accurate and complete job specifications. When the job requirements and contents are vague, the likelihood of finding a satisfactory candidate is considerably lessened. Neither present employees, agencies, schools, or advertising can supply their maximum recruiting assistance when the information supplied is insufficient and not clearly stated. Another improvement possibility is the avoidance of delay in hiring the likely candidate. In too many cases a qualified candidate is lost because of a lack of promptness in dealing with the applicant from the time of application to the time the decision to hire or not to hire is rendered. A third area is developing the reputation of the particular office as being a good place to work. The office possessing this valuable public good will commonly have a satisfactory group from which outstanding candidates can be selected.

SELECTION OF OFFICE HELP

Selection means "making a choice by preference." This choice by preference is based on comparison between two factors: (1) what the job requires for successful execution, and (2) what the applicant has to offer. For the most part, the better the balance between these two factors, the better the selection work and the more likely is the attainment of a satisfactory working force. Under job requirements are such attributes as the amount of formal education, knowledge, experience, and physical considerations. Under what the applicant offers are his fund of knowledge, experience, intelligence, physical attributes, and personality.

This matching of the job requirements with the capabilities the applicant has to offer is not to be thought of as an exacting operation. On the contrary, it is quite flexible. Job requirements should be used as a guide. Frequently a satisfactory person does not have the *exact* qualifications desired, but most human beings are flexible. It should also be remembered that many jobs change with time.

VOCATIONAL REQUIREMENTS

For certain types of common office work, it is possible to establish vocational requirements which can facilitate employment procedures. Especially since about 1950 various associations interested in office management have been active in establishing minimum standards of qualifications for various common office jobs. For example, the suggested minimum vocational requirements for the job of beginning stenographer is to type at a rate of 55 words per minute on straight copy material for a 10-minute period, with 5 errors or less; to perform shorthand writing at 100 words per minute; to transcribe notes of unfamiliar material at the rate of 35 words per minute for a 10-minute period, and to produce work of mailable quality; to transcribe from a machine, at the rate of 1 cylinder per hour, cylinders of approximately 10–12 letters, each letter consisting of two to three paragraphs. The education required is high school; the physical characteristics, apparent good health, good vision, good hearing, and good eye-hand co-ordination; the mental characteristics, knowledge of good spelling and grammar, accuracy, and adaptability. To date, progress is being made in getting office managers to request employees who meet these standards, and schools to train toward them. Thus, some uniformity in requirements is being established, and sizable savings both to schools and employers should be realized.

TOOLS OF PERSONNEL SELECTION

There are a number of selection tools that assist in matching what the applicant has to offer with what the job requires. For purposes of this book, however, the discussion of the various selection tools will be confined to these five: (1) application form, (2) interview, (3) references, (4) physical examination, and (5) tests.

APPLICATION FORM

The application form is a written record providing a means of securing and maintaining the more obvious personnel information, such as identification, education, work history, and activities of the applicant. It is particularly helpful in the employment procedure and is also useful as a reference for pertinent facts concerning the employee which are frequently needed in situations arising from employer-employee relations.

It is imperative to know what to ask and what not to ask in an application form. Sufficient information should be obtained; superfluous information should be avoided. All questions asked should serve a definite purpose in evaluating the candidate's possible value to the enterprise.

In many offices it is desirable for the office manager to design his own application form. Some idea of what to ask can be gained through a study of forms used by other companies. These forms, however, have been designed to fit a particular need and are not necessarily completely adaptable to another office. It is also possible to secure standard forms, but, again, their content may not be exactly suited to the specific needs of the office.

The number of questions depends upon the particular needs of the office. However, in general, the essential information on the application form includes:

1. *Filing and reference data:* for maintaining the record in the file, for finding after it has been filed, for identifying the persons responsible for the record, and for identifying the form itself.
2. *Personal identification of the applicant:* data which correctly identifies (not describes) the applicant.
3. *Description and personal history of the applicant:* including physical description, family status, general habits, character, clubs and associations to which applicant belongs, and other recreational activities.
4. *Education and specialized training:* the extent and kind of formal schooling and training.
5. *Previous experience and employment record:* the jobs the applicant has held, details about his employment history, and his present circumstances.
6. *Type of employment desired and working conditions required:* what job, salary, hours, and location the applicant wants.
7. *References:* character references other than relatives or previous employers who are included in No. 3 and No. 5.[1]

The sequence of the data does not necessarily have to be that of the order shown in the above list. Experience shows that it is probably best to have questions arranged in an order which will help in directing the conversation of the subsequent employment interview.

For the higher-level jobs, it is often quite helpful to ask several questions designed to gain some insight into the candidate's general attitude toward life and his ability to write and to organize material. To illustrate, questions such as the following might be asked: "In narrative form give us a resumé of your major accomplishments, hopes, and ambition." "Will you tell us about your special qualifications not covered elsewhere in this application?" "What unusual business situations have you encountered, and what did you do about them?"

INTERVIEW

The interview, one of the basic tools in the selection process, provides the opportunity for meeting the applicant and observing his verbal ability, appearance, general personality, and attitude, as well as the chance to "get together and talk it over." The face-to-face meeting with the applicant offers possibilities of information afforded by no other means.

The objectives of the employment interview have been well expressed by W. V. Bingham, who said: "The functions of the employ-

---

[1] Frank M. Knox, "A Guide to Personnel Record Keeping," *Personnel* (New York: American Management Association), November, 1942, p. 544.

ment interview are: to get information, to give information, and to make a friend."[2] This two-way transmission of information, plus the achieving of a favorable impression upon the applicant, are fundamental to good interviewing, and unless these conditions are achieved the interview is not wholly satisfactory. The exchange of information is essential to intelligent selection. "To make a friend" reflects the interviewer's ability to gain public good will by securing a favorable attitude of the applicant toward the company, whether he is hired or not.

Content of Interview.   Effective interviewing contains an artistic element—an ability to talk with people in a free, easy, and understanding manner and at the same time to obtain definite information. The interview is far more than just a "look-over" for appearance. Carefully worded and timed questions can, for example, bring out a consistent pattern revealing important clues concerning the applicant. These clues, properly interpreted, plus information from the other selection means, including application blanks, references, and tests, frequently point to certain facts that assist the work of selection. For example, during the interview does the candidate's answers indicate a lack of self-confidence by expressing himself timidly, or blaming others for his own misfortunes? What about his attitude? Does he appear to like routine work? Does he resent close supervision? Does he hold his former teachers in low esteem?

Improving the Interview.   Various devices can be used to improve interviewing technique. First, it is a good practice for the interviewer to have a list of items which he wishes to cover. This can be made out before each interview, or a standardized list can be employed as a guide for all interviews. Finding out the accuracy and quality standards on previous jobs held by the candidate, the supervisory practices liked, the grades received at school, and the responsibilities in addition to family are illustrative of areas to cover that will make for effective interviewing. Second, rating charts can be used. By this means a written record of the relative intensities of the important factors is made by the interviewer. The chart actually helps to crystallize the interviewer's thinking by focusing his attention on the important items. Without rating charts, the opinions and reactions of the interviewer might be too general and hazy for practical use. A third interviewing aid is oral trade questions. An idea of the candidate's competency is obtained through use of these questions, which are concerned with

---

[2] W. V. Bingham, "The Three Functions of the Interview in Employment," *Management Review,* Vol. XV, No. 1 (January, 1926), p. 36.

names of office machines, office operations, general knowledge of office jobs, and the like. Fourth, an interviewer's guide designed to help secure essential information can be used. This guide is actually a part of the interview itself and serves as a control to assure a complete, well-rounded interview. The interviewer asks the questions on the guide and records the answers given by the applicant as favorable or unfavorable. The list covers some thirty-five questions pertaining to the applicant's work, family, and social and personal history.[3] Fifth, interviewing practices shown by experience to be effective should be followed. These include:

1. Put the applicant and yourself at ease.

2. Explain clearly what the job is—the duties, responsibilities, chances for promotion, working conditions, and so forth. If possible, read or let the candidate read the job description.

3. Use language appropriate to the educational and experience background of the applicant, and that does not reveal your own attitude.

4. Encourage the applicant to talk by asking questions that begin with why, when, and how. Avoid questions that can be answered by a "Yes" or "No."

5. Interrupt the applicant only when what is being said is irrelevant. Start speaking after the applicant has paused for at least ten seconds.

6. Let the applicant ask questions.

7. Grant sufficient time for the interview, but do not prolong to the point of boredom or useless repetition.

8. Keep your interviews fresh—periodically change the questions and the sequence in which they are asked.

REFERENCES

Managers usually like to obtain information on the applicant from previous employers and responsible persons currently acquainted with him. Reference checking is a helpful means in appraising not only the candidate's co-operation and dependability but also contributes a great deal to the candidate's probable skill, interests, and abilities. On the other hand, there are many who believe references are frequently unreliable. Members of this school claim inaccurate evaluations are provided, either excessive praise or excessive criticism is supplied.

The value of references depends upon the knowledge and character

---

[3] For further information see "The Diagnostic Interviewer's Guide" published by E. F. Wonderlic, 750 Grove Street, Glencoe, Illinois. Also the "Interviewer's Guide" by Fergason Personnel, 330 S. Wells St., Chicago, Illinois.

of the person supplying the reference information. Qualifications include being fully familiar with the demands of the job, knowing the candidate extremely well, informing with absolute honesty, and exercising sound evaluating judgment. These qualifications appear to be filled best by professional people and by former employers.

In a great majority of cases, agreement on these points exists: (1) references from former employers are more reliable than those supplied by personal friends of the candidate, (2) telephone reference inquiries produce better results than mail, and (3) reference information should be obtained *before* a full interview. Former employees can verify dates of employment, salaries, type and quality of work performed, and attendance record. Personal friends tend to supply favorable generalizations, but these usually represent the candidate's qualifications as the friend sees it. In the case of reference information from teachers, it is best to inquire for description of the candidate's actions rather than to supply a behavior evaluation. The teacher may not know the latter, but can and will supply accurate data on the types of courses taken by the candidate, grades received, school disciplinary actions that were taken, attendance record, and extracurricular activities.

The use of the telephone for obtaining reference checks has grown in popularity. For office applicants it is especially effective. Most applicants for office jobs are local people, and telephoning is fast and inexpensive. Other considerations are: a depth of detail can be acquired, questions to disclose the basis of the data supplied can be asked, and people given as reference are usually more willing to speak frankly than to put the same comments in writing.

When writing is preferred, it is advisable to use a reference form consisting of a well-designed combination letter and questionnaire that requests answers to specific questions designed to expedite better selection. For example, it is best to ask for factual information—periods of employment, duties, and salaries; make questions specific—not "In your opinion does Miss —— work well with groups of people?" but "Has Miss —— had any conflicts with teachers or fellow classmates while attending school?"; and assure the respondent that his answers will be considered confidential.

PHYSICAL EXAMINATION

The main purpose of the physical examination is to determine the type of work the applicant is best suited physically to perform. It is a selection device and should not be used for seeking out hidden ailments in the applicant.

Results of the physical examination should show one of several situations: (1) that the candidate is physically able to do certain types of work; (2) that he is fit for limited service only in specific jobs; (3) that with certain adjustments and treatments, he will be suited for jobs of a particular sort; or (4) that he is physically unfit, and proper corrective action cannot be made.

Physical examinations help to raise the standard of physical fitness, to increase work output, to lower accident rates, to decrease turnover, and to lessen the amount of absenteeism caused by sickness. For continued health maintenance it is best to make periodic physical checkups among present employees at intervals of not more than one year. To be really worth while, the examination must be complete; half-examinations and "hurry up" affairs are of questionable value, particularly from the long-range point of view. Careful examination of the eyes is of special importance for office workers. Medical findings should be carefully recorded and held in strict confidence.

TESTS

Tests are measurements of personnel aspects secured by scientific methods of observing and recording in certain standard situations. The measurements are normally qualitative and seek to determine the degree or intensity of the attribute being measured. The qualities or personal characteristics measured are believed to be definitely related to success in performing the work. Tests determine what a candidate can do, but not what he will do. The test score is actually a probability grade. It is not a mark of certainty but an indication of the probability of the candidate's success or failure as determined by his possession of the attributes measured and the importance of these attributes in the work accomplishment.

Tests are constructed according to one of two basic approaches, the realistic and the factorial. Under the realistic approach, those factors which appear most important for the job are listed, then a test is drawn up to measure these particular factors. Under the factorial approach, certain factors make up all job requirements; for example, a certain amount of interest, intelligence, and reliability are required for any job. Tests are made to measure these common factors, and the amount of each factor the applicant possesses is compared with the predetermined common factor requirement of the job.

Several terms in connection with tests should be familiar to the office manager. These include:

1. *Validity of Test.* This refers to the relationship between the test score and accepted or known facts about the attribute measured by the test. To illustrate: the most desirable employees among the present employees should make a high score; the average employees, a lower score; and the least desirable employees, the lowest score.

2. *Reliability of Test.* This deals with the consistency of test in yielding similar results when given on different occasions. In other words, the same approximate results should always be obtained with the same group and the same test.

3. *Standardization of Test.* When a test has been found, through a process of experimentation, to have both validity and reliability, the test is commonly referred to as a standardized test.

4. *Norms of Test.* A series of numbers indicating performance scores of large numbers of persons who have taken the test are called "norms." They serve as guides for comparison of scores.

Testing is a specialized field, and best results are usually obtained when the work is performed by qualified testing experts. Trained personnel, either on a part- or full-time basis, can be engaged.

TYPES OF TESTS

There are on the market today a great number of tests designed to measure the many different attributes considered significant in personnel work. A complete list of these tests is beyond the scope of this book.[4] Some tests are designed to measure the acquired skill and knowledge of the applicant, while others examine his potentialities. For greatest proficiency most office work necessitates certain skill and personality attributes plus an ability to perform several or all of the following: typing, stenography, arithmetic computations, spelling, correct grammar, and reading comprehension. There are tests covering specialized fields of activity such as banking and insurance. Also, some tests consist of a battery of individual tests, while others are made up of a single test sheet.

The National Business Entrance Tests, sponsored jointly by the National Office Management Association and the United Business Education Association, offer a battery of tests covering machine calcu-

---

[4] For an informative volume giving voluminous help in locating, identifying, and evaluating tests and books on testing, see Oscar Krisen Buros (ed.), *The Fourth Mental Measurements Yearbook* (Highland Park, N.J.: Gryphon Press, 1953). Also recommended is Herbert Moore, "Experience and Employment Tests," *Studies in Personnel Policy No. 32* (New York: National Industrial Conference Board, 1941).

lation, stenography, typing, bookkeeping, filing, and business fundamentals. Those who pass these tests are given a card or certificate of proficiency which is evidence of having successfully passed certain standardized clerical tests.

A twelve-hour examination program is utilized for Certified Professional Secretary candidates. The examination, prepared annually, consists of personal adjustments and human relations, economics and business organization, business law, secretarial accounting, stenography, and secretarial procedures. Successful candidates are given a CPS identifying card and are permitted to wear a CPS pin.[5]

Among the many types of single trait tests, the following are probably of greatest importance in office management: (1) the intelligence test, (2) the clerical test, (3) the personality test, and (4) the interest test. Figure 25–2 shows a comparison of these four types of tests revealing for each one the contribution, general content, basic implication, names, and main purpose. A brief discussion of each of these types of tests follows.

Intelligence Test. The measurement of mental quickness and mental capacity is the objective of the intelligence or mental alertness test. This test serves to indicate one's adequacy in a number of types of work and is very useful for office work. However, it is generally agreed that intelligence tests are not adequate in themselves as a basis for selection. Mental ability is but one of several attributes contributing to success on the office job.

Clerical Test. These tests are designed to measure the degree of achievement possessed by candidates for clerical work. This type of test is of great value in office work, for it can help evaluate the ability to do such things as filing, copying, typing, and taking shorthand. From these tests, candidates having at least a certain minimum ability can be selected. Figure 25–3 illustrates portions of a written clerical test.

Another type of clerical test measures the competence of applicants for stenographic positions by presenting the test materials on standard phonograph records. The Seashore-Bennett Stenographic Proficiency Test is of this type. The test consists of five letters, varying in length and complexity, which have been carefully selected to represent typical business correspondence. An alternate set of five letters is also provided. This permits retesting, or the use of one set for hiring and the

---

[5] For further information on the National Business Entrance Tests, write The National Office Management Association, Willow Grove, Pa.; for information on the Certified Professional Secretary, write National Secretaries Association, 222 W. 11th Street, Kansas City, Mo.

Name	Contribution	General Content of Test	Basic Implications	Examples of Standard Tests	Main Purpose of Test
Intelligence and Mental Alertness Tests	Indicates one's adequacy in a number of types of work.	Problems on information and of judgment and reasoning. Questions dealing with contrast or comparison. Memory tasks.	What a person has absorbed is a fair indication of what he will or can absorb. Differences in background are not taken into consideration. Little indication of how the indicated ability may be applied.	Army Alpha (Original and Several Revisions) Benge Test of General Knowledge The Henmow-Nelson Test of Mental Ability The O'Rourke General Classification Test Otis Self-Administering Test of Mental Ability The Pressey Senior Classification and Verification Psychological Corporation Scott Company Mental Alertness Test	To make preliminary selection. To gain an insight to the applicant's ability to understand and to manage ideas.
Trade and Clerical Tests	Helps to show the degree of achievement possessed by a candidate for this specific type of work.	Questions appraising vocabulary level. Ability to notice details. Problems in simple calculations and arithmetic reasoning. Competency in performing clerical work.	Candidate having achievement of certain level and above will probably execute the job requirements most effectively.	Benge's Clerical Test Blackstone Stenographic Proficiency Tests Minnesota Vocational Test for Clerical Workers National Business Entrance Tests O'Rourke's Clerical Aptitude Test Psychological Corporation Shellow's Intelligence Test for Stenographers Thurstone Examination in Clerical Work, Form A	To determine applicant's knowledge of a specific trade or profession. To select candidates having at least a certain minimum of relative ability to perform work in a particular field.
Personality Tests	Indicates the presence or absence of traits, or group of traits.	Single item questions which are answered with "Yes," or "No." Single words suggested—applicant names words which he associates with this single word.	Applicant will and can answer questions honestly and that the make-up of the personality in relation to situational demands of the jobs are definitely related.	Beckman Revision of Allport A-S Test California Test of Personality Heidbreder's Personal Traits Rating Scale, Form 2 Humm-Wadsworth Temperament Scale Laird's Personal Inventory C-2	To appraise those qualities which are pivotal in a situation and probably will determine the degree of future success of candidate on the job.
Interest Tests	Aims to determine the extent of the candidate's genuine interest in a particular type of work.	Questions to indicate the correct use or identity of machines and devices.	One's latent or developed interest in a certain type of work is closely related to the energy, persistence, and contribution which he gives to that work.	Brainard-Steward Specific Interest Inventory Strong's Vocational Interest Blank, Form A Thurstone Vocational Interest Schedule	To determine the degree of interest which a candidate has for different types of work.

FIG. 25-2. Comparison of various tests on significant factors.

Write opposite each name below the number of the file drawer in which that record should be filed.

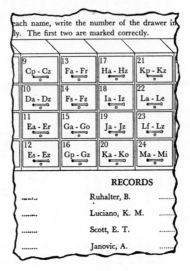

each name, write the number of the drawer in ly. The first two are marked correctly.

9 Cp - Cz	13 Fa - Fr	17 Ha - Hz	21 Kp - Kz
10 Da - Dz	14 Fs - Fz	18 Ia - Iz	22 La - Le
11 Ea - Er	15 Ga - Go	19 Ja - Jz	23 Lf - Lz
12 Es - Ez	16 Gp - Gz	20 Ka - Ko	24 Ma - Mi

RECORDS

....   Ruhalter, B.   ....

....   Luciano, K. M.   ....

....   Scott, E. T.   ....

....   Janovic, A.   ....

Write your answer to each problem on the line at the right.

6. How many notebooks can be bought for $3.00 at the rate of 2 for $.50?.. _____

7. At 8 a.m. the barometric pressure was 30.6 and at 11 a.m. the pressure was 31.8. Assuming a constant rate of increase, what time was it when the pressure was 31.0?.. _____

8. A man earned $28 and saved $7. What percent of his earnings did he save?............................ _____%

In the following list, when the spelling of any word is incorrect, cross it out and write the correct spelling in the space following word. If word is correct, do nothing.

assure..   immediatly...

foriegn..   morgage...

responsability..   bookeeping...

Some of the following sentences are grammatically incorrect. Each incorrect sentence contains only one such error. If sentence is incorrect, cross out the wrong word and write the correct word at the end of the line.

6. I have drank all my milk now.. _____

7. Will you bring this to the office across the street?.. _____

8. Neither the president nor the manager are taking a vacation............................ _____

FIG. 25-3. Portions of a general clerical test.

other for training or for upgrading purposes. The dictated material is
played on the phonograph, and the applicant takes down the dictation
in shorthand and later transcribes it. A portion of the general introduction and instructions to the person taking the test is as follows:

> This is going to be a test to see how well you can write shorthand. Before
> beginning, I want to tell you about the test, and also let you become accustomed
> to my voice. The test will consist of several letters. The dictation will be typical
> of the kind you will have to take as a stenographer. I have a few more instruc-
> tions to give you, so suggest that you get warmed up by taking notes on the rest
> of my remarks. Begin now.
>
> . . . .
>
> After each letter I will give you half a minute to go back over your notes.
> You may not have time to read over the whole letter, but you will have time
> to. . . .[6]

Personality Test. Knowledge of the presence or absence of traits
or a group of traits contributing to the applicant's personality is sought
by this type of test. These traits are evidence of attitudes reflected in
the applicant's conduct. Measurement of such things as emotionalism,
dominance, and self-confidence are made.

Interest Test. Tests designed to measure the extent of the candidate's genuine interest in a particular type of work are called interest
tests. Advocates of this type of test believe that a person knows best,
likes best, and devotes most effort to the type of work in which he has
the greatest interest. The value of the test is based on this assumption.
No doubt there is a close relationship between ability and interest,
but having the interest does not always mean that the ability too is
present. A person must have more than the interest to succeed on a
job. However, one probably likes what he can do well, or efforts are
more commonly devoted to the work that one likes. To this extent,
identifying and measuring interests are important in selection work.

ADMINISTERING THE SELECTION PROGRAM

Some administrators of the selection program are unwisely looking
for perfection in candidates hired. Such an approach is totally unrealistic. The superior and practical viewpoint is to seek adequacy in the
really important attributes, outstanding excellence in a few others, but
recognizing certain deficiencies and the need to be satisfied with less
than perfection. Subsequent training and supervising are quite likely
to correct the known inadequacies.

It is also well to avoid arbitrary generalizations for selection pur-

---

[6] The Psychological Corporation, *The Seashore-Bennett Stenographic Proficiency Test*
(New York, 1946), p. 1.

poses. Some definite guides, of course, must be established, but flexibility in their application should be followed. Frequently, the generalizations are not factually based; they lack validity and seriously curtail the size of the selection pool. Among the more common unrealistic selection generalizations are formal educational requirements, experience, age, and appearance.

Promotability of the candidate should be viewed in its true perspective. Typically, not all office candidates aspire to management positions. In tight office labor markets, the pressing problem is to select a person who can do the immediate job. Those having the ability and desire to advance can be selected by other methods.

Finally, a balance among the various selection tools should be maintained. All have their place, each either supplements or confirms the information supplied by the other. For example, from the interview can be obtained information for selection that is not secured from tests. The application form should supply data that is best suited for this media, and tests should provide new data as well as supplement information revealed by the application form.

PERSONNEL SELECTION AND LABOR TURNOVER

Labor turnover has to do with addition to and subtraction from the working force over a specific period of time. As already stated, it is a normal state of affairs for some individuals to leave and others to enter the employ of an office, and this will take place regardless of the quality of personnel selection.

A certain amount of personnel change is probably desirable, but if at all possible, it is usually to the best interests of the enterprise to keep its employees. Stability of the working force gives a personnel continuity and experience which generally is advantageous. Furthermore, the full benefits of effective recruitment, selection, placement, and training are jeopardized if individuals are hired, work a while, and then leave. Also, the total dollar cost incurred to put a person on the payroll and take him off represents a sizable amount. Various studies indicate the expense range from about $400–$600.

Employee Termination. It is important to know the cause of every employee termination. With such information, it is possible to take remedial action, if practical and necessary, and to determine an enlightened personnel policy. The reason for an employee's leaving is frequently difficult to ascertain. The real reason might be a hidden one, perhaps not uncovered during an exit interview. To obtain correct information commonly requires careful probing and investigating. Employees leaving should be classified as (1) quits—termination at employee's request, (2) layoff—temporary cessation of employment at instigation of employer, or (3) discharge—termination at employer's request. Sometimes these data, segregated by office divisions, sex, age, salary group, and length of service, will reveal possible avenues for reducing the labor turnover.

Labor turnover is commonly related directly to selection or placement practices. This relationship in the office deserves special analysis because of prevailing circumstances found there. The preponderance of female help in offices gives rise to normal terminations due to marriage, having families, home duties, and moving because husband is being transferred. However, hiring women with these turnover risks may constitute the most practical solution to the recruiting and selecting efforts, and such employees may represent a highly satisfactory work group while they are employees.

Measurement of Labor Turnover. There are a number of ways to compute a labor turnover value. Net labor turnover is a common measurement for determining the movement of labor. This is equal to the number of replacements hired multiplied by 200 divided by the sum of the working force at the beginning of the period considered and those at the end of the period. Mathematically it is expressed as:

$$\text{Net labor turnover} = \frac{R \times 200}{F_b + F_e}$$

where

R = Number of replacements hired,
F_b = Total working force at beginning of period,
F_e = Total working force at end of period.

Usually a period of one year is used, although net labor turnover can be figured for any desired period. In some instances a formula is used which takes into account separations, rather than replacements. Also, separations may be classified into those which are avoidable and unavoidable to the employer.[7]

QUESTIONS

1. Name and discuss the four major aspects of recruiting office employees.
2. In what ways do you believe the recruiting of office employees can be improved? Are you of the opinion that these improvement means are practical and can be accomplished? Explain.

---

[7] See Gordon S. Watkins, Paul A. Dodd, Wayne McNaughton, and Paul Prasow, *The Management of Personnel and Labor Relations* (New York: McGraw-Hill Book Co., Inc., 1950), pp. 278–79.

3. Are the tools of personnel selection helpful when a company with four different job openings has only one applicant? Explain.

4. You are in need of a file clerk, a junior accountant, and a messenger boy. How would you recruit candidates for these office jobs?

5. Discuss the importance and influence of vocational requirements upon the selection of office employees.

6. Stage an interview with an applicant for the job of "cost clerk." Bring out the important factors that make an interview successful. Summarize your techniques.

7. Give three different types of information usually requested on an application form, and for each type explain how it can be used to help select a candidate for a given office job.

8. Evaluate the use of references as an aid in the selection of office employees.

9. Assume that an office manager has a limited budget and can use only three types of tests for personnel selection purposes. Which three types of tests do you believe he should use? Substantiate your answer.

10. A friend of a present employee has been interviewed, and tested, and her references checked. She is recommended to the supervisor of Department "K-5," who hires her. At the end of a four-week period, it appears she cannot perform the work satisfactorily. Is the personnel selection, supervision, company, or employee at fault? Explain your answer.

11. As the manager of the employee selection program of Protective Insurance Company, what basic viewpoints or guides would you take into account in administering your work?

12. Do you agree with the following: "The astute office manager will try to keep labor turnover of the office at a minimum and to find out the real reason for each employee's termination. High labor turnover indicates ineffective managerial actuating efforts."

CASE PROBLEMS

CASE 25–1.   FAIRMONT COMPANY

The following appeared in the classified help wanted—women advertisements of a daily newspaper in a large city.

General Office
Varied office duties, ex. opportunity, must be reliable, age 19–25, steady work, liberal employee benefits.
Write LMH 518 NEWS

PROBLEMS:

1. Do you believe this advertisement will probably recruit desirable candidates? Discuss.

2. In your opinion, in what ways could this advertisement be improved? Substantiate your viewpoints.

CASE 25-2.   THE SYCAMORE INSURANCE COMPANY

The manager of the audit department believes that the selection procedure for office personnel needs revision. The personnel for this department consists of the following: (1) *checkers* who review all premium computations to see that all the various factors have been included and are in accordance with the current state regulations, (2) *calculators* who check the mathematical accuracy of the premium computations and adjustments made by the checkers, (3) *typists* who write the letters and endorsements, (4) *billers* who make out the billing after the premium computations have been checked, and (5) *file clerks* who file policies and handle all other filing duties.

At the present time all applicants are secured from recommendations of present employees and newspaper advertisements. Each applicant fills out a long and detailed application form. A messenger is then given the filled-in form and conducts the applicant to the supervisor of the unit in which the applicant desires to work. The form is given to the supervisor, and the applicant is introduced. Then the interview follows. On an average, the time taken for an interview is about fifteen minutes. Usually the decision to hire or not is made at the end of the interview. References are confined to those from former employees and are sometimes telephoned as a part of the interview, depending upon the desires of the supervisor. In the case of calculators and typists, certain trade tests are used to determine the applicant's proficiency.

PROBLEMS:

1. Are you inclined to agree with the manager of the audit department? Why?

2. In what specific ways do you believe the present recruitment and selection procedure can be improved? Justify your viewpoints.

3. What major obstacles do you anticipate might be encountered in efforts to adopt your suggested improvements? Discuss how you would try to overcome these obstacles.

CASE 25-3.   CENTRAL MANUFACTURERS, INC.

Mr. Horace Novell, the employment manager of the Central Manufacturers, Inc., Jersey City, New Jersey, has a number of jobs to be filled. This is mainly a result of the company's recently buying a small competing firm and relocating this business in the present building of the Central Manufacturers, Inc.

The following list shows the jobs to be filled and the sources of applicants:

Job to Be Filled	*Source of Applicant*
A. Assistant purchasing agent	1. Educational institutions
B. Auditor	2. Commercial employment agencies and the United States Employment Service
C. Bookkeeper	
D. Cashier	3. Equipment manufacturers' training schools
E. Company doctor	
F. Factory guard	4. Advertising
G. File clerk	5. Applicants recommended by employees
H. Interviewer for personnel department	6. Present employees through promotions
I. Junior cost accountant	7. Management consulting and public accounting firms

Job to Be Filled—Continued

  J. Locksmith
  K. Maintenance man for specialized
     office equipment
  L. Mechanical engineer to learn ma-
     chine design
  M. Office manager
  N. Receptionist
  O. Research chemist
  P. Sales trainee
  Q. Scrubwoman
  R. Systems analyst
  S. Training director
  T. Typist

PROBLEMS:

1. In each case match the job to be filled with the probable best sources of applicants.

2. What tools of personnel selection (application form, interview, etc.) would you be most likely to use for candidates recommended by employees? For those from commercial employment agencies? For those secured by advertising? Explain your answer in each case.

CASE 25–4. MANHATTAN COMPANY

Labor turnover data for this company for the year ending are:

Department	January 1	Hired	Left	December 31
Accounting	17	1	2	16
Central service unit	22	12	9	25
Credit	7	1	0	8
Order	4	2	1	5
Personnel	14	6	4	16
Production	219	18	40	197
Purchasing	6	0	0	6
Sales	21	9	7	23
Total	310	49	63	296

PROBLEMS:

1. Compute the net labor turnover rate by departments and in total for the Manhattan Company for the year.

2. What interpretation do you derive from these data? Explain.

3. What information not included in the turnover data would be helpful in an analysis of the Manhattan Company's labor turnover? Discuss.

Chapter · 26

Training of Office Employees

Undertake something that is difficult; it will do you good. Unless you try to do something beyond what you have already mastered, you will never grow.

—RONALD E. OSBORN

ONE OF the vital areas of managerial actuating is employee training. To contribute their maximum assistance toward achieving office objectives, employees require both the know-how and the know-why of their respective jobs. Motivating efforts are strongest when each employee is able and willing to perform his particular task.

Employee training is an everyday activity in most enterprises. Employees acquire their training either by means of planned and well-administered programs or by a hit-and-miss method which includes learning by mistakes, by trial and error, and by absorption. Since training goes on continually, progressive managers have set up definite training programs so that proper direction and control can be given to make the employees more useful to the enterprise.

DEFINITION AND CHALLENGE OF TRAINING

Training is a planned development of people. It is an enlargement of work habits which are useful in solving office production problems. It assists people to acquire skill through the use of what they have learned.

The subject of training is widely discussed, and almost all managers agree that it is necessary and proper. This might lead to the belief that effective training is universal among offices. However, in quite a number of cases, this is not the case. Well planned, really serious training is absent in far too many offices. Especially in periods of labor shortages do employers get anxious to keep employees "at productive work," and to start new employees on their jobs with little, if any, time devoted to company training. In these instances office training typically

507

is considered a very worth-while activity and is going to be done *in the future*—it has not won present formal installation and promotion. But progress is being made and will continue especially as office training methods are improved, as the benefits of training become more pronounced, as greater acceptance of the importance of the human element in the office is won, and as managers assume greater responsibility for training.

INDUCTION OF EMPLOYEE

Proper induction of an employee is vital and can be considered the initial training effort. Included in this aspect of training are the welcoming of the new employee to the company, explaining the office rules and regulations, acquainting him with the employees' benefits, informing of the company's policies and operations, and telling what is expected of him as an employee. The new office employee's impression of the company is frequently formed during the first several hours at the new job. A good start is almost imperative for the achievement of good future relations and might well contribute abundantly to the employee's progress and success.

A responsible person should be designated to take charge of the new employee when he first reports for work. It is a good idea to start off by telling him something about the office such as what work is done in the office, what general procedures are used, and general information concerning working hours, overtime, salary plans, tardiness, absence, personal telephone calls, social activities, lunch time, and location of eating places and rest rooms. Frequently, an employees' manual or policy handbook is of great help to the inductee, but this is not a substitute for personalized induction efforts. Much of the material in the handbook will merit oral discussion with the new employee. Important points can be emphasized, and the explanations handled informally in a friendly, helpful manner.

Employee induction is more than a survey of the policies and practices followed in an office. It is actually job integration which includes acquainting and adjusting the new employee to the work climate of the office.

Introductions should be made to the new employee's department head, fellow employees, and those supervisors with whom he will be associated. If it is possible, an introduction to one of the officers is also helpful, as this gives the new employee a feeling of worth and helps him to visualize the extent of the company.

The employee should then be returned to his department, where either the department head or an appointed person shows him his workplace and explains the new job in a brief but complete manner. Experience shows it is a good idea to give the employee some job which he can do without too much instruction and then to leave him by himself. This gives the new employee a chance to digest some of the new surroundings. Follow this up with contacts about every hour or so throughout the rest of the day. Encourage the new employee to ask questions. During subsequent days the responsibilities and duties of his particular job and its relation to the company are developed. This is accomplished either on a full-time basis covering a specific period or by means of selected intermittent training sessions, depending upon the type and program of training in the particular enterprise.

VALUE OF TRAINING

Training is one of the criteria for judging the manager's concept of what really constitutes management-in-action. For example, an office manager can make out a report himself, or he can help an employee to learn how to make it out. Likewise, the manager can do work over himself which has been done incorrectly, or he can point out the error to the employee and train that employee to do the work correctly. One who really manages makes use of training to help him manage. Planning, organizing, actuating, and controlling are each helped by training. For example, the creating of effective plans, the building of a satisfactory organization structure, the delegating of authority, the stimulating of employees, and the seeing that objectives are achieved via the planned avenues are all assisted by good training.

A well-trained group of office employees will usually show a greater increase in, and a higher quality of, work output than will an untrained group. Employees do a more intelligent job and make fewer mistakes when they possess the know-how, have an understanding of their jobs and of the interdependence of one job and another, and know the "why" of the company's policies and procedures. Furthermore, morale can be boosted *after* the employee knows what to do.

In addition, the responsibility of supervision is lessened. Training does not eliminate the need for good supervision, but it reduces the requirement for detailed and constant supervision. A well-trained office employee is more self-reliant in his work, because he knows what to do and how to do it. Under such conditions, close supervision is ordinarily not mandatory.

Also, the best available methods of performing the work can be standardized and made available to all employees. High levels of performance become the rule rather than the exception. The advantages of past knowledge and experience can be retained.

These values, however, are not obtained without a price. Certain difficulties and possible losses are incurred and should be recognized in any training program. First of all, regular office work is likely to be interrupted or delayed by time spent in training. The output of the trainee might be temporarily reduced. Also, training might foster the dependence upon others for solutions to challenges which the employee should think through for himself. Self-reliance and capacity for new ideas might be stifled. Furthermore, competent training leaders are difficult to obtain. When mediocre instruction is utilized, not only may the results of the training be below what is expected but it may prove harmful.

OBJECTIVES OF TRAINING

The objectives of training efforts depend upon the particular needs of the enterprise. Comparing respective job requirements to the qualifications of the employee performing the jobs will reveal certain areas in which training might prove helpful. Also, a careful analysis of the type and number of errors being made will show specific needs for training. Future plans of the company, anticipated increases in personnel, and changes in methods of procedures are other sources for determining the objectives of a training program. To illustrate, programing studies for employees are usually conducted prior to the installation of electronic data processing machines.

At the risk of some repetition the following are offered as a guide in determining the objectives of training efforts. Each employee should have (1) complete knowledge of what constitutes his job and what its relationship is to other jobs in the organization, (2) knowledge of the best methods of doing his job, (3) an opportunity to do the job under normal working conditions, (4) knowledge of operating policies and of the procedures of doing his job, and (5) ample opportunity for recognition and advancement when satisfactory ability is demonstrated.

All too frequently knowledge of the job content is left to chance or to the belief that with time the employee will pick up the required knowledge. A manager should use a well-planned training program to get job-content information to each employee. Improved relations are a certainty when the employee understands completely what his job is, the relationship of his work to other work in the department, and, in time, that of his department to the entire organization structure.

Each employee should have knowledge of the best methods of doing his job. It is not sufficient for managers alone to know the best methods; a manager must see to it that the employees know, for only then is maximum efficiency in work output possible.

Knowledge must be applied to have practical value. Application requires skill, and the opportunity to develop this is equally important as acquiring the knowledge. A trainee may be able to read the charts, recite the answers, and describe perfectly how the work is performed. But in addition to these accomplishments he needs on-the-job experience so that he can be a part of actually performing the job.

Up-to-date knowledge of operating policies and procedures is another important and common objective in office training. Information on personnel practices should be made known to all. Likewise, the general scope of desired public relations and the quality of paper work required are among the types of information which should be a part of every employee's knowledge.

Each employee should have ample opportunity for recognition and advancement when ability is demonstrated. Employees want to acquire proficiency in order that they may be more valuable to the enterprise. This may take the form of improved status, public recognition, promotion, or increased earnings. These must be available if the results of training are to be fully satisfactory. It is a mistake for an enterprise to train an employee for a better job or to improve or add to his knowledge and skill without subsequently offering him a job on which he can use the newly acquired ability, either in the present or at some near future date, within or outside the enterprise.

FUNDAMENTALS OF TRAINING

Most employees are acquiring knowledge and skill most of the time. This appears to be a natural process, but the acquisition need not necessarily be applicable to the employee's job. The sources can be personal performance, behavior of other employees, hearing, observing, and imitating. These means are commonly referred to as "experience." It places a strong emphasis on what is practical and is conditioned extensively by experiment and accident. As such, it is not an efficient means.

Intentional efforts to teach someone can be far more effective, providing the efforts are properly managed. Beginning with what the trainee now knows and can perform, it is possible to determine what the trainee must know and be able to do in order to perform successfully particular work assignments. The differential between what is now known and what is needed constitutes the gap which training seeks to fill. This gap is reduced gradually, because learning is a gradual process. An employee learns bit by bit, not all at once. Knowing the gap to be filled and considering the gradual doses which can be absorbed by the trainee and in what sequence, the formal training operation can be set in motion. Usually tie-ins or association of new concepts with knowledge or skills already possessed by the trainee prove effective in training work.

There are, however, basic considerations to the activity of acquiring knowledge and skill. Of prime importance is the trainee's personal interest in wanting to learn. Economic or social gains may motivate him, but a stimulus must be present. Necessarily, people start from where they are in any training effort, and they are most likely to want to learn when they see what is taught is helpful to them. In addition, the trainee must be in a receptive mood, emotionally settled and free from worries, personal troubles, and anxieties. Lastly, it must be recognized that the trainee must learn for himself; he must subject himself to the learning process. The instructor's role is primarily one of guidance and stimulation.

TYPES OF TRAINING

Training can be classified in many ways. One useful classification is training for present jobs and training for future jobs. Another is training for any or all of the following: job knowledges, job skills, and attitudes. Still another is training for basic information, for personal development, and for specific production in definite work application. A useful list showing the range and types of training may be outlined as follows:

Pre-employment Training. This deals with the type and amount of instruction needed by inexperienced employees prior to their entering the office. This training is generally provided by educational institutions outside the enterprise, such as public schools, universities, business colleges, night schools, and correspondence courses. Pre-employment training is generally broader and more fundamental than the other types of training. Likewise, it often is of a theoretical nature in contrast to the practical aspect of the other types; it seeks to provide an intellectual background and to develop the art of thinking and reasoning.

Induction Training. The objective of induction training is to provide the new employee with the information necessary for a complete knowledge and understanding of practices and procedures of the enterprise. It provides the employee with a picture of the organization structure, the employee's place in it, the job he is expected to do, and the importance of his job to other jobs. It is the initial indoctrination process to which each new employee is subjected. It is specific and applies only to the particular enterprise which the employee has joined.

On-the-Job Training. This type of training aims to give the employee the necessary skill required for a specific job. It seeks to fill the gap between what ability the worker can supply and what ability the job requires. The job can be either that of the present or future assignment. In some cases the job is of a higher grade than the employee's present one; in other words, the employee is being prepared for promotion. The make-up of on-the-job training takes many different forms, including lectures in specific subjects, practice on new machines, job rotation—including all jobs of a certain group—special assignments of a temporary nature, understudying a junior executive, special courses, reading assignments, and special work shops by professional associations. On-the-job training stresses just that—on the job—but some of the training may be acquired, in part, outside the enterprise. The entire program, however, should be carefully coordinated.

Supervisory Training. One of the most important types of training in any enterprise is supervisory training. Training of supervisors is vital because of their essentiality in management. Special courses in supervisory training have been designed, and many of these are generally considered effective. Discussion of supervisory training is included in the chapter on office supervision, Chapter 29.

Figure 26–1 indicates the type of training which is given to employees of different classifications or circumstances. For example, the new employee is given induction training and on-the-job training. The former provides information relative to his new job and to the policies and practices of the company; the latter includes specific training to help him acquire necessary skill.

PLANNING THE TRAINING PROGRAM

A good training program requires careful planning and should be built in such a way that each component and type of training is coordinated into a smooth-working, unified training plan. Usually the program should be tailor-made to suit the particular needs of the enterprise.

With the training objectives as a background, the following segments should be given careful consideration in planning the training program: (1) the trainees, (2) the instructor, (3) the training period, (4) the training material, and (5) the training methods.

TYPES OF TRAINING GIVEN TO VARIOUS CLASSIFICATIONS OF EMPLOYEES

Classification of Employee	Type of Training	Training Required
New	Induction	To give information relative to the job, the policies and practices of the company.
	On-the-job	Specific training in the important details of employee's job. To help employee acquire the necessary knowledge and skill.
Seasoned	On-the-job	To instruct on changes in procedures, routines, policies, and new equipment. Also to prepare for jobs of higher grade (promotion).
Transferred	Induction	To give information relative to new duties and work environment.
	On-the-job	Specific training in the important details of the new job. To help employee acquire the necessary knowledge and skill.
Supervisor	Supervisory	To give information relative to the theory and practical application of supervisory techniques.

FIG. 26–1.

Trainees.   Proper selection of employees to train is of major importance if permanent, gainful results are to be obtained. A trainee should be trained for the kind of job he likes and is fitted to perform. In this respect, training is closely related to the selection of personnel. Evidence is quite conclusive that careful screening of candidates for training raises the effectiveness of the training work.

In the case of supervisory training, it is best to include all supervisors and those considered for promotion to such posts. Excluding some employees on the basis that they do not need the training or that they are already doing their work satisfactorily is a poor policy. The reasons for this statement are best stated by the following: ". . . Even the outstanding supervisor can profit from a well-organized, properly conducted training program. We have observed that their participation and contribution are of real benefit to less qualified supervisors. Nor should any supervisor be excluded because 'he's beyond all help.' If this is really so, he should not be occupying a supervisory post."[1]

Instructor. A key figure in a good training program is the instructor. A capable teacher contributes immeasurably to the success of a training program. Qualified instructors may be obtained from inside or outside the company; however, many office employees are not good teachers. The efficient employee does not necessarily have the ability to teach. Instructors need many qualifications besides knowing how to do the work. A good teacher has the skill to instruct and is tolerant, understanding, and patient. Also important is an appreciation for the value of the training work in relation to the enterprise and an understanding of what the employee goes through in order to acquire the skill and knowledge which the program is designed to achieve.

Training Period. The length of the training period depends upon the skill to be acquired, the trainee's learning capacity, and the training media used. For example, a simple indoctrination program for clerks may require an hour a day over a period of a week, while a course in accounting machines may be given 1½ hours a week for 16 weeks. The use of effective visual material usually helps to reduce the training time. In the experience of a large Chicago bank, for example, the instruction time for a savings teller's job was reduced from 30 days to 10 days, and for a commercial department bookkeeper's job from 12 weeks to 6 weeks. The bank's training director estimates that effective visualization reduces the teaching time on an average of 50 per cent.[2]

In order to maintain interest and to secure greatest accomplishment, it is recommended that no single session last longer than 1½ hours. The best practice is to pay employees for training time if the course relates in any way to their work. Many states have laws or rulings affecting training time, and, in addition, certain federal laws are applicable. Controversial issues are likely to appear if the employee does any productive work during the training time, if the training is outside regular working hours, or if the training work is intended to train the employee for a new or additional skill.[3]

---

[1] Raymond J. W. O'Toole, "Training Supervisors Today for the Responsibilities of Tomorrow," *Annual Conference Proceedings, Life Office Management Association, 1947* (New York), p. 26.

[2] A. Gordon Bradt, "Putting the 'See' in Personnel Training," *Burroughs Clearing House* (Detroit: Burroughs Adding Machine Co.), September, 1951, p. 32.

[3] Federal and prevailing state laws should be checked to help determine whether trainee or company time should be used.

Training Material. A text or some written material is usually desirable as a basis for instruction, review, and reference. For most subjects a satisfactory book can be selected, but in instances where the course content is of a special nature, it may be well to prepare material for this specific use. A complete outline of the entire course should be made with the main topics included under each meeting or session. When a text is used, the parts to be covered must be clearly indicated; and assignments which require some preparatory time should be made for every meeting. This helps to keep the program on schedule, points the meeting toward definite subjects, and usually assists in the progress and satisfaction of the trainee.

Training Methods. The method of training is of vital consideration in the planning of any training program. There exists today many different schools of thought about the method of training. However, the objective should be foremost in determining the form of training to provide. Fundamentally all instruction should (1) proceed from the known to the unknown, (2) go from the simple to the complex, and (3) follow the order of "prepare, present, and apply."

Training methods can be classified into eight major groups: lectures, demonstrations, conferences, problem solving, role playing, coaching and counseling, guided experience, and actual practice. Choice of training method depends upon many factors, including the objectives of the training, the number of trainees, the preferences of the instructor, the type of material to be covered, the cost, the time allotted, and the wishes of the trainees.

The lecture is an effective means of initially explaining the material to the trainees. It should be carefully prepared, reinforced by the use of charts, sketches, and models, and presented by a qualified speaker. Demonstrations provide forceful presentation of how the job is done. This means stresses learning by eye, rather than by ear, and is especially helpful for jobs where physical skills are vital. The conference method permits trainees to express themselves orally and to exchange thoughts, and enables the instructor to judge the trainee's understanding of the subject material. The conference method is especially popular in supervisory training.

Problem solving is effective when the problems are well selected and bring out pertinent considerations to the work at hand. In short, solving the problems should meet specific development needs such as an ability to analyze and relate given facts, to determine the problem to be solved, to read and to substantiate the recommended actions to be taken. Unless a developmental need is met, this method of training may be inadequate, time consuming, and ineffective. Role playing narrows the gap between talking about what should be done and actually doing it. For training purposes, the playing out of a typical problem situation can be quite effective. It is especially helpful in situations involving employee relations. The method permits the trainees to participate, to gain an insight into their own behavior, and to look at the problem from many different viewpoints.

Coaching and counseling are normally work-centered and fact-centered individual efforts aimed to convey useful work information and to improve skill. Coaching emphasizes "setting up the plays," but permitting the employee to carry them out as best he can. Motivation and practical instruction are essential. The instructor must have the respect of the trainee, understand how he feels, and possess an ability to use analogies and demonstrations. Counseling stresses the assisting of an employee to recognize his strengths and weaknesses in fulfilling the requirements of his job. The counselor spends most of his time listening. His role is to help the trainee help himself, to become independent in his own right, and to build confidence in himself. The amount of direction and assistance given depends upon the individual being counseled. Both coaching and counseling emphasize a person-to-person individualized relationship. Essentially it is an informal rather than a formal method of training.

The guided experience method utilizes evaluation of the trainee to reveal his weaknesses, then the causes of these weaknesses are decided, and experience to remedy them are planned. Extreme care is taken to select the proper work assignments so that the trainee's shortcomings are ultimately removed. The assignments vary and include such things as writing reports, serving on committees, solving specific problems, performing research work, and working on normal day-to-day tasks. Like coaching and counseling, the guided experience method can be considered a highly personalized, informal type of training.

The last training method to be discussed is actual practice which stresses the performance of the office work. "Learning by doing" might be used to describe this method, which is believed by many to be the most important of all training methods. Each employee learns how to apply what he knows to the problem that confronts him at the particular time.

COST OF TRAINING

Training costs money. Many analyses of its cost are unrealistic in that comparisons are made between the expenditures of "no training" —actually a misleading term—and that of a formal training program.

The fact is that training costs are tangible and intangible. Erroneously the latter group are commonly ignored in the cost of training.

Under tangible training costs are training materials, nonproductive time of trainee, and nonproductive time of employee instructor or fee charged, if an outsider. Under the intangible classification are such things as a longer time for the trainee to attain a reasonable level of production, loss of employees seeking better job opportunities, time of experienced employees asked "show me how to do this" by the trainee, loss due to work spoilage and errors, practicing of poor work methods, and improper work viewpoints and attitudes permitted to develop and spread.

Training is a necessity in modern management, and reasonable expenditures for it should be made. The amount depends upon the needs and the aims of the office. However, whatever the costs, they should be kept under control. Management members should have some idea of what is being accomplished for the expenditures being made. This brings up the question of training effectiveness.

EFFECTIVENESS OF TRAINING

From the managerial viewpoint, it is an excellent idea to measure the effectiveness of training efforts. The evaluation, however, must be in terms of a particular training problem. This problem may be expressed in the form of questions, such as:

1. Has the training increased production?
2. Has there been a decrease in the number of errors?
3. Has the number of accidents decreased?
4. Has there been a reduction in labor turnover?
5. Has there been a reduction in absenteeism, requests for transfers, and number of grievances?
6. Has the amount of material spoilage been reduced?

It is usually best to measure effectiveness by departments or by some homogeneous group, for the problems of measurement become quite complex when the entire office is considered. It is advisable to make comparisons between office groups as units. A good procedure is to use as a control one group which is characterized by little or no formal training, by training of a particular type, or by a different method of training. Special care should be exercised to see that the groups compared are reasonably similar with respect to such factors as age, sex, time of week, month, or year.

Evaluating the results of training is not, however, a simple matter. Many companies make little effort to evaluate training results as such, or they are satisfied with general over-all indications of the training's worth. It is difficult to differentiate what factors contribute to increased production and employee development. Many of the products of training are intangible and are extremely difficult to measure. However, many personnel practices tend to measure indirectly, at least in part, the results of training, including such practices as employee merit rating, periodic personnel reviews, and keeping employees informed.

Training can be overdone to the point that the efforts and costs in its behalf exceed the highest estimates of benefits within a reasonable period. Training should be carefully managed; it should not be engaged in simply because "it is the thing to do." It is a continuous, not an "off-and-on," activity. It can start on a small scale and subsequently increase as the benefits become known and the needs and progress of the enterprise dictate. As a guide, these points should be kept in mind: (1) office training is desirable and necessary and is performed regardless of whether a formal program is carried on or not; (2) office training must be tailor-made to fit the specific need of the enterprise; (3) the questions of what, when, where, and how the office training should be conducted requires answering; (4) office training should be based on the needs of the office as shown by job analysis, prevalence of errors, low work output, and employees' attitudes; (5) office training should be preceded by careful selection of trainees; and (6) the training of office supervisors is vital.

QUESTIONS

1. What interpretation do you give to the following statement: "One who really manages makes use of training to help him manage."

2. What are the five objectives of office training efforts, regardless of the type, location, or size of the office?

3. Can the gap between the beginner and the average employee be filled by proper training? The gap between the average and the expert employee? Explain your answers.

4. Do you agree with the statement: "In the office, it is advisable that the new employee be let alone during the first day on the job. This permits adjustments to new surroundings in a manner that is not only acceptable, but also normal, to the new employee"?

5. Carefully identify each of the following:
    a) Guided experience method of training.
    b) Training.
    c) On-the-job training.
    d) Intangible costs of training.

6. Do you believe an employee-training program is a good investment? Why?

7. Enumerate and discuss some important reasons why an office manager may be disinclined to sponsor a training program for his employees.

8. Evaluate and justify the use of coaching and counseling as office training methods.

9. A new employee has just completed a two weeks' indoctrination training program given by a bank. The training director of the bank has rated the new employee as unsatisfactory, basing his opinion on the training results. Should the new employee be placed on the job, asked to repeat the training, or dropped from the payroll? Explain your answer.

10. What is your reaction to the following: "Although well-planned office training helps employees to acquire skills and to develop themselves, it can be engaged in to an excessive degree especially in old, well-established offices"?

11. Give an example illustrating an occasion when you would recommend the use of role playing in office training. When you would recommend the use of lectures? The use of actual practice?

12. As an office manager, would you try to evaluate the effectiveness of office training programs? Why?

CASE PROBLEMS

CASE 26–1.   SERBUR TEXTILES, INC.

As an industry, textiles have been suffering from overproduction and soft prices. Sales volume is down. Business activity has been declining for Serbur Textiles, Inc. Currently its sales are 30 per cent less than they were two years ago, and Mr. Benjamin Geiss, the treasurer, believes adjustments in the company's personnel must be made in order to keep the company solvent and competitive. Accordingly he has suggested, among other reductions, that four members of the office training unit be laid off indefinitely. This would leave the director of the unit and an assistant remaining. Mr. Geiss points out that the office force as a whole has been reduced nearly 20 per cent during the past eighteen months and with this smaller work force plus the fact that relatively few new employees are being hired—only in cases of absolute necessity—a reduction in training personnel is a logical place to trim costs.

Objections to Mr. Geiss's plans are voiced by the office manager, Mr. Julius Lieberman, who explains that office training is vital and that competent instructors skilled in office training work are difficult to replace. The instructors would certainly find employment elsewhere, and thus a great permanent loss to the company would be suffered. Mr. Lieberman suggests trimming costs elsewhere—areas where the situation is not so critical.

Mr. Geiss counters with the statement that the pruning of any organization structure is difficult—every function and every employee seems essential. He cannot see where office training is going to be needed for months to come. He also questions the contribution that this training unit has made. As best he can make out the company's cost for processing various paper work has been about the same for the past four years, except where new office machines were installed. He requests Mr. Lieberman to send him a report indicating what office personnel should be reduced and specific data to show that the office training unit should remain as is.

PROBLEMS:

1. What do you think about the viewpoints of Mr. Geiss? Discuss.
2. Point out the major contents of the report that Mr. Lieberman is to prepare.
3. What action do you feel the company should take? Why?

CASE 26-2. STANLEY MANNING

Stanley Manning, an office supplies salesman of the Evergreen Equipment Company, was attending evening university classes, studying accounting. One day, while making a call upon an automobile parts manufacturer, Stanley mentioned to the buyer that he was looking for a job in the accounting field where he could apply his new knowledge. During the conversation, Stanley was informed that a junior accountant's job was open with the manufacturer. Subsequently, Stanley talked with the office manager and secured the job.

He was placed with an outstanding accountant in the department. By observing and asking questions of this older employee, it was believed that Manning would learn to perform his work competently. Soon after acquiring his new job, he was asked to help out in the cashiering department and was informed what to do by the head cashier. Manning was told that he could then relieve in the cashiering department when necessary.

After three months in the accounting department, Manning did not seem to have acquired needed skill and knowledge for that department. He made some costly mistakes, was inclined to work slowly, and failed to ask questions about the work not familiar to him. At this time one of the cashiers became ill and Manning was requested to help out there until the cashier returned. Three weeks elapsed, and it was then announced that the cashier would not return. The office manager informed Manning that he would be given a two weeks' intensive and specific training in the details of the cashiering work. Manning said his major interest was accounting, not cashiering, but the office manager explained that cashiering was where he was needed and that it offered him greater promotional opportunities.

Subsequently, Manning completed the cashiering training and after three months in the department was rated "satisfactory" by the head cashier. He was given an increase of $20 per month which was greater than the rate of newly hired junior accountants. However, Manning was dissatisfied. He told the office manager that accounting was his chosen work and requested a transfer. The office manager replied that the cashiering work was going smoothly and he thought it best to continue the present arrangement.

Stanley Manning returned to his job. After thinking the situation over for several hours, he decided to quit his job. He informed the office manager who said he was sorry to see Stanley leave.

PROBLEMS:

1. Do you believe Stanley Manning is taking the correct action? Why?
2. Evaluate the office training work of this company.
3. What action do you feel the office manager should take? Why?

Chapter · 27

Office Safety

Forgive many things in others; nothing in yourself.
—AUSONIUS

PROVIDING a safe place in which to work and promoting safe work habits are conducive to favorable motivation of employees. Losses caused by accidents are costly not only from the humanitarian but also from the economic viewpoint. Office accidents represent an inexcusable waste of experienced employees. Even slight injuries received in an office can result in loss of working time and the disrupting of normal working conditions. Managerial attention must be paid to safety in the office.

RESPONSIBILITY FOR SAFETY

The keynote in office safety is safe equipment and machinery combined with employee co-operation. This resolves ultimately into primarily a managerial responsibility. It is up to the managers to provide a safe working place and to see that safety measures are recognized and enforced. It is the responsibility of the managers to see that office work is not held up because of accidents, that costs are not increased because of accidents, and that losses which result from accidents, and which cannot be recovered, are not incurred.

To be sure, the intelligent and continuous co-operation of employees with management measures is essential for an effective safety program. But the chief responsibility for safety rests with managers, who must take the initiative and carry the program through if successful accident-prevention work is to be achieved. Aggressive action is required. The mere moral attitude of wanting to do the right thing is not enough. Wishing for fewer accidents does not prevent, for example, the order clerk from tripping on an uneven, worn, or loose floor covering and suffering a serious fall.

ACCIDENT OCCURRENCE

Accidents can and do happen to office employees; they enjoy no automatic exemption. These accidents come about in a number of ways. For example, typewriters, calculators, and other office machines frequently need cleaning. Some cleaning fluids are inflammable, and cases are on record where the fumes from the cleaning fluid were ignited by a spark from the electric motor of the machine, resulting in a sudden flash fire which caused severe burns to office employees. Severe falls and injuries have resulted from slipping on highly polished

Courtesy: GM Folks, General Motors Corp., Detroit

FIG. 27–1. Accidents are caused by carelessness. The practices illustrated commonly result in accidents. These pictures are especially posed for accident-prevention promotional work.

floors and running on stairways by women in high-heeled shoes. Reclining too far back in a chair can result in the occupant's being thrown with considerable force, and serious, sometimes permanent, injuries have been suffered by office employees in this way. Illustrations of practices that frequently result in accidents are shown in Figure 27–1.

A CAUSE FOR EVERY ACCIDENT

Accidents do not just happen; they are caused. There is a reason for every accident that happens. The cause of every accident is some defect of action or lack of action which must be corrected in order to prevent a recurrence of the accident. Falling down a stairway is not a cause; it is a result—an accident. The causes are loose papers on the stair treads, inadequate lighting on the stairway, or the employee's failure to watch where he is stepping. These conditions must be rectified in order to achieve better safety results.[1]

Some writers have classified the causes of accidents under three headings: mechanical, physiological, and psychological. These terms are self-explanatory. Under mechanical causes, for example, are classified such things as improper lighting, unguarded machines, and technical defects in equipment. Physiological causes include bad eyesight and age of employees, while psychological causes cover such things as the employee's tendency to take unnecessary chances, horseplay, and temporary emotional and mental disturbances. These causes are interrelated and must be attacked jointly in most practical activities designed to reduce accidents.

MANAGERIAL COURSE OF ACTION

Experience and records show that accidents can be reduced; in fact, many can be prevented entirely. The best course of action for preventing accidents depends upon the circumstances in each particular case. Some advocate the so-called "triple *E*" program, which consists of engineering, education, and enforcement. That is, the first step is to engineer all equipment and machines with safety guards, cutoff switches, and other devices to make them as safe as is technically possible. Next, education to all employees is provided, to instill work habits and practices for winning high safety achievements. Last, enforcement insures that safety regulations are carried out.

An effective managerial course of action for achieving safety in the office consists of the following:

1. Plan effective safety actions.
2. Organize the safety efforts by allotting the work and establishing the relative authority and responsibility among the safety personnel.
3. Actuate all employees by promoting a feeling of safety among them.
4. Control the safety work by means of adequate records and the consideration of cost.

---

[1] For an excellent discussion of this subject, see Rollin H. Simonds and John V. Grimaldi, *Safety Management* (Homewood, Ill.: Richard D. Irwin, Inc., 1956), chap. iv.

PLAN EFFECTIVE SAFETY ACTIONS

Before hazards causing accidents can be eliminated, they must be identified. Available safety information reveals that the main types of office accidents have to do with slipping, tripping, handling materials, being hit by falling objects, and striking against objects. Among the more common hazards which result in office accidents are:

Defective electric cords lying across aisles, and loose connections
Paper clips and thumb tacks on the floor
Loose linoleum or carpeting
Slippery floors
Open desk drawer or file drawer
Tilting backwards too far in office chair
Sharp burrs on edges of metal office equipment
Sharp pointed pencils placed in upright position in handkerchief coat pocket
Broken glass desk top
Exposed moving parts of office machines
Splinters and loose veneer on wood desks and chairs
Bottles, papers, or books stacked on top of filing cabinets
Protruding pencil sharpeners and power and telephone outlets
Reading while walking
Running in aisle, on stairways, or through doorways

Especially helpful in locating and knowing what hazards to eliminate in a given office is a check list. An illustration of such a form is shown in Figure 27–2. In addition, an analysis of the accident reports can help in locating areas that need attention.

With factual data as a background, steps can be taken to incorporate each of the following safety actions into the program.

Education of Employees to Possible Dangers. Each employee should be made thoroughly aware of all the possible dangers of his job. All the details that make for safety should be carefully explained. These efforts can be planned and made a regular part of the job process and the training work. In this manner the correct and usual way of doing the job, which is also the safe way, becomes habitual. Safety is built right into the job—it is a part of the job. Simple visual aids to help in this work are shown in Figure 27–3.

Provision of Safe Work Areas. Safety planning should include all necessary provisions for safe working places and equipment for employees. Office floors should be covered with nonslippery material; adequate lighting should be provided; desks and chairs should be free of sharp edges.

Promotion of First-Aid Service. Adequate first-aid service should be included in the safety planning. Insistence upon first-aid treatment for minor injuries means little if adequate facilities are not available. When these facilities are provided, managers show that they wish all injured employees to receive treatment promptly. Furthermore, such provisions reflect adequate safety planning by the managers.

Availability of Safety Clothing. The use of special clothing and protective equipment designed to protect employees from injuries is another area to be included in safety planning. Finger guards should

---

OFFICE SAFETY INSPECTION DATA

Carefully inspect the office, and for each question, check whether a hazard exists. If "Yes," briefly note the important details.

QUESTION	Does Hazard Exist?		COMMENTS (GIVE LOCATION AND DETAILS.)
	Yes	No	
1. Are aisles obstructed?............................			
2. Do pencil sharpeners project over desk or table?...			
3. Are file drawers kept closed when not in use?......................................			
4. Are machines properly guarded?...................			
5. Are glass desk tops broken?......................			
6. Are there any sharp metal projections on any equipment?...............................			
7. Is electrical wiring concealed?.....................			
8. Are office accessories insecurely placed?.............			
9. Are papers and waste properly disposed of?........			
10. Are facilities for smokers adequate?...............			
11. Are materials stacked on desks or cabinets?...			
12. Are extension cords used extensively?.............			
13. Are floors too highly polished?...................			
14. Is carpeting loose or worn?.....................			

FIG. 27–2.   Portion of a form designed to assist in determining safety hazards.

---

be furnished to employees doing work where the chances of suffering paper cuts are quite high. Likewise, plastic aprons should be available to employees working around large quantities of ink, glue pots, and cleaning solutions.

Inclusion of Good Housekeeping Practices.   Good housekeeping in the office is essential for good safety work. The habit of orderliness and cleanliness should be included in safety planning, and adequate provisions made for its promotion and follow-up. Stairways should be kept clear of all loose objects; aisles should be marked for traffic lanes; an adequate number of wastepaper baskets should be furnished; and regular clean-up service should be provided. A clean, orderly office

Courtesy: National Safety Council, Chicago

FIG. 27–3. Visual aids to help educate the office employee to possible dangers on the job.

sets a good example for the employee and helps to keep the office personnel safety-minded.

ORGANIZING AND THE SAFETY WORK

It is important that there be a recognized head of office safety work. This person should be given complete responsibility for the direction and guidance of all office safety efforts. The person in charge might be the office manager himself, or the office manager might appoint a subordinate to the job. Generally, the safety director need not spend all of his time on safety, but it is advisable for him to devote a certain amount of time regularly to the program.

Importance of Supervisors. Department heads are the key personnel in accident-prevention work. In many respects the success of the entire safety program depends upon the supervisors. The entire program is promoted by the co-operation of the department heads, and they can do more than anyone else toward keeping the employees safety-minded. Furthermore, supervisors can correct unsafe conditions; they can see that safety rules are followed, that first aid is provided in case of accident, and that proper reports are filled out.

Safety Committees. Because participation promotes acceptance for safety efforts, safety committees with rotating memberships are recommended. A five-member committee, with membership rotating bimonthly, usually works out very well. The system of replacements should be such that not more than two new members are added at any one time, thus insuring that the remaining three members are familiar with the work of the committee.

The work of this group is advisory. It fulfills a staff function to the safety head and submits suggestions for the reduction of accidents within the office. Frequently the safety committee may also:

1. Make regular inspections of the office.
2. Supervise the maintenance and use of first-aid equipment.
3. Make fire-prevention inspections.
4. Sponsor accident-prevention contests.
5. Help prepare safety rules.
6. Review safety suggestions made by the employees.
7. Supervise the display of safety materials on the bulletin boards.
8. Accumulate and transmit safety training material to the other employees.[2]

ACTUATING ALL EMPLOYEES BY PROMOTING SAFETY CONSCIOUSNESS

The mental attitude of the employee toward safety is exceedingly important in accident-prevention work. There is a great deal of truth in the saying: "The best safety device in all the world is located an inch or two above the eyebrows." The employee who "thinks safety" and who has developed a safety consciousness "from the ears up" has gone a long way toward preventing accidents.

All efforts designed to keep safety on the employee's mind and to keep accident prevention a live subject in the office will help substantially in the safety program. Although it may seem strange, it is a common occurrence for people to be careless. Safety-mindedness requires alert-mindedness. Safety work is a continuous process, requiring constant reminders to the employee to work safely, to avoid taking chances, and to keep safety foremost among his thoughts. The task is not an easy one, but persistence and steadfastness of purpose will achieve good results.

It is a truism that, for the most part, people attach the same degree of importance to activities as do their leaders. If the managers think, believe, and are actively engaged in accident-prevention work, then this same spirit will be picked up by the employees. The safety example set by managers is important in attaining a good safety record.

Explain Safety Rules. Safety rules should be explained, and the reasons for their rigid enforcement given to the employees. The entire safety program can be seriously handicapped if there is any let-

---

[2] National Safety Council, Inc., *Industrial Safety Guide* (Chicago, 1946), p. 3.

down in either the education or the enforcement of safety rules. Quite often having the rules in writing is helpful and can be fulfilled by issuing mimeographed, typewritten, or printed forms.

Inform Office Employees of Safety Fundamentals.   This can take various forms, including articles in company papers, talks at meetings, informal suggestions to employees, movies, and safety instruction cards. This latter medium provides the employee with pertinent suggestions about safety and serves as a series of timely reminders, help-

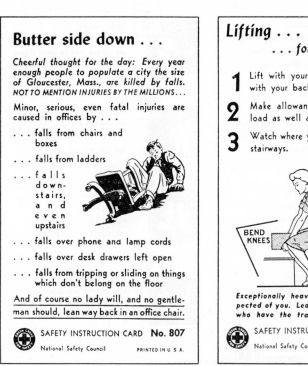

Butter side down . . .

Cheerful thought for the day: Every year enough people to populate a city the size of Gloucester, Mass., are killed by falls. NOT TO MENTION INJURIES BY THE MILLIONS...

Minor, serious, even fatal injuries are caused in offices by . . .

. . . falls from chairs and boxes

. . . falls from ladders

. . . f a l l s
d o w n -
s t a i r s ,
a n d
e v e n
upstairs

. . . falls over phone and lamp cords

. . . falls over desk drawers left open

. . . falls from tripping or sliding on things which don't belong on the floor

And of course no lady will, and no gentleman should, lean way back in an office chair.

SAFETY INSTRUCTION CARD   **No. 807**
National Safety Council   PRINTED IN U S A.

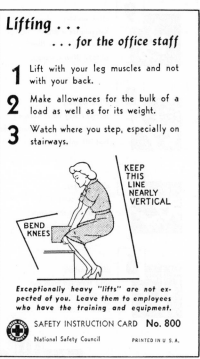

Lifting . . .
. . . for the office staff

1 Lift with your leg muscles and not with your back.

2 Make allowances for the bulk of a load as well as for its weight.

3 Watch where you step, especially on stairways.

KEEP
THIS
LINE
NEARLY
VERTICAL

BEND
KNEES

Exceptionally heavy "lifts" are not expected of you. Leave them to employees who have the training and equipment.

SAFETY INSTRUCTION CARD   **No. 800**
National Safety Council   PRINTED IN U S A.

Courtesy: National Safety Council, Chicago

FIG. 27–4. Safety instruction cards.

ing to keep safety on the minds of the employees. Figure 27–4 shows several examples of safety instruction cards.

Employ Bulletin Boards.   Pictures, posters, and cartoon sketches can also be used to arouse the employee's interest in safety. It is usually best to have this material specific in nature, telling the employee what to do under particular conditions. Giving the employee general safety cautions and slogans is probably of limited value. Also, it is usually well to supplement this type of safety promotion with intensive individual follow-up. The bulletin boards used should be located in

Courtesy: National Safety Council, Chicago

FIG. 27–5. An effective safety poster.

areas that are frequently seen, accessible, and in full view. A poster with exceptionally lively layout is shown in Figure 27–5.

Promote Safety Contests. This approach stresses the competitive spirit and usually relies upon the employee's desire to excel. An award in the form of a plaque, banner, special pin, or money may be given the individual, group, or department having the best safety record for a given period. A reversal of this technique can also be used, and it is generally effective. In this case a booby prize is given the unit having the poorest safety record, with the requirement that this "award" be displayed prominently. This approach appeals to the employee's pride and to his desire to escape any designation which makes him look ridiculous. Like all promotional plans, safety contests must be publicized and made acceptable to the employees.

OFFICE SAFETY WORK AND CONTROLLING

Effective accident-prevention work requires that adequate records be kept of all accidents. It is important to know what accidents happened, where, and when. Adequate records will also show the type of injuries and the conditions which caused them. By studying such data, a manager is able to take intelligent corrective action and knows where to stress safety efforts.

Content of Safety Records. Safety records should include such things as the date of the accident, the employee's name, the department, the injury suffered, a concise description of the accident, and a report of the action taken to prevent a recurrence. Other information might be added, depending upon the experience and the use which it is desired to make of these data.

Safety Indexes. There are also two widely used and accepted indexes in safety statistics. These are: (1) the frequency rate, and (2) the severity rate. These names are self-explanatory, as the frequency rate measures the occurrence of accidents and the severity rate measures the seriousness of accidents. The indexes are used to show the relative values and trends within any group and the comparisons among different groups.

a) Frequency Rate. The frequency rate can be defined as the number of disabling injuries suffered per million man-hours worked. The formula is:

$$\text{Frequency rate} = \frac{\text{Number of disabling injuries} \times 1,000,000}{\text{Total number of man-hours worked}}$$

Disabling injuries are frequently referred to as "lost-time accidents arising out of and in the course of employment." The National Safety Council classifies the following types of injuries as disabling injuries:

1. Death.
2. Permanent total disability: Any injury or combination of injuries suffered in one accident which permanently and totally in-

capacitates an employee from following any gainful occupation. Loss of both eyes or of both hands are examples.

3. Permanent partial disability: Any injury suffered in one accident which results in the loss of any member or part of a member of the body but which does not result in death or permanent total disability.

4. Temporary total disability: Any injury suffered in one accident which results in no permanent injury but which prevents the injured person from returning to a regularly established job within twenty-four hours after the start of the shift during which he was injured.

The total number of man-hours is best obtained from payroll records or time cards. If these are unavailable, the number can be estimated by multiplying the average number of employees by the average number of hours worked during the period considered.

b) Severity Rate. The severity rate is the number of days charged as a result of injuries per million man-hours worked. The formula is:

$$\text{Severity rate} = \frac{\text{Time charged (in days)} \times 1,000,000}{\text{Total number of man-hours worked}}$$

Days charged are sometimes called "days of disability." However, the time charged away from the job does not accurately measure the severity of the accident. Therefore, tables have been set up indicating an arbitrary number of days which should be used for various types of accidents. For example, an accident resulting in death or in permanent total disability is charged at the rate of 6,000 days for each case. This is approximately twenty years. A permanent partial disability resulting in the loss of a hand is charged at 3,000 days.

Available safety data show that the office frequency rates and severity rates are among the lowest of any industry classification. This is shown in Figure 27–6. It is encouraging to note that the rates are declining for every industry—safety is progressing.

ACCIDENT COSTS

Costs are another means of controlling safety, inasmuch as the amount of expenditure has some relationship to the efforts directed to this area. Budgets over these costs are desirable, and actions to get the most benefits for a given expenditure should be encouraged.

It is a well-known fact that accidents are expensive. The loss might be in money, skill, time, human suffering, work output, or interruption in the flow of work. The hidden or incidental costs of accidents are much greater than the measurable direct costs. Such things as the cost

THREE-YEAR FREQUENCY AND SEVERITY RATES OF SELECTED INDUSTRIES

INDUSTRY	FREQUENCY RATES					SEVERITY RATES				
	1950–52	1951–53	1952–54	1953–55	1954–56	1950–52	1951–53	1952–54	1953–55	1954–56
Offices............	1.31	1.69	2.48	2.71	1.40	120	90	170	174	115
Automobile.......	4.26	3.80	3.27	2.99	2.76	430	390	350	332	296
Chemical..........	5.42	5.03	4.64	3.90	3.73	710	730	670	642	535
Construction......	18.90	17.53	16.72	17.84	18.77	2530	2310	2280	2275	2352
Lumbering........	41.02	37.06	33.42	30.83	27.09	4120	3880	3670	3631	3163
Printing and publishing..........	8.09	7.94	7.06	6.59	6.45	370	430	320	257	165
Steel..............	4.40	4.15	3.92	3.98	3.87	1200	1130	1060	953	888
Tobacco..........	5.41	4.92	4.32	3.82	3.50	210	190	200	151	137

Compiled from Accident Facts (Chicago: National Safety Council, Inc., 1953, 1954, 1955, 1956, 1957)

FIG. 27–6. Comparison of safety statistics.

of hiring and training new employees, the interference to production, and the loss of good will are sizable expenses not generally thought of in connection with the costs of accidents. According to reliable estimates, there is a ratio of four to one between hidden costs and direct costs of accidents.[3] This means that total accident costs are far greater than most people realize.

QUESTIONS

1. Support the belief that there should be a safety program for office employees.
2. Explain why office safety ultimately resolves into a managerial responsibility.
3. Select one of the two illustrations shown in Figure 27–1. Assume you are an office supervisor and observe the condition shown by your selected illustration. What action would you take? Be specific.
4. Do you agree with the statement: "Office safety is readily accepted by the employee mainly because it is for his own benefit. Rigid enforcement of safety regulations smacks of the dictator approach. An employee is a human being and does not have to be pushed into being a safe employee."
5. Assume you have just been appointed safety head in an office employing 150 people. What steps would you take to initiate an effective safety program?
6. Discuss several major ways in which office employees can be motivated to practice safe work habits.
7. Are committees effective in promoting safety among office employees? Substantiate your answer.

[3] See H. W. Heinrich, *Industrial Accident Prevention* (3rd ed.; New York: McGraw-Hill Book Co., Inc., 1950), pp. 37–46.

8. Explain the meaning of the statement: "The best safety device is located an inch or two above the employee's eyebrows."

9. Referring to Figure 27–2, how helpful do you believe the use of a questionnaire like this actually is in efforts to prevent accidents and injuries? Give reasons for your answer.

10. Discuss the work of controlling as applied to office safety.

11. Comment on the statement: "Safety instructions should be integrated with office training, regardless of the particular job and the trainee."

12. With reference to office safety, in your own words explain what is meant by a frequency rate of 8.0? A severity rate of 160.0? If the severity rate is divided by the frequency rate, such as 160.0 divided by 8.0, giving a value of 20.0, what is the meaning of the value, 20.0? Discuss.

CASE PROBLEMS

CASE 27–1. WESTERN MARBURY COMPANY

Several months ago the office manager announced that smoking by the office employees at the workplaces during working hours would be permitted by the company. This decision came about when it was found that a great deal of working time was lost by crowding into the rest rooms "for smokes" during working hours. The employees had asked that the ban on smoking in the office be lifted and had been quite aggressive in securing the present concession of smoking being permitted at the desks.

Ten days ago a fire started in the purchasing division of the company's office. Two employees suffered minor burns in extinguishing the flame, and some damage was done to a desk and to carpeting. An investigation revealed that the cause was carelessness on the part of an employee, who had placed a lighted cigarette on the edge of his desk. The lighted cigarette had fallen into a wastebasket filled with papers, and the fire had started.

The following day, the office manager issued a memorandum to every office employee requesting full co-operation in helping to keep the office a safe place in which to work. The employees were urged to be especially careful about smoking in the office, and it was explained that a serious fire could mean a loss of jobs and valuable property. In addition, an attractively illustrated poster was put on the office bulletin board suggesting, "Be careful. Watch where you place your lighted matches and cigarettes. Help avoid a serious fire which might result in physical injury to you and the loss of your job." At the same time, the office manager personally spoke with all the office supervisors requesting that they stress office safety to their respective employees and especially caution them about the handling of lighted matches and cigarettes.

Yesterday, a repetition of the fire incident again occurred in the office. This time the fire was in the cost accounting division. The fire got a fairly good start and damaged one corner of the office. The damage is estimated at about $1,800. The cause is not known. The supervisor of the cost accounting division feels it might be similar to that of the previous fire, but he has no proof of this. Close questioning of the three employees who work in the area where the fire started does not reveal any careless use of matches or cigarettes.

PROBLEMS:

1. What are your reactions to the handling of the situation by the office manager after the first fire? Explain.
2. Should the office manager continue to allow smoking in the office? Discuss.
3. What action do you recommend that the office manager now take? Why?

Chapter · 28

Office Trade-Unionism

You can employ men and hire hands to work for you, but you must win their hearts to have them work with you.
—WILLIAM J. H. BOETCKER

TRADE-UNIONS among office employees have existed for a number of years. Among the oldest are the editorial employees of some newspapers, organized around 1890; the National Association of Letter Carriers, created in 1892; and the Brotherhood of Railway and Steamship Clerks, organized in 1899. These early unions were loosely organized, judged in terms of present-day standards; but they were unions and their members were clerical employees.

GROWTH OF OFFICE UNIONIZATION

During the following several decades, other office unions came into being, among which are the following: the National Federation of Post Office Clerks (organized in 1906), the American Federation of Teachers (1916), the National Federation of Federal Employees (1917), and the American Federation of Governmental Employees (1932).

Since about 1935 there has been increased interest in the unionization of office employees. Stimulus was brought about by the National Industrial Recovery Act of 1933 and, in particular, by the National Labor Relations Act of 1935. Today, the American Federation of Labor–Congress of Industrial Organization (AFL–CIO) has established strong office employees' unions. In addition, there are a number of independent unions not affiliated with the AFL–CIO. In addition, the memberships of many nonclerical unions include office employees. This is illustrated by the following list which is indicative, not complete, but helps to show the breadth of office unionism as well as the dispersion of office employees.

AFL–CIO:

Allied Trade Council
Amalgamated Clothing Workers
American Communications Association
Hotel and Restaurants Employees Union
Industrial Union of Marine and Shipbuilding Workers of America
International Brotherhood of Electrical Workers of America
International Brotherhood of Teamsters, Chauffeurs, Warehousemen and
    Helpers of America
International Chemical Workers Union
Office Employees International Union
Oil Workers International Union
Textile Workers Union of America
Transport Workers Union of America
United Automobile, Aircraft and Agricultural Implement Workers of
    America
United Farm Equipment and Metal Workers of America
United Office and Professional Workers of America
United Steel Workers of America
Utility Workers Union of America

Independent:

Associated Unions of America
Communication Workers of America
National Federation of Salaried Unions

CURRENT STATUS OF OFFICE UNIONISM

Various estimates place the percentage of union to total office employees in the range between 3–6 per cent. This may appear minor, but it is a composite figure for all office employees, and in certain enterprises the extent of office unionization assumes a prominent position.

The growth in office unionization has been relatively slow compared to that of factory employees. There are many reasons for this, including:

1. *Social status of the office employee.* Identification of office employees is with "those in the know." The typical office employee works in street clothes, is around, sees, and sometimes meets the executives of the company.

2. *Line of demarcation between the office and the factory employees.* Traditionally, the office employee believes his work to be of a higher sort. His work is of a dignified type. It offers prestige and is generally looked up to.

3. *The conservative nature of most office employees.* They are in-

clined to stay with the old rather than to try out the new. In addition, about two thirds of the office employees are women, many of whom are interested in working in offices for only a limited period of time.

4. *Receiving certain benefits of unionism without being members.* In many instances the benefits negotiated by unions of nonoffice employees are passed along to the office employees of that enterprise. This practice has been termed "a free ride" for the office employees. The practice may be questioned, but it does exist.

5. *Satisfactory working conditions.* Most office employees feel that they work in an area which is cleaner than that in which many other employees work. Also, they may consider the work safer and not as physically tiring.

6. *The dispersion of office employees.* In many enterprises the ratio of office to total employees is about 5–15 per cent. This scattered distribution of relatively small groups has made for difficulty in unionization activities.

BASIC REASONS WHY OFFICE EMPLOYEES JOIN UNIONS

The interest in unions on the part of office employees can be attributed to several factors. In the first place, favorable labor legislation has made it possible to organize.[1] Employees are now assured the right to engage in this activity. Also, in certain areas unions have been active in organizing office employees. Such things as conversations with employees, speeches at meetings, and the distribution of union literature are used in this connection. In addition, office employees have witnessed the success of factory employees in collective bargaining, and undoubtedly this has suggested that perhaps they too should be members of a union. The unions' winning of greater economic security has no doubt been enticing. In the opinion of many, the fact that since about 1940 many office salary rates have not increased comparably to those of most union members is one of the foremost reasons for office employees joining unions. Another basic reason is that the union offers a vehicle for reaching managers about grievances and personal needs. Furthermore, employees want more to say about their work and the conditions under which it is performed. They feel that with a union they are assured some participation in decision making and must be consulted before certain changes are made. Finally, an increasing gap between the office employees and the managers has made for an interest in unions. As a result of office growth, the em-

---

[1] The legal aspects of unionism are discussed later in this chapter.

ployee might have the feeling of isolation and sense a loss of close association with management members. Under such conditions, the employee might turn to group action for relief.

OPERATION IN THE UNIONIZED OFFICE

When a union exists in an office, managers are required to bargain with the authorized representatives concerning "wages and other conditions of employment." In other words, a process which might be called "collective co-operation" is used whereby employers and representatives of employees arrive at agreements covering compensation and the conditions under which employees will work. This usually means that policies concerning matters such as wages, discharge, discipline, and transfer must be discussed with the union representatives and incorporated into a mutually agreed-upon labor contract. Subsequently, decisions utilizing these policies are made by management members but are frequently subject to question by and explanation to the union, via an established grievance procedure. The net effect is to challenge the decision-making process of management members, regardless of the level of management. The union wants to be consulted and to present its views in matters affecting its members during the decision-making process so that the decision reached will be in keeping with its views. To reiterate, the ultimate decision is made by a management member, but from the practical viewpoint, the decision must be acceptable to the employees in order to be entirely effective.

CHARACTERISTICS OF CONTRACTS

The majority of current office-union contracts are tailor-made to suit the special conditions of the individual offices. There is, however, some similarity of contracts, since most of them cover the same subject topics. Most contracts contain clauses covering such matters as recognition of the union, union status, union security, salaries, hours of work, seniority, employment procedures, transfers and dismissals, grievance procedures, penalties, maternity leaves, and severance pay. A discussion of several of these subjects follows.

Union-Recognition Clause. A recognition of the union clause points out that the union named in the contract is fully recognized by the employer; frequently it also states what jobs and what employees are covered by the contract. Sometimes a statement is included to the effect that the union will not accept into membership those employees in the excluded groups.

Status of Union. Union status concerns the relationship of members of the union with the company. In general, there are three kinds of union status:

1. Union shop—nonunion members may be hired, but after a certain period, they must, as a requirement of employment, become union members.

2. Maintenance of membership shop—all employees are not required to join the union, but all present union members must retain membership during the time when the contract is in force.

3. Exclusive bargaining shop—the union is recognized as the exclusive bargaining agent for all employees, but no employee is compelled to join it or to remain a member.[2]

Wage Rates. Clauses on wage rates frequently include the recognition of job classifications and wage rates for each class. Minimum rates only might be stated. Uniform adjustments, either in amount or percentage, may be provided, and the effective date of such adjustments may be included.

The following is a typical contractual statement pertaining to wages.

Section 2. The wage schedules as set forth in this schedule, attached hereto as Exhibit B and made a part hereof, shall apply and be in effect as of July 1, 1958, and shall remain in effect for the life of this agreement.

Section 3. Overtime compensation and deductible time lost shall be computed by dividing the monthly salary by one hundred seventy-three and one third ($173\frac{1}{3}$) to arrive at an hourly rate to be used for such computations.

Layoffs and Seniority. While most unions favor the governing of layoffs and rehires on seniority, they will grant a statement to the effect that seniority shall govern when the employee involved has the ability to do the work under question. Questions arising in connection with seniority are sometimes clarified by the practice of preclassifying employees either by occupation or by departments or divisions. In this way, employees making up a fairly comparable group are associated together.

To illustrate:

Section 3. A reduction in working forces resulting in demotions and layoffs will normally be on a departmental seniority basis except for stenographers and filing clerks, who will be on a company-wide basis.

---

[2] The Labor Management Relations Act of 1947 outlawed in interstate commerce (1) the closed shop—in which the employer agrees to hire only union members, and all employees must continue their good standing in the union during their terms of employment; and (2) the preferential shop—in which preference in hiring and in layoff are given union members.

Penalty Clauses. Penalty provisions provide punishment for members who violate parts of the contract. Penalties might be in the form of reductions in pay, temporary or permanent layoffs, or less severe disciplinary measures, depending upon the nature of the violation.

CONTRACT LIMITATIONS

It is not feasible to write a collective-bargaining contract which covers every possible source of difference between the employer and the employee. A brief contract stating the points in simple terms usually is sufficient. Attempts to cover all contingencies in great detail will result in complicating the contract and in making it extremely difficult to interpret. Arguments about language technicalities lead to disputes which usually cause trouble.

There must be a spirit of co-operativeness on the part of both interested parties; they must want the contract to work. When both parties have this attitude, even the skimpy and legally poorly written contract can help to expedite harmonious relations. Without this attitude the success of a well-written contract can be seriously curtailed.

In many respects questions involving the legal rights are peripheral quizzes—they do not penetrate to the real core of management-union co-operation. Managerial actions and techniques conducive to production and mutual co-operation are paramount considerations as well as the union's appreciation of the inherent characteristics and conditions under which the office must operate. Recognition must be given to the development of the various elements affecting the general background in which the contract is made. The status of the American worker is changing. A far-reaching social change is progressing in the form of a labor movement. Today enlightened managers accept the doctrine that they have economic as well as social responsibilities.

LABOR MANAGEMENT RELATIONS ACT OF 1947

This law is commonly referred to as the Taft-Hartley Act and is the federal legislation under which management-union co-operation is administered. By this law, a National Labor Relations Board was established with the power to hear testimony, render decisions, and decide the appropriate unit for purposes of collective bargaining. The Board serves mainly in a judiciary capacity. A General Counsel and his staff prosecute the cases brought before the Board. Among the other important provisions of this law are unfair labor practices, strike controls, and checks on unions.

Unfair Labor Practices.   The Taft-Hartley Act forbids unfair labor practices by the employer and also by unions or their agents. The former or employer list includes (1) interfering or restraining employees from forming or joining a labor union, (2) dominating or influencing a labor organization, (3) discriminating in the hiring or in the conditions of employment of any employee because he is a member of a union, (4) terminating employment or discriminating against employee for any charge or testimony given under this law, and (5) refusing to bargain collectively with representatives of his employees.

Practices which constitute unfair labor practices by unions or their agents include: (1) coercing or restraining employees in connection with their joining a union, (2) charging "excessive or discriminatory" union initiation fees (the meaning of "excessive or discriminatory" is determined by the Labor Board in cases where there is an authorized union-shop contract), (3) refusing to bargain collectively with the employer, (4) participating in jurisdictional strikes, and (5) practicing "featherbedding," i.e., making the employer pay for services not performed.

Charges of unfair labor practices on the part of either employer or union are investigated, complaints issued, and prosecution carried on before the National Labor Relations Board by the General Counsel, who has exclusive authority to prosecute unfair labor practices. He is appointed by the President and has general supervision over all attorneys employed by the Board, excepting trial examiners and legal assistants to Board members.

Basing its decision on the preponderance of evidence and testimony, the Board decides whether any defendant named in the complaint is guilty of an unfair labor practice. If he is not guilty, the findings are stated and an order is issued dismissing the complaint. If he is guilty, the Board states its findings and causes a cease and desist order, prohibiting the continuation of the unfair practice, to be served on the guilty party. For enforcement of its orders, the Board has the power to petition the Circuit Court of Appeals with jurisdiction where the unfair labor practice occurred.

Strike Controls.   The Taft-Hartley Act provides that a sixty-day notice must be given the other party before the normal termination of a labor contract. The Federal Mediation and Conciliation Service must be notified at least thirty days after the sixty-day notice if no agreement is reached. This provision is, of course, intended to help settle the differences of opinion. Lockouts and strikes are prohibited during the notice period. There is no compulsory arbitration or court-injunction right against a legitimate noncritical strike, i.e., one not threatening "national health and safety" or affecting an entire industry.

In contrast, threatening lockouts or strikes affecting "national health and safety" or an entire industry may be delayed eighty days by the President of the United States in this manner: A board of inquiry may be appointed to determine the facts involved in the dispute. A report stating these facts, along with each party's statement of its position, is filed with the Federal Mediation and Conciliation Service, and the contents are made known to the public. In addition, the President at this time may, through the Attorney General, seek a court injunction against the lockout or strike. If the injunction is issued, there follows a period of sixty days in which to bring about a settlement. If this is not reached, the National Labor Relations Board holds, within the ensuing fifteen days, a company-by-company election on each employer's last offer of settlement and certifies same within five days to the Attorney General, who then moves to dissolve the injunction. Then the President submits a comprehensive report of the proceedings to Congress, along with any recommendation which he deems fitting and proper for appropriate action.

Checks on Unions.   In order for a union to take advantage of the National Labor Relations Board under this Act, that is, seek a Board election or file an unfair labor practice with the Board, the union must previously file (1) pertinent union information, and (2) non-Communists affidavits by each officer of the union.

The pertinent union information is filed annually with the Secretary of Labor. The report must include name, title, compensation, and allowances for each of the union's three principal officers and for any other officer or agent of the union if the aggregate compensation and allowances of any one of these persons exceeds $5,000 for the preceding year. The report must also include the manner of election or appointment of these officers or agents; the amount of initiation fees and regular dues; a statement showing the procedure followed for such things as qualifications for union membership, levying of assessments, authorization for bargaining demands, for strikes, for disbursement of union funds, and for the basis for expulsion of members; and a report showing receipts and expenditures for the fiscal year and total assets and liabilities at the end of the fiscal year. All union members have a right to a copy of their unions' financial report.

The affidavits by union officers can be filed either contemporaneously with a union action privileged by the Act or within the preceding twelve-month period. The affidavit is a sworn written statement signifying that the union officer is not a member or affiliate of the Communist party and does not believe in, belong to, or support any organization believing in or teaching the overthrow of the United States government by force or by illegal or unconstitutional methods.

Other Major Provisions of the Act. Additional important provisions of the Act include the following:

1. Union-shop agreements must be in accordance with the prevailing state law and are void in states that forbid them.

2. An employee or a group of employees can petition that the union's authorization to enter into a union-shop contract be withdrawn; such a petition must contain the signatures of 30 per cent of the employees represented by the union. However, only one election on union security can be held each year.

3. In instances of authorized union-shop contracts, the failure of a member to pay union dues and initiation fee is the only cause for loss of good standing with the union for which an employer can be forced to discharge an employee.

4. Union dues checkoff is allowed only with the employee's written consent.

5. If the majority of professional workers desire a union, they can be represented, if they wish, by a union other than that representing the production workers.

6. The individual employee can present grievances direct to his supervisor, providing the union representative is informed and given an opportunity to be present. Settlement of the grievance can be made if such settlement is not contrary to any terms of the existing union contract.

7. The employer can refuse to bargain with a union of foremen or supervisors. They can have their union, but the employer need not bargain with them if he does not choose to do so.

8. Unions as well as employers can sue and be sued for violations of contract under this Act. Judgments against unions must be collected from them, not from the individual employee.[3]

HANDLING OF CONTROVERSIES

Ideally, the manager and the union representative should solve their differences by means of interpreting the labor contract, bargain-

---

[3] An excellent source on this subject is Selwyn Torff, *Collective Bargaining: Negotiations and Agreements* (New York: McGraw-Hill Book Co., Inc., 1953).

ing, or mutual agreement. In practice, however, this does not always take place. Hence, to handle controversies several methods are available, including:

By mediation. Both parties agree to use a third party, or mediator, in order to compromise or reach an agreement. He may relay one party's opinion to the other or act as a chairman in getting the parties together to relate their beliefs and opinions. In addition, the mediator may define the basis of the dispute and show the legal meaning of the agreement, thus indirectly demonstrating how settlement might be reached.

By conciliation. Each party may ask for a conciliator who serves as an intermediate and seeks to settle the dispute. In contrast to that of the mediator, the work of the conciliator is aggressive; he may be said to take the offensive. The conciliator may induce one party to accept certain requests of the other or may give advice as to the manner of settling the dispute. To bring about agreement, conciliators depend upon such things as their ability, prestige, and knowledge of all facts in the case. They have no legal power to compel acceptance of any terms.

By arbitration. The parties may use voluntary arbitration to settle their differences. To do this, both parties agree to submit the case to a neutral, impartial third party or umpire. It is usually agreed that the arbitrator's findings will be accepted as final.[4]

In actual practice, the terms "mediation" and "conciliation" are used synonymously. As previously stated, the Taft-Hartley Act provides that a thirty-day notice of a change in or termination of a labor contract must be filed with the Federal Mediation and Conciliation Service. This makes it possible for the Service to get the differences settled before an open break has occurred.

THE CHALLENGE OF BARGAINING

Fundamentally, the aims of management members and of unions are reconcilable. It may at first appear that the differences in goals between the two are very great. But when the aims of each are analyzed, they appear compatible and able to exist in harmony. Figure 28–1 shows diagrammatically the position of collective bargaining in relation to the major goals of managers and of unions.

To bring about greater improvement, harmony, and mutual benefit in management-union co-operation, the major areas requiring satisfactory solution deal with (1) more intense utilization of competent manpower in working and thinking about labor relations, (2) the

---

[4] K. Braun, *The Settlement of Industrial Disputes* (Philadelphia: Blakiston Co., 1944), p. 29.

"Arbitration" as discussed here applies to reaching a contract agreement and is not the common type of arbitration which deals with the interpretation and application of existing contracts to specific disputes.

rights of management, (3) recognition of all interested parties, (4) the scope and viewpoint of labor relations, and (5) the basis for conducting collective bargaining.

More Intense Utilization of Competent Manpower. This area is probably of greatest importance. The more intense application of the best minds toward finding ways and means to assist management-union co-operation appears fundamental to its continued progress. Time will bring improvement, particularly if members of management, unions, government, and the public give sufficient time and ef-

Goals of Managers		*Goals of Unions*
1. An equitable income for the owners.		1. Security of employment.
2. A reasonable income for contingencies, expansion, and improvements.		2. Wages consistent with a decent standard of living and commensurate with the quality and quantity of work output.
3. Good reputation for products or services.	Collective bargaining resolves and harmonizes for mutual benefit	3. Consultation and opportunity for suggestions in shaping policies.
4. Reputation as a good place to work.		4. Employee recognition and status for work well done.
5. Favorable attitude of the public.		5. Good working conditions.

FIG. 28–1.

fort toward finding satisfactory solutions. The answers might be found, in part, by smoothing out the business cycle, improving management techniques, training more efficient employees, and broadening the educational backgrounds of managers and of labor leaders.

Rights of Management. This is a vital area. Management members desire freedom to meet their responsibilities and resent any restrictions in carrying out functions which they believe essential for performing their job. Traditionally, managers want no restrictions on their right to hire, fire, discipline, and maintain order and efficiency. On the other hand, unions feel that one of their main functions concerns the welfare of their members. They are interested in all matters which involve the employee; conditions of employment, they reason, are of vital concern to them.

Experience shows that the planning and the executing done by managers determines to a significant degree what action the union takes. By and large, unions are opportunistic and operate on a basis of practical consequences. It is possible to include in the contract the principal managerial rights and specify these as managerial functions, but acceptance by the union is a debatable question and depends upon individual circumstances and precedents and the character of the rights. There are some who feel that a policy of specifying managerial functions has a limiting effect, since unions might claim participation in matters not specifically stated. However, this might be handled by an additional statement to the effect that all existing functions now carried out by members of management shall remain functions of members of management.

Recognition of All Interested Parties. It is well to note that there are actually *three, not two,* interested parties in a labor contract: (1) the employees represented by the union, (2) the owners represented by managerial personnel, and (3) the consumers, or general public. The negotiators are usually only the managers and the union representatives, but their agreements should be consistent with the public interest. Disagreements resulting in strikes or shutdowns obviously affect public interest. Likewise, agreements which are contrary to the public interest can be very damaging; their effects, although more subtle, are probably of greater duration than those of disagreements.[5]

Scope and Viewpoint of Labor Relations. Generally speaking the manager's viewpoint of labor relations is of limited scope in comparison with that of unions. Many managers think of management-union co-operation as limited to their particular shop or office, the whole subject being concerned with their employees. In contrast, many unions are typically interested in all employees throughout an entire industry or occupation. They want to maintain their organizational strength and to secure protection from other unions. This explains, for example, the demands for uniformity of wages among similar employees, for the union shop, and for the maintenance of membership clauses.

---

[5] O. Fairweather and L. Shaw, "Minimizing Disputes in Labor Contract Negotiations," *Labor and Contemporary Problems* (Durham, N.C.: Duke University Law School), Spring, 1947, pp. 305 and 328.

Basis for Conducting Collective Bargaining. Most managers would like to operate on the familiar business basis. The process is orderly, and contracts represent agreements satisfactory to both, which in case of violation means redresses enforceable by court action. However, evidence seems to indicate that in some instances unions are not certain that the traditional business code is the best medium. They are driven by a passion for improvement of the employees' lot and, in many respects, believe collective bargaining and the attainment of satisfactory management-union co-operation are more in the nature of a social and political procedure than a business procedure. That is, they feel the relationship of employees to employer is basically different from that of the typical business process.

SUGGESTIONS FOR IMPROVEMENT

There is probably no single course of action that can or should be recommended, but certain approaches seem to be in order. Although somewhat idealistic in their make-up, the following suggestions appear essential and form the basis for realistic progress.

Management members should take the offensive and acquire an enlightened view of their role in collective bargaining. They should find out the real reasons behind the union demands. Management must be active, not passive. It should supply intelligent leadership and play an important part in pioneering in and seeking for improved methods and relationships.

Managers and unions should both strive further to recognize fully the problems of each other. Neither party should ask for concessions which, if granted, jeopardize the existence of the other. Both should seek for something workable, as any other approach leads to strife.

In addition, closer association should be developed among managers, employees, and the unions. Managers should know the employees, employees should know the managers, and both should know the union. They should know each other as fellow human beings working together. A spirit of co-operation and understanding must prevail; for all three are bound together, and they must strive for mutual, not separate, survival.

Both managers and unions should be capable and willing to accept complete responsibilities. Agreements made in good faith should be carried out, and any subsequent adjustments found desirable should be made in accordance with the mutually agreed-upon procedure.

Also, it must be realized that time is required to bring about changes in things. This is especially true with matters pertaining to management-union co-operation. Both parties must allow time for ideas to be absorbed. Improvements do not just happen overnight; they evolve; they take time.

QUESTIONS

1. Do you feel that the extent of office unionization will increase, decrease, or remain about the same? Why?

2. What interpretation and significance do you attach to the statement: "Unions offer an effective vehicle to nonmanagement members for reaching managers about grievances and personal needs."

3. Of the various reasons given in this chapter for the relatively slow growth of office unionism, which one do you believe is probably most important? Why?

4. In your opinion do trade-unions help, hinder, or have no effect upon the actuating efforts of a manager? Elaborate on your answer.

5. What are some important employer unfair labor practices forbidden by the present federal labor law?

6. Discuss the subject "rights of management" with specific reference to its effect upon labor-management relations.

7. In a unionized office should an office employee bring his work problems to his supervisor, the union steward, or a member of the personnel department? Justify your answer.

8. In company "RST" the office employees are nonunion and the factory employees are members of a union. Recently, as a result of collective bargaining, a 4 per cent increase in wages was given factory employees. At the same time a like increase was given office employees.
   a) Do you feel the office employees are justified in accepting this increase?
   b) How can the managers of the company justify the increase to office employees?
   c) Should the office employees join the union?
   Give reasons for your answers.

9. Relate briefly the meaning of each of the following:
   a) Union shop.
   b) Mediation.
   c) "Collective co-operation."
   d) Closed shop.

10. Is the work of the office manager changed by the existence of a union in the office? Explain.

11. Should the present federal labor law be modified so that management members would be required to file annually the same type of pertinent data concerning themselves as is now required of union representatives? Why?

12. What do you believe should be done to resolve the differences of opinion regarding the basis under which collective bargaining is conducted? Elaborate your answer.

CASE PROBLEMS

CASE 28–1. THE CHANDLER MANUFACTURING COMPANY

Hilda Zimmerman worked twenty-two months as a file clerk before being laid off. Her rate of pay was $1.35 an hour. She was soon recalled and given the job of general clerk at a pay rate of $1.15 an hour. About a week later during a lunch recess, Hilda met a friend, Ethel Kessler, who had been working as a clerk in the production planning department of the company. Hilda brought Ethel to the employment manager about a year ago and helped her get the job. During the conversation, Hilda learned that Ethel had been laid off but was recalled two days ago and was now working as a clerk in records retention at $1.25 per hour with a promise of 8 cents increase after six months if her work was satisfactory.

Hilda reported the circumstance as a grievance to her union steward who took the case to the assistant personnel manager who handled such matters. The steward contended that Hilda should be given the records-retention job instead of Ethel because of Hilda's seniority and her desire and capacity to do the work.

The assistant personnel manager denied the requests stating the situation was investigated thoroughly before action was taken. The records of Hilda Zimmerman showed she was rated "fair" in co-operation with others and "poor" in dependability. An interview with the filing supervisor revealed that Hilda seemed to waste time, do a lot of complaining about the work assigned to her, and when informed of her unsatisfactory rating, said she would try to do better, but no improvement was accomplished.

PROBLEMS:

1. What action should the steward take? Why?

2. What action should the company take? Why?

3. Other than pay, what important factors do you feel might be important in this case? Explain.

CASE 28–2. MARION MAYO PRODUCTS COMPANY

The office employees of this company belong to a local union, No. 351, which is affiliated with a large nationally known union. The existing labor contract contains the following clauses dealing with vacations.

Article XI. Vacations

SECTION 1. Employees with two (2) years and less than five (5) years service with the Company shall be entitled to two (2) weeks vacation with pay each calendar year and employees with five (5) or more years service with the company shall be entitled to three (3) weeks vacation with pay each calendar year.

Vacation pay will be computed on the basis of a forty (40) hour week at regular weekly straight time rates.

SECTION 2. Employees who voluntarily quit or who are discharged for just cause shall lose all claim to any vacation with pay.

Employee Myrtle Briggs, an accounting machine operator, in good union standing, has been with the company for three years and five months. To go with friends on a trip to Canada for her vacation, Miss Briggs has decided to take her vacation the first two weeks in July, and so informs her union steward who is making up a vacation list to turn over to the union's office committee for presentation to the office manager.

However, before the list was completed the office manager posted on the bulletin board a vacation listing showing, for each employee, the amount of vacation due and the designated time assigned for the vacation. For Myrtle Briggs, the period given was the last two weeks in August.

Miss Briggs became upset when she saw the listing, complained to her supervisor, and was told the posted listing was official. The schedules were arranged by the office manager and were to be considered final.

Several days later, Miss Briggs asked her supervisor for permission to speak with the office manager regarding her vacation period. The request was granted. The office manager told Miss Briggs that he would like to grant her request but could not for two reasons. First, to make changes would set a bad precedent and open the door for more changes. Second, special care was taken in preparing the list so that the various types of office skills would be available at all times to continue getting out the work. Miss Briggs stated that she had told her steward she wanted the first two weeks in July, and nothing had been said at that time that she could not have it. The office manager replied, "The union has nothing to do with the scheduling of vacations. It is strictly a managerial prerogative."

Upon returning to her department, Miss Briggs related to her steward what had taken place. The steward said she did not see where one employee made that much difference, that vacation schedules were of union interest, and that the matter would be investigated.

Several weeks passed. On the Monday morning beginning the first two weeks in July, Myrtle Briggs did not report for work. Not until two weeks later did she return, stating that she had taken the trip as planned, had had a perfectly wonderful time, and was glad to get back to work.

PROBLEMS:

1. What is your general opinion of employee Myrtle Briggs? Why?
2. What action do you recommend by the office manager? Discuss.

Chapter · 29

Office Supervision

The efficiency of most workers is beyond the control of the management and depends more than has been supposed upon the willingness of men to do their best.

—Sumner H. Slichter

The supervisor is a key figure in the managerial work of actuating. Almost every plan, policy, and decision originated at the top of the organization structure must filter down through the supervisory level. Because of his strategic location both to influence and to implement the many actuating techniques, the supervisor is extremely influential in motivating employees, in training them, in handling cases of tardiness, in promoting safety, and in building teams which carry out specific duties.

Actually the accomplishment of satisfactory office production and the establishing of a favorable work climate depend in large measure upon the quality of office supervision. The supervisor is charged with seeing that the work in his unit is performed within reasonable time and at reasonable cost. Many of the problems and hurdles interfering with getting the office work accomplished involve questions of supervision. Likewise, it is the supervisor who through his knowledge and skill maintains work relationships with employees that stimulate them favorably.

THE SUPERVISOR'S STATUS

The supervisor represents the focal point about which the top managers' wishes are distributed and the operative employees' desires are concentrated. He is the point of contact between management members and nonmanagement members. To many employees the supervisor represents management.

Usually, a supervisor is thought of as being below the executive level. The supervisor's work is similar to that of the executive; but the scope of the work, the matters on which decisions must be made, and the general over-all executive work are not as broad in the case of the supervisor as in the case of the executive. For convenience, a "supervisor" can be defined as *a management member working at an organizational level where personal oversight of tasks assigned to small groups is assumed in order to assure satisfactory performance.*

DUTIES OF THE SUPERVISOR

The supervisor's job is to direct the activities within his group and to develop the employees under him. Fundamentally, this resolves into the ability to get work performed properly by others. This is the heart of supervisory success. A person who insists upon doing everything himself never makes a satisfactory supervisor. Many failures in supervision are in getting things done through people. It is not always the employee's fault, which is the common explanation.

The precise duties of a supervisor differ from one job to another, but in general there are certain universal duties carried out by a supervisor. Probably foremost is that dealing with subordinates. The supervisor is expected to utilize his employees' capacities and interests effectively. He assigns employees definite work, points out certain goals, and gets them to want to perform an accurate and satisfactory volume of work. Various means can be used by the supervisor, depending mainly upon the type of employee, the work situation, and the kind of office work.

Most supervisors are called upon to review and evaluate the work performance of their employees, to answer questions concerning the methods-in-action to accomplish the work, and to instruct and give direction and orders in achieving the work. These duties can be grouped and identified as performing technical matters. The complexity of these technical elements varies considerably among supervisory jobs. Normally supervisors of unskilled or highly routine work require the least technical competence, while those in charge of highly skilled or professional work require the most.

The supervisor's manner of dealing with subordinates and in performing the technical considerations of his job give rise to the supervisor's duty of utilizing effective human relations. Strictly speaking this is not in addition to but rather an integral part of dealing with subordinates and of performing technical matters. The practice of human relations is not performed in isolation by the supervisor but is integrated with his choice of whom to assign the work, what motivating forces to be used, and how best to explain technical situations about the work. The supervisor's duty is to create employee interest in the objectives of his office unit, practice friendliness and fairness, give clear instructions, keep the employee informed of new developments, and express genuine interest in the employee's welfare.

In addition, many supervisors have the duties and devote a sizable portion of their time to improving work methods and training employees. The extent of these activities will depend upon the individual situation. Where highly developed staff units in these areas exist, the need may be relatively small, but even in such cases at least a modicum of method improving and training are a part of the supervisor's job.

THE SUPERVISOR AS MANAGEMENT MEMBER

An office supervisor needs the active backing and support of his superiors. They must feel that supervision is vital in the enterprise and give help and assurance to those at the supervisory levels. The policies and practices established by the top management group should keep the supervisor's situation in mind. Preferably the supervisors should have the opportunity to participate in managerial meetings, to voice their viewpoints, and to be recognized as belonging to the management group. Such action lends emotional support, fosters close co-operation among supervisors, and helps them to gain the feeling of security, of belonging, and of support which are essential to the carrying out of effective supervision.

It is insufficient to give lip service to such a program. Too frequently office supervisors are considered management members by decree alone. Nothing tangible is done to make supervisors a part of management or to make them feel that they are. A recognition of certain factors by top management members is necessary. These include written statements outlining the supervisor's authority and responsibility, adequate compensation, recognition of individual performance, direct two-way flow of management information, and education in the profession of management. These activities, along with other important ones and the tools for achieving them, are shown in graphic form in Figure 29–1.

THE WORK OF THE SUPERVISOR

A variety of ways are possible in which to classify the work of the supervisor. Figure 29–2 is a reprint from a handbook for supervisors of a well-known company. In this illustration the classification of responsibilities of supervisors are divided into six main types, and under each type the important responsibilities are listed. Since the supervisor is a management member, the format of the fundamental func-

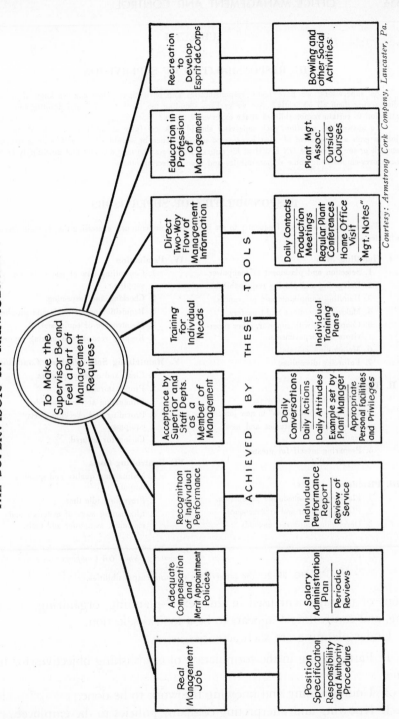

THE SUPERVISOR IN MANAGEMENT

Courtesy: Armstrong Cork Company, Lancaster, Pa.

FIG. 29-1. The supervisor in management.

SUBJECT I

THE RESPONSIBILITIES OF SUPERVISION

As supervisors, we have many responsibilities and obligations. How can we know if we are discharging them all efficiently? Are we perhaps spending too much time on, and devoting too much attention to certain responsibilities at the expense of others?

To answer this question, each supervisor should look carefully at the requirements of his own job to gain a perspective of what is expected of him. Then he should ask himself is he is spending enough or too much time ON EACH of his duties. In this way he may discover that unwittingly he has been over-emphasizing some responsibilities and even neglecting others.

RESPONSIBILITIES OF SUPERVISORS

We must check ourselves frequently to see if we are conscientiously exercising the six main responsibilities which are:

I. Handling Men
1. Selection and placement of manpower.
2. Delegating and placing responsibilities.
3. Handling complaints and grievances.
4. Making promotions and transfers.
5. Cooperating with superior, other supervisors and departments.
6. Maintaining morale.
7. Enforcing discipline.

II. Training
1. Instructing new employees.
2. Instructing "old hands" in new jobs.
3. Developing understudies and new leaders.
4. Preparing myself for greater responsibilities.

III. Planning
1. Planning and scheduling production.
2. Planning layout and arrangements.
3. Developing improved methods.

IV. Production
1. Controlling flow of materials and supplies.
2. Checking and inspecting.
3. Requisitioning materials and supplies.
4. Maintenance of equipment.
5. Keeping records and making reports.

V. Maintaining Safe Working Conditions
1. Clean and orderly quarters.
2. Proper storage.
3. Eliminating accident hazards.
4. Providing and checking safety equipment.
5. Caring for injured.

VI. Controlling Costs
1. Maintaining quality and quantity output.
2. Preventing idle time.
3. Eliminating waste of materials and machines, manpower and tools.

Courtesy: Shell Oil Company, Inc., New York

FIG. 29–2. The supervisor's six main responsibilities.

tions of management used in this text—planning, organizing, actuating, and controlling—appears to be a logical selection.

Under planning are such activities as:

1. Participating in the formulation of establishing objectives for his unit.

2. Understanding and knowing the work to be done.

3. Knowing and interpreting company policies to the employee.

4. Keeping up with new developments.

Organizing efforts by the supervisor include:

1. Delegating work to others.
2. Allocating the work among members of the unit.
3. Placing similar work in the same unit.
4. Establishing proper authority relationships among members of a unit.

The supervisor's managerial actuating efforts deal with:

1. Informing employees of changes.
2. Disciplining the employee.
3. Developing understudies.
4. Securing teamwork and harmony among employees.
5. Increasing the value of the employee.

Controlling encompasses the following work by the supervisor:

1. Following stated practices and procedures.
2. Evaluating work output in terms of cost.
3. Checking accuracy and quantity of work.
4. Minimizing peak work loads.

Further discussion of the supervisor and each of the fundamental functions of management is warranted and is included in the immediate following pages.

THE SUPERVISOR AND PLANNING

Effective supervision requires thorough planning. The successful supervisor has found that planning enables him to gain his goal with a minimum of effort. Planning helps the supervisor to maintain the proper balance in his work; major objectives are given the major portion of his time and effort. Also, planning makes for orderliness in supervision; actions are thought through. Likewise, areas of nonaction are predetermined. The supervisor knows what he is going to do and when he is going to do it.

Failure of the supervisor to plan his work results in inefficiencies and makes the job of supervision more difficult. Frequently the lack of planning results in a failure to meet expectancies or to anticipate and to prevent supervisory problems before they occur. Other indications of lack of planning are tardiness in getting work accomplished, excessive costs, not enough time to finish the work, low morale, lack of direction to the group, waste of material, loss of employees' time, and an absence of over-all co-ordinated effort.

THE SUPERVISOR AND ORGANIZING

In a relatively small enterprise the manager, who in many cases is also the owner, maintains close supervisory relations with each employee. He is in a position to exert a real influence upon the employee's development to meet job requirements, and to keep him informed about changes and progress of the business. But with growth of the company and the resultant spreading of the gap between top management members and nonmanagement members, it is generally agreed that supervisors must narrow the gap and conduct many of the needed managerial relations with employees.

The size and complexity of the enterprise, as well as the viewpoint toward employees, tend to modify the supervisor's organizational status and his authority. Unfortunately in many offices it is not clear what the office supervisor is expected to do. The former concept of the supervisor "running his unit," with complete authority to hire, fire, change work sequence, make improvements, and handle operations in any way believed satisfactory, has changed considerably in many offices. This lack of a clear-cut understanding is due to the very nature of the job—the fact that the work of supervision is so varied, the scope so large, and the activities involved so numerous. However, the transition can be said to have been brought about by the use of staff members to assist and to render advice to the supervisor in carrying out his work. In some cases, it is believed that the work of office supervising has become so complex that expert help to the supervisor is an absolute necessity. In contrast, others are of the opinion that staff helpers usurp authority and take over activities which constitute the fundamental duties of the supervisor. For example, in many offices the supervisor does not interview and select new employees but he does have a voice in the final hiring.

SELECTION OF OFFICE SUPERVISORS

Effective supervision can be said to start with the methods used for supervisory selection. From what has already been discussed, it follows that a supervisor's qualifications are different from those of an operative employee. The employee having the longest service, the highest production volume, or the longest no-tardiness and no-absenteeism record is not necessarily the best selection for a supervisory job. Much of the work the supervisor is called upon to perform differs from that of the operative employee.

The first step in the selection of office supervision is to determine the background and characteristics needed for the supervisory jobs. Such information can be used to set the minimum employment qualifications and standards. Realistic preparation of these data should be followed.

The actual task of selection is assisted by use of any one or all of the following: (1) appraisals of the candidates, (2) written tests, (3) interviews, and (4) evaluation of experience and training. The first, or appraisal of candidates, can take many different forms, including inquiry of the candidate's present superior, talking with those acquainted with the candidate's work performance, and discussing with friends the candidate's activities in clubs and other groups outside the office.

Written tests are increasing in usage, but they probably do not yet qualify as a common means for office supervisory selection. Tests are designed to measure both work, personality, and technical factors. They provide a means to screen initially a large number of candidates, and they stress objective evidence instead of someone's opinion and judgment. However, considerable criticism has been leveled against tests in which it is pointed out that they concentrate on selected areas rather than the "entire man," that some candidates are practically certain not to reveal their true ability by written word, and that the candidates answer test questions for a prescribed situation in one way, yet for the same situation perform in a different way under actual working conditions.

As pointed out in Chapter 25, interviewing is perhaps the most common means of selection, and this statement includes supervisory selection. The face-to-face meeting, the opportunity to clarify ambiguous written statements, and the flexibility to shape it to the individual case make for the wide use and popularity of the interview method.

Finally, the evaluation of experience and training provides a practical element to the selection method followed. A detailed investigation of the candidate's work history is sometimes undertaken. Thus, elements which might be overlooked in the other selection approaches are brought into the program. Knowledge of the enterprise and technical competence are illustrative of these elements.

THE SUPERVISOR AND ACTUATING

As already pointed out, the ability of a supervisor to apply actuating efforts to his employees is a vital portion of his job. At this point, attention is directed to actuating work applied to supervisors by their superiors.

In many respects the training of office supervisors is similar to that discussed in Chapter 26. However, discussion of certain aspects unique to supervisory training warrant review at this time. Top managers are interested in having a comprehensive training program for office supervisors for many reasons, including: improvements in both the quantity and quality of work, better understanding of company policies, effective development of employees, improvement in employee-employer relations, and reductions in labor turnover and operating costs.

Strictly speaking, any educational activity designed to prepare the candidate for supervisory work or to improve the supervisor in carrying out his duties successfully can be termed "supervisory training." The field is quite broad and deals with many, yet related, subjects. Supervisory training is not confined to learning to perform a set of movements more efficiently but includes the development of attitudes, control of emotions, and the broadening of one's views.

To keep the supervisor fully informed constitutes one of the biggest problems in securing effective supervision. Conditions are constantly changing, new developments are taking place, and in most cases, the supervisor finds himself confronted with new personnel, new attitudes, and new problems.

Among the many means of supervisory training are included:

1. *Company supervisory schools* in which organized classes in problems of supervision are studied.

2. *Individual study* of the various available materials on theories and practices of supervisory work.

3. *Conferences and seminars* that afford discussions with supervisors of other departments, group training, and an opportunity to talk over problems of mutual interest.

4. *Dramatized meetings* in which supervisors act out their problems, this acting out to be followed by discussions and comments to bring out possible improvements in the handling of problems.

5. *Observation of and talks with employees* to gain a better insight into their jobs and their attitudes.

6. *Interviews with top management members* to gain advice and suggestions regarding what supervisory action might be taken under various circumstances.

7. *Involvement in an actual situation,* handling the work of supervision on a learn-by-doing technique. Usually some background data are desirable before using this means of obtaining information.

When a series of meetings constitute the supervisory training program, a format something like the following might be followed:

Session	Topic
1.	Introduction to entire course. Preliminary remarks
2.	Management principles and functions
3.	Planning your work
4.	Organizing your work
5.	Actuating others to do the work
6.	Controlling your work
7.	The responsibilities of the supervisor
8.	Gaining desirable attitudes
9.	Developing leadership
10.	Handling orders and instructions
11.	Administering effective discipline
12.	Administering effective discipline
13.	Job analysis and evaluation
14.	Job analysis and evaluation
15.	Merit rating
16.	Merit rating
17.	Controlling costs
18.	Controlling costs
19.	Examination
20.	Review

TRAINING WITHIN INDUSTRY FOUNDATION

Excellent work in supervisory training is being accomplished by the members of the Training Within Industry Foundation, a nonprofit organization which advocates gaining maximum results from employed people through better supervision. Years of intensive research and many office tryouts with groups of supervisors have helped develop highly successful training programs for supervisors. Among the more important for normal office use are:

1. *Job Instruction.* The "JI" course consists of five 2-hour sessions and is intended to give skill in instructing. It is especially helpful where there is work involving long break-in periods, numerous errors, or difficulty in getting the office work out on time. To illustrate the content, the course consists of four main parts: (1) preparing the employee, (2) presenting the operation, (3) trying out the performance, and (4) following up on performance.

2. *Job Relations.* Known as the "JR" course, this also consists of five 2-hour sessions. It helps provide skill in leadership and is recommended where there are too many misunderstandings among employees and complaints are numerous in the human relations area.

3. *Job Methods.* This "JM" program likewise is five 2-hour sessions. It gives skill in improving methods through practice sessions and on-the-job coaching. This program is effective in finding better methods of accomplishing office work.

4. *Job Economics Training.* Known as the "JET" course, this requires five 1½-hour sessions and provides the basic principles upon which the American economy operates.

5. *Discussion Leading.* This "DL" course of four 3-hour sessions is designed to give skill in getting participation in meetings and in discussing thoroughly matters of common interest.

6. *Program Development.* The "PD" course is intended for the instruction of one person in a company who has responsibility for designing and conducting training programs in his company or some unit thereof. The normal time required for this course is 5 days, dispersed among 2 or 3 weeks, to permit specific application of program material to the trainee's company.

THE SUPERVISOR AND CONTROLLING

Controlling of the supervisor's efforts is needed to assure that a proper balance is maintained among the various facets of the supervisory work. An equitable appraisal of all the integrated parts must be made and compared with established levels of satisfactory performance.

Data on important factors such as cost, quantity of work achieved, quality of work, number of grievances, number tardy, number absent, and labor turnover rates are illustrative. Trends in these data are significant. Also changes in some factors may help predict future changes in others—frequently before either the difficulty or favorable accomplishment is revealed by standard operating reports.

DECISION MAKING AND LEADERSHIP IN SUPERVISION

From what has been stated it follows that the supervisor should possess decision-making and leadership qualities. The office supervisor must be able to reach decisions in the light of major objectives, policies, and facts in a given case. It is axiomatic that decisions should be based on facts, not guesses. However, it is not always possible to get all the facts, and in such instances the available facts plus judgment must serve as the basis for the decisions. It is usually best to make decisions as close to the organizational point of action as possible. This means that when supervisors have adequate information, they should make decisions at their work level. However, if they do not have complete information, the question should be referred to the next higher level in the organization for decision.

Confidence, enthusiasm, and willing co-operation are gained through leadership. The differences among individuals are recognized and utilized, teamwork is fostered, and the development of individual employees is promoted. The most appropriate means to utilize will vary with the particular circumstances, but, in general, effective techniques include keeping all members of a group informed, answering all questions forthrightly, offering constructive criticism, listening to the employee's "side of the story," and giving assistance in thinking out a satisfactory means for overcoming areas of weakness. Evidence shows that high-producing office groups are those in which emphasis is placed upon the employee, not the product as such; general rather than close supervision is practiced; and most of the supervisor's time is spent in supervising and practicing effective leadership.[1]

NEEDS OF THE SUPERVISOR

A particularly helpful listing of the needs of the supervisor indicates five basic needs. Two of these concern *what he must know*. Their exact content varies from one office to another, depending upon the nature of the office and its work. The other three basic needs concern what the supervisor *must be able to do*. These are fairly constant regardless of the office and its type of work.

The five basic needs are:[2]

1. *Knowledge of the Work.* Knowledge of materials, office forms, equipment, routines, and manner in which results are used are included in this need. Much of this knowledge might be acquired while one is serving in a nonsupervisory capacity. The supervisor should know enough about the detail work that is done to provide the necessary leadership to those performing the tasks and to plan and organize their work so that orderly and reasonable rates of accomplishment are realized.

2. *Knowledge of Responsibilities.* This includes comprehension of the company's policies, rules, and regulations, of the extent of the supervisor's authority and responsibility, and of matters on which he can make final decisions. An acquaintance with basic information about organization, management, collective bargaining, communication, budgeting, and any area of direct or indirect concern in the particular supervisory job appears to be a minimum requirement.

3. *Skill of Instructing.* Whether a supervisor gives specific instructions on a particular task or makes assignments in fairly broad terms, it is necessary that he pass along his knowledge to others. This, in turn, calls for skill in instructing and is a prime means for making supervision more effective. Generally, an employee is more satisfied, has

---

[1] Daniel Katz, Nathan Maccoby, and Nancy Morse, "Productivity, Supervision, and Morale in an Office Situation," Part I (Ann Arbor: Survey Research Center, University of Michigan), December, 1950, pp. 62–63.

[2] The five points have been adapted from *A Program for Supervisors in the Federal Service,* Supervision Improvement Program (Washington, D.C.: U.S. Civil Service Commission), August, 1944, p. 2.

greater interest, and will be more industrious when informed clearly what work is wanted and how it is to be performed. This means that the supervisor should have skill in instructing, so that a well-trained work force is available.

4. *Skill of Improving Methods.* Better utilization of materials, machines, and manpower is the constant aim of progressive managers. Some methods of performing work are inherited; others are hastily thrown together; while still others are copied from similar operations. All can be improved. Skill in analyzing, supplemented by ingenuity, usually results in improved ways of performing work.

5. *Skill of Working with People.* This sometimes suffers as a result of the pressure and volume of day-to-day work. Working with and getting along with people are vital to the supervisor. This emphasizes the important areas of understanding the behavior and attitudes of individual employees and of recognizing basic human motivations.

SECURING EFFECTIVE SUPERVISION

Much material is available concerning how to be an efficient supervisor. Some of it is quite idealistic and contains many platitudes. The subject is broad, but the following ten points are included in order to indicate, in general, the type of activity which is recommended.

1. *Treat all workers alike—show no favoritism.* The successful supervisor operates objectively; his personal likes and dislikes are not permitted to influence his work.

2. *Practice consultative supervision.* This practice includes talking things over with the employees and giving them an opportunity to suggest the best way to accomplish a task. Such a procedure makes for a co-operative work force and recognizes the fact that no one has a monopoly on good ideas.

3. *Enforce all rules and regulations promptly.* Usually nothing is gained by delaying action in cases where violations are involved. In fact, delay might be interpreted as a lack of decisiveness and an inability to cope with the situation.

4. *Keep your instructions simple and repeat them frequently to the new employee.* Good supervision requires mutual understanding between the supervisor and the employee. In addition, a patient, helpful attitude must be assumed, particularly in working with the employee who is not yet fully familiar with all the job requirements.

5. *Insist upon and stress the need for each employee to give a full day's work for a full day's pay.* Satisfactory work outputs are the chief responsibility of every supervisor.

6. *Watch waste—material loss and time loss.* One of the chief foes of efficiency is waste. Guarding against this enemy will add significantly to the work output.

7. *Keep fully informed on company policies and their interpretations.* The supervisor is constantly called upon to interpret company policies to the employees. Knowing the policies and keeping informed of any changes and additions is a supervisory "must."

8. *Secure employees' opinions regarding supervision.* Through some means, such as attitude surveys, spot interviews, casual conversations, and discussion groups, find out what is bothering the employees and what "gripes" are developing. Adequate and correct information at the right time and place may avoid much needless trouble.

9. *Develop capable assistants.* Good management requires that qualified replacements be available to maintain the supervisory force at a satisfactory number and caliber. Failure to develop an understudy jeopardizes the supervisor's chances for promotion.

10. *Let top management members know what you are doing and why.* Because supervision is vital to the enterprise, top management members should know what supervisory action is taking place. Effective supervision requires complete backing by these members, and one of the best ways to retain this endorsement is to tell them what is going on, along with the various reasons why.

QUESTIONS

1. Does the fact that to many employees the supervisor represents management make the supervisor a manager? Why?
2. What is your concept of an office supervisor's duties?
3. What difference does it make in an office whether supervisors are considered members of management? Justify your answer.
4. Discuss some personal attributes that appear to be closely related with supervisory success.
5. Justify your viewpoint toward this quotation: "With more and more specialists and expert staff people being used in the modern office organization structure, the importance and status of the office supervisor has decreased. She is not as important as formerly. In many cases she decides virtually nothing, her superiors telling her what to do."
6. Mention some activities an office supervisor performs in the area of organizing. Of controlling.
7. An office supervisor tells you he is refraining from developing an understudy because he feels that success in such an undertaking will mean the loss of his (the supervisor's) job. As office manager, how would you cope with this situation? Explain.

8. Referring to Figure 29–1, what Training Within Industry Foundation courses might be used to improve the supervisor's ability to discharge each of the six responsibilities of supervisors listed?

9. The eleven office supervisors of Zoreb Manufacturing Company have just completed a supervisory course of twenty meetings similar to the listing shown in this chapter (p. 561). You as a management trainee are requested to formulate a follow-up course to consist of twelve meetings, each 1½ hours in length. List the topics and indicate the means of training you would recommend. Justify your program giving reasons for your selections.

10. Draw up a program for the recruitment and selection of office supervisors for a large office. Assume candidates will be recruited from both within and outside the enterprise.

11. As an office manager, what practical recommendations would you make to assure more efficient supervisory services? Explain.

12. Do you feel that the selection of supervisors is basically any different from that of nonsupervisory members? Should it be? Why?

CASE PROBLEMS

CASE 29–1.   STRAYER MANUFACTURING COMPANY

Herman Ellinger, supervisor of the accounting department, has turned in his resignation, with regret, in order to become a member of a public accounting firm in which he is promised an ownership interest. His assistant, Arvid Juhl, age sixty-one, has been offered the supervisor's job, but he has rejected it explaining that he does not wish to take on this responsibility at his age and honestly feels it should be given to someone else. Several attempts to persuade Juhl to change his mind and accept the promotion have failed.

The accounting department consists of sixteen employees exclusive of the supervisor and the assistant. Of these sixteen employees, ten are women. The oldest, from the viewpoint of company service, is Mary Ann Gebhardt, age fifty-two, who has been with the company twenty-eight years. She is well thought of, an excellent worker, accurate, and dependable. The second oldest from the employment standpoint is Hazel Sims, having been a company employee for twenty-four years. She is forty-nine, quiet, reserved, has little to say, works steady, and accomplishes much work.

Henry Crawford, age thirty-seven, has seventeen years of company service, the longest of any male employee in the accounting department. He completed two years of college before joining the company and for the past seven years has been attending evening university classes and expects to receive his degree with a major in accounting a year from next June. He is ambitious and is for one Henry Crawford, first and last. Close associates say he is rather blunt in his conversations and expects things to be done immediately. Crawford does not get along too well with Arvid Juhl. From the viewpoint of age, John Donner is the oldest, being forty-four. He joined the company in 1948, is a satisfactory accounting department employee, but in the opinion of Mr. Ellinger, should not be appointed the new supervisor.

The president of the company has stated informally that perhaps a new man should be brought in from the outside. However, the president indicates he is not fully familiar with the situation and has no definite opinion or suggested decision concerning it.

PROBLEMS:

1. What is the major problem in this case? The minor problems?

2. Discuss your recommended action to resolve the company's major problem as you see it.

3. What person or persons (title or titles) should probably carry out your recommended action? Explain.

CASE 29–2. STABILITY NATIONAL BANK

An operator of one of the proofing machines in the central proof section is Gladys Swasey. She is twenty-four years of age, married, competent, and a steady worker. Satisfactory operators for this type of work appear to be scarce.

For the past two weeks, Gladys Swasey has been coming in late. The records show that she has been twelve to fifteen minutes tardy every morning.

The supervisor of the section calls her to his desk and has a talk with her about the tardiness. She says she is sorry, but the reason is that her husband's starting time has been changed and it is difficult to get him to start early enough to get her to work on time. In addition, one morning last week they had trouble getting the car started, although they were ready to go in ample time for her to reach the bank on time.

The following morning, Gladys Swasey arrives on time, and the same is true for the remaining two mornings of the week. However, the following week she arrives five minutes late on Monday, eight minutes late on Tuesday, and fifteen minutes late on Wednesday and Thursday. It is now Friday morning, and Gladys Swasey has just entered the office. She is fifteen minutes late.

PROBLEMS:

1. Enumerate the major actions which might be taken to correct this situation. Discuss.

2. What action do you recommend that the supervisor take? Why?

Chapter · 30

Developing Office Executives

Many persons wonder why they don't amount to more than they do, have good stuff in them, energetic, persevering and have ample opportunities. It is all a case of trimming the useless branches and throwing the whole force of power into the development of something that counts.

—W. J. JOHNSTON

WITH REVOLUTIONARY changes and developments taking place in the office, there is a constant, pressing need for executive leaders capable of handling the complex affairs of today's modern office and to insure the continuity of good office management. Executive ability is in great demand. What most enterprises need, especially in the office, is a steady stream of creative personnel with broad knowledge, down-to-earth practicality, a deep understanding of human motivations, a capacity for independent thinking, and an ability for identifying and solving problems.

OVER-ALL QUALIFICATIONS

Interestingly, there is no universal agreement regarding what general qualities constitute the basis for executive success. Apparently there are many factors, and these vary depending upon the particular circumstances. However, it appears that the requirement is less on filling the human mind with facts and more on developing the ability to think clearly and systematically, to exercise judgment, and to make decisions involving almost limitless numbers of considerations.

The office executive becomes more of a generalist, not a specialist, as he advances to a top-flight position. Actually he cannot function effectively in a top management position if the essence of what he brings and does to it is his specialty. The inherent nature of the fundamental functions of management make this so.

TECHNICAL SKILL

From what is known, although admittedly probably incomplete, it appears that three basic skills are common to most successful executives. Included are skills in technical, visualization, and human relations. Under technical skill are included such things as effective application of one's knowledge of specific techniques in record keeping, office practices, office layout, and the like. Essentially, technical skill deals with tangible operations and is the most common type of skill possessed. It is probably most important for lower executive level tasks. The belief is now quite prevalent that the management member whose main skill is technical and who possesses only a minimum competence in visualization and human relations skills may not be able to advance above the lower level of supervision.

SKILL IN VISUALIZATION

This skill deals with the capacity to picture mentally the managerial operations, to envision their relations, to exercise creativeness, and to evolve means for accomplishing definite goals. Visualization skill is not visionary. In contrast, it is highly practical. But it involves intangibles, it includes perception of the management process, and it implies possession of an all-inclusive conceptual viewpoint and understanding about all the elements through which the major tasks will be accomplished.

Visualization skill is especially important for the office executive. Many times the office job setup encourages the employee to think in terms of details. If the person keeping the records is also made responsible for seeing to it that action is taken on them, he will usually develop his visualization skill. He releases himself from the idea that something useful is being supplied by simply compiling a mass of data and acquires the basic concept of reasons why the records are kept and how best they can be utilized and by whom.

SKILL IN HUMAN RELATIONS

Since the executive achieves goals through the efforts of others, it follows that skill in human relations is essential to executive ability and growth. Much of the discussion in this section of the book deals with this topic, but for emphasis it can be repeated that skill in human relations deals with manager-nonmanager relationships, the general attitude toward people, the evaluating of human motivations, and the winning of loyalty, support, and willing co-operation.

DEVELOPING EXECUTIVE SKILLS

Most efforts designed to develop executives concentrate upon improvement in skills of visualization and of human relations. In part, this is probably due to the fact that most executive candidates acquire technical skill as a necessary ingredient to gain and retain employment. The immediate need for the other skills is not quite so evident, and relatively speaking they are newer fields of endeavor.

The discussion here will be limited to four common means of developing executive skills. The first is *coaching*. This means is personalized, flexible, practical, and effective. It provides on-the-job experience plus guidance from experienced minds. The second means is the *understudy method*. The executive trainee works as an assistant or helper to an executive and thus acquires familiarity with the work and practices of his superior. As the need arises, informal interviews are held between the executive and the trainee. Experience with executive-in-action events is gained, and acquaintance with the atmosphere and position in which the trainee will eventually perform are acquired. However, on major problems the trainee should be required to submit complete data affecting the issue along with his recommendations for action. In this way, thinking is stimulated and the accepting of responsibility is encouraged.

Job rotation is a third method of executive development. The rotating of executive trainees among different organizational units on a "merry-go-round" basis provides the trainees with over-all knowledge of the enterprise, the work done by each unit, and the opportunity to participate in the affairs of the various units. This method assists the individual to think in terms of universal managerial principles rather than in the immediate activities at hand. Fourth and last is the *conference method*. An exchange of opinions and ideas among the trainees is the heart of the conference method. A group leader asks provocative questions and maintains order. Available written cases or descriptions of situations within the enterprise are used to point up the discussions. The trainees are encouraged to express themselves freely. No approved solution or "this is the way to think about it" material is furnished. Listening, participating, expressing one's thoughts, developing teamwork, broadening of viewpoints, and developing tolerance are among the objectives of this method. The size of the group is normally limited to about twenty participants who are seated around a conference table with the conference leader located at one end.

EXECUTIVE'S UTILIZATION OF TIME

An important consideration in the potentiality and effectiveness of an executive is the utilization of his time. Mastery of the fundamental skills is insufficient, wise use of time on the job is also required. Some office executives complain about the lack of time to do all that is expected of them, but the president of the respective companies hasn't any more time yet accomplishes much more. Why is this? In part, because of better time utilization.

One of the best ways for an executive to utilize his time effectively is to practice delegation. This was discussed in Chapter 21 under the managerial function of organizing. Delegating work to subordinates and controlling their performance are key considerations in executive success. When an executive tries to do all the work himself, he indicates a lack of understanding and applying management.

To make their time more useful, successful executives concentrate on essentials—the really important tasks. They perform key tasks only and do not let themselves get involved in endless details. Thinking is directed along the broader concepts, not to narrow defined limits. And unnecessary work is quickly identified as such and abolished.

The common office slogan "Do it now" can be overdone, but it has virture in that it seeks to eliminate the practice of delay. For most people, including executives, the completion of a task once it is started makes for efficient time utilization. Tasks not quite finished are the vexation of many executives. Using adequate management, staying with a job until it is finished, and not giving in to interruptions are key habits to be followed.

The budgeting of one's time is also a timesaver. The time-minded executive decides what tasks he has to perform, estimates the time for each, and schedules these time periods through his workday. This approach helps utilize time more effectively and establishes goals that are achieved during the day, thus providing a sense of satisfaction to the executive.

The last suggestion is to acquire speed in reading and become more selective in what is read. Few adults receive reading training beyond the elementary school level. Many executives read at this pace, which is a serious detriment to their efficiency of time utilization. Data based on accelerated reading courses indicate an average increase of about 75 per cent in the reading efficiency of their members. When such increases can be achieved, the executive can utilize his time more effectively.

GAINING TOP MANAGEMENT ENTHUSIASTIC SUPPORT FOR OFFICE MANAGEMENT

The remainder of this chapter will be devoted to the important subject of gaining the enthusiastic support of top managers for office management. In the final analysis, the failure of an office manager to realize the zenith of his job possibilities is due, in most cases, to an inability to show, and to convince, top management members of the vital nature of office management work.

BEING SOLD COMPLETELY ON THE IMPORTANCE OF OFFICE MANAGEMENT

First, and above all else, the office manager must be sold completely on the essentiality of office services. He must be convinced in his own mind that the office is a vital part of the organization structure and that the managing of the office work is fundamental to the success of the enterprise. The following is appropriate on this point: "In selling an idea to the top executive, you must first be sold yourself. That is axiomatic. I believe you all know that. You must have a knowledge of the details. You must be in a position to answer questions. You must anticipate questions before you present any new idea to the top executive. You should know what he is going to ask. Don't go up with half finished reports."[1]

Furthermore, the office manager must be confident. He must believe intently and feel very strongly that top management members can be convinced. He must also realize completely the importance of office management. His attitude must be one of enthusiasm and positive assurance that office work is a cardinal activity in every enterprise and that the management of these clerical activities is one of the key forces in successful operation.

RECOGNIZING TOP MANAGEMENT MEMBERS' VIEWPOINTS

In order to get other people to believe and to think as you want them to, it is usually helpful to find out first something about their characteristics, such as their interests, activities, problems, desires, and attitudes. With this information as a background, an intelligent approach can be made. Appeals can be focused on what are probably the most responsive factors, that is, those lines having greatest interest to

---

[1] Wilbur F. Lawson, "How to Sell Office Management to the Top Executive," *Annual Conference Proceedings, National Office Management Association, 1941* (Philadelphia), p. 7.

the top manager. It resolves into *not* what the office executive wants to do but what the enterprise needs to have done.

Effective Basic Appeals. The appeals and aims based on top executives' characteristics are numerous and vary with the type of personnel and enterprise. However, among the most desired aims which top managers are usually interested in achieving for the enterprise are: improved service, lower costs of operation, and increased net income.

With a little imagination, the office manager usually can show very easily how his proposal will improve service. Since all office work is a service function to the enterprise, it follows that service is one appeal that the office manager can and should use in practically all his efforts. Service is the one thing he has to offer.

When stressing reduced costs of operation, it is always well to point out the benefits and to show their relationship to the current costs of operation. Care should also be taken to include the initial cost of making the change and to explain how this is absorbed and how much time this will take after the proposal is adopted.

The use of sales psychology is effective in expressing the savings. As a general rule, the amount should not be given in terms of dollars as such, since statements of this sort frequently do not have a motivating spark. A more effective way is to express the savings as the net income on a certain size of order. To illustrate, merely stating, "The savings to be realized are $6,300 per year," is not nearly as effective as the statement, "The savings to be realized from this proposal are greater than the net income realized on an order of $95,000." Both statements mean the same thing, but the second one is much more effective. Along this line of thought it is helpful to keep in mind that annual sales of approximately $50,000 are required to support the labor costs of one clerk.

When lower cost of operation and savings are stressed, it is well to suggest a means for checking or verifying the effectiveness of the proposal. Top executives typically want proof. Explain how the indicated results can be substantiated, who would be responsible for this work, and approximately what it will cost.

The amount of net income can be influenced by the activities of the office manager. Usually office work affects net income by any or all of the following: (1) reduction in office expenses; (2) elimination of office waste, including that of material, equipment, space, and human energy; (3) use of more efficient office machines and equipment; (4) increase in office employees' productivity; and (5) redesign of office forms and procedures.

Other Major Considerations. The general attitudes of top management members must also be considered in any attempt to recognize their viewpoints. Of necessity, they are concerned with over-all operations; they must retain a perspective of all activities. The office manager should keep this in mind and, if possible, always indicate the advantages to all parts of the organization structure in any plan submitted. In other words, the office manager should show not only how just one unit is benefited, the office, for example, but also how others, such as purchasing, production control, sales, and personnel, are helped.

Presentations of single, isolated ideas are unlikely to win approval by top executives. The proposal should be related to something already recognized, and preferably should be beneficial to a maximum number of persons or activities of the enterprise.

The office manager should also recognize that there is a certain amount of human resistance to almost anything new. Many people favor a *status-quo* policy—a sort of "do-not-disturb-things, let-them-be-as-they-are" attitude. Especially is this true if there are no complaints and things are running quite smoothly. The feeling is: "Why take a chance? Let well enough alone." Being human, some members of top management have this complacent attitude; however, the possibility of this condition's existing in any particular case should be realized and taken into account by the office executives.

KEEPING CONSTANTLY PREPARED

To sell top management members, the office executive must: (1) keep himself in such a position that he can act at the opportune time, and (2) know what to do when that time arises. Both concepts must be kept in mind by the office executive if he hopes to succeed in gaining top managers' acceptance and support.

Act at the Opportune Time. The office manager should use his time for managing, not for executing the actual clerical work. He should give himself time for the constructive and creative aspects of his job. He must think ahead, give direction, and motivate the entire office work force. The details and technical aspects should be delegated to staff members.

Furthermore, the office manager should mingle with members of the management field. Since office work affects all phases of an enterprise, it is important that the office manager attend, within the enterprise, the committee and other group meetings at which discussions and decisions regarding policies take place. Whenever possible, he should participate and bring out the consideration for and the importance of the office work. Membership in the various management associations is also recommended. Contacts with management people help to give the office executive the management viewpoint as well as to keep him abreast of developments in the field.

In addition, the office manager must recognize that *there is a proper time for the presentation of every idea or plan submitted to top management members.* Usually this is when they are in a receptive mood and are open to, or even request, suggestions regarding the particular subject at hand. To force any plan upon top managers might mean rejection and complete defeat of the whole idea. Sometimes it is well to draw up an entire plan, to *file it away,* and to let it stay filed away until the proper time, as determined mainly by top managers, arrives.

Know What to Do. Equally important to the factor of being free to act at the opportune time is knowing what to do when the proper time arrives. First, the office manager should avail himself of the many ideas found in management literature, including books, magazines, company papers, and special bulletins. *But he must have more than the idea; he must also know how to employ the idea effectively in his office.* This is the important thing, and it requires study, imagination, and a thorough thinking through of the idea.

Second, the office manager should use research. He should find out, through scientific methods, for example, what improvements can be made; and he should know the wishes of the employees. Facts, not opinions, should be sought; and upon these facts his suggestions and recommendations to top management members should be based.

Third, the office manager must maintain adequate records of all office activities so that he can speak correctly about what his segment of the organization is doing. In short, he should know what services he is providing. It is well to write these data in an easily readable and attractive style, so that it is possible to inform top managers quickly and precisely of the activities of the office. Having data in black and white will also help to dispel, for example, the erroneous notion that frequently exists that certain office jobs are being done by the personnel or sales units when in reality the office unit is performing the functions and is being charged with the costs.

FORMULATING A PLAN

The best technique is to submit a plan, request approval, and give reasons why it should be adopted. This approach is vastly superior to that of advising a top manager that a problem exists and asking what should be done about it.

Remember that, all things considered, the advantage lies on the side that takes the initiative. An army with unrivaled offensive power is usually the victor; a basketball team with a terrific offense is extremely difficult to defeat. Games are usually not won by the team which can't score. Using this as an analogy, when an office manager submits a plan to top managers and asks for approval, he is taking the initiative. When he does this, his chances for successfully selling top executives are much greater than when he waits to be told what to do or adopts a policy of guarding or of constantly defending his past actions.

One more thing to remember in formulating a plan is to select the work which offers the greatest possibilities for improvement. Make the whole plan worth while. Top executives usually like to deal with issues of major significance. They expect issues of a minor sort to be handled by the persons to whom authority has been delegated.

Very frequently it helps to review past recommendations that have been accepted by top management members. In this way some insight is gained into what types of subjects are most likely to be viewed favorably. Similar programs used by other enterprises, and the results obtained, are also helpful. They permit a comparison, which is usually an effective persuasion device. In the case of new ventures, case histories are of especially great assistance, for they demonstrate what others have done and give assurance to the recipient of the suggested program.

SELLING EMPLOYEES FIRST

The office manager might first try to sell his proposition to top management members and, after gaining their acceptance, tell the employees the "what and how" of the plan. However, the reverse of this procedure is usually better. Sell the employees first. Top executives will probably talk with the employees before any decision is reached, and it is well to have the employees "for" the plan. Care should be taken to avoid any coercion of top management members or any impression of ideas are being put in the employees' heads which are fundamentally not in keeping with the top executives' thinking. The office manager should condition his plan to the point where he is reasonably certain it will be accepted when top members of management give the "go ahead" signal.

Among the effective appeals to employees are: an easier way to do the job, improved working conditions, fewer chances for making errors, opportunity to gain job security, increase in earnings, and opportunity for advancement. These are the types of things in which the employee is most interested.

Finally, the office manager must carefully organize and think through his selling program to the employees. It must be factually complete and logical in its development, yet include emotional appeal. Possible objections of employees should be anticipated, and the ways of overcoming and answering them should be worked out *before* the program is launched.

SELLING TOP MANAGEMENT MEMBERS

If the office manager has adequately prepared his case by following, with some degree of proficiency, the steps already discussed, he will find that the work of actually selling top management members is not particularly difficult. Probably 90 per cent of the job is preparation; the remaining 10 per cent is the actual sales effort. These three considerations merit top priority: (1) use dramatic presentations, (2) employ top management language, and (3) give due regard to top managers' individual attitudes.

Office management is intangible; hence, for others to gain a concept of it, dramatization or striking expressive action should be used. Present losses can be portrayed, for example, in a chart showing dollar bills burning or showing a silent partner marked "Inefficiency" or "Waste" at the side of each employee, or some such idea. Top managers will grasp and understand these dramatic effects. The unusual is remembered. In addition, all material should be drawn up in an interesting, readable style. The format should be attractive, and a little color and art work usually are well worth the cost and effort.

The second consideration, employing top management language, is also important. Special office management jargon frequently confuses and seldom convinces. Special terms, operations, and identities of the office may be commonplace to those in office work but not to the members of top management. It is also best not to bring in special or unusual analyses and detailed data, as they slow up the advance. The best procedure is to have the data available but to produce them only when requested or when they will aid in answering a specific question which has been asked.

The final suggestion concerns giving due regard to any "sacred cow" of top managers. Quite often certain subjects, activities, or beliefs hold a particular meaning or fondness for top executives, and the office manager will do well not to trespass on these ideas. Normally this offers no hardship, for he can usually shape his presentation exclusive of these particular notions.

In conclusion, the office manager can promote his profession tremendously through careful and diligent application of proven techniques. Knowing the technical aspects of his job are important but not sufficient. He should also know how to present ideas to members of top management and motivate them to act in the manner he desires. Development of this ability plus the accelerating growth in all clerical activities destine office management to become of increasing importance in the future.

QUESTIONS

1. Discuss several means for developing visualization skill in an office executive trainee.
2. Explain why a specialist advanced to a top management job must bring more than his specialty to it.
3. The statement has been made by some practicing office managers that the professionalization of office managers is the best way to promote the field of office management. Do you agree with this viewpoint? Explain.
4. Discuss specific practices an office executive can follow in order to utilize his time effectively.
5. Is there any difference in meaning between selling and actuating top management members? Office nonmanagement members? Explain your answers.
6. How effective do you feel the conference method is for training office executives? Elaborate on your answer.
7. "The advantage usually lies on the side taking the initiative." Explain, citing examples from your own experience.
8. In each of the following cases, give an example of how an office manager might use dramatization in his efforts to gain support of top executives:
   a) The need for additional office space.
   b) The purchase of three new accounting machines.
   c) The elimination of private secretaries for top executives.
   d) The giving of pay increases to all office employees.
9. Suppose an office manager always focuses his efforts on the wants of top management members. List and discuss the advantages and the disadvantages to the office manager of such an approach.
10. In making a presentation dealing with office work and its management to top managers, what in your opinion are the best approaches to use? Give reasons for your answers.
11. Elaborate on the statement: "There is a proper time for the presentation of every idea submitted to top management members."
12. Does the fact that office work is a service function increase or decrease the importance of gaining recognition of top management members by the office manager?

CASE PROBLEMS

CASE 30–1.   REILLY MANUFACTURING COMPANY

Two weeks ago, office manager Bernard Zwick sent a report to the president pointing out the importance of paper work and the need to purchase six office machines and to hire more clerks. The report was neatly typed, well organized, and totaled about seventy-five double-spaced typewritten pages. As yet, Mr. Zwick has received no answer. He made an appointment with the president for the following day. Entering the president's office, this conversation took place:

MR. ZWICK: Hello, Mr. Copeland. How are you?

MR. COPELAND: Hello, Mr. Zwick. Won't you be seated?

MR. ZWICK: Thanks. Mr. Copeland, I know you're a busy man and I won't take much of your time. I want to talk with you about the report I sent you. What did you think of it?

MR. COPELAND: Well, frankly I haven't read it yet. What's the gist of it?

MR. ZWICK: I'm trying to improve our office so we can give better service.

MR. COPELAND: I see. You're doing an excellent job of managing the office, Mr. Zwick. I have heard no complaints. Things seem to be moving along very well. You mentioned better service. What did you have in mind?

MR. ZWICK: Well, I thought an analysis of our sales might be helpful.

MR. COPELAND: Did you speak with Jim Wells (sales manager) about this?

MR. ZWICK: No, sir. I noticed that some of our old customers we used to bill are no longer buying. Perhaps a list of such accounts would prove helpful.

MR. COPELAND: Who are some of them?

The secretary enters the office, interrupting the conversion, and says, "A Mr. Byron McGovern is here to see you regarding the new stock issue."

MR. COPELAND: Oh, yes. Thanks. Tell him I'll see him in a few minutes. . . . Will you excuse me, Mr. Zwick? It is quite urgent that I see Mr. McGovern.

PROBLEMS:

1. What is the problem facing Mr. Zwick?
2. What should he do about it? Discuss fully.

CASE 30–2. GULF GROCERY WHOLESALE COMPANY

Total management personnel from the supervisory level up is eighty-seven men and women. Main organization units include office, purchasing, personnel, order-handling, stock, and delivery. The company's executive committee wishes to initiate a formal executive development program. Business is expected to increase on the average of 7 per cent per year for the next decade. The company operates in six states and sells grocery items to over 1,400 retail grocery outlets.

PROBLEMS:

1. Outline the general features of your recommended program, noting the probable schedule of events.
2. Will any special development training be given office management personnel? Why?

machines and to his more clerks. The report was neatly typed, well organized and spaced about seventy-five double-spaced typewritten pages. As yet, Mr. Zwick has received no answer. He made an appointment with the president for the following day. Concluding the president's office, this conversation took place:

Mr. Zwick: Hello, Mr. Copeland. How are you?

Mr. Copeland: Hello, Mr. Zwick. Won't you be seated.

Mr. Zwick: Thanks, Mr. Copeland. I know you're a busy man and I won't take much of your time. I want to talk with you about the results of your work. What did you think of it?

Mr. Copeland: Well, frankly I haven't read it yet. What's the gist of it?

Mr. Zwick: I'm trying to improve our office so we can give better service.

Mr. Copeland: I see. You're doing an excellent job of managing the office.

Mr. Zwick: I have heard no complaints. Things seem to be moving along very well. You mentioned better service. What did you have in mind?

Mr. Zwick: Well, I thought ... [illegible] ...

Mr. Copeland: ... [illegible] ...

Mr. Zwick: Simply I suggest ... [illegible] ...

Mr. Copeland: Why not some of them?

[Here, someone enters the office, interrupting the conversation and asks Mr. Copeland ... [illegible] regarding the new work.]

Mr. Copeland: Yes, thank you. Tell him I'll see him in a few minutes.

Well, as I was saying, Mr. Zwick, it is quite obvious ... [illegible] Mr. Manager.

Problems:

1. What is the problem here, Mr. Zwick?
2. What should be done to correct this?

CASE No. — . SELF-SERVICE WHOLESALE GROCERY

Food management personnel from the [illegible] have investigated several other systems. In an association using indoor open, self-service cash-and-carry, order-handling stock, and delivery. Ed company's executives conducted a survey to initiate a formal executive development program. Increase in payroll or increase on the average of [illegible] cent per year for five years. The wholesale operations in six states and sells grocery items in over 1,400 retail grocery outlets.

Problems:

1. Outline the general features of your recommended program, using the probable schedule of events.
2. Will any special development training be given? State what manufacturer procedures will apply.

PART VI......

Controlling the Work of the Office

Controlling, a fundamental function of office management, con-
sists of determining what is being accomplished, evaluating it,
and if necessary applying corrective measures. It can be viewed
as the familiar management "follow-up" either to confirm opera-
tions taking place according to plans or to reveal deviations that
need remedial actions so that the specific goals are achieved.
Controlling is applied to one or all of the following factors:
(1) quantity of work, (2) quality of work, (3) use of time, and
(4) cost. Controlling is extensive; there is no single type of man-
agerial control that is all-inclusive. Some have to do with the
amount of work accomplished, while others concern the accuracy
to be achieved, the practices to follow, or the dollars to expend.
The following eight chapters deal with the most important aspects
of managerial controlling as applied to office work.

Chapter · 31

Standards and
Standardization in the Office

Progress is not made by taking pride in our present standards,
but by critically examining these standards, hypothetically setting higher standards and attempting to achieve them.

—J. L. ROSENSTEIN

THE FIRST two steps in any controlling work is to
determine what is being accomplished and to evaluate this accomplishment. Preferably this is expressed in terms of definite measurable units.
Without knowledge of accomplishment and evaluation, any control effort has a hollow ring. It is the essence of what is being done and
how well it is being done.

Fundamental to these accomplishment and evaluation tasks of controlling are standards. *A standard is something established either by
custom or authority in order to gauge such things as quality, performance, and service of any factor used in management.* A standard is a
reference line of management; or it may be thought of as a basis of
reckoning, i.e., a basis of comparison. Most standards represent the best
current knowledge of an item or practice formulated and accepted to
meet the needs of present conditions.

IMPORTANCE OF STANDARDS

The use of standards is the keystone of modern management. As
stated above, standards serve as an accepted basis against which an
actual action or object may be judged, thus providing a sound comparison between similar types. In this manner the work of controlling is
facilitated. However, standards are also important to the other fundamental functions of management, including planning, organizing, and
actuating. For example, in planning, standards are the essential media

for determining what components are required for establishing the sequence of successive operations. In other words, standards provide the common language for carrying out managerial work in areas such as expressing what is to be done, discussing, allocating, and instructing.

BASES FOR STANDARDS

Standards are set by managers from three different sources: past experience, estimate or guess, and scientific procedure. Standards set from past experience mean that in determining the standard, past records or practical knowledge gained from actual working experience are used. Standards set by estimate or guess are arrived at either from carefully thought-out guesses or from rough appraisals of what the standard should be. Standards set as a result of scientific procedures mean that science and the scientific method were used in determining these standards.

EXTENT OF STANDARDS

Standards apply to all factors of an enterprise. For example, there exist, in management, standards for each of the six M's—i.e., Men, Materials, Machines, Methods, Money, and Markets. This means that modern managers have established recognized bases of reference for each of the six factors. For example, concepts such as "standard" material and "standard" machine are common in the office, but less commonly identified standards are "standard" man and "standard" money. The concept of a standard man is frequently used in personnel work when considering what qualifications a man must possess to fill a particular job, while standards in money or the financial part of an enterprise are very well illustrated by expressions of standard costs.

In many offices the basic types of standards, along with the type of area covered by each, are shown by the following:

Basic Standard	Area
Work	Measurements of the quantity and the quality of accomplishment
Tools	Desk, file, machine
Conditions	Amount of space, equipment layout, lighting, floor covering
Process	Filing methods, mail distribution, handling accounts receivable, duplicating process

Under tools, for example, a standard for a machine might designate the type to be used for certain work. This would be a standard for purpose of controlling. In this connection a complete inventory of all machines in the office would be taken. Such things as the number, model, name of manufacturer, location in the office, estimate of condition of unit, purchase price, and date of purchase would be determined. In most cases it is desirable to put a company number on each unit by means of tag, sticker, or decalcomania, to permit permanent identification. If not immediately available, the manufacturer may be written to for some of this information. Commonly a file is maintained with a separate card for each machine. Among the most important types of data to be retained are a detailed description of the unit, the type of work for which it is used, the date of manufacture, and a record of maintenance work and expenses. Periodic checkups in the file should be made about every twelve to eighteen months.

MEANS OF EXPRESSING STANDARDS

Various means for expressing standards can be used, including the following:

1. *Written specifications:* simply a detailed statement of the requirements that must be followed or that must be met by the factor under consideration. Figure 31–1 shows a Standard Practice Bulletin for writing how a specific type of office work is to be performed.

2. *Model:* a typical sample, a minature representation, or an exact representation of a specimen of the factor considered standard.

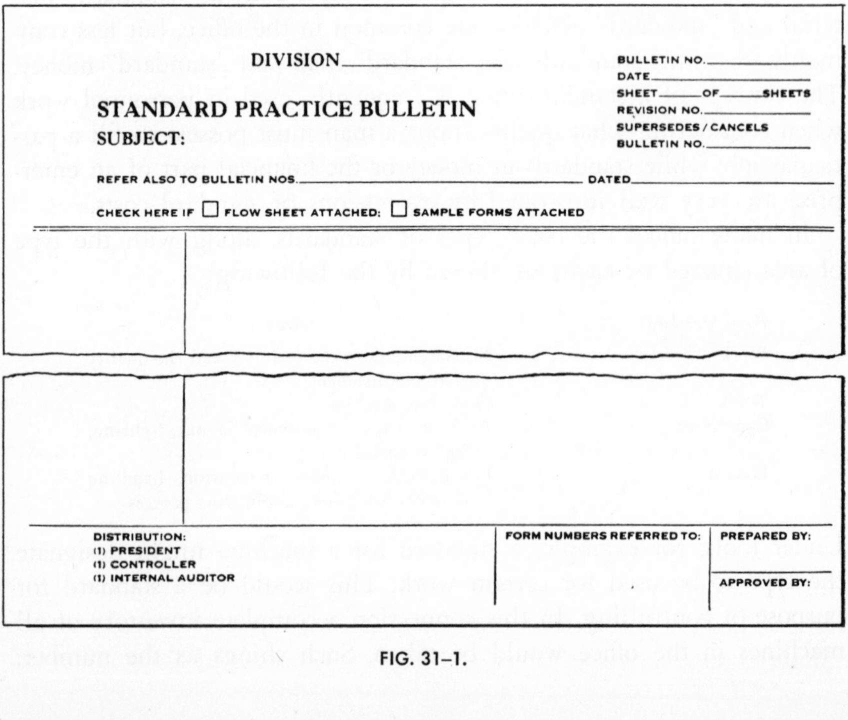

DIVISION ______

STANDARD PRACTICE BULLETIN

SUBJECT:

BULLETIN NO. ______
DATE ______
SHEET ___ OF ___ SHEETS
REVISION NO. ______
SUPERSEDES / CANCELS
BULLETIN NO. ______

REFER ALSO TO BULLETIN NOS. ______ DATED ______

CHECK HERE IF ☐ FLOW SHEET ATTACHED: ☐ SAMPLE FORMS ATTACHED

DISTRIBUTION:
(1) PRESIDENT
(1) CONTROLLER
(1) INTERNAL AUDITOR

FORM NUMBERS REFERRED TO:

PREPARED BY:

APPROVED BY:

FIG. 31–1.

3. *Accepted rule or regulation:* an established course or guide prescribed by authority.

4. *Unwritten customary procedure:* the habitual usage or generally recognized practice as shown by past experiences.

5. *Verbal communication:* the conveyance of thoughts and opinions concerning the standard by means of spoken words.

Convenience has tended to associate or group certain of these means with certain factors employed by managers. For example, a standard method is usually expressed by one of three means—a written specification, an unwritten customary procedure, or a verbal communication. In contrast, a standard material might be expressed by any of these means plus a model. Figure 31–2 shows the means most commonly

Factor	Written Specification	Model	Accepted Rule or Regulation	Unwritten Customary Procedure	Verbal Communication
Men	X	...	X*	X	X
Materials	X	X	...	X	X
Machines	X	X	...	...	...
Methods	X	...	...	X	X
Money	X	...	X	X	...

* Particularly in the case of government and public institutions.

FIG. 31–2. The means most commonly used to express standards according to the factors of management.

used to express standards according to factors. To illustrate, for machines the standard is usually expressed by a written specification or by a model. A methods standard expressed by means of a written specification is illustrated by Figure 31–3. In this case, the method is precisely stated; it tells exactly what to do and minimizes the possibility of misunderstanding.

STANDARDS AND PERFECTION

The establishment of a standard does not mean that perfection has been reached. For example, a material standard for paper designated by an office *does not* imply that paper meeting all those particular specifications is the best paper obtainable; it may actually be paper of an inferior quality. What the standard actually means is that paper of these specifications is the type desired by the manager and is satisfactory for the specific purpose in mind, taking into account such things as the type of printing press, the price range, and the desired finished product. Material standards specifying a low grade of material are not uncommon, for they simply reflect a manager's belief that for the process and use to which the material is going to be subjected, the low grade of material is best.

Experience shows that after a standard has been set it is common to try to improve the standard and to move it toward perfection. This is as it should be, for progress in management is dependent in large

---

Every error which is made in posting a passbook or ledger card must be corrected by an adjusting entry on the savings machine, as described in the following paragraphs. No erasures are permitted.

If the wrong old balance is posted in the machine, the correction should be made as follows:

1. If the old balance is picked up incorrectly and detected immediately, the Clear and Sub-Total lever is merely brought to the "Clear Balance" position and the balance cleared.

2. If the error is found after posting the old balance and the deposit or withdrawal, but before extending the new balance, the incorrect old balance is to be set up and the Overdraft key depressed (with the book and card out of the machine), and the correct old balance is to be set up on the Old Balance key. The book and card are then to be inserted and the correct new balance extended.

3. If the error is not detected before the new balance is posted, the correct old balance is to be picked on the Old Balance key (with the book and card out of the machine). If the entry was a deposit, the amount is to be recorded under the Overdraft key. The card and book are then to be inserted and set to the line immediately below that on which the incorrect balance appears and the correct new balance extended. The word "Balance" is to be written beside it and an ink line drawn through the incorrect balance.

4. If the error is not detected until the cards are proved at the end of the day, the procedure in (3) above is to be followed, except that the card only can be corrected. A Caution signal should be placed on the card so that the book will be corrected when next presented. The customer should be advised of the error and asked to present his passbook for verification as soon as possible.

Source: "Manual for Savings Tellers" (Boston: First National Bank of Boston, 1943), pp. M1 and M2

FIG. 31–3. A methods standard in the form of a written specification.

measure upon improvements in standards. In addition, the setting of a standard seems to place a level below which future standards will not be set; that is, once a standard is set, changes are discouraged that are not in the direction of improvement.

INTERDEPENDENCE OF STANDARDS WITHIN AN ENTERPRISE

Standards are changed not only because improvements are made but also because, within an enterprise, standards are interdependent. For a given task in an office, assume standards have been set up for the material, machine, and method. These three standards are interdependent and may be called "associated standards." The employee, in order to accomplish the task, must use the standard material in the standard machine and follow the standard method. Figure 31–4 in the second column illustrates the present standards for the material, machine, and method. It can be seen that the employee is to use 12-pound, $8\frac{1}{2} \times 11$-inch paper in a $11\frac{1}{4}$-inch roll typewriter and that he is to make five copies, using $\frac{1}{2}$-inch spacing between vertical columns.

Factor	Present Standards	Standards after Changes	Reasons for Changes in Standards
Material	12# White Bond Paper. Size $8\frac{1}{2}'' \times 11''$	16# White Bond Paper. Size $17'' \times 22''$	New sheet size requested by top management members. Larger sheets necessitate heavier paper.
Machine	$11\frac{1}{4}''$ Roll Typewriter	$19\frac{1}{4}''$ Roll Typewriter	Larger roll needed to accommodate new paper size.
Method	Insert paper in machine, make 5 copies, leave $\frac{1}{2}''$ spacing between vertical columns.	Insert paper in machine, make 4 copies, leave 2'' spacing between vertical columns.	Number of copies reduced from 5 to 4 because of heavier paper used. Increased spacing improves appearance of sheet.

FIG. 31–4. Illustrating the interdependence of associated standards. The standard for material was changed upon request of top management members. This change in the standard for material necessitated a change in the standard for machine and also in the standard for method.

Now suppose that a change is made in the standard of the material from 12-pound, $8\frac{1}{2} \times 11$-inch paper to 16-pound, 17×22-inch paper. In order to handle this new weight and size paper, it is necessary to change the machine standard from a $11\frac{1}{4}$-inch to a $19\frac{1}{4}$-inch roll typewriter and to change the method standard from making five copies to four copies and from allowing $\frac{1}{2}$-inch spacing to a 2-inch spacing between vertical columns. These changes in standards and the reasons for making them are shown in concise form in Figure 31–4.

In general, a manager should review all standards when any one standard is revised. This is especially important for associated standards, but it also applies for standards of the same group. To repeat, *standards are not independent: they are interdependent.*

It will be found that frequently when only the one standard is changed, the associated standards remain entirely compatible with the revised standard. But a manager doesn't know this until he reviews and studies all the associated standards after each revision. In similar vein, a change in any one of the standards of a *similar group* necessitates a review of all standards in that group. For example, *all methods standards* should be reviewed whenever a change is made in any one methods standard, because in this way possible sources of improvement and the bettering of all methods standards can be discovered and adopted.

AMERICAN STANDARDS ASSOCIATION, INC.

Since 1947, the American Standards Association, Inc., with assistance by the National Office Management Association, has directed its efforts to the establishing of office standards. The American Standards Association does not set standards; it provides the machinery whereby every group concerned in any project has a right to participate in the setting of the standards. The program includes the establishment of office standards for each of the following major groups: office equipment and furniture, paper for office use, office supplies, business machines, personnel, physical and physiological factors, and office forms, records, and procedures. Figure 31–5 shows an office standard for basic sheet sizes and standard stock sizes for bond papers and index bristols. By its use the task of decision making by the office manager is simplified and cost reduction is encouraged.

ADVANTAGES OF STANDARDS

The advantages of the use of standards in management are tremendous and include:

1. *Aid managing.* The performance of the management process is expedited by the use of standards. Identification and measurement of quality, performance, and capacity of the factors used by a manager constitute the supports upon which the managerial functions can be predicated.

2. *Provide a common basis for understanding.* Standards provide a common terminology, or a common language, between the employee and supervisor or between the buyer and seller. Through the use of standards it is possible to determine exactly what is being discussed or investigated.

3. *Aid in securing co-ordination.* Standards serve as focal points around which revolve most problems of management. The synchronization of the various factors used by a manager depend, in the final analysis, upon the synchronization or interplay of the various standards which are brought together.

Division 2
Paper
NOMA
N2.1 - 1955
•
ASA
Reg. U. S. Pat. Off.
X2.2.1 - 1955
*UDC 676.3.001.3/389.172
•

NOMA
OFFICE STANDARD

Basic Sheet Sizes and Standard Stock Sizes
for Bond Papers and Index Bristols
(An American Standard)

1. Scope

1.1 The scope and purpose of this standard is to list the basic sheet sizes and standard stock sizes of bond papers and index bristols in order to encourage the use of normally available sizes.

2. Definitions

2.1 For purposes of this standard, the terms listed below are defined as follows:

2.1.1 Basic Sheet Size, as defined in the Dictionary of Paper* is a certain sheet size recognized by buyers and sellers as the one upon which its basic weight is figured. Usually, it is also the one which prints, folds, and trims most effectively.

2.1.2 Standard Stock Sheet Sizes are the sizes of paper normally stocked by most paper merchants and most paper mills and from which the sizes commonly used in the office are cut with a minimum of waste.

2.1.3 Bond Paper° is a grade of writing or printing paper originally used where strength, durability, and permanence are essential requirements, as in government bonds and legal documents. Its use has extended into other fields, such as business letterheads and forms, where strength and permanence, though important properties, are not so essential; this accounts for the wide range of quality in this type of paper. These qualities are obtained through the use of rag pulp, bleached chemical wood pulps, and mixtures of these fibers in the manufacturing process. Although bond paper is a typical writing paper, almost all of it is subjected to some form of printing before use. Therefore, it must have good printing qualities which, however, are not as important as writing and erasing qualities, clean-

liness, formation, finish, color and freedom from fuzz. It is usually made in basis weights from 13 to 24 pounds (17 in. x 22 in. per 500 sheets).

2.1.4 Index Bristols* are bristols used principally for index records, business and commercial cards. They are a group of cardboards made on the Fourdrinier or cylinder machine of homogeneous stock (such as rag, sulphite, or bleached sulphate pulp) or by pasting together two or more plies of the same kind of paper, and finished and sized for pen and ink work. The usual basis weights are 180, 220, 280, 340, and 440 pounds (25.5 in. x 30.5 in. per 1000 sheets).

*The Dictionary of Paper, published under the auspices and direction of the American Paper and Pulp Association, 122 East 42nd Street, New York, N. Y. (Copyright Second Edition 1951.)

3. Standard Stock Sheet Sizes†

(All Dimensions in Inches)

Bond Papers (Rag Content or Chemical Wood Pulp)	Index Bristols (Rag Content or Chemical Wood Pulp)
17 x 22‡	20½ x 24¾
17 x 28	22½ x 28½
19 x 24	22½ x 35
22 x 34	25½ x 30½‡
24 x 38	
28 x 34	
34 x 44	

† The Standard Stock Sheet Sizes listed in this standard, except for the 22½ x 35 size Index Bristol, are identical with those listed in Simplified Practice Recommendation R22-40 for Paper of the U. S. Department of Commerce.

‡ Basic Size.

NOTE: When the direction of the grain is important, it should be specified.

• **Approved as American Standard by the American Standards Association, Inc.—Aug. 16, 1955**
• **Sponsor: National Office Management Association.**   *Universal Decimal Classification

NATIONAL   OFFICE   MANAGEMENT   ASSOCIATION
WILLOW GROVE, PA.

Courtesy: American Standards Association, Inc., New York; and National Office Management Association, Willow Grove, Pa.

FIG. 31–5.   A written office standard.

4. *Reduce waste.* Standards help to determine definite requirements. Losses resulting from obsolete equipment, inefficient methods, and excess materials are kept at a minimum when good standards are employed and strictly enforced.

5. *Promote better utilization of employees.* Standards help to achieve the goal of utilizing personnel within carefully defined and

known limits. Executives are encouraged to do executive work—not routine work. Likewise, supervisors are expected to carry out the job of supervising—not that of an operative employee with only the title of supervisor.

6. *Encourage simplicity.* Standards tend to eliminate the unusual and complicated procedures. Under standards, all office paper work of a similar nature is similarly written and similarly distributed. The office forms used are simple, so that there is no question about what is wanted, what has been done, or what is to be done.

7. *Act as stimuli to research.* Standards help to localize areas within which improvements might be made. They serve to help state the problem and to assist the researcher in concentrating on a problem of relatively limited scope.

8. *Provide effective connecting links between the findings of research and the application of research results.* Standards serve as the contact points for the application of research findings. New discoveries and improvements are introduced via the standards, and in this manner the beneficial contributions of research are utilized with a minimum of time and effort.

9. *Provide interchangeability of part and machine.* Each component may be so specified and accurately determined by the use of standards that it is entirely feasible to use any one of a group of similar components. By means of standards, it is possible to insure that all of part "X" will be identical within the limits set up by the standards.

10. *Make mass production possible.* Standards permit the handling of each component separately; thus, specialization may be practiced and the gains thereof realized. Difficult and complex jobs requiring long and strenuous training periods are reduced by the use of standards to relatively simple tasks, yet at no sacrifice in the total amount of work accomplished.

OFFICE STANDARDIZATION

Uniformity is the meaning of standardization. For example, when a company adopts certain stated standards regarding the type and size of desks it will use, the practice is known as standardization. In many instances standardization deals with an industry, not with just one enterprise. Both the needs and the benefits of standardization are in proportion to the complexity of managing the particular enterprise or industry.

Typically a number of considerations must be included in standardizing upon an office item. For desks, the considerations might include size, appearance, utility, comfort, interchangeability, construction, maintenance, depreciation, and initial cost. How much weight to give to each of these factors is primarily a question of judgment, although weights in proportion to the relative costs of the factors might be developed.

STANDARDIZATION OF STATIONERY AND SUPPLIES

For illustrative purposes, consider the standardization of office stationery and supplies. The first step to consider would be the kinds of materials most suited for the particular needs. This information would be obtained by means of discussion, exchange of information and ideas, comparative tests, contacts with associations interested in standards, and the establishing of specifications. Subsequently, inspection of receivables to specifications, survey of stock stored to reduce stock carried on hand, and stores records and practices would be studied for standardization of possible improvements.

In all this work perhaps hundreds of different items would be included, items such as paper, erasers, paper clips, pencils, pens, ink, carbon paper, stencils, rubber bands, staplers, typewriter ribbons, and adhesive tape. Consideration would be given to the nomenclature of these items with the goal of simplifying it, to size and color, to the utility, to the quality by grades, to cost, and to deterioration or shelf life. The task, while not especially difficult, would be time consuming and involves securing agreement among people, ferreting and organizing facts about various product lines.

ECONOMIC AND SOCIAL ASPECTS OF OFFICE STANDARDIZATION

From an *economic* viewpoint, there is little doubt that office standardization is beneficial. Such economic factors as simplified control, greater quantities of work achieved, the advancement of office production techniques, and the assistance in managerial decision making are among the virtues generally pointed out.

However, from the *social* viewpoint, there has been much discussion regarding the real benefits of standardization. Some writers argue very fervently that it has been highly beneficial to the employees, while others quite vehemently contend that standardization has resulted in genuine losses to the employees' best interests.

From the social point of view those favoring standardization claim: First, the level of the *skilled* worker has been raised, as shown by the trend to higher real wages for skilled employees over a period of years.[1]

---

[1] By the term "real wage level" is meant a level based on what the wages will buy in terms of commodity prices. In contrast, the term "actual wage level" means a level based on the amount of money wages only, without regard to what can be purchased with that amount of money.

Furthermore, the level of the *semiskilled* worker has also increased, and he too enjoys a higher real wage level. Second, many tasks remain fundamentally the same whether they are standardized or not. The standard permits a measurement of performance and does not change the basic nature of the task. Third, the adoption of standardization by enterprises actually results in the worker's gaining greater freedom. This is true because a uniformity among similar jobs is approached which makes the services of the worker in demand among more employers. Fourth, the employee can better improve his position, for he can concentrate his efforts within a certain area and also demonstrate his improvement against a definitely known measurement of achievement. Furthermore, the employee enjoys greater safety and frequently, after a time, can execute the requirements of the job with less expenditure of effort.

Those who contend that the use of standardization is to the employees' disadvantage cite the following reasons to support their beliefs: First, the whole business of standardization tends to deprive the worker of his dignity and rightful position. He sacrifices valuable skill and loses interest and enthusiasm for his work. Second, the range within which the employee may exercise his skill is narrowed. He is told exactly what to do, and his individual initiative is stifled. Third, the employee loses an understanding of his efforts in the over-all picture of total activities. He has less opportunity to see the relative importance of his contribution to the completed product or service. Fourth, the employee may become an undesirable citizen of his community. His interest and outlook have been impeded; his life becomes dull and drab; and he fails to participate actively in any community activities.

QUESTIONS

1. Can controlling take place without the use of a standard? Elaborate on your answer.
2. In your opinion what means are probably the most common for expressing office standards?
3. Do standards imply perfection? Explain your reply.
4. Discuss the extent and importance of standards in the field of office management.
5. Why is it important to review all standards when one standard is revised? Illustrate your answer by an example taken from your experience or by an incident with which you are familiar.
6. Explain how standards help an office manager to co-ordinate his activities.
7. With reference to Figure 31–5, explain how the use of this standard helps an office manager in his work.

8. In your opinion, what are the three most important advantages of standards in office management? Point out and discuss your major reasons for selecting these three advantages.

9. Comment fully on the statement: "Standards are the foundation upon which a manager builds, and there is nothing more important in management than standards."

10. Clearly point out the relationship between office standards and standardization.

11. Do you favor office standardization? Cite reasons to support your viewpoint.

12. Write out a standard with which you are familiar and explain how it probably helps in the management of the factor concerned. It is suggested that you select any common factor in office work which you have performed or observed in school, at work, or at home.

CASE PROBLEMS

CASE 31–1.   BENTON-DONOHUE COMPANY

For the past several months, Mr. Richard E. Schubert, the office manager, has been giving serious consideration to the establishing of standards for posture chairs which his company purchases. Mr. Schubert believes that standards are necessary for three chair classifications—executive, supervisory, and clerical. For each of these groups a particular model, design, upholstery, and color would be determined and used throughout the entire office.

To substantiate his viewpoint, Mr. Schubert points out that the use of such standards would greatly improve the appearance of the office and save much time in purchasing. Also, chair purchases could be made at better prices for the company. But probably of even greater importance is the elimination of comparison of chairs by employees of the same general organization level. For example, one supervisor would not compare his chair to that of another supervisor and feel that he had a better or an inferior chair by comparison. Chair equality would be attained.

The controller suggests that the employees of each office division should be permitted to select the chairs they want. In other words, chair standards should extend within an office division only. Any other standards arrangement would conflict with personnel interests and possibly with the type of work performed. Furthermore, he believes that the company should give its chair business to several suppliers. Competition should be encouraged; otherwise the company might find itself at the mercy of one supplier.

The president of the company doesn't see anything wrong with employees of the same organization level using different chairs, and he asks two questions of the office manager: first, "How are you going to determine the standards for chairs in our office?" and, second, "What are the tangible savings from adopting the use of chair standards?" As the president sees it, the answer to question No. 1 is so involved that the company should not undertake the project. In addition, many employees would question the results and their use regardless of what would be determined. In answer to the second question, it appears that additional expenditures, not savings, would be incurred. Not one, but groups of chairs would probably have to be purchased, if chair standards were adopted. Also, the possibility of taking advantage of lower prices on the chair market would be minimized, and further improvements in chair design and manufacture would be discouraged.

PROBLEMS:

1. Do you agree with the viewpoint of the controller? Discuss. Of the president? Discuss.

2. What action do you recommend that the office manager take? Why?

Chapter · 32

Quantity and Quality Control

The most important part of every business is to know what ought to be done.

—COLUMBELLA

IN MOST offices the volume of work is likely to be quite large during some periods and, conversely, quite small during other periods. This fluctuation appears to be in the general nature of office work which is of a service and facilitating type, influenced in volume by factors outside the office.

Controlling efforts are complicated by this fluctuating characteristic. A steady, even flow of office work is best for the application of the control process. Hence, various means to minimize the fluctuations have been devised and will be discussed in this chapter. These efforts are controlling actions over quantity from the broad, over-all office viewpoint. Focusing attention to limited areas as, for example, controlling dealing with the amount of work accomplished with a certain procedure or by a single office employee are discussed subsequently in Chapters 33 and 34.

PATTERNS OF FLUCTUATION

A study of the demands upon an office over a comparatively long period of time will usually reveal a rhythmic pattern in office activities. For example, it may be found that peak loads are generally experienced on the first day of each week, every Friday, or the last few days of each month. Figure 32–1 shows a graphical representation of an office work load having rhythmic weekly peaks.

In such cases as the one illustrated, controlling can be directed to help take care of the peak periods, since these are known in advance and an adequate means for handling them can be determined. In other

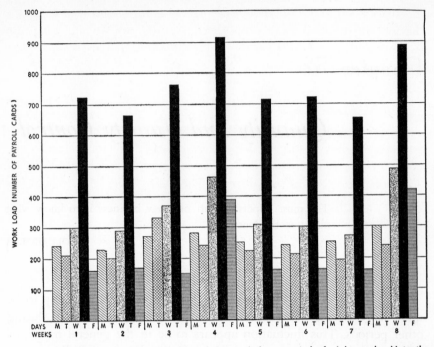

FIG. 32–1. Office work load by days of the week for a period of eight weeks. Note the weekly rhythmic pattern, with the peak load occurring on Thursday of each week. Proper control will take care of these periodic peak loads.

cases, however, the demands upon an office are continually changing, and where this condition exists, the work of controlling is extremely difficult. Special control efforts may be required to meet the situation.

PROBLEMS INCURRED

Perhaps the most important problem incurred by the fluctuation of office work is that of getting the work finished when it is needed. Adequate control can assist tremendously in this respect. Also, work fluctuation creates a feast or famine situation in the factors utilized in performing the work. For any given period, how many people to hire, what machines to employ, and which methods to adopt are typical questions. On the one hand, the reduction of idle machine and personnel time are paramount, while, on the other hand, lack of sufficient capacity in machine or man power is of foremost consideration. Another disturbing problem is the designating and the handling of rush or special work. In most instances this designation means little in determining work priority, because the terms are applied to practically all the work. Furthermore, the supplying of accurate information concerning the status of certain work in the office is complicated by work fluctuation. Information about such things as the progress of a particular job, the number of units completed, and the probable finishing time is not readily supplied when the work volume is characterized by steep peaks and deep troughs.

CONSIDERATIONS IN CONTROL EFFORTS OVER WORK FLUCTUATION

Certain fundamentals must be taken into account in controlling office work fluctuation. Among the more important requirements are:

1. *The controlling should help in getting the work accomplished.* Controls are a means, not an end. The controlling efforts should be selected and utilized on the basis of achieving the goal, not perpetuating a control mechanism or program as such.

2. *All control efforts should be carefully co-ordinated, so that both unity and a minimum of wasteful overlapping efforts are achieved.* Controlling of work fluctuation cannot be left to the individual employee. When this is done, sporadic, unbalanced, and somewhat haphazard results are common. Generally, the best practice is to have the controlling under the direction of one individual or a division designated to handle this function.

3. *All management members must realize that the controlling efforts are intended to help them.* The controlling should be constructive in its ultimate effect, and as a result management members should be able to give more attention to such duties as getting the work out, handling grievances, making decisions, improving methods, and reducing costs.

4. *Complete data on personnel, machines, procedures, and cost must be known.* Intelligent controlling can take place only when adequate knowledge and information about the things being controlled are available and supplied. As stated in Chapter 31, these data may be in the form of standards.

5. *The office work should be expressed in readily measurable units.* Some expression for describing accurately the quantity of work is necessary. Control efforts are usually most effective when applied to a specific amount of work which is known and understood by all affected by it.[1]

6. *Knowledge of time standards for all major operations within the office should be available.* The reasonable time expectancies for completion of work are basic tools to control work fluctuation. Knowing when, how much, and for how long the controlling efforts are applied,

---

[1] Measuring and timing office work is the subject of Chapter 36.

are decisions which should be guided by the utilization of office time standards.[2]

7. *The sequence of operations on each type of work should be established and utilized.* In many instances the office procedure will supply this information, but details covering a specific job or a portion of the entire work are sometimes also necessary. This is especially true in the case of congested or "bottleneck" areas.

8. *Accurate and fast means of communication between the one doing the controlling and the employee doing the actual physical office work must be provided.* In the smaller office, or where the supervisor initiates his own means of control, no particular difficulty is encountered with this requirement. However, when centralized controlling is used, fast intercommunication service is necessary between the line operators and the controlling unit.

MEANS OF CONTROLLING OFFICE WORK FLUCTUATION

The question now arises: "What specifically can the office manager do in order to meet the problems inherent in the fluctuation of the office work volume?" The answer lies in employing one or several means at his disposal. The choice depends upon his preference and the circumstances of the particular office. Eight possibilities are discussed on the following pages.

EMPLOYMENT OF PART-TIME HELP

This possible solution is self-evident and will not be treated in any detail here. In certain cases, the use of part-time help is entirely satisfactory, but experience seems to indicate that, in general, part-time help may not be as reliable, efficient, and co-operative as regular employees. Also, the cost of recruiting, hiring, and training part-time employees might be excessive. Flexibility of the work force, however, is gained by the use of part-time people.

OVERTIME WORK

Although commonly resorted to, this solution to the problem of work fluctuation is not entirely satisfactory. For occasional overloads it may represent the simplest solution. However, when the amount of work during regular hours is light and frequent peak loads are common, the working of overtime is open to serious questions as the best way of handling the problem. For one thing, overtime increases unit labor cost considerably. Consider a common case in which an employee

---

[2] *Ibid.*

works all day Saturday, or 8 hours overtime. These 8 hours are paid for at the rate of time and one half. In effect, these overtime hours increase the unit labor cost by 8.33 per cent, which is a substantial amount. This increase can be calculated thusly: Including overtime the employee is paid for 52 hours $(40 + 8 \times 1\frac{1}{2})$, whereas 48 (8×6) productive hours are supplied. The labor payment is therefore 52 divided by 48, or 1.0833, or an increase of 8.33 per cent.

There is also the question of employee fatigue. Over an extended period, there is reasonable question whether the rate of output during the overtime hours will be the same as that during the regular work hours. The rate of production during overtime tends to fall below the normal production rate. Most office managers will concur in the statement that an office employee working an extra two or three hours after a normal eight-hour working day will not produce an extra two eights or three eights of a normal day's work. The amount will be less—in some instances, considerably less.

Furthermore, legal restrictions must be taken into account. Federal and state laws regulate the type of work and the hours which an employee can work in certain occupations. Where female employees are involved, the regulatory statutes may be of especial importance.

FORMING MOBILE UNITS

In some offices it is possible to form "flying squadron" units which are moved from area to area to help handle excessive work loads. Generally speaking, the office must be fairly large to utilize this method. However, the same idea is used informally in most small offices by shifting the employees around when and as the work requires.

The mobile unit arrangement necessitates employees with comprehensive training in a number of different types of office work. Hiring and maintaining such employees present some difficulties, but can be managed satisfactorily.

CALLING SERVICE BUREAUS TO DO THE WORK

Office overloads or work which is of a special nature can be handled by outside enterprises which specialize in this type of work. Most of these so-called "service bureaus" are independently owned business firms, but some are units of office machine manufacturers. Service bureaus are located in all major cities throughout the United States, several are nation-wide in scope. Some are specialists operating, for example, punched-card installations only, but many offer complete services in typing, calculating, tabulating, filing, transcribing, duplicating, and direct mailing. Service bureaus offer vast experience and competent, specialized personnel to handle complex jobs. The service is fast. For example, one service bureau completed for a client, inventory calculations involving 3,500 hours of work within three working days. Typical of the type of work handled are letters, reports, production cost analysis, pension calculations, labor distribution studies, payrolls, and market research tabulations. In view of the service provided, the cost of service bureaus is usually reasonable.

It should be observed that these outside service bureaus are useful to the office manager for more than meeting peak loads or emergency problems. They are also helpful when purchase of particular office machines cannot be justified by the office because of its size or the amount or character of the work. Also, a service bureau can be engaged to serve as a laboratory to test the value of a new means of handling office work before the necessary equipment is purchased.

STRESS CENTRALIZATION IN ORGANIZATION

As pointed out in Chapter 19, one of the strongest justifications for centralization in office organizing is the more effective handling of peak loads. When the excess work is (1) mainly basic activities such as typing, computing, copying, sorting, and filing, and (2) concentrated in different departments at different times, the centralized organization approach has real merit.

USE OF CYCLING

Cycling is an arrangement whereby papers are processed throughout a period according to an orderly plan rather than as a group, for example, at the beginning or end of each period. In other words, by means of cycling, the work is spread out evenly throughout the period. The practice of cycling has been used in connection with the mailing of statements and is commonly referred to as cycle billing. The same practice, however, can be applied to other types of office work.

Cycling has been used for a long time by public utility companies in sending out their bills for service. Meters are read, for example, in a certain section of the city, bills mailed, and payments specified by a certain date. Several days later, other meters in another section of the city are read, bills mailed, and payments requested by a date which is a few days after that of the previous group.

During recent years many department stores have adopted cycle billing. Under this plan each account is posted once a month, but statements are mailed for a different section of accounts on different days throughout the month. The accounts can be divided into twenty or fewer groups, depending upon such things as the volume of postings, the number of accounts, and the number of trays required to house the accounts.

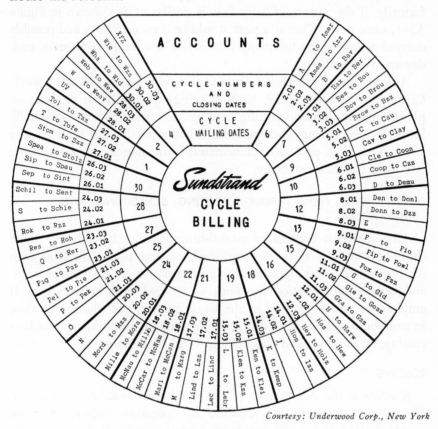

Courtesy: Underwood Corp., New York

FIG. 32–2. Chart used to establish cycles in a cycle billing system.

Figure 32–2 shows a chart which gives the divisions for twenty cycles. Going from the outer to the inner circle of this chart, the data represented are, respectively: the accounts, the cycle numbers and closing dates, and the cycle mailing dates. For example, to the right of and slightly above the center of the chart, accounts "Cle to Coon" have cycle number 6.01. The "6" of this number indicates that the closing date is the sixth of the month. The cycle mailing date is 10, i.e., the tenth of the month, which allows four days after closing accounts to prepare the statements for mailing to customers.

MAINTAIN WORK BACKLOG

This means utilizes a reservoir of work so to speak in order to level out the peaks and valleys of the office work flow. When certain work can be postponed, or moved up, this approach works out quite satisfactorily. If the pattern of work flow is similar to that shown in Figure 32–1, some of the Thursday peak would be done on Friday and possibly delayed as late as the following Monday. The attempt is to make each day an average day.

An alternate approach is to mix urgent with nonurgent office work. Certain tasks of the office, such as bringing records up to date, replenishing supplies, and putting headings on certain papers, can usually be performed during slack periods. When work having high priority is received, it is processed immediately—the nonurgent work being laid aside for the time being.

ORDERLY WORK FLOW THROUGH ROUTING, SCHEDULING, AND DISPATCHING

This approach consists of establishing specific channels by which the office work is to be accomplished, placing time values on each successive step so arranged, receiving information on progress of work, and issuing authorization for work to proceed from step to step. It emphasizes the controlling of the work quantity and the use of time in work performance. Each of the major components of this approach—routing, scheduling, and dispatching—will be discussed.

ROUTING

Routing is the determining of the route or channel through which the work travels and the sequence of operations required for the completion of the work. For most offices, routing is determined by the procedure used. In some instances the choice of a particular machine or of a certain area may be fixed by the routing process, but this is the exception rather than the rule with most office work.

Figure 32–3 illustrates a form of office route sheet. The departments and the operations to be performed are listed in sequence; in the case illustrated, they begin with "sort" by department No. 7 and finish with "ship" by department No. 5. According to this figure, the work is ready to be delivered to department No. 22 as indicated by the check marks in the first column. The machine or equipment to be used is indicated by data in the fourth column. The starting time and the amount of time allowed for each operation are also included.

Frequently, the office work is placed in a heavy manilla envelope with the route sheet attached on the outside. A copy of the sheet is retained by the person or department doing the central control work. In some instances the form of the route sheet is printed on the envelope to prevent possible loss of the route sheet in the office.

ROUTE SHEET

Form: *177B5*　　　　　　No. *3375*　　　　　　Starting Time: *2:30 P.M.*
Description: *House Orders for Kansas City Branch*　　Starting Date: *12/13*
Quantity: *350*　　　　　　　　　　　　　　　　　Written By: *TSD*

Deliver To	Department	Operation	Machine	Time per 100 Pcs.		Time for This Job	
				Hrs.	Min	Hrs.	Men
✓	7	Sort			6		21
✓	13	Post Prices	#4B	2	30	8	45
✓	13	Check			40	2	20
	22	Type	#241RR(Regular)	5	12	18	12
	22	Check			55	3	13
	5	Ship			30	1	45

FIG. 32–3. Illustration of a route sheet for office work.

SCHEDULING

Scheduling is the assigning of time values to the work sequence— the determination of when each operation starts and when it should be completed. The extent to which office work can be scheduled depends upon the individual circumstances; but usually a great deal can be scheduled, including billing, key punching, tabulating, transcribing, check writing, order writing, and inventory taking.

The common practice in scheduling is to work backwards from the time specified for completion. An allowance is made for each operation required by the work, and in this manner a starting time is determined. For example, if the time set for completion of a job is 4:00 P.M., Thursday, June 12, and the work requires eighteen hours' time, this means that the work should start eighteen hours before that time and date, or 2:00 P.M., Tuesday, June 10.[3]

[3] This is based on working hours from 8:00 to 12:00 noon and from 1:00 to 5:00 P.M., five days a week.

The Folder System.   In certain instances a simple and quite effective informal method of scheduling office work can be used advantageously. This is known as the folder system. Under this plan a given number of units of work are placed in a folder. These are distributed by the supervisor, who notes to whom the work is given, the starting time, and the machine or workplace used. Upon return of the completed work, the time is noted and the process is repeated. The supervisor is the key person under this plan. He has knowledge of the work on hand, the amount completed, the amount in process, and when it should be finished.

Use of Visible Index Cards.   The data necessitated by more formal and complete scheduling, usually for fairly large quantities of work, can be handled on cards. When cards are used, a visible-index type providing signals for control purposes works out very well.[4] A separate card is made out for each machine, desk, or workplace. The signals featured by this type of equipment are moved to specific positions along the margin of the card to designate specific scheduled times. Scanning the cards quickly reveals what equipment is available for work and what jobs are currently being worked on.

Use of Charts.   Another effective means of recording scheduling data is by the use of charts. One of the original types, called the "Gantt Chart," was devised by Henry L. Gantt. The basic principle used is that work planned and work accomplished are shown on the same chart in relation to each other and also in their relation to time. The items are listed in a column, with corresponding capacities or data on maximum scheduling loads shown in an adjacent column. Other columns are used for time units, such as hours, days, weeks, or months.

Figure 32–4 shows a Gantt Chart representing the scheduling of work for Department 13, in which six posting machines are used. In this figure a main time column represents one week, as shown by the date filled in at the right and top of each time column. To illustrate, the column headed "Dec. 3" means the week ending December 3. In this case there are five divisions under each main time column; the divisions represent the five working days in the week. The data for each machine are shown in the identified horizontal sections of the chart, i.e., machine No. 1–N by the top horizontal section, machine No. 2–B by the second horizontal section, etc. For each machine the work scheduled by weeks is indicated by the light line and the total cumulative work scheduled by the heavy line. Thus, for posting machine No. 4–B, work time scheduled for the week ending December

---

[4] See Chapter 7 for discussion on visible equipment for filing.

17 is three days, which represents 960 postings (3×320); and the total amount of time scheduled for this machine for the six weeks' work is twelve days. The V mark on the top of the chart shows that the chart represents the status as of that date, which, in the illustration, is December 14. This type of Gantt Chart is termed a "Load Chart," since it graphically represents the load assigned to each machine and likewise reveals the idle or available time. Successive additions can be made on the chart by extending the proper lines; a redrawing is not necessary.

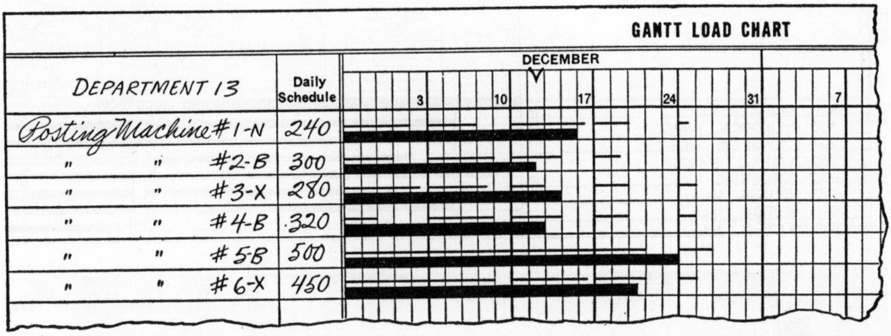

FIG. 32–4. Gantt Load Chart showing graphically the degree of utilization of machines, idle time, and time available for scheduling.

The "Combination Visible Card-Gantt Chart" is another type of scheduling chart, which is increasing in use, and combines the principles of the visible card and the Gantt Chart. This newer chart has the general appearance of a large, visible card file with the overlapping card pockets hanging vertically. See Figure 32–5.

The scheduled items, such as operations, machines, or work stations, are shown in the extreme left column of the chart; time is indicated along the horizontal axis. A separate pocket is used for each scheduled item. At the extreme left of each pocket is placed a card which gives frequently used information about the scheduled item, with the identifying data appearing in the visible margin. The remaining portion to the right in each pocket is used to show graphically the scheduled operations and times allotted for the particular item. To do this, two types of cards are used: time insert cards and operation cards.

Operation cards are printed card forms used to indicate data concerning the operation and the time scheduled for the operation on the time scale. The information about the operation is written on the card. The scheduled time information is shown in the botton margin of the card. Time insert cards are printed strips of paper which are placed in the visible margin to show the time scale along the horizontal axis.

The strips are folded lengthwise with the turned-up stub showing the printed scale.

When the operation card is tucked in the visible margin and behind the insert card, only the colored strip of the operation card is visible; and the length of this strip indicates the amount of time required to

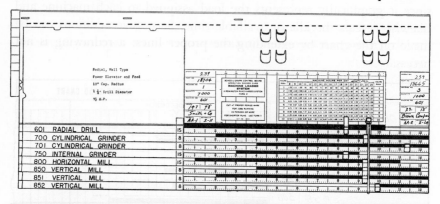

Courtesy: Remington Rand, Inc., New York

FIG. 32–5. *Top:* Close-up of scheduling chart. *Bottom:* Installation in office of a large manufacturer.

do the work. The exact placement of the card is determined by the scale of the insert card in the visible margin. Since a colored strip indicates scheduled time, it follows that white space indicates free or unscheduled time.

DISPATCHING

Dispatching is the putting into action and adequately following up the routing and scheduling plans; it is the signaling to go ahead and the checking to see that action is taking place when and where it is wanted.

Dispatching in the office is usually quite simple. It is frequently done informally by the supervisor; however, when the volume and different kinds of office work warrant, employees doing only dispatching work can probably be employed advantageously. Quite often it is desirable to use a central-control board which graphically visualizes the dispatching of the many different jobs which are started, moved through the office, and completed.

Types of Dispatching Control Boards. There are many types of control boards, including the three-hook, grooved-strip, spring-clip, and peg-string types. The discussion here will be confined to the grooved-strip and the peg-string boards, since they are probably most adaptable to office work.

The grooved-strip board has horizontal cardholder strips for insertion of tickets representing work lots. The extreme left column is used for work-lot numbers, and the remaining columns are headed by department names. Cards are made out for each work lot. As the work progresses the cards are moved on the board to correspond with the correct department location of the work. In some instances, the time is shown horizontally. When this is done, separate tickets can be made for each operation on each work lot as well as for the scheduled starting and finishing times indicated on each card. In this manner the helpfulness of the board is increased by showing the scheduling function.

The usual pattern of the peg-string board is to have controlled items on the left side and such things as time, operations, and departments in separate sections across the top. The board has a series of small holes into which pegs are inserted. For each item in the left column, there are two horizontal rows of holes. The top row is used to indicate the scheduled operations; the bottom for the actual progress. Thus, comparison between the two is easily made.

To show the scheduled operations, a peg with a string attached is inserted in the proper hole corresponding to the operation and time value. The string, which extends from the left of the board to the peg, is always taut, thus giving the impression of a horizontal line. Pegs inserted in the bottom row of holes shows the actual progress. To expedite quick reference, an assortment of different pegs, having contrasting colors, shapes, and markings on the top, are employed.

A quick glance at the board shows the times for dispatching, what work is behind schedule, and what work is ahead of schedule. A

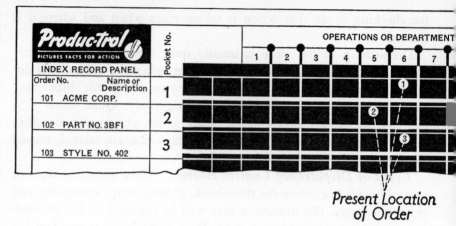

FIG. 32–6.   A close-up view of the peg-string board.

vertical cord representing a specific time and date, frequently a "today line," is used to assist in visualizing these conditions. Each day, for example, the cord is moved to the right to a distance equal to one day on the time scale. All data are kept up to date on the board by moving the pegs to the proper positions representing the current condition.

Figure 32–6 shows a close-up view of the peg-string board. The first line, pocket No. 1, covers order No. 101. The large round peg shows that this order is in department No. 6. To the right and under July, the small round peg indicates that the order was received July 11. The peg with the string attached to it is shown under July 25, which is the scheduled completion date of the current operation. The "today line" is at July 21. Hence, this order is to be completed in four days. In contrast, order No. 103 in the third pocket was scheduled for completion on July 16 and is five days behind schedule. This order is in department No. 6, which should be consulted to determine what can be done to get the order moving. The square pegs to the extreme right of the board indicate the scheduled dates for finishing the orders. Order No. 101, for example, is to be completed August 12.

QUALITY CONTROL

One of the important areas in which control efforts are made in an office is quality of work. Poor quality impedes the essential services of an office. A poorly typed letter, an incorrectly executed office form, an error in extending the cost data, or a misspelled name on a customers' list represents waste, because time and energy have been expended but full measures of returns for those expenditures have not been realized. Some of the work must be done over, some can be "fixed up"

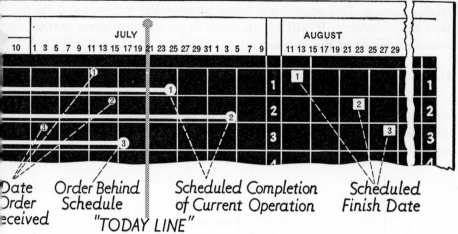

Courtesy: Wassell Organization, Westport, Conn.

by additional expenditure of time and energy, and some is used "as is" —with errors or misstatements undetected, and promising the possibility of subsequent waste.

Generally speaking, lack of adequate control over quality can result in three types of losses. Paper work errors can cause a wrong decision to be made. Failure to process an inquiry properly might result in the loss of the prospective sale from a very important customer. Also, poor quality can result in loss of good will. A customer's payment improperly posted, or an incorrect billing are examples. Furthermore, loss in time and money is incurred in detecting and correcting office errors. Frequently this loss is unnoticed, but nevertheless it is present.

APPROACHES TO CONTROL OVER OFFICE QUALITY

Faced with the necessity of maintaining a satisfactory level of quality, the office manager can select one of several alternatives. The approach to be used depends upon individual considerations. Usually the particular type of office work, the personnel, the cost of maintaining quality, and the possible effect of an error in the work are given high priority. First, a practice of checking every segment of all work can be followed. This constitutes 100 per cent inspection—i.e., each letter or each column of figures is gone over to verify the correctness of the work. Second, a policy of either spot or sample checking can be followed. In the case of spot checking, every third or perhaps fifth document or segment of work is checked. For sample checking, a group which is representative of the total is determined statistically and is subsequently checked to determine the quality level of the total work being performed. Third, the office work can be inspected by means of statistical quality control. This approach is based on statistical methods and the laws of probability. It will be discussed in elementary terms in the remaining pages of this chapter.

STATISTICAL QUALITY CONTROL

Natural phenomena and their relationships are statistical in character. Repeated productive operations of the same thing will provide a distribution of values. This can be evidenced either by measurement on each of a quantity of similar items or by repeated measurements

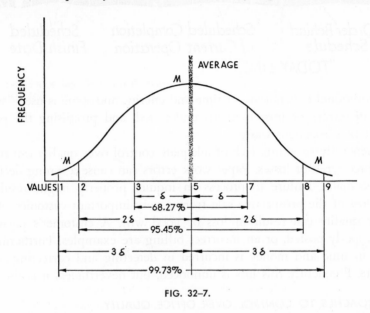

FIG. 32–7.

of the same thing on the same item. This follows because of the inherent characteristics of the measuring method.

The distribution of values can be shown graphically by means of a curve, with the values represented on the horizontal scale and the frequency of the values on the vertical scale. For our purposes here it can be stated that when the phenomena are natural, sufficiently large, and of random selection, most of the values will cluster in the center around a representative average value, while other values in the group will tend to taper off to the left and to the right of this average. The result is what the statistician calls a normal, or bell-shaped, curve, as shown by the curve, *MMM,* in Figure 32–7. To illustrate, if the errors of inventory recorders are counted, it will be found that most commit, let us say, five errors, while a few commit three, and still fewer commit one error. Likewise to the right (or greater than five errors), there will be some with seven errors, and a few with nine errors.

Based on statistical mathematics and the laws of probability, the statistician can determine the normal dispersion or spread of these data. Commonly, a value known as a standard deviation is calculated. Within a standard deviation to the left and to the right of the average are contained 68.27 per cent of the values of the series. Within two standard deviations to the left and to the right are 95.45 per cent, and within three standard deviations, 99.73 per cent of the values. These concepts are shown in Figure 32–7.

CHANCE AND ASSIGNABLE CAUSES

These statistical relationships are utilized in developing effective means to control the quality of work. For a series of data, it is known statistically what variations from the average can be expected on account of the inherent characteristics of the phenomena. Variation within a definable area is inevitable and is the result of chance. However, variation outside the definable area can be discovered and subsequently corrected. In other words, statistical quality control reveals when a variation is due to other than chance, i.e., when an assignable cause is present. But it does not tell what the cause is. Investigation and analysis are required to find and remove the assignable cause.

CONTROL CHART

A graphical device known as a "control chart" is constructed and used for plotting data and showing variations from the acceptable goal or standard. The values of the limits placed on the chart are determined statistically. In this work, the statistical concepts of the normal curve, the average or normal quality value, and the limits of variations that are due to chance are determined.

Figure 32–8 illustrates a control chart. This can be thought of as developed from a normal, or bell-shaped, curve placed on its side, so that the area in which variations due to chance occur is represented by a horizontal band. In this illustration, this band is from 3.0 to 7.0 errors. The average or normal expectancy due to the inherent nature of the work is 5.0 errors; however, the quality of the work will vary from 3.0 to 7.0 errors because of chance. It is inevitable and is not assignable to a cause. When the quality measurement goes outside this pattern of variations—for example, as indicated by points 1 and 2—the cause is not chance but an assignable influence which should be discovered and eliminated. It might, for example, be a defective tabulating key mechanism on the typewriter, paper slipping in the machine, or a space bar that is not working properly.

In a control chart the frequency of plotting the data depends upon the quality and the value of the product controlled. Usually the values are obtained from a sample of the work—that is, a representative number of the total are selected and checked. This may be once every fifteen minutes, or perhaps once a day. The value of these selected units is representative statistically of the total being processed.

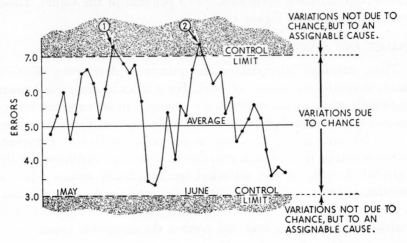

FIG. 32–8.   A control chart.

A different control chart is usually established for each control station. This is done because the work being quality controlled at one station may differ considerably from that at another station.

It should be noted that statistical quality control stresses preventive rather than remedial action. When more than 7.0 errors were found in a batch of work, indicated by point 1 in Figure 32–8, the work is stopped, and the reason for this assignable amount of errors discovered and corrected before the work is permitted to continue. A large quantity of work is not processed and subsequently much of it found defective. Statistical quality control emphasizes a look see while the work is being done, not a look-see after the work is completed. Also, the trend of the readings is usually indicative. For example, the increasing readings climaxing to point 2 in Figure 32–8, point to the occurrence of such a reading as 2 outside the control limits. Many feel that trends leading to readings near the control limits can be used as signals to look for an assignable cause without waiting for the actual reading to exceed the control limits.

PROGRAM TO FOLLOW UNDER STATISTICAL QUALITY CONTROL

To exercise control over quality by means of statistical quality control, it is first necessary to find out the current quality level of the operation. A fact-finding survey of from two to four weeks is recommended, the exact time depending upon the variety and complexity of the work being done. A description of the error, its probable cause, and an estimate of the time required to correct it provide additional information helpful in determining the areas in which quality control is needed.

The quality levels and the control limits should then be determined. It is usually best to concentrate on the key areas or locations. This tends to give control over the entire work of the office. Some errors can be eliminated entirely by the use of such techniques as process improvement, machine operation, and simplified office forms. When the error can be eliminated—i.e., all the factors causing it, the need to control such errors is likewise eliminated.

The next step is to establish the sampling plans so that economical and statistically sound representations of the total values will be used. This resolves itself into a problem of statistics, but a practical understanding of the included problem is necessary.

Installation of the program is usually a simple task, but close supervision and the availability of expert assistance, if needed, should be supplied. Like all new programs, that of statistical quality control gives rise to questions and to situations demanding on-the-job decisions.

Review of the program should be made periodically to check on results and make minor adjustments deemed advisable. Of course, if the nature of the work changes, the quality control efforts usually must also be changed accordingly. To reiterate, statistical quality control shows how much variation can and should be expected from the average. It is therefore unwise to censure the employee for making more than the average number of errors as long as the number made is within the control limits. When the measurements go beyond these limits, the assignable cause should be discovered and eliminated.

QUESTIONS

1. Discuss briefly the major problems created by fluctuation of office work.
2. As an office manager, would you favorably view working your employees overtime to meet work requirements? Justify your stand.
3. Identify each of the following:
   a) Assignable cause in statistical quality control.

  b) Cycle billing.
  c) Service bureau.
  d) "Folder system" of office work scheduling.
4. Are routing, scheduling, and dispatching interrelated or independent functions? Substantiate your answer, using an illustration.
5. Generally speaking, under what specific conditions would you recommend the use of part-time office help? Of mobile units within the office? Of no organized attempt to regulate the work output?
6. For each of the following, indicate what means probably would be used to handle the peak office work load caused by—
  a) Finishing a payroll by Friday morning of each week.
  b) Issuing statements to customers the first of each month by a large department store.
  c) Completing an inventory over a week end for a large manufacturing company.
  d) Issuing licenses to car owners of a state during the first two months of the year.
7. An office manager believes that scheduling all the work in his office would cost more than the advantages to be gained from such scheduling efforts. He feels, however, that scheduling certain operations only would be possible from the standpoint of cost. In your opinion would the scheduling of certain operations only probably prove satisfactory? Why or why not?
8. Point out the relationship, if any, in each of the following pairs:
  a) Scheduling and office machines.
  b) Routing and office layout.
  c) Standards and office work fluctuation.
  d) Quality control and dispatching.
9. Distinguish carefully between the use of a peg-string board and that of a visible card-Gantt Chart for scheduling office work.
10. An office manager receives daily reports on the results of statistical quality control work in key locations of the office. Aside from quality information, in what ways can the office manager use these reports to improve the accomplishment of the office work? Discuss.
11. Many feel that office work must be 100 per cent accurate and free from mistakes. In the light of statistical quality control, is this belief reasonable? Should an office manager expect this degree of quality? Discuss.
12. Does statistical quality control stress remedial or preventive action? Use Figure 32–8 in explaining your answer.

CASE PROBLEMS

CASE 32–1. STEADMAN COMPANY

For the past few weeks, the volume of office work has increased about 18 per cent. Unfinished work is piling up, and the office manager does not know if a temporary peak or a permanent new office work level is being attained. Data on the present office force are:

Type of Work	Three Accountants	Six Typists	Seven Clerks	Receptionist and Switchboard Oper.
Accounting..........	100	...	...	...
Typing..............	...	190	22	5
Filing..............	12	19	196	...
Miscellaneous.......	8	31	62	35
Hours per week......	120	240	280	40
Aver. hr. pay rate....	$2.35	$1.80	$1.40	$1.50

The sales manager suggests that the office staff work overtime in order to complete the work. He realizes that time and one half will be paid for overtime hours, but in his opinion this is the best answer.

The office manager personally dislikes the idea of overtime. He wants to go home to his family at the regular quitting time. Also, he will not receive overtime pay himself, because of his payroll classification. He favors hiring extra help.

The president of the company suggests that a service bureau be used to handle the overload. A friend of the president has told him that a service bureau, the Keystone Office Services, does excellent work and gives fast service. If the work is brought to its office, the bureau charges for accounting work, $4.00 per hour, for typing and general clerical, $2.75 an hour; or it will send help to the client's office, for which the charge is $4.50 and $3.50, respectively, an hour per employee supplied by Keystone.

PROBLEMS:

1. What important factors should be considered in arriving at a decision? Discuss.

2. What action should the office manager take? Justify your answer.

CASE 32–2.   ROSS MANUFACTURING COMPANY

Billings are processed by a series of operations, some of which are performed manually and some by machine. Briefly, the cost of the finished product is calculated, discount extended to give the net price, after which the freight charges are added. About 750 billings are prepared daily. The managers have decided against mechanizing this work due to adjustments required and the initial expense. At present, a complete inspection is made of one billing selected at random from each batch of 25 billings. Each such inspection costs 18 cents. Incorrect work is found in one out of every 30 batches. Subsequently, all the billings in that batch are inspected. This costs $1.55 for each billing in the batch. The higher cost is due to the inconvenience of removing the work from the line and reworking the incorrect billing which commonly requires telephoning and assembling required information.

An employee suggests that batches of 50 billings each would be just as effective as the present system and would reduce inspection costs. However, the supervisor believes smaller batches should be used—perhaps 5 or 10 to a batch—contending this would improve inspection and lower inspection costs. A second employee claims 100 per cent inspection is the only sure way to know all billings are correct, but this is not needed since the company's experience is that on the average only one error exists in a reworked batch. This amounts to one erroneous billing in 750 which in his opinion is extremely accurate work.

PROBLEMS:

1. With whom are you inclined to agree: the first employee, the second employee, or the supervisor? Why?

2. Evaluate the present quality control practices employed by the company for its billings.

Chapter · 33

Controlling and Improving
Office Procedures

Work Simplification philosophy, techniques, and participation
with know-how, provide an effective approach to eliminate
waste and at the same time help root out many deep seated
causes of internal strife, replacing them with understanding
and confidence.

—BEN S. GRAHAM

EVALUATING THE office work being accomplished,
as included in the controlling function of management, quite frequently
leads to the belief that the work can be done in an improved, simpler,
and better manner. In fact, over a period this viewpoint becomes
so prevalent that full acceptance is given this challenging statement—
inherent in most human efforts is waste of many kinds. However,
dynamic, not static, office procedures control will stimulate thoughts
and efforts leading into actions which help to minimize waste and
to increase office work efficiency.

PROCEDURES CONTROL

As pointed out in Chapter 12, an office procedure concerns the way
of doing a major phase of an office activity. Hence, it follows that
control of procedures means literally the ascertaining, evaluating, accepting, or rejecting of the manner or the means of office work performance. In other words, in procedures control the evaluation and
corrective follow-up are centered around processing.

There is unanimity of approval that office procedures *which are
necessary* should be performed in the most effective way. Appraisal
in terms of objective accomplishment is sometimes used. If the predetermined goal is gained, the procedure is considered satisfactory.

This goal achievement criteria is sometimes employed to emphasize elimination of nonproductive or wasteful elements of a procedure, that is, those parts not contributing directly to the desired end results. Examples include delays at desks, waiting for instructions, and long moves from work station to work station.

ELIMINATION OF WASTE

The elimination of waste is the foremost goal. Waste exists (1) in doing unnecessary office work, and (2) in doing necessary office work inefficiently. Each of these groups offers a tremendous challenge to everyone interested or employed in office work.

The evaluating of office procedures, seeking to improve their effectiveness, and eliminating waste, leads logically to the subject of work simplification which is extremely important. In fact, the remainder of this chapter and the next chapter deal with this subject. To reiterate, dynamic procedures control leads to work simplification, but the two terms are not synonymous. Work simplification is a broader and more fundamental concept, as will be shown in the immediate following pages.

WORK SIMPLIFICATION

A helpful definition is: "Work Simplification is the organized application of common sense by everyone to eliminate waste of any kind—waste time, energy, space, material, equipment, and so forth."[1] Basically it deals with creating an improved process or an easier and better way of doing necessary office work, but from the practical viewpoint it actually is more than this. It is also a philosophy to utilize "the organized application of common sense by everyone," and encompasses an attitude, thinking, and action about getting work accomplished. It transcends all work in all places at all times. It seeks to conduct office functions in the least laborious, least elaborate, least intricate manner consistent with the stated objectives. It concerns quantity of work, quality of work, the use of time, and the cost. It affects all expenditures made in accomplishing work—it is not limited to any one area of endeavor. As included in the above definition, its goal is "to eliminate waste of any kind."

Work simplification can be applied to a procedure, method, form, arrangement, machine, or type of equipment. In this book, work

---

[1] Ben S. Graham, Chairman, Future Demands Committee, The Standard Register Company, Dayton, Ohio, in a statement to the author, November 5, 1952.

simplification is first discussed in relation to an entire office procedure. The application of work simplification to an individual's job is treated in the following chapter. It is believed that this is the correct order— i.e., first simplify the procedure and then simplify the elements making up the procedure. To reverse this order would mean that individual jobs would be improved before determining whether they are necessary.

Work simplification deals with such things as the number of copies made, the make-up and size of the form, the type of machine used, the skill required to do the work, who sees the form and what he does with it, and how long it remains at each desk. The possibilities for securing work simplification are limited only by the ability, imagination, and aggressiveness of the person doing the simplification work. There is no secret formula.

Many office procedures have been studied over and over again, and improvements have resulted from each study. The best way is a theoretical concept. Waste in office work will always be found as work requirements change, new machines are developed, new materials become available, and informed office personnel aggressively seek improvements.

PRINCIPLES OF WORK SIMPLIFICATION

Over a period many lists of principles or guides of work simplification have been compiled. Some are quite lengthy, but for purposes here five principles will be discussed.

1. *Promote participation with know-how by every office employee by means of training in and encouraging the use of work simplification.* Enthusiastic employees with initiative and imagination in formulating the means and in co-operating in efforts to eliminate waste are of fundamental importance. A will to want an improved procedure to work satisfactorily and an understanding of the reasons for developing procedural improvement to eliminate waste are cardinal considerations in any work simplification program. For the most part, these are not won by having an expert simplify the work and by then telling the employees how the work should be done. In contrast, these considerations are won by encouraging employee participation in the work simplification efforts, for in this way employee interest, self-expression, acceptance, and co-operation are motivated and utilized.

But participation alone is insufficient. Nothing is more frustrating to the employee than to be asked to take part in an activity about which he knows little or nothing. This means the know-how must be supplied. Information and examples must be made available to him or, in other words, training is provided. Thus the "participation with know-how" is supplied.

The best improvements in the manner of office work performance may produce discouraging results because of employee attitudes and reactions. This has been summarized in four words, "employee resistance to change," but such a phrase assumes that resistance to change is a cause, which, in fact, is questionable.[2]

Most office employees dislike being "pushed around," being criticized, and not being informed of developments of changes which affect them. Factors such as these constitute the cause of resistance to change. In addition, fear of the unknown effect of improvements contributes to the employee's resistance. At the bottom of this is the employee's natural suspicion of what might happen to him as a result of the change. Typical of these fears are the questions: "Will my job be eliminated?" "Will lower prestige and loss of esteem by fellow employees result?" "Will my favorite desk location be lost?" "Is a loss in pay involved?" These fears must be eliminated in order to gain the full benefits of procedural improvements.

The question can be posed: "How can the real causes of resistance to change be overcome?" The answer is primarily employee participation with know-how in the work simplification program. A person will usually accept what he himself proposes. Give the employee the technique and the means for improving office work; the resultant improvement will usually have acceptance and the strong will to make it work satisfactorily. Even though the improvement does not represent the zenith of what probably can be done, it is well to remember that an average improvement with employee acceptance and enthusiasm will commonly outproduce a superior improvement with employee passive resistance.

In addition, frank information pointing out the need for improvements to keep the enterprise competitive or to give greater security to the employee should be provided. It is not necessary that an office employee lose his job as a result of work simplification. A policy of retraining and transferring to other jobs can be followed. In many cases the normal labor turnover will take care of the number of employees needed; those leaving the company are not replaced. But

---

[2] Ben S. Graham, Chairman of the Future Demands Committee, The Standard Register Company, is a leading exponent of the school of thought that believes the so-called "employee resistance to change" is an effect, not a cause. The background for the discussion here is based upon the thoughts advanced by Mr. Graham.

these facts should be explained in simple language to the employees so that they know what is going on and where they fit into the picture. Also, the ideas of acquiring a real sense of accomplishment and of getting things done the simple way are strong appeals to many office employees.

2. *Make the series of activities productive and simple.* Activities should bring the work closer to the end product, that is, they should contribute toward accomplishing the desired goal. As far as possible those contributing directly to the goal or so-called productive elements of a procedure should be maximized and, conversely, the nonproductive elements reduced to an absolute minimum. Normally this provides for the greatest productivity. However, in most procedures there are usually nonproductive elements that cannot be eliminated entirely, some are required to maximize the productive elements.

The more effective activities or series of activities are usually simple in their make-up. Involved ways of performing work should be avoided because they invariably include waste especially of time and of quality. The specific goals for performing most office work are relatively simple, and the process can be simple. But there is some tendency to get imbued with details, or excessively concerned with the frills. These must be guarded against and eliminated for improved work efficiency.

3. *Reduce distances traveled to the shortest amounts feasible.* Movement of papers or of people are costly and wasteful, since the great majority of such activities do not represent purposive effort. Therefore movements should be closely scrutinized, and if not essential, they should be eliminated. For office procedures, distances must be traveled, but these should be reduced to a minimum.

It is usually better to move the paper than the person. Sometimes the machine can be brought to the work, or mechanical handling devices such as conveyors, pneumatic tubes, and gravity feeds to deliver or to take away the papers can be used. When messengers are employed perhaps more items per trip are in order. Different arrangements of the office layout might also offer worth-while improvements.

4. *Arrange activities to provide a smooth flow from one clerical step to another or a rhythmic pattern for an employee at a workplace.* Excessive amounts or spurts of unduly heavy work loads tend to discourage the office employee. As a result, the feeling of never "getting on top of the work" or of having a sense of accomplishment plagues the employee. In contrast, the situation of carefully throttling the work in order to keep busy is equally annoying. A steady, constant

flow of work which is adequate and reasonable is especially significant in determining the most satisfactory office procedure.

Provide for a steady, constant flow of the work whenever possible. Once the paper work starts "through the mill," it should continue to progress until the completion of the procedure. Delays and hesitations should not be permitted. Get the work to flow. The following ditty illustrates this very well:

> When you have a plan
> With perfect FLOW,
> You reduce the times
> You "stop" and "go."[3]

For the individual employee, a rhythmic pattern of work actions should be encouraged by the arrangement of the work. Getting a swing or emphasis upon certain parts of the work helps to lessen fatigue and monotony. Motions along curved, not straight, lines should be used.

5. *Provide employees with pleasant physical surroundings and comfortable correct workplaces.* Almost every day additional evidence is found demonstrating that pleasant physical working conditions add materially to employees' satisfaction and productivity. Waste is decreased. Adequate light, for example, is an important factor in keeping errors in office work at a minimum.

An employee should be comfortable. This means that his chair, desk, table, or machine should be of such dimensions that the work can be accomplished with ease, that is, without excess physical exertion or strain. When possible, it is usually desirable to have the employee sit part of the time and stand part of the time. Some change is apparently necessary for maximum comfort.

TOP MANAGEMENT SUPPORT

A work simplification program should have the approval and support of the top managers for full benefits to be derived. They must be convinced that work simplification is the means to pursue to get rid of waste. Support from the top not only gives prestige and status to the program but it also serves to inform all members of the enterprise that work simplification is in keeping with the mode of operation the top managers want to exist.

---

[3] Lynell R. Cooper, "Product Analysis for Efficient Manufacturing," *Modern Management* (New York: Society for Advancement of Management, Inc.), October, 1947, p. 21.

NOMINAL HEAD OF PROGRAM

It is usually advisable to have one person in the office serve as nominal head of the work simplification program and responsible for co-ordinating the various efforts, stimulating interest in the program, and acting in the capacity of a clearing house for the various projects. Specifically, the day-to-day activities of this head include conducting all or some of the training sessions, counseling trainees and graduates of the training, publicizing the work simplification program, making periodic reports to top managers on the progress of the program, and budgeting the program's expenses.

A satisfactory arrangement is to have the person in charge report to a committee made up of the office manager and several department heads. By this means, proposed changes can be talked over, and an exchange of ideas is provided for. This medium also serves as a basis for keeping the department heads informed about procedural improvement, as well as for reminding them of the importance of effective procedures in office work. It may be desirable to have a member of top management on the committee so that vested interests on the lower levels will not be perpetuated.

If the volume of work warrants, a work simplification organizational unit staffed with full-time employees can be formed. Regardless of the organizational arrangement the principle of "participation with know-how" should be followed. Outside consultants can be used to bring in specialized knowledge, broad, fresh, and objective viewpoints. They are especially effective in training employees in the techniques of work simplification.

THE FIVE-STEP PATTERN

An effective approach used in work simplification consists of five steps including:

1. Select the office work to be improved.
2. Get all the facts about this work.
3. Analyze and evaluate these facts.
4. Devise the improvement.
5. Apply the improved way of accomplishing the office work.

Experience has shown this pattern to be an excellent basis for simplifying any work. Discussion of each step follows.

SELECT THE OFFICE WORK TO BE IMPROVED

Generally speaking, this is a trouble-giving situation such as the time taken to do the work is excessive, costs are unduly high, or the end result seems unjustifiable. It may be work that limits other office work or one in which labor requirements appear way out of proportion.

Whatever the office work selected, it must be defined. This brings objective clarity to the work simplification. In far too many instances attempts to simplify work are made without first gaining a clear concept of the work objective. The defining of the work assists in its simplification because all efforts can be concentrated and directed toward this goal. Questions to help in formulating the definition include: What is the end result of this work? Is it essential? Is this end result achieved now in part or in total by another procedure?

GET ALL THE FACTS ABOUT THIS WORK

The next step is to find out how the work is currently being handled. Details of the present procedure are obtained from available record sources, i.e., job descriptions, charts, lists, outlines, and sample forms. Supplemental information can be obtained from talks with members of management. This is followed by an inspection of the actual procedure in action so that the type of work and the equipment used can be observed.

All the facts are needed to perform a competent analysis. For example, it is insufficient to note, "Purchasing Department copy filed." Additional information required is: How many are filed per day or month? Is this a full-time job for one employee? Are any not filed? Why? Are they filed alphabetically?

To aid in getting all the facts and to gain a clear comprehension of them, graphic representations or charts have been developed. Charts show the complete action in concise form; they bring out the salient points vital in the analysis. There are many different types of charts that can be used, the major ones used for office procedures are shown in Figure 33–1. For each chart, the objective, suggested usage, and illustration are given. Observe that each of these charts has a particular purpose and value, and it is neither necessary nor practical to use every type of chart in a particular study. Frequently more than one chart is used, and the right combination of several charts usually reveals information and clues for work simplification. More will be discussed about charts later in this chapter.

OBJECTIVE	CHART TO USE	CHART ILLUSTRATION
TO IDENTIFY AND ANALYZE THE VARIOUS DETAILED STEPS OF THE WORK PROCESS	PROCESS CHART IDENTIFIES THE VARIOUS STEPS AND DIFFERENTIATES PRODUCTIVE FROM NONPRODUCTIVE ELEMENTS	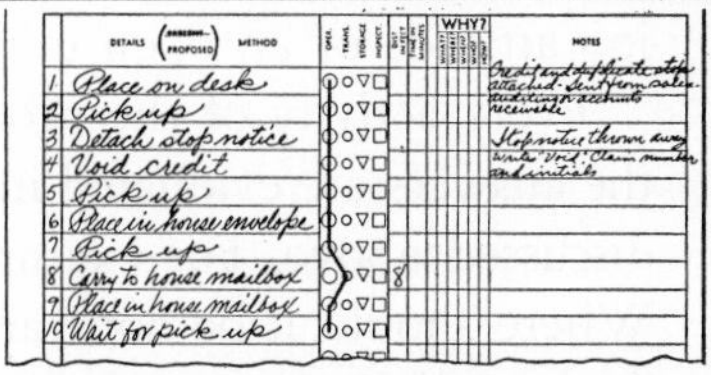
TO IMPROVE THE ARRANGE- MENT OF PHYSICAL FACILITIES	MOVEMENT DIAGRAM INDICATES MOVEMENT OF A PERSON OR A PAPER IN CONNECTION WITH PERFORMING WORK	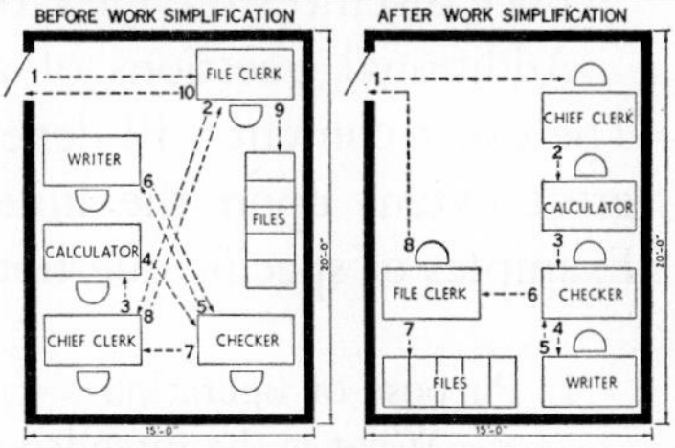
TO DETERMINE WHAT TYPES OF JOBS ARE PERFORMED AND WHO DOES THEM	WORK-DISTRIBUTION CHART— BASICALLY A SPREAD SHEET OF SUMMARIZED DATA	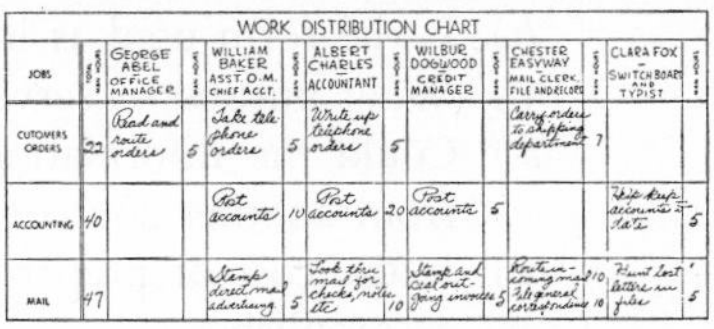
TO ANALYZE THE DISTRIBUTION AND USE OF COPIES OF A MULTI-COPY OFFICE FORM	PROCEDURE FLOW CHART SHOWS NUMBER OF COPIES, WHO PREPARES, AND WHERE THEY ARE USED	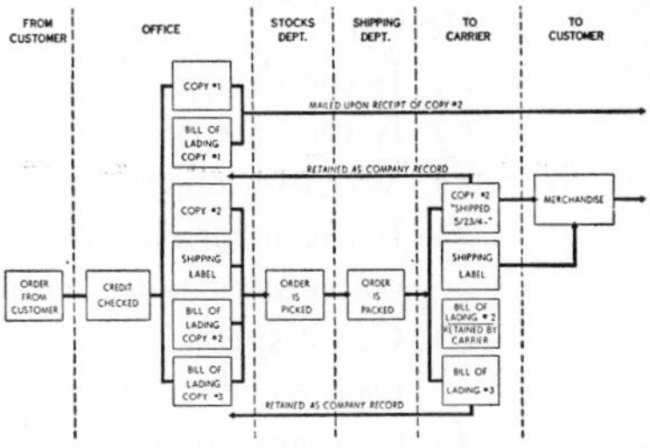

FIG. 33–1. Various types of charts used in simplifying office procedure.

ANALYZE AND EVALUATE THESE FACTS

Using the factual information about the entire procedure as a guide, the next step is to analyze and evaluate these facts. This phase of work simplification might be described as one of challenging or of questioning each detail of the work. For this purpose questions pertaining to Why, What, Where, When, Who, and How are extremely helpful. The facts obtained in step No. 2 show what is done, where, when, by whom, and how. To this the big Why must be added. In other words, the questioning now is, What is being done and Why, Where should it be done and Why, When should it be done and

Why, Who should do it and Why, and How should it be done and Why. The use of these questions has been referred to as a questioning attitude or an open mind. It is essential in work simplification.

Every activity of the procedure is subjected to this questioning, and the answers are evaluated in terms of the work simplification principles discussed above. For example, the answers to the double question of Where should it be done and Why, should comply with the principle, "reduce distances traveled to the shortest amounts feasible."

Additional questions of a more specific nature can also be asked. The exact content will depend upon the individual case and to a very great extent upon the initiative and imagination of the questioner. Examples of specific questions include:

1. Purpose of operation
    a) What is the intended use of the form?
    b) Is the form used as intended?
    c) What purpose is served by the report?
    d) Could the information given on the form or the report be obtained from another source?
    e) Is the cost of preparing the form or report justified by the results it accomplishes?
2. Design
    a) Is the design of the form such that no portion is unused?
    b) Is the size of the form best suited to its use?
    c) Would a change in color of the form facilitate its use?
    d) Is the information by which the form will be filed located in the most convenient place from a filing standpoint?
    e) Can a special type of form, such as Activisible, Kardex, or Keysort, be used to advantage?
    f) Can large forms be designed so that when folded they will fit in standard files?
3. Process analysis
    a) Is the operation duplicated at any point in the procedure?
    b) Should the form be filed permanently or temporarily or be destroyed?
    c) Can two or more records be produced at one writing by combining forms?
    d) Can the copying of information be eliminated by using original records?
    e) Is information compiled in the manner best suited for subsequent sorting, filing, or use?
    f) Should permanent records be made on a 35 mm. film to conserve filing space?
4. Inspection
    a) Is the form or work legible?
    b) Is the form or report easy to interpret?
    c) How is work checked for errors?

d) Is it important that all parts of the work be "letter perfect"?

e) Would the use of mechanical devices improve the accuracy of the work to a desirable extent?

5. Material

a) Is the paper stock used for the form the best suited for its purpose?

b) Is the size of the form most economical from a material standpoint?

c) How can waste of forms and office supplies be reduced?

d) Are office materials analyzed for suitability and ordered in most economical quantities?

6. Material handling

a) Can the flow of a form through the procedure be expedited by improved office layout?

b) Can the amount of time the form is delayed while awaiting action be reduced?

c) Is messenger service adequate?

d) Can pneumatic tubes or other forms-conveying systems be used to advantage?

e) Should special arrangements be made for keeping forms clean during handling in the shop?[4]

DEVISE THE IMPROVEMENT

Improvement is obtained by seeking to eliminate, combine, change, or simplify the steps of the procedure. Answers to, "What is being done and Why?" may point out activities that are unnecessary and can be eliminated. If so, eliminate them for this is the zenith of work simplification. Figure 33–2 illustrates the What and Why ques-

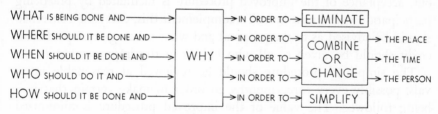

FIG. 33–2. Questions used in work simplification.

tion leading to elimination. Likewise, as shown in the figure, questions of Where and Why, When and Why, and Who and Why will suggest combining or changing of procedural elements as to place, time, and person, respectively. An improved procedure will result. How and Why emphasizes simplifying the activity.

As in the previous step, the devising of the improvement is conducted along the lines in conformity with work simplification principles.

[4] H. B. Maynard and G. J. Stegemerten, *Guide to Methods Improvement* (New York: McGraw-Hill Book Co., Inc., 1944), pp. 25, 28, 31, 35, 39, 40, 45, and 46.

For example, the answer to When-Why suggesting a change in the time scheduling of the task are guided by consideration for "arranging activities to provide a smooth flow."

The sequence of the questioning and subsequent improvement action is logical and practical. If the activity can be eliminated, there is no need to study it further for possible combination or change. Likewise the Who-Why question precedes the How-Why because the former might lead to improved labor utilization, and this should be determined before the manner of doing the work is improved.

APPLY THE IMPROVED WAY OF ACCOMPLISHING THE OFFICE WORK

This last step includes obtaining approval for the installation of the improved procedure, installing it, checking to see if the estimated decrease in waste is being realized, and following up periodically to uncover further possible improvements that may be developed. A common practice is to have a form filled out comparing pertinent information of the present with that of the proposed procedure. Savings expected in terms of man-hours, equipment, material, and dollars are the type of information included. Such information is essential for obtaining approval for the installation of the new procedure.

Acceptance of the improved way is sometimes predicated upon the results of a test installation. In this way, weaknesses can be spotted and corrected, and the assured savings can be validated. As already pointed out, acceptance of the improved procedure is facilitated by practicing participation with know-how. To complement this, everyone concerned should be advised as to the proposal and what is being attempted. Full credit should be given to all who helped in the improvement.

The simplified procedure should be reviewed at reasonable intervals, possibly every three months, in order to make certain that it is being followed. The value of the improved procedure is minimized if it is only partly followed. It is important to know how the procedure is working out and if its action is effective. In short, in order to improve procedures it is necessary to have due regard for results of their execution.

CHARTS IN PROCEDURES WORK

The balance of this chapter will be given to the important charts used in work simplification of office procedures. Included in this discussion are the process chart, movement diagram, work-distribution chart, and procedure flow chart.

PROCESS CHART

A process chart shows in detail the successive steps in a process; it is probably one of the most helpful tools in work simplification. The steps are indicated by brief statements and symbols arranged vertically in chronological order, with the first step at the top of the sheet. There are four commonly used symbols: (1) a large circle ○ for an operation such as writing, posting, sorting, and filing; (2) a small circle ○ for transportation such as movement of paper from place to place or the walking of an individual; (3) an inverted triangle ▽ for storage or delay such as an office form remaining in place awaiting further action; and (4) a square ☐ for inspection which includes checking or verifying, but not changing the paper. To illustrate, signing a letter constitutes an operation and would be represented by a large circle. Sending the letter to another office unit is a transportation and is shown by a small circle. Filing the letter is represented by a storage triangle. Checking the letter for errors constitutes inspection and is represented by a square.

The arrangement of these simple symbols gives a clear picture of the office procedure. In addition, it is customary to include the time required, the distance covered if movement is involved, and a summary by type of action.

Sometimes the "do" operations or those constituting the actual work and adding value to the product are distinguished from the "make-ready" and "put-away" operations, which are, respectively, the preparatory and the cleaning-up types that add cost but not value to the product. The distinction is by means of coloring the large circles for the "do" operations. Some recommend refinement of the "do" operations. For this purpose, two concentric large circles are used to indicate a "do" operation which is the origin of the record, and a large circle with three or four diagonal lines within it designate a "do" operation adding information to a record. In addition, developments to use a set of symbols more meaningful have taken place. In this respect, an arrow is used for transportation and a large D for delay which is considered an avoidable delay and distinct from a storage which is intentional.

A process chart can be drawn for an entire procedure covering many departments, or it may be confined to a part of a procedure. The details will vary accordingly, but a process chart always shows the basic types of actions throughout the area covered.

Figure 33–3 illustrates a process chart. It shows the process of stop-

MARSHALL FIELD & COMPANY
FLOW PROCESS CHART

JOB *Stopping any incorrect Charge Credit*

SUBJECT CHARTED *Credit form*

CHARTED BY *Ethel Marable*

DATE *November 19—*

DEPT. *Customer's Service* SEC *Adjusting*

SUMMARY			
METHOD	PRES.	PROPD.	SAVG.
NO. OF OPERATIONS	17		
NO. OF TRANSPORTATIONS	7		
NO. OF STORAGES	5		
NO. OF INSPECTIONS			
MAN HOURS OR MINUTES			
DISTANCE TRAVELED	92 ft.		

	DETAILS (PRESENT / PROPOSED) METHOD	OPER.	TRANS.	STORAGE	INSPECT.	DIST. IN FEET	TIME IN MINUTES	WHAT?	WHERE?	WHEN?	WHO?	HOW?	NOTES
1	Placed on desk	○	○	▽	□								Credit and duplicate Stop attached—sent from Sales Auditing or accounts receivable
2	Picked up	○	○	▽	□								
3	Placed in drawer	○	○	▽	□	2							
4	Waits	○	○	▽	□								Time indefinite—may have other work of priority nature
5	Taken out of drawer	○	○	▽	□	2							
6	Placed on desk	○	○	▽	□								
7	Waits	○	○	▽	□								makes out request for claim which acts as out-of-file notice
8	Attached to request	○	○	▽	□								
9	Carried to central files	○	○	▽	□	15							
10	Placed in basket	○	○	▽	□								
11	Waits	○	○	▽	□								For central file clerk
12	Picked up	○	○	▽	□								
13	Carried to file cabinet	○	○	▽	□	25							
14	Waits	○	○	▽	□								Looking for claim under correct name
15	Attached to claim	○	○	▽	□								
16	Carried to out basket	○	○	▽	□	25							
17	Placed in basket	○	○	▽	□								
18	Waits	○	○	▽	□								for pick up
19	Picked up	○	○	▽	□								
20	Carried to desk	○	○	▽	□	15							
21	Placed on desk	○	○	▽	□								
22	Stop taken from claim	○	○	▽	□								Original stop now placed on claim
23	Credit voided	○	○	▽	□								write "Void", claim number and initials
24	Picked up	○	○	▽	□								
25	Placed in house envelope	○	○	▽	□								
26	Picked up	○	○	▽	□								
27	Carried to house mailbox	○	○	▽	□	8							
28	Placed in house mailbox	○	○	▽	□								
29	Wait for pickup	○	○	▽	□								

24-01-01 Form 187

Courtesy: Marshall Field & Company, Chicago

FIG. 33–3. A fill-in type of process chart covering the work of stopping an incorrect charge credit.

ping an incorrect charge account in a large department store. It is drawn for the credit form papers. This work is brought about by the following situation.

An article of merchandise is purchased by a customer, Mrs. John T. Smith, with a charge account. The merchandise is returned, but the clerk incorrectly writes Mrs. John F. Smith on the credit memorandum. Later, the customer telephones and informs the Adjusting Department

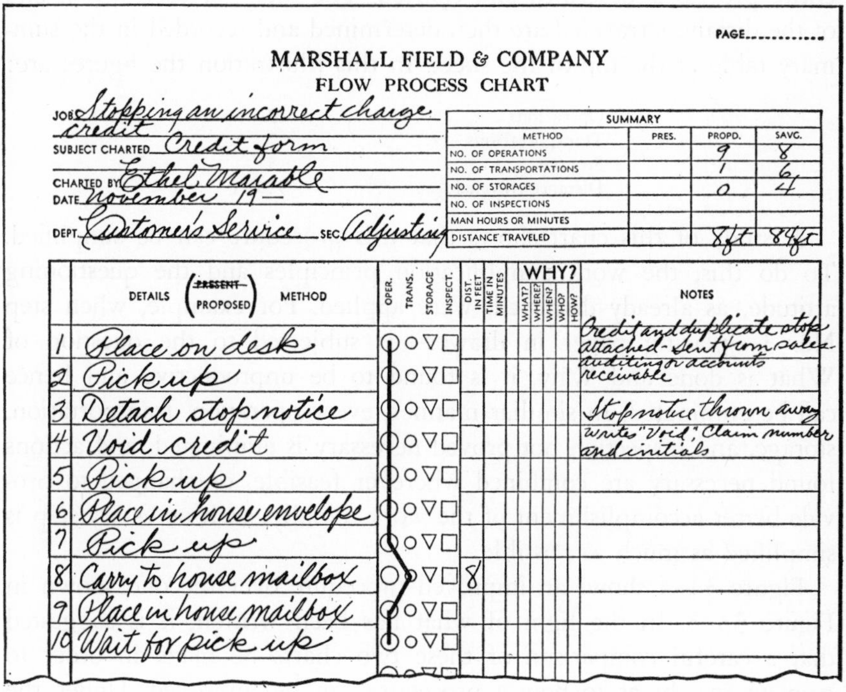

Courtesy: Marshall Field & Company, Chicago

FIG. 33–4. An improved procedure over that shown in Fig. 33–3.

of the store that the name is not Mrs. John F. Smith, but Mrs. John T. Smith. Meanwhile, the credit memorandum is in process in either the Sales Auditing Department or the Accounts Receivable Department, both located several floors away from the Adjusting Department. Hence, a "stop notice" is prepared and a duplicate copy sent to Sales Auditing or Accounts Receivable telling them not to bill the credit memorandum made out to John F. Smith. This stop notice, along with the credit memorandum to John F. Smith, is returned to the adjuster who handled the telephone call.

The placing of the credit memorandum and stop notice on the desk constitutes step No. 1 of the chart illustrated in Figure 33–3. Therefore, on the line No. 1, this action is briefly described in the column to the left. This action is an operation in that something happens to the papers; hence, it is represented by a large-circle symbol and is indicated on the chart by filling in the large circle under "operation" on line No. 1. Appropriate notes are made in the column to the right.

Next, the forms are picked up. Hence, on line No. 2, this action is expressed and represented by a large circle. In a similar manner, the entire process is described and charted. The totals of each action and of the distances traveled are then determined and recorded in the summary table at the top of the sheet. In this illustration the figures are:

> Operations......................17
> Transportations.................. 7
> Storage......................... 5
> Distance traveled...............92 feet

A study of this chart shows that this procedure can be simplified. To do this, the work simplification principles and the questioning attitude, as already discussed, were applied. For example, when step No. 3—placing paper in drawer—is subjected to the question of What is done and Why, it is found to be unproductive and hence can be eliminated. In similiar manner, every operation, transportation, storage, and inspection not proved necessary is eliminated, and actions found necessary are combined wherever feasible, or changed to provide better accomplishment of the work. Finally, each necessary step is simplified as much as possible.

Figure 33–4 shows an improved procedure over the one shown in Figure 33–3. In the light of what has been written, it is suggested that a careful comparison of these two charts be made in order to gain an insight as to how a procedure can be improved. Under the new procedure, credits are voided with a claim number on them and sent to Sales Auditing or Accounts Receivable. The stop notice can be discarded, since its duplicate is already on claim. The elimination of requests to pull claims out of the central file accounts for getting rid of steps No. 7 through No. 21 of the original procedure. Also, steps No. 3 through No. 6 have been eliminated; they were simply delaying actions brought about by the make-up of the original procedure. The improved procedure requires eight less operations, six less transportations, four less storages, and less than 10 per cent of the former distance traveled.

MOVEMENT DIAGRAM

A movement diagram portrays motion through space. It is drawn on a scaled layout of the office floor plan so that the movement can be measured and viewed in proper relationship with the physical factors. These charts are helpful in spotting backtracking, visualizing the physical motion involved, and locating congestions and bottlenecks.

Movement diagrams are of two types: those showing paper movement and those showing employee movement. The entire chart should be of one type or the other. Attempting to follow first one and then the other on the same chart leads to confusion. As the name implies, paper movement charts depict the successive lines of travel for a paper form, i.e., from desk to desk or from department to department. Figure 33–5 illustrates paper movement diagrams, showing the movements before and after work simplification.

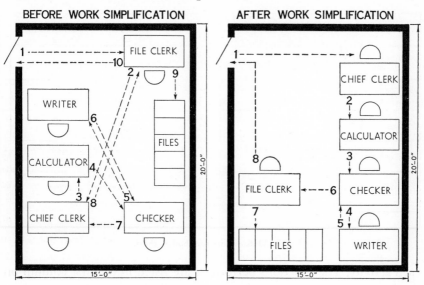

FIG. 33–5. Paper movement diagrams.

In many instances, however, the paper is not moved by simply handing it to the person at the adjacent desk or by messenger service; it is carried by the person last working on it to the next successive station. This is part of the procedure. It is therefore apparent that an analysis of employee movement is equally as important as an analysis of paper movement. Charts showing employee movement are especially helpful where the work is nonrepetitive and where the employees operate over a large area. The employee movement chart is similar in appearance to the paper movement chart.

WORK-DISTRIBUTION CHART

Proper distribution of work, facts on who is doing what, and the full utilization of labor skills on tasks for which they are best suited are fundamental to good management. In order to know what types of jobs are done and who performs them, a work-distribution chart can be used. This is basically a spread sheet which shows, for a given time period—usually a week—the type of work and the time spent on each job by each employee in the office unit under review. The basic information can be obtained from the supervisor or the employees. Probably more objective data are obtained by observing each employee and recording information on his activities. However, this approach is relatively expensive.

Figure 33–6 shows a work-distribution chart. A vertical column is used for each employee, along with one to indicate the time spent on

OFFICE FUNCTIONS	TOTAL MAN HOURS	LOIS MILLER Unit Supervisor	MAN HOURS	BETTY HEIDT Stenographer	MAN HOURS	RUTH TORFF Order Clerk	MAN HOURS	EDITH WRIGHT File Clerk	MAN HOURS	SYLVIA GAZEL Telephone Switch board Operator	MAN HOURS
Correspondence	54	Read and route Dictation	9 10	Takes dictation Transcribes	10 20	Types labels and materials for files	5				
Computing	32	Figures prices	3	Figures prices	2	Figures prices	15	Figures prices	12		
Filing	21					Files correspondence Finds letters in file	2 5	Files correspondence Finds letters in file Classifies correspondence	4 6 4		
Handling mail	26	Opens mail Time stamps mail	2 5	Stamps mail	2	Opens mail	5	Stamps mail	4	Opens mail Stamps mail	3 5
Miscellaneous	67	Answers questions Answers telephone inquiries Supervises	8 2 1	Cleans typewriter Gets supplies Arranges advertising stuffing material	1 2 3	Answers telephone inquiries	8	Errands for postage stamps and supplies Maintains tickler file for follow-ups	2 8	Operates switch- board	32
	200		40		40		40		40		40

FIG. 33–6.   Work-distribution chart.

each activity. The functions performed are listed in the first column on the left. This chart gives a graphic, over-all picture of the work done and the relative amounts of time put on each job. It shows, for example, whether major activities are given the most time or, in contrast, how much time is being spent on relatively unimportant functions. It reveals whether special skills are being wasted, whether too many employees are performing the same function, and whether an employee is doing too many unrelated tasks.

PROCEDURE FLOW CHART

This type of chart is very effective where multiple copy forms are used. It depicts graphically the distribution and subsequent steps for each form from physical inception to permanent storage or destruction. Generally this type of chart is not difficult to construct.

Figure 33–7 shows a procedure flow chart of work performed for handling uniform express receipt-collect shipments. Four separate writings are required for each package. These include separate typings for each of two labels, a packing slip and duplicate, and the copies of the uniform express receipt-collect. As indicated in the chart, the labels are put on the package. One copy of the packing slip is sent to the Billing Department for filing, the other copy placed in the package. Other operations can be determined from the chart.

A procedure to accomplish the same objective, but with much waste eliminated, is shown in Figure 33–8. As illustrated, a seven-part form is written at one time from the sales order. The writing is checked, and then the copies are sent to the Shipping Department, where they are distributed and used as indicated on the chart. The total number of operations has been reduced from thirty to seventeen, a saving of nearly 45 per cent. Waste elimination has been achieved by giving special attention to making activities productive, combining operations, eliminating others, and increasing the accuracy.

QUESTIONS

1. Name and discuss two principles of work simplification that you feel are of outstanding importance.
2. Discuss the importance of having top management members support for a work simplification program.
3. Should office work simplification be applied first to a procedure and then to methods, or vice versa? Why? Are there any outstanding exceptions to your answer? Explain.
4. As a junior accountant in an office, would you favor or disfavor work simplification in this office? Why? What significance is your answer from the viewpoint of the manager of this office? Explain.
5. Is it practical to simplify office procedures without the use of charts? Why?
6. Can all the elements of a procedure be productive? Explain.
7. In your opinion, do office employees resist change to procedural improvements? Discuss.
8. Identify each of the following by a simple statement:
   a) A "do" operation.
   b) Questioning attitude.
   c) Work simplification.
   d) Control of office procedures.
   e) A process chart.
9. Explain Figure 33–2 in your own words.
10. In your opinion, is the questioning approach probably most effective in dealing with process charts, work distribution charts, or procedure flow charts? Justify your answer.
11. Do you agree with the statement: "Whenever a change is made in an office

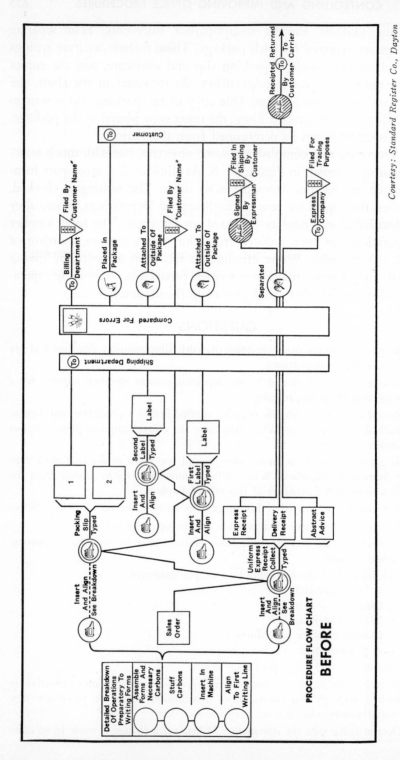

FIG. 33-7. A procedure flow chart before work simplification.

Courtesy: Standard Register Co., Dayton

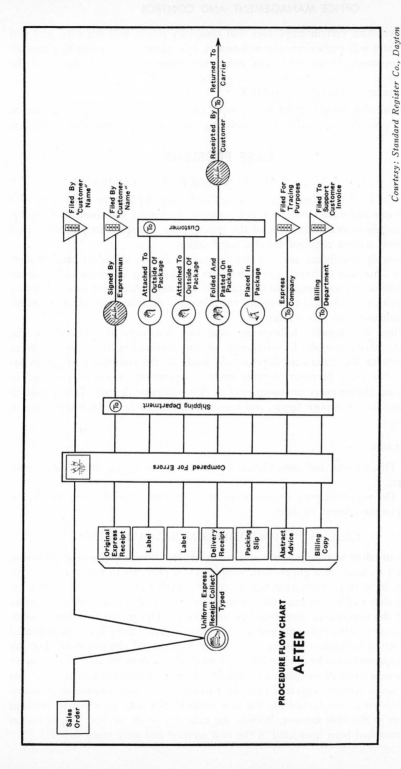

PROCEDURE FLOW CHART

AFTER

Sales Order

Uniform Express Receipt Collect Typed

- Original Express Receipt
- Label
- Label
- Delivery Receipt
- Packing Slip
- Abstract Advice
- Billing Copy

Compared For Errors

To Shipping Department

Signed By Expressman — Filed By "Customer Name"

Filed By "Customer Name"

Attached To Outside Of Package

Attached To Outside Of Package

Folded And Pasted On Package

Placed In Package

To Customer

To Express Company — Filed For Tracing Purposes

To Billing Department — Filed To Support Customer Invoice

Receipted By Customer — Returned To Carrier

Courtesy: Standard Register Co., Dayton

FIG. 33–8. The improved procedure over that shown in Fig. 33–7, after work simplification.

procedure, certain employees will complain, others will not care, and still others will enthusiastically welcome it. It is usually impossible to please all employees all the time. The most expeditious course is to make all the changes for improvement in a procedure at one time and thus gain the benefits as quickly as possible"?

12. Normally, should all the major types of charts used in work simplification of procedures be utilized in analyzing a specific office procedure? Explain.

CASE PROBLEMS

CASE 33-1.   TALLMAN INSURANCE COMPANY

In the local Cleveland branch office's collection department, consisting of a supervisor and three clerks, it is believed too much time is consumed in typing. An analysis showed that most of the typing time was spent in preparing paid premium reports required by the home office.

Monthly statements are sent for premiums due to all agents and brokers except "Account Current" agents who are those doing a considerable volume of business, and who render to the company a monthly Account Current showing premiums written and balances due the company. Account Current agents remit in accordance with this account.

When the monthly billings are sent out, one copy is retained for the branch office's records. Upon receipt of the remittances from the agent in payment of the statement, deposits are made in the company's premium account. For every premium deposit made, a typewritten report is prepared in duplicate, listing every premium paid in that particular deposit. This deposit is balanced to the deposit figure, and then sent immediately to the home office in Baltimore.

PROBLEMS:

1. Discuss your recommendation for reducing the typing time. Justify your answer.

2. Do you anticipate resistance to your recommendation from either the clerks or the agents? Explain.

CASE 33-2.   TOSTOMERO MUSIC PUBLISHERS

In an effort to reduce waste and cut costs, Mr. Benito Grassi, the president, decided to institute a paper-work simplification program in this company. An expert in work simplification was hired for a period of six months. It was believed that within this time the program could be well established, and further use of the expert's services would be unnecessary. During the first day at work, the expert observed the entire office and finally selected the job of opening mail and sorting the contents as the first job for analysis and simplification. The job was improved considerably, and the new method was demonstrated by the expert to the supervisor of the mail department, who agreed that the new method was a big improvement. Together they went to one of the four employees performing this work and showed her the new method. She was requested to perform the job in the new manner. Within the next day or so, all four employees on this work had been instructed in the new method and were using it.

For the following two weeks production records kept by the supervisor of the mail department showed that the productivity of the four employees increased approximately 30 per cent. It was found that the mail work for the day was nearly finished by mid-afternoon. Three of the girls were sent to the shipping department, where they were given work of verifying the sheet music gathered for an order against the items called for on that order.

The expert, quite pleased with the achievements to date, reviewed other jobs for analysis. He wrote a short note to Mr. Grassi informing him of the success of the program. The following day he received a telephone request from the mail department supervisor to come to that department at once. The expert complied, and the supervisor related that the four girls had come to him in a group asking for more money. He told them the plan was to give them an increase but they had beat him to it. Beginning a week from next Monday their pay would be raised from $60 to $70 a week. The supervisor inquired of the expert if this was correct. The expert assured him that was the amount the company agreed upon.

"Did the girls react favorably to the pay increase?" asked the expert.

"They seemed to be satisfied. They didn't say much of anything."

Over the next six weeks, the production of the four girls decreased until it was practically the same as it had been before the simplified method was installed. The decline was fairly uniform for each of the four employees. The expert checked the operators several times and observed that the employees were still using the new method. He spoke to them individually, but none had any complaints, nor did any have an explanation for the current level of production.

PROBLEMS:

1. Discuss the important ramifications of this problem.
2. Evaluate the work of the expert. Explain.
3. What action do you now recommend for the company? Why?

CASE 33–3.   DELANEY ENGINEERING COMPANY

Draw a procedure flow chart of the following:

1. Orders of the Delaney Engineering Company are received direct either from the customer or the company branch salesmen.

a) The order is first checked by the Order Department.

b) If it is clearly defined and is for standard parts, it is typed immediately. Eight copies are made.

c) If the order is not clear, i.e., wording is ambiguous, part must be identified, etc., it is sent to the Engineering Department for specifications before typing.

2. The order typist assigns an order number, keeping a record of the customer's name and the number assigned.

3. This order record is made in duplicate. The original is sent to the Billing Department, where it is filed according to order number. The second copy is retained by the Order Department and filed alphabetically by customer's name.

4. The original or invoice copy of the order is retained by the Billing Department until evidence has been received that the order has been shipped.

a) It is then filed by invoice number for ten years along with the original order record sent by the Order Department.

5. The second copy is the shipping order.

a) It is routed through the Credit Department for a credit check. During this work it may be passed on as open account; passed on a C.O.D. basis; or held for further credit information.

b) From the Credit Department, it goes to the Production and Stores Department, where the material is secured and sent to the Shipping Department.

c) After the order is shipped, this second copy is returned to the Billing Department and filed by number with the original order record sent by the Order Department.

6. Copy No. 3 is a tissue copy which is retained by the Shipping Department for permanent record.

7. Copy No. 4 is a tissue copy which is sent by the Shipping Department to the Order Department as evidence of shipping. It is filed with the original order data under the customer's name.

8. Copy No. 5 is another tissue copy which is enclosed with shipment by the Shipping Department when the order is shipped.

9. Copy No. 6 is sent to the Credit Department. If credit is satisfactory, this copy is sent to the customer acknowledging his order. If there is any question about method of payment, the Credit Department holds the entire order packet pending satisfactory credit arrangements.

10. Copies Nos. 7 and 8 are sent to the branch sales office and to the salesmen respectively. They are mailed out immediately after the order is written up by the Billing Department.

Chapter · 34

Simplifying Office Methods

All the problems of the world could be settled easily if men were only willing to think.

—Dr. Nicholas Murray Butler

AFTER THE necessary office work has been simplified into the best procedure, each step or series of steps performed by an individual employee should be carefully analyzed to find out the best way of accomplishing the work. The efforts of simplification are now concentrated upon the work done by an employee in a particular procedure.

Improvement in the performance of an employee's task is obtained by following the same fundamental approach already discussed in the preceding chapter under "procedures." The same principles and techniques of work simplification apply to the individual office employee's task as well as to office procedures. Facts are obtained, charts are used to visualize the work, every detail of the task is questioned to uncover clues for improvement, employee participation is encouraged, and greater productivity and accuracy are sought. The goal is to eliminate waste.

MOTION STUDY

When improvement efforts are concentrated on the task of an employee performing a given type of work, the term "motion study" is commonly used to identify these efforts. In this sense, motion study designates the analytical method applied to a part, while work simplification is applied to the whole or series of parts. However, this is a question of terminology. As stated above, work simplification applies equally to the entire procedure or any part of it, including the work done by the individual employee.

The fundamental basis of all physical work is the execution of motions. Task performance usually involves physical movements on the part of the employee. For example, movements by the left hand and arm or by the right fingers and wrist are typical movements for many office tasks.

Frank B. and Lillian M. Gilbreth, pioneers in this area of management, define motion study as follows: "Motion study consists of dividing work into the most fundamental elements possible; studying these elements separately and in relation to one another; and from these studied elements, when timed, building methods of least waste."[1] In other words, it is the careful analysis of an employee's motions with the view of finding the best way of doing the task, i.e., eliminating waste of all kind.

One of the prime ways of eliminating waste is to eliminate unnecessary motions. Those movements which do not contribute to the fulfillment of the task are discarded. Only the essential motions are retained, and these are arranged to accomplish the work with a minimum of time, effort, and fatigue. This results in greater output per employee and in a reduction of fatigue and waste. The gains possible from motion study are tremendous, for as the Gilbreths wrote:

> The greatest waste in the world comes from needless, ill-directed, and ineffective motions. These motions are unnecessary and preventable. Their existence in the past was excusable, because there was no knowledge of how to dispense with them. That excuse no longer obtains. The methods and devices of waste elimination are known and are being constantly used. But the knowledge of how to make these great world-wide economies is being disseminated at an astonishingly slow pace.[2]

Motion study is not speed-up. Motion study does not imply speeding up the movements of the employee; rather it implies an increase in the rate of work production. There is a significant difference between these two concepts, and this difference should be clearly understood. Speeding up the employee means to hurry *all* the steps, *both the necessary and the unnecessary ones.* In contrast, increasing the rate of production through motion study means *performing only the necessary steps in a normal manner.*

APPROACH TO SIMPLIFY EMPLOYEE TASK

Since the approach followed for simplifying an employee's task is similar to that for improving an office procedure, discussed in detail in Chapter 33, the material of this chapter is concentrated on

---

[1] Frank B. and Lillian M. Gilbreth, *Applied Motion Study* (New York: Macmillan Co., 1919), p. 43.

[2] *Ibid.,* p. 57.

pointing out considerations and information especially helpful in simplifying the office employee's task. The basic five-step pattern of work simplification will be followed, but the discussion under each will be material not yet presented in this book. For reference purposes this five-step pattern or work simplification approach includes: (1) select the work to be improved, (2) get all the facts about this work, (3) analyze and evaluate these facts, (4) devise the improvement, and (5) apply the improved way of accomplishing the work.

START WITH REPETITIVE TASKS

In selecting the work to be improved it is best to start with repetitive tasks. They lend themselves most readily to analysis, since they occur in volume and over a period of time, making a detailed study possible. Furthermore, they offer large savings possibilities. The savings on each task performance might be small, but the doing of the task over and over again results in cumulative savings of a sizable amount.

In the experience of one company, the annual savings amount to $340 per office task improved. This may appear relatively small, but on the average over 150 such improvements are developed each year, making a yearly savings of over $50,000—a truly worth-while goal.

Selecting repetitive tasks for simplification does not mean that special tasks do not warrant study. *Any task can be improved with sufficient study.* In many instances worth-while savings on regular tasks have been made from analysis of special tasks. Actually, the job selected and the extent and thoroughness of the analysis depend upon a number of things, such as the continuity of the work, the amount of processing required, the total cost or number of people engaged in the work, the value connected with the paper handled, and the interest of the operative employee, supervisor, or analyst.

GETTING ALL THE FACTS

As in the case of procedural improvement, it is necessary to have all the facts about the work to make a proper and meaningful analysis. This information is obtained from a number of sources. Of particular interest here is the use of charts, among which the more common include the left- and right-hand chart, the production study chart, and the operator-machine chart. See Figure 34–1. All of these pertain to the individual employee performing a specific task. They differ in content and make-up, but not in purpose, from the charts used for procedural analysis. A detailed discussion of these charts along with examples are included at the end of this chapter.

OBJECTIVE	CHART TO USE	CHART ILLUSTRATION
TO ANALYZE THE HAND MOTIONS OF THE OPERATOR	LEFT AND RIGHT HAND CHART SHOWS THE DETAILED MOTIONS OF EACH HAND IN PERFORMING THE WORK	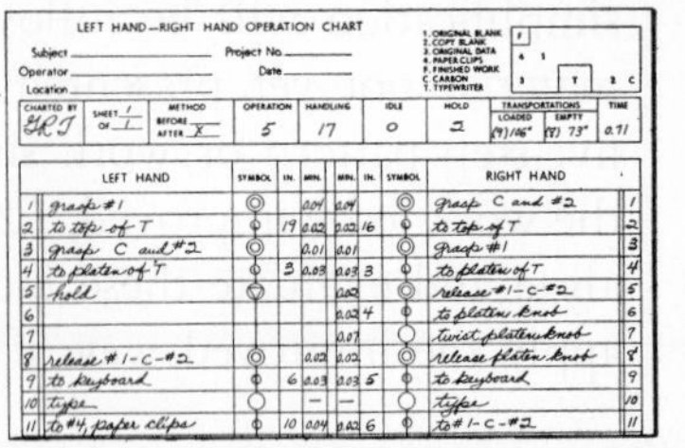
TO STUDY HOW AN EMPLOYEE SPENDS HIS TIME	PRODUCTION STUDY CHART SHOWS AN EMPLOYEE'S TIME BY ACTIVITIES	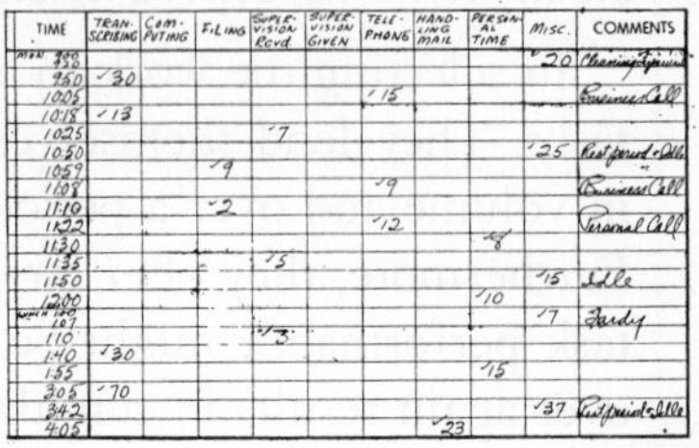
TO SHOW THE WORK RELATIONSHIPS BETWEEN OPERATOR AND MACHINE	OPERATOR-MACHINE CHART SHOWS CORRELATION BETWEEN OPERATOR AND MACHINE IN PERFORMING THE WORK.	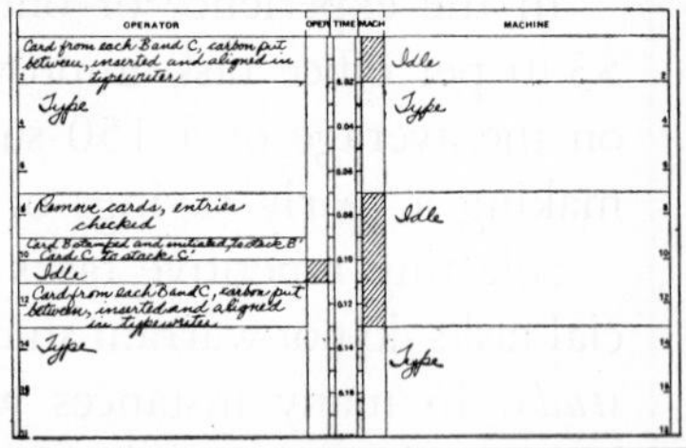

FIG. 34–1. Various types of charts used in simplifying office methods.

THERBLIGS

To assist in analyzing the facts, the Gilbreths developed the idea that all motions are made up of elements called "therbligs" (coined from the spelling of the name Gilbreth backwards, except for the *th*).[3] Most manual work consists of a relatively few basic motions repeated again and again. Gilbreth designated seventeen therbligs; other motion analysts have arrived at a slightly different number. Figure 34–2 shows sixteen commonly used fundamental motions as classified by Professor Ralph M. Barnes.

The use of therbligs is helpful in detailed studies and refinements. However, motion analysts frequently do not use the therbligs as such,

[3] There is a difference of opinion as to the correct definition of a therblig. Some writers call it an elementary motion, while others feel that it is fundamental but of a compounded, not an elemental, nature and concerns work accomplishment.

Name of Fundamental Motion	Symbol	Description
Select	St	Select refers to the choice of one object from among several.
Grasp	G	Grasp refers to taking hold of an object.
Transport loaded	TL	Transport loaded refers to moving an object from one place to another.
Position	P	Position consists of turning or locating an object in such a way that it will be properly oriented to fit into the location for which it is intended.
Assemble	A	Assemble consists of placing one object into or on another object with which it becomes an integral part.
Use	U	Use always consists of manipulating a tool, device, or piece of apparatus for the purpose for which it was intended.
Disassemble	DA	Disassemble consists of separating one object from another object of which it is an integral part.
Inspect	I	Inspect consists of testing a piece to determine whether or not it complies with standard size, shape, color, or other qualities previously determined.
Pre-position	PP	Pre-position refers to positioning an object in a pre-determined place in such a way that it may be grasped in the position in which it is to be held when it is needed.
Release load	RL	Release load refers to that part of the cycle during which the hand is letting go of the object grasped, allowing it to slip out of the hand.
Transport empty	TE	Transport empty consists of moving the empty hand in reaching for an object.
Rest for over-coming fatigue	R	Rest for overcoming fatigue is a fatigue or delay allowance provided to permit the worker to recover from the fatigue incurred by his work.
Unavoidable delay	UD	Unavoidable delay refers to a delay beyond the control of the operator.
Avoidable delay	AD	Avoidable delay refers to any delay of the operator for which he is responsible and over which he has control.
Plan	Pn	Plan refers to a mental reaction which precedes the physical movement, that is, deciding how to proceed with the work.
Hold	H	Hold denotes the retention of the object after it has been grasped, no movement of the object taking place.

Source: Ralph M. Barnes, "Work Methods Manual" (New York: John Wiley & Sons, Inc., 1944), p. 68

FIG. 34–2. Names, symbols, and descriptions of commonly used fundamental motions. The motion "select" is sometimes segregated into three separate motions: "search," "find," and "select."

but they do employ them as fundamental to their thinking. For example, it is generally recognized that economy in motion is realized when both the right and left hand start their therbligs at the same time. The motion economist will strive to attain this condition, but he might not make a therblig analysis.

THE QUESTIONING APPROACH

The questioning approach is advantageous in seeking simplification of office methods. It is actually more of attitude than of technical knowledge. It can be developed by anyone who approaches the job with an open mind and who believes that the manner of doing the work can be improved. Each detail of the work manner is questioned for its essentiality, possible change, combination with other motions, or simplification. The questions of What-Why, Where-Why, and so forth, are utilized as previously discussed and illustrated. (See Fig. 33–2.)

Additional questions of a method-improving nature and with purposeful intent should be developed and used. They should lead to betterment, not just a conglomeration of queries. Generally speaking, good questions are required in order to get good answers. The following list includes a number of selected questions which are worded to provide practicality and to furnish answers that are useful in bringing out possibilities for improvement.[4]

Questions regarding setup or workplace layout:

1. Is the recipient of the form provided with a proper place to keep it?
2. Are pens, pencils, erasers, forms properly prepositioned?
3. Are desk tops and drawers kept in an orderly condition so that time spent looking for lost articles is reduced to a minimum?
4. Is a desk necessary, or could the work be done as well on a flat-top table?
5. Should a specially designed table be provided to facilitate the use of office machines?

Questions regarding tools and equipment:

1. Can gathering or sorting aids be used?
2. Should a machine replace hand methods?
3. Are office machines properly maintained by qualified maintenance men?
4. Can any foot-operated devices, such as a foot-operated stapler, be used?
5. Is the type of typewriter suitable for the use to which it is put?

Questions regarding working conditions:

1. Are unnecessary noises and disturbances eliminated?
2. Is privacy assured for telephone conversations of a confidential nature?
3. What precautions are taken to prevent the spread of colds and other infectious diseases throughout the office?
4. Are suitable facilities provided for personal belongings?
5. Could certain clerical operations, such as payroll work, be handled to better advantage on a three-shift basis?

---

[4] Adapted from H. B. Maynard and G. J. Stegemerten, *Guide to Methods Improvement* (New York: McGraw-Hill Book Co., Inc., 1944), pp. 51, 56, 60–61.

DEVELOPING THE IMPROVED METHOD

This can be viewed as consisting basically of two closely interrelated functions: (1) improving the employee's motions, and (2) providing a suitable workplace area. In the former the step-by-step examination to eliminate, combine, change, or simplify the motions is followed. To assist in these efforts various lists of guides have been developed. Figure 34–3, for example, shows helpful suggestions to follow in improving office methods.

HELPFUL HINTS
TO
SIMPLIFY YOUR JOB

1. Have source document and end result in same format, if possible.
2. Use pre-computed tables or graphic indicators.
3. Avoid writing the same information twice.
4. When a pencil is satisfactory, use it in preference to making insertions into a typewriter.
5. Use a file copy in preference to making entry in register.
6. Make only the number of copies that are needed and used.

FIG. 34–3. Points to remember in simplifying an office method.

There exist fundamental guides to assist in acquiring the most efficient motion patterns. These guides are universal—they apply to all motion cycles. By following these guides, the greatest savings in motion expenditures will be realized. The list includes:

1. Both hands should preferably begin their therbligs simultaneously.
2. Both hands should preferably complete their therbligs at the same instant.
3. Both hands should not be idle at the same instant except during rest periods.
4. Motions of arms should be in opposite and symmetrical directions instead of in the same direction, and should be made simultaneously.
5. Hesitation should be analyzed and studied, its causes accounted for, and if possible eliminated.
6. Shortest time demonstrated in one part of a study should be used as a mark to attain, and reason for other times required in other parts of the study should be known.
7. Number of therbligs required to do work should be counted, for the best way is almost always a sequence of the fewest therbligs.
8. The best sequence of therbligs in any one kind of work is useful as suggesting the best sequence in other kinds of work.

9. Every instance where delay occurs suggests advisability of providing some optional work that will permit utilizing the time of delay, if so desired, or of making fatigue study of the interval.
10. Variations of time required for any single therblig should be arrayed and causes recorded.
11. Lateness of various parts of the anatomy as compared with other portions should be recorded.
12. All material and tools should be located within the normal grasp area.
13. Motions should be confined to lowest possible classifications in order to reduce fatigue, as listed below giving the least fatigue and most economical first.
    1st. Finger motions.
    2nd. Finger and wrist motions.
    3rd. Finger, wrist, and lower arm motions.
    4th. Finger, wrist, lower arm and upper arm motions.
    5th. Finger, wrist, lower arm, upper arm and body motions.
14. Tools and materials should be located as to permit proper sequence of therbligs. The part required at the beginning of the cycle should be next to the point of release of the finished piece from the former cycle.
15. Sequence of motions should be arranged to build rhythm and automaticity into the operation.
16. Hands should be relieved of all work that can be done by feet or other parts of the body.
17. Tools and materials should be prepositioned as much as possible to reduce the search, find and select therbligs.
18. Gravity feed containers should be used to deliver the material as close to the point of assembly or use as possible. This delivery point should be near the height at which it is assembled in order to eliminate any lifting or change in direction in carrying the parts to the assembly.
19. Ejectors should be used to remove the finished part.
20. Use "drop delivery" whereby the operator may deliver the finished article, by releasing it in the position in which it was completed, without moving to dispose of it.

NOTE: Improvement of methods and conditions necessitate repetition of trial motion and time studies. During these trials, details of work manipulation are perfected and tested by comparing time. When no further improvement is possible, final records of method and time are made.

The position in which work is placed when it is deposited for operator is most important.[5]

PROVISION OF SUITABLE WORKPLACE AREA

In motion economy, the providing of a suitable workplace area is of equal importance with analyzing the employee's motions. The best

[5] Allan H. Mogensen, *Common Sense Applied to Motion and Time Study* (New York: McGraw-Hill Book Co., Inc., 1932), pp. 98–99.

With reference to No. 13 in this list, regarding the classification of motions, an interesting and highly informative discussion of leg, body, and knee motions is made by Maynard, Stegemerten, and Schwab, *Methods-Time Measurement* (New York: McGraw-Hill Book Co., Inc., 1948), pp. 105–20.

motion cycle and the maximum elimination of waste are not possible unless the proper workplace area is provided.

In considering the workplace area, there are usually many possibilities for improvement. Among the most important are:

1. *Place only what is needed for the task on the desk or table top.* Do not clutter up the work area with such things as paper clips, pads, miscellaneous folders, magazines, and books which are not required in performing the task. Supplies and tools not needed should not be in the employee's way. When they are allowed to remain, inefficient motions as well as unsightly work areas are evident.

2. *Keep the employee's supplies and tools not needed for the particular task in desk drawers or in cabinets.* Supplies and tools should be stored neatly and systematically; the arrangement used depends upon the individual circumstances. Materials placed in cabinets should be indexed according to some simple plan that facilitates finding.

3. *Utilize the normal and the maximum working areas.* The *normal* working area for the right hand on a desk top, for example, is the area determined by swinging the extended right hand and forearm only across the desk. The pivoting is at the elbow, with the upper arm being relaxed at the side of the body. The arm tends to swing out a little at the outer end of the arc. In a similar manner, the normal working area for the left hand is determined. These two normal areas overlap in front of the employee, and this overlapping area represents the location in which work requiring both hands can be performed most readily.

The *maximum* working areas are the areas determined by swinging the extended hand and entire arm, pivoting at the shoulder. Figure 34–4 shows graphically the normal and maximum working areas with dimensions for an average employee.

Paper being worked on should be located within the arcs of the normal working areas common to both hands. Supplies should also be conveniently located, i.e., within the normal and never outside the maximum working areas. It should be noted that the periphery of this area is arc-shaped and not rectangular. The arrangement of the supplies and tools should also follow a pattern determined by motion principles.

4. *Provide a comfortable and effective arrangement.* For minimum fatigue, the chair should support the employee slightly above the small of the back and should permit him to sit erect with his weight supported by the bone structure of the body. It is desirable that the height of the seat and of the back, and the relative position of the back to the seat, be adjusted in order to meet individual needs. Correct

chair height is achieved when the weight at the knees is supported by the feet and when no pressure exists between the upper leg and the front edge of the seat. The back support should be such that the occupant can sit back in the chair.

The height of the workplace should be such that comfortable support is given the underside of the forearm at a point slightly below the elbows. In cases where the hands are self-supported and a desk or table is used, the workplace should be of such height that the hands work at a level slightly higher than that of the elbows.

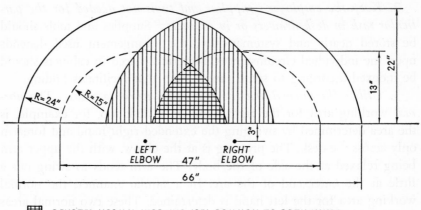

⊞ DENOTES NORMAL WORKING AREA COMMON TO BOTH HANDS

⊞ DENOTES MAXIMUM WORKING AREA COMMON TO BOTH HANDS

FIG. 34–4. Illustration of normal and of maximum working areas.

In typing, for example, the forearms should be parallel to the slope of the keyboards with the wrists slightly lower than the knuckles. The typist should sit in a position that will cause her upper arms to slope slightly forward. Sitting erect in the chair directly in front of the machine with feet flat on the floor makes it possible to type comfortably and easily.

The use of functional office equipment can also be cited. For example, a desk with a recessed portion on one end, to permit a Comptometer keyboard to be on the same level as the desk top, adds to the employee's comfort and efficiency. Sometimes it is helpful to do away with a portion of a worktable top so that a particular piece of required equipment can be located in the most convenient area and at the right height.

Materials and devices normally required in the execution of the work should be provided and conveniently arranged. This includes such things as supplying devices to hold papers while typing; locating frequently used supplies such as paper clips, stapler, and rubber stamps on a rotor where easy access is possible; and putting reference materials, including books, catalogues, and lists, on convenient racks within easy reach or vision of the operator.

The arrangement of unitizing can also be followed. Under this plan, each operating unit is considered a separate entity and is supplied individually with all the tools and supplies necessary for its work. The required papers, books, supplies, and the like are located on a wall rack or in a floor cabinet near the operator's desk. For the most part, this arrangement brings best results when a large portion of the office consists of widely dispersed and fairly independent units, although it is not limited to this particular type of setup.

APPLICATION OF THE NEW METHOD

After an improved method has been worked out, it is a relative simple matter to apply it, providing the employee has participated in the simplification work and has an understanding of and confidence in the management members of the enterprise, as discussed in the preceding chapter. There is no adequate substitute for gaining and maintaining wholesome understanding between the management and non-management members. The purpose of methods improvement should be clearly set forth, and the reasons for its importance in the enterprise made crystal-clear to every employee. Along this line it is frequently helpful to show examples of what has been accomplished with methods improvements in other offices, and to indicate that it is one of the media through which the combination of high wages and low hours has come about.

Everyone must realize the importance of motions in performing office work and see possibilities for improvement. This includes all department heads, division heads, supervisors, and operative employees. To achieve this goal, training groups can be held; meetings with department heads and supervisors are common. They can be conducted separately for each group or combined into one group, depending upon the individual circumstances. In certain instances supervisors may not partake freely in the discussions if management heads are also present. When this condition exists, separate groups can be formed, but management heads should never be excluded from the program; otherwise, they may lose touch with the progress and fail to see the supervisor's viewpoint.

THE LEFT- AND RIGHT-HAND CHART

An important tool of methods improvement is the left- and right-hand chart which shows the actions and motions of each hand. In this case six symbols are used including:

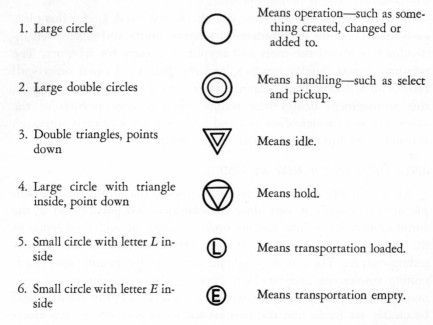

1. Large circle — Means operation—such as something created, changed or added to.

2. Large double circles — Means handling—such as select and pickup.

3. Double triangles, points down — Means idle.

4. Large circle with triangle inside, point down — Means hold.

5. Small circle with letter *L* inside — Means transportation loaded.

6. Small circle with letter *E* inside — Means transportation empty.

Some believe it is best to observe the actions of both hands and to indicate these data on the chart as the work progresses. Others prefer to prepare the chart by following the actions of the right hand only, the actions of the left hand only, and then combining the two charts in order to show the relationships existing according to time of execution. Attention must be given to details. A few seconds saved on an action or the elimination of a short movement, perhaps 3 or 4 inches, may seem small; but when the task is repeated over and over again, the cumulative savings in fatigue and time become highly significant.

An Original Method Described. Figure 34–5 illustrates a left- and right-hand operation chart for typing, in duplicate, original sales data sent in by field representatives. The workplace layout is sketched at the top of the chart. A number or code system can be used to identify the various materials and equipment used. Also, provisions for the inclusion of other pertinent data are made at the top of the sheet. Of special interest is the summary information which shows the total actions by type along with the distance the hands travel and the time taken to perform the task.

In this case the task begins with the operator reaching with the right hand to the pile of copy blanks positioned to the right and forward of the typewriter. This action is "transportation empty," since the hand is empty, and is indicated on line No. 1 by a small circle with an *E* inside under the symbol column for the right hand. The description "to No. 2" is written in the description column on the right. In making this transportation the hand travels 20 inches, and this is recorded in the distance column, right hand, on line No. 1. While this is going on, the left hand is idle, so a double triangle is inserted under the symbol column of the left hand and the word "idle" written in the description column on the left.

Next, the right hand grasps a copy blank. This is a handling action and is shown by large double circles on line No. 2 under the right hand. "Grasp No. 2" is written on the same line under the description column. During this particular operation the left hand was idle. Since this is the same as the previous entry for the left hand, no new symbol is necessary on the chart.

In a similar manner each step of the operation is observed and noted on the form. It is important that all details be included and that extreme care be exercised to insure accuracy in this work.

Improving an Original Method. A study of Figure 34–5 shows that the method can be improved. In this figure it should be observed that the right hand moves first to No. 2, the copy blank pile. The analyst will question the necessity and purpose of this action. He will ask questions such as, "Is this necessary?" "What is its purpose?" and others which will help to achieve improvement. Also, he will observe that the right hand successively makes six transportations—three empty and three loaded—all to the same general area. Are these necessary? Can they be eliminated, combined, or simplified? Can they be made productive? Further, it will be observed that in the beginning the right hand is occupied while the left hand is idle. As already pointed out, motion economy results from both hands moving simultaneously in opposite directions. Therefore, arrangements should be made to have both hands moving at the same time and in opposite directions if possible. By following this minute and careful consideration of each action, the analyst is able to simplify the work, make it easier to do, and eliminate waste.

Figure 34–6 shows a method improvement for accomplishing the

LEFT HAND—RIGHT HAND OPERATION CHART

Subject_____ Project No._____
Operator_____ Date_____
Location_____

1 = ORIGINAL BLANK
2 = COPY BLANK
3 = ORIGINAL DATA
4 = PAPER CLIPS
F = FINISHED WORK
C = CARBON
T = TYPEWRITER

	F		1
		4	2
3		T	C

CHARTED BY	SHEET 1 OF 1	METHOD BEFORE X AFTER___	OPERATION	HANDLING	IDLE	HOLD	TRANSPORTATION		TIME
GRT			6	23	4	3	LOADED (10) 131"	EMPTY (12) 136"	1.25 (X)

(X) NO TYPING

#	LEFT HAND	SYMBOL	IN.	MIN.	MIN.	IN.	SYMBOL	RIGHT HAND	#
1	idle	▽			0.05	20	E	to #2	1
2					0.02		○	grasp #2	2
3					0.05	16	L	to top of T	3
4					0.01		○	release #2	4
5					0.04	9	E	to C, carbon paper	5
6					0.02		○	grasp C	6
7					0.04	13	L	to top of T	7
8					0.01		○	release C	8
9					0.06	25	E	to #1	9
10					0.02		○	grasp #1	10
11					0.06	25	L	to top of T	11
12					0.02		○	release #1	12
13	grasp #1-C-#2	○		0.01	0.01		○	grasp #1-C-#2	13
14	to platen of T	L	3	0.03	0.03	3	L	to platen of T	14
15	hold	▽			0.02		○	release #1-C-#2	15
16					0.02	4	E	to platen knob	16
17					0.07		○	twist platen knob	17
18	release #1-C-#2	○		0.02	0.02		○	release platen knob	18
19	to keyboard	E	6	0.03	0.03	5	E	to keyboard	19
20	type	○		—	—		○	type	20
21	to #1-C-#2	E	6	0.03	0.03	5	E	to T platen knob	21
22	grasp #1-C-#2	○		0.02	0.02		○	grasp platen knob	22
23	remove #1-C-#2	○		0.05	0.05		○	twist platen knob	23
24	to top of T	L	3	0.03	0.02		○	release platen knob	24
25	hold	▽			0.03	3	E	to top of T	25
26					0.03		○	grasp C	26
27					0.05	13	L	to "C" on desk	27
28	release #1-C-#2	○			0.02		○	release C	28
29	to paper clips, #4	E	15	0.06	0.05	13	E	to top of T	29
30	grasp paper clip	○		0.02			▽	idle	30
31	to #3, original data	L	10	0.04					31
32	grasp #3, original data	○		0.03					32
33	to top of T	L	20	0.05					33
34	release original data card on #1-#2	○		0.02	0.02		○	grasp #1-#2	34
35	attach clip	○		0.04			▽	hold #1-#2	35
36	to "F" on desk	L	25	0.06			○	release	36
37	release	○		0.02			▽	idle	37
38	to T	E	25	0.06			▽		38

FIG. 34-5.

same work. The new work layout is sketched at the top of the sheet. Idle time has been eliminated, and simultaneous hand motions have been made a part of the method. The two transportations—empty and loaded—to the copy blanks and the two transportations to the

LEFT HAND—RIGHT HAND OPERATION CHART

Subject _____ Project No._____
Operator _____ Date_____
Location _____

1. ORIGINAL BLANK
2. COPY BLANK
3. ORIGINAL DATA
4. PAPER CLIPS
F. FINISHED WORK
C. CARBON
T. TYPEWRITER

| CHARTED BY | SHEET 1 OF 1 | METHOD BEFORE___ AFTER X | OPERATION 5 | HANDLING 17 | IDLE 0 | HOLD 2 | TRANSPORTATIONS LOADED (9) 106" EMPTY (8) 73" | TIME 0.71 |

#	LEFT HAND	SYMBOL	IN.	MIN.	MIN.	IN.	SYMBOL	RIGHT HAND	#
1	grasp #1	◎		0.04	0.04		◎	grasp C and #2	1
2	to top of T	⊕	19	0.02	0.02	16	⊕	to top of T	2
3	grasp C and #2	◎		0.01	0.01		◎	grasp #1	3
4	to platen of T	⊕	3	0.03	0.03	3	⊕	to platen of T	4
5	hold	▽			0.02		◎	release #1-C-#2	5
6					0.02	4	⊕	to platen knob	6
7					0.07		○	twist platen knob	7
8	release #1-C-#2	◎		0.02	0.02		◎	release platen knob	8
9	to keyboard	⊕	6	0.03	0.03	5	⊕	to keyboard	9
10	type	○		—	—		○	type	10
11	to #4, paper clips	⊕	10	0.04	0.02	6	⊕	to #1-C-#2	11
12	grasp paper clip	◎		0.02	0.01		◎	grasp #1-C-#2	12
13	to #3, original data	⊕	8	0.03	0.02		○	pull #1-C-#2 from T	13
14	grasp #3, original data	◎		0.03	0.02	2	⊕	to top of T	14
15	to top of T	⊕	18	0.04	0.01		◎	release #1-C-#2	15
16	release on top #1-C-#2	◎		0.02	0.03		◎	grasp C	16
17	grasp #3 and #1-C-#2	◎		0.04	0.05	12	⊕	to "2" on desk	17
18	hold	▽		0.02	0.02		◎	release	18
19					0.03	16	⊕	to left hand	19
20					0.02		◎	grasp clip	20
21					0.04		○	attach to #3, #1-#2	21
22	to "F" on desk	⊕	25	0.06	0.02		◎	release	22
23	to #1 on desk	⊕	10	0.04	0.03	16	⊕	to "2" on desk	23

FIG. 34–6.

carbon paper have been combined. A comparison study between the two charts will reveal other work simplification accomplishments.

PRODUCTION STUDY CHART

The production study chart shows how an employee spends his working time and the major functions performed. Either the employee can record his activities or the supervisor or an analyst can obtain the data by means of observation. In any event, the employee should be informed of the study, its purpose, and told why and how the recordings are made. For meaningful results, the job content should be fairly consistent from day to day and the observed employee should neither hasten or retard his normal efforts. The data should be collected for several consecutive days, preferably a week, in order to arrive at what would seem to be a normal pattern.

Recording the Data. There are several ways in which the information of a production study chart can be recorded. One method consists of using graph paper with sections representing time units throughout the working day. These sections are filled in with colored pencil according to a color-identification key for the various functions performed. Another method consists of simply marking down in tabular form the various types of work done and the time each job is started and finished.

Figure 34–7 illustrates an effective form for a production study chart for office work. The usual identification data—employee name, date, and the like—are shown at the top. A series of vertical columns are used for the various functions, with the extreme left column utilized for time and the extreme right for comments. Since the study begins at 9:00 A.M. Monday, the insertion "Mon.9.00" is written on the first line under the "Time" column. The employee is observed cleaning her typewriter, so a check mark ($\sqrt{}$) is made on the first line under "Miscellaneous" and "cleaning typewriter" is written under "Comments." She finishes this task at 9:20 A.M. and begins transcribing. Hence, "9.20" is written on the first line under "Time," and a check mark is made under "Transcribing" on line two. She stops transcribing at 10:05 A.M. to telephone. Hence, on line three a check mark is made under "Telephone," and the entry "10.05" is made in the "Time" column. In a similar manner entries are made throughout the entire day.

Performing Calculations. The calculations for figuring the elapsed time per function can be made as the study progresses or at the completion of all observations. In the illustration, the ordinary 60-minute watch has been used. For the first line the elapsed time between 9.00 and 9.20 is 20 minutes, which is recorded in the same square as the check mark under "Miscellaneous." For the second line the elapsed time is 9.50 minus 9.20, or 30 minutes. The itemized totals are shown at the bottom of the form along with the percentage figures. For example, the total time spent on transcribing is 143 minutes.

This constitutes 34.1 per cent of the total day's working time, calculated by dividing the transcribing time, 143 minutes, by the total day's working time, 420 minutes.

These types of data are important in work simplification effort. They tell what the status of the jobs is at present and give, per em-

PRODUCTION STUDY CHART

Date 3/21 Employee's Name *Nancy Taussig* Sheet 1 of 5 Sheets
Study By ERH Division or Unit *Transcription – 32*
Computations By ERH Job Title *Transcriber*

TIME	TRAN-SCRIBING	COM-PUTING	FILING	SUPER-VISION Rcvd.	SUPER-VISION GIVEN	TELE-PHONE	HAND-LING MAIL	PERSON-AL TIME	MISC.	COMMENTS
MON. 9:00 9:20									√20	Cleaning typewriter
9:50	√30									
10:06						√15				Business Call
10:18	√13									
10:25				√7						
10:50									√25	Rest period or idle
10:59			√9							
11:08						√9				Business Call
11:10		√2								
11:22						√12				Personal Call
11:30								√8		
11:35				√5						
11:50									√15	Idle
12:00								√10		
LUNCH 1:00 1:07										
1:10			√3						√7	Tardy
1:40	√30									
1:55									√15	
3:05	√70									
3:42									√37	Rest period or idle
4:05							√23			
4:15								√10		
4:25						√10				Business Call
4:45		√20								
4:58									√13	Idle
5:00									√2	Cleaning up desk
TOTALS	143	—	31	15	—	46	23	43	119	420
PER CENT	34.1	—	7.4	3.6	—	11.0	5.4	10.1	28.4	100.0%

FIG. 34–7. Chart showing how an employee spends her working time. Data are secured by observing the employee.

ployee, a picture of the over-all work pattern which might form the basis for remedial supervision, equalization of the work load, and further analysis to improve efficiency. They can also be used to supply basic information for the construction of a work distribution chart.[6]

[6] See Chapter 33 for discussion of work distribution chart.

For example, a production study chart may reveal that a typist, with a typing speed of 50 words per minute, spends only 50 per cent of her time typing. The remaining 50 per cent is spent on other activities, most of which are nonessential including positioning papers in typewriter, checking work, removing papers from typewriter, separating copies, cleaning typewriter, answering telephone, filing papers, and getting information from supervisor. In this case the effective typing production is at a rate of only 25 (50 per cent of 50) words per minute. In too many offices the sole emphasis is upon the speed of the operator. True, this is important, but when the methods analysis reveals only 50 per cent of the employee's particular skill being utilized, it is a challenge to the manager to eliminate such waste. The production study chart reveals such situations and assists in correcting them.

OPERATOR-MACHINE ACTIVITY CHART

As the name implies, this chart shows the relation between the operator and the machine. Its use is somewhat limited in office methods, owing to the general nature of most office activities. It is chiefly employed to determine idle machine time and the number of machines which one operator can reasonably handle.

Figure 34–8 shows an operator-machine activity chart. Pertinent data and a sketch of the workplace layout are included at the top. Time is represented by vertical distance on the scale shown in the center column of the sheet. For example, 2-scale units represent two minutes, 4-scale units four minutes, etc. The activities of the operator are listed in the left column, those of the machine on the right.

The vertical height of each spacing in these respective columns is determined by the time devoted to the particular activity. For example, in the illustration the first action by the operator was to "take a card from each B and C, put a carbon between, insert and align in typewriter." This required two-tenths (0.2) minutes, so a horizontal line was drawn two units down from the beginning horizontal line. During this time the typewriter was idle; hence a horizontal line was drawn across the right column under "machine," two units from the same beginning line, and "idle" written in the space so formed.

Next, the operator typed. This action continued five-tenths (0.5) minutes, so a horizontal line was drawn across the "operator column" five units below the last horizontal line, or in this case opposite the "7" mark on the time scale. The space so formed was marked "type." Since the typewriter action stopped at the same time, a horizontal line was also drawn across the "machine" column opposite "7" on the time scale, and the space above was marked "type." In a similar manner, the entire chart was constructed.

This method can be improved very easily. The use of multicopy stub sets with interleaved carbon offers one possibility. This would re-

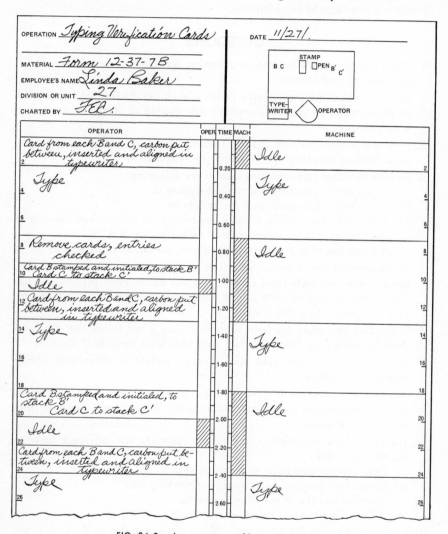

FIG. 34–8. An operator-machine activity chart.

duce the labor time per unit and increase the operating time of the machine—both contributing to greater efficiency. However, a more significant improvement would be the use of continuous strip office forms with carbon interleaved, thus permitting the operator to type continuously until a quantity of work is finished. The checking and separating of the forms could subsequently be handled on this quantity. This method would provide a smooth and rhythmic flow of work, permit specialization upon the immediate task, and eliminate unnecessary reaching, as well as excessive finger and arm motions. Elimination of much waste would be achieved.

QUESTIONS

1. Discuss eight guides in achieving motion economy, using illustrations to demonstrate your answers.

2. In your opinion, for a given type of office work can the method followed in its performance be improved without first getting all the facts about that work? Discuss.

3. How is it possible for motion study to bring about greater work accomplishment without speeding up the employee? Explain.

4. List the therbligs performed for each of the following:
   a) An executive receiving a letter and signing it.
   b) A shipping clerk answering the telephone.
   c) A stenographer folding a letter, inserting it in an envelope, sealing it, and placing it in the outgoing mail basket on her desk.
   d) A typist inserting a card in a typewriter, preparatory to typing.

5. From question No. 4 above, select one of the activities listed and chart it, using a left- and right-hand chart. Point out the motions depicted on the chart which in your opinion can be eliminated, changed, combined, or simplified in performing this work.

6. If an office procedure has been simplified, does it not follow that the components making up that procedure have also been simplified? Explain.

7. Does motion economy take into account individual differences among employees? Explain.

8. Analyze your motions in typing a letter, or taking notes from a reference book, or sorting and then filing cards in a file. What do you conclude from your study? Discuss.

9. For each of the following pair, carefully point out the difference between the two identities:
   a) Operator-machine chart and motion study.
   b) Normal working area and maximum working area.
   c) Therblig and the What-Why questions.
   d) A "handling" and a "transportation loaded."

10. Comment fully on the following: "For a given quantity of work, it is entirely possible for methods improvements to reduce employee fatigue in performing that quantity. But methods improvements usually result in increasing the amount of work performed, and as a result employee spends the same amount of energy or more than before the improvement. Hence, the employee is quite likely to be just as fatigued under the improved method as before the improvement."

11. Explain why you agree or disagree with the statement: "To acquire and

maintain high work output the office manager should emphasize, for employment applicants, high occupational accomplishments such as 55 words per minute typed, 200 papers filed per hour, and so forth, provide periodic training designed to maintain this high skill, and pay higher than the prevailing comparable pay for similar work in the community. These are the keys to office efficiency."

12. As an office manager would you agree to the suggestion that the employees fill out the data on their own respective production study charts and turn these data in to you for analysis and interpretation? What would be the advantages under such an arrangement? The disadvantages?

CASE PROBLEMS

CASE 34–1. ODGEN PRODUCTS COMPANY

For each shipment received, two stapled copies of the receiving slip are sent to the inventory control clerk who performs the following operations: (1) unstaples copies placing copy No. 2 in stack at upper right of desk and placing copy No. 1 in front of her on desk; (2) notes vendor's name and type of material; (3) searches through master list (usually 5–6 typewritten sheets kept to her left on desk) for matching name and material, and when found, writes date of arrival opposite proper name on master list; (4) reaches for proper rubber stamp from tray containing some twenty different stamps in front of her and at back area of desk top; (5) presses proper stamp on inking pad to her left front, and stamps copy No. 1 receiving slip; (6) turns left while remaining seated to file at right angle to her desk and seeks matching inventory card, or cards, if more than one item on the slip (cards are arranged alphabetically by product name); (7) finds card, pulls from file, takes stapler from top right desk drawer and staples slip and card; and (8) replaces stapler in desk drawer and places stapled packet in stack to her right below the No. 2 copy stack.

PROBLEMS:

1. From the viewpoint of work simplification, describe, using a proper chart to assist, an improved method for performing this work.

2. Explain your recommended action in getting your suggested method adopted.

CASE 34–2. SUPREME TABLE COMPANY

The work of employee Beverly Carlson consists of gathering four cards and stapling them together to form a packet. The cards are made of a stiff, medium-weight type of paper material. The work area and the present method of performing the job is depicted by the left- and right-hand chart on page 662.

The office manager requests that the manner of doing this job be improved and assigns you this task. Preliminary investigations show that the card material must be picked up individually. It will not slide or bend easily.

PROBLEMS:

1. Using the chart of the present method as a guide, point out the areas in which you believe improvements can be made. Explain.

LEFT HAND—RIGHT HAND OPERATION CHART

Subject_____ Project No._____
Operator_____ Date_____
Location_____

STAPLER | 4 | 3 | BASKET
| 2 | 1 |

OPERATOR

CHARTED BY	SHEET 1 OF 1	METHOD BEFORE X AFTER___	OPERATION 3	HANDLING 14	IDLE 3	HOLD 4	TRANSPORTATIONS LOADED (7) 136"	EMPTY (7) 136"	TIME —
ae3									

LEFT HAND	SYMBOL	IN.	MIN.	MIN.	IN.	SYMBOL	RIGHT HAND
Idle	▽				28	⊖	To stack 4
						◎	Grasp 4
					24	⊕	To left hand
Grasp 4	◎					◎	Release
Hold	▽				28	⊖	To stack 3
						◎	Grasp 3
					28	⊕	To left hand
Grasp 3	◎					◎	Release 3
Hold	▽				12	⊖	To stack 2
						◎	Grasp 2
					10	⊕	To left hand
Grasp 2	◎					◎	Release 2
Hold	▽				12	⊖	To stack 1
						◎	Grasp 1
					12	⊕	To left hand
Grasp 1	◎					◎	Grasp 4 - 3 - 2
Jog to even edges	◯					◯	Jog to even edges
Idle	▽					◎	Release 4 - 3 - 2 - 1
To stapler	⊕	10			18	⊕	To stapler
Hold	▽				7	⊖	To stapler handle
						◯	Press handle
To basket at right	⊕	34			22	⊖	To desk top
Release	◎					▽	Idle
To desk top	⊖	27					

SUMMARY

	L.H.	R.H.	TOTAL
Operation	1	2	3
Handling	5	9	14
Idle	2	1	3
Hold	4	0	4
Trans. (Loaded)	2	5	7
Trans. (Empty)	1	6	7
Distance	71 inches	201 inches	272 inches

2. Draw a left- and right-hand chart of your improved method, and indicate the savings to be gained from your proposed method.

CASE 34–3. MILDRED CLEVENGER

With her approval and knowledge, typist Mildred Clevenger was observed during a workday by analyst Herman Wright for the purpose of making a production study chart. The data recorded included the following: Miss Clevenger read the newspaper till 9:00 A.M., the official starting time. Promptly at 9:00 A.M., she checked her typewriter and arranged work on her desk; at 9:12, conversed with a messenger boy; at 9:21, answered a business telephone call; at 9:29, typed; at 10:05, talked with supervisor; at 10:20, idle; 10:30, rest period; at 10:45, typed; at 11:13, made a personal telephone call; at 11:42, typed; at 12:00, lunch; at 1:00, typed; 1:55, idle; at 2:12, answered a business telephone call; at 2:24, idle; at 2:35, typed; at 3:00, rest period; at 3:15, typed; at 3:25, made a personal telephone call; at 3:55, typed; at 4:17, took typed material to advertising department; at 4:35, typed; at 4:41, answered a business telephone call; at 4:55, put work away and covered typewriter; and at 5:00, official quitting time, left desk.

PROBLEMS:

1. Draw the production study chart.
2. Calculate the itemized totals of the activities taken by Mildred Clevenger.
3. What interpretations do you make from these data? Discuss.
4. What action do you recommend as a result of the factual data assembled? Why?

Chapter · 35

Office Forms

Censure is often useful, praise often deceitful.
—WINSTON CHURCHILL

ESSENTIAL TOOLS of most clerical work are office forms. They assist in recording transactions, transmitting information, expediting filing, supplying control data, and reducing clerical errors. Office forms are the raw materials of the office; they are the means by which paper work service and help is provided administration.

The design, use, and cost of office forms in any given office are vital because both the efficiency and economy of the office are greatly affected by the office forms utilized. Adequate controlling of office forms is therefore mandatory for good office management.

DEFINITION AND REASONS FOR USE

An office form is a printed piece of paper which provides space for entering records, information, or instructions which are to be conveyed to other individuals, departments, or enterprises. Office forms are used in various sizes, designs, types of paper, and number of copies. Common examples include cost tickets, expense accounts, factory orders, requisitions, sales data, purchase orders, invoices, and credit memos.

Office forms are used because they meet the demands of modern office activity. More specifically the use of office forms:

1. *Reduces copying.* Office forms are particularly helpful where several copies are necessary. The monotonous work of copying, as well as the chance of committing errors in copying, is eliminated. Items common to many transactions are printed on the form.

2. *Insures uniformity.* Forms give standard appearance to the format of records. Identification and recognition of data are made easier; filing and sorting are simplified.

3. *Serves as work guides.* An office form guides the office employee in his work. He knows where to begin and what he is doing,

664

and understands what he is expected to do. His job is made easier.

4. *Gives official sanction.* An office form gives a mark of approval to written work which is viewed as authentic when appearing on a printed office form.

5. *Implements mechanical operations.* For office mechanization, the paper on which data are recorded must meet certain machine requirements, such as a definite size, a certain arrangement of information, uniformity of spacing, and provisions for punching and notching. Forms meet these requirements, and thus facilitate the use of office machines.

CHALLENGE OF OFFICE FORMS IN OFFICE MANAGEMENT

In nearly all enterprises, forms have a tendency to continue indefinitely regardless of need. The root of much office efficiency stems from this situation. In many instances an outmoded form is extended deep traditional and almost reverent consideration. To question its value or suggest the possibility of its elimination amounts to heresy.

There is also a tendency, almost an obsession in some cases, to start new forms regardless of whether the information desired is now contained in existent forms or can be secured by a slight modification in these forms. The viewpoint can be described as narrowed to the particular needs for a particular problem of a particular person. Individualism is emphasized to the exclusion of practically all other considerations.

Based on the results of a survey, two out of every three executives believe that there is an operation in their respective enterprises where greater efficiency could result if the proper office form could be developed.[1] This certainly indicates ample opportunity for improving office work through the media of forms.

FORMS CONTROL

One of the best ways to combat these inefficiencies and to improve office form usefulness is to utilize controlling over forms. By means of forms control a manager seeks to (1) use and retain only those forms which are necessary, (2) insure that the needed forms are designed properly to give greatest assistance at the least cost, (3) produce the required forms by the most appropriate process, (4) distribute forms to those having justifiable reasons for receiving them, (5) study proposed or revised forms for essentiality, and (6) review

---

[1] A market study, "How Business Forms Are Bought and Used" (Washington, D.C.: *U.S. News and World Report,* January, 1954).

periodically all forms in use in order to keep them in line with current needs of the enterprise.

It is in order to point out that forms control applies to the forms' design, production, and use, after the procedure and methods have been selected. Control over procedures and methods was discussed in the two preceding chapters. Nor is forms control inclusive of work measuring and timing control. This latter area is the subject of the next chapter. However, to reiterate, all are controlling, all are important, and all are interrelated.

The City of New York uses thousands of forms which cost nearly $2 million annually. Late in 1951, it launched a city-wide Forms Control Program having these objectives:[2]

1. Control of the design, adoption, procurement, and use of forms.
2. Co-ordination of form design and control with systems, methods, and procedures.
3. Standardization of sizes, papers and other physical aspects of forms.
4. Standardization of forms commonly used by various agencies.
5. Elimination of unnecessary and obsolete forms.
6. Improvement in the functional efficiency and appearance of forms.
7. Combination or consolidation of different forms performing the same or similar functions.
8. Effectuation of economies possible through proper controls.

It can readily be seen that forms control is a huge task. Yet it can be reduced to three major steps: centralize, analyze, and standardize.

CENTRALIZE

In every enterprise a qualified person should be appointed to head the work of forms control. In many cases this person will be the office manager. This person should have the authority to purchase forms and to design, review, pass on, or reject any and all forms in the enterprise. Competent help should be assigned to the forms control organizational unit, and it should be given sufficient status so that others will take it seriously. The members must work well with those of the other organizational units, and their suggestions must be encouraged.

To centralize forms control the following steps are taken:

1. Announce to all employees and explain the existence of the forms control unit, its function and authority. Be specific as to who is the head of it.

---

[2] The City of New York, Bureau of the Budget, *Manual of Form Design,* October, 1953. These objectives are taken from the Preface. This manual was edited by Dr. Herman Limberg.

2. Freeze all form activity at its status quo. Announce that any additions or changes must be taken up and cleared through the forms control unit.

3. Obtain at least two copies of every office form used in the enterprise. File one copy in a centralized form control file. Use the other for purposes of analysis as described below.

4. File each form in the centralized file according to function. This will bring together every form that is similar in nature regardless of its design, its name, or where it is used. Representative of the functions of forms include: to report, request, record, instruct, order, authorize, cancel, acknowledge, and claim. The functional arrangement assists analysis.

5. Secure a listing of all the office procedures used in the enterprise.

6. Mark all forms in the centralized file according to the procedure in which they are used.

ANALYZE

The second major step in a forms control program is analysis. To obtain needed inventory data concerning forms, use of the record sheet as shown in Figure 35–1 is helpful. Also, questionnaires sent to those using the forms frequently prove effective. It is helpful for the person

FORM NUMBER | SIZE | PUNCHING

FORM TITLE

PROCESS – ☐ PENRULE ☐ LETTERPRESS ☐ LITHOGRAPH ☐ OFFSET

PRINTED – ONE/TWO SIDES HEAD TO HEAD/FOOT | PERFORATING

PAPER –	WEIGHT	GRADE	KIND	COLOR PAPER	COLOR INK
SHEET 1					
SHEET 2					
SHEET 3					
SHEET 4					
SHEET 5					
SHEET 6					
SHEET 7					
SHEET 8					
SHEET 9					
SHEET 10					

BINDING

CARBON

DATE	VENDOR	QUANTITY	PRICE PER M	STARTING NUMBER	LAST NUMBER DEL'D

SPECIAL INSTRUCTIONS

Courtesy: American Sales Book Co., Inc., Subsidiary of Moore Corp., Ltd., Niagara, N.Y.

FIG. 35–1. Forms control record.

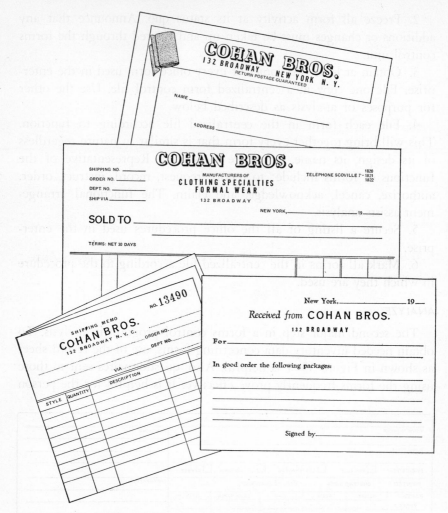

Courtesy: American Sales Book Co., Inc., Subsidiary of Moore Corp., Ltd., Niagara, N.Y.

FIG. 35–2. Forms used by a clothing manufacturer. *Top to bottom:* shipping label, invoice, shipping memo, and packing slip.

in charge of forms control to meet separately with each department head and discuss improvements. These meetings can be followed by group meetings for all department heads in order to decide what improvements can be made in forms that affect more than one department.

Each form should be analyzed to determine if it can be: (1) eliminated, (2) combined with others, or (3) improved. Here again, emphasis should be given to functional considerations. The form's adequacy to meet the work requirements consistent with efficient man-

FROM

COHAN BROS.

132 BROADWAY
NEW YORK N.Y.

TO

RETURN POSTAGE GUARANTEED 25103

RECEIVED FROM
COHAN BROS.

132 BROADWAY - NEW YORK N.Y.

IN GOOD ORDER THE FOLLOWING PACKAGES

No. 25103   DATE

FIRM   PER

PACKING SLIP

SHIP VIA
ORDER No.   DEPT. No.
LOT No. QUANTITY 29 30 32 34 35 36 37 38 39 40 42 44 46 48 50

COHAN BROS.

132 BROADWAY
NEW YORK N. Y.
DATE

MANUFACTURERS OF
CLOTHING SPECIALTIES
FORMAL WEAR

SOLD TO

TELEPHONE
SCOVILLE 7-1820
1821
1822

No. 25103

SHIP VIA
ORDER No.   DEPT. No.

SALESMAN
TERMS NET 30 DAYS

LOT No. QUANTITY 29 30 32 34 35 36 37 38 39 40 42 44 46 48 50 UNIT PRICE EXTENSION TOTAL

Courtesy: American Sales Book Co., Inc., Subsidiary of Moore Corp., Ltd., Niagara, N.Y.

FIG. 35–3. A combination of the four forms shown in Fig. 35–2. Now the same amount of work is accomplished in one typing operation instead of in four.

agement is of foremost importance. Results achieved are sometimes amazing. In the case of one prominent Chicago company the total number of office forms was reduced from 1,182 to 368.

Figures 35–2 and 35–3 show how forms can be combined to improve office efficiency. Originally, four separate forms—shipping label, invoice, shipping memo, and packing slip—were typed separately. In the improved design, the four forms are combined and require only one typing. In the illustration a copy has been raised to show the shipping label in the upper left corner, the receiving memo in the upper right, and the packing slip below. These are separated by tearing apart at the perforations.

In addition, consideration of the size of the forms—correctness for filing, cut without waste, and easy folding, for enclosure in an envelope—is included. Also, the weight of paper for the original and each carbon copy, the direction of the grain, the use of color and its essentiality in the particular form are carefully reviewed. Specifications are checked—the type of ink, punches, and perforations are investigated. The ordering quantities and rates of consumption are compared.

STANDARDIZE

The final major step in forms control is standardization. A form should become standard when, after thorough study, it has been ascertained to be the one best suited to meet the company's requirements. Standardized forms are desirable because they give uniformity, stability, and continuity to forms control efforts.

This does not mean that the work of form control becomes static. Quite the contrary; it is dynamic. As the needs of the company change, the forms used will also change. The person in charge of forms control work must recognize this fact.

Standardized forms expedite training, help insure measurable results of accomplishment, and promote the maintenance of satisfactory outputs. In the majority of cases it is desirable to standardize the size of paper, paper stock, and printing style. Forms of an odd size should be avoided because they involve difficulties in office handling as well as paper waste in manufacturing. Standardizing paper stock and printing style simplifies ordering, eliminates chances for error, and insures uniformity of records—an important consideration when forms are retained over a period of years.

SPECIFIC WAYS OF IMPROVING OFFICE FORMS

More needs to be said regarding the improvement of office forms as developed under the second step of analyze. The person in charge of the forms control program should enlist the help of form-design engineers. These men are trained and experienced in this type of work and are usually able to suggest improvements in a form. Most companies manufacturing office forms offer design services and are very willing to be of help. In addition, the employee who will use the form can frequently offer helpful suggestions as well as evaluate a proposed form. A check list such as that shown by Figure 35–4 assists in forms-

HAMMERMILL FORM ORDER SHEET • PART 1

a *5 minute* FORM CHECK LIST

[A quick and easy method of checking the efficiency and economy of any form—new or old—before placing your printing order. Read the text at the bottom of this sheet.]

Necessity

		OK	?
1	Has the entire system been checked and would a written procedure for the use of this form help put it into more efficient operation?		
2	Are all copies of the form or report necessary?		
3	Have the actual users of this form been consulted for suggested improvements, additional requirements and possible eliminations?		
4	Can the data furnished by this form be combined with some other form or can some other form be eliminated or consolidated with it?		
5	Has everyone responsible for the form or the form system approved it?		

Purpose

		OK	?
6	If form is to be sent from one person to another, are proper spaces for "to" and "from" provided?		
7	Will routing or handling instructions printed on each copy be helpful?		
8	Should this form be consecutively numbered, or have a place for inserting a number?		
9	If this is an Outside Contact Form, should it be designed to mail in a window envelope?		
10	If this form is to take information from, or pass information to, another form, do both have the same sequence of items?		
11	Have we taken into consideration the number of forms which will be used in a given time (4 to 12 months)—the possibility of changes, and how long the form will remain in use?		

Size and Arrangement

		OK	?
12	Is the size right for filing, attention value, ample room for information and to cut without waste?		
13	Is all recurring information being printed, so that only variable items need be filled in?		
14	Has space been provided for a signature?		
15	Is spacing correct for handwriting or typewriting? (The Hammermill Form Layout Sheet will help check this.)		
16	Are the most important items, which should be seen first, prominently placed? (Near the top, if practicable.)		

Wording

		OK	?
17	Does the form, by title and arrangement, clearly indicate its purpose?		
18	Is there a proper space for the date?		
19	Is the form identified by company name and firm name or code number to aid reordering?		
20	If this is a revised form, can it be distinguished from the previous form?		

Paper and Printing

(SPECIFICATIONS)

		OK	?
21	Should the form be on colored paper to speed up writing, distribution, sorting and filing; to designate departments or branch offices; to indicate days, months or years; to distinguish manifold copies; to identify rush orders?		
22	Have we specified paper which will be thoroughly satisfactory, economical enough for form use, consistent in performance and surely available for later reorders?		
23	Is proper weight of paper used for original and each carbon copy? (Bond Substances 9, 13, 16 and 20. Ledger Substances 24, 28 and 32. Mimeo-Bond Substances 16 and 20. Spirit and Gelatin Duplicator Substances 16 and 20.)		
24	Are detailed specifications complete? (Paper, type, ink, rules, punch, perforate, score, fold, gather, pad, carbon sheet, stitch, etc.)		
25	Can other forms, printed on the same paper as this one, be ordered now to reduce production costs?		
26	Have requirements been estimated correctly and is the quantity to be ordered most economical? (Consider probability of revision and rate of use.)		

Remarks ON POINTS QUESTIONED (?)

Pt. #

DATE_____ 19____   SIGNED_____

HOW TO USE THIS FORM Run through this list and appraise a new or revamped form point by point with an initial (rather than a check mark) either in the column headed "OK" or "?." This will help in working out the most efficient form size and specifications and the best working arrangement of items and copy. Points marked (?) for further study can then be appraised systematically and discussed with those who will regularly use the form. Findings and further details can be elaborated upon in the column for "Remarks" at bottom of the second column.

To pin down responsibility, the person or persons giving the final OK should place their initials opposite the remarks. The whole Check List should be filed with a copy of the form for future reference.

Courtesy: Hammermill Paper Company, Erie, Pa.

FIG. 35–4. A form check list which aids in improving office forms.

improvement efforts. In this list, twenty-six pertinent questions are classified under five main headings: the necessity, purpose, size and arrangement, wording, and paper and printing of the form. Use of this list helps reveal information which is basic to improvement and to show the present weaknesses of the existing form. A separate sheet is recommended for each form analysis.

The work of improving office forms can be conveniently considered in terms of functional considerations and physical considerations. The former deals with factors such as the way the form is used, its purpose, the information supplied on it, and the number of copies required. Physical considerations include the ink, print type, paper, and size.

FUNCTIONAL CONSIDERATIONS

Greater economies can be secured through functional considerations than through physical considerations. To reiterate, form improvement should, therefore, be evaluated primarily in terms of the amount of effort required to use the form. Various estimates show that for each dollar spent for office forms, somewhere between $15 to $25 is spent to process these forms. Taking the average of $20, this means that a five-copy form costing $60.00 per thousand involves a processing cost of $1,200.00. A 10 per cent reduction in these processing costs, a reasonable possibility, is equivalent to twice the total physical costs of the form.

There are seven factors that merit discussion here, including:

1. *Purpose of the Form.* The foremost consideration is to determine the job for which the form is to be used. An office form is actually a road map of a job: it shows the flow and sequence of the work. A form should start where the job starts, stop where the job stops, and include the necessary intermediary steps according to the most efficient logical sequence of operations. The form directs employees from the beginning to the end of the job.

2. *What Information to Include.* Knowing the purpose of the form, the next step is to decide what information the form should include. Help along this line can be secured by answering questions such as these:

> What information is needed to accomplish the stated purpose?
> Is the information really vital?
> How is it to be used?
> Who uses it and in what manner?

A complete list of the items to be included is prepared. Then a careful review of this list should be made in order to eliminate duplications and information not absolutely necessary.

3. *Sequence of Items.* The order should be mainly that of the normal flow of the work, and related items should be grouped. When items are transcribed from one form to another, the items should be arranged in the same sequence on both forms. If instructions are necessary, they should be located just above the portion of the form

to which they refer. This helps to have them read at the proper time, which is just before filling in the form. All instructions should be brief and to the point.

4. *General Pattern of the Form.*   The method of completion is important. If the work is to be done manually, ample writing space is necessary and horizontal lines on the form are desirable. Spacing should be three or four lines to the inch.

If the work is to be done by machine, the form should be spaced in accordance with the demands of the machine. The data should be arranged to utilize a tabular alignment, and horizontal lines on the form should be omitted. The following illustrates correct and incorrect arrangement when a machine is used:

Correct	*Incorrect*
Name:	Name _____
Address:	Address _____
S. S. Number.	S. S. Number _____
Age:	Age _____

An excellent illustration showing the improvements possible by proper arrangement of necessary information and the use of space is shown by the before and after comparisons in Figures 35–5 and 35–6. The old form was $11 \times 8\frac{1}{2}$ inches and contained numerous opportunities for improvement, as noted on the illustration. In contrast, the new form is smaller, $8\frac{1}{2} \times 8\frac{1}{2}$ inches, yet is far more effective.

The use of "boxed style" should be employed whenever appropriate. This style saves filling-in time, conserves space, and improves legibility. It is helpful to provide a reference number for each space to be filled in. By this means, tabulation, comparison, and interpretation of data are expedited. Where long sentences are necessary, it is desirable to have them printed in columnar form instead of across the full width of the sheet, as this expedites reading and makes for better appearance. However, when the information to be filled in is lengthy, the boxed style is usually inappropriate; the regular or "open style" is better. An illustration of a form featuring the boxed style for answers and numbers to expedite machine tabulation is shown in Figure 35–7 (p. 676).

5. *Adequate Identification.*   The form name should suggest its purpose. For example, the title "Sales Records" is not complete; "Weekly Sales Records by Territories" is more descriptive. Usually the center or the upper left corner is preferable for the location of the name of the company and the upper right area for reference data in filing.

Numbering all forms helps identify them and serves as a quick reference. The identification number should be in a convenient location, preferably near the title. In the case of multiple forms, it is usually advisable to number each copy for handy reference. Quick identification can also be gained by using different colors of papers.

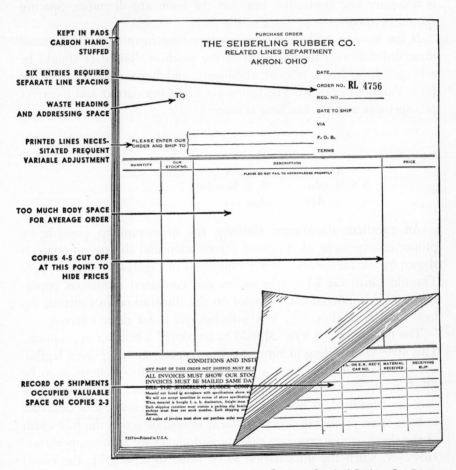

FIG. 35–5. Original form before redesign.

Courtesy: Standard Register Co., Dayton

6. *Number of Copies.* Whether a single or multiple copy form should be used depends mainly upon two considerations: (1) who requires a copy, and (2) when the copy is needed. Multiple forms afford a quick means of supplying many copies. However, it is best to keep the number of copies at a minimum. Only the required number of copies should be made, and extreme prudence and care in this

respect is recommended, as excess papers tend to clutter up an office and contribute to inefficiency.

7. *Type of Form.* There are in general five different types or arrangements of office forms: single, stub type, continuous stub type,

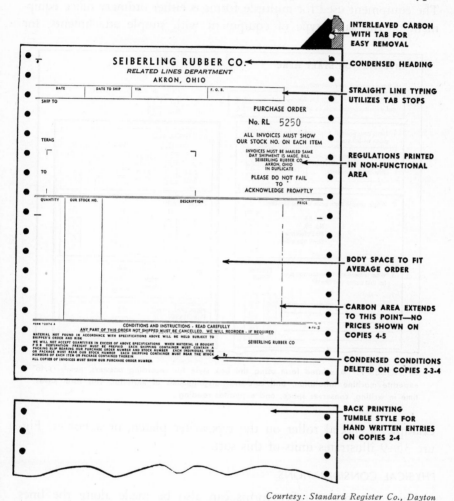

Courtesy: Standard Register Co., Dayton

FIG. 35–6. Form after redesign.

fan or **Z** arrangement, and continuous semi-strip arrangement. The single type is used where the original copy only is required, as, for example, in the case of an employment application form. When necessary, copies can be obtained simply by using carbon sheets and as many form sheets as required. Many single unit forms are used in an office.

The other four arrangements mentioned above are multiple forms. Illustrations and features of each are shown in Figure 35–8.

Multiple forms require only one writing, minimize mistakes, help attain uniformity, improve departmental co-ordination, and save time. The equipment used for multiple forms is either ordinary office equipment or the same type of equipment with simple attachments, for

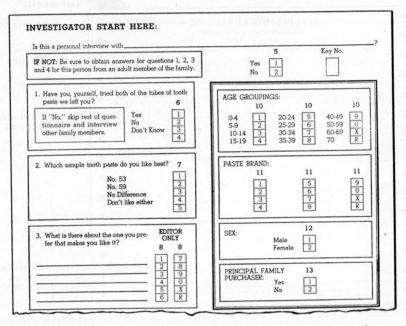

FIG. 35–7. A printed form using the box style for recording answers, numbers to expedite machine tabulation, and columnar arrangement of material. This form saves time in writing, conserves space, and expedites reading.

example, a special roller on the typewriter platen, or a holder. Figure 35–9 illustrates units of this sort.

PHYSICAL CONSIDERATIONS

Improvements in office forms can also be made along the lines of ink, print type, paper, and means of carbonizing copies. Although technical in nature, the office manager should possess some knowledge of them.

1. *Ink.* The ink selected should provide proper contrast to the paper and should give a clear, uniform, and smooth imprint. Certain printing processes require a certain type of ink. Use of more than one color of ink adds to the cost of the form.

One of the latest "inks" is a magnetic oxide coated on plastic film.

Can be made with stub at top, bottom, either side, or top and bottom. The latter is used when set must be separated into two sections after initial writing for subsequent fill-ins. Carbon is fastened to stub, is used once, and can be of same or different widths and lengths to permit selective copying.

STUB TYPE UNIT ARRANGEMENT

This is the same as the stub type unit arrangement except that the bottom sheet of each set is attached to the following set by perforations.

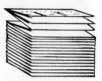

CONTINUOUS STUB TYPE UNIT ARRANGEMENT

These are provided in continuous strips with perforated accordian folds at left and right edges. The arrangement is available in either packs or rolls. Being joined at alternate sides, the forms can be separated from the strip but still retained in sets. The fan arrangement is available with or without interleaved carbon.

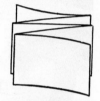

FAN OR Z ARRANGEMENT

This arrangement is similar to the continuous stub type except for the absence of stubs. The forms are perforated at fold. Depending upon method and equipment used, these may be utilized either with or without carbon interleaving.

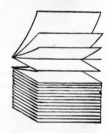

CONTINUOUS SEMI-STRIP ARRANGEMENT

FIG. 35–8. The main types or arrangements of multiple office forms.

When a typewriter key, for example, strikes this magnetic ink ribbon, an impression is made on paper as a deposit of magnetic material. Subsequently the deposit can be read by electronic means used to put various counting and sorting mechanisms into action.

2. *Print Type.* The print type should be selected primarily on the basis of readability, with some thought given to making the printed page distinctive. For any one form, it is best to keep the type sizes and type styles to a minimum. Items of equal importance should be printed

This attachment, called a "dual feed," makes it possible to produce two records in one operation. Common information is typed on two forms of different size, with independent spacing as the work requires.

This device provides vertical tab spacing. The lever at the left is pulled down, causing the next form to be drawn to exact positioning for typing.

A pack holding refold tray for convenience in use of continuous multiple form.

FIG. 35–9.

in the same type throughout the entire form. Normally, italic and bold-face type should be used for emphasis, but confined to those items or words where special stress is required. See Appendix C, page 746, for further information.

3. *Paper.* Acquaintance with the more salient facts about paper used in forms is desirable. The five important properties of paper are: weight, grade, grain, color, and size.

a) Weight. Paper is usually sold by weight. Normally the mill supplies paper in standard sizes according to the different grades and the intended purposes for which the paper is to be used. To illustrate, the purposes and corresponding sizes are shown in this table:

Use of Paper	Size
Bonds, ledgers, general writing	17″ × 22″
Book papers and offset pages	25″ × 38″
Cover stock	20″ × 26″
Newsprint	24″ × 36″
Bristol board	22½″ × 28½″

A ream is the common measurement for quantity of paper and is approximately 500 sheets. For example, bond paper listed as 17″ × 22″—20 means that 20 pounds of this grade and size paper includes approximately 500 sheets. Likewise, bond paper 17″ × 22″—13 means that 13 pounds of this grade and size paper contain approximately 500 sheets. Comparing these two, the latter sheets would be thinner, since, based on the same size and approximate quantity, their weight is less (13 pounds) compared to the former (20 pounds).

The lightest paper which will give satisfactory results should be used. Among the factors which determine the proper weight of paper are: number of copies, amount of handling, purpose of the form, how filed—on edge or side, length of time retained, and whether printed on one or two sides. The following weights are usually recommended:

Application	Weight of Paper Recommended
Legal documents	28 pound
Ledgers	24 pound
Letterheads	20 pound
When 1–4 copies are made	16 pound
When 5–8 copies are made	13 pound
When over 9 copies are made	tissue

b) Grade. The grade of paper means the quality and is chiefly based on the kinds of materials used in the manufacturing process. Paper is made from rags, mechanical wood pulp, sulphite wood pulp, soda wood pulp, and sulphate wood pulp, which are used in varying amounts depending upon the kind of paper.

The grade of paper selected for a form depends upon such things as the life of the form, the amount of handling, and the appearance. The following table can be used as a guide:

Life of Form	Grade of Paper
1–5 years	100 per cent sulphite
6–12 years	50 per cent sulphite and 50 per cent rag
Over 12 years	100 per cent rag

c) Grain.   Like wood, paper has a grain characteristic. The direction of the grain is determined by the alignment of the fibers making up the paper. The expression, "with the grain," signifies the longitudinal direction of most fibers. Grain direction is the result of the manufacturing process.

The grain of paper is important because it determines the rigidity of paper. Some processes require that the grain of the paper run with the length of the printing roll. The grain should be parallel to the typewriter platen, because the paper then rolls around the platen better and there is less tendency for the sheets to slip. Paper folds more easily and quickly when it is parallel with the grain. Furthermore, when the graining runs vertically on forms posted by machine or filed on edge, there is less tendency for the forms to buckle and curl.

d) Color.   The possibility of using colored paper for office forms should be considered. This frequently affords an effective medium for securing a strong appeal, a unique identification, and a simple means of facilitating the handling of forms. However, colored paper usually costs more than white.

e) Size.   The size of the paper form is determined by such things as the amount of information, the economical paper size, the size and types of office equipment and machines, and the mechanical requirements. The limitations of the printing process must, of course, be considered in determining the physical dimensions of a form.

For purposes of economy and to eliminate waste, forms in the process of development should be made to be cut from stock sizes of paper. It is advisable to discuss the subject of economical stock sizes with the prospective supplier.

4. *Means of Carbonizing Copies.*   The providing of carbon paper for use with the forms can be achieved in several ways: (1) inserting carbon by hand, (2) one-use carbon interleaved into the form, (3) carbon in the machine—using a simple "floating carbon" device, and

(4) spots of wax carbon applied to the back of the form during the manufacturing process.

As indicated in Figure 35–8 some multiple forms provide one-use carbon paper interleaved into position. When the fan and continuous semi-strip arrangements are used without carbon interleaving, the "floating carbon" device can be used. In this case, the forms slip over the carbon sheets which remain in the machine, and these sheets are used many times over until the impressions indicate the need for a carbon change. The fourth method, application of spots of wax carbon, makes it possible to apply the carbon to certain parts of a form, thus permitting only certain portions of the original writing to appear on the copies. Frequently price information or specification data do not appear on all copies, since this information has little value for the purpose of some copies. A similar result can be achieved in the other carbon methods by cutting off certain carbon sheets or blacking out, with a solid mass of dots or other marks, that portion of the form which is not to receive an impression. The carbon mark is not visible on the blackened area.

One of the newer developments in carbonizing is the carbonless "NCR paper" of the National Cash Register Company. Colorless chemicals on the paper itself eliminate the necessity for carbon paper. For an office form the bottom side of the first sheet is coated with one chemical and the top side of the second sheet with another chemical. Writing on the first sheet reproduces instantly on the second sheet, and similar reaction takes place between the remaining sheets of the pack. "NCR paper" is available in quantities for processing into office forms. Among the advantages cited for its use are very clear copies are obtained, smears and smudges are eliminated, and hands and clothing are not soiled.

QUESTIONS

1. Normally, is the greatest cost in designing, in manufacturing, or in using an office form? What importance does your answer have upon the managing of office work?
2. Can an office form meet approval after a thorough analysis, yet contribute to office inefficiency because the whole manner of getting the office work accomplished is outdated? Explain.
3. Are you of the opinion that an office forms control program can be carried too far and conducted too aggressively? Substantiate your answer.
4. Why should an office manager be concerned with the subject of office forms?

5. Should office forms be developed to meet the requirements of office procedures, or vice versa? Why?

6. In the step of centralizing under forms control, why should a copy of each form be filed according to function? What other ways of filing could be followed? Why not use them?

7. Why is standardization a major step in forms control?

8. Since in most offices there is a general tendency to start new office forms, would a practical and satisfactory control over forms result from declaring periodically a "holiday period" during which no new form could be launched in an office? Elaborate on your answer.

9. Should descriptions of merchandise, discount terms, or special instructions ever be preprinted on invoice forms? Explain.

10. Referring to Figure 35–4, explain how this form check list is used to improve office forms.

11. Discuss the various means of carbonizing copies of office forms.

12. What are some important properties of paper which should receive consideration in the determination of an office form?

CASE PROBLEMS

CASE 35–1.   COLLINS–ROTHROCK CORPORATION

"You ask about our inventory records, Mr. Hanson," stated Edward Cooney, Purchasing Director of the Collins–Rothrock Corporation. "I shall relate our experience to you."

"Our office was frequently uncovering errors in inventory records recorded manually by stock clerks. The errors were generally due to arithmetic inaccuracies in addition of incoming stock or subtraction of issues to operations. It was thought that the design of the 8 × 5 card could be modified in such a way as to make it easier for the recorder to check his own work. At that time, the card we were using provided individual columns for receipts, date, order number, quantity disbursed, and the balance on hand. This design necessitated horizontal computation. The quantities in the receipts or disbursements columns were added or subtracted, as the case might be, from the balance-on-hand column. The necessary movement of the eyes and the retentive effort in carrying mentally the proper figures to the balance column were both tiring and confusing."

"A modified card form design was created providing for computations vertically; that is, receipts, disbursements, and balance on hand were to be recorded one below the other as is done in simple arithmetic. Receipts of stock were to be recorded in black, and disbursements or issues of material from stock were to be recorded in red. A balance figure was to be shown after each transaction recorded. We have found that the new card works out very well, and our employees are enthusiastic about its use."

PROBLEMS:

1. Draw the new card for inventory records as you envision it from the remarks of Mr. Cooney.

2. Point out its major advantages. Its disadvantages.

CASE 35–2. GENERAL DISTRIBUTORS OF ILLINOIS

Launched in 1947, this mail-order house has enjoyed a steady growth in business. The customer's order blank, enclosed in the company's catalog and also sent to prospective customers upon request, is shown in the accompanying illustration. It is desired to revise this form to expedite order handling. Among the favorable suggestions are: (1) include statement that a 25 per cent deposit is required on all C.O.D. shipments; (2) show catalog number and the page

number from which item is ordered; (3) provide spacing for taxes which are 10 per cent on certain items providing purchases are not made for resale as, for example, is the case with orders from retailers who do not pay the tax; (4) add provision for order-picker to check off items as they are assembled for shipment; (5) simplify the identifying and shipping instructions and subsequent work in which it is used for processing order; and (6) show that company pays freight anywhere in the U.S.A. on all orders of $50 or more.

PROBLEMS:

1. Draw the order blank that you recommend for this company.
2. Point out the advantages of your recommended order blank.

CASE 35–3.   WINCHESTER METAL PRODUCTS COMPANY

Believing some inefficiency exists in the paper work of the company, the general manager appointed a committee of three, the office manager, the assistant production control manager, and the assistant purchasing agent, to conduct a forms survey and advise him what action should be taken. Employees were informed of the study and its purpose, and emphasis was given to the intention that no employee would lose his job as a result of this study.

Discovered were some sixty-seven forms in use by the office force, all of which the office employees said were essential either for office use or to assist the factory in its work. The sixty-seven forms represent an accumulation over the past ten–fifteen years. During this time, some of the forms have been altered in design, but none eliminated.

PROBLEMS:

1. Comment fully on the approach and the means utilized by the company in trying to improve its efficiency.

2. What recommendation should the committee make? Why?

3. What course of action should the general manager follow? Explain.

Chapter · 36

Measuring and Timing Office Work

A man doesn't begin to attain wisdom until he recognizes he is no longer indispensable.

—RICHARD E. BYRD

IN THE LAST four chapters consideration has been given to the work quantity and quality, manner of performance, and office forms. These are vital in office managerial controlling, but their full significance requires additional concepts, namely, measuring and timing. That is, the answers to the questions of controlling, "What is being done?" and "Is this satisfactory?" necessitate knowledge of (1) how much work, and (2) within what time limits is the work accomplished.

MEASURING OFFICE WORK

To measure means to determine quantity. In office management the major interest is with (1) measurement of work, and (2) measurement of time. For control purposes these two measurements are tied together; for example, so many orders written within a given time. The number of orders written becomes more meaningful when tied with the quantity of time.

Measurement of work concerns accomplishment or productivity. It has to do with results; it does not deal with the amount of energy expended, although in many cases this may be in direct proportion to the work output. Measurement provides data showing the amount of work done, and this information is helpful in determining whether the office is being managed efficiently, and the amount of work achieved by each employee.

Much of the work in an office can be measured fairly accurately

685

and inexpensively. The extent in any given case will depend upon the particular type of office tasks performed, but usually from two thirds to three fourths of all work in an office can be measured. In a well-known mail-order house, for example, 83 per cent of all clerical work is under a work measurement plan, including such work as mail opening, order reading, accounting, billing, corresponding, and addressing. This is not to imply that most offices have work measurement for about 80 per cent of their operations. Actually the figure is far less. But the belief is too prevalent that work measurement cannot be used in office operations. Resistance against such measurement frequently is quite strong.

It is true that difficulty in measurement is encountered when the office work is nonrepetitive and irregular, and is primarily mental rather than manual. These are impediments, but when study and analysis are applied with the ultimate objective of measuring the office work, surprisingly useful and reliable results are achieved. It is erroneous to accept the belief that work measurement cannot be set for clerks.

MEASURING UNIT

To measure requires a recognizable unit. There are many different units that can be used, the selection depending mainly upon the type of office work. For example, typewritten work can be measured by typing area or sheets, and purchase orders by the number written. Sometimes the quantity can be determined very easily by means of counting devices on machines, and frequently the relationship of the weight of paper to the amount of work can be employed. Other examples of measuring units in the office are the number of invoices written, the amount of postage (dollar value) used on outgoing mail, the weight of incoming mail handled, the reams of paper used in duplicating work, the number of pay checks prepared, the inches of card stacks filed, and the number of credit investigations made.

The unit used should be easy to identify, count, and understand. For each related application it should possess uniformity of scope and definition. Generally speaking the unit preferred is that which comes into existence as a by-product of an essential clear-cut office operation. This characteristic aids identifying and counting.

In some instances, the selection of a satisfactory unit is extremely difficult, while in other cases, there are several available and acceptable units. In the latter case, for example, typewritten work can be measured in units of (1) pages, (2) standard-length lines, (3) key strokes, (4) square inches of typed material, or (5) cylinders or disks from which material is transcribed. The choice is guided by the individual characteristics of the work under consideration. No one unit is best under all conditions. For example, the number of pages is satisfactory providing the pages are approximately uniform in the amount of typed material and in difficulty.

Accurate measurement is desirable and should be sought, but in the case of office work, this can be carried to uneconomical extremes. Too precise or too detailed measurements can result in bulky and sometimes cumbersome data which are ineffective in practical application.

COMPOSITE WORK MEASUREMENT UNITS

Because in many cases office work contains a number of variables and the job of an office employee may consist of several related but independent tasks, the use of a composite unit to measure office work is sometimes used. For example, orders from customers may be measured in units consisting of 200 orders or what is sometimes called "a block of orders." The content of the individual orders may vary considerably, but the content of 200 orders will normally be quite like that of another 200 orders. Thus a work measurement unit possessing reasonable comparability is provided.

Also, the work measurement can be considered over a period of time, i.e., for ten or fifteen days. During such a period, the average make-up of the composite unit will be fairly constant, that is, comparing one fifteen-day period with another fifteen-day period.

The *work unit* is another composite means of office work measurement.[1] The entire office or a portion of it can be used. The work of the office included is expressed in a single unit which is considered the most important item and the one upon which most all other work depends. To illustrate, the incoming order might be considered the single unit of measurement. Credit investigation, correspondence, billing, and the like are tied up with the handling of the incoming order. These activities increase as the incoming orders increase, and vice versa. In some offices the incoming order may not be the best single unit of measurement. In such cases the unit might be any of the following:

---

[1] This plan was developed by Mr. W. H. Leffingwell. See Leffingwell and Robinson, *Textbook of Office Management* (3d ed.; New York: McGraw-Hill Book Co., Inc., 1950), pp. 534–38 for detailed discussion.

number of policies handled, applications processed, orders received, items on order, units shipped, sheets duplicated, bills sent out, requisitions made, or checks written.[2]

The work unit can be weighted according to the relative difference in the unit's content. That is, a unit may be classified as "class A" and given a weight of 1 point. Another unit, because of its content, is given classification "B," having a weight of 2 points. Work on a "B" unit might be longer and involve more work. Likewise "class C" might be given a value of 3 points. Thus, recognition is given to the relative importance of the unit, so that the work measurement reflects a more accurate quantity.

TIMING OFFICE WORK

Common practice associates time measurement, or the aspect of duration, with the work measurement. Time is an all-important factor. To punch a given number of cards or to file a definite quantity of orders is an accomplishment, but the important question is—within what time limits can this be done? How long should it take? How much time should elapse from the start to the finish? Time is the element which is basic and common to all work.

For any given case it is customary to identify the measurement of work and also that of time as "time study." Formally defined, *time study is the determination of a satisfactory work output and of the time required to complete a given number of work units regularly.* The unit may be an entire task or any part thereof. Time is usually expressed in minutes per piece or 100 pieces or at a rate of so many pieces per hour.

The values from time study are called "time standards" and are used by managers as bases of reference for controlling. More specifically time standards help the manager of office work in that:

1. *A basis for work distribution is provided.* Time standards give the office manager the means for determining the volume of work and the number of employees required to get the work out. They afford the establishment of a "fair day's work," and they make it possible to plan the office operations.

2. *The office work can be scheduled.* Knowledge of the time to be allocated to different tasks expedites the arrangement of the order of work according to a predetermined timetable. By this means full utilization of all production factors can be more nearly attained. Available

---

[2] H. M. Kaiser, "Measuring Office Output for Effective Control," *Office Management Series No. 90, American Management Association* (New York, 1940), p. 15.

times of machines or of employees for emergency or special rush jobs can be readily determined, as well as information on the starting and completing dates for the various tasks, all of which helps the office to provide excellent service to the remaining parts of the enterprise.

3. *Effectiveness of department, division, or individual can be determined.* An indication of what the working force should accomplish is provided. The question is not, "Is the employee always busy?" but "What does the employee accomplish?" The actual productivity compared with standard productivity is known. It is therefore possible to distinguish the efficient from the inefficient employee or group. Remedial action to improve the work of the inefficient personnel can be taken.

4. *Control over costs can be exercised.* Time standards make it possible to compare standard against actual costs. Some control can thus be used effectively, since information as to where costs are out of line is supplied.

5. *Morale and labor relations are improved.* With time studies the employee knows what is expected of him, and this makes office work more interesting. Having an objective—an end in view—lends encouragement so that office work does not seem like an endless mass of detailed work. Generally, the employee will be happier and do better work when he knows what and how much he is supposed to do and upon what basis his efforts will be judged. Time standards remove favoritism; they provide factual information and treat all employees alike. In addition, by means of standards, basic data can be obtained which are extremely helpful in considering employee promotions and in formulating training programs.

METHODS FOR DETERMINING OFFICE TIME STANDARDS

Standard times for office operations can be determined in six different ways. These are by (1) subjective judgment, (2) past performance records, (3) work sampling and statistical means, (4) stopwatch study, (5) standard data from time study, and (6) standard time data. A discussion of each follows.

SUBJECTIVE JUDGMENT

Time standards set through subjective judgment are sometimes referred to as rule-of-thumb standards. They are based only on the experience and guess of the management member. It is strongly recommended that the manager refrain from the use of such time standards.

Even when an accurate guess in establishing the standard has been made, it is extremely difficult to explain and justify the estimate. Frequently, disagreement over the guess arises and may cause problems and trouble that will outweigh any value the subjective judgment standard might have had.

PAST PERFORMANCE RECORDS

Under this plan a count is made of work done on a particular class, unit, or item of office work. It is a recording of what is happening. To illustrate, assuming billings written as the unit, the records will show accomplishments day by day or week by week as follows: the number of units on hand at the beginning of the period; the number received during the period; the number completed; and the number at the end of the period. These are basic data; and after a short lapse of time it is possible, with some adjustment, to arrive at a quantity of work which should be completed within a given period of time.

Under this plan each employee records the amount of work completed and the time taken to do it. Simple forms can be used, and cooperation of the employee is essential. To secure this, it is well to explain carefully and in some detail the purpose, operation, and need of the plan.

Standards arrived at from this approach have management value.[3] They are indicators of work and time requirements and can be used in managerial controlling. However, they are really records of what is being done, and standards so determined have one outstanding shortcoming: *They frequently represent "what is," rather than "what should be."*

In most cases the measurement of time for a *work unit* is based on past performance records. The time standard, expressed as clerical minutes per unit (C.M.U.), is obtained by dividing, for the office or portion being considered, the total clerical minutes worked by the weighted number of units completed. A time period of one week is most satisfactory. Expressed by formula the expression is:

$$\frac{\text{Clerical minutes}}{\text{per unit}} = \frac{\begin{array}{c}\text{Total number of clerks} \\ \text{for office considered}\end{array} \times \begin{array}{c}\text{Minutes in} \\ \text{work week}\end{array}}{\text{Weighted number of units completed}}$$

If 14 clerks work 40 hours a week and complete orders classified as follows:

---

[3] For example, they are usable in federal offices where watch time study is prohibited by clauses in appropriation bills.

1,000 class A, weight 1,
50 class B, weight 2,
100 class C, weight 3,

the value of the clerical minutes per unit is:

$$\text{C.M.U.} = \frac{14 \times 40 \times 60}{(1,000 \times 1) + (50 \times 2) + (100 \times 3)}$$

$$\text{C.M.U.} = \frac{33,600}{1,400}$$

$$\text{C.M.U.} = 24.$$

The *work unit* time standard gives the office manager a rough idea of what is accomplished and within what time expenditure. Areas or portions of the office needing attention can be located, as well as those in which the output is satisfactory or above a predetermined clerical-minutes-per-unit value.

WORK SAMPLING AND STATISTICAL MEANS

Work sampling is a method employing random observations whereby the ratio of delays and of elements of work to the total process time is determined. It is based on the law of probability. That is, the chance occurrences in the sample tend to follow the same distribution pattern as that of the total universe of work being studied. The technique consists of intermittent but frequent spot checking of the activity of one or more office employees and the recording of the activity at the moment it is observed. From this work sample, the time spent on each type of operation in relation to the total time available is determined.

Work sampling data can be secured by means of observations by the supervisor. It can be carried to any desired degree of detail, is economical, and measures cyclic effect, a very important concept in most office work. From work sampling data, it is possible to determine effective utilization of time, causes and extent of interference with effective accomplishment, and flow of work through an office. There are many who believe work sampling is one of the most practical and economical means for appraising the time required to perform clerical work.

A convenient method for measuring typing work is the "Type Timer," a simple and accurate chart on transparent plastic. By placing over the typed area, the numbers indicating the typing time required can be determined by reading directly from the chart. Allowances are provided for such things as the number of copies, size of type, and whether source material is handwritten, in print, transcribed from shorthand notes, or from transcribing machine. The "Type Timer" is available from the M. Wiberg and Company, Highland Park, Illinois.

STOP-WATCH STUDY

This means of determining time standards emphasizes a relatively precise measurement of a particular task or an individual segment of office work. The time standard developed from this source applies to specific work done under specific conditions such as workplace, method, and material. It is not a universal time standard. The work selected for study should be repetitive and of sufficient volume to warrant careful analysis. The proper workplace should be resolved, and the work motions economized. There is no point in establishing carefully set time values for work that is performed ineffectively and that is soon to be improved. The variable job elements which are affected by changing conditions must be placed under control and preliminary analyses completed, so that the standards arrived at will be meaningful and valid.[4] It should be noted that stop-watch study is also helpful in determining waste, many studies in fact being made for this purpose.

The equipment needed for a stop-watch study includes a stop watch, a time-study form, a clip board to hold the form, and a pencil. The stop watch should be one which reads directly in one-hundredths (0.01) of a minute. Keeping all values in minutes and hundredths of minutes simplifies calculations. The watch should also provide means for snapping back the hands to zero after each reading if the "snapback" method is desired. A time-study form provides for a neat and orderly arrangement of the data, and its use avoids a great deal of unnecessary writing. The clip board usually provides a space for holding the watch and also serves as a backing when writing on the form.

STEPS IN STOP-WATCH STUDY

1. *Advise the employees that time studies are to be made.* Include facts concerning the purpose, method, personnel doing the work, and the like. Frequently it is desirable to have some of the employees help in the time-study work. When offices are unionized, it is well to discuss these matters fully with the union representatives and to enlist their co-operation in the time study.

2. *Identify and carefully note what is the beginning and the end of the task to be studied.* It is usually helpful to have the end of the task cycle followed immediately by a repetition of the task cycle. When the

---

[4] D. S. Valentine, "Setting Standards for Work Performance," *Office Management Series No. 121, American Management Association* (New York, 1948), pp. 20–22.

selected task cycle requires the exclusion of work or time between the cycles, difficulties in the handling of subsequent calculations may be encountered.

3. *Select an employee who appears to be above average.* This above-average type is selected because he will have the best motions and rhythm in his work. This does not mean, however, that the time standard to be determined will require an above-average worker. Discussion of this point is given later in this chapter. Advise the supervisor and let the employee know that he is to be studied. Tell him the answer to any question he might ask about time study. Do not proceed until the employee's complete co-operation has been secured. When ready, take a position a little to one side of and behind the employee. Do not stand in front of him. To become familiar with the task, watch the completion of it several times.

4. *Divide the task into its elements or the smallest motions that can be observed and read.* List these elements on the form sheet and describe each one accurately. To illustrate, the elements used in posting material-requisition notices on card files are:

a) Read identification on material requisition.

b) Find proper card-file drawer.

c) Pull drawer out.

d) Find proper card.

e) Enter data in handwriting on card.

f) Check appropriate square on material requisition and initial.

g) Close file drawer.

h) Pick up and place material requisition in outgoing-mail basket located at right back of table top. These elements are listed along the top of the form shown in Figure 36–1.

5. *Record time observations on the form.* Put the starting time of the study in the space provided (upper left of Fig. 36–1). Make certain the stop-watch hands are set at zero. Start the stop watch at the beginning of the first element; and at the completion of this element, note and record the watch reading on the first line in the first column under the letter "R," which stands for Reading. At the completion of the second element, note the watch reading and record on the first line of the second column under the letter "R." In similar manner, read and record the watch readings for each of the elements.

In Figure 36–1 the reading at the completion of element one is 12; at the end of element two, 21; at the end of element three, 25; at the end of element four, 50; and so on.

At the end of the last element, let the watch continue to run and in like manner repeat the task cycle-recording readings on the second line. Continue this procedure until a sufficient number of cycles have been timed to indicate some commonness in the elapsed time per element. Usually about eight to ten cycles should be recorded.[5]

Variations from the proper sequence are recorded as "repeats" on the immediate line below, or, in the case of interruptions, by footnoting

STUDY NO. 14   DATE 10-1   SHEET NO. 1   OF 1 SHEETS
STUDY STARTED 8:30 A.M.   STUDY ENDED 8:41 A.M.
OPERATION: POST MATERIAL REQUISITION NOTICES ON CARD FILES

Element column headings:

1. READ IDENTIFICATION ON MATERIAL REQUISITION
2. FIND PROPER CARD FILE DRAWER
3. PULL DRAWER OUT
4. FIND PROPER CARD
5. ENTER DATA BY HAND-WRITING ON CARD
6. CHECK MARK APPROPRIATE SQUARE ON MATERIAL REQUISITION AND INITIAL
7. CLOSE FILE DRAWER
8. PICKUP AND PLACE MATERIAL REQUISITION IN CLERICAL-MAIL BASKET

	1 (T/R)	2 (T/R)	3 (T/R)	4 (T/R)	5 (T/R)	6 (T/R)	7 (T/R)	8 (T/R)
1	12 / 12	9 / 21	4 / 25	25 / 50	35 / 85	13 / 98	5 / 103	7 / 10
2	12 / 22	8 / 30	5 / 35	23 / 58	40 / 98	13 / 211	5 / 16	7 / 23
3	11 / 34	8 / 42	5 / 47	22 / 269 (A 364)	37 / 401	12 / 13	4 / 17	6 / 23
4	14 / 37	9 / 46	8 / 55	PULLED WRONG DRAWER - CLOSED IT				
5			6 / 61	24 / 85	35 / 520	13 / 33	4 / 37	9 / 46
6	12 / 58	9 / 67	5 / 72	23 / 95	37 / 632	13 / 45	5 / 50	7 / 57
7	13 / 70	10 / 80	4 / 84	24 / 708	38 / 46	11 / 57	5 / 62	8 / 70
8	12 / 82	9 / 91	6 / 97	23 / 820	36 / 856 (B 881)	5 / 98	5 / 913	
9	11 / 24	8 / 42	5 / 47	25 / 72	39 / 101	13 / 24	4 / 28	7 / 1035
TOTALS T.	0.97	0.62	0.40	1.89	2.97	1.00	0.37	0.51
NO. OF VALUES USED	8	7	8	8	8	8	8	7
AVERAGE (SELECTED) T	0.121	0.089	0.050	0.236	0.371	0.125	0.046	0.074
TOTAL RATING FACTOR	1.11	1.11	1.11	1.11	1.11	1.11	1.11	1.11
ELEM. BASE TIME	0.134	0.099	0.056	.262	0.412	0.139	0.051	0.082
OCCURR. PER UNIT	1	1	1	1	1	1	1	1
BASE TIME PER UNIT	0.134	0.099	.056	1.262	0.412	0.139	0.051	0.082

FOREIGN ELEMENTS:
A: 269 / 364 = 95 — MADE ERROR-ERASURE AND CORRECTION
B: 856 / 881 = 25 — REQUISITION NOTICE DROPPED ON FLOOR
C: 120

RATING FACTOR 1.11

OPERATOR'S NAME: BETTY SMITH   OPERATOR'S NO.: 429   OBSERVER: GRT.

Designed by H. B. Rogers, 7-6-44. 1944 NORTHWESTERN UNIVERSITY

FIG. 36–1. Time-study data sheet for an office task.

and explaining in the space located on the extreme right of the form. To illustrate, referring to Figure 36–1 again, on the third line under element five, an interruption occurred and is footnoted by letter "A." At the right of the form a description is given that the employee made an error, erased, and corrected. This "foreign element" took place between watch readings of 269 and 364, or a total of 95, which is actually $^{95}/_{100}$ of a minute. Another interruption is shown by footnote "B" on the eighth line under element six.

---

[5] Some engineers claim that readings should be taken for at least 15–20 minutes. The number of cycles which represents a reliable sample can be determined mathematically. See the article by M. E. Mundel, "How Many Readings for a Time Study?" *Modern Management* (New York: Society for Advancement of Management, Inc.), August, 1949, pp. 21–22.

SKILL			EFFORT		
+ 0.15 + 0.13	A 1 A 2	SUPERSKILL	+ 0.13 + 0.12	A 1 A 2	KILLING
+ 0.11 + 0.08	B 1 B 2	EXCELLENT	+ 0.10 + 0.08	B 1 B 2	EXCELLENT
+ 0.06 + 0.03	C 1 C 2	GOOD	+ 0.05 + 0.02	C 1 C 2	GOOD
0.00	D	AVERAGE	0.00	D	AVERAGE
− 0.05 − 0.10	E 1 E 2	FAIR	− 0.04 − 0.08	E 1 E 2	FAIR
− 0.16 − 0.22	F 1 F 2	POOR	− 0.12 − 0.17	F 1 F 2	POOR
CONDITIONS			CONSISTENCY		
+ 0.06	A	IDEAL	+ 0.04	A	PERFECT
+ 0.04	B	EXCELLENT	+ 0.03	B	EXCELLENT
+ 0.02	C	GOOD	+ 0.01	C	GOOD
0.00	D	AVERAGE	0.00	D	AVERAGE
− 0.03	E	FAIR	− 0.02	E	FAIR
− 0.07	F	POOR	− 0.04	F	POOR

Courtesy: Stewart M. Lowry, Harold B. Maynard, G. J. Stegemerten, "Time and Motion Study" (New York: McGraw-Hill Book Co., Inc., 1940), p. 233

FIG. 36–2. Performance rating chart.

6. *Evaluate the employee's skill, effort, working conditions, and consistency during the study.* These factors, observed while the operator was doing the work, are recorded on the left side of the form in Figure 36–1. As a guide, a leveling chart is usually used such as that shown in Figure 36–2. The algebraic values of the ratings are obtained from this chart, and in the case illustrated the following will apply:

Attribute	Rating	Algebraic Value
Skill..............................	B2	+0.08
Effort or speed.......................	C2	+0.02
Conditions...........................	D	0.00
Consistency or rhythm................	C	+0.01
Total...............................	....	+0.11

This total added algebraically to unity gives 1.11, which is the leveling or rating factor and is indicated on the form near the bottom of the lefthand column in Figure 36–1.

7. *Calculate the time elapsed for each element* by subtracting the preceding from the immediately following cumulative reading and recording under the appropriate column headed "T," which stands for Time. To illustrate, in Figure 36–1 on the first line, the value 9 under "T" in element two is obtained by subtracting 12 from 21; the value 4 under element three is obtained by subtracting 21 from 25. Other values of time elapsed for each element are obtained in like manner.

8. *Calculate the time standard by:*

a) Finding the representative, observed, elemental time. To do this, study the time taken by elements shown by each vertical column under "T," strike out the abnormal times, and find the average—usually the arithmetic average of the remaining times. In the illustration given in Figure 36–1, the abnormal time of 18 for element two on line 9 has been discarded. The average of the selected T values is 0.089, as shown near the bottom of the column. This was calculated by dividing 0.62 by 7.

b) Apply the leveling factor. To do this, multiply the average T value by the leveling factor. In the case illustrated, this is 0.089 times 1.11, which gives 0.099, the elemental base time. Since the T value occurs once per unit, the base time per unit is the same, namely 0.099, which is written on the bottom line of the column.

c) Add allowances for personal needs, fatigue, unavoidable delays, and the like. This can be expressed either as a lump percentage or as separate percentages for each allowance. This is shown in Figure 36–3. The sum of the base time per unit is 1.235. An allowance of 20 per cent as a lump sum has been added, and the new value is 1.482. This is, of course, in minutes. Expressed as units per hour, the value is 40.5. Figure 36–3 also illustrates other pertinent data which are included on the time-study sheet. Information regarding the conditions, the material used, and a sketch of the workplace area is usually included for identification and future reference.

STANDARD DATA FROM TIME STUDY

Time standards derived from either this source or the next source to be discussed, standard time data, are predetermined time values for definite elements or basic motions. These data are expressed by tables of values, algebraic equations, and graphic curves. By their use the time standard can be set before the work is actually performed. To do this, the necessary elements or basic motions making up the task are determined, and the standard time for each element is added, to give a total standard time value for the particular task. It is an analytical and detailed approach which synthesizes an operation time. It avoids the stop watch which is sometimes objectionable, reduces the judgment required, and expedites the establishing of standards especially when a variety of sizes or qualities on the same product are included.

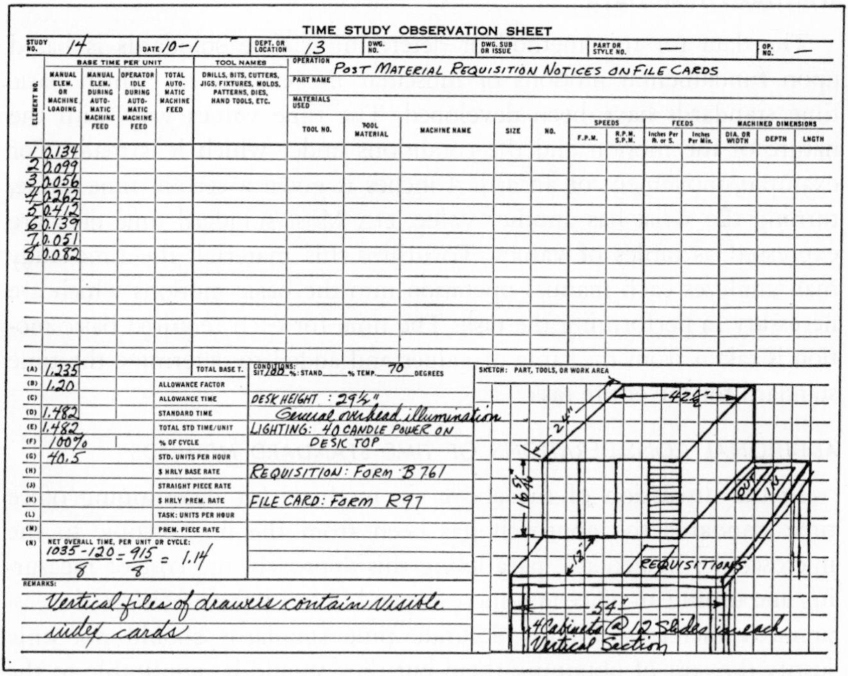

FIG. 36–3.   Reverse side of time-study data sheet shown in Fig. 36–1.

From the data of many actual time studies it is possible to determine the basic allowable times for elements which are common to many tasks.[6] To do this, relationships between time and some meaningful variable, such as distance, size, or weight, are determined. For example, consider the element "pulling file drawer out." From many actual time studies, the time values for this element are obtained. Some of these values will be for pulling file drawers out a distance of 6 inches, others 10 inches, still others 14 inches, etc. By mathematical analysis of these

---

[6] "Elemental motions" as used here means the smallest motions that can be observed and read for time. It does not mean elementary motions or therbligs, which are discussed in the preceding chapter. Therbligs usually are of too short a duration to be measured by a stop watch.

data, the relationship between time and distance traveled for the element "pulling file drawer out" can be determined. From this relationship the amount of time for this element can be predetermined, based on the distance the drawer travels. In similar manner, relationships can be determined for the size of the drawer and the weight of material in it. The relationships so developed, as previously stated, can be expressed as tables of values, as equations, or as graphs.

STANDARD TIME DATA

The data for this method of determining time standards is based upon fundamental motions or muscular movements for which basic time standards have been developed. The time values vary with the nature of the motion and the conditions under which it is made. For example, movement of an arm 4 inches is given a certain time value, turning the wrist has another value, etc. Most standard time data are expressed as tables of values. To utilize this material, the time-study man analyzes each manual operation into the basic motions which are necessary in performing the task. The time for each required basic motion is taken from the table of values and added to determine the time standard for the entire task.

ADDITIONAL CONSIDERATIONS OF TIME STANDARD METHODS

In the discussion of the above six methods for determining office time standards the approach has been from the macroscopic to the microscopic. In general, paralleling this approach, the cost of measuring and timing an office task increases and likewise the precision of measurement increases. Highly accurate time standards should not only justify the cost of obtaining them but they should be applicable to the particular office situation. The use of an exact predetermined time standard may not bring forth best results if applied to work having strong cyclic characteristics. In similar manner, time standards based on past performance records may prove of little help in controlling.

The selection of the means of determining the office standard must be made with great care. From the over-all viewpoint, stop-watch study or predetermined time values are desirable when the following office conditions are met: (1) the tasks are well defined, (2) there is consistency in the work flow, (3) uniformity in physical characteristics of the office work is present, and (4) specific quantities of work exist.

EXAMPLES OF OFFICE TIME STANDARDS

The following office time standards have value in connection with various types of office work. They are included here to be helpful in a comparative way only. They were determined for conditions prevailing in a particular office and should be used as guides, not goals.

Units
Per Hour

I. Typing

Type name and account number on card... 180
Type labels from typewritten copy... 135
Type ledger cards... 105
Type report, double space on 8½ × 11-inch paper, one original and one carbon copy   10
Type address on envelope.. 85

II. Calculating and Checking

Compute products of 3-digit number by 3-digit number, using machine............. 500
Add 20 numbers in a column, each number is 3-digits, by machine.................. 2
Compare columns of figures on tape or report, with columns of figures in like order.
  (Number of digits per figure compared equals 5.).............................4,800
Count items on a tape, or lines on a sheet......................................9,400

III. Accounting

Pull from source, post account to ledger sheet by machine, and replace sheet........ 130
Make entries in ledger (manual)... 40

IV. Filing and Sorting

Sort correspondence papers for filing... 480
File correspondence papers in alphabetical file................................... 180
Sort 5 × 3-inch cards alphabetically.. 300
Locate and pull addressing plates from alphabetical file.......................... 420

V. Miscellaneous

Hand fold 8½ × 11-inch sheet with one fold......................................1,200
Seal ordinary envelope (manual)... 450
Assemble three sheets of paper, 8½ × 11 inches, and insert in large 9 × 12-inch
  envelope... 575

QUESTIONS

1. Indicate what measuring unit you would recommend and your reasons why for each of the following:

   a) Duplicating of a monthly report.
   b) Typing billings to customers.
   c) Opening of first-class mail.
   d) Receiving office visitors and sorting 3 × 5-inch cards alphabetically.

2. What is meant by a composite work-measurement unit in connection with office work and how is it used?

3. In your opinion does measurement of work or measurement of time pose the bigger problem in the setting of office time standards? Explain.

4. Is the setting of time standards a responsibility solely of a manager? Why?

5. Why should a time study be made only after the proper workplace has been provided and the motions economized? Are there any exceptions?

6. Name and discuss four major advantages in having time standards. Are these advantages to managers exclusively, to nonmanagement members exclusively, or to both managers and nonmanagement members? Explain.

7. Carefully distinguish between the concepts in each of the following pairs:

a) Work sampling and standard time data.
b) Time study and stop-watch study.
c) Time standards and definition of task.
d) Leveling factor and allowance for personal needs.

8. Explain the following: "Past performance records are actually 'what is' rather than 'what should be.'"

9. In your opinion, should the person determining the time standard for a task be able to perform that task within the time set by him as the time standard? Why or why not?

10. Do you agree with the statement: "Stop-watch study for determining time standards is s scientific process"? Explain your answer.

11. Since time standards represent the time required for the average employee, why not select in stop-watch study an average employee and time him?

12. Discuss your reactions to the following: "Although the timing of office activities has been given much attention in recent years, the determining of valid office time standards has witnessed little progress. This condition, however, should not be discouraging to the office manager because in most cases adequate control over office work is possible by means of sound simplification of procedures and proper design and usage of office forms."

CASE PROBLEMS

CASE 36–1.   THE DODSON COMPANY

Five employees type billings. To satisfy requirements for foreign shipments, stub-type unit arrangement forms are used for foreign customers, while the continuous semistrip arrangement forms are used for domestic customers. A cursory examination shows that the number of items on a billing is usually 1, 2, or 3 with occasional billings for 4 and 5, and rarely for 6 or more items.

On Tuesdays and Wednesdays the work load appears greatest. On Fridays the load is normally light; however, the employees appear busy, but fewer billings are written on this day. Items on the foreign billings show little change from month to month, while on domestic billings there is a great variety of items ordered from week to week. Two of the operators receive 15 per cent more pay than the others, although all have been with the company about the same period.

PROBLEMS:

1. To expedite work allocation, describe your recommendation for measuring the work of the billing clerks.

2. Do you feel that both managers and operators will accept your recommendation? Why?

CASE 36–2.   DIXON SERVICE COMPANY

The following time data concerns the work of posting visible file records. Company practices allow 15 per cent for personal needs, delays, and rest periods.

STUDY NO.	32-014			STYLE OR PART NO.
DATE	March 27			
SHEET NO.	1			OPERATION NO.
OF	1 SHEETS			PART NAME
STUDY STARTED	10:50 A.M.			
STUDY ENDED	10:59 A.M.			OPERATION Purchasing-
ELAPSED TIME HRS/MIN	9			Posting inventory file records

Element descriptions:
1. Reads pertinent data from Prod. copy at top of stack
2. Pulls out proper file tray
3. Finds proper card
4. Enters data on card
5. Closes file tray
6. Places top Prod. copy in folder
7. Puts folder in Desk Bin returns hands to next Prod. copy

DESCRIP-TION / RATING / SKILL / SPEED		1 T	1 R	2 T	2 R	3 T	3 R	4 T	4 R	5 T	5 R	6 T	6 R	7 T	7 R	FOREIGN ELEMENTS R	T	DESCRIPTION
Maximum	A1 (1)	09		15		19		42		46		56		70		A 200/300	100	File tray jammed
	A2 (2)	80		85		90		120		24		35		50		B 346/431	85	Error in entry- erased
Excellent	B2 (3)	62		67		72		200		B303		12		27		C		
Good	C2 (4)	36		43		46		B464		68		79		93		D		
Standard	D (5)	504		11		14		45		49		60		76		E		
Fair	E2 (6)	88		94		99		629		33		45		60		F		
Poor	F2 (7)	71		77		82		708		13		23		39		G		
Very Poor	G1 (8)	50		57		62		89		94		806		21		H		

DESCRIPTION / RATING CONDITIONS / EFFORT:
Ideal A (10); Excellent B (11); Good C (12); Standard D; Fair E (13); Poor F (14)

	1	2	3	4	5	6	7
TOTALS T.							
NO. OF VALUES USED							
AVERAGE (SELECTED) T							
RATING							
TOTAL RATING FACTOR							
ELEM. BASE TIME							
OCCURR. PER UNIT	1	1	1	1	1	1	1
BASE TIME PER UNIT							

OPERATOR'S NAME Susan Lanski
OPERATOR'S NO. 137 M ( ) F (X)
OBSERVER P.E.J.
APPROVED W.S.

Designed by H. B. Rogers. 7-8-44. Revised 7-28-47

1944 NORTHWESTERN UNIVERSITY

USS 1144—25M

PROBLEMS:

1. Compute the time standard for the indicated work in postings per hour.

2. How many postings would you expect for a regular eight-hour day? Explain.

CASE 36–3. BYRNES MANUFACTURING COMPANY

Data helpful for certain analysis work are typed on 5 × 3 cards at the time the purchase orders are prepared. In the upper right corner of each card is a coded number like 37–41–5882. The first portion of the number indicates the type of material, the second portion the vendor's identity, and the third portion the manufacturing order on which the material will be used.

These cards are manually sorted to numerical sequence. Used for this work is a cabinet with eleven horizontal shelves. From top to bottom of the row to the left are shelves 1, 2, 3, and 4; correspondingly the row to the right consists of shelves 5, 6, 7, and 8, and the center row of shelves 9, 0, and S. The latter is the storage area to hold unsorted cards.

Sorting is done from right to left, first by the unit digit, then by the tens digit, and so forth. The operator keeps her eye on the number area of the cards on the central unsorted stack, or shelf S. The location and identity of each shelf is memorized. The top unsorted card is grasped using one hand, moved to the proper shelf, and released. While the one hand is returning, the other hand grasps the second unsorted card and moves it to its proper shelf. This continuous motion is used until all the cards are sorted to the first digit. Then the work is repeated for the second digit, and so forth, until the sorting is completed.

Assume that the time taken to place a batch of 400 cards on shelf S is 0.20 minutes; to sort with either hand, 0.03 minutes; to collect the sorted cards and return to shelf S, 0.16 minutes. These times are for an operator working under excellent conditions who has good, but not quite excellent, skill, average speed, and excellent rhythm. An allowance factor of 18 per cent is believed equitable.

PROBLEMS:

1. Compute the time standard (in cards per hour) for this work.

2. Will this time standard rate apply when the total number of cards to be sorted is either 100 or 1,988? Why?

Chapter · 37

Office Manuals

There is really no unsurmountable barrier save your own inherent weakness of purpose.

—RALPH WALDO EMERSON

To ASSIST in obtaining the desired control of the employees' efforts in an enterprise, it is necessary that each employee be fully informed regarding his duties and responsibilities, the regulations under which he shall work, and the policies and practices of the enterprise for which he is working. This information should be given in a simple, direct manner and by a uniform, authoritative, yet relatively inexpensive, means. It should convey the information quickly and accurately. One of the best media for getting these data to the employee is the office manual.

DEFINITION OF OFFICE MANUAL

An office manual is a written record of information and instructions which concern and can be used to guide the employee's efforts in an enterprise. Actually, it is a guidebook—a source for data believed essential for the highest performance of the job. It is a device to help in the orientation of employees. It can help to make instructions definite, to state policies and procedures, to fix responsibility, and to show how the employee can contribute to the achievement of company objectives as well as to his relationship with other employees. Fundamentally, manuals relieve management members of having to repeat similar information, explanations, or instructions. Uniformity, accessibility, and deliberation are among the advantages of a manual. In many enterprises manuals are considered "musts."

TYPES OF OFFICE MANUALS

Different offices find they have need for different manuals. The type is determined by answering the question, "What is the purpose to be served?" In some instances a single purpose only is served, while in others several purposes are to be fulfilled. The number and the kind of purposes are determined by the individual circumstances.

Manuals can be written to cover a variety of subjects, including policies, organization structure of the enterprise, employment, indoctrination, job instruction, standard work practices, history of the enterprise, and specialized or departmental practices such as in the accounting, engineering, purchasing, or sales department. However, for convenience, the major types of manuals along with their respective purpose can be set forth as follows:

Type of Manual	*Purpose*
Manual of Policies	To state the policies of the enterprise or office.
Manual of Operations, or Standard Practices Manual, or Job Instruction Manual	To inform employees of established methods, procedures, and standards.
Manual of Office Rules and Regulations or Handbook on Employment	To give concise information on benefits, operating rules, and employment regulations.
Historical Manual	To provide historical information about the enterprise.
General Manual	To supply selected items from any area or subject deemed desirable and helpful in the work performance.

MANUAL OF POLICIES

As set forth in Chapter 12, a policy is a basic guide to action. It prescribes the over-all boundaries within which activities are to take place and, hence, reveals broad managerial intentions or forecasts broad courses of managerial action likely to take place under certain conditions. To illustrate, promoting employees solely on the basis of merit is a policy. It states the guide for promoting, but it does not tell who will be promoted, Likewise, the payment of salaries above the prevailing amounts in the community for similar work, consistent with the economic well-being of the enterprise, is another example of a policy. Knowing the policies of an enterprise provides the main framework around which all actions are based. Policies furnish the background for an understanding of why things are done as they are.

A manual of policies puts into writing the policies of an enterprise. It has been said that a policy does not really exist unless it is in writing. To decide each case on its individual merits and to convey this decision verbally is not in keeping with modern management thinking. Proponents of a manual of policies cite these advantages: (1) written policies require managers to think through their courses of action and to predetermine what actions will be taken under various circumstances, (2) a general program of action for many matters is provided and only the unusual or exceptional matter requires the attention of the top managers, (3) a framework is provided within which the manager can operate freely, and (4) written policies help to insure an equitable treatment to all employees.

On the other hand, there are those who object to having a manual of policies. Among the important points they mention are: (1) policies are extremely difficult to write accurately and completely—the interpretation of words and phrases sometimes leads to serious misunderstandings; (2) written policies make it difficult to keep policies flexible, as is frequently required by changing conditions; and (3) knowledge of policies should be confined to those persons charged with their execution—the top executive, department heads, or supervisors, as the case might be.

MANUAL OF OPERATIONS

A manual can serve as a convenient source for information on how the work is to be done. The authorized steps can be listed; and supplementary information, in the form of diagrams, sketches, and charts, can be included in order to clarify the data. The standards and guides to be followed are usually included.

As already stated, a manual with this type of information is commonly referred to as a Manual of Operations, a Standard Practices, or a Job Instruction Manual. Actually the contents of such a manual can be pointed toward any one or all of the following:

1. *Individual Tasks and Jobs.* Illustrative of this type of manual is one which explains how to operate and use an adding machine. The importance of keeping accurate records can be emphasized and information included describing the parts and operations of an adding machine, practice lessons, and an explanation of the practices of the company. A glossary of terms is sometimes included to clarify the work as illustrated in Figure 37–1.

2. *Departmental Practices.* Manuals of this type contain a statement of the duties of the department. Its divisions are defined, the supervisors listed, and their responsibilities indicated, along with outlines and procedures for operating. The work of departments such as sales, purchasing, accounting, and research is often set up and described in departmental manuals.

3. *General Practices in a Special Field.* This type of manual is becoming more popular, for it furnishes valuable general information which is usable in special lines of work. Its adoption is mainly in large

MANUAL OF INSTRUCTION
FOR
ADDING MACHINE OPERATORS

The glossary consists of terms most commonly used in the Central Proof Division and has been prepared for the use of listing clerks. Every effort has been made to define these terms in words familiar to you. The definitions are not technical, but are given as generally accepted meanings, and the use of some of them should be avoided whenever possible, as they are considered "shop" language.

Accounts Receivable.—A section of the Bookkeeping Division where the Bank accumulates for certain customers miscellaneous charges which may cover services rendered or expenses incurred. The total is charged to the customer's account or billed monthly.

All Clearings.—A deposit consisting of checks drawn on Chicago banks. Such deposits are identified by a blue pencil marking.

Balance Table.—A designated table where clerks verify that finished work received from the adding machines is in balance or that work not in balance has been properly approved. (Grand total of checks equal grand total of credits.)

Block.—A term used to designate a method of assembling deposits or other incoming work in groups of various sizes for proving purposes.

Block Number.—An identifying number assigned to a block. The checks, credits, master tapes, makeups and production record card should all bear the block number.

Books.—Checks drawn on this Bank.

Cash Substitution Ticket.—A form which is substituted for coin and currency received in deposits. The cash substitution ticket, which is placed in the deposit in lieu of the currency or coin, enables the deposit to be properly balanced.

Source: "Manual of Instruction for Adding Machine Operators" (Chicago, Continental Illinois National Bank and Trust Company of Chicago), January, 1943, p. 33. Reproduced here by special permission.

FIG. 37–1. Portion of a page from an office manual for adding-machine operators.

offices, although in certain instances the small office can benefit from manuals of this type.

MANUAL OF OFFICE RULES AND REGULATIONS

Manuals are an excellent media in which to explain employee benefit plans, including such things as group insurance, hospitalization, and savings facilities. Questions regarding the use of the company library, cafeteria, and recreation club can also be answered. In addition, the prescribed guides for conduct are included and cover such items as sick allowances, the use of rest periods, conduct regarding smoking, solicitation for money in the office, the sale of tickets, hours of employment, holidays, vacations, office etiquette, rest periods, telephone usage, and recreational provisions. As already stated, a manual of this type is identified either as a Manual of Office Rules and Regulations or a Handbook on Employment. However, for psychological reasons the manual may be given a title like, "You and the XYZ Company," or "Getting Along at XYZ." Such a manual helps to orientate and to inform the employee by giving him specific answers to all the elements of his work surroundings, thus promoting understanding and harmoni-

---

GENERAL OFFICE ROUTINES

DESKS—Keep your desk clean. It's a workbench, not a catchall. Never allow a lot of old-fashioned relics to accumulate on it. File everything away in its natural place, and dispose of obsolete matter. (The job of filing is an important one and is not to be neglected or allowed to pile up.)

Avoid having decorations on the desk that might tip and spill, such as flower containers, ink bottles, sponge cups, etc. Keep such things in safer places.

Clear all desks and tables before leaving the building. Any papers or letters of a confidential nature must be put away, never left on the desk top. All lights are to be turned off, fans and ventilators disconnected, and blinds raised. Typewriters should be covered when not being used.

DUSTING—Each office is to be thoroughly dusted each morning—during the day too if necessary. No one need resent dusting—it's part of the job.

Pens should be filled, pencils sharpened and water bottles filled first thing in the morning. See to it that ash trays are kept clean throughout the day. If blotters are used, make sure soiled ones are replaced.

Typewriters should be dusted morning and night, type cleaner applied weekly.

SUPPLIES—If you are responsible for handling supplies for the office, check them regularly and make sure that you are not running low. Keep a list at your desk of supplies that will soon need to be requisitioned (use form 527 for ordering). All requisitions must be authorized by the department head.

HOURS—Arrange hours if possible so the office will not be unattended at any time. If it is impossible for someone to be present during lunch hour, do not leave without making arrangements with someone else to take any important calls.

CALLERS—It is much better to have an understanding with your superior regarding his wishes in the matter of announcing callers, the persons he wishes to see and those he does not, rather than to guess at the proper procedure in each instance.

Keep an accurate, up to date list or notebook of telephone numbers and addresses, business as well as personal. Such a list should be readily accessible. Add to it regularly so it will be of value both to you and your superior.

Source: Secretaries' and Stenographers' Handbook (Chicago: Butler Brothers, 1946), p. 20
Reproduced here by special permission.

FIG. 37–2. Page of a manual used by a large national distributor of general merchandise.

ous relationships. Figure 37–2 shows a sample of the type of information included in this kind of manual.

HISTORICAL MANUAL

Many employers feel that it is important to give employees information regarding the history of the company—its beginning, growth, accomplishments, present management, and current status. This gives the employee an insight into the tradition and thinking behind the enterprise with which he is associated. It probably makes for better understanding, increases morale, and helps the employee to feel that he belongs—that he is a part of the company. Giving employees a "picture of the whole" helps him to fit himself into the total picture. Manuals, of course, are excellent means for conveying this type of information to employees. The "story" of the enterprise usually can be told on several pages, and quite frequently it can be a part of a message written by a major officer. Historical information is commonly included as the introductory portion to a manual of office rules and regulations.

GENERAL MANUAL

This type of manual represents a combination of any two or all of the types discussed above. The company's needs, the size of the enterprise, and the philosophy of the top managers usually determine the make-up. The contents of a general manual might include the following:

1. *Title page*—giving the name of the manual, name of the company, and date of publication.

2. *Ownership page*—stating "This book is the property of the _____ _____ in Department _____."

3. *Foreword*—setting forth the purpose of the manual, suggesting its careful use, and inviting constructive criticisms.

4. *Table of Contents*—listing the selections making up the book, along with the proper page numbers.

5. *Company History and Policies*—outlining briefly the start and subsequent development of the company, telling about its products or services, and giving concise statements and terse discussions of company policies. Frequently this portion of the manual is issued over the signature of the president or some other major officer.

6. *Job Instruction and Execution*—explaining what the job is, how it is done, and the like. Organization charts, diagrams, and sketches should be used. Illustrations of properly executed forms and records are also helpful.

7. *Rules and Regulations*—including the approved standards for employees' conduct and the basis for disciplinary action.

8. *Index*—providing a complete and handy reference to all the material in the manual. In the case of large organizations, a list of officers and personnel of branch offices might be included as a separate section of the index.

SOURCES FOR MANUAL MATERIAL

Probably one of the best sources of material for a manual is manuals used by other enterprises. Looking over what has been included in manuals of another company suggests what topics might be covered. However, the manual should be personalized to meet the particular needs of an enterprise.

Additional data can be secured from a number of other sources. Such data might include: (1) minutes of board of directors' meetings, (2) reports of executive conferences, (3) speeches and published articles of executives, (4) bulletins and company circulars, (5) agreements with employees and contracts with unions, (6) grievance records, (7) company magazines or similar publications, and (8) interviews with executives, especially the personnel manager, training director, and supervisors.

Experience shows that, with time, it will be desirable to eliminate certain material and to add other material. The additional material might be secured from the above sources or, because of the unique nature of the information, may be secured from a special source. For example, instructions in the correct use of a new office machine would probably be secured from the manufacturer or seller.

PREPARATION OF MANUALS

Some orderly process must be followed in the preparation of manuals if they are to be inclusive and to be completed within a reasonable period of time. The process followed depends a great deal upon the individual in charge of this work. In general, however, it will be helpful to follow a procedure along these lines:

1. *Announce to all members of the enterprise that a manual is to be prepared.* Encourage their suggestions and ideas as to what should be included. Appointing a committee of employees often encourages their participation in the preparation of the manual. As a result, better understanding and greater acceptance and use are usually gained. Special attention should be directed to supervisors for they are usually rich sources of excellent material.

2. *Draw up a list of all the subjects to be covered by the manual.* The purpose of the manual, the cost, and managerial judgment will determine, for the most part, what items are included. Proper subheadings should be made under each main topic, and the list should be arranged according to the contemplated main divisions or sections of the manual.

A big timesaver in this respect is to use a separate card for each topic and file behind guides. By this means material can be classified quickly and the list or outline changed with a minimum of effort.

A logical arrangement of the material is most commonly used, but this sequence is not necessarily the most effective in all cases. Consideration should be given to placing the vital information or that which is most interesting in the beginning, using the last portion of the list for data of less importance.

3. *Write the information under each subject.* Check the source data to help insure accuracy in all writing. Source material can be numbered and indexed, and this means of identification tied in with the writing by means of marginal notes. Keep the prospective reader in mind—write so he will want to read the manual and understand what it is intended to mean. A simple, friendly, and sincere style is best. Short words and sentences should be employed. Include charts, diagrams, and examples of proper forms, letters, and reports in order to gain greater clarity. These illustrations should be in an inexpensive, rough form until it is decided, as described below, whether they will be included in the final manual. All material should be presented in the normal-flow-of-work sequence. The amount of detail depends upon the importance of the subject.

4. *Prepare a limited number of copies for key executives, supervisors, employee or union representatives, and several key employees.* Have them read the manual and submit criticisms and suggestions. Quite often, better ways of expression are found in this way. Sometimes subjects can be combined, major items previously overlooked can be added, minor points strengthened, and the entire manual improved.

5. *Revise the manual and give it to top management members for approval.* Corrections and suggestions from the previous step are incorporated. It is well to include a separate statement to the effect that the entire contents are in agreement with the philosophy of top management members and are acceptable to the employees.

6. *Send the approved manuscript to the printer or the party doing the actual mechanical production work.* The manual can be published by any of several different methods, including mimeographing, multilithing, or letterpress printing.[1] The quantity, appearance, and cost will probably determine the process used. Details regarding size, paper, and type of binding must also be decided. Generally it is well to seek competent advice in these matters.

---

[1] See Chapter 9 for discussion of duplicating processes.

The size $6\frac{1}{4} \times 4\frac{1}{2}$ inches is excellent for a booklet intended for carrying in the pocket. If the manual is to be used as a reference book on a desk, an $11 \times 8\frac{1}{2}$-inch size is very satisfactory. Other popular sizes include $9\frac{1}{8} \times 6$ inches, $8\frac{1}{2} \times 5\frac{1}{2}$ inches, and $5\frac{1}{8} \times 3\frac{3}{4}$ inches. Pages of these sizes can be cut, with minimum waste, from sheet sizes usually carried by the printer.[2]

The number and size of the pages in the booklet generally determine the weight of paper used. When the number of pages does not exceed about twenty-four, a thick paper can be used; but where a greater number of pages are involved, a thinner stock is used, to eliminate unnecessary bulk. For page sizes under about $8\frac{1}{2} \times 5\frac{1}{2}$ inches, a paper of about 60 pounds is used. When the size is greater, paper of about 70 pounds is employed.

It is advisable to set off the reading material by headings. These can be made to stand out on the page by the use of white space around them, or color may be employed. Color increases the cost, but in many cases the effect brought about by such things as a colored border, headline, or illustration justifies the additional expense. Additional suggestions are shown in Figure 37–3.

The type of binding may be either side or saddle wire stitching, screw post, prong fasteners, ring binder, and wire or plastic edge binding. The choice will depend primarily upon usage, amount of material, appearance, and cost.[3]

DISTRIBUTION OF MANUALS

It is paramount that the distribution of the manuals provide a copy to everyone concerned with and in need of the information the manual contains. The extent of distribution depends upon the size of the enterprise; in most cases one copy of the manual should be available for ready reference in at least each department or division. In cases where manuals pertain to specific jobs, copies should be readily available to every employee on such jobs.

To increase the readership of the manual, it is sometimes given to the employee only during an interview. His attention is directed to specific pages, and he is encouraged to read the entire booklet. In some

[2] In the case of loose-leaf and many bound manuals, it is customary to give the dimension of the binding side first. Thus, an 11×8-inch size means the binding is on an 11-inch side. The dimensions used in this discussion follow this practice. In contrast, and at times somewhat confusingly, in specifying dimensions of index cards the horizontal dimension is named first, followed by the vertical dimension. For example, an 8×5 card means 8 inches horizontally and 5 inches vertically.

[3] See Chapter 35, p. 679, for detailed discussion of this subject.

cases, depending upon the type manual, it is mailed to the employee's home with an accompanying letter. Forewarning of the manual to be used as the subject for a forthcoming meeting or group discussion is a very effective means of encouraging readership. In addition, sometimes the employee is requested to sign and to return an enclosed card in the manual as evidence of reading the complete booklet, and in other

---

PAGE SIZE—

If printed, the 6 × 9-inch page size is effective. This is the typical book size.

If typed, the 8½ × 11-inch page size will be preferred by most employees.

ARRANGEMENT OF MATERIAL—

Place sections most frequently used at front of manual.

Related sections should be placed close together and interrelated by cross references.

Set sections apart by stiff divider page of different colored paper.

Either tab sections for ready reference or use a divider page size to facilitate a margin index.

REMEMBER TO—

Make the cover attractive by using a clear, brief title and well-selected art work.

Include a table of contents and an index so that the reader can quickly find that for which he is looking.

FIG. 37–3. Helpful suggestions for preparation of manuals.

instances, questions are asked on the card to measure the employee's understanding of the manual contents.

MANUAL MAINTENANCE

The problem of keeping the manual up to date is ever present. In most enterprises changes are taking place constantly, owing to new work being added or improvements in current work being made. Revisions of and additions to manuals are constantly in process. New pages must replace the old and be distributed to all holders of the manuals. These changes may be covered either by single sheets or by entire supplements. Frequently, amendments are written on colored paper to attract attention to the change. Also, notations made in red ink in the manual will point out those parts which have been changed, omitted, or amended. When many changes cause the manual to be difficult to read and use, it should be rewritten.

All revisions should clear through a central control unit so that proper authorization and conformity in results are obtained. If this is not done, needless confusion and misunderstanding will result. The revised sheets should follow the established form of the manual. New material will probably be added every three to six months, together with certain modifications in the old material. Many managers advocate the use of a form of binder which facilitates the insertion of revised sheets.

EVALUATION OF USE OF MANUAL

From what has already been written, it follows that manuals are excellent tools of managerial control and that beneficial results accrue from their use. There are some, however, who do not support the use of manuals for any of a number of reasons. Among the more common adverse criticisms are that manuals "cost too much," "are too much work," "stifle initiative," or "won't work in our case."

In some cases these objections are no doubt justifiable, but for most enterprises the use of manuals is beneficial. Manuals inform and therefore help the employee to evaluate what he is accomplishing and to take corrective steps if needed. The manual information evolves from the co-operation of the employer and employee and represents tried and tested data. In this connection, the willingness of the management members to accept and utilize employee's suggestions in the manual formulation and the manner of the manual's announcement to the employees contribute greatly to the way in which the manual is accepted. Normally a sincere verbal statement describing the manual and explaining how it will help both the employee and employer is sufficient. Periodic revisions of the manual foster the progressive spirit—the will to improve current practices is encouraged. Manuals also help to set up and to define the boundary and scope of operations of each management area. Employees know within what defined area they can operate, and freedom within that area is insured. When changes are necessary, decisions and amendments can be made quickly and adequately by the person having the proper authority. This adds up to a highly effective working force.

QUESTIONS

1. If the office manager of a medium-sized office was limited to one type of manual, what type would you recommend? Why?
2. It has been suggested that a manual be written that would be adaptable for use by all offices. Spaces for individualized "fill-ins" would be provided do you believe such a manual is feasible? Explain.

3. In your opinion, could an effective manual of operations be prepared by asking each employee to write a complete description of his various duties and the manner in which they are performed? Elaborate on your answer.

4. What kinds of information should be in an office manual?

5. Are you of the opinion that for most offices a manual is beneficial? Substantiate your answer.

6. Discuss the subject of manual maintenance.

7. Generally speaking do you favor an office having a manual of policies? Justify your answer.

8. Distinguish carefully between the elements in each of the following pairs:

   a) Manuals and managerial orders.
   b) A policy manual and an operations manual.
   c) An $11 \times 8\frac{1}{2}$-inch manual and an $8\frac{1}{2} \times 11$-inch manual.
   d) Managerial controlling and manuals.

9. Enumerate and discuss briefly the major steps in the preparation of a manual.

10. As an office manager, would you favor having a requirement that all revisions of all manuals clear through a central control unit? Why?

11. Is an office manual of greater importance in a large or in a small office? Justify your answer.

12. Do you feel that office manuals reduce the need for training of office employees? Explain.

CASE PROBLEMS

CASE 37–1.   MEREDITH-PIEDMONT WOOD FURNITURE COMPANY

Eighty-five persons are employed in the office consisting of the following organization units: office services, correspondence, order-billing, accounting, purchasing, filing, and records retention. The office manager believes that having an office manual would help in informing office employees about their work and in achieving a well-co-ordinated office force. He requests authorization to proceed with actions to write, print, and distribute such a manual.

In contrast, the president of the corporation takes the viewpoint that (1) an office manual would represent an additional expenditure for which little return would be realized; (2) it would tend "to freeze" activities as they now are, i.e., retard progress; and (3) he questions whether it would be used, since the corporation has never had a manual.

PROBLEMS:

1. Write the preface to the proposed manual and prepare the table of contents.

2. Evaluate the president's viewpoints.

3. What action should the office manager take? Why?

CASE 37–2.   NEWCOMB COMPANY

The office manual of the Newcomb Company, of Louisville, Kentucky, contains information on the general rules and regulations and the operating standards and requirements of the company. As original orders and routines have been modified or replaced, pages in the manual have been canceled by writing "Void" across the appropriate sheet or sheets.

Each key employee has a copy of the manual at his desk, and no one is permitted to remove it. At present the manual contains about 400 pages and is in the form of a post binder about 6 × 4 inches in size.

As department heads or other executives originate, adopt, or change a standard procedure, rule, or regulation, they place a copy of the change in their own manual and send additional copies of the change through the intercompany messenger service to all holders of company manuals. For official sanction a change must bear the signature of a department head or other executive.

Within the past sixty days several cases have occurred when conflicting orders were followed by different employees. In one instance, the error is estimated to have cost the company $800. The difficulty was traced to the fact that a revised sheet was not placed in the manual of a supervisor. There is some doubt that the revised sheet was ever sent to the supervisor, who insists no copy of the particular revision was received.

In another case, the payment for merchandise shipped to a foreign country was improperly handled. The junior accountant who handled the transaction explained that he had asked his supervisor for instructions in the matter. Together they looked through the manual but could find no reference to the subject at hand. They then decided to handle the situation in what they believed the best manner possible. Unfortunately, their action was not in keeping with company requirements, and much needless correspondence with the customer followed. Investigation of the case showed that nearly a page and a half in the manual covers the subject. The employees had simply failed to find it. When asked why the office manager or the treasurer of the company was not consulted regarding proper disposition, the junior accountant explained that at the time the decision had to be made the office manager was attending an important meeting and could not be interrupted, and the treasurer was out of the city. His story was confirmed in full by his supervisor.

The president of the company has recently expressed the opinion that perhaps the use of the office manual should be abolished and the existing manuals destroyed. He favored a strengthening of formal lines of supervision and indicated that a manual never has replaced, doesn't now replace, and never will replace competent organization and supervision.

The office manager stated that from his observation the manuals were helpful in getting out the office work. They covered the great majority of situations. Of special importance was their use in training. For example, new employees spend their first day reading the general rules and regulations and studying the sections covering the operation procedures applicable to the job for which they are engaged.

PROBLEMS:

1. Can the company's office manual and its use be improved? Why? Be specific and complete.

2. Do you agree with the president of the company? Why, or why not?

3. As the office manager, what action would you take? Discuss.

Chapter · 38

Office Costs and Budgets

He is already poverty-stricken whose habits are not thrifty.
—T. T. MUNGER

O FFICE OPERATING effectiveness is frequently expressed by means of cost which is a common medium used for managerial controlling. Implied in every office accomplishment are the questions of not only when it was done, and where, and how, but also at what cost. Getting the office work completed is important; however, of still greater significance from the viewpoint of controlling is getting the work completed at a certain cost. Insight into labor efficiency, machine efficiency, and "overhead" efficiency can be secured through careful analysis of cost data.

Managerial success in many cases lies in understanding the nature of true costs. Knowledge of what things cost and how these costs are figured and evaluation of the final results in terms of costs are fundamental factors in the effective use of management. In addition, the question of costs must be answered if the enterprise is to continue. Cost knowledge is essential to survival, at least from a long-range point of view.

DEFINITION OF COST

In this discussion the concept of cost is confined to monetary expenditures. It is recognized that the term "cost" is commonly used to mean an outlay not only of money but also of time and labor. However, this implies simply that time and labor can be expressed in units of money. *Cost is the dollar amount expended for the ownership, use, or service of every component making up and employed in the execution of the work.* Cost is a matter of money outlay for manual or mental work accomplished, planned, or in process of being achieved.

IMPORTANCE OF COST

Since cost is basic and common to nearly all business activities, it follows that cost information can be put to a great number of uses. Prudence demands, however, that a limit be set on its use, with the boundaries determined either by the cost of using the cost data or by the employment of other techniques and indexes believed to be superior under the particular circumstances.

In many cases the making of a managerial decision is influenced to a considerable degree by the consideration of cost information. Questions as to whether to install a new procedure, to purchase a new office machine, to perform a new service, or to revise a form design are

COST SAVINGS ESTIMATE

DEPARTMENT NO. ___78___

DATE _9/7/58_

DESCRIPTION _Adopt work layout and method described by M-240_

NOTE: ALL COSTS FOR ONE YEAR

COSTS	PRESENT	PROPOSED	SAVINGS
LABOR	$2875	$2130	+$745
MATERIAL	925	800	+ 125
MACHINE TIME	750	1035	- 285
OTHER (WRITE IN)			
TOTAL	$4550	$3965	$585

ACTION ___Recommended and approved on Oct. 3, 1958 by executive committee, R. C. McGinnis, Chairman.___

APPROVED AND PUT INTO EFFECT BY ___CRW.___

FIG. 38–1.   A cost-savings estimate.

decided with the aid of cost information. Sometimes the question is answered almost entirely on the basis of cost. In addition, cost also helps justify a managerial action. Recommendations for a change usually include the cost before and the cost (estimated) after the change is effected. Likewise, if an alteration has been made, the wisdom of this move is frequently confirmed by a before-and-after cost picture. Figure 38–1 illustrates one type of form that can be used.

Cost serves as an effective median for co-ordinating managerial activities. For example, it is helpful in determining the program of action that will achieve the required results, yet maintain the proper balance. The selection and extent of managerial efforts, their timing, and direction can be executed in an orderly manner. Actions predicated on guesses or on hit-and-miss bases are minimized.[1]

---

[1] The budget, discussed later in this chapter, is also helpful in utilizing cost data for effective managerial purposes.

It is by means of cost that an office manager keeps informed of basic bench marks of the office operations. Many of the items in the reports dealing with accomplishments and in the ordinary financial statements are expressed in cost. The number of employees; supplies used; inventory on hand, in-process, or finished; charge for floor space occupied; charge for office machines usage; and the like are expressed in dollar values, estimated from cost information.

Another reason for the importance of cost is its use to supply clues to places where waste can be reduced or eliminated. While curbing waste is a desired result of all controlling, it is especially so in the case of cost. The very nature of cost information focuses attention on what was paid out and what was received. This leads to waste reduction. To illustrate, a study of duplicating costs might uncover uneconomical runs and the use of improper paper for the specific purpose. In addition, cost information reveals fluctuations in cost which can be followed up by investigations to determine the reasons. It may be found, for example, that too much material was purchased at one time or, contrariwise, that insufficient quantities are being bought.

To reiterate, cost is not an objective in itself but a guide to help manage, especially in the activity of controlling, the various activities in order that the aims of the enterprise will be realized. It is simply a means, but an important one, used by a manager. Suggested by the use of cost information is the maintaining of satisfactory cost levels and in many instances the reducing of costs. The satisfactory level is one that is compatible with the successful operation of the office. Progressive reductions in the amount of cost appear to be a normal state of affairs in a progressive economy. The eternal challenge is to perform the office work better and at less cost. This leads to the subject of cost control.

COST CONTROL

As pointed out throughout this book, controlling consists basically of determining what's being done, evaluating it, and taking corrective action if necessary. The same holds true for cost control. For the discussion here, these five steps will be considered in order: (1) assemble facts on cost, (2) know what cost is satisfactory, (3) compare actual cost with the cost deemed satisfactory, (4) take remedial action if necessary, and (5) provide adequate and proper follow-up.

ASSEMBLE FACTS ON COST

The initial step in cost control is to get together the facts on cost, classify as to type, and arrange so that handy reference and quick comparisons can be made. Sources of cost information include ledgers, cost journals, payroll records, purchases, and records of service charges. To expedite this work it is usually advisable to concentrate the efforts in several selected areas.

In assembling the factual cost information, it is well to take into account these considerations:

1. *The data should be accurate, timely, and identified.* In the modern office, frequent changes may be made in the efforts to improve operations. These changes are sometimes of a major sort and necessitate a new collection of cost data in order to reflect an accurate measurement of current expenditures. Even in the case of minor adjustments, the resultant effect may be sufficiently large to invalidate a considerable portion of previous cost information. Cost data should be closely affiliated and apply to the current situation; otherwise, their value is questionable.

There are so many different kinds of cost that the term "cost" in and of itself is practically meaningless. The variety of costs is almost endless, the different kinds depending upon the degree and type of work covered. To facilitate understanding, information concerning "cost of what to whom" is needed.

Several common identification arrangements will be given. The first, based on the factors or elements of material, labor, and overhead include:

Element	*Segregation and Meaning*
Material cost.........	Direct material cost—expenditures for materials which are or become a part of the product (office forms and letterheads).
	Indirect material cost—expenditures for materials which are not a part of the product but necessary in the carrying out of the work (typewriter ribbons, erasers).
Labor cost...........	Direct labor cost—expenditures for labor attributable to and having a bearing upon the product or service (billing-machine operator, typist).
	Indirect labor cost—expenditures for labor not attributable to or in an unbroken connection with the product or service (methods man, janitor).
Overhead cost........	Expenditures which do not belong exclusively to any part of the material or labor (rent, light, heat, managerial expense, telephone).

The second arrangement utilizing a functional basis consists of:
Total costs made up of—

    I. Production costs, under which are
        A. Production overhead costs
        B. Office cost consisting of
            1. Office overhead cost

　　2. Prime office costs
　　　　a) Direct office material cost
　　　　b) Direct office labor cost
　II. Sales cost, under which are
　　A. Sales overhead cost
　　B. Promotion, travel, and advertising cost
　　C. Salesmen's compensation cost
　　　　1. Wage payment cost
　　　　2. Commission and bonus cost

This outline is for illustrative purposes only and is not complete.

2. *The data should apply to well-defined components.* Usually in studying cost data, the most important figures are not the totals but the individual cost figures—those covering each component of those which collectively make up the total cost. Sufficient details must be included in all cost information to maximize its managerial value. No single factor tells the whole cost story.

In addition, the "cost per unit" should be used. The unit cost is the important concept. Comparison of a $300 actual cost with a $200 expected cost is not valid. If the work accomplished is 150 units and the expected output was 100 units, the true values become:

$$\text{Actual} = \frac{\$300}{150 \text{ units}} = \$2.00 \text{ per unit,}$$

$$\text{Expected} = \frac{\$200}{100 \text{ units}} = \$2.00 \text{ per unit,}$$

which demonstrates that the actual unit cost did not exceed but is equal to the expected cost.

3. *The identification and presentation form must be simple and complete.* The operation covered should be clearly specified, so that the data are identified with the correct kind of cost. Such things as date, location of operation, operation number, and other pertinent information should be included. The arrangement can be in properly headed, simple, tabular columns. However, in special cases it might be advisable to have the data in coded form in order to preserve its confidential nature. Either cards or letter-size paper can be used, depending upon the custom and individual requirements.

KNOW WHAT COST IS SATISFACTORY

This can be determined in a number of ways. The amount may be arrived at from past experience, giving due consideration to general economic changes and conditions. A general evaluation of what is received for a given expenditure may also be used. However, probably most satisfactory are standard costs, and, if available, they should be employed.

Standard cost is a computed predetermined cost which represents the amount of expenditure for direct material, direct labor, and overhead considered normal for the performance of the work. Theoretically, when the work is done by a standard employee with standard material and under standard conditions, the total dollar expenditure should be the standard cost. This is clearly stated in the following:

> Sound quantity standards are the foundation of any control plan. The contribution of the engineer and production man in the determination of proper allowances for labor times or material quantities is vital to the setting of proper standards for control.
>
> A standard cost is the monetary expression of these quantity standards. With the establishment of a standard price per unit of standard time or standard quantity, a quantity standard can be expressed in dollars.[2]

In some cases the standard cost being established some time ago must be adjusted to reflect current conditions. These adjustments are called variances and are applied to the cost standard to determine the cost currently considered acceptable. Variances may be either positive, i.e., added to the standard, or negative, i.e., subtracted from the standard.

The use of standard costs gives rise to several outstanding advantages, including (1) basic references are provided to orientate managerial efforts, (2) strict accountability for deviations from the established standard cost can be placed on those responsible for the deviations, and (3) cost analysis is simplified. In contrast, standard cost usage has its shortcomings. For example, the units of expression are dollars and, hence, subject to fluctuating value; personnel must be especially trained for standard-cost work so that proper interpretation and use of the standard data are made, and in cases of special work, standard-cost data cannot be used unless serious adjustments are made. While all these objections are valid, they are not particularly serious. Dollar values tend to remain *relatively* the same even though they do fluctuate in absolute value. It is probably true that some guide to acceptability, although it be found wanting in many respects, is better than none at all. Also, most efforts to guide the performance of work must, of practical necessity, be tempered with judgment.

---

[2] Theodore Lang, *Cost Accountants' Handbook* (New York: Ronald Press Co., 1944), p. 14.

COMPARE ACTUAL COST WITH COST DEEMED SATISFACTORY

This shows whether expenditures are greater, the same, or less than an acceptable level. It indicates the performance efficiency expressed in dollars. If the expenditure is less than the amount considered satisfactory, an investigation is made to determine if the work performed was of acceptable quality and quantity and if the satisfactory cost level is proper. On the other hand, where the actual cost exceeds the established satisfactory level, an investigation might be made to check the satisfactory level or, more likely, to analyze the actual cost to see in what way it can be brought into line.

The comparison work is expedited by cost reports giving detailed information on expenditures and compiled at the end of each day, week, or month. For maximum assistance the report should show the plus or minus deviations from the standard for each item and, what is very important, should include sufficient data to establish trends. In many instances the comparison of actual with standard cost is included under budgetary control which is discussed later in this chapter.

TAKE REMEDIAL ACTION IF NECESSARY

For the most part this includes efforts to reduce expenditures in those cases where actual costs are exceeding the satisfactory cost level. In many cases the data apply to what has already happened, so that the remedial action is for some future date. However, it is vital to evaluate costs and to seek the reasons for present values. To illustrate, investigation of an increasing trend in office personnel costs may reveal poor selection techniques and high turnover. The remedial action might include a testing program, retraining of interviewers, and specific employee training efforts.

Although costs are detailed in terms of specific office functions, it is necessary to retain the over-all viewpoint in deciding the remedial action. A reduction in one expense might increase another, making a total net gain in expenses. For example, centralized office costs may be reduced, but the work has been shifted to branch offices where the costs increase. Other illustrations are reducing the amount of light resulting in an increase of time required to do the work, eliminating interoffice telephone service with the resultant increase in time spent by employees in delivering messages personally.

Another consideration is to utilize all time and space savings effected. There is no gain doing work in less time or in less space unless the savings are transferred to other work. For example, a job may be improved to the point where what formerly was an eight-hour task becomes a six-hour task, thereby saving two hours. But actually there is no saving unless these two hours are used to perform other work. Likewise, an office machine may save the time of one person out of three; but unless the third person is transferred and put to other work, the net result costwise is not a saving but only a machine added.

PROVIDE ADEQUATE AND PROPER FOLLOW-UP

To make cost control effective, it is necessary (1) to check up and see that the remedial steps are followed, and (2) to know, as a consequence of these revisions, what the new results will be. The first point is achieved through personal means—observation and working with supervisors. For the latter point, some simple type of reporting can be instituted. For these reports to have greatest value, they should be made on a weekly and, in some instances, on a daily basis. It is important to know immediately if costs are getting back into line. Receiving reports at relatively long intervals of time might mean needless continuation of costly practices or receipt of information when it is too late to do anything about it.

Cost control is a job that never ends. It varies in intensity with the particular needs of the enterprise, the skill of the personnel assigned and interested in it, and the beliefs of the top management members. It takes time and is laborious work, but it is well worth the effort. Best results are usually obtained from continuous, not sporadic, efforts.

EMPLOYEES ARE KEY TO COST REDUCTION

Certain items normally offer greater cost reduction possibilities than others. Those representing the big items, the ones on which the most money is now being spent, and those of a cumulative and repetitive nature, usually offer the best opportunities for lowering costs. Some research and probing may be required to find this type of information for a particular office.

In most offices, however, the major expense is wages and salaries —employees are the key cost. A breakdown of total office expenses under typical conditions is shown by Figure 38–2. In other words, nearly three out of every four office dollar costs are for people. To increase efficiency, this suggests the use of less employees, or the more efficient use of those presently employed. Stressing people as the core of office cost reduction, Fred E. Shelton, Jr., suggests careful examina-

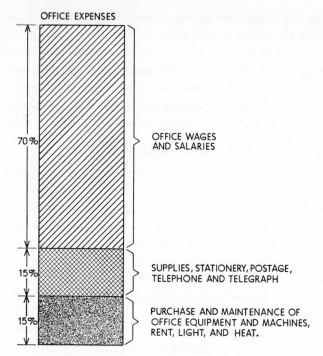

FIG. 38–2. Wages and salaries are the key costs of an office.

tion of four areas: (1) office supervision, (2) habit patterns, (3) servile attitudes, and (4) methods of administration.[3]

COST-CONSCIOUSNESS AMONG EMPLOYEES

Cutting cost is not a job restricted to managers. It is a job in which every employee can and should participate. Interest in costs is fundamental because it is a means contributing to employee security. To reduce costs is a way of keeping an enterprise fit so it can continue to operate successfully and to meet its responsibilities.

Cost information can be used to develop a cost-consciousness among employees. A feeling of the importance of cost and its use throughout the entire enterprise must be achieved in order for cost to have greatest value. Every member on the payroll, from the top executive to the lowest employee, should be made aware of and encouraged to think in terms of cost. When the employees are cost-minded, a basic and broad beginning toward improving operations has been accomplished. Thinking in terms of cost is necessary for greatest efficiency.

[3] Fred E. Shelton, Jr., "Wanted. Cost Reduction," *Office Executive* (Willow Grove, Pa.: National Office Management Association) June, 1956, pp. 9–11. This is an excellent article. Mr. Shelton, Jr., is office manager of the Standard Register Company, Dayton, Ohio.

To accomplish this aim, suggestions pointing out possibilities for lowering office expenses are helpful. Figure 38–3 shows this in graphic form and brings out the fact that cost permeates all office activities. Every employee has the opportunity to be cost-minded and to reduce costs. In addition, accurate cost information should be disseminated to all supervisors and employees who are charged with those costs and for which they are responsible. By this means, cost is given important and meaningful status. Employees are quick to recognize this and will seek to use cost as a guide in their everyday tasks.

OFFICE BUDGETS

Among the important responsibilities of an office manager is the maintenance of a proper balance among all office activities and the achievement of objectives within certain predetermined limits. To help accomplish these goals and exercise the necessary controlling, the office manager can use a budget.

BUDGET DEFINED

A budget has been defined in a variety of ways; one definition is: "A budget is a forecast, in detail, of the results of an officially recognized program of operations, based on the highest reasonable expectation of operating efficiency."[4] Actually there are two concepts involved, the budget and budgetary control. Each of these can be defined formally in the following manner: *A budget is a device consisting of an orderly arrangement of statistical data determined by computed guesses and covering all phases of the enterprise for a definite future period of time.* On the other hand, *budgetary control is the process of using the budget by comparing actual results with the computed guesses in order to correct either the estimates or the causes of the differences.*

The budget and budgetary control are interrelated and must always be considered jointly. A budget without budgetary control is useless from the managerial viewpoint; and budgetary control without a budget is meaningless.

KINDS OF BUDGETS

It is possible to draw up a budget for almost any department or division of an enterprise. Frequently, separate budgets are made for sales, production, purchasing, finance, labor, and general expense.

---

[4] J. R. Bartizal, *Budget Principles and Procedures* (New York: Prentice-Hall, Inc., 1942), p. 1.

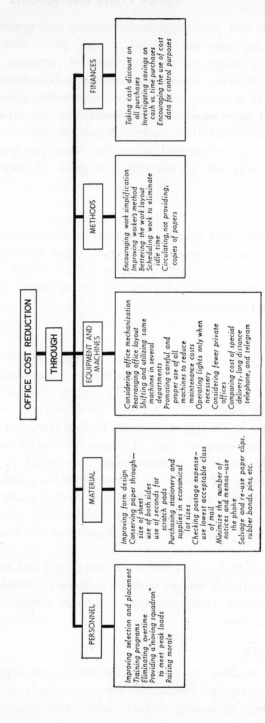

FIG. 38-3. Possibilities for the reduction of office costs.

These are then combined into one budget, which is sometimes termed the "master budget" or simply the "budget."

A budget can be expressed in dollars, physical units, or any other term which is useful and convenient to use. The dollar is probably the most frequently used. Quite often, where physical units are employed, the dollar values are also shown. When this practice is followed, it should be noted that not only units but also unit cost, i.e., price, must be forecast. Price forecasting is particularly difficult in times of rising or declining prices. For example, in the case of a purchasing budget, serious difficulties can be encountered, and, likewise, in the case of a labor budget, wage rates must be intelligently estimated.

It is sometimes desirable to show in a budget not only the allowances at a certain level of activity but also the allowances at various other levels. Such a budget is referred to as a *step budget,* and its value lies in predetermining and in thinking through the action to be taken should variations from the estimated goal arise. Actually the work of preparing a step budget is not as difficult as it may at first appear. Deviations are estimated from the allowances for the established goal. Some items will vary directly with the volume; others will tend to rise or fall with the operating level, but not in direct proportion to it; others will remain the same regardless of the operating level.

PREPARATION OF THE BUDGET

An interesting graphic representation showing the sequence of budget preparation is shown in Figure 38–4. The total estimated income is determined from expected sales and other sources of income. From this total estimated income are subtracted the expenses of sales, production, purchasing, and general expenses. This gives the estimated net income or loss, which can be reflected in the financial budget, an estimated balance sheet, and an estimated earnings statement. The chart shows some of the details included under each individual budget.

Usually the sales budget is developed first, since in many cases all other activities are predicated on what the sales-expectancy picture is. Using the predicted sales as a basis, the plan for production, purchasing, and the like can be drawn up.

However, in some cases this approach is reversed. The beginning is made by estimating the approximate income needed to provide a fair return on capital invested in the enterprise; then one works back to determine the sales required, the production, and so on. There are variations of these two approaches, as well as other methods.

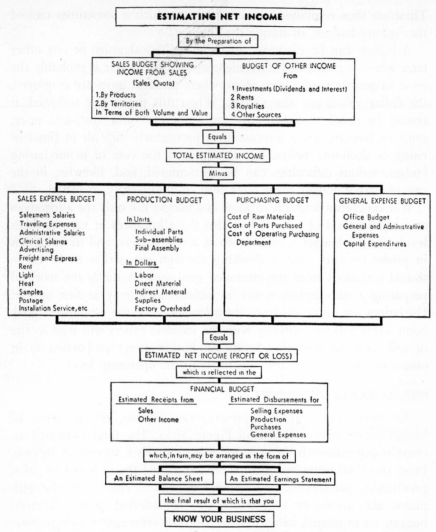

Courtesy: *Art Metal Construction Co., Jamestown, N.Y.*

FIG. 38–4. A normal sequence of budget preparation. The chart shows the co-ordination of the various individual budgets and the type of information found in each one.

Most procedures for budget making consist of a series of steps somewhat like the following:

1. A conference of top management members is held to discuss trends and general outlook and to formulate broad policies regarding activities throughout the coming year.

2. The basis for the entire program, including sales and net income, or some other entity, is first drawn up by the executive in charge

of the particular activity. It is then submitted for discussion and approval to the remaining top management members.

3. Each department head then prepares a budget for his own separate activity, guided by the data in the basic budget.

4. These budgets covering separate departments are submitted to the officer in charge of the budget. Generally, this is the controller or the budget officer.

5. A conference between the designated officer and each department head is then held for the purpose of thoroughly discussing and, when necessary, revising the respective, individual department budget. Sometimes a budget committee is used, in which case the budget officer transmits the estimates to the committee along with his recommendations.

6. After a tentative agreement on each individual budget has been reached, the master budget meeting is called. At this time each individual budget is submitted and discussed. If necessary, adjustments are made and final approval is obtained. This approval is generally contingent upon a final O.K. by the general manager or the president.

7. When finally determined, the budget is written up in its approved form, and copies are sent to all persons charged with carrying out a major portion of the plan. In like manner copies covering specific parts of the master budget are distributed to lesser executives who are responsible for the execution of a particular portion of the plan.

ALL BUDGETS CONCERN THE OFFICE MANAGER

The office manager should use all the budgets employed in an enterprise to find out the plan or projected trends in operations which will affect the amount of office work. Such things as an increase in advertising literature to be mailed, a change in the number of bills payable, the development of new sales markets, a new policy regarding billing practices, and a reduction in the number of purchasing orders constitute the type of information he needs to know in order to have the office provide its necessary functions.

Ordinarily the office manager is active in the preparation of (1) the cash budget, and (2) the office expense budget. In the case of the cash budget, the extent of office activities affects the cash requirements of the enterprise. The purchase and trade-in of office machines and equipment, the expansion or contraction of any office function in order to keep it in balance with changes elsewhere in the enterprise, or simply action to cut down office expenditures are illustrations of the office's influence on the cash budget.

The office expense budget is the individual budget covering office activities and is one in which the office manager is vitally interested. Typical items include supervision, clerical payroll, stationery, supplies, postage, telephone and telegraph service, reception and messenger service, purchase and maintenance of office machines and equipment, rent, and light. As already indicated, comparisons are made with the estimated amounts.

Figure 38–5 shows a portion of an office expense budget. In this case entries of actual expenditures have been made for the months of January and February. Expenses for February are nearly $400 in excess of the estimate. A study of the itemized data for this month shows that clerical payroll, machine and equipment purchases, and supervision payroll are the items chiefly responsible for the increase. Further investigation of these expenses should be made.

THE BUDGET PERIOD

The data of a budget apply to a definite period of time. The length of this period varies, however, because of several important considerations, one of which is the ability to make reasonable forecasts covering conditions affecting the work. All comparisons are made with the forecast data. It follows, therefore, that for valid comparison the budget should cover only a reasonable future period, usually one year or less.

Another consideration is the normal cycle for completion of the work. The period selected should be long enough to include seasonal or any characteristic variations so that the "up and down" changes are covered. In other words, the budget cycle should cover the sales and production cycles.

The length of the fiscal period should also be taken into account. Many budgets are concerned with income and expenditure and are expressed in dollar units. In these cases the budget period should coincide with or fit into the time pattern already existing for other financial controls.

Also, the intended use of the budget influences the budget period selected. For example, if the budget is to serve as a quarterly check, the time period should include a three-month period. If the purpose is a semiannual check, a six-month period will be used.

The most common period covered is one year, with breakdowns for quarterly and monthly periods. The year usually coincides with the calendar year, although if operations are on a fiscal basis, the fiscal

OFFICE EXPENSE BUDGET FOR THE YEAR 195—

ITEM	JAN. Estimate	JAN. Actual	FEB. Estimate	FEB. Actual	NOV. Estimate	NOV. Actual	DEC. Estimate	DEC. Actual	TOTAL Estimate	TOTAL Actual
1. Stationery and envelopes	$ 75	$ 68	$ 35	$ 83	$ 50		$ 35		$ 250	
2. Supplies	50	35	35	21	35		35		400	
3. Postage	35	35	35	35	35		35		420	
4. Telephone and telegraph	185	173	185	186	185		185		2,220	
5. Reception and messenger service	450	440	450	440	500		500		5,700	
6. Magazine and book subscription	18	18		18					50	
7. Maintenance of machines and equipment*	40	53	40	62	40		40		480	
8. Purchase of machines and equipment*	440	291		165	200				2,400	
9. Rent	80	80	80	80	80		80		960	
10. Light	22	21	20	21	20		26		216	
11. Traveling expenses*	80	135	80	40	80		80		960	
12. Employee's welfare	50	60	50	47	50		50		550	
13. Clerical payroll*	3,750	3,870	3,750	3,920	4,000		4,000		46,750	
14. Supervision payroll*	1,140	1,140	1,140	1,170	1,300		1,300		15,000	
15. Miscellaneous (list)	25		25		25		25		300	
Install new electric outlet				18						
Fix door at north exit		3								
Total	$6,440	$6,387	$5,890	$6,288					$76,656	

* These items must be justified by details on supplementary sheets.

FIG. 38-5. An office expense budget. Supplementary sheets are used to show the details of certain items which are selected on the basis of judgment and experience.

year is used. Customarily, the forecasts are subjected to revision and addition either monthly or quarterly as new conditions become known.

REVISION OF BUDGET

Generally, the forecast will be made during November and December for the following year. Then the revising and adjusting can follow any of a number of plans, but the following three are the most frequently used.

1. *Periodic Budgeting.* This plan provides for major revisions three times a year—in March, June, and September—for the remaining months of the year. For example, in March a reforecast for the period April through December is made. If needed, revisions can be made at other times of the year as well.

2. *Progressive Budgeting.* This arrangement furnishes definite times for major revisions throughout the year, such revisions covering definite periods following the revision date. For example, assume that revision times are bimonthly or at the end of February, April, June, August, October, and December and that the period covered is six months. At the end of February, revisions would be made for the following six-month period, March through August; at the end of April revisions are made for the period May through October; and so on. Revisions made at times other than the definite dates usually apply to the current budget only.

3. *Moving Budgeting.* Under this plan a forecast for twelve months is maintained by adding a month as each month is completed. To illustrate, at the completion of October, 1953, a forecast for October, 1954, is added; therefore the twelve-month forecast would cover November, 1953, through October, 1954. Revisions in the forecasts covering the intervening months are made when necessary.

USE AND EVALUATION OF BUDGETS

To a great extent the budget's practical use and effectiveness are predicated on the interest and enthusiasm of the executives and supervisors. If they have had a part in its formulation and want to make it operative, the use of the budget will normally be successful. Periodic statements and comparisons should be issued so that all management personnel are informed and their interest maintained. Enforcement of the budget is achieved by making individuals responsible for carrying out the prescribed operations. In the final analysis there is no substitute for this fixing of responsibility. Sometimes certain conditions need to be corrected to attain the goal set up by the budget. But, when fixed responsibility is placed with the individual, these conditions will be either corrected or promptly reported to the manager for remedial action.

Budgets provide important advantages to an office manager. Of major significance is that assistance is supplied in achieving a desired balance among the various office activities. The over-all viewpoint is encouraged. Facilitating the delegation of authority to division heads and supervisors is also worthy of mention. In addition, the use of a budget helps to reveal weaknesses in the office organization structure. Those units in which expenditures are excessively high can be signaled out for managerial attention. Furthermore, emphasis to planning and especially to orderly controlling is assisted by the budget's formulation and use. Also, the decision making of a management member is expedited and is facilitated by the factual information and records of accomplishment shown by the budget.

On the other hand, it should be noted that a budget is a managerial tool—a means of assistance to a manager, not management itself. Budgets are not automatic in their operation. Care in their compilation and wise, meaningful interpretation of the data are required. In addition, the use of budgets requires time. Current ills are not "blitzed" by budgets. The discovery, correction, or elimination of undesirable conditions is not an overnight job. It cannot be hurried. Finally, budgets are limited by the accuracy of the forecasts. Reviews about every month or three months should be scheduled so that new developments or changes of conditions are reflected in the budget.

QUESTIONS

1. Cite the major reasons for cost being important in office management.
2. Elaborate on the statement: "There are so many different kinds of cost that the term 'cost' is practically meaningless."
3. State concisely the meaning and give an example of each of the following: (a) unit cost, (b) indirect material cost, (c) cost-consciousness by employee, and (d) cost control.
4. An office manager devotes considerable attention and diligently applies various control media—including effective routing, scheduling, simplifying of work, time standards, and manuals—to the efforts of getting the office work accomplished. Will the effective use of these controls exclude the need for cost control? Why?
5. Discuss the importance of employees as the key to reducing office costs.
6. What are the outstanding advantages in using standard costs for office controlling purposes?
7. Which of the following can serve as objectives of an office manager:

(a) costs, (b) reduction of costs, (c) budgets, and (d) standard cost. Explain your answers.

8. Are budgets limited by the accuracy of the forecasts? Why?

9. Do you agree with the statement: "All budgets concern the office manager"? Explain your answer.

10. As an office manager, what basic arrangement for revising the budget would you follow? Why?

11. Explain the following: "A budget requires a considerable period of time to become an accurate control mechanism."

12. Miss "A" believes that if an item is in the budget, it is sufficient justification for spending that amount in order to utilize funds advantageously and keep them in balance. In contrast, Miss "B" claims that, whenever possible, savings on every budget item should be made in order to keep costs at a minimum. With whom do you agree? Give your reasons.

CASE PROBLEMS

CASE 38-1.   OFFICE MANAGEMENT ASSOCIATION OF AMERICA

A series of five one-day clinics dealing with office management problems is being considered by this association. To acquire enrollees it is proposed to send direct-mail pieces to 400 executives and 600 association members. For the former a cost of 13 cents each is estimated, and for the latter 8 cents each. The meetings will be held in the association's conference room so there is no rent to be paid. The instructor for each meeting will be given $50 per day, and the rental of a projector is estimated at $15 a day. Tentatively the registration fee is $37.50 for the five sessions. This includes luncheons as well as coffee during the morning and afternoon breaks at each session. Cost of a luncheon is $3 a plate, for the coffee 50 cents per session per registrant. Estimated miscellaneous expenses of $400 for up to and including 50 registrants cover the cost of class materials, mailing clinic reminders to enrollees, lunch for instructors, advertising, and incidentals. For over 50 registrants to and including 125 registrants, the estimated miscellaneous expenses are $600.

PROBLEMS:

1. Draw up the budget for the clinics using the bases of 25, 50, 75, and 100 registrants.

2. What interpretations do you make from these budget data?

CASE 38-2.   APEX FINANCE COMPANY

In the collection department of this company are four bookkeepers, paid $375 each a month, and one credit clerk, who receives $285 a month. They are expected to handle 20,000 accounts per year. It is not anticipated that the requirements of the company will exceed this amount for some years to come. This standard is believed equitable, but for the past several months the rate of output has been around 1,500 per month. To meet the required standard rate of 20,000 accounts per year, the bookkeepers are working overtime. In addition to labor costs, there are also the following annual costs in connection with the handling of the accounts: postage, $312.00; office forms, $211.75; miscellaneous supplies, $125.00; and overhead expenses allocated to this department, $522.00.

The office manager, Mr. Jeffrey Morgan, wants to reduce costs on getting this work accomplished. Accordingly he called the representatives of several office machine manufacturers and found that a machine to do the bookkeeping work would cost the company $2,650 a year, including depreciation, maintenance costs, interest on capital invested, etc. This figure is based on a ten-year period. An operator to run the machine will cost $5,200 a year. The operator would perform all credit work in connection with accounts handled. By use of the machine a production of 16,000 accounts per year is estimated. However, two employees in addition to the machine operator would be required. Each of these two employees would be paid $300 per month.

Furthermore, mechanization would necessitate new forms costing $475 a year. The cost of other supplies would remain the same. Mr Morgan was informed by the treasurer of the company that the same overhead costs would continue to be charged the department whether a change in the manner of doing the work was made or not. At some future date an adjustment might be made, but for the present, the same overhead cost should be included.

Mr. Morgan also spoke with a representative from the Voss Office Services and received a quotation of $123.70 per hundred accounts to do the work. This quotation includes pickup and delivery of the work that would be done in the offices of the service bureau company.

PROBLEMS:

1. Evaluate the viewpoint and action of the office manager.

2. Compute the cost of performing the work under the present plan and under each of the suggested plans.

3. What is your recommendation to this company? Why?

Appendixes

APPENDIX A

History of
Office Management

The written word became a fact about 7000 B.C. This was the real beginning of record keeping; now some tangible things, such as a sign indicating ownership or a picture conveying some sort of information, could be set down in writing for the purpose of aiding memory.

The oldest known documents of the Babylonian civilization, whose history goes back to about 4000 B.C., are written in cuneiform or wedge-shaped characters which were derived from the more primitive pictorial writing. The written documents were mostly on tablets of clay; the written characters were impressed into the clay while it was wet, and then the clay was dried in the sun. Records were made of such things as the king's public activities, the transactions of commercial houses, and the laws and judgments of the court. Contracts of all sorts were made and guaranteed. Complete archives of these materials have been found in Babylonia.

Egyptian hieroglyphs, developed around 2200 B.C., were written on sheets of papyrus stretched over a frame, and brushes and pens made from reeds were the instruments of writing. Complete records were kept of such things as harvesting operations, payment of taxes, and accounts of workers, including hours worked and wages paid. These records were made primarily to assist in tax collections. Both the Egyptians and the Babylonians used a column arrangement in their written records. Accounts were divided into income and expenditures, each in a separate column; in addition, accounts were divided into cash or credit, very much as they are in many present-day systems of finance.

GREEK AND ROMAN OFFICE WORK

Office work was also important during the great Greek and Roman civilizations of ancient times. Here again, extensive commerce, banking activities, and taxation required a great deal of office work. The Romans were especially meticulous in keeping detailed records. In their records of landownership, for example, were included not only information regarding size and boundaries but also such things as the number of trees and vines, the extent of pasture, and the amount of woods and water on the land.

As early as 500 B.C. the Greeks used the abacus, a device for performing calculations by sliding balls in grooves or on individual rods within a frame.[1] The abacus, really one of the first office appliances, is credited as a Chinese invention. It was not used extensively in Europe until the end of the fifteenth century. The abacus, or *suan pan,* as the Chinese call it, is still widely used in China and Japan, and occasionally in the United States one may see a local Chinese laundryman figure bills by use of this calculating device. The sight is extremely fascinating, for his speed and accuracy rival that of the modern calculating machine. The accompanying figure shows an abacus.

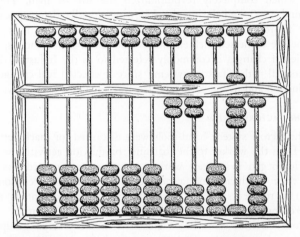

The abacus was one of the first ways of calculating.

ARABIC NUMERALS IN EUROPE

Arabic numerals, which offered a mathematical decimal system with place values, came to Europe from the Arabs. No doubt Arabic numerals were known in certain areas of Europe prior to the beginning of the thirteenth century, but in the year 1202 a book on arithmetic, entitled *Liber Abaci,* was written that was destined to change European mathematical customs. In it the author, Leonard Piscanos (an Italian) pointed out the distinct advantages of the Arabic numerals, including such things as the saving of time and space, the simplifying of work in addition and subtraction, and the possibility of solving problems of multiplication and division in writing.

INFLUENCE OF CHURCH UPON OFFICE WORK

Much of the clerical work performed during the Middle Ages was in connection with the church. The word "clerk" stems from the same source as "clergy"; both come from a Greek word meaning "a certain portion." The church maintained vital statistics of the community, such as births and marriages; and in

---

[1] D. E. Smith, *History of Mathematics* (Boston: Ginn & Co., 1925), Vol. II, pp. 161–64.

return for these services the priest's portion or allotment of the crop or return was given. With the passing of time the term "clerk" became associated with one who kept records, or one who performed work which required writing.

INDUSTRIAL REVOLUTION

Down through the middle of the eighteenth century, people of western Europe went on using the same methods and implements to produce the necessities of life that their forefathers had used for some 2,500 years. During all this time, there had been no significant progress in the methods of tilling soil, harvesting crops, weaving cloth, or working wood and metal.

Then, within a short period of time, there appeared in England a series of inventions which completely revolutionized the life of man. This new era started around 1760, and during the following decades there appeared fundamental and far-reaching changes for supplying the wants of man. The world had never before witnessed such enormous changes in such a short span of time.

This series of changes is commonly referred to as the Industrial Revolution. Some writers call it the "factory system," since it effected real changes in methods of production and in the economic structure of industrial society.

EFFECT OF THE FACTORY SYSTEM

Under the factory system, hand tools were discarded for machinery; skill was transferred from the worker to the machine; production activities were centralized; factories began to appear; workers came to be removed from the consumers of their products; and a new class of owners of economic wealth appeared. The repercussions of these changes were momentous and vitally affected the economical, the political, and the social aspects of man.

Production activities came to be clustered in fairly large groups, and the activities themselves, together with commerce, began to gain wider influence. This expansion brought with it a growth in office work; but, by and large, paper work was regarded as a necessary evil, inasmuch as it did not produce directly a physical, usable article.

STATUS OF OFFICE WORK

Relatively little was done at this time to better the general status of office work or to improve its efficiency. Its role in business was confined mainly to simple record keeping and the collecting and copying of legal evidence which could be used in possible legal cases.

However, during this time there were several important inventions which resulted in improving the performance of office work. The first of these was the invention of the copying press by James Watt in 1780. The only known method of duplicating a record up to that time was to copy it by hand. Watt's invention made it possible to secure accurate impressions with the use of low-skilled help and in a small fraction of the time previously required. But the copying press was also slow in being adopted, and it was not until around 1870, or nearly a hundred years after its invention, that the copying press became generally used.

Another important contribution to office work was the invention of a commercially successful typewriter by two Americans, Sholes and Glidden, around the year 1873. This made mechanical writing possible and greatly improved the quality and quantity of written work. It also served to break down opposition to office mechanization and to pave the way for the adaptation of other office machines which were to appear beginning around 1890, such as the adding, addressing, and tabulating machines.

Office people were not easy to convince of the advantages of performing office work by machine instead of by hand. For example, criticisms of the typewriter included the time occupied in the spacing and setting of a letter, the clicking noise, the easily detected errors, the cost of the machine, and its upkeep. Even twenty-five years after the first typewriter was put on the market, it was still universally expected that an office worker should have a good Spencerian hand. In fact, most letters during the 1890's were still written by hand, and in many instances this work was done by skilled office workers known as "amanuenses."

OFFICE MANAGEMENT OF THE EARLY TWENTIETH CENTURY

About the beginning of the twentieth century, office work gradually started to gain recognition as important work. The concept of business office work as consisting of reading the mail, writing a few letters, and putting unpaid bills in one empty cigar box and paid bills in another gave way to the fuller realization and understanding of the tasks performed in the office.

There are several major reasons for this enlightened view. In the first place, it became increasingly difficult for the owner or active head of an enterprise to retain the whole range of ideas, facts, and plans either in his own head or on papers in his desk. It was just too big a job. Many enterprises already were quite large, and many more were expanding at a rapid rate. The importance of having good written records and someone to specialize in handling this work was beginning to be realized.

Second, it was recognized that enterprises outlived individuals. In order to have a permanent and continuing account of the enterprise's activities, the work of making written records was set up as a distinct activity, delegated to a responsible individual.

Third, business enterprises were giving an increased amount of attention to economies in production and distribution. It became imperative to have records of operations and transactions so that managers could give intelligent direction. It became increasingly important to know where the enterprise was, how it got there, and where it was probably heading. In addition, these records were helpful in instituting the necessary measures of managerial control.

During the period about 1900–1915, office work was dominated by various systems which were intended to make the operation of office work efficient. These systems were of all sorts and varieties and almost always included the use of specially designed cards and books. Sometimes unique office gadgets were included.

Also during this time, tidbits of office wisdom, such as "Do It Now," "Put It in Writing," and "Make Memorandums in Duplicate," were widely distributed and for the most part carefully followed. This prevailing custom seems to indicate that performing an office task immediately upon the first recognition of it and making a written record of everything were among the essentials of good office work. It is doubtful, however, that all these systems and slogans increased the efficiency of the office. They probably helped get the work performed and finished with less effort; but, by their use, many tasks which should have been completely eliminated were retained and carried out with diligent regularity.

The mechanization of the office continued, and more and more work was adapted to machines. Vast improvements were made in the types of office machines that already existed, and many new machines were added to the list. Likewise, office equipment such as desks, chairs, filing cabinets, and typewriter stands was improved and designed to give more and better service.

THE PERIOD 1916–30

During this period, management engineers attained enviable achievements in improving quality and method in the factory. These successes inspired similar research in office products and methods. A general movement to improve office work was launched, and notable progress was made. Among the newer achievements in the office were such things as budgetary control, improved procedures for determining costs, distribution-analysis records, calculating machines, multiple duplicating equipment, and accounting machines.

Beginning with the 1920's there has been an increasing use of scientific management applied to office work. Scientific management had already gained significant headway in the factory, and the tangible evidence of its success in the shop naturally suggested its use in the office. The person charged with managing the office was becoming genuinely concerned with such questions as "What is the real purpose of the office records and accounts?" "What are the best methods of performing the work?" "How long should it take to do the work?"

DEVELOPMENTS DURING 1931–50

Since the early 1930's the trend toward increased control of business by government has stimulated an increase in office work. Government has enacted legislation providing for a steadily growing number of regulatory measures, such as those affecting working hours, wages, and conditions, the social security of the worker, the selling of securities, and the payment of taxes. To comply with the many new regulatory measures, enterprises found it necessary to have very complete and accurate records of all activities. Likewise, government itself found it necessary to set up and to maintain a vast number of new accounts in order to administer the provisions of the various laws. The influence of government, therefore, has helped to accelerate the growth and the importance of office work and also of office management.

In addition, the growth in the amount and importance of office work is attributable to other important factors, among which are: (1) the increase in insurance and advertising activities, (2) the development of modern accounting techniques, (3) the acceptance and extensive use of credit and installment selling, and (4) the expansion of small enterprises to national operations. Additional factors could be mentioned, but they would serve only to emphasize the point that the trend of office work, both in volume and value, has been definitely upward.

The office continued to grow in importance during World War II. More and more recognition was given the person charged with the management of office work. The concept of an office manager was no longer confined to that of a loyal and faithful clerk who had served many years and who knew all the details of every office operation. Office managers were achieving more complete executive status.

The tremendous growth in our economy during this period served to emphasize further the work and the management of the office. The importance of the human element in the office and means for achieving better work relationships were stressed. In addition, new types of records and improved methods were developed.

STATUS OF OFFICE MANAGEMENT SINCE 1951

Progress continues to be achieved in the office management field. Much more emphasis is being given to mechanization, with many speculations as to the make-up of the future office and its automation. Laborsaving equipment appears destined to become more commonplace in the office of tomorrow. The use of color is becoming more prevalent, and much attention is being given to providing pleasant, invigorating office surroundings. This is in keeping with the increasing attention to the office employee and to the subject of human relations. In addition, more functional and more analytical approaches are influencing the thinking in office management. They are taking over from the traditional approach.

However, there is still need for further development of successful techniques especially applicable to office work. The principles of good factory management can serve as excellent idea sources for office improvements, but modifications are frequently in order; it does not necessarily follow that the techniques for carrying out these principles are the same in the shop and in the office. There are several reasons for this. In the first place, office work and shopwork are not exactly alike—they have significant differences. Office work usually involves a greater proportion of mental effort; it is more likely to occur in concentrated amounts, i.e., characterized by periodic peak loads; and its make-up is much more of a nontangible nature. Furthermore, experience has shown that in cases of shop production, even when the setups are similar, identical techniques of management do not always bring about the same results. All this would seem to indicate that some questioning can be made of a general practice permitting managerial techniques of shopwork to be applied without change or adjustment to office work.

The management of office work is moving ahead. It is making significant advances, and the progress will continue. The importance of office work, the necessity for its effective management, and full recognition of its essentiality by top management members, destine its continued gain.

APPENDIX B

Important Postal Regulations

* Rates shown are those in effect on January 1, 1959.

FIRST-CLASS MAIL

This includes material sealed against postal inspection and all written material, whether written wholly or in part by hand or by typewriter. Examples are letters, carbon copies, executed forms, and any material enclosed in business reply envelopes. The rates for first-class mail sent to any place in the United States or its possessions are as follows:

Airmail	7 cents for each ounce or fraction
Letter	4 cents for each ounce or fraction
U.S. postal card	3 cents each
Post card	3 cents each

Letters mailed without postage or a sufficient amount of stamps are returned to the sender for postage, if the local return address is shown. If not, local mail is delivered collect and nonlocal mail is held at the addressee's post office for postage, notice being sent to the addressee. When deficient postage is collected, there is also a penalty of one cent for each ounce or fraction. First-class letters are returned, if an address is given. However, undeliverable postal and post cards are not returned unless the return address is shown on the address side in the upper left-hand corner, along with a statement that return postage is guaranteed.

SECOND-CLASS MAIL

Unsealed newspapers and periodicals come under this classification. The post office should be consulted for publisher's rates.

THIRD-CLASS MAIL

For regular mailing, circulars and form letters cost 3 cents for the first two ounces or fraction and $1\frac{1}{2}$ cents for each additional ounce or fraction. For catalogues with 24 or more pages the rate is 3 cents for the first two ounces or fraction, and $1\frac{1}{2}$ cents for each additional ounce or fraction. The weight limit is up to but not including 16 ounces.

In many offices, bulk mail permitted under "Sec. 34.66 P.L. and R." is an important part of this classification. A permit for use must be obtained at the post office, and the fee is $10 per calendar year. Savings are possible under bulk mailing. For not less than 200 separately addressed identical pieces or not less than twenty pounds, the rate for merchandise and miscellaneous printed material is 14 cents per pound or fraction, but not less than 2 cents for each piece if not over 1.714 ounces. For catalogues of 24 or more pages, the cost is 10 cents per pound or fraction, but not less than 2 cents for each piece if not over 2.4 ounces.

Bulk mail cannot be registered, insured, or sent C.O.D., nor can uncanceled stamps be used. The mail must be separated by state and post office, tied in bundles, and mailed at the post office.

FOURTH-CLASS MAIL

This is commonly referred to as parcel post and includes printed matter, merchandise, and all mailable matter weighing more than eight ounces, with the exception of that classified as first or second class. For most parcels the weight limit for fourth-class mail is forty pounds per parcel in the first and second zones, and twenty pounds in the third to the eighth zones. The size is also limited to 72 inches length and girth combined. For example, a parcel 24 inches long, 10 inches wide, and 14 inches high measures 72 inches $(24 + 10 + 10 + 14 + 14)$ in length and girth combined.

The rate for fourth-class mail is based on the weight and the distance—within what zone or number of miles the package is to be delivered. Special rates, below those of regular fourth class, apply to books.

OTHER POSTAL CONSIDERATIONS

Special Delivery means mail will receive immediate delivery at the post office of the addressee. An additional fee is charged, and the words "Special Delivery" should be marked directly above the address.

Special Handling applies to fourth-class mail only and means that for payment of a special fee the mail will receive the most expeditious handling and transportation. "Special Handling" should be marked directly above the address.

Return of Undeliverable Mail. The following postal procedures should be observed:

First-class mail...............	Is returned—no charge, but must include sender's return address on every piece.
Transient second-, third-, and fourth-class mail..............	Is returned when marked "Return Postage Guaranteed" under sender's return address.

The post office provides several methods to large mail users who employ third-class mail and who wish to keep their mailing list corrected and up to date. The method depends upon the instructions to the postmaster given on the envelope.

An effective method is to have printed in the bottom left-hand corner "Form 3547 Requested." This means the sender will either (1) pay for the receipt of Form 3547, which gives the new address of the addressee, or (2) pay for the return of an undeliverable piece when a forwarding address is unknown. If the new address is not local to that of the addressee's post office, the piece is destroyed unless the addressee has left instructions that he will pay for mail forwarded. On the other hand, if the piece is of obvious value, it is returned to the sender, who pays postage at the regular third-class rate.

Type Styles and Sizes Used for Office Forms

10 PT. GARAMOND CAPS AND SMALL CAPS ARE SHOWN HERE
1234567890

10 Pt. Powell Caps and Lower Case Are Shown Here
1234567890

10 Pt. Alternate Gothic Caps and Lower Case Are Shown Here
1234567890

10 PT. HESS BOLD CAPITALS ARE SHOWN HERE
1234567890

10 Pt. Poster Bodoni Caps and Lower Case Are Shown Here
1234567890

12 Pt. Sans Serif Bold Caps and Lower Case Are Shown Here
1234567890

12 Pt. Sans Serif Bold Italic Caps and Lower Case Are Shown Here
1234567890

12 PT. COPPERPLATE GOTHIC CAPITALS ARE SHOWN HERE
1234567890

14 Pt. Cheltenham Bold Condensed Caps and Lower Case Are Shown Here
1234567890

18 PT. No. 66 GOTHIC CAPS ARE SHOWN HERE
1234567890

inches	12 POINT	14 POINT	16 POINT	18 POINT	20 POINT	22 POINT	24 POINT	26 POINT
	1	1	1	1	1	1	1	1
	2	2	2	2	2	2	2	2
	3	3	3	3	3	3	3	3
	4	4	4	4	4	4	4	4
	5	5	5	5	5	5	5	5
	6	6	6	6	6	6	6	6
1	7	7	7	7	7	7	7	7
	8	8	8	8	8	8	8	8
	9	9	9	9	9	9	9	9
	10	10	10	10	10	10	10	10
	11	11	11	11	11	11	11	
	12	12	12	12	12	12		
2	13	13	13	13	13			
	14	14	14	14				
	15	15	15					
	16	16	16					
	17	17						
	18	18						
3	19	10						
	20							
	21							
	22							

Number of lines per inch according to popular type points. Based on type set without any extra leading (spacing between the lines).

Index

A

Absenteeism, 452–53
Acceptance of employee
 of methods analysis, 619, 651
 of procedural analysis, 619, 628
Accidents
 cause of, 523–24
 cost of, 532–33
 frequency rate of, 531–32
 hazards of, 525
 managerial action to reduce, 524
 measurement of, 531–32
  frequency rate, 531–32
  severity rate, 532
 occurrence of, 523
 in the office, 522
 records of, 531
 severity rate of, 532
Accounting machines, 264
 classification of, 265–66
 descriptive, 267–70
 features of, 265
 nondescriptive, 266–67
 operations performed by, 264–65
 types of, 264
 window-posting, 269
Acoustic material, 344
Activity; *see* Functions
Actuating
 and correspondence, 85
 definition of, 21
 and duplicating, 170–71
 and mail handling, 187
 in office management, 23, 29
 and personnel management, 451
 and records retention, 157
 and report writing, 65
 research in, 460
 responsibility of, 446
 suggestions for motivating, 448
Adding machine, 102–3
Addition, 98
Addressing machines, 84, 271–74
 application of, 271, 273–74
 attachments for, 271, 273
 types of, 271
Administering
 personnel relations, 451
 program, 501–2
Aim, importance of, in management, 20

Air conditioning, 339–40
Alphabetical filing, 114–17
Alternates in planning, 217
American Federation of Labor (AFL), 536–37
American Management Association, 43
American Standards Association, 588
Analysis
 defined, 40
 of job, 403–4
 of methods, 646
 of office forms, 667–69
 of procedures, 625–27
 in scientific method
  detailed, 40
  preliminary, 39–40
Answering device for telephone, 206
Apeco duplicating process, 165
Application form, 491–92
Approach of questioning in work simplification, 625–26
Approaches to management, 45
Arrangement of work
 parallel, 400–401
 serial, 399
Artificial lighting systems, 331–33
Associated standards, 537
Audits, of filing, 140
Ausonius, 522
Authority
 channels of, 436
 characteristics of, 411–12
 coequality with responsibility, 437
 defined, 411
 delegation of, 413
  implications of, 413
  problem of, 414
 horizontal, 412
 line, 416
 and organization structure, 412
 span of, 414
 staff, 416
 vertical, 412
Automatic answering device (telephone), 206
Automatic electronic computer; *see* Automation in office *and* Electronic computer
Automatic typing machine, 81–84

749